K.M. F. Max Muller

The Science Of Language Vol-I

K.M. F. Max Muller

The Science Of Language Vol-I

ISBN/EAN: 9783741103469

Manufactured in Europe, USA, Canada, Australia, Japa

Cover: Foto ©Andreas Hilbeck / pixelio.de

Manufactured and distributed by brebook publishing software (www.brebook.com)

K.M. F. Max Muller

The Science Of Language Vol-I

THE
SCIENCE OF LANGUAGE

FOUNDED ON

LECTURES DELIVERED AT THE ROYAL INSTITUTION

IN 1861 AND 1863

BY

F. MAX MÜLLER, K.M.

IN TWO VOLUMES.—VOL. I

LONGMANS, GREEN, AND CO.
39 PATERNOSTER ROW, LONDON
AND BOMBAY
1899

BIBLIOGRAPHICAL NOTE

First printed, January, 1891;
Re-issued in Collected Edition of Prof. Max Müller's Works,
and reprinted, January, 1899.

PREFACE.

Changes in the New Edition.

MY Lectures on the Science of Language were delivered at the Royal Institution in London in the years 1861 and 1863. They have since passed through many editions, and in every succcssive edition I have tried to remove whatever seemed to me either doubtful or wrong. But, after the two volumes had been stereotyped, I found it very troublesome to do this, except on a very limited scale, so that it became almost impossible to keep my lectures abreast with the advance of philological science which, particularly of late years, has been very rapid.

It is difficult indeed for an author who lives beyond the number of years generally allotted to scholars, to know what to do with his old books. After his death, they take their place on the peaceful shelves of a library, and he himself is no longer held responsible for defects which at the time when they were written were inevitable. But so long as he is alive, the author is expected to keep his books up to the highest mark, and he is blamed if he lends the authority of his name to opinions which he himself has ceased to hold.

When therefore a new edition of my Lectures became necessary once more, I insisted on the destruction of the old stereotype plates, and I determined to make one more attempt to render these volumes as correct as I could. I found it necessary not only to strike out many things, but likewise to add, and, in some cases, to re-write many pages. I left out what was peculiar to the form of lectures, and in order to keep this new edition more clearly distinct from former editions, I have changed the title from 'Lectures on the Science of Language,' to 'The Science of Language, founded on Lectures delivered at the Royal Institution in the years 1861 and 1863.'

I did not attempt, however, to change altogether the original character of my book, and though I should gladly have written a new work on the Science of Language instead of remodelling the old, my age and my many occupations rendered such an idea impossible.

What will, I believe, strike my present and future readers as the most serious defect in this new edition of my Lectures on the Science of Language, is the elaborate character of many arguments in support of theories which are now accepted by almost everybody, but which thirty years ago were novel and startling, and required to be defended against numerous gainsayers. I shall mention a few of them.

The Science of Language as different from Comparative Philology.

The very idea that, by the side of Comparative Grammar, there was room for a Science of Language, treating not only of vowels and consonants and the laws of phonetic change, but of the nature, the origin, and development of human speech, was received very coldly at first. With the exception of Heyse's *System der Sprachwissenschaft*, 1856, no such attempt had been made before. My own teachers and friends, such as Professors Bopp, Benfey, Curtius and others, looked upon my attempt to establish the general principles of a Science of Language and to connect the discoveries of Comparative Philology with the great problems of philosophy, as at all events premature, while philosophers by profession resented most strongly the intrusion of a new Saul among the old prophets of Logic, Psychology, and Metaphysics.

All this is changed now. Book after book has been published on *Language and the Study of Language*, on *the Life and Growth of Language*, on *the Origin of Language*, on *the Principles of Comparative Philology*, on *the Principles of the History of Language*, in which many of the problems first mooted in my Lectures have been most ably and far more fully discussed. The Science of Language, as founded on Comparative Philology, will, I believe, hold its place for ever as an independent science, and some of the most eminent philosophers of the day have given it the warmest welcome. That it is as essential to the critical philosopher as logic and psychology, is no longer doubted, while some of the more far-seeing thinkers have readily admitted that it will hereafter form the only solid basis of all sound philosophy. It may truly be said therefore that there was no longer any need for pleading so elaborately for the admission of the Science of Language, as a real science, among the most important of academic studies. All I can say is, *Forsan et haec olim meminisse juvabit.*

And if the title of a Physical Science has been less readily granted to the Science of Language, this is chiefly due to a radical difference of opinion among philosophers, who regard man either as the acme of nature, or as totally unconnected in his mental functions with the rest of the animal world. No one has insisted more strongly than I have on the line of demarcation that separates man and beast, namely language, but no one has been more anxious at all times to render unto nature the things which are of nature, and unto mind the things that are of the mind. No doubt nature may be defined so as to exclude the Science of Language from the narrower circle of the Physical Sciences. With the wider meaning assigned to nature in our days, however, I hold as strongly as ever that the study of human speech may claim not only admission to, but the highest place among the Physical Sciences.

Bow-wow and Pooh-pooh Theories.

Though the problem of the origin of language was expressly excluded from my lectures (it has since been fully treated in my 'Science of Thought'), I had to explain what I considered to be the constituent elements of human speech, namely roots, and not the mere imitations of sounds or interjectional cries. I was told at the time that my repeated argumentations against what I called the Bow-wow and Pooh-pooh theories were only a slaying of the slain, and if that seemed to be so thirty years ago, how much more must it seem to be so at present. And yet I could not entirely suppress those portions of my book. It was a surprise to me when I delivered my lectures that the so-called onomatopœic theory should in our times still count a few, but very valiant supporters. But though it may be true that that theory in its crudest form is no longer held by anybody, yet, in a slightly modified form it has been broached again and again.

How little the real problem that has to be solved had been understood, was shown once more when my friend, Professor Noiré, now no longer among us, announced what I consider the best, if not the only possible solution of the problem of the origin of roots. He saw clearly that what had to be explained was not the origin of such imitative sounds as cuckoo or bow-wow. Who could ever have been in doubt as to their origin? What had to be explained was the genesis of conceptual sounds, or, if you like, of sonant concepts. Noiré showed that our first concepts arose by necessity from the consciousness of our own repeated or continuous acts. They could not be our acts, unless we were conscious of them, and our consciousness of them became conceptual as soon as we became conscious of many successive acts as one action. He further showed how these concepts of our own acts might become, so to say, sonant through the *clamor concomitans*, that is, the sounds which involuntarily accompany the simplest acts of man. If *mar*, for instance, was one of the many sounds that accompanied the act of rubbing or grinding, then it could serve as the sonant sign of our consciousness of that continuous or repeated act. It would be from the first a conceptual, not a merely perceptual sound.

No doubt, this may be called a mere theory, a mere possibility. Though language might have arisen in that way, it did not follow that it could not have arisen in any other way. But when it became clear to me that what we had obtained as the result of our scientific analysis of language, namely the roots, were exactly what Noiré postulated, sounds expressive of the simplest acts of man, I said both εὕρηκας and εὕρηκα. One of the oldest riddles of the world seemed to me solved, and solved without a residue.

Nothing could be simpler, nothing more convincing, to those who knew what the *punctum saliens* of our problem really was. But so completely was Noiré's theory, the Synergastic Theory, misunderstood that it was actually taken by some philosophers for a mere repetition or subdivision of the onomatopœic theory. This convinced me that the old leaven was still at work, and that what seemed to myself also, while revising my lectures, an uncalled-for slaying of the slain, might nevertheless be useful even at present, if only as the record of a once hotly contested fight.

Starting from the conviction that the Science of Language should be treated as one of the Physical Sciences, I proceeded to explain in what sense it seemed to me to require a physiological foundation.

Phonetics the Foundation of Comparative Philology.

To many of my younger readers the elaborate arguments in favour of phonetic studies as the only safe foundation of philological studies, contained in the second volume of my lectures, may seem at present supererogatory. Here again it is now admitted by almost everybody that a knowledge of Phonetics is essential to a sound study of Comparative Philology. But when I tried for the first time to make the researches of Johannes Müller, Brücke, Czermak and others, subservient to the Science of Language, I was severely blamed by Professor Benfey, in his review of my Lectures (*Göttinger Gelehrte Anzeigen*, 1867), for this innovation, and for encumbering Comparative Philology with such heterogeneous subjects as Phonetics. Now all this is changed. Phonetic studies are not only recognised as an essential part of Comparative Philology, but they are cultivated for their own sake, and have often been carried to such excess that we have lately been warned by our friends against the danger of 'trying to listen too much to the growth of phonetic grass.'

Phonetic Laws invariable.

It followed almost by necessity from my treatment of the Science of Language, or, at least, of one portion of it, as a Physical Science, that I had to insist so strongly and repeatedly in the course of my Lectures on the invariability of phonetic laws. Here it may seem that I spoke rather too dogmatically when I declared 'that we might as well think of changing the laws which control the circulation of our blood as of altering the laws of speech.' This statement aroused at the time strong opposition, and I do not mean to defend it now in all its crudity. The term 'law' as applied to the changes of language requires a more careful definition. These laws are not universal laws, like the law of gravitation. They belong to the class of empirical laws, 'uniformities which observation or experiment has shown to exist, but on which,' as Mill remarks, 'we hesitate to rely in cases varying much from those which have been actually observed, for want of seeing any reason why such a law should exist.'[1]

We know, for instance, that in Sanskrit no word can end in two consonants. Yet there are a few exceptions, such as ûrk, strength, or amârt, from mrig. There are eleven consonants only that can be

[1] Mill, *Logic*, iii. 16. 1.

final in Sanskrit, k, ṅ, *t*, *n*, t, n, p, m, l, *h*, *m*, while in Greek no more than three consonants can stand at the end of a word, n, r, s. But here again there is an exception, namely the κ in οὐκ and ἐκ. Now we cannot discover any reason why the Greeks should not have tolerated more than three consonants at the end of their words, considering how we ourselves use almost any consonant as final. But it can easily be imagined how much the whole character of a language is determined by these phonetic restrictions. There are other combinations of consonants to which the Greeks object, such as *mr*, *ml*, *ns*. Again, we cannot tell why, and we must remember that Argives and Cretans tolerated participles in *ns* such as τιθένς, while all other Greeks rejected them, and changed τιθένς or τιθέντς into τιθείς.

These are therefore hardly to be called laws, for we cannot give any reason why they are obeyed in one place and defied in another; we cannot trace them back to more general, ultimate laws,—or at least we have not yet succeeded in doing so.

Curtius and those who followed him, though they insisted very strongly on a strict observance of phonetic laws, always allowed what they called sporadic cases, that is, exceptions not yet accounted for. These sporadic cases have formed of late years a favourite trysting-place for the old and the new schools. The new school maintains, as I did many years ago, that phonetic laws admit of no exceptions whatever, and that, if they did, language would not be a subject fit for a really scientific treatment. These may seem brave words, but as a fundamental principle, they ought to be accepted by all students of language. But even the most extreme supporter of this general principle has to limit it, by adding, as Professor Brugmann does, that it is only within the same linguistic sphere and at the same time that phonetic change takes place with rigid consistency.[1] With this limitation the general principle would probably be excepted at present as almost a truism. And if in another place, Professor Brugmann says that all which he and his friends have been contending for is that 'all words undergo the same change, if the letters stand under the same conditions,' who would now deny this? The difficulty, however, remains, how to ascertain what letters stand under the same conditions, nay, how to discover what these conditions are in their endless variety. Each language has its own phonetic idiosyncrasies, the dialects of each language go their own way, nay, we know that even families and individuals have often their own peculiar pronunciation.

Dialectic Growth.

I tried to comprehend all these disturbing influences under the general name of *Dialectic Growth*, using Dialectic in a very wide, but, I believe, in its original sense. Dialects begin with the casual conversation of individuals. They continue as the conversational language of families, clans, villages, some-

[1] Brugmann, *Zum heutigen Stand der Sprachwissenschaft*, p. 78.

times of tribes, confederacies, and states. Though for a time unobserved, they continue to be the feeders of language in ancient even more than in modern times. Having followed for a time their own independent course, many of these dialectic contributions differ of necessity from the general character of the broad stream of language into which they are absorbed. There are besides in every language what may be called survivals, old-fashioned words and forms which are retained unchanged in their time-honoured character, while all the rest follow the changing fashion of the day.

Contact of different languages.

Still more violent disturbances are caused by the historical contact and conflict between nations speaking different or distantly related languages. The wide difference between Old High-German and Gothic cannot be explained by the slow process of phonetic decay only, but must be accounted for by the contact between Low German and High German tribes, and finally by the political displacement of the former by the latter. The English of Alfred would never have become the English of Chaucer but for the misusage it received by Danish and Norman conquerors. Nor should we be able to account for the strange aspect of French, unless we knew how Latin, having suffered already by the ill-treatment of Roman legionaries and the Celtic inhabitants of Gaul, was finally knocked to pieces by German Franks. It is when people accustomed to one language have to express themselves in another, as in the contact between Latin, Celtic, and Teutonic in Central Europe, or between English and Norman French in England, that the greatest phonetic disintegration takes place.

We may, no doubt, stand on our right and declare that all the disturbances caused by these events are themselves amenable to general rules, that exceptions cease to be exceptions, as soon as we can account for them, and that sporadic cases are no longer sporadic, if we can bring them under a new law. That is so; that is in fact the true meaning of *Exceptio probat regulam*.[1] The exception, if accounted for, proves the correctness of the law of which it forms an exception. On this point, therefore, the old and the new schools could hardly differ. Their real difference is one of scientific temper rather than of principle. The young enthusiast says, there must be a reason for everything that seems anomalous and sporadic in language; the old observer says, there may be. They both look for an explanation, and they both rejoice when it is found, just as Adams and Leverrier rejoiced when the anomalies in the movements of Uranos were accounted for by the discovery of the new planet, Neptune.

---

[1] What is thought to be an exception to a principle is always some other and distinct principle cutting into the former; some other force which impinges against the first force, and deflects it from its direction. Mill, *Logic*, iii. 10. 4.

But though exceptions to the laws of phonetic change can thus be accounted for by dialectic influences, there still remained the question why there should be any phonetic change at all. This question also I tried to answer from a physiological point of view, and perhaps in fuller detail than would be necessary at present.

For a long time the usual phrase in linguistic works was, *k* becomes *g*, *t* becomes *d*, *s* becomes *r*; but how one letter could become another letter was never so much as asked. Then came the time when Curtius introduced the name *Verwitterung*, which means decay, or wear and tear, produced on stone by the influence of the weather. That again was a metaphorical expression, and did not give us a *vera causa*. I believe I was the first to suggest the prosaic reason that all phonetic change was due to laziness, to an economy of muscular effort required in pronouncing vowels and consonants. If this explanation should have been suggested before by others, I claim no priority, nor should I, at present, gain much credit for it. The chief objection raised against my explanation was that in many cases these phonetic changes could not possibly be said to facilitate pronunciation. In Grimm's Law, for instance, to put *th* for *t* could not be considered an alleviation, for to many people the pronunciation of *th* is by no means easy. The transition of *th* into *d* might be called a relief, but the transition of *d* into *t* was the very opposite of an alleviation of utterance.

But this was the very point I wished to establish. There are phonetic changes due to laziness, as when we pronounce *night* for *knight*, *lord* for *hláford*, *Woosta* for *Worcester*. But there are others that require a very different explanation. The changes comprised under the name of 'Grimm's Law' could never be classed as due to phonetic decay. They are collateral, dialectic varieties, fixed among different German tribes, according to the phonetic idiosyncrasies of each, and determined by influences totally different from muscular economy. No one could say that it required a greater effort to pronounce a tenuis than an aspirata or a media, for we see that the Gothic speakers pronounced all these varieties with equal facility. I therefore entered very fully, perhaps too fully, into the question why each of these German tribes had fixed on tenuis, media, and aspirata in their own way, and in a way so different from Sanskrit, Greek, Latin, Celtic, and Slavonic. I am assured that this distinction also between phonetic decay and dialectic growth is now generally admitted and requires no further proof. But I must say that in several recent publications this distinction is by no means strictly observed. We are treated again and again to transitions of one consonant into another by what are called 'almost imperceptible changes.' With these almost imperceptible changes, almost everything becomes possible in the history of language.

False Analogy.

Among the causes producing change in language, whether we call that change growth or decay, I had to point out one more, which I called *False Analogy*. In this case the facts themselves to which I appealed have never been contested, but the name itself has been strongly condemned. I am not one of those who consider that a name is of little consequence, and I quite see that False Analogy is an expression that may produce a wrong impression. When I appealed [1] to such forms as Ital. *essendo* from *essere*, like *credendo* from *credere*, Span. *somos, sois, son*, as if we had in Latin *sumus, sutis, sunt*, as the result of false analogy, I did not thereby wish to dispute the right of language to give birth to such grammatical monsters. We must admit that, in language, whatever is is right, and that without the far-reaching influence of analogy, language would never have become what it is. I laid myself particular stress on the levelling influence exercised by children on the spoken, and afterwards on the written language. But though *bad, badder*, and *baddest*, I *goed*, I *coomed*, I *catched*, may in time become classical, I thought that for the present they might be put down as the result of a mistaken analogy on the part of our juvenile offenders. So far back as 1856 I had

[1] Last ed. i. p. 74; new ed. vol. ii. pp. 220, 221.

directed¹ attention to what may be called Germanisms in French. These also may be treated as the result of a mistaken analogy; for instance, in such words as *contrée, Gegend, avenir, Zukunft,* &c. If I was wrong, from the grammarian's point of view, in qualifying all such analogies as false, I am now quite prepared to recognise that even mistaken analogy is a legitimate principle in the development of language, though I must add that to appeal to it too often as a panacea for all etymological troubles may become a new source of danger to our studies.

The lessons of Modern Languages.

There is one more point which at the time when I published my lectures had to be established by the strongest arguments—I mean the true importance of the study of modern languages. There was then a strong prejudice against mixing up modern with ancient philology. The Comparative Grammar of the Romanic languages by Professor Dietz was read with a kind of patronising interest, but as to placing it by the side of Bopp's Comparative Grammar of the Aryan languages, that was not to be thought of. The principle of Geology which I applied to the Science of Language,² namely that we must begin with what is known and then proceed to what is unknown, was by no means accepted as a matter of course, whereas now, who is there to doubt it?

---

[1] Kuhn's *Zeitschrift*, vol. v. p. 11, *Über deutsche Schattirung Romanischer Worte.*

[2] *Lectures*, vol. ii. p. 13.

I mention all this, not in order to claim the merit of having initiated these various theories, but simply in order to explain why much that must now seem superfluous and tedious in my Lectures was absolutely necessary thirty years ago. Whoever studies the history of any science, or whoever has been able himself to watch the progress of a science for a long number of years, knows but too well how little there is that can really be called original. Leibniz knew the importance of modern languages as well as any one of us. 'We must begin,' he wrote, 'with studying the modern languages which are within our reach, in order to compare them with one another, to discover their differences and affinities, and then to proceed to those which have preceded them in former ages, in order to show their filiation and their origin, and then to ascend step by step to the most ancient of tongues, the analysis of which must lead us to the only trustworthy conclusions.'[1] But in the course of time many things that were known are forgotten again, what was accepted for a time is rejected and has to be re-established, and the progress of human knowledge seems often like the motion of a pendulum, or rather like a spiral movement, returning again and again to the same point, and yet, we may hope, attaining at each turn to a higher elevation.

[1] *Lectures on the Science of Language*, vol. ii. p. 13.

Progress of Comparative Philology.

There have been of late repeated complaints, chiefly on the part of classical scholars, that Comparative Philology has produced nothing really new since the days of Bopp, Pott, and Grimm, while on the other hand we have been told that new eras are constantly dawning upon us, and that everything written before each successive era is perfectly antiquated, prescientific, antediluvian. The truth lies, as usual, between the two extremes. Comparative philologists have not been idle, though, of course, after a new world has once been discovered, we must not expect immediately another Columbus. There has been neither stagnation, nor have there been any cataclysms. Like every vigorous science, the Science of Language has grown and is growing with that steady continuity which is the surest sign of a healthy life.

Relationship of Languages.

Let us look at some of the more important problems. The relationship of languages has not been much modified of late years, and the principles of classification have remained much the same. Thirty years ago, it was a recognised principle that languages must be classified according to their grammar, not according to their dictionary, because, though the dictionary might be mixed, the grammar could never be so. After a time this statement seemed too dogmatic, and very learned books were written to prove that no language was entirely unmixed, and that even grammatical forms might be borrowed from one language by another. But soon there followed a reaction, the pendulum swung back, and it was perceived that, though ready-made grammatical forms might in certain cases be borrowed, and new grammatical forms be created by analogy, yet there was this difference, that in every language the real grammatical elements are historical survivals of an earlier stage during which living elements became formal, and that such grammatical forms must grow, and can never be borrowed.

There has been no lack of new pedigrees for the Aryan family of speech by Schleicher, Schmidt, Fick, and others, but on this point also we seem to have come back to the conviction that beyond the broad fact of the bifurcation into a North-Western and South-Eastern division, it is impossible to determine how long after that event certain members of the North-Western branch remained united, before they became finally settled as independent national languages. The germs of the differences between the Aryan languages have in many cases been traced back to a period previous even to the first Aryan Separation.[1]

Home of the Âryas.

The question as to the *Original Home of the Âryas* is of small importance to the student of Comparative

---

[1] See Inaugural Lecture, *On the Results of Comparative Philology*, 1872 (*Selected Essays*, vol. i. p. 174).

Philology, but it is attractive in the eyes of the general reader. Much light has been shed on it by various scholars, much darkness also has been thrown over it by unscholarly writers. But how much the materials have increased, how much more is now known about it than formerly, may best be seen in Schrader's *Prehistoric Antiquities of the Aryan Race*, 1890, in which that question is very ably and carefully discussed.[1]

Phonetic Laws.

The greatest progress, however, has been made in the critical treatment of what are called *Phonetic Laws*. The discoveries in this department are less startling and attract less attention outside the narrow circle of scholars. But they are nevertheless of the greatest value, and give evidence, not only of minute accuracy in observation, but of brilliant genius in combination. We have been taught that many phonetic changes which were thought to be impossible are possible, and that many which we thought possible are impossible. Etymologies that were almost universally accepted have been rejected, others little dreamt of have been firmly established.

Three Periods of Comparative Philology.

In one sense it may truly be said that we have entered into a third period of Comparative Philology,

---

[1] See also, *Biographies of Words and the Home of the Aryas*, 1888.

a period by no means less important than the two which preceded it. It is necessary in every branch of scientific research to take stock from time to time, and all the more so in a new and constantly progressing science. There have been three such stock-takings in Comparative Philology. The first was represented by Bopp's Comparative Grammar, 1833 to 1852, third edition 1868-71; the second by Schleicher's *Compendium*, first edition 1862, fourth edition 1876; the third by Brugmann's *Grundriss der Vergleichenden Grammatik*, the first volume of which was published in 1886, the second in 1889.

A mere comparison of these three works will prove that the progress of Comparative Philology has been rapid, but, at the same time, continuous. Schleicher has not superseded Bopp, nor Brugmann Schleicher, but as Schleicher's work added not only to the strength of the foundations, but also to the height of the building, so has Brugmann's work increased its depth, its height, and its width. The disappointment which has been expressed at Brugmann's *Grundriss* seems to me hardly justified. If people expected an entirely new revelation, a temple built on the ruins of ancient systems, a complete annihilation of Bopp, Grimm, Pott, Benfey, Schleicher, Curtius, and all the rest, no doubt they have been disappointed. Brugmann's work is written in a critical, but at the same time in an historical spirit. The facts on which it rests are on the whole the same which had been brought together by the industry of his predecessors, but their treatment shows a decided advance.

Nothing is more troublesome and more thankless than to prepare a complete and accurate survey of the work done by our predecessors and fellow-workers, and to award to friends and foes that amount of praise and blame which they and their labours seem to deserve in our own eyes. We should therefore be all the more grateful to those who, like Bopp, Schleicher, and Brugmann, undertake from time to time that laborious and often invidious task. If we consider that Brugmann's *Grundriss* represents the results of a period filled with the many original contributions of such men as Ascoli, Bartholomae, Bréal, Bugge, Collitz, Dowse, Fick, Henry, Hübschmann, Kluge, Merlo, Osthoff, Rhys, Saussure, Sayce, Schmidt, Schrader, Stokes, Sweet, Verner, Windisch and many others, while Brugmann himself has probably contributed more original research than any one else, we certainly have a right to place his work by the side of Bopp's and Schleicher's great works. But though it marks a new period, we may hope nevertheless that it may prove but a stepping-stone in the triumphant advance of the Science of Language.

As my lectures are chiefly concerned with the general principles of the Science of Language, I found it impossible to give so full an account of the labours of Brugmann and other more recent scholars as they deserve. When treating of purely phonetic questions, such as Grimm's Law for instance, I have tried to supplement what I had formerly written by giving a short account of the later discoveries of Grassmann, Verner, Paul, and others. In other cases I have simply, in deference to more recent discoveries, left out etymologies no longer tenable, or supplied their place by others of a less doubtful character. But some of the most important discoveries, such as the original Aryan system of vowels, their influence on preceding consonants, the true meaning of nasalisation, of Guna and Vriddhi, names which I still venture to retain,[1] the different classes of gutturals, and the far-reaching action of the Aryan accent, could be but rarely alluded to in these lectures, which are chiefly intended to give results now generally accepted, to define the limits of the Science of Language, to determine its relation to other sciences, to exhibit its materials, to describe and justify its principles, and to point out the high aims of which we ought never to lose sight.

I cannot close this preface without expressing my gratitude for the kindness and indulgence with which these lectures have been received by scholars and students in every part of the world. They have more than realised the objects which I had in view in writing them. Again and again I have received letters from unknown friends, suggesting improvements, correcting mistakes, and furnishing new materials for my studies. To all of these I tender my warmest thanks. I ought to mention, however

[1] See Appendix to *Science of Thought*, p. 619.

more particularly two scholars who have rendered me valuable assistance while I was carrying this new edition through the Press, the Rev. A. L. Mayhew and Dr. Joseph Wright. The former pointed out to me many etymologies, now antiquated or replaced by better ones; to the latter all the credit is due, if the ever-shifting and changing spelling of Anglo-Saxon and other Teutonic words has been rendered uniform in this new edition, according to the standard of spelling now generally approved in England.

F. MAX MÜLLER.

IGHTHAM MOTE, KENT:
   Aug. 30, 1890.

PREFACE TO THE FIRST EDITION.

MY Lectures on the Science of Language are here printed as I had prepared them in manuscript for the Royal Institution. When I came to deliver them, a considerable portion of what I had written had to be omitted, and, in now placing them before the public in a more complete form, I have gladly complied with a wish expressed by many of my hearers. As they are, they form only a short abstract of several courses delivered from time to time in Oxford, and they do not pretend to be more than an introduction to a science far too comprehensive to be treated successfully in so small a compass.

My object, however, will have been obtained, if I should succeed in attracting the attention, not only of the scholar, but of the philosopher, the historian, and the theologian, to a science which concerns them all; and which, though it professes to treat of words only, teaches us that there is more in words than is dreamt of in our philosophy. I quote from Bacon: 'Men believe that their reason is lord over their words, but it happens, too, that words exercise a reciprocal and reactionary power over our intellect.' 'Words, as a

Tartar's bow, shoot back upon the understanding of the wisest, and mightily entangle and pervert the judgment.'

M. M.

OXFORD: *June* 11, 1861.

PREFACE TO THE FIFTH EDITION.

THE fifth edition of my Lectures on the Science of Language has been carefully revised, but the main features of the work have not been altered. I have added some new facts that seemed to me essential for strengthening certain arguments, and I have omitted or altered what was really no longer tenable. But I have not attempted to re-write any portion of my Lectures, or to give to them that form which I should wish to give to them, if now, after the lapse of five years, I had to write them again.

In one or two cases only, where my meaning had been evidently misapprehended even by unprejudiced critics, I have tried to express myself more definitely and clearly. Thus in my last Lecture, where I had to speak of the origin of roots, I had quoted the opinion of the late Professor Heyse of Berlin, but I never meant to convey the impression that I adopted that opinion. I look upon it as a mere illustration, and nothing more, and I never held myself in any way responsible for it.

Nor did I wish to attach any mysterious meaning to the purely preliminary definition which I gave of roots, by calling them 'phonetic types.' I might have called them phonetic moulds, or typical sounds, as well as phonetic types; and all that I wished to convey by this expression was that roots are like firm moulds in which all words are cast; that they are like sharply cut types of which numerous impressions have been taken; that, in fact, every consonant and every vowel in them is settled, and that therefore no etymology is admissible which does not account for every link in that long chain of changes which connects, for instance, the Sanskrit root vid, to know, with the English adverb *historically*. It is the definiteness of these roots which alone has imparted definiteness to etymological research, and it was this important characteristic, their definiteness, which I wished to impress on my hearers by using the name of phonetic types. In etymological researches it matters little what opinion we hold on the origin of roots, as long as we agree that, with the exception of a number of purely mimetic expressions, all words, such as we find them, whether in English or in Sanskrit, encumbered with prefixes and suffixes, and mouldering away under the action of phonetic corruption, must in the last instance be traced back, by means of definite phonetic laws, to those definite primary forms which we are accustomed to call roots. These roots stand like barriers between the chaos and the cosmos of human speech, and they alone prevent that 'ugly rush' which would follow, and which has followed, wherever words have been derived straight from imitations of the sounds of nature or from interjections.

There is, no doubt, a higher interest which leads the philosopher to inquire into the nature of these phonetic types, and tempts him to transcend the narrow limits of the purely positive science of language. I value as much as any one the labours of Mr. Wedgwood and the Rev. F. W. Farrar in their endeavours to trace the origin of roots back to interjections, imitations, or so-called vocal gestures. I believe that both have thrown much light on a very difficult problem, and as long as such researches are confined to the genesis of roots, without trenching on etymology in the ordinary sense of that term, I mean, on the formation and the history of words, Mr. Farrar is quite right in counting me not as an opponent, but as a neutral, if not an ally.

M. M.

St. Ives, Cornwall:
20th Sept. 1866.

PREFACE TO THE SIXTH EDITION.

IN revising once more the two volumes of my Lectures on the Science of Language, I have fully availed myself of the help and counsel of my numerous reviewers and correspondents. As my Lectures were reprinted in America, and translated into German, French, Italian, Hungarian, and Russian, the number of reviews, essays, and even independent books which they have elicited has become considerable, and the task of examining them all was not an easy, nor always a grateful one. Yet I have but seldom read a review, whether friendly or unfriendly, without being able to correct a mistake, or without feeling called upon to improve a sentence that had been misunderstood, to soften an expression that had given offence, to insert a new fact, or to allude to a new theory. Although my general views on the Science of Language have remained unchanged, the mere number of pages will show how many additions have been made, while a careful reader will easily discover how much has been changed, and, I hope, improved in my Lectures since they were first delivered at the Royal Institution in 1861 and 1863.

Though I have protested before, I must protest once more against the supposition that the theory on the origin of language which I explained at the end of my first course, and which I distinctly described as that of Professor Heyse of Berlin, was ever held by myself. It is a theory which, if properly understood, contains some truth, but it offers an illustration only, and in no way a real solution of the problem. I have abstained in my Lectures from propounding any theory on the origin of language, first, because I believe that the Science of Language may safely begin with roots as its ultimate facts, leaving what lies beyond to the psychologist and metaphysician; secondly, because I hold that a theory on the origin of language can only be thoroughly treated in close connection with the theory on the origin of thought, i.e. with the fundamental principles of mental philosophy. Although in treating of the history of the Science of Language I found it necessary in my Lectures to examine some of the former theories on the origin of language, and to show their insufficiency in the present state of our science, I carefully abstained from going beyond the limits which I had traced for myself. Much has been written during the last ten years on the origin of language, but the only writer who seems to me to have approached the problem in an independent, and at the same time a truly scientific spirit, is Dr. Bleek, in his essay *Über den Ursprung der Sprache*, published at the Cape in 1867. I am not surprised that his essay should have been received with marked favour by the most eminent physiologists, but I think, nevertheless, that in the minds of philosophical readers it will leave a strong conviction that researches into the origin of language transcend the domain of the physiologist as well as of the philologist, and require for their solution a complete mastery of the problems of psychology. At all events it seems now generally admitted that a mere revival of the mimetic or onomatopœic theory on the origin of words would be an anachronism in the history of our science. That Mr. Darwin in his fascinating work 'On the Descent of Man' should incline towards the mimetic theory is but natural, though it seems to me that even if it were possible to revive the theories of Demokritos and Epikuros, language, articulate and definite language, language derived, as it has been proved to be, not from shrieks, but from roots, i. e. from general ideas, would still remain what I called it in my first course of Lectures, *our Rubicon which no brute will dare to cross* (vol. i. p. 403).

On other points I think that those who have done me the honour of carefully examining and freely criticising my Lectures will find that not one of their remarks has been neglected; and I can honestly say that, where I have retained my own opinions against the arguments of other scholars, it has not been done without careful consideration. In some cases my critics will see that I have given up positions which they had proved to be no longer tenable; in others, I have indicated, by a few additional words, that I was prepared for their objections, and able to meet them; in others, again, the fact that I have left what I had written without any change must show that I consider their objections futile. It would have been easy to answer some of my rather over-confident critics, and I confess it was sometimes difficult to resist the temptation, particularly when one finds oneself blamed, as happens not unfrequently, for having followed Copernicus rather than Ptolemæus. 'Οψιμαθεῖς *quam sint insolentes non ignoras*. But controversy, particularly in public, is always barren of good results. I can now look back on five and twenty years of literary work, and whatever disappointment I may feel in seeing how little has been done and how much more remains to be done, and probably never will be done, I have at least this satisfaction, that I have never wasted one hour in personal controversy. I have grappled with opinions, but never with their propounders; and, though I have carefully weighed what has been proved against me, I have never minded mere words, mere assertions; still less, mere abuse.

If I may call attention to a few of the more important passages where the reader of this new edition will find new information, I should point out the following. In the first volume, p. 242 *seq.* [p. 281 of present edition], the statements on the relation of Pehlevi to Zend have been re-written in accordance with the new results that have been obtained by a more careful study of Pehlevi texts and inscriptions. In the second volume, pp. 15-23 [pp. 15-24], the question of the origin of the participle in *-ing* has been more fully treated. On p. 33 [p. 35] will be found an interesting letter on ceremonial pronouns in Chinese, by M. Stanislas Julien. The analysis and classification of vowels and consonants, on pp. 123-168 [pp. 108-136], has been carefully revised in accordance with the latest researches on this interesting subject. On pp. 139-141 [pp. 136-140] will be found my reply to Professor Czermak's important essay, *Über den Spiritus asper und lenis*. His independent testimony (p. 143, *note* 49) [p. 140, *note* 2], that the emissions of breath (the sibilants, etc.) are to be subdivided, exactly like the checks of breath (the *mutae*), into *soft* and *hard*, will show that my own division of these sounds was not unfounded, while his experiment, described on pp. 159 and 160 [p. 147], explains, and to a certain extent justifies, the names of *hard* and *soft* by the side of *surd* and *sonant*.[1] In the Fifth Lecture, *On Grimm's*

---

[1] As a specimen of the over-confident and unsuspecting criticism described above, I quote some extracts from the *North American*, in many respects, I believe, one of the best American reviews: 'But specially

Law, I have endeavoured to place my explanation of the causes which underlie that law in a clearer light, and I have answered some important arguments that had been advanced against my theory, particularly that founded on the historical changes in the names of places, such as *Strataburgum* and *Strazpuruc*.

Professor Max Müller's account of the *spiritus asper* and the *spiritus lenis*, and his explanation of the difference between such sounds as *z*, *v*, *b*, on the one hand, and *s*, *f*, *p*, on the other, is to be rejected. We have a right to be astonished that he revives for these two classes of letters the old names "*soft*" and "*hard*," which have happily for some time been going out of use, and fully adopts the distinction which they imply, although this distinction has been so many times exploded, and the difference of the two classes shown to consist in the intonation or non-intonation of the breath during their utterance. It is in vain that he appeals to the Hindu grammarians in his support: they are unanimous against him—not one of them fails to see and define correctly the difference between "sonant" and "surd" letters.'

I do not blame a writer in the *North American Review* for not knowing that I myself have run full tilt against the terminology of 'hard' and 'soft' consonants as unscientific (unwissenschaftlich), and that I was one of the first to publish and translate in 1856 the more scientific classification into 'surd' and 'sonant,' consonants as contained in the Rigveda-prâtiçâkhya. But the Reviewer might surely have read the *Lecture* which he reviewed, where on page 130 (now page 144), I said: 'The distinction which, with regard to the first breathing or spiritus, is commonly called *asper* and *lenis*, is the same which, in other letters, is known by the names of *hard* and *soft*, *surd* and *sonant*, *tenuis* and *media*.'

The same Review says: 'The definition of the *wh* in *when*, as a simple whispered counterpart of *w* in *wen* instead of a *w* with a prefixed aspiration, is, we think, clearly false.' Now on a question concerning the correct pronunciation of English, it might seem impertinence in me were I not at once to bow to the authority of the *North American Review*. Still the writer might have suspected that on such a point a foreigner would not write at random, and if he had consulted the highest authorities on phonetics in England, and, I believe, in America too, he would have found that they agree with my own description of the two sounds of *w* and *wh*. See *Lectures*, vol. ii. p. 148, note 55 [p. 146, *note* 2].

My derivation of *Earl*, *Graf*, and *King*, which had been challenged, have been defended on pp. 280, 281, and 284 [pp. 317-322], and the question whether the reported initial digamma in the name of Helena renders a comparison between Helena and Saramâ impossible has been fully discussed on pp. 516 *seq.* [pp. 586 *seq.*]

Lastly, I wish to call attention to a letter with which I have been honoured by Mr. Gladstone (vol. ii. pp. 440-444) [pp. 507-511], and in which his opinions on the component elements of Greek Mythology, which I had somewhat misapprehended, will be found stated with great precision.

M. M.

Oxford: *April* 1871.

CONTENTS.

CHAPTER I.

THE SCIENCE OF LANGUAGE A PHYSICAL SCIENCE.

                                                                                                    PAGE

Name of the science of language — The physical sciences — The three stages, empirical, classificatory, theoretical — The empirical stage — Practical character of the science of language — Language the barrier between man and beast — The classificatory stage — The theoretical stage — The science of language a physical science 1-27

CHAPTER II.

THE GROWTH OF LANGUAGE IN CONTRADISTINCTION TO THE HISTORY OF LANGUAGE.

Objections — Language the work of man — Has language a history? — Changes in language — Growth of language, not history — Language independent of political history — Causes of change in language — Phonetic decay — No phonetic decay in Chinese — Phonetic decay in Sanskrit — Grammatical forms produced by phonetic decay — Dialects — Two kinds of dialects — Dialect, the natural state of language — Wealth of dialects — Growth *versus* history of language — Latin and Neo-latin — Influence of literature — Growth of language, its true meaning — History of language, its true meaning — Recapitulation — Grammar, the principle of classification — No mixed language 28-87

CHAPTER III.

THE EMPIRICAL STAGE.

Language studied in India and Greece — Empirical stage — Grammar — Study of foreign languages — Interpreters — Travels of Greek philosophers — Barbarians learning Greek — Berosus, Menander, Manetho — Scholars at Alexandria — The article in Greek — Cases — Dionysius Thrax — Teachers of Greek at Rome — Greek influences at Rome — Crates of Pergamus — Carneades — Alexander Polyhistor — Varro, Lucilius, Cicero — Caesar, de Analogia — Grammatical terminology — Genitive case . . 86–122

CHAPTER IV.

THE CLASSIFICATORY STAGE.

Grammatical study of Sanskrit — The facts of grammar — Grammar in Chinese — Grammar in Finnish — The origin of grammatical forms — Historical study of languages — Lineal relationship — Collateral relationship — Classification of languages — Barbarians — Influence of Christianity — Work done by missionaries — Semitic languages — Hebrew, the primitive language — Leibniz — Leibniz collects materials — Adelung . . . 123–161

CHAPTER V.

THE DISCOVERY OF SANSKRIT.

Imperfect classification — The language of India — Vedic Sanskrit — Asoka's inscriptions — Grammatical and ungrammatical Prâkrits — Grammatical Prâkrits — Ungrammatical Prâkrits, Asoka's inscriptions — The Gâthâ dialect — Ancient Apabhramsas — Two classes of Asoka's inscriptions — Introduction of writing — Difficulty of writing a spoken language — Renaissance of Sanskrit literature — The modern vernaculars — Sinhalese . . 162–184

CHAPTER VI.

SANSKRIT AS KNOWN OUTSIDE INDIA.

PAGE

Jewish testimonies — Greek accounts of India — Chinese accounts of India — Persian accounts of India — Arab accounts of India — Alberuni — Akbar — European accounts of India — St. Francis Xavier — Filippo Sassetti — Roberto de' Nobili — Heinrich Roth — Scholars of the eighteenth century — Père Calmette — Père Pons — Paolino da S. Bartolomeo — Marco della Tomba — E. Hanxleden — Asiatic Society of Calcutta — Similarity between Sanskrit, Greek, and Latin — Père Coeurdoux — Halhed — Sir William Jones — Lord Monboddo — Dugald Stewart — Frederick Schlegel 185–230

CHAPTER VII.

GENEALOGICAL CLASSIFICATION OF LANGUAGES.

The founders of Comparative Philology — The proper place of Sanskrit in the Aryan family — The position of Provençal among the Romanic languages — Genealogical classification — English and Anglo-Saxon — Continental Saxon, Low German — Frisian — Dutch, Flemish, Old Frankish — High German — No Prototeutonic language — Ulfilas — Gothic — Scandinavian — The Edda — Italic class — Hellenic class — Celtic class — Windic class — Albanian — South-Eastern division — Indic class — Iranic class — Was Zoroaster a historical character? — Was Zoroaster the author of the Avesta? — Pehlevi — Kurdish — Balûchi — Language of Afghans and Dards — Armenian — Gipsies — South-Eastern and North-Western branches 231–290

Note on the Origin of the name Ârya 291

Note on August Friedrich Pott 303

Note on Ulfilas 307–312

CHAPTER VIII.

THE SEMITIC FAMILY.

PAGE

Comparative study of the Semitic languages — Division of the Semitic family — Aramaic — Chaldee and Syriac — Hebraic — Arabic — Himyaritic inscriptions — Ethiopic — Family likeness of the Semitic languages 313-324

CHAPTER IX.

ANALYSIS OF LANGUAGE.

Radical and formal elements — All cases originally local — Verbal terminations — Yes'r and Yes'm — East Indies and West Indies — Grammatical terminations — The Romanic future — The Teutonic weak preterite — Aryan civilisation — Horne Tooke — The root AR — The root SPAS — Classes of roots — Number of roots — Demonstrative roots — Composition 325-384

CHAPTER X.

MORPHOLOGICAL CLASSIFICATION.

Families and classes of languages — Distant relationship — Morphological classes — Three stages, radical, terminational, inflectional — Transition from one stage to another — *Radical stage* — *Terminational stage* — Rask's and Prichard's classification — Vocalic harmony — Nomad languages — Agglutination and inflection 385-405

CHAPTER XI.

URAL-ALTAIC FAMILY.

The five classes of the Ural-Altaic family — Samoyedic, Tungusic, Mongolic, Turkic, Finno-Ugric — Samoyedic class — Altaic languages — Tungusic class — Mongolic class — Turkic class — Turkish grammar — Finno-Ugric class — Castrén's classification —

Hunfalvy's classification — Budenz's classification — Donner's classification — Finno-Ugric family — Spreading of the Finno-Ugric languages — Geographical distribution — The Fins and their literature — The Ests and their literature — Finno-Ugric philology 406–442

CHAPTER XII.

SURVEY OF LANGUAGES.

The Northern and Southern divisions of the Turanian class — South-Turanian languages — Tamulic languages — Munda languages — Taic languages — Bhotiya languages — Languages of Farther India — Languages of the Caucasus — Egypt — Sub-semitic languages — Languages of Africa — America — Oceanic languages — *Inflectional stage* 443–454

CHAPTER XIII.

THE QUESTION OF THE COMMON ORIGIN OF LANGUAGES.

The exhaustive character of the morphological classification — Common origin of languages — Language and race — Comparative philology — Biblical genealogies — Formal relationship of languages — True meaning of the problem of the common origin of languages 455–476

CHAPTER XIV.

THE THEORETICAL STAGE.

The problem of the origin of language — Man and Brute — Language, the barrier between man and brute — Roots — The Bow-wow and Pooh-pooh theories — The *Primum cognitum* — Adam Smith — Leibniz — The *Primum appellatum* — Reason and language — Roots as phonetic types — Origin and confusion of tongues 477–536

INDEX 537

THE SCIENCE OF LANGUAGE.

CHAPTER I.

THE SCIENCE OF LANGUAGE A PHYSICAL SCIENCE.

Name of the Science of Language.

THE SCIENCE OF LANGUAGE is a science of very modern date. We cannot trace its lineage much beyond the beginning of our century, and it is scarcely received as yet on a footing of equality by the older branches of learning. Its very name is still unsettled, and the various titles that have been given to it in England, France, and Germany are so vague and varying that they have led to the most confused ideas among the public at large as to the real objects of this new science. We hear it spoken of as Comparative Philology, Scientific Etymology, Phonology, and Glossology. In France it has received the convenient, but somewhat barbarous, name of *Linguistique*. If we must have a Greek title for our science, we might derive it either from *mythos*, word, or from *logos*, speech. But the title of *Mythology* is already occupied, and *Logology* would jar too much on classical ears. We need not waste our time in criticising these names, as none of them has as yet received that universal sanction which belongs to the titles of other modern sciences, such as Geology or Comparative Anatomy; nor will there be much difficulty in christening our young science after we have once ascertained its birth, its parentage, and its character. I myself prefer the simple designation of the Science of Language, though I fear that in these days of high-sounding titles, this plain name will hardly meet with general acceptance.

The Physical Sciences.

From the name we now turn to the meaning of our science. But before we enter upon a definition of its subject-matter, and determine the method which ought to be followed in our researches, it will be useful to cast a glance at the history of the other sciences, among which the science of language now, for the first time, claims her place. The history of a science is, as it were, its biography; and as we buy experience cheapest in studying the lives of others, we may, perhaps, guard our young science from some of the follies and extravagances inherent in youth by learning a lesson for which other branches of human knowledge have had to pay more dearly.

The Three Stages, Empirical, Classificatory, Theoretical.

There is a certain uniformity in the history of most sciences. If we read such works as Whewell's *History of the Inductive Sciences* or Humboldt's *Kosmos*, we find that the origin, the progress, the causes of failure and success have been the same for almost every branch of human knowledge. There are three marked periods or stages in the history of every one of them, which we may call the *Empirical*, the *Classificatory*, and the *Theoretical*. However humiliating it may sound, every one of our sciences, however grand their present titles, can be traced back to the most humble and homely occupations of half-savage tribes. It was not the true, the good, and the beautiful which spurred the early philosophers to deep researches and bold discoveries.

The Empirical Stage.

The foundation-stone of the most glorious structures of human ingenuity in ages to come was supplied by the pressing wants of a patriarchal and semi-barbarous society. The names of some of the most ancient departments of human knowledge tell their own tale. Geometry, which at present declares itself free from all sensuous impressions, and treats of its points and lines and planes as purely ideal conceptions, not to be confounded with the coarse and imperfect representations as they appear on paper to the human eye—geometry, as its very name declares, began with measuring a garden or a field. It is derived from the Greek *gé*, land, ground, earth, and *métron*, measure. Botany, the science of plants, was originally the science of *botánē*, which in Greek does not mean a plant in general, but fodder, from *bóskein*, to feed. The science of plants would have been called Phytology, from the Greek *phytón*, a plant.[1] The founders of Astronomy were not the poet or the philosopher, but the sailor and the farmer. The early poet may have admired the 'mazy dance of planets,' and the philosopher may have speculated on the heavenly

[1] See Jessen, *Was heisst Botanik?* 1861.

harmonies; but it was to the sailor alone that a knowledge of the glittering guides of heaven became a question of life and death. It was he who calculated their risings and settings with the accuracy of a merchant and the shrewdness of an adventurer; and the names that were given to single stars or constellations clearly show that they were invented by the ploughers of the sea and of the land. The moon, for instance, the golden hand on the dark dial of heaven, was called by them the Measurer—the measurer of time; for time was measured by nights, and moons, and winters, long before it was reckoned by days, and suns, and years.

Moon[1] is a very old word. It was *mône* in Anglo-Saxon, and was used there, not as a feminine, but as a masculine; for the moon was originally a masculine, and the sun a feminine, in all Teutonic languages; and it is only through the influence of classical models that in English moon has been changed into a feminine, and sun into a masculine. It was a most unlucky assertion which Mr. Harris made in his *Hermes*, that all nations ascribe to the sun a masculine, and to the moon a feminine gender.[2] The fact is that in all Teutonic languages the sun was originally a feminine, the moon a masculine. In the mythology of the Edda, *Mâni*, the moon, is the son,

---

[1] Kuhn's *Zeitschrift für vergleichende Sprachforschung*, b. ix. s. 140. In the Edda the moon is called *ârtali*, year-teller; a Bask name for moon is *argi-izari*, light-measure. See *Dissertation critique et apologétique sur la Langue basque*, p. 28.

[2] Horne Tooke, p. 27, note. Pott, *Studien zur griechischen Mythologie*, 1859, p. 304. Grimm, *Deutsche Grammatik*, iii. p. 349. Bleek, *Ueber den Ursprung der Sprache*, p. xviii. (Kapstadt, 1867.) Schultze, *Fetischismus* (1871), pp. 242-252.

Sôl, the sun, the daughter of *Mundilföri*. In Gothic *mêna*, the moon, is masculine; *sunnô*, the sun, feminine.[1] In Anglo-Saxon *môna*, gen. *mônan*, the moon, is masculine; *sunne*, gen. *sunnan*, the sun, feminine. As late as the fourteenth century we find Chaucer alluding to the sun as feminine in the rubric to his first conclusion of the Astrolabe, ' to fynde the degree in which the sonne is day by day, after *hir* cours abowte.'[2] In Old Saxon, too, *sunna* is feminine, *mâno* masculine, and in Swedish and Danish *sol* and *måna* retain the same gender. The Lithuanians also give the masculine gender to the moon, *mênů*; the feminine gender to the sun, *saule*: and in Sanskrit, though the sun is ordinarily looked upon as a male power, the most current names for the moon, such as *K̀andra*, *Soma*, *Indu*, *Vidhu*, are masculine. We are told[3] that, according to Accadian views, the moon existed before the sun, and was called the father of the gods, while, according to Semitic views, the sun came first and held the most prominent place among the gods. Hence in Accadian the moon was conceived as a man, the sun as a woman, while in Babylonian the sun was masculine, and the moon feminine. The names of the moon are frequently used in the sense of month, and these and other names for month retain the same gender. Thus *mênôths* in Gothic, *mônađ* in Anglo-Saxon are both masculine. In Greek we find *mēn*, and the Ionic *meis*, for month, always used in the masculine gender. In Latin we have the deri-

---

[1] Ulfilas uses besides, *sáuil*, probably neuter, and *sunna*, masculine. See Grimm, *Deutsche Grammatik*, iii. p. 350.
[2] Chaucer's *Treatise on the Astrolabe*, ed. Skeat, p. 14.
[3] Sayce, *Hibbert Lectures*, pp. 156, 165.

vative *ménsis*, month, and in Sanskrit we find mâs for moon, and mâsa for month, both masculine.[1]

Now, this mâs in Sanskrit is clearly derived from a root MÂ, to measure, to mete. In Sanskrit, I measure is mâ-mi; thou measurest, mâ-si; he measures, mâ-ti (or mimî-te). An instrument of measuring is called in Sanskrit mâ-tram, the Greek *métron*, our metre. Now, if the moon was originally called by the farmer the measurer, the ruler of days and weeks and seasons, the regulator of the tides, the lord of their festivals, and the herald of their public assemblies, it is but natural that he should have been conceived as a man, and not as the love-sick maiden which our modern sentimental poetry has put in his place.

It was the sailor who, before entrusting his life and goods to the winds and the waves of the ocean, watched for the rising of those stars which he called the Sailing-stars or *Pleiádes*,[2] from *plein*, to sail.[3] Navigation in the Greek waters was considered safe after the return of the Pleiades; and it closed when they disappeared. The Latin name for the *Pleiades* is *Vergiliæ*,[4] from *virga*, a sprout or twig. This name

---

[1] See Curtius, *Grundzüge der griechischen Etymologie*, No. 471.
[2] Ideler, *Handbuch der Chronologie*, b. i. s. 241, 242. H. F. Perthes, *Die Plejaden*, p. 14, note.
[3] See, however, Pott, *Etymologische Forschungen*, vol. ii. 1, p. 892. Πληϊάδες, wild doves.
[4] In the Oscan Inscription of Agnone we find a Jupiter Virgarius (djuvef verehasiof, dat. sing.), a name which Professor Aufrecht compares with that of Jupiter Viminius, Jupiter who fosters the growth of twigs (Kuhn's *Zeitschrift*, i. s. 89).—See, however, on Jupiter Viminius and his altars near the Porta Viminalis, Hartung, *Religion der Römer*, ii. 61. The Zulus called the Pleiades the *Isilimela*, the digging-stars, because, when they appear, the people begin to dig. See Calaway, *The Religious System of the Amazulu*, part iii. p. 397.

was given to them by the Italian husbandmen, because in Italy, where they became visible about May, they marked the return of summer.[1] Another constellation, the seven stars in the head of Taurus, received the name of *Hyades* or *Pluviæ* in Latin, because at the time when they rose with the sun they were supposed to announce rain. The astronomer retains these and many other names; he still speaks of the pole of heaven, of wandering and fixed stars,[2] yet he is apt to forget that these terms were not originally the result of scientific observation and classification, but borrowed from the language of those who were themselves wanderers on the sea or in the desert, and to whom the fixed stars were in full reality what their name implies, stars driven in and fixed, by which they might hold fast on the deep, as by heavenly anchors.

But although historically we are justified in saying that the first geometrician was a ploughman, the first botanist a gardener, the first mineralogist a miner, it may reasonably be objected that in this early stage a science is hardly a science yet: that measuring a field is not geometry, that growing cabbages is very far from botany, and that a butcher has no claim to the title of comparative anatomist. This is perfectly true, yet it is but right that each science should be

[1] As to their number, see M. M., *Introduction to Rig-veda*, vol. iv. p. xxxvii, and Whitney, *Journ. American Orient. Soc.* viii. p. 79.

[2] As early as the times of Anaximenes of the Ionic, and Alkmaeon of the Pythagorean, schools, the stars had been divided into travelling (ἄστρα πλανώμενα or πλανητά), and non-travelling stars (ἀπλανεῖς ἀστέρες or ἀπλανῆ ἄστρα). Aristotle first used ἄστρα δεδεμένα, or fixed stars. (See Humboldt, *Kosmos*, vol. iii. p. 28.) Πόλος, the pivot, hinge, or the pole of heaven.

reminded of these its more humble beginnings, and of the practical requirements which it was originally intended to answer. A science, as Bacon says, should be a rich storehouse for the glory of God, and the relief of man's estate. Now, although it may seem as if in the present high state of our society students were enabled to devote their time to the investigation of the facts and laws of nature, or to the contemplation of the mysteries of the world of thought, without any side-glance at the practical results of their labours, no science and no art have ever prospered and flourished among us, unless they were in some way subservient to the practical interests of society. It is true that a Lyell collects and arranges, a Faraday weighs and analyses, an Owen dissects and compares, a Herschel observes and calculates, without any thought of the immediate marketable results of their labours. But there is a general interest which supports and enlivens their researches, and that interest depends on the practical advantages which society at large derives from these scientific studies. Let it be known that the successive strata of the geologist are a deception to the miner, that the astronomical tables are useless to the navigator, that chemistry is nothing but an expensive amusement, of no use to the manufacturer and the farmer—and astronomy, chemistry, and geology would soon share the fate of alchemy and astrology. As long as the Egyptian science excited the hopes of the invalid by mysterious prescriptions (I may observe by the way that the hieroglyphic signs of our modern prescriptions have been traced back by Champollion to the real hieroglyphics of Egypt[1])—and as long as it instigated the avarice of its patrons by the promise of the discovery of gold, it enjoyed a liberal support at the courts of princes, and under the roofs of monasteries. Though alchemy did not lead to the discovery of gold, it prepared the way to discoveries more valuable. The same with astrology. Astrology was not such mere imposition as it is generally supposed to have been. It is counted a science by so sound and sober a scholar as Melancthon, and even Bacon allows it a place among the sciences, though admitting that 'it had better intelligence and confederacy with the imagination of man than with his reason.' In spite of the strong condemnation which Luther pronounced against it, astrology continued to sway the destinies of Europe; and a hundred years after Luther, the astrologer was the counsellor of princes and generals, while the founder of modern astronomy died in poverty and despair. In our time the very rudiments of astrology are lost and forgotten.[2]

Even real and useful arts, as soon as they cease to be useful, die away, and their secrets are sometimes lost beyond the hope of recovery. When after the Reformation our churches and chapels were divested

[1] Bunsen's *Egypt*, vol. iv. p. 108.
[2] According to a writer in *Notes and Queries* (2nd Series, vol. x. p. 500), astrology is not so entirely extinct as we suppose. 'One of our principal writers,' he states, 'one of our leading barristers, and several members of the various antiquarian societies, are practised astrologers at this hour. But no one cares to let his studies be known, so great is the prejudice that confounds an art requiring the highest education with the jargon of the gipsy fortune-teller.' See also H. Phillips, Jr., *Medicine and Astrology*, a paper read before the Numismatic and Antiquarian Society of Philadelphia, June 7, 1866.

of their artistic ornaments, in order to restore, in outward appearance also, the simplicity and purity of the Christian church, the colours of the painted windows began to fade away, and have never regained their former depth and harmony. The invention of printing gave the death-blow to the art of ornamental writing and of miniature-painting employed in the illumination of manuscripts; and the best artists of the present day despair of rivalling the minuteness, softness, and brilliancy combined by the humble manufacturer of the mediæval missal.

Practical Character of the Science of Language.

I speak somewhat feelingly on the necessity that every science should answer some practical purpose, because I am aware that the science of language has but little to offer to the utilitarian spirit of our age. It does not profess to help us in learning languages more expeditiously, nor does it hold out any hope of our ever realising the dream of one universal language. It simply professes to teach what language is; and this would hardly seem sufficient to secure for a new science the sympathy and support of the public at large. There are problems, however, which, though apparently of an abstruse and merely speculative character, have exercised a powerful influence for good or evil in the history of mankind. Men before now have fought for an idea, and have laid down their lives for a word; and many of the problems which have agitated the world from the earliest to our own times, belong properly to the science of language.

Much of what we now call mythology was in truth

a disease or affection (πάθος) of language. A myth means a word, but a word which, from being a name or an attribute, has been allowed to assume a more substantial existence. Many of the Greek, the Roman, the Indian, and other heathen gods are nothing but poetical names, which were gradually allowed to assume a divine personality never contemplated by their original inventors. *Eos* was a name of the dawn before she became a goddess, the wife of *Tithonos*, or the dying day. *Fatum*, or fate, meant originally what had been spoken; and before Fate became a power, even greater than Jupiter, it meant that which had once been spoken by Jupiter, and could never be changed, not even by Jupiter himself. *Zeus* originally meant the bright heaven, in Sanskrit Dyaus; and many of the stories told of him as the supreme god, had a meaning only as told originally of the bright heaven, whose rays, like golden rain, descend on the lap of the earth, the *Danaë* of old, kept by her father in the dark prison of winter. No one doubts that *Luna*, for *losna*, originally *louxna*, was simply a name of the moon; but so was likewise *Lucina*.[1] *Hekate*, too, was an old name of the moon, the feminine of *Hekatos* and *Hekatebolos*, the far-darting sun; and *Pyrrha*, the Eve of the Greeks, was nothing but a name of the red earth, and in particular of Thessaly. This mythological disease, though less virulent in modern languages, is by no means extinct even now.

[1] Luna is not, as commonly supposed, a contraction of *lucna*, but, as is shown by the dialectic form *losna*, it must be derived from *louxna*, like Zend *raokhshna*; cf. *inlustris*, for *inluxtris*. Hegmann, *Das L der indogerm. Sprachen*, 1873, p. 33.

During the middle ages the controversy between Nominalism and Realism, which agitated the church for centuries, and finally prepared the way for the Reformation, was again, as its very name shows, a controversy on names, on the nature of language, and on the relation of words to our conceptions on one side, and to the realities of the outer world on the other. Men were called heretics for believing that words such as *justice* or *truth* expressed only conceptions of our mind, not real things walking about in broad daylight.

In modern times the science of language has been called in to settle some of the most perplexing political and social questions. 'Nations and languages against dynasties and treaties,' this is what has remodelled, and will remodel still more, the map of Europe. There was a time when comparative philologists in America have been encouraged to prove the impossibility of a common origin of languages and races, in order to justify, by scientific arguments, the unhallowed theory of slavery. Never do I remember to have seen science more degraded than on the title-page of an American publication in which, among the profiles of the different races of man, the profile of the ape was made to look more human than that of the negro.

Language the Barrier between Man and Beast.

Lastly, the problem of the position of man on the threshold between the worlds of matter and spirit has of late assumed a very marked prominence among the problems of the physical and mental sciences. It has absorbed the thoughts of men who, after a long life spent in collecting, observing, and analysing, have brought to its solution qualifications unrivalled in any previous age; and if we may judge from the greater warmth displayed in discussions ordinarily conducted with the calmness of judges and not with the passion of pleaders, it might seem, after all, as if the great problems of our being, of the true nobility of our blood, of our descent from heaven or earth, though unconnected with anything that is commonly called practical, have still retained a charm of their own—a charm that will never lose its power on the mind and on the heart of man. Now, however much the frontiers of the animal kingdom have been pushed forward, so that at one time the line of demarcation between animal and man seemed to depend on a mere fold in the brain, there is *one* barrier which no one has yet ventured to touch—the barrier of language. Even those philosophers with whom *penser est sentir*,[1] who reduce all thought to feeling, and maintain that we share the faculties which are the productive causes of thought in common with beasts, are bound to confess that *as yet* no race of animals has produced a language. Lord Monboddo, for instance, admits that *as yet* no animal has been discovered in the possession of language, 'not even the beaver, who

---

[1] 'Man has two faculties, or two passive powers, the existence of which is generally acknowledged: 1, the faculty of receiving the different impressions caused by external objects, physical sensibility; and 2, the faculty of preserving the impressions caused by these objects, called memory, or weakened sensation. These faculties, the productive causes of thought, we have in common with beasts. . . . . Everything is reducible to feeling.'—*Helvetius.*

of all the animals we know, that are not, like the orang-outangs, of our own species, comes nearest to us in sagacity.'

Locke, who is generally classed together with these materialistic philosophers, and who certainly vindicated a large share of what had been claimed for the intellect as the property of the senses, recognised most fully the barrier which language, as such, placed between man and brutes. 'This I may be positive in,' he writes, 'that the power of abstracting is not at all in brutes, and that the having of general ideas is that which puts a perfect distinction between man and brutes. For it is evident we observe no footsteps in these of making use of general signs for universal ideas; from which we have reason to imagine that they have not the faculty of abstracting or making general ideas, since they have no use of *words* or any other general signs.'

If, therefore, the science of language gives us an insight into that which, by common consent distinguishes man from all other living beings; if it establishes a frontier between man and the brute, which can never be removed, it would seem to possess at the present moment peculiar claims on the attention of all who, while watching with sincere admiration the progress of comparative physiology, yet consider it their duty to enter their manly protest against a revival of the shallow theories of Lord Monboddo.

The Classificatory Stage.

But to return to our survey of the history of the physical sciences. We had examined the empirical

stage through which every science has to pass. We
saw that, for instance, in botany, a man who has travelled
through distant countries, who has collected a
vast number of plants, who knows their names, their
peculiarities, and their medicinal qualities, is not yet
a botanist, but only a herbalist, a lover of plants, or
what the Italians call a *dilettante*, from *diletture*, to
delight in a subject. The real science of plants, like
every other science, begins with the work of classification.
An empirical acquaintance with facts rises to
a scientific knowledge of facts as soon as the mind discovers
beneath the multiplicity of single productions
the unity of an organic system. This discovery is
made by means of comparison and classification. We
cease to study each flower for its own sake; and by
continually enlarging the sphere of our observation,
we try to discover what is common to many and offers
those essential points on which groups or natural
classes may be established. These classes again, in
their more general features, are mutually compared;
new points of difference, or of similarity of a more
general and higher character, spring to view, and
enable us to discover classes of classes, or families.
And when the whole kingdom of plants has thus been
surveyed, and a simple tissue of names been thrown
over the garden of nature; when we can lift it up, as
it were, and view it in our mind as a whole, as a system
well defined and complete, we then speak of the
science of plants, or botany. We have entered into
altogether a new sphere of knowledge, where the individual
is subject to the general, facts to law; we discover
thought, order, and purpose pervading the

whole realm of nature, and we seem to perceive the dark chaos of matter lighted up by the reflection of a divine mind. Such views may be right or wrong. Too hasty comparisons, or too narrow distinctions, may have prevented the eye of the observer from discovering the broad outlines of nature's plan. Yet every system, however insufficient it may prove hereafter, is a step in advance. If the mind of man is once impressed with the conviction that there must be order and law everywhere, it never rests again until all that seems irregular has been eliminated, until the full beauty and harmony of nature has been perceived, and the eye of man has, as it were, caught the eye of God beaming out from the midst of all His works. The failures of the past prepare the triumphs of the future.

Thus, to recur to our former illustration, the systematic arrangement of plants which bears the name of Linnæus, and which is founded on the number and character of the reproductive organs, failed to bring out the natural order which pervades all that grows and blossoms. Broad lines of demarcation which unite or divide large tribes and families of plants were invisible from his point of view. But in spite of this, his work was not in vain. The fact that plants in every part of the world belonged to one great system was established once for all; and even in later systems most of his classes and divisions have been preserved, because the conformation of the reproductive organs of plants happened to run parallel with other more characteristic marks of true affinity. It is the same in the history of astronomy.

Although the Ptolemæan system was a wrong one, yet even from its eccentric point of view, laws were discovered determining the true movements of the heavenly bodies. The conviction that there remains something unexplained is sure to lead to the discovery of our error. There can be no error in nature; the error must be with us. This conviction lived in the heart of Aristotle when, in spite of his imperfect knowledge of nature, he declared 'that there is in nature nothing interpolated or without connection, as in a bad tragedy;' and from his time forward every new fact and every new system have confirmed his faith.

The object of classification is clear. We understand things if we can comprehend them; that is to say, if we can grasp and hold together single facts, connect isolated impressions, distinguish between what is essential and what is merely accidental, and thus predicate the general of the individual, and class the individual under the general. This is the secret of all scientific knowledge. Many sciences, while passing through this second or classificatory stage, assume the title of comparative. When the anatomist has finished the dissection of numerous bodies, when he has given names to every organ, and discovered the distinctive functions of each, he is led to perceive similarity where at first he saw dissimilarity only. He discovers in the lower animals rudimentary indications of the more perfect organisation of the higher; and he becomes impressed with the conviction that there is in the animal kingdom the same order and purpose which pervades the endless variety of plants or any other realm of nature. He learns, if he did not know it before, that things were not created at random or in a lump, but that there is a scale which leads, by imperceptible degrees, from the lowest infusoria to the crowning work of nature—man.

The Theoretical Stage.

In this way the second or classificatory leads us naturally to the third or final stage—the theoretical, or metaphysical. If the work of classification is properly carried out, it teaches us that nothing exists in nature by accident; that each individual belongs to a species, each species to a genus; and that there are laws which underlie the apparent freedom and variety of all created things. This has given to the study of nature a new character. After the observer has collected his facts, and after the classifier has placed them in order, the student asks what is the origin and what is the purpose of all this? and he tries to soar, by means of induction, or sometimes even of divination, into regions not accessible to the mere collector. In this attempt the mind of man no doubt has frequently met with the fate of Phaeton; but, undismayed by failure, he asks again and again for his father's steeds. Physical science would never have been what it is without the impulses which it received from the philosopher, nay, even from the poet and the dreamer.

Copernicus, in the dedication of his work to Pope Paul III. (it was commenced in 1517, finished 1530, published 1543), confesses that he was brought to the discovery of the sun's central position, and of the diurnal motion of the earth, not by observation or analysis, but by what he calls the feeling of a want of symmetry in the Ptolemaic system. But who had told him that there *must* be symmetry in all the movements of the celestial bodies, or that complication was not more sublime than simplicity? And the solution of his perplexities was suggested to Copernicus, as he tells us himself, by an ancient Greek philosopher, by Philolaos, the Pythagorean. No doubt with Philolaos the motion of the earth was only a guess, or, if you like, a happy intuition, not, as it was with Tycho de Brahe and his friend Kepler, the result of wearisome observations of the orbits of the planet Mars. Nevertheless, if we may trust the words of Copernicus, it is quite possible that without that guess we should never have heard of the Copernican system. Truth is not found by addition and multiplication only. When speaking of Kepler, whose method of reasoning has been considered as unsafe and fantastic by his contemporaries as well as by later astronomers, Sir David Brewster remarks very truly, 'that, as an instrument of research, the influence of imagination has been much overlooked by those who have ventured to give laws to philosophy.' The torch of imagination is as necessary to him who looks for truth, as the lamp of study. Kepler held both, and more than that, he had the star of faith to guide him.

Let us quote in conclusion the testimony of Alexander von Humboldt as to the value of imagination, or even of faith and superstition, in the progress of human knowledge. 'At the limits of exact knowledge,' he writes, 'as from a lofty island-shore, the eye loves to glance towards distant regions. The images which it sees may be illusive; but like the illusive images which people imagined they had seen from the Canaries or the Azores, long before the time of Columbus, they may lead to the discovery of a new world.'

In the history of the physical sciences, the three stages which we have just described as the empirical, the classificatory, and the theoretical, appear generally in chronological order. I say, generally, for there have been instances, as in the case just quoted of Philolaos, where the results properly belonging to the third have been anticipated in the first stage. To the quick eye of genius one case may be like a thousand, and one experiment, well chosen, may lead to the discovery of an absolute law. Besides, there are great chasms in the history of science. The tradition of generations is broken by political or ethnic earthquakes, and the work that was nearly finished has frequently had to be done again from the beginning, when a new surface had been formed for the growth of a new civilisation. The succession, however, of these three stages is no doubt the natural one, and it is very properly observed in the study of every science. The student of botany begins as a collector of plants. Taking each plant by itself, he observes its peculiar character, its habitat, its proper season, its popular or unscientific name. He learns to distinguish between the roots, the stem, the leaves, the flower, the calyx, the stamina, and pistils. He learns, so to say, the practical grammar of the plant before he can begin to compare, to arrange, and classify. Again, no one can enter with advantage on the third stage of any physical science without having passed through the second. No one can study *the* plant, no one can understand the bearing of such a work as, for instance, Professor Schleiden's *Life of the Plant*,[1] who has not studied the life of plants in the wonderful variety, and in the still more wonderful order, of nature. These last and highest achievements of inductive philosophy are possible only after the way has been cleared by previous classification. The philosopher must command his classes like regiments which obey the order of their general. Thus alone can the battle be fought and truth be conquered.

The Science of Language a Physical Science.

After this rapid glance at the history of the other physical sciences, we now return to our own, the science of language, in order to see whether it really is a science, whether it may be classed as one of the physical sciences, and whether it can be brought back to the standard of the inductive sciences. We want to know whether it has passed, or is still passing, through the three phases of physical research; whether its progress has been systematic or desultory, whether its method has been appropriate or not. But before we do this, we shall, I think, have to do something else. You may have observed that I always took it for granted that the science of language, which is best known in this country by the name of Comparative Philology, is one of the physical sciences, and that therefore its method ought

---

[1] *Die Pflanze und ihr Leben*, von M. J. Schleiden, Leipzig, 1858.

to be the same as that which has been followed with so much success in botany, geology, anatomy, and other branches of the study of nature. In the history of the physical sciences, however, we look in vain for a place assigned to comparative philology, and its very name would seem to show that it belongs to quite a different sphere of human knowledge.

There are two great divisions of human knowledge, which, according to their subject-matter, may be called *physical* and *historical*. Physical science, it has been said, deals with the works of God, historical science with the works of man. Thus the science of optics, including all the laws of light and colour, is a physical science, whereas the science of painting, with all its laws of manipulation and colouring, being that of a man-created art, is a purely historical science.[1] Now if we were to judge by its name, comparative philology, like classical philology, would seem to take rank, not as a physical, but as an historical science, and the proper method to be applied to it would be that which is followed in the history of art, of law, of politics, and religion. However, the title of comparative philology must not be allowed to mislead us. It is difficult to say by whom that title was invented; but all that can be said in defence of it is, that the founders of the science of language were chiefly scholars or philologists, and that they based their inquiries into the nature and laws of language on a comparison of as many facts as they could collect within their own special spheres of study. Neither in Germany, which may well be called the birthplace of

[1] *Intellectual Repository*, June 2, 1862, p. 217.

this science, nor in France, where it has been cultivated with brilliant success, has that title been adopted. It will not be difficult to show that, although the science of language owes much to the classical scholar, and though in return it has proved of great use to him, yet comparative philology has really nothing whatever in common with philology, in the usual meaning of the word. Philology, whether classical or oriental, whether treating of ancient or modern, of cultivated or barbarous languages, is no doubt an historical science, in the strictest sense of the word. Language is here treated simply as a means. The classical scholar uses Greek or Latin, the oriental scholar Hebrew or Sanskrit, or any other language, as a key to an understanding of the literary monuments which bygone ages have bequeathed to us, as a spell to raise from the tomb of time the thoughts of great men in different ages and different countries, and as a means ultimately to trace the social, moral, intellectual, and religious progress of the human race. In the same manner, if we study living languages, it is not for their own sake that we study grammars and vocabularies. We do so on account of their practical usefulness. We use them as letters of introduction to the best society or to the best literature of the leading nations of Europe. In comparative philology the case is totally different. In the science of language, languages are not treated as a means; language itself becomes the sole object of scientific inquiry. Dialects which have never produced any literature at all, the jargons of savage tribes, the clicks of the Hottentots, and the vocal modulations of the Indo-Chinese are as important, nay, for the solution of some of our problems, more important, than the poetry of Homer, or the prose of Cicero. We do not want to know languages, we want to know language; what language is, how it can form an instrument or an organ of thought; we want to know its origin, its nature, its laws; and it is only in order to arrive at that knowledge that we collect, arrange, and classify all the facts of language that are within our reach.

And here I must protest, at the very outset of these lectures, against the supposition that the student of language must necessarily be a great linguist. How is he to find time for acquiring what is called a practical knowledge of the hundreds of languages with which he has to deal? He does not aspire to be a Mithridates or Mezzofanti. His knowledge should be accurate, but it cannot possibly be that familiar knowledge which we can acquire in a life-time of six or seven languages, whether dead or living.

It is the grammar and the dictionary, not the literature, which form the subject of his inquiries. These he consults and subjects to a careful analysis, but he does not encumber his memory with paradigms of nouns and verbs, or with long lists of words which have never been used for the purposes of literature. It is true, no doubt, that no language will unveil the whole of its wonderful structure except to the scholar who has studied it thoroughly and critically in a number of literary works representing the various periods of its growth. Nevertheless, short lists of vocables, and imperfect sketches of a grammar, are in many instances all that the student can expect to obtain, or can hope to master and to use for the purposes he has in view. He must learn to make the best of this fragmentary information, like the comparative anatomist, who frequently learns his lessons from the smallest fragments of fossil bones, or the vague pictures of animals brought home by unscientific travellers. If it were necessary for the comparative philologist to acquire a critical or practical acquaintance with all the languages which form the subject of his inquiries, the science of language would simply be an impossibility. But we do not expect the botanist to be an experienced gardener, or the geologist a miner, or the ichthyologist a practical fisherman. Nor would it be reasonable to object in the science of language to the same division of labour which is necessary for the successful cultivation of subjects much less comprehensive. Though much of what we might call the realm of language is lost to us for ever, though whole periods in the history of language are by necessity withdrawn from our observation, yet the mass of human speech that lies before us, whether in the petrified strata of ancient literature or in the countless variety of living languages and dialects, offers a field as large, if not larger, than any other branch of physical research. It is impossible to fix the exact number of known languages, but their number can hardly be less than nine hundred.[1]

That, before the beginning of our century, this vast field should never have excited the curiosity of the

[1] Balbi in his *Atlas* counts 860. Cf. Pott, *Rassen*, p. 230; *Etymologische Forschungen*, ii. 83. (Second Edition.)

natural philosopher may seem surprising, more surprising even than the indifference with which former generations treated the lessons which the very stones seemed to teach of the life still throbbing in the veins and on the very surface of the earth. The saying that 'familiarity breeds contempt' would seem applicable to the subjects of both these sciences. The gravel of our walks hardly seemed to deserve a scientific treatment, and the language which every ploughboy can speak could not be raised without an effort to the dignity of a scientific problem. Man had studied every part of nature, the mineral treasures in the bowels of the earth, the flowers of each season, the animals of every continent, the laws of storms, and the movements of the heavenly bodies; he had analysed every substance, dissected every organism, he knew every bone and muscle, every nerve and fibre of his own body to the ultimate elements which compose his flesh and blood; he had meditated on the nature of his soul, on the laws of his mind, and tried to penetrate into the last causes of all being—and yet language, without the aid of which not even the first step in this glorious career could have been made, remained unnoticed. Like a veil that hung too close over the eye of the human mind, it was hardly perceived. In an age when the study of antiquity attracted the most energetic minds, when the ashes of Pompeii were sifted for the playthings of Roman life; when parchments were made to disclose, by chemical means, the erased thoughts of Grecian thinkers; when the tombs of Egypt were ransacked for their sacred contents, and the palaces of Babylon and Nineveh forced to surrender the clay diaries of Nebuchadnezzar; when everything, in fact, that seemed to contain a vestige of the early life of man was anxiously searched for and carefully preserved in our libraries and museums—language, which in itself carries us back far beyond the cuneiform literature of Assyria and Babylonia and the hieroglyphic documents of Egypt; which connects ourselves, through an unbroken chain of speech, with the very ancestors of our race, and still draws its life from the first utterances of the human mind—language, the living and speaking witness of the whole history of our race, was never cross-examined by the student of history, was never made to disclose its secrets until questioned, and, so to say, brought back to itself within the last fifty years, by the genius of a Humboldt, Bopp, Grimm, Bunsen, and others. If we consider that, whatever view we take of the origin and growth of language, nothing new has ever been added to the substance of language,[1] that all its changes have been changes of form, that no new root or radical has ever been invented by later generations, as little as one single element has ever been added to the material world in which we live; if we bear in mind that in one sense, and in a very just sense, we may be said to handle the very words which issued from the mouth of man, when he gave names to 'all cattle, and to the fowl of the air, and to every beast of the field,' we shall perceive, I believe, that the science of language has claims on our attention, such as few sciences can rival or excel.

[1] Pott, *Etym. Forsch.* ii. 220.

CHAPTER II.

THE GROWTH OF LANGUAGE IN CONTRADISTINCTION TO THE HISTORY OF LANGUAGE.

Objections.

IN claiming for the science of language a place among the physical sciences,[1] I was prepared to meet with many objections. The circle of the physical sciences seemed closed, and it was not likely that a new claimant should at once be welcomed among the established branches and scions of the ancient aristocracy of learning.[2]

---

[1] Schleicher, *Die Darwinische Theorie*, 1863, p. 7, has since adopted the same view. '*Glottic*,' he says, 'or the Science of Language, is therefore one of the natural sciences; its method is on the whole the same as that of the other natural sciences.'

[2] Dr. Whewell classes the science of language as one of the palaitiological sciences; but he makes a distinction between palaitiological sciences treating of material things, for instance, geology, and others respecting the products which result from man's imaginative and social endowments, for instance, comparative philology. He excludes the latter from the circle of the physical sciences, properly so called, but he adds: 'We began our inquiry with the trust that any sound views which we should be able to obtain respecting the nature of truth in the physical sciences, and the mode of discovering it, must also tend to throw light upon the nature and prospects of knowledge of all other kinds—must be useful to us in moral, political, and philological researches. We stated this as a confident anticipation; and the evidence of the justice of our belief already begins to appear. We have seen that biology leads us to psychology, if we choose to follow the path; and thus the passage from the material to the immaterial has already unfolded itself at one point; and we now perceive that there are several large provinces of speculation which concern subjects belonging to man's immaterial nature, and which are governed by the same laws as sciences altogether physical. It is not our business to dwell on the

Language the Work of Man.

The first objection which was sure to be raised on the part of such sciences as botany, geology, or physiology is this:—Language is the work of man: it was invented by man as a means of communicating his thoughts, when mere looks and gestures proved inefficient; and it was gradually, by the combined efforts of succeeding generations, brought to that perfection which we admire in the Veda, the Bible, the Koran, and in the poetry of Homer, Dante, Shakespeare, and Goethe. Now it is perfectly true that if language be the work of man, in the same sense in which a statue, or a temple, or a poem, or a law are properly called the works of man, the science of language would have to be classed as an historical science. We should have a history of language as we have a history of art, of poetry, and of jurisprudence, but we could not claim for it a place side by side with the various branches of natural science. It is true, also, that if you consult the works of some of the most distinguished modern philosophers you will find that whenever they speak of language, they take it for granted that language is a human invention, that words are artificial signs, and that the varieties of human speech arose from different nations agreeing on

prospects which our philosophy thus opens to our contemplation; but we may allow ourselves, in this last stage of our pilgrimage among the foundations of the physical sciences, to be cheered and animated by the ray that thus beams upon us, however dimly, from a higher and brighter region.'—*Indications of the Creator*, p. 146. See also *Darwinism tested by the Science of Language*, translated from the German of Professor A. Schleicher by Dr. Al. V. W. H. Bikkers (London: Hotten, 1869), and my review of this work in 'Nature,' No. 10, Jan. 6, 1870.

different sounds as the most appropriate signs of their different ideas. This view of the origin of language was so powerfully advocated by the leading philosophers of the last century, that it has retained an undisputed currency even among those who, on almost every other point, are strongly opposed to their teaching.

A few voices have, indeed, been raised to protest against the theory of language being originally invented by man. But they were chiefly the protests of theologians who, in their zeal to vindicate the divine origin of language, were carried away far beyond the teaching of the Bible which they were anxious to defend. For in the Bible it is not the Creator who gives names to all things, but Adam. 'Out of the ground,' we read, 'the Lord God formed every beast of the field, and every fowl of the air; and brought them unto Adam to see what he would call them: and whatsoever Adam called every living creature that was the name thereof.'[1]

With the exception of this small class of philosophers, more orthodox even than the Bible,[2] the

[1] Genesis ii. 19.
[2] St. Basil was accused by Eunomius of denying Divine Providence, because he would not admit that God had created the names of all things, but ascribed the invention of language to the faculties which God had implanted in man. St. Gregory, bishop of Nyssa in Cappadocia (331–396), defended St. Basil. 'Though God has given to human nature its faculties,' he writes, 'it does not follow that therefore He produces all the actions which we perform. He has given us the faculty of building a house and doing any other work; but we, surely, are the builders, and not He. In the same manner our faculty of speaking is the work of Him who has so framed our nature; but the invention of words for naming each object is the work of our mind.' See Ladevi-Roche, *De l'Origine du Langage*, Bordeaux, 1860, p. 14; also Horne Tooke, *Diversions of Purley*, p. 19.

generally received opinion on the origin of language is that which was held by Locke, which was powerfully advocated by Adam Smith in his *Essay on the Origin of Language*, appended to his *Treatise on Moral Sentiments*, and which was adopted with slight modifications by Dugald Stewart. According to them, man must have lived for a time in a state of mutism, his only means of communication consisting in gestures of the body, and in changes of the countenance, till at last, when ideas multiplied that could no longer be pointed at with the fingers, 'they found it necessary to invent artificial signs of which the meaning was fixed by mutual agreement.'

We need not dwell on minor differences of opinion as to the exact process by which this artificial language is supposed to have been formed. Adam Smith would wish us to believe that the first artificial words were *verbs*. Nouns, he thinks, were of less urgent necessity because things could be pointed at or imitated, whereas mere actions, such as are expressed by verbs, could not. He therefore supposes that when people saw a wolf coming, they pointed at him, and simply cried out 'He comes.' Dugald Stewart, on the contrary, thinks that the first artificial words were nouns, and that the verbs were supplied by gesture; that, therefore, when people saw a wolf coming, they did not cry 'He comes,' but 'Wolf, Wolf,' leaving the rest to be imagined.[1]

But whether the verb or the noun was the first to be invented is of little importance; nor is it possible for us, at the very beginning of our inquiry into the

[1] Dugald Stewart, *Works*, vol. iii. p. 27.

nature of language, to enter upon a minute examination of a theory which represents language as a work of human art, and as established by mutual agreement as a medium of communication. While fully admitting that if this theory were true, the science of language would not come within the pale of the physical sciences, I must content myself for the present with pointing out that no one has yet explained how, without language, a discussion, however imperfect, on the merits of each word, such as must needs have preceded a mutual agreement, could have been carried on. But as it is my chief object to prove that language is not a work of human art, in the same sense as painting, or building, or writing, I must ask to be allowed, in this preliminary stage, simply to enter my protest against a theory, which, though still taught in the schools, is nevertheless, I believe, without a single fact to support its truth.

Has Language a History?

There are other objections, however, besides this, which would seem to bar the admission of the science of language to the circle of the physical sciences. Whatever the origin of language may have been, it has been remarked with a strong appearance of truth, that language has a history of its own, like art, like law, like religion; and that, therefore, the science of language belongs to the circle of the *historical*, or, as they used to be called, the *moral*, in contradistinction to the *physical* sciences. It is a well-known fact, which recent researches have not shaken, that nature is incapable of progress or improvement. The flower which the botanist observes to-day was as perfect from the beginning as it is to-day. Animals which are endowed with what is called an artistic instinct, have never brought that instinct to a higher degree of perfection. The hexagonal cells of the bee are not more regular in the nineteenth century than at any earlier period, and the gift of song has never, as far as we know, been brought to a higher perfection by our nightingale than by the Philomele of the Greeks. 'Natural History,' to quote Dr. Whewell's words,[1] 'when systematically treated, excludes all that is historical, for it classes objects by their permanent and universal properties, and has nothing to do with the narration of particular or casual facts.' Now, if we consider the large number of tongues spoken in different parts of the world with all their dialectic and provincial varieties, if we observe the great changes which each of these tongues has undergone in the course of centuries, how Latin was changed into Italian, Spanish, Portuguese, Provençal, French, Roumanian, and Roumansch; how Latin again, together with Greek, the Celtic, the Teutonic, and Slavonic languages, together likewise with the ancient dialects of India and Persia, points back to an earlier language, the mother, if we may so call it, of the whole Indo-European or Aryan family of speech; if we see how Hebrew, Arabic, and Syriac, with several minor dialects, are but different impressions of one and the same common type, and must all have flowed from the same source, the original language of the Semitic race; and if we add to these two, the Aryan and Semitic, at least one more well-established class

[1] *History of Inductive Sciences*, vol. iii. p. 531.

of languages, the Turanian, comprising the dialects of the nomad races scattered over Central and Northern Asia, the Tungusic, Mongolic, Turkic, Samoyedic, and Finnic,[1] all radii from one common centre of speech: if we watch this stream of language rolling on through centuries in three mighty arms, which, before they disappear from our sight in the far distance, may possibly show a convergence towards one common source: it would seem, indeed, as if there were an historical life inherent in language, and as if both the will of man and the power of time could tell, if not on its substance, at least on its form.

Changes in Language.

And even if the mere local varieties of speech were not considered sufficient ground for excluding language from the domain of natural science, there would still remain the greater difficulty of reconciling the historical changes affecting every one of these varieties with the recognised principles of physical science. Every part of nature, whether mineral, plant, or animal, is the same in kind from the beginning to the end of its existence, whereas few languages could be recognised as the same after the lapse of but a thousand years. The language of Alfred is so different from the English of the present day that we have to study it in the same manner as we study Greek and Latin. We can read Milton and Bacon, Shakespeare and Hooker; we can make out Wycliffe and Chaucer; but when we come to the

---

[1] Names in *ic* are names of classes as distinct from the names of single languages.

English of the thirteenth century, we can but guess its meaning, and we fail even in this with works previous to Orm and Layamon. The historical changes of language may be more or less rapid, but they take place at all times and in all countries. They have reduced the rich and powerful idiom of the poets of the Veda to the meagre and impure jargon of the modern Sepoy. They have transformed the language of the Zend-Avesta and of the mountain records of Behistûn into that of Firdûsi and the modern Persians; the language of Virgil into that of Dante, the language of Ulfilas into that of Charlemagne, the language of Charlemagne into that of Goethe. We have reason to believe that the same changes take place with even greater violence and rapidity in the dialects of savage tribes, although, in the absence of a written literature, it is extremely difficult to obtain trustworthy information. But in the few instances where careful observations have been made on this interesting subject, it has been found that among the wild and illiterate tribes of Siberia, Africa, and Siam, two or three generations are sufficient to change the whole aspect of their dialects. The languages of highly civilised nations, on the contrary, become more and more stationary, and sometimes seem almost to lose their power of change. Where there is a classical literature, and where its language has spread to every town and village, we can hardly understand how any further changes should take place. Nevertheless, the language of Rome, for so many centuries the queen of the whole civilised world, was deposed by the modern

Romance dialects, and the ancient Greek was supplanted in the end by the modern Romaic. And though the art of printing and the wide diffusion of Bibles and Prayer-books and newspapers have acted as still more powerful barriers to arrest the constant flow of human speech, we may see that the language of the authorised version of the Bible, though perfectly intelligible, is no longer the spoken language of England. In Booker's *Scripture and Prayer-book Glossary*[1] the number of words or senses of words which have become obsolete since 1611, amount to 388,[2] or nearly one fifteenth part of the whole number of words used in the Bible. Smaller changes, changes of accent and meaning, the reception of new, and the dropping of old words, we may watch as taking place under our own eyes. Rogers[3] said that 'cóntemplate is bad enough, but bálcony makes me sick,' whereas at present no one is startled by cóntemplate instead of contémplate, and bálcony has become more usual than balcóny. Thus *Roome* and *chaney*, *laylor* and *goold*, have but lately been driven from the stage by *Rome*, *china*, *lilac*, and *gold*; and some courteous gentlemen of the old school still continue to be *obleeged*

---

[1] *A Scripture and Prayer-Book Glossary*: being an explanation of obsolete words and phrases in the English Bible, Apocrypha, and Book of Common Prayer, by the Rev. J. Booker: Dublin, 1862. *The Bible Word-book*, a glossary of Old English Bible words, by J. Eastwood and W. Aldis Wright: Cambridge, 1866.

[2] *Lectures on the English Language*, by G. P. Marsh: New York, 1860, pp. 263 and 630. These lectures embody the result of much careful research, and are full of valuable observations. They have lately been published in England, with useful omissions and additions by Dr. Smith, under the title of *Handbook of the English Language*.

[3] Marsh, p. 532, *note*.

instead of being *obliged*.[1] *Force*,[2] in the sense of a waterfall, and *gill*, in the sense of a rocky ravine, were not used in classical English before Wordsworth. *Handbook*,[3] though an old Anglo-Saxon word, has but lately taken the place of *manual*; and a number of words such as *cab* for cabriolet, *buss* for omnibus, and even a verb such as *to shunt*[4] tremble still on the boundary line between the vulgar and the literary idioms. Though the grammatical changes that have taken place since the publication of the authorised version are yet fewer in number, still we may point out some. The termination of the third person singular in *th* is now entirely replaced by *s*. No one now says *he liveth*, but only *he lives*. Several of the strong imperfects and participles have assumed a new form. No one now uses *he spake*, and *he drave*, instead of *he spoke*, and *he drove*; *holpen* is replaced by *helped*; *holden* by *held*; *shapen* by *shaped*. The distinction between *ye* and *you*, the former being

---

[1] Trench, *English Past and Present*, p. 210, mentions *great*, which was pronounced *greet* in Johnson's time, and *tea*, which Pope rhymes with *obey*.

[2] Marsh, p. 589.   [3] Sir J. Stoddart, *Glossology*, p. 60.

[4] In Halliwell's *Dictionary of Archaisms* 'to shunte' is given in the sense of to delay, to put off:—

'Schape us an ansuere, and schunto yow no lengere.'
Morte Arthure, MS. Lincoln, f. 67.

Also in the sense of to shun, to move from (North):—

'Then I drew me down into a dale, whereas the dumb deer
Did shiver for a shower; but I shunted from a freyke.'
Little John Nobody, c. 1550.

In *Sir Gawayne and the Green Knight*, ed. R. Morris, Sir Gawayne is said to have shunt, i.e. to have shrunk from a blow (v. 2280; see also 2268, 1902). In the *Early English Alliterative Poems*, ed. R. Morris, Abraham is said to sit *schunt*, i.e. a-skant or a-slant (B. 605, p. 56). See Mr. R. Morris' remarks in the Glossary, p. 190; and Herbert Coleridge, Glossary, s.v.

reserved for the nominative, the latter for the other cases, is given up in modern English; and what is apparently a new grammatical form, the possessive pronoun *its*, has sprung into life since the beginning of the seventeenth century. It never occurs in the authorised version of the Bible;[1] and though it is used ten times by Shakespeare, Ben Jonson does not recognise it as yet in his English Grammar.[2]

It is argued, therefore, that as language, differing thereby from all other productions of nature, is liable to historical alterations, it is not fit to be treated in the same manner as the subject-matter of all the other physical sciences.

There is something very plausible in this objection, but if we examine it more carefully, we shall find that it rests entirely on a confusion of terms. We must distinguish between historical change and natural growth. Art, science, philosophy, and religion all have a history; language, or any other production of nature, admits, strictly speaking, of growth only.

---

[1] It was supposed to occur in the authorised version of 1611, in Leviticus xxv. 5, but the right reading here was *it*, as may be seen from the following extracts given by Lord Carysfort:
Wickliffe.—Thingis that the erthe frely bryngith forth, thou shalt not recpe.
Coverdale, 1535.—Loke what groweth of *it* self after thy harvest, &c.
Cranmer, 1541.—That whiche groweth of *the* owne accorde, &c.
Genevan, 1560.—That which groweth of *it* owne accorde of thy harvest, &c.
The Bishops', 1568.—That which groweth of *the* owne accorde of thy harvest, &c.
King James's, 1611.—That which groweth of *it* owne accord of thy harvest, &c.

[2] 'Foure Possessives: My, or Myne; Plurall, Our, ours. Thy, thine; Plurall, Your, yours. His, Hers, both in the plurall making, Their, theirs.' See *The English Grammar made by Ben Jonson*, 1640, chap. xv.

Growth of Language, not History.

Let us consider, first, that although there is a continuous change in language, it is not in the power of any man either to produce or to prevent it. We might think as well of changing the laws which control the circulation of our blood, or of adding one cubit to our stature, as of altering the laws of speech, or inventing new words according to our own pleasure. As man is the lord of nature only if he knows her laws and submits to them, the poet and the philosopher become the lords of language only if they know its laws and obey them.

When the Emperor Tiberius had made a mistake and was reproved for it by Marcellus, another grammarian of the name of Capito, who happened to be present, remarked that what the emperor said was good Latin, or, if it were not, it would soon be so. Marcellus, more of a grammarian than a courtier, replied, 'Capito is a liar; for, Cæsar, thou canst give the Roman citizenship to men, but not to words.' A similar anecdote is told of the German Emperor Sigismund. When presiding at the Council of Constance, he addressed the assembly in a Latin speech, exhorting them to eradicate the schism of the Hussites. 'Videte Patres,' he said, 'ut eradicetis schismam Hussitarum.' He was very unceremoniously called to order by a monk, who called out, 'Serenissime Rex, schisma est generis neutri.'[1] The emperor, however, without losing his presence of mind, asked the impertinent monk, 'How do you know it?' The old

---

[1] As several of my reviewers have found fault with the monk for using the genitive *neutri*, instead of *neutrius*, I beg to refer them to Priscianus, lib. vi. cap. i. 220; and cap. vii. 243. The expression

Bohemian schoolmaster replied, 'Alexander Gallus says so.' 'And who is Alexander Gallus?' the emperor rejoined. The monk replied, 'He was a monk.' 'Well,' said the emperor, 'and I am emperor of Rome; and my word, I trust, will be as good as the word of any monk.' No doubt the laughers were with the emperor; but for all that, *schisma* remained a neuter, and not even an emperor could change its gender or termination.

The idea that language can be changed and improved by man is by no means a new one. We know that Protagoras, an ancient Greek philosopher, after laying down some laws on gender, actually began to find fault with the text of Homer, because it did not agree with his rules. But here, as in every other instance, the attempt proved unavailing. Try to alter the smallest rule of English, and you will find that it is physically impossible. There is apparently a very small difference between *much* and *very*, but you can hardly ever put one in the place of the other. You can say 'I am very happy,' but not 'I am much happy,' though you may say 'I am most happy.' On the contrary, you can say 'I am much misunderstood,' but not 'I am very misunderstood.' Thus the western Romance dialects, Spanish and Portuguese, together with Walachian, can only employ the Latin word *magis* for forming comparatives:—Sp. *mas dulce*; Port. *mais doce*; Wal. *mai dulce*: while French, Provençal, and Italian only allow of *plus* for the same

---

generis neutrius, though frequently used by modern editors, has no authority, I believe, in ancient Latin. See Ausonius, *Epig.* 50. Servius, ad *Aen.*, i. 703.

purpose; Ital. *più dolce*; Prov. *plus dous*; Fr. *plus doux*. It is by no means impossible, however, that this distinction between *very*, which is now used with adjectives only, and *much*, which precedes participles, should disappear in time. In fact, 'very pleased' and 'very delighted' are expressions which may be heard in many drawing-rooms. But if that change take place, it will not be by *the will* of any individual, nor by *the mutual agreement* of any large number of men, but rather in spite of the exertions of grammarians and academies.

And here you perceive the first difference between history and growth. An emperor may change the laws of society, the forms of religion, the rules of art: it is in the power of one generation, or even of one individual, to raise an art to the highest pitch of perfection, while the next may allow it to lapse, till a new genius takes it up again with renewed ardour. In all this we have to deal with the conscious and intentional acts of individuals, and we therefore move on historical ground. If we compare the creations of Michael Angelo or Raphael with the statues and frescoes of ancient Rome, we can speak of a history of art. We can connect two periods separated by thousands of years through the works of those who handed on the traditions of art from century to century; but we shall never meet here with the same continuous and unconscious growth which connects the language of Plautus with that of Dante. The process through which language is settled and unsettled combines in one the two opposite elements of necessity and free will. Though the individual seems to be the prime agent in producing new words and new grammatical forms, he is so only after his individuality has been merged in the common action of the family, tribe or nation to which he belongs. He can do nothing by himself, and the first impulse to a new formation in language, though always given by an individual, is mostly, if not always, given without premeditation, nay, unconsciously. The individual, as such, is powerless, and the results apparently produced by him depend on laws beyond his control, and on the co-operation of all those who form together with him one class, one body, or one organic whole.

Language independent of Political History.

There is another objection which we have to consider, and the consideration of which will again help us to understand more clearly the real character of language. It has been said that although language may not be merely a work of art, it would, nevertheless, be impossible to understand the life and growth of any language without an historical knowledge of the times in which that language grew up. We ought to know, it is said, whether a language which is to be analysed under the microscope of comparative grammar, has been growing up wild, among wild tribes without a literature, oral or written, in poetry or in prose; or whether it has received the cultivation of poets, priests, and orators, and retained the impress of a classical age. Again, it is only from the annals of political history that we can learn whether one language has come in contact with another, how long this contact has lasted, which of the two nations stood higher in civilisation,

which was the conquering and which the conquered,
which of the two established the laws, the religion.
and the arts of the country, and which produced the
greatest number of national teachers, popular poets,
and successful demagogues. All these questions are
of a purely historical character, and the science which
has to borrow so much from historical sources, might
well be considered an anomaly in the sphere of the
physical sciences.

Now, in answer to this, it cannot be denied that
among the physical sciences none is so intimately
connected with the history of man as the science of
language. But a similar connection, though in a less
degree, can be shown to exist between other branches
of physical research and the history of man. In
zoology, for instance, it is of some importance to know
at what particular period of history, in what country,
and for what purposes certain animals were tamed
and domesticated. In ethnology, a science, we may
remark in passing, quite distinct from the science of
language, it would be difficult to account for the
Caucasian stamp impressed on the Mongolian race in
Hungary, or on the Tatar race in Turkey, unless we
knew from written documents the migrations and
settlements of the Mongolic and Tataric tribes in
Europe. A botanist, again, comparing several specimens of rye, would find it difficult to account for their
respective peculiarities, unless he knew that in some
parts of the world this plant has been cultivated for
centuries, whereas in other regions, as for instance in
Mount Caucasus, it is still allowed to grow wild.
Plants have their own countries, like races; and the

presence of the cucumber in Greece, the orange and cherry in Italy, the potato in England, and the vine at the Cape, can be fully explained by the historian only. The more intimate relation, therefore, between the history of language and the history of man is not sufficient to exclude the science of language from the circle of the physical sciences.

Nay, it might be shown that, if strictly defined, the science of language can declare itself completely independent of history. If we speak of the language of England, we ought, no doubt, to know something of the political history of the British Isles, in order to understand the present state of that language. Its history begins with the early Britons, who spoke a Celtic dialect; it carries us on to the Saxon settlements, the Danish invasions, the Norman conquest: and we see how each of these political events contributed to the formation of the character of the language. The language of England may be said to have been in succession Celtic, Saxon, Norman, and English. But if we speak of the history of the English language, we enter on totally different ground. The English language was never Celtic, the Celtic never grew into Saxon, nor the Saxon into Norman, nor the Norman into English. The history of the Celtic language runs on to the present day. It matters not whether it be spoken by all the inhabitants of the British Isles, or only by a small minority in Wales, Ireland, and Scotland. A language, as long as it is spoken by anybody, lives and has its substantive existence. The last old woman that spoke Cornish, and to whose memory a monument has been raised at Paul, represented by

herself alone the ancient language of Cornwall. A
Celt may become an Englishman, Celtic and English
blood may be mixed: and who could tell at the
present day the exact proportion of Celtic and Saxon
blood in the population of England? But languages
are never mixed. It is indifferent by what name the
language spoken in the British Islands be called,
whether English or British or Saxon; to the student
of language English is Teutonic, and nothing but
Teutonic. The physiologist may protest, and point
out that in many instances the skull, or the bodily
habitat of the English language, is of a Celtic type;
the genealogist may protest and prove that the arms
of many an English family are of Norman origin;
the student of language must follow his own way.
Historical information as to an early substratum of
Celtic inhabitants in Britain, as to Saxon, Danish,
and Norman invasions, may be useful to him. But
though every record were burnt, and every skull
mouldered, the English language, as spoken by any
ploughboy, would reveal its own history, if analysed
according to the rules of comparative grammar.
Without the help of history, we should see that
English is Teutonic, that like Dutch and Frisian it
belongs to the Low-German branch; that this branch,
together with the High-German, Gothic, and Scandinavian branches, constitute the Teutonic class;
that this Teutonic class, together with the Celtic,
Slavonic, the Hellenic, Italic, Iranic, and Indic classes,
constitute the great Indo-European or Aryan family
of speech. In the English dictionary the student of
the science of language can detect, by his own tests,

Celtic, Norman, Greek, and Latin ingredients, but not a single drop of foreign blood has entered into the organic system of English speech. The grammar, the blood and soul of the language, is as pure and unmixed in English as spoken in the British Isles, as it was when spoken on the shores of the German Ocean by the Angles, Saxons, and Juts of the continent.

Causes of change in Language.

But if the changes in language are not produced, like the changes in politics or art, by the deliberate acts of free individuals, and if they can be studied, and ought to be studied, quite independently of the history of the times during which they take place, the question that has to be answered is, What is the cause of these changes? Though it may be quite true that language cannot be changed or moulded by the taste, the fancy, or genius of any individual man, it is equally true that it is through the instrumentality of man alone that language can be changed. If language grows, it can grow on one soil only, and that soil is man. Language cannot exist by itself. To speak of language, as Frederick Schlegel did, as a tree sending forth buds and shoots in the shape of terminations of nouns and verbs,[1] or, as Schleicher did, as a thing by itself, as an organic thing living a life of its own, as growing to maturity, producing offspring, and dying away, is sheer mythology; and though we cannot help using metaphorical expressions, we should

[1] Horne Tooke, p. 629, *note*, ascribes this opinion to Castelvetro, without, however, giving any proof that the Italian scholar really held this view. In its most extreme form this view was supported by Frederick Schlegel.

THE GROWTH OF LANGUAGE.

always be on our guard against being carried away by the very words which we are using.

The changes of language, which no one can deny, which take place before our eyes, and have taken place during all periods of history, are due to two principal causes,

1. *Dialectic Regeneration.*
2. *Phonetic Decay.*

Phonetic Decay.

I begin with the second as the more obvious, though in reality its operations are mostly subsequent to the operations of dialectic regeneration, and in some cases may even be traced back to it. I think it may be taken for granted that everything in language had originally a meaning. As language can have no other object but to express our meaning, it might seem to follow almost by necessity that language could originally contain neither more nor less than what was required for that purpose. It would also seem to follow that if language contains no more than what is necessary for conveying a certain meaning, it would be impossible to modify any part of it without defeating its very purpose. This is really the case in some languages which for this, if for no other reasons, form a class by themselves, sometimes called *isolating*, or distinguished from *agglutinative* and *inflectional* languages. In Chinese, for instance, *ten* is expressed by *shĭ*.

No Phonetic Decay in Chinese.

It would be impossible to change *shĭ* in the slightest way without making it unfit to express *ten*. If instead of *shĭ* we pronounced *t'sí*, this would mean *seven,* but not *ten.* But now, suppose we wished to express double the quantity of ten, twice ten, or twenty. We should in Chinese take *eúl,* which is two, put it before *shĭ,* and say *eúl-shĭ,* twenty. The same caution which applied to *shĭ,* applies again to *eúl-shĭ.* As soon as you change it, by adding or dropping a single letter, it is no longer twenty, but either something else or nothing. We find exactly the same in other languages which, like Chinese, are called monosyllabic. In Tibetan, *chu* is ten, *nyi* two; *nyi-chu,* twenty. In Burmese *she* is ten, *nhit* two; *nhit-she,* twenty.

Phonetic Decay in Sanskrit.

But how is it in English, or in Gothic, or in Greek and Latin, or in Sanskrit? We do not say *two-ten* in English, nor *duo-decem* in Latin, nor *dvi-dasa* in Sanskrit.

We find [1] in

Sanskrit	Greek [2]	Latin	English
vim̃sati	veikati	viginti	twenty.

Now here we see, first, that the Sanskrit, Greek, and Latin are only local modifications of one and the same original word; whereas the English *twenty* is a new compound, and like the Gothic *twai tigjus* (two decads), the Anglo-Saxon *twen-tig,* framed from Teutonic materials; products, in fact, of what I call dialectic regeneration.

We next observe that the first part of the Latin *viginti* and of the Sanskrit *vim̃sati* contains the same number, which from *dvi* has been reduced to

---

[1] Bopp, *Comparative Grammar,* § 320. Schleicher, *Deutsche Sprache,* s. 233. [2] Lakonic form for *eikosi.*

vi. This is not very extraordinary. *Dvi* is not easy to pronounce; at all events *vi* is easier. In Latin *bis*, twice, stands likewise for an original *dvis*, and that corresponds to the English *twice*, the Greek *dis*. This *dis* appears again as a Latin preposition, meaning *a-two*; so that, for instance, *discussion* means, originally, striking a-two, different from *percussion*, which means striking through and through. Well, the same word, *dvi* or *vi*, we have in the Latin word for twenty, which is *vi-ginti*, the Sanskrit vimsati.

The second part of *vi-ginti* can hardly be anything else but a remnant of a word for ten, Sanskrit dasan, or for decad, Sanskrit dasat or dasati. But the loss of the first syllable da is anomalous, and so is the nasal in the first syllable of Sanskrit vimsati, and in the second syllable of Latin *vi-ginti*, confirmed by the α in Greek εἴκατι. This *ginti* cannot well be taken as a dual, because the dual weakens rather than strengthens its base;[1] still, *vi-ginti*, twenty, must be accepted as a corruption, and a very old corruption, of two words meaning *two* and *ten*.

Now there is an immense difference—I do not mean in sound, but in character—between two such words as the Chinese *eúl-shí*, two-ten, or twenty, and those mere cripples of words which we meet with in Sanskrit, Greek, and Latin. In Chinese there is neither too much, nor too little. The word speaks for itself, and requires no commentary. In Sanskrit, on the contrary, the most essential parts of the two component elements are gone, and what remains is a

[1] See Benfey, *Vocativ*, p. 9; *Das Zahlwort Zwei*, p. 27; Corssen, *Krit. Ntr.* 06. In Sanskrit the Nom. Dual is nâmnî, the Nom. Plur. nâmâni.

kind of metamorphic agglomerate which cannot be explained without a most minute microscopic analysis. Here, then, we have an instance of what is meant by *phonetic corruption*; and you will perceive how, not only the form, but the whole nature of language can be affected by it. As soon as phonetic corruption shows itself in a language, that language has lost what we considered to be the most essential character of all human speech, namely, that every part of it should have a meaning. The people who spoke Sanskrit were as little aware that vimsati meant *twice ten* as a Frenchman is that *vingt* contains somehow the remains of what is now *deux* and *dix*. Language, therefore, has entered into a new stage as soon as it submits to the attacks of phonetic change. The life of language has become benumbed and extinct in those words or portions of words which show the first traces of this phonetic mould. Henceforth those words or portions of words can be kept up artificially or by traditions only; and, what is important, a distinction is henceforth established between what is substantial or radical, and what is merely formal or grammatical in words.

Grammatical Forms produced by Phonetic Decay.

For let us now take another instance, which will make it clearer how phonetic corruption leads to the first appearance of so-called grammatical forms. We are not in the habit of looking on *twenty* or German *zwanzig* as the plural of a word for ten. But how was a plural originally formed? In Chinese, which from the first has guarded most carefully against the taint of phonetic corruption, the plural is formed in the most sensible manner. Thus, man in Chinese is *jin*; *kiai* means the whole or totality. This added to *jin* gives *jin-kiai*, which is the plural of man. There are other words which are used for the same purpose in Chinese; for instance, *péi*, which means a class. Hence *i*, a stranger, followed by *péi*, class, gives *i-péi*, strangers. The same process is followed in other cognate languages. In Tibetan the plural is formed by the addition of such words as *kun*, all, and *t'sogs*, multitude.[1] Even the numerals, *nine* and *hundred*, are used for the same purpose. We have similar plurals in English, but we do not reckon them as grammatical forms. Thus, *man-kind* is formed exactly like *i-péi*, stranger-kind; *Christendom* is the same as all Christians, and *clergy* is synonymous with *clerici*. In Bengali we find *dig*[2] added to a noun to give it plural meaning, in Hindi *lok* or *log*, world, and similar words.[3] And here again, as long as these words are fully understood and kept alive, they resist phonetic corruption; but the moment they lose, so to say, their presence of mind, phonetic corruption is apt to set in, and as soon as phonetic corruption has commenced its ravages, those portions of a word which it affects retain a merely artificial or conventional existence, and may dwindle down to grammatical terminations.

Phonetic decay may therefore be considered as one of the principal agents which change isolating into agglutinative, and agglutinative into inflectional languages.

[1] Foucaux, *Grammaire Tibétaine*, p. 27, and Preface, p. x.
[2] On the origin of this *dig*, see my essay on Bengali in the *Transact. of the Brit. Assoc.* for 1847, p. 337.
[3] Kellog, *Grammar of Hindi*, p. 74.

CHAPTER II.

But in order to explain how the principle of phonetic decay leads to the formation of grammatical terminations, let us look to languages with which we are more familiar. Let us take the French adverb. We are told by French grammarians [1] that in order to form adverbs we have to add the termination *ment*. Thus from *bon*, good, we form *bonnement*; from *vrai*, true, *vraiment*. This termination does not exist in Latin. But we meet in Latin [2] with expressions such as *bonâ mente*, in good faith. We read in Ovid, 'Insistam forti mente,' I shall insist with a strong mind or will, I shall insist strongly; in French, 'J'insisterai fortement.' Glosses in mediæval MSS. are introduced by *aut, vel, seu, id est, hoc est*, or by *in aliâ mente*, and this comes to mean *autrement* or *otherwise*.[3] Therefore, what has happened in the growth of Latin, or in the change of Latin into French, is simply this: in phrases such as *forti mente*, the last word was no longer felt as a distinct word, it lost its independent accent, and at the same time its distinct pronunciation. *Mente*, the ablative of *mens*, was changed into *ment*, and was preserved as a merely formal element, as the termination of adverbs, even in cases where a recollection of the original meaning of *mente* (with a mind), would have rendered its employment perfectly impossible. If we say in French that a hammer falls *lourdement*, we little suspect that we ascribe to a piece of iron a heavy mind. In Italian, though the adverbial termination *mente* in *chiaramente*

---

[1] Fuchs, *Romanische Sprachen*, s. 355.
[2] Quintilian, v. 10, 52. 'Bonâ mente factum, ideo palam; mala, ideo ex insidiis.'
[3] Grimm, *Rechtsalterthümer*, p. 2.

is no longer felt as a distinct word, it has not as yet been affected by phonetic corruption; and in Spanish it is sometimes used as a distinct word, though even then it cannot be said to have retained its distinct meaning. Thus, instead of saying, 'claramente, concisamente y elegantemente,' it is more elegant to say in Spanish, ' clara, concisa y elegante mente.'

It is difficult to form any conception of the extent to which the whole surface of a language may be altered by what we have just described as phonetic change. Think that in the French *vingt* you have the same elements which exist in *deux* and *dix*; that the second part of the French *douze*, twelve, represents the Latin *decim* in *duodecim*; that the final *ente* of *trente* was originally the Latin *ginta* in *triginta*, Spanish *treinta*, which *ginta* was again a derivation and abbreviation of the Sanskrit *dasa* or *dasat*, ten. Then consider how early this phonetic disease must have broken out. For in the same manner as *vingt* in French, *veinte* in Spanish, and *venti* in Italian presuppose the more primitive *viginti* which we find in Latin, so does this Latin *viginti*, together with the Greek *eikosi*, and the Sanskrit vimsati presuppose an earlier language from which they are in turn derived, and in which, previous to *viginti*, there must have been a more primitive form *dvi-ginti*, and previous to this again, another compound as clear and intelligible as the Chinese *cál-shĭ*, consisting of the ancient Aryan names for two, *dvi*, and ten, dasati. Such is the virulence of this phonetic change, that it will sometimes eat away the whole body of a word, and leave nothing behind but decayed fragments. Thus *sister*, which in Sanskrit is svasar,[1] appears in Pehlvi and in Ossetian as *cho*. *Daughter*, which in Sanskrit is duhitar, has dwindled down in Bohemian to *dci* (pronounced *tsi*).[2] Who would believe that *tear* and *larme* are derived from the same source; that the French *même* contains the Latin *semetipsissimus*; that in *aujourd'hui* we have the Latin word *dies* twice;[3] or that *to dowal*, a verb in ordinary use among the joiners in Yorkshire, is the same as the English *to dovetail*? Who would recognise the Latin *pater* in the Armenian *hayr*? Yet there is no difficulty in identifying *père* and *pater*; and as several initial *h*'s in Armenian correspond to an original *p* (*het* = *pes*, *pedis*; *hing* = Greek *pente*, five; *hour* = Greek *pyr*, fire), we can easily understand how the Armenian *hayr* is really a parallel form of the Latin *pater*.[4]

Dialects.

We have now to consider the influence of Dialectic Regeneration on the growth or change of language. But before we can do this we must first try to understand clearly what we mean by dialect. We saw that language has no independent substantial existence. Language exists in man, it lives in being spoken, it dies with each word that is pronounced, and is forgotten. It is really a mere accident that language should ever

---

[1] Sanskrit s = Persian *h*; therefore svasar = *krahar*. This becomes *chohar*, *chor*, and *cho*. Zend, qanha, acc. qanharem; Persian, *khaher*. Bopp, *Comp. Gram.* § 35.
[2] Schleicher, *Beiträge*, b. ii. s. 392: *dci* = *dûyte*; gen. *decre* = *dûytere*. See Poncel, *Du Langage*, p. 208.
[3] *Hui* = *hodie*, Ital. *oggi* and *oggidì*; *jour* = *diurnum*, from *dies*.
[4] See M. M.'s *Letter to Chevalier Bunsen*, On the Turanian Languages, p. 67.

have been reduced to writing, and have been made the vehicle of a written literature. Even now the largest number of languages are unwritten, and have produced no literature. Among the numerous tribes of Central Asia, Africa, America, and Polynesia, language still lives in its natural state, in a state of continual combustion; and it is there that we must go if we wish to gain an insight into the growth of human speech previous to its being arrested by any literary interference. What we are accustomed to call languages, the literary idioms of Greece and Rome and India, of Italy, France and Spain, must be considered as artificial, rather than as natural forms of speech. The real and natural life of language is in its dialects, a name which in its widest sense comprises provincialisms, brogue, *patois*, *jargon*, or any other variety that affects the general progress of language, down to the idiom of families and individuals; and in spite of the tyranny exercised by the classical or literary idioms, the day is still very far off which is to see the dialects, even of classical languages, such as Italian and French, entirely eradicated. About twenty of the Italian dialects have been reduced to writing, and made known by the press.[1] Formerly four varieties of French were recognised, *Norman*, *Picard*, *Burgundian*, and *French* of Ile de France. But Champollion-Figeac reckoned the most distinguishable dialects of France as fourteen.[2] Along the Italian Riviera nearly every bay has its own dialect; in Norway every valley speaks its own Norse.[3] The number of

[1] See Marsh, p. 678; Sir John Stoddart's *Glossology*, s. 31.
[2] *Glossology*, p. 33.
[3] Ellis, *Annual Address*, 1877.

modern Greek dialects[1] is carried by some as high as seventy, and though many of these are hardly more than local varieties, yet some, like the Tzaconic, differ from the literary language as much as Doric differed from Attic. In the island of Lesbos, villages distant from each other not more than two or three hours have frequently peculiar words of their own, and their own peculiar pronunciation.[2]

But let us take a language which, though not without a literature, has been less under the influence of classical writers than Italian or French, and we shall then see at once how abundant the growth of dialects. The Frisian, which is spoken on a small area on the north-western coast of Germany, between the Scheldt and Jutland, and on the islands near the shore, which has been spoken there for at least two thousand years,[3] and which possesses literary documents as old as the twelfth century, is broken up into endless local dialects. I quote from Kohl's *Travels*. 'The commonest things,' he writes, 'which are named almost alike all over Europe, receive quite different names in the different Frisian Islands. Thus, in Amrum, *father* is called *aatj*; on the Halligs, *baba* or *babe*; in Sylt, *foder* or *vaar*; in many districts on the mainland, *täte*; in the eastern part of Föhr, *oti* or *ohitj*. Although these people live within a couple of German miles from each other, these words differ more than the Italian *padre* and the English *father*. Even the names of their districts and islands are

[1] *Glossology*, p. 29.
[2] *Nea Pandora*, 1859, Nos. 227, 229; *Zeitschrift für vergleichende Sprachforschung*, x. s. 190.
[3] Grimm, *Geschichte der Deutschen Sprache*, s. 668; Marsh, p. 379.

totally different in different dialects. The island of *Sylt* is called *Söl, Sol,* and *Sal.*' Each of these dialects, though it might be made out by a Frisian scholar, is unintelligible except to the peasants of each narrow district in which it prevails. What is therefore generally called the Frisian language, and described as such in Frisian grammars, is in reality but one out of many dialects, though, no doubt, the most important; and the same holds good with regard to all so-called literary languages.[1]

Klaus Groth writes: 'The island of Frisian speech on the continent of Schleswig, between Husum and Tondern, is a very riddle and miracle in the history of language, which has not been sufficiently noticed and considered. Why should the two extreme ends only of the whole Frisian coast between Belgium and Jutland have retained their mother-speech? For the Ost-Frisians in Oldenburg speak simply Platt-Deutsch like the Westphalians and ourselves. Cirk Hinrich Stüremburg's so called Ost-Frisian dictionary has no more right to call itself Frisian than the Bremen dictionary. Unless the whole coast has sunk into the sea, who can explain that close behind Husum, in a flat country as monotonous as a Hungarian Pussta, without any natural frontier or division, the traveller on entering the next inn may indeed be understood if he speaks High or Low German, nay, may receive to either an answer in pure German, but hears the host and his servants speak in words that sound quite strange to him? Equally strange is the

[1] See *De Friske Findling, dat sen freske sprekkwurde,* fon M. Nissen; Stedesand, 1873-83.

frontier north of the Wiede-au, where Danish takes the place of Frisian. Who can explain by what process the language has maintained itself so far and no farther, a language with which one cannot travel above eight or ten square miles? Why should not these few thousand people have surrendered long ago this "useless remnant of an unschooled dialect," considering they learn at the same time Low and High German, or Low German and Danish! In the far-stretching straggling villages a Low German house stands sometimes alone among Frisian houses, and *vice versâ*, and that has been going on for generations. In the Saxon families they do not find it necessary to learn Frisian, for all the neighbours can speak Low German; but in the Frisian families one does not hear German spoken except when there are German visitors. Since the seventeenth century German has hardly conquered a single house, certainly not a village.'[1]

It has been one of the most fatal mistakes in the science of language to imagine that dialects are everywhere corruptions of the literary language. Even where there has been a literary language, dialects are by no means mere modifications of it. In England,[2]

[1] *Illustrirte Deutsche Monatshefte*, 1869, p. 330.

[2] 'Some people, who may have been taught to consider the Dorset dialect as having originated from corruption of the written English, may not be prepared to hear that it is not only a separate offspring from the Anglo-Saxon tongue, but purer, and in some cases richer, than the dialect which is chosen as the national speech.'—Barnes, *Poems in Dorset Dialect*, Preface, p. xiv.

'En général, l'hébreu a beaucoup plus de rapports avec l'arabe vulgaire qu'avec l'arabe littéral, comme j'aurai peut-être l'occasion de le montrer ailleurs, et il en résulte que ce que nous appellons l'arabe vulgaire est également un dialecte fort ancien.'—Munk, *Journal asiatique*, 1850, p. 229, *note*.

the local patois have many forms which are more
primitive than the language of Shakespeare, and the
richness of their vocabulary surpasses, on many points,
that of the classical writers of any period. Dialects
have always been the feeders rather than the channels
of a literary language; anyhow, they are parallel
streams which existed long before the time when one
of them was raised to that temporary eminence which
is the result of literary cultivation.

Two Kinds of Dialects.

What Grimm says of the origin of dialects in
general applies only to such as are produced by
phonetic corruption, and even to them partially
only. 'Dialects,' he writes,[1] 'develop themselves
progressively, and the more we look back in the
history of language the smaller is their number, and
the less definite their features. All multiplicity
arises gradually from an original unity.' So it
seems, indeed, if we build our theories of language
exclusively on the materials supplied by literary
idioms, such as Sanskrit, Greek, Latin, and Gothic.[2]
But what were these very languages before they had
been fixed by literary cultivation? Are we to suppose that in India,—a country as large almost as
Europe, and divided by mountains, forests, and deserts,—one and the same language was spoken when
the poets of the Veda sang their first hymns to cele-

[1] *Geschichte der Deutschen Sprache*, s. 833.

[2] How much truer is Grimm's account of the dialects of Märchen:—
Vorrede, p. xv: 'Diese Abweichungen erschienen mir merkwürdiger
als denen, welche darin blosz Abänderungen und Entstellungen eines
einmal dagewesenen Urbildes sehen, da es im Gegentheil vielleicht nur
Versuche sind, einem im Geist blosz vorhandenen Unerschöpflichen auf
mannigfachen Wegen sich zu nähern.'

brate the power of their gods? Does not Greece show us, even in its literature, a variety of local dialects? and does what we call the classical Latin pretend to be anything but one out of the many dialects of Latium, spoken by the patrician families of Rome? Mehlhorn, one of the most thoughtful of Greek grammarians, says very truly (*Greek Grammar*, § 40): 'that it is unscientific to treat dialects as deviations from the Attic κοινή. Each race had its own right, and if the Lacedaemonian said παρσένος we may say, for the sake of brevity, that it stands for παρθένος, but both forms have the same right and must be classed as co-ordinate. The word πέλεθρον has the same right as πλέθρον, and the latter may as rightly be called a shortening of the former, as the former a development of the latter. Certain combinations of consonants are avoided by all Greeks, such as μρ, μβ, μλ, but ενς in τιθένς, etc., was tolerated by Argives and Cretans, though rejected by all other Greeks. To Attic ears φιλέουσι sounded too soft, not so to Ionic.'[1]

Wherever we have an opportunity of watching the growth of literary languages, we find that dialects existed previous to their formation. Every literary language is but one out of many dialects; nor does it at all follow that, after one of them has thus been raised to the dignity of a literary language, the others should suddenly be silenced or strangled like the brothers and play-fellows of a Turkish Sultan. On the contrary, they live on

[1] All the changes which Greek grammarians comprehend under Metalepsis (§ 108), are treated as dialectical by Mehlhorn, while Curtius and others prefer to look on labialism (k and p) and dentalism (t and p) as successive modifications.

in full vigour, though in comparative obscurity; and
unless the literary and courtly languages invigorate
themselves by a constantly renewed intercourse with
their former companions, the popular dialects will
sooner or later assert their ascendancy. Literary
languages, such as Sanskrit, Greek, and Latin, are
the royal heads in the history of language. But as
political history ought to be more than a chronicle of
royal dynasties, so the historian of language ought
never to lose sight of those lower and popular strata
of speech from which these dynasties originally sprang,
and by which alone they are supported.

Dialect, the Natural State of Language.

Here, however, lies the difficulty. How are we
to prove the existence of these prehistoric dialects?
We may indeed argue *a priori* and show how it
stands to reason that dialects must have existed before uniform literary languages. Language existed at
first in individuals, in families, in clans, and in tribes,
and though in order to understand and to be understood, each individual had to adapt his language to
that of his neighbours, yet a far more considerable
liberty was probably allowed to every speaker in
chosing his own way of expressing himself. Hardly
any one even now speaks like everybody else. Individuals, families, towns, provinces, have their own
peculiarities, and nothing bewrays a man so easily as
his language. I cannot tell what it is, but having
been away for fifty years from my native town of
Dessau, I quickly recognise a German who comes from
that small town. In each family, even now, a father's
language differs from that of the mother, that of the

children, particularly of young children, from that of their parents. The very nature of speech therefore would lead to dialectic variety; and this in early times, when language moved within very narrow bounds, might soon change the whole surface of language. So far even *a priori* arguments would lead us to admit that from its very first beginning language existed in the form of dialects.

But history also tells us of the large number of dialects spoken in countries where we imagine that one language only prevailed.

We are told by Pliny,[1] that in Colchis there were more than three hundred tribes speaking different dialects; and that the Romans, in order to carry on any intercourse with the natives had to employ a hundred and thirty interpreters. This is probably an exaggeration; but we have no reason to doubt the statement of Strabo,[2] who speaks of seventy tribes living together in that country, which, even now, is called 'the mountain of languages.'

Our chief dependance, however, must be placed on the accounts which missionaries give us of languages which were still, so to say, in a state of nature, spoken, not written, and which they could watch in their transition to a literary stage. I asked Mr. W. Gill, who had spent all his life among tribes still being in a dialectic stage of language, to observe the changes which were taking place before his eyes. The following are some

[1] Pliny, vi. 5; Hervas, *Catalogo*, i. 118.
[2] Pliny depends on Timosthenes, whom Strabo declares untrustworthy (ii. p. 93, ed. Casaub). Strabo himself says of Dioskurias, συνέρχεσθαι ἐς αὐτὴν ἑβδομήκοντα, οἱ δὲ καὶ τρισκόσια ἔθνη φασὶν οἷς οὐδὲν τῶν ὄντων μέλει (x. p. 498). The last words refer probably to Timosthenes.

of the remarks he sent me, curiously confirming what had been anticipated :

'When a chief or priest uttered a witticism or invented a new phrase it was at once caught up and passed current, at first with the addition of " na mea e !"="as so-and-so says." As time passed on, the addition was dropped, and the saying was incorporated with the language. This process is still going on. Mispronunciations, imperfect articulations of words arising from loss of teeth in old men who from their former rank or prowess are entitled to respect, sometimes give rise to similar changes. In the olden times the desire on the part of the priests to conceal their oracles from the vulgar tended to corrupt the language. A frequent source of change was the arrival of drift natives. Scarcely ever did a drift canoe touch at Mangaia, but it left permanent traces upon the language of the islanders. In translating ancient songs, it sometimes happens that words now perfectly obsolete are found in cognate dialects. When visiting the Ellice Islanders, confessedly descendants of the Samoans, I found that their dialect is much nearer to that of the Hervey Group than the parent stock. This is to be accounted for by the fact that in a large body of natives intertribal wars, the ever-increasing ceremonial of heathen worship, the aspiring of chiefs to distinction, and especially their passion for great public assemblies, at which professed orators are pitted one against another—all occasioned divergence from the original tongue and refinements upon it. In smaller communities there were necessarily fewer inducements to changes of any sort, just as we know that the old Saxon plural (housen) yet lingers amongst the villagers of our own land.

'Your remarks on the rapid changes taking place in the dialects of illiterate tribes (*Science of Language*, vol. i. p. 37; also vol. ii. pp. 36, 37) are strikingly confirmed by the changes now going on in the dialects spoken at Tahiti and other islands in Eastern Polynesia. The language spoken at Tahiti at the commencement of the present century varies considerably from that spoken to-day. In numerous smaller islands, christianised by teachers from Tahiti, the original dialects have been swept away. In the Ellice Group the Samoan is superseding the original tongue. So, too, of several islands which have been instructed by teachers from Rarotonga. If the race should exist a century hence, very few dialects will survive the wholesale destruction now going on. The dialects that will live are those in which the Bible has been translated. It is for this reason that I desiderate a careful collection of words in ALL the known dialects of the great Polynesian family, for the purposes of science.'

The same excellent missionary in Mangaia, told me how, at the time of his arrival in that island, several local different dialects were spoken there, but that through his learning one of them and using it for his translations and in his schools, this so-called missionary dialect has become the recognised language of the whole population.

Mr. Trumbull,[1] in his Preface to Roger Williams' *Key* (p. 7) *into the Language of America*, writes, 'And this special value of Roger Williams's Key is enhanced by the fact that it was compiled before the language of the Narragansetts had been essentially modified by intercourse with the English, or by the influence of Eliot's and other printed translations into Massachusetts dialect. To such modifications all unwritten languages are subject, and the Indian languages of America were, from their structure, peculiarly so. That it did in fact take place in New England, and as a consequence of the printing of the Indian Bible, is not doubtful, though we have no means of ascertaining whether or not it extended to the Narragansett tribe. Experience Mayhew, writing from Martha's Vineyard in 1722, states that the language of that island and that of Natick were then " very much alike," but adds,

[1] *A Key into the Language of America*, in Publications of the Narragansett Club, Providence 1866.

"indeed the difference *was* something greater than now it is, before our Indians had the use of the Bible and other books translated by Mr. Eliot; but since that the most of the little differences that were betwixt them, have been happily lost, and our Indians speak, but especially write, much as those of Natick do."'

Gabriel Sagard, who was sent as a missionary to the Hurons in 1626, and published his *Grand Voyage du Pays des Hurons*, at Paris, in 1631, states that among these North American tribes hardly one village speaks the same language as another; nay, that two families of the same village do not speak exactly the same language. And he adds what is important, that their language is changing every day, and is already so much changed that the ancient Huron language is almost entirely different from the present. During the last two hundred years, on the contrary, the languages of the Hurons and Iroquois are said not to have changed at all.[1] We read of missionaries[2] in

---

[1] *Du Ponceau*, p. 110. Mr. Horatio Hale, who has lately obtained a vocabulary of a remnant of the Hurons, the Wyandot tribe, declares it to be the oldest branch of the primitive language from which the Iroquois dialects are derived.

[2] S. F. Waldeck, *Lettre à M. Jomard des Environs de Palenque, Amérique centrale*. ('Il ne pouvait se servir, en 1833, d'un vocabulaire composé avec beaucoup de soin dix ans auparavant.') 'But such is the tendency of languages, amongst nations in the hunter state, rapidly to diverge from each other, that, apart from those primitive words, a much greater diversity is found in Indian languages, well known to have sprung from a common source, than in kindred European tongues. Thus, although the Minsi were only a tribe of the Delawares, and adjacent to them, even some of their numerals differed.'—*Archæologia Americana*, vol. ii. p. 160.

'Most men of mark have a style of their own. If the community be large, and there be many who have made language their study, it is only such innovations as have real merit that become permanent. If it be small, a single eminent man, especially where writing is unknown,

Central America who attempted to write down the language of savage tribes, and who compiled with great care a dictionary of all the words they could lay hold of. Returning to the same tribe after the lapse of only ten years, they found that this dictionary had become antiquated and useless. Old words had sunk to the ground, and new ones had risen to the surface: and to all outward appearance the language was completely changed.

Nothing surprised the Jesuit missionaries so much as the immense number of languages spoken by the natives of America. But this, far from being a proof of a high state of civilisation, rather showed that the various races of America had never submitted, for any length of time, to a powerful political concentration, and that they had never succeeded in founding great national empires. Hervas reduces, indeed, all the dialects of America to eleven families [1]—four for the

---

may make great changes. There being no one to challenge the propriety of his innovations, they become first fashionable and then lasting. The old and better vocabulary drops. If, for instance, England had been a small country, and scarce a writer of distinction in it but Carlyle, he without doubt would have much altered the language. As it is, though he has his imitators, it is little probable that he will have a perceptible influence over the common diction. Hence, where writing is unknown, if the community be broken up into small tribes, the language very rapidly changes, and for the worse. An offset from an Indian tribe in a few generations has a language unintelligible to the parent-stock. Hence the vast number of languages among the small hunting tribes of Indians in North and South America, which yet are all evidently of a common origin, for their principles are identical. The larger, therefore, the community, the more permanent the language; the smaller, the less it is permanent, and the greater the degeneracy. The smaller the community, the more confined the range of ideas, consequently the smaller the vocabulary necessary, and the falling into abeyance of many words'—Dr. Rae, *The Polynesian*, No. 23, 1862.

[1] *Catalogo*, i. 393.

south, and seven for the north; but this could be done only by the same careful and minute comparison which enables us to class the idioms spoken in Iceland and Ceylon as cognate dialects. For practical purposes the dialects of America are distinct dialects, and the people who speak them are mutually unintelligible.

This is confirmed by one of the latest and most competent observers, Dr. Brinton. In his *Myths of the New World* (p. 8), he writes 'The American Indians exhibit an almost incredible laxity. It is nothing uncommon for the two sexes to use different names for the same object, and for nobles and vulgar, priests and people, the old and the young, nay, even the married and single, to observe what seem to the European ear quite different modes of expression. Families and whole villages suddenly drop words and manufacture others in their places out of mere caprice or superstition, and a few years separation suffice to produce a marked dialectic difference.' And Mr. Leland, who has been spending several years among the woods and lakes of Main, tells the same story, namely, that 'when the old men talk together the younger only understand half of what they say. The earlier language had interminably long names, the generation which comes shorten them. Old Passamaquoddy Indians still use " chew-dech-a-lòh " for yes; their sons say " A-ha." '[1]

We hear the same observations everywhere where the rank growth of dialects has been watched by intelligent observers. If we turn our eyes to Burmah,

[1] *The American*, 22 Dec. 1883, p. 169.

we find that the Burmese language has produced a considerable literature, and is the recognised medium of communication not only in Burmah, but likewise in Pegu and Arakan. But the intricate mountain ranges of the peninsula of the Irawaddy[1] afford a safe refuge to many independent tribes, speaking their own independent dialects; and in the neighbourhood of Manipura alone, Captain Gordon collected no less than twelve dialects. 'Some of them,' he says, 'are spoken by no more than thirty or forty families, yet so different from the rest as to be unintelligible to the nearest neighbourhood.' The Rev. N. Brown, the excellent American missionary, who has spent his whole life in preaching the Gospel in that part of the world, tells us that some tribes who left their native village to settle in another valley became unintelligible to their forefathers in two or three generations.[2]

In the North of Asia the Ostiakes, as Messerschmidt informs us, though really speaking the same language everywhere, have produced so many words and forms peculiar to each tribe, that even within the limits of twelve or twenty German miles, communication among them becomes extremely difficult. Castrén, the heroic explorer of the languages of northern and central Asia,[3] assures us that some of the Mongolian dialects are actually entering into a new phase of grammatical life; and that while the literary language of the Mongolians has no terminations for the persons of the verb, that characteristic

---

[1] *Turanian Languages*, p. 114. [2] *Ibid.* p. 233.
[3] *Ibid.* p. 30.

feature of Turanian speech had lately broken out in the spoken dialects of the Buriates and in the Tungusic idioms near Njertschinsk in Siberia.

One more observation of the same character from the pen of Robert Moffat, in his *Missionary Scenes and Labours in Southern Africa*. 'The purity and harmony of language,' he writes, 'is kept up by their pitchos or public meetings, by their festivals and ceremonies, as well as by their songs and their constant intercourse. With the isolated villagers of the desert it is far otherwise; they have no such meetings; they are compelled to traverse the wilds, often to a great distance from their native village. On such occasions fathers and mothers, and all who can bear a burden, often set out for weeks at a time, and leave their children to the care of two or three infirm old people. The infant progeny, some of whom are beginning to lisp, while others can just master a whole sentence, and those still further advanced, romping and playing together, the children of nature, through their live-long day, *become habituated to a language of their own*. The more voluble condescend to the less precocious; and thus, from this infant Babel, proceeds a dialect of a host of mongrel words and phrases, joined together without rule, and *in the course of one generation the entire character of the language is changed.*'

Wealth of Dialects.

Such is the life of language in a state of nature;[1] and, in a similar manner, we have a right to conclude

[1] See Schelling, *Works*, vol. i. p. 114. On Lituanian dialects see *Mittheilungen der Lith. Lit. Gesellschaft*, 1885, 5 Heft.

languages grew up which we only know after the bit and bridle of literature were thrown over their necks. It need not be a written or classical literature to give an ascendancy to one out of many dialects, and to impart to its peculiarities an undisputed legitimacy. Speeches at pitchos or public meetings, popular ballads, national laws, religious oracles, exercise, though to a smaller extent, the same influence. They will arrest the natural flow of language in the countless rivulets of its dialects, and give a permanency to certain formations of speech which, without these external influences, could have enjoyed but an ephemeral existence. Though we cannot fully enter, at present, on the problem of the origin of language, yet this we can clearly see, that whatever the origin of language, its first tendency must have been towards an unbounded dialectic variety. To this there was, however, a natural check, which prepared from the very beginning the growth of national and literary languages. The language of the father became the language of a family; the language of a family that of a clan.[1] In one and the same clan different families would preserve among themselves their own familiar forms and expressions. They would add new words, some so fanciful and quaint as to be hardly intelligible to other members of the same clan. Such expressions would naturally be suppressed, as we

---

[1] Derham mentions the case of a lady who died at the age of 93, and had given birth to 16 children, of whom 11 married. Upon her death she had 114 grandchildren, 228 great-grandchildren, and 900 great-great-grandchildren. If we take the age of the lady upon her first marriage at 17, then she had within 76 years, 1258 descendants. Lobscheid, *Engl. and Chin. Dictionary*, 1866.

suppress provincial peculiarities and pet words of our own, at large assemblies where all clansmen meet and are expected to take part in general discussions. But they would be cherished all the more round the fire of each tent, in proportion as the general dialect of the clan assumed a more formal character. Class dialects, too, would spring up; the dialects of servants, grooms, shepherds, and soldiers. Women would have their own household words; and the rising generation would not be long without a more racy phraseology of their own. Even we, in this literary age, and at a distance of thousands of years from those early fathers of language, do not speak at home as we speak in public.

We can hardly form an idea of the unbounded resources of dialects. When literary languages have stereotyped one general term, their dialects will supply fifty, though each with its own special shade of meaning. If new combinations of thought are evolved in the progress of society, dialects will readily supply the required names from the store of their so-called superfluous words. There are not only local and provincial, but also class dialects. There is a dialect of shepherds, of sportsmen, of soldiers, of farmers.[1]

[1] "Our fine dictionary words are mere dead sounds to the uneducated, which fail to awaken in *their* minds any living and breathing reality. So they call up new ones for themselves, mostly of a grotesque order, certainly, but as full of life and spirit as a brigade of shoe-blacks. With them a thing is not "overpowering," but it is a "*stunner;*" it is not "excellent," but "*a regular fizzer;*" and it does not "proceed satisfactorily," but it "goes like *one o'clock*" (i.e with as little delay as a workman gets off to dinner when the clock strikes *one*). With the same love of grotesque imagery, the navvy calls bacon with streaks in it "*tiger;*" and the Parisian cabman speaks of taking a glass of absinthe, in allu-

I suppose there are few persons who could tell the exact meaning of a horse's poll, crest, withers, dock, hamstring, cannon, pastern, coronet, arm, jowl, and muzzle. Where the literary language speaks of the young of all sorts of animals, farmers, shepherds, and sportsmen would be ashamed to use so general a term.[1] 'The idiom of nomads,' as Grimm says, 'contains an abundant wealth of manifold expressions for sword and weapons, and for the different stages in the life of their cattle. In a more highly cultivated language these expressions become burthensome and superfluous. But in a peasant's mouth, the bearing, calving, falling, and killing of almost every animal has its own peculiar term, as the sportsman delights in calling the gait and members of game by different names. The eye of these shepherds, who live in the free air, sees further, their ear hears more sharply— why should their speech not have gained that living truth and variety?'[2]

Thus Dame Juliana Berners, lady prioress of the nunnery of Sopwell in the fifteenth century, the

sion to its green tinge, as "*choking a parrot*." To say that this is not poetry, because it is vulgar, is very much like saying that a block of coal isn't carbon, because it is not a diamond. A great deal of the imagery in the Old Norse Sagas is as really slang as anything in the speech of a London street boy or a member of Congress. To take a single instance, an Icelandic poet speaks of the beginning of battle as the time "when the *black legs begin to swing;*" the said black legs being nothing more or less than the handles of the battle-axes.'

[1] See A. B. Meyer, *Mafoor und andere Papua Dialecte*, p. 6.

[2] Many instances are given in Pott's *Etym. Forsch.* pp. 128–169. Grimm *Geschichte der Deutschen Sprache*, p. 25, ' Wir sagen: die stute fohlt, die kuh kalbt, das schaf lammt, die geiss zickelt, die sau frischt (von frisching, frischling), die hündin wolft (M. H. D. erwirfet das welf); nicht anders heisst es französisch la chèvre chèvrote, la brebis agnèle, la truie porcèle, la louve louvète, etc.'

reputed author of the *Book of St. Albans*,[1] informs us that we must not use names of multitudes promiscuously, but we are to say, 'a congregacyon of people, a hoost of men, a felyshyppynge of yomen, and a bevy of ladyes; we must speak of a herde of hartys, swannys, cranys, or wrennys, a sege of herons or bytourys, a muster of pecockys, a watche of nyghtyngalys, a flyghte of doves, a clateryngc of choughes, a pryde of lyons, a slewthe of beerys, a gagle of geys, a skulke of foxes, a sculle of frerys, a pontifycalyte of prelates, a bomynable syght of monkes, a dronkenshyp of coblers,' and so of other human and brute assemblages. In like manner in dividing game for the table, the animals were not carved, but 'a dere was broken, a gose reryd, chekyn frusshed, a cony unlacyd, a crane dysplayed, a curlewe unioyntyd, a quayle wynggyd, a swanne lyfte, a lambe sholderyd, a heron dysmembryd, a pecocke dysfygured, a samon chynyd, a hadoke sydyd, a sole loynyd, and a breme splayed.'

Growth versus History of Language.

Let us now look again at what is commonly called the history, but what ought to be called, the natural growth of language, and we shall easily see that it consists chiefly in the play of the two principles which we have just examined, *phonetic decay* and *dialectic regeneration* or *growth*.

[1] 'The Book containing the Treatises of Hawking, Hunting, Coat-Armour, Fishing, and Blasing of Arms, as printed at Westminster by Wynkyn de Worde; the year of the incarnation of our Lord 1486.' (Reprinted by Harding and Wright: London, 1810.)

Latin and Neo-Latin.

Let us take the six Romanic languages. It is usual to call these the daughters of Latin. I do not object to the names of parent and daughter as applied to languages; only we must not allow such apparently clear and simple terms to cover obscure and vague conceptions. Now if we call Italian the daughter of Latin, we do not mean to ascribe to Italian a new vital principle. Not a single radical element was newly created for the formation of Italian. Italian is Latin in a new form. Italian is modern Latin, or Latin ancient Italian. The names *mother* and *daughter* only mark different periods in the growth of a language substantially the same. To speak of Latin dying in giving birth to her offspring is again pure mythology, and it would be easy to prove that Latin was a living language long after Italian had learnt to run alone. Only let us clearly see what we mean by Latin. The classical Latin is one out of many dialects spoken by the Aryan inhabitants of Italy. It was the dialect of Latium, in Latium the dialect of Rome, at Rome the dialect of the patricians. It was fixed by Livius Andronicus, Ennius, Nævius, Cato, and Lucretius, polished by the Scipios, Hortensius, and Cicero. It was the language of a restricted class, of a political party, of a literary set. Before their time, the language of Rome must have changed and fluctuated considerably. Polybius tells us (iii. 22), that the best-informed Romans could not make out without difficulty the language of the ancient treaties between Rome and Carthage. Horace admits (*Ep.* ii. 1, 86), that he could not understand the old Salian poems, and he hints

that no one else could. Quintilian (i. 6, 40) says, that
the Salian priests themselves could hardly understand
their sacred hymns. If the plebeians had obtained
the upperhand instead of the patricians, Latin would
have been very different from what it is in Cicero;
and we know that even Cicero, having been brought
up at Arpinum, had to give up some of his provincial
peculiarities, such as the dropping of the final s, when
he began to mix in fashionable society, and had to
write for his new patrician friends.[1] After having
been established as the language of legislation, religion,
literature, and general civilisation, the classical Latin
dialect became stationary and stagnant. It could not
grow, because it was not allowed to change or to
deviate from its classical correctness. It was haunted
by its own ghost. Literary dialects, or what are
commonly called classical languages, pay for their
temporary greatness by inevitable decay. They are
like artificial lakes at the side of great rivers. They
form reservoirs of what was once living and running
speech, but they are no longer carried on by the main
current. At times it may seem as if the whole stream
of language was absorbed by these lakes, and we can
hardly trace the small rivulets which run on in the
main bed. But if lower down, that is to say, later in
history, we meet again with a new body of stationary
language, forming or formed, we may be sure that its
tributaries were those very rivulets which for a time

---

[1] Quintilian, ix. 4. 'Nam neque Lucilium putant uti eadem (s) ultima, cum dicit Serenu fuit, et Dignu loco. Quin etiam Cicero in Oratore plures antiquorum tradit sic locutos.' In some phrases the final s was omitted in conversation; e. g. *abin* for abisne, *viden* for videsne, *opu'st* for opus est, *conabere* for conaberis.

were almost lost from our sight. Or it may be more accurate to compare a classical literary idiom to the frozen surface of a river, brilliant and smooth, but stiff and cold. It is mostly by political commotions that this surface of the more polite and cultivated speech is broken and carried away by the waters rising underneath. It is during times when the higher classes are either crushed in religious and social struggles, or mix again with the lower classes to repel foreign invasion; when literary occupations are discouraged, palaces burnt, monasteries pillaged, and seats of learning destroyed—it is then that the popular, or, as they are called, the vulgar dialects, which had formed a kind of undercurrent, rise beneath the crystal surface of the literary language, and sweep away, like the waters in spring, the cumbrous formations of a bygone age. In more peaceful times, a new and popular literature springs up in a language which *seems* to have been formed by conquests or revolutions, but which, in reality, had been growing up long before, and was only brought out, ready made, by historical events. From this point of view we can see that no literary language can ever be said to have been the mother of another language. As soon as a language loses its unbounded capability of change, its carelessness about what it throws away, and its readiness in always supplying instantaneously the wants of mind and heart, its natural life is changed into a merely artificial existence. It may still live on for a long time, but while it seems to be the leading shoot, it is in reality but a broken and withering branch, slowly falling from the stock from which it sprang.

The sources of Italian are not to be found in the classical literature of Rome, but in the popular dialects of Italy. English did not spring from the Anglo-Saxon of Wessex only, but from the dialects spoken in every part of Great Britain, distinguished by local peculiarities and modified at different times by the influence of Latin, Danish, Norman, French, and other foreign elements. Some of the local dialects of England, as spoken at the present day, are of the greatest importance for a critical study of English; and a French prince, now living in this country, deserves great credit for collecting what can still be saved of them. Hindustani is not the daughter of Sanskrit as we find it in the Vedas, or in the later literature of the Brahmans: it is a branch of the living speech of India, springing from the same stem from which Sanskrit sprang, when it first assumed its literary independence.

Influence of Literature.

While thus endeavouring to place the character of dialects, as the feeders of language, in a clear light, I may appear to some of my readers to have exaggerated their importance. No doubt, if my object had been different, I might easily have shown that, without some kind of literary cultivation, language would never have acquired that settled character which is essential for the communication of thought; that it would never have fulfilled its highest purpose, but have remained the mere jargon of shy troglodytes. But as the importance of literary languages is not likely to be overlooked, whereas the importance of dialects, as far as they sustain the growth of language, had never been pointed out, I thought it better to dwell on the advantages which literary languages derive from dialects, rather than on the benefits which dialects owe to literary languages. For a proper understanding of the growth of language, it is impossible to exaggerate the importance of the constant undergrowth of dialects. Remove a language from its native soil, tear it away from the dialects which are its feeders, and you arrest at once its natural growth. There will still be the progress of phonetic corruption, but no longer the restoring influence of dialectic regeneration. The French of Canada has preserved peculiarities which were recognised at the time of Molière, but have long vanished from Parisian French. If Canadians pronounce *loi* and *roi* like *loué* and *roué*, so did Molière, nay so did Lafayette as late as 1830.[1] The language which the Norwegian refugees brought to Iceland has remained almost the same for seven centuries, whereas, on its native soil, and surrounded by local dialects, it has grown into two distinct languages, the Swedish and Danish. In the eleventh century the languages of Sweden, Denmark, and Iceland are supposed[2] to have been identical; nor can we appeal to foreign conquest, or to the mixture of foreign with native blood, in order to account for the changes which the language underwent in Sweden and Denmark, but not in Iceland.[3]

---

[1] See Brachet, *Etymol. Dictionary*, p. lix.
[2] Marsh, *Lectures*, pp. 133, 368.
[3] 'There are fewer local peculiarities of form and articulation in our vast extent of territory (U.S.), than on the comparatively narrow soil of Great Britain.'—Marsh, *Lectures*, p. 667.

Growth of Language, its true meaning.

We now have to consider once more that important principle which underlies the growth of language, whether it takes place by phonetic decay or by dialectic regeneration, namely that such growth is entirely beyond the control of individual speakers. When we speak of laws, or rules, or tendencies which control the growth of language, what we really mean is simply that they control those who speak the language, and that their sway is often as irresistible as the sway of natural laws.

History of Language, its true meaning.

But though it is wrong to speak of a history of language, if we take history in its strict sense, as referring always to the actions of free agents, I am quite ready to admit that growth also is by no means free from objections, if we take it in its proper sense, as applying to the development of organic beings only. We speak, however, of the growth of the successive strata of the earth, and we know what we mean by it; and it is in this sense, but not in the sense of growth as applied to a tree, that we have a right to speak of the growth of language. If that modification which takes place in time by continually new combinations of given elements, which withdraws itself from the control of free agents, and can in the end be recognised as the result of natural agencies, may be called growth; and if so defined we may apply it to the growth of the crust of the earth, the same word in the same sense will be applicable to language, and will justify us, I think, in removing the science of language from the pale of the historical to that of the physical sciences.

Recapitulation.

In thus considering and refuting the objections which have been, or might be, made against the admission of the science of language into the circle of the physical sciences, we have arrived at some results which it may be useful to recapitulate before we proceed further. We saw that whereas philology treats language only as a means, comparative philology chooses language as the object of scientific inquiry. It is not the study of one language, but of many, and in the end of all, which forms the aim of this new science. Nor is the language of Homer of greater interest, in the scientific treatment of human speech, than the dialect of the Hottentots.

We saw, secondly, that after the first practical acquisition and careful analysis of the facts and forms of any language, the next and most important step is the classification of all the varieties of human speech, and that only after this has been accomplished, would it be safe to venture on the great questions which underlie all physical research, the questions as to the what, the whence, and the why of language.

We saw, thirdly, that there is a distinction between what is called history and growth. We determined the true meaning of growth, as applied to language, and perceived how it was independent of the caprice of man, and governed by laws that could be discovered by careful observation. Though admitting that the science of language was more intimately connected than any other physical science with what is called the political history of man, we found that, strictly speaking, our science might well dispense with that auxiliary, and that languages can be analysed and classified on their own evidence, particularly on the strength of their grammatical articulation, without any reference to the individuals, families, clans, tribes, nations, or races by whom they are or have been spoken.

Grammar, the principle of classification.

In the course of these considerations, we had to lay down two axioms, to which we shall frequently have to appeal in the progress of our investigations. The first declares grammar to be the most essential element, and therefore the ground of classification in all languages which have produced a definite grammatical articulation; the second denies the possibility of a mixed language.

No Mixed Language.

These two axioms are, in reality, but one, as we shall see when we examine them more closely. There is hardly a language which in one sense may not be called a mixed language. No nation or tribe was ever so completely isolated as not to admit the importation of a certain number of foreign words. In some instances these imported words have changed the whole native aspect of the language, and have even acquired a majority over the native element. Thus Turkish is a Turanian dialect; its grammar is purely Tataric or Turanian; — yet at the present moment the Turkish language, as spoken by the higher ranks at Constantinople, is so entirely overgrown with Persian and Arabic words, that a common clod from the country understands but little of the so-called Osmanli, though its grammar is the same as the grammar which he uses in his Tataric utterance. The presence of these Persian and Arabic words in Turkish is to be accounted for by literary and political, even more than by religious influences. Persian civilisation began to tell on the Arabs from the first days of their religious and military conquests, and although the conquered and converted Persians had necessarily to accept a large number of religious and political terms of Arabic, i. e. Semitic, origin, it would appear from a more careful examination of the several Persian words admitted into Arabic, that the ancient Aryan civilisation of Persia, reinvigorated by the Sassanian princes, reacted powerfully, though more silently, on the primitive nomadism of Arabia.[1] The Koran itself is not free from Persian expressions, and it contains even a denunciation of the Persian romances which circulated among the more educated followers of Mohammed.[2] Now the Turks, though accepting a Semitic religion, and with it necessarily a Semitic religious terminology, did not accept that religion till after it had passed through a Persian channel. Hence the large number of Persian words in Turkish, and the clear traces of Persian construction and idiom even in Arabic words as used in Turkish. Such Aryan words as *din*, faith, *gaur*, an

---

[1] Reinaud, *Mémoire sur l'Inde*, p. 310. Renan, *Histoire des Langues sémitiques*, pp. 292, 379, &c. Spiegel, *Avesta* (Uebersetzung), vol. i. p. 39.
[2] Cf. *Über die Fremdwörter im Korán*, by Dr. R. Dvorák, Wien; *Academy*, Aug. 3, 1886, p. 242.

infidel, *oruj*, a fast, *namáz*, prayers, used by a Turanian race, worshipping according to the formularies of a Semitic religion, are more instructive in the history of civilisation than coins, inscriptions, or chronicles.[1]

There is, perhaps, no language so full of words evidently derived from the most distant sources, as English. Every country of the globe seems to have brought some of its verbal manufactures to the intellectual market of England. Latin, Greek, Hebrew, Celtic, Saxon, Danish, French, Spanish, Italian, German — nay, even Hindustani, Malay, and Chinese words — lie mixed together in the English dictionary.[2] On the evidence of words alone it would be impossible to classify English with any other of the established stocks and stems of human speech. Leaving out of consideration the smaller ingredients, we find, on comparing the Teutonic with the Latin, or Neo-Latin or Norman-French elements in English, that the latter have a decided majority over the home-grown Saxon terms. This may seem incredible; and if we simply took a page of any English book, and counted therein the words of purely Saxon and Latin origin, the majority would be no doubt on the Saxon side.

---

[1] 'It is doubtful whether the Arabs, in their low state of civilisation, would have made such rapid progress, and the fact that most, and the most famous of their learned men were of foreign or mostly of Persian origin, as well as the coincidence of the beginning of Arabic literature with the victory of the Abbassides, the supporters of the Semitic element in the Islam, speaks against it.'—Weil, *Geschichte der Chalifen,* ii. p. 83. Ibn Chaldun, in Slane's Preface to *Ibn Chalikan,* vol. ii. English translation.

[2] For a complete analysis of native and foreign elements in English, see Skeat's *Etymological Dictionary,* pp. 747-761.

CHAPTER II.

The articles, pronouns, prepositions, and auxiliary verbs, all of which are of Saxon growth, occur over and over again in one and the same page. Thus, Hickes maintained that nine-tenths of the English dictionary were Saxon, because there were only three words of Latin origin in the Lord's prayer. Sharon Turner, who extended his observations over a larger field, came to the conclusion that the relation of Norman to Saxon was as four to six. Another writer, who estimated the whole number of English words at 38,000, assigned 23,000 to a Saxon, and 15,000 to a classical source. On taking, however, a more accurate inventory, and counting every word in the dictionaries of Robertson and Webster, M. Thommerel established the fact that of the sum total of 43,566 words, 29,853 came from classical, 13,230 from Teutonic, and the rest from miscellaneous sources.[1] On the evi-

---

[1] Some excellent statistics on the exact proportion of Saxon and Latin in various English writers, are to be found in Marsh's *Lectures on the English Language*, pp. 120 seq. and 181 seq. Dr. J. M. Weisse adds the following statistics:

Averaging the words in Noah Webster's *Dictionary*, 1861, he found:—
    55,524 Graeco-Latin words.
    22,220 Gotho-Germanic (mostly Anglo-Saxon).
       443 Celtic.
        98 Slavonic.
     1,724 Semitic (Hebrew and Arab.).
    —————
    80,009

Averaging the words in Walker's *Pronouncing Dictionary*, 1852, he found:—
    56,108 Graeco-Latin.
    21,777 Gotho-Germanic (mostly Anglo-Saxon).
      461 Celtic.
      768 Semitic.
    —————
    79,114

Thomas Shaw, in his *Outlines of English Literature*, p. 44, says,

dence of its dictionary, therefore, and treating English as a mixed language, it would have to be classified, together with French, Italian, and Spanish, as one of the Romanic or Neo-Latin dialects. Languages, however, though mixed in their dictionary, can never be mixed in their grammar. Hervas was told by missionaries that, in the middle of the eighteenth century, the Araucans used hardly a single word which was not Spanish, though they preserved both the grammar and the syntax of their own native speech.[1]

This is the reason why grammar is made the criterion of the relationship and the base of the classification in almost all languages; and it follows.

'The English now consists of 38,000 words.' An anonymous writer observes: There are in the English language:

   20,500 nouns.
    40 pronouns.
   9,200 adjectives.
   8,000 verbs.
   2,600 adverbs.
    69 prepositions.
    19 conjunctions.
    68 interjections.
     2 articles.
   ―――――
   40,498

All these calculations, however, have now become antiquated, considering that the new *Oxford Dictionary* promises to bring the number of words in the English Language to 250,000.

[1] 'En este estado, que es el primer paso que las naciones dan para mudar de lengua, estaba quarenta años ha la araucana en las islas de Chiloue (como he oido á los jesuitas sus misioneros), en donde los araucanos apénas proferian palabra que no fuese española; mas la proferian con el artificio y órden de su lengua nativa, llamada araucana.' —Hervas, *Catalogo*, tom. i. p. 16. ' Este artificio ha sido en mi observacion el principal medio de que me he valido para conocer la afinidad ó diferencia de las lenguas conocidas, y reducirlas á determinadas clases.'—*Ibid.* p. 23.

therefore, as a matter of course, that, according to the strict principles of the science of language, it is impossible to admit the existence of a mixed idiom. The fact that some languages, such as Turkish and even German have sometimes adopted foreign words with their own grammatical terminations, does not in the least affect the principle here laid down, not even, if by a kind of false analogy, such terminations were attached to native words. Because we can say in German *à la* Bismarck, it does not follow that *à la* has become part and parcel of the German language. Because in English we can say *bearable* as well as *tolerable*, it does not follow that *able* is a Teutonic suffix. We may form whole sentences in English consisting entirely of Latin or Romance words; yet whatever there is left of grammar in English bears unmistakable traces of Teutonic workmanship. What may now be called grammar in English is little more than the terminations of the genitive singular and nominative plural of nouns, the degrees of comparison, and a few of the persons and tenses of the verb. Yet the single s, used as the exponent of the third person singular of the indicative present, is irrefragable evidence that, in a scientific classification of languages, English, though it did not retain a single word of Saxon origin, would have to be classed as Saxon, and as a branch of the great Teutonic stem of the Aryan family of speech.

In ancient and less matured languages, grammar, or the formal part of human speech, is far more abundantly developed than in English; and it is, therefore, a much safer guide for discovering a family

likeness in scattered members of the same family.
There are languages in which there is no trace of
what we are accustomed to call grammar; for instance, ancient Chinese; there are others in which
we can still watch the growth of grammar, or, more
correctly, the gradual lapse of material into merely
formal elements. In these languages new principles
of classification will have to be applied, such as
are suggested by the study of natural history; and
we shall have to be satisfied with the criteria of
a morphological affinity, instead of those of a genealogical relationship.

I have thus answered, I hope, some of the objections which threatened to deprive the science of language of that place which she claims in the circle of
the physical sciences. We shall now see what the
history of our science has been from its beginning to
the present day, and how far it may be said to have
passed through the three stages, the empirical, the
classificatory, and the theoretical, which mark the
childhood, the youth, and the manhood of every one
of the natural sciences.

CHAPTER III.

THE EMPIRICAL STAGE.

Language studied in India and Greece.

THOUGH as a general rule each physical science begins with analysis, proceeds to classification, and ends with theory, yet, as I pointed out before, there are exceptions to this rule, and it is by no means uncommon to find that philosophical speculations, which properly belong to the last or theoretical stage, were attempted in physical sciences long before the necessary evidence had been collected or arranged. Thus, we find that the science of language also, in the only two countries where we can watch its origin and history—in India and Greece—rushes at once into theories about the mysterious nature of speech, and cares as little for facts as the man who wrote an account of the camel without ever having seen the animal or the desert. The Brahmans, in the hymns of the Veda, raised language to the rank of a deity, as they did with all things of which they knew not what they were. They addressed hymns to her, in which she is said to have been with the gods from the beginning, achieving wondrous things, and never revealed to man except in part. In the Brâhmaṇas, language is called the cow, breath the bull, and their young is said to be the mind of man.¹ Brahman, the highest being, is said to be known through speech, nay, speech itself is called the Supreme Brahman.² At a very early period, however, the Brahmans recovered from their raptures about language, and set to work with wonderful skill dissecting her sacred body. Their achievements in grammatical analysis (vyâkarana), which date from the sixth century B.C., are still unsurpassed in the grammatical literature of any nation. The idea of reducing a whole language to a small number of roots, which in Europe was not attempted before the sixteenth century by Henry Estienne,³ was perfectly familiar to the Brahmans at least 500 B.C.

The Greeks, though they did not raise language to the rank of a deity, paid her, nevertheless, the

---

[1] Colebrooke, *Miscellaneous Essays*, i. 32. The following verses are pronounced by Vâk, the goddess of speech, in the 125th hymn of the 10th book of the Rig-veda: 'Even I myself say this (what is) welcome to gods and to men: "Whom I love, him I make strong, him I make a Brahman, him a great prophet, him I make wise. For Rudra (the god of thunder) I bend the bow, to slay the enemy, the hater of the Brahmans. For the people I make war; I pervade heaven and earth. I bear the father on the summit of this world; my origin is in the water in the sea; from thence I go forth among all beings, and touch this heaven with my height. I myself breathe forth like the wind, embracing all beings; above this heaven, beyond this earth, such am I in greatness."' See also Atharva-veda, iv. 30; xix. 9, 3. Muir, *Sanskrit Texts*, part iii. pp. 108, 150.

[2] Brih in Briha-spati, the same as Vâkas-pati, lord of speech, is the root of the Lat. *verbum* and of the English *word*. The Vedic brih represents vridh, from which the nominal base vridha, i. e. Gothic *waúrd*, Lit. *vardas*, name. Brah-man comes from the same root.

[3] Sir John Stoddart, *Glossology*, p. 276. The first complete Hebrew Grammar and Dictionary of the Bible were the work of Rabbi Jonâ, or Abul Walîd Merwân Ibn Djanâh, in the middle of the eleventh century. The idea of Hebrew roots was explained even before him by Abu Zacariyya 'Hayyudj, who is called the first Grammarian by Ibn Ezra. Cf. Munk, *Notice sur About Walid, Journal asiatique*, 1850, avril.

greatest honours in their ancient schools of philosophy. There is hardly one of their representative philosophers who has not left some saying on the nature of language. The world without, or nature, and the world within, or mind, did not excite more wonder and elicit deeper oracles of wisdom from the ancient sages of Greece than language, the image of both, of nature and of mind. 'What is language?' was a question asked quite as early as 'What am I?' and 'What is all this world around me?' The problem of language was in fact a recognised battle-field for the different schools of ancient Greek philosophy, and we shall have to glance at their early guesses on the nature of human speech, when we come to consider the third or theoretical stage in the science of language.

Empirical Stage.

At present, we have to look for the early traces of the first or empirical stage. And here it might seem doubtful what was the real work to be assigned to this stage. What can be meant by the empirical treatment of language? Who were the men that did for language what the sailor did for his stars, the miner for his minerals, the gardener for his flowers? Who was the first to give any thought to language? —to distinguish between its component parts, between nouns and verbs, between articles and pronouns, between the nominative and accusative, the active and passive? Who invented these terms, and for what purpose were they invented?

We must be careful in answering these questions,

for, as I said before, the merely empirical analysis of language was preceded in Greece by more general inquiries into the nature of thought and language; and the result has been that many of the technical terms which form the nomenclature of empirical grammar, existed in the schools of philosophy long before they were handed over, ready made, to the grammarian. The distinction of noun and verb, or more correctly, of subject and predicate, was the work of philosophers. Even the technical terms for case, number, and gender were coined at a very early time for the purpose of entering into the mysteries of thought; not for the practical purpose of analysing the forms of language. This, their practical application to the spoken language of Greece, was the work of a later generation. It was the teacher of languages who first compared the categories of thought with the realities of the Greek language. Aristotle himself may have learnt many of his lessons from language, but it was the grammarian who transferred the terminology of Aristotle and the Stoics back from thought to speech, from logic to grammar; and thus opened the first roads into the impervious wilderness of spoken speech. In doing this, the grammarian had to alter the strict acceptation of many of the terms which he borrowed from the philosopher, and he had to coin others before he could lay hold of all the facts of language even in the roughest manner. For, indeed, the distinction between noun and verb, between active and passive, between nominative and accusative, does not help us much towards a scientific analysis of language. It is no more than a first grasp, and it can only be compared with the most elementary terminology in other branches of human knowledge. Nevertheless, it was a beginning, a very important beginning; and if we preserve in our histories of the world the names of those who are said to have discovered the physical elements, the names of Thales and Anaximenes and Empedocles, we ought not to forget the names of the discoverers of the elements of language—the founders of one of the most useful and most successful branches of philosophy—the first Grammarians.

Grammar.

Grammar then, in the usual sense of the word, or the merely formal and empirical analysis of language, owes its origin, like all other sciences, to a very natural and practical want. The first practical grammarian was the first practical teacher of languages, and if we want to know the beginnings of the science of language, we must try to find out at what time in the history of the world, and under what circumstances, people first thought of learning any language besides their own. At *that* time we shall find the first practical grammar, and not till then. Much may have been ready at hand through the less interested researches of philosophers, and likewise through the critical studies of the scholars of Alexandria on the ancient forms of their language as preserved in the Homeric poems. But rules of declension and conjugation, paradigms of regular and irregular nouns and verbs, observations on syntax, and the like, these are the work of the teachers of languages, and of no one else.

Now, the teaching of languages, though at present so large a profession, is comparatively a very modern invention. No ancient Greek ever thought of learning a foreign language. Why should he? He divided the whole world into Greeks and Barbarians, and he would have felt himself degraded by adopting either the dress or the manners or the language of his barbarian neighbours. He considered it a privilege to speak Greek, and even dialects closely related to his own were treated by him as mere jargons. It takes time before people conceive the idea that it is possible to express oneself in any but one's own language. The Poles called their neighbours, the Germans, *Niemiec, niemyi* meaning *dumb*;[1] just as the Greeks called the barbarians *Aglossoi*, or speechless. The name which the Germans gave to their neighbours, *walh* in Old High-German, *wealh* in Anglo-Saxon, from which the modern *Welsh* (A.S. *wælisc*), is supposed to be the same as the Sanskrit *mlekkha*, and, if so, it meant originally a person who talks indistinctly.[2]

Study of Foreign Languages.

Even when the Greeks began to feel the necessity

[1] The Turks applied the Polish name *Niemiec* to the Austrians. As early as Constantinus Porphyrogeneta, cap. 30, Νεμίτζοι was used for the German race of the Bavarians (Pott, *Indo-Germ. Sp.* s. 44; Leo, *Zeitschrift für vergleichende Sprachforschung*, b. ii. s. 258). Russian, *njemez'*; Slovenian, *němec*; Bulgarian, *němec*; Polish, *niemiec*; Lusatian, *njemc*, mean German; Russian, *njemo*, indistinct; *njemyi*, dumb; Slovenian, *něm*, dumb; Bulgarian, *něm*, dumb; Polish, *njemy*, dumb; Lusatian, *njemy*, dumb.

[2] Leo, *Zeitschrift für vergl. Sprachf.* b. ii. s. 252. Beluch, the name given to the tribes on the western borders of India, south of Afghanistán, has likewise been identified with the Sanskrit m l e k k h a.

of communicating with foreign nations, when they felt a desire of learning their idioms, the problem was by no means solved. For how was a foreign language to be learnt as long as either party could only speak their own? The problem was almost as difficult as when, as we are told by some persons, the first men, as yet speechless, came together in order to invent speech, and to discuss the most appropriate names that should be given to the perceptions of the senses and the abstractions of the mind. At first it must be supposed that the Greeks learned foreign languages very much as children learn their own. The interpreters mentioned by ancient historians were probably children of parents speaking different languages. Cyaxares, the king of Media, on the arrival of a tribe of Scythians in his country, sent some children to them that they might learn their language and the art of archery.[1] The son of a barbarian and a Greek would naturally learn the utterances both of his father and mother, and the lucrative nature of his services would not fail to increase the supply. We are told, though on rather mythical authority, that the Greeks were astonished at the multiplicity of languages which they encountered during the Argonautic expedition, and that they were much inconvenienced by the want of skilful interpreters.[2] We need not wonder at this, for the English army in the Crimea was hardly better off than the army of Jason; and such is the variety of dialects spoken in the Caucasian Isthmus, that it is still called by the inhabitants 'the Mountain of Languages.'

[1] Herod. lib. i. cap. 73.   [2] Humboldt's *Kosmos*, vol. ii. p. 141.

Interpreters.

If we turn our eyes from these mythical ages to the historical times of Greece, we find that trade gave the first encouragement to the profession of interpreters. Herodotus tells us (iv. 24), that caravans of Greek merchants, following the course of the Volga upwards to the Ural mountains, were accompanied by seven interpreters, speaking seven different languages. These must have comprised Slavonic, Tataric, and Finnic dialects, spoken in those countries in the time of Herodotus, as they are at the present day. The wars with Persia first familiarised the Greeks with the idea that other nations also possessed real languages. Themistocles studied Persian, and is said to have spoken it fluently. The expedition of Alexander contributed still more powerfully to a knowledge of other nations and languages. But when Alexander went to converse with the Brahmans, who were even then considered by the Greeks as the guardians of a most ancient and mysterious wisdom, their answers had to be translated by so many interpreters that one of the Brahmans themselves remarked, they must become like water that had passed through many impure channels.'[1]

---

[1] This shows how difficult it would be to admit that any influence was exercised by Indian on Greek philosophers. Pyrrhon, if we may believe Alexander Polyhistor, seems indeed to have accompanied Alexander on his expedition to India, and one feels tempted to connect the scepticism of Pyrrhon with the system of Buddhist philosophy then current in India. But the ignorance of the language on both sides must have been an almost insurmountable barrier between the Greek and the Indian thinkers. (*Fragmenta Histor. Græc.* ed. Müller, tom. iii. p. 243 *b*; Lassen, *Indische Alterthumskunde*, b. iii. s. 380.)

CHAPTER III.

Travels of Greek Philosophers.

We hear, indeed, of more ancient Greek travellers, and it is difficult to understand how, in those early times, anybody could have travelled without a certain knowledge of the language of the people through whose camps and villages and towns he had to pass. Many of these travels, however, particularly those which are said to have extended as far as India, are mere inventions of later writers.[1] Lycurgus may have travelled to Spain and Africa, he certainly did not proceed to India, nor is there any mention of his intercourse with the Indian Gymnosophists before Aristocrates, who lived about 100 B.C. The travels of Pythagoras are equally mythical; they are inventions of Alexandrian writers, who believed that all wisdom must have flowed from the East. There is better authority for believing that Democritus went to Egypt and Babylon, but his more distant travels to India are likewise legendary. Even Herodotus, though he travelled in Egypt and Persia, never gives us to understand that he was able to converse in any but his own language.

Barbarians learning Greek.

As far as we can tell, the barbarians seem to have possessed a greater facility for acquiring languages than either Greeks or Romans. Soon after the

---

[1] On the supposed travels of Greek philosophers to India, see Lassen, *Indische Alterthumskunde*, b. iii. s. 379; Brandis, *Handbuch der Geschichte der Philosophie*, b. i. s. 425. The opinion of Dugald Stewart and Niebuhr that the Indian philosophers borrowed from the Greeks, and that of Görres and others that the Greeks borrowed from the Brahmans, are examined in my Essay on Indian Logic, in Dr. Thomson's *Laws of Thought*.

Macedonian conquest we find [1] Berosus in Babylon, Menander in Tyre, and Manetho in Egypt, compiling, from original sources, the annals of their countries.[2] Their works were written in Greek, and for the Greeks. The native language of Berosus was Babylonian, of Menander Phenician, of Manetho Egyptian.

Berosus, Menander, Manetho.

Berosus was able to read the cuneiform documents of Babylonia with the same ease with which Manetho read the papyri of Egypt. The almost contemporaneous appearance of three such men, barbarians by birth and language, who were anxious to save the histories of their countries from total oblivion, by entrusting them to the keeping of their conquerors, the Greeks, is highly significant. But what is likewise significant, and by no means creditable to the Greek or Macedonian conquerors, is the small value which they seem to have set on these works. They have all been lost, and are known to us by fragments only, though there can be little doubt that the work of Berosus would have been an invaluable guide to

---

[1] See Niebuhr, *Vorlesungen über alte Geschichte*, b. i. s. 17.

[2] The translation of Mago's work on agriculture belongs to a later time. There is no proof that Mago, who wrote twenty-eight books on agriculture in the Punic language, lived, as Humboldt supposes (*Kosmos*, vol. ii. p. 184), 500 B.C. Varro, *de R. R.* i. 1, says: 'Hos nobilitate Mago Carthaginiensis praeteriit Poenica lingua, quod res dispersas comprehendit libris xxiix., quos Cassius Dionysius Uticensis vertit libris xx., Graeca lingua, ac Sextilio praetori misit : in quae volumina de Graecis libris eorum quos dixi adjecit non pauca, et de Magonis dempsit instar librorum viii. Hosce ipsos utiliter ad vi. libros redegit Diophanes in Bithynia, et misit Dejotaro regi.' This Cassius Dionysius Uticensis lived about 40 B.C. The translation into Latin was made at the command of the Senate, shortly after the third Punic war.

the student of the cuneiform inscriptions and of Babylonian history, and that Manetho, if preserved complete, would have saved us volumes of controversy on Egyptian chronology. We learn, however, from the almost simultaneous appearance of these works. that soon after the epoch marked by Alexander's conquests in the East, the Greek language was studied and cultivated by literary men of barbarian origin. though we should look in vain for any Greek learning or employing for literary purposes any but his own tongue. We hear of no intellectual intercourse between Greeks and Barbarians before the days of Alexander and Alexandria. At Alexandria, various nations, speaking different languages, and believing in different gods, were brought together. Though primarily engaged in mercantile speculations, it was but natural that in their moments of leisure they should hold discourse on their native countries, their gods, their kings, their lawgivers, and poets. Besides, there were Greeks at Alexandria who were engaged in the study of antiquity, and who knew how to ask questions from men coming from any country of the world. The pretension of the Egyptians to a fabulous antiquity, the belief of the Jews in the sacred character of their law, the faith of the Persians in the writing of Zoroaster, all these were fit subjects for discussion in the halls and libraries of Alexandria. We probably owe the translation of the Old Testament, the Septuagint, to this spirit of literary inquiry which was patronised at Alexandria by the Ptolemies.[1] The writings of Zoroaster also, the Zend-

---

[1] Ptolemæus Philadelphus (287–246 B.C.), on the recommendation of

Avesta, would seem to have been rendered into Greek about the same time. For Hermippus, who is said by Pliny to have translated the writings of Zoroaster, was in all probability Hermippus,[1] the Peripatetic philosopher, the pupil of Callimachus, one of the most learned scholars at Alexandria.

Scholars at Alexandria.

But although we find at Alexandria these and similar traces of a general interest having been excited by the literatures of other nations, there is no evidence which would lead us to suppose that their languages also had become the subject of scientific inquiry. It was not through the study of other languages, but through the study of the ancient dialects of their own language, that the Greeks at Alexandria were first led to what we should call critical and philological studies. The critical study of Greek took its origin at Alexandria, and it was chiefly based on

---

his chief librarian (Demetrius Phalereus), is said to have sent a Jew of the name of Aristeas, to Jerusalem, to ask the high priest for a MS. of the Bible, and for seventy interpreters. Others maintain that the Hellenistic Jews who lived at Alexandria, and who had almost forgotten their native language, had this translation made for their own benefit. Certain it is, that about the beginning of the third century B.C. (285), we find large portions of the Hebrew Bible translated into Greek by different hands. See, however, Kuenen, *Religion of Israel*, iii. p. 207.

[1] Pliny, xxx. 2. 'Sine dubio illa orta in Perside a Zoroastre, ut inter auctores convenit. Sed unus hic fuerit, an postea et alius, non satis constat. Eudoxus qui inter sapientiæ sectas clarissimam utilissimamque eam intelligi voluit, Zoroastrem hunc sex millibus annorum ante Platonis mortem fuisse prodidit. Sic et Aristoteles. Hermippus qui de tota ea arte diligentissime scripsit, et vicies centum millia versuum a Zoroastre condita, indicibus quoque voluminum ejus positis explanavit, præceptorem a quo institutum disceret, tradidit Azonacem, ipsum vero quinque millibus annorum ante Trojanum bellum fuisse.' See Bunsen's *Egypten*, Va, 101.

the text of Homer. The general outline of grammar existed, as I remarked before, at an earlier period. It grew up in the schools of Greek philosophers.[1] Plato knew of noun and verb as the two component parts of speech. Aristotle added conjunctions and articles. He likewise observed the distinctions of number and case. But neither Plato nor Aristotle paid much attention to the forms of language which corresponded to these forms of thought, nor had they any inducement to reduce them to any practical rules. With Aristotle the verb or *rhêma* is hardly more than predicate, and in sentences such as 'the snow is white,' he would have called 'white' a *rhêma*. The first who reduced the actual forms of language to something like order were the scholars of Alexandria. Their chief occupation was to publish correct texts of the Greek classics, and particularly of Homer. They were forced, therefore, to pay attention to the exact forms of Greek grammar. The MSS. sent to Alexandria and Pergamus from different parts of Greece varied considerably, and it could only be determined by careful observation which forms were to be tolerated in Homer and which were not. Their editions of Homer were not only *ekdoseis*, a Greek word literally rendered in Latin by *editio*, i.e. issues of books, but *diorthôseis*, that is to say, critical editions. There were different schools, opposed to each other in their views of the language of Homer. Each reading that was adopted by Zenodotus or Aristarchus had to be defended, and this could only be done by establishing general rules on the grammar of the Homeric poems.

[1] M. M.'s *History of Ancient Sanskrit Literature*, p. 163.

The Article in Greek.

Did Homer use the article? Did he use it before proper names? These and similar questions had to be settled, and as one or the other view was adopted by the editors, the text of these ancient poems was changed by more or less violent emendations. New technical terms were required for distinguishing, for instance, the article, if once recognised, from the demonstrative pronoun. *Article* is a literal translation of the Greek word *árthron*. *Arthron* (Lat. *artus*) means the socket of a joint. The word was first used by Aristotle, and with him it could only mean words which formed, as it were, the sockets in which the members of a sentence moved. In such a sentence as 'Whoever did it, he shall suffer for it,' Greek grammarians would have called the demonstrative pronoun *he* the first socket, and the relative pronoun *who* the second socket;[1] and before Zenodotus, the first librarian of Alexandria, 250 B.C., all pronouns were simply classed as sockets or articles of speech. It was he who first introduced a distinction between personal pronouns or *antōnymíai*, and the mere articles or articulations of speech, which henceforth retained the name of *arthra*. This distinction was very necessary, and it was, no doubt, suggested to him by his emendations of the text of Homer, Zenodotus being the first who restored the article before proper names in the Iliad and Odyssey. Who, in speaking now of the definite or indefinite article, thinks of the origin and original meaning of the word, and of the time

[1] Ἄρθρον προτασσόμενον, ἄρθρον ὑποτασσόμενον.

which it took before it could become what it is now, a technical term familiar to every school-boy?

Cases.

Again—to take another illustration of the influence which the critical study of Homer at Alexandria exercised on the development of grammatical terminology—we see that the first idea of numbers, of a singular and a plural, was fixed and defined by the philosopher. But Aristotle had no such technical terms as singular and plural; and he does not even allude to the dual. He only speaks of the cases which express one or many, though with him *case* or *ptôsis* had a very different meaning from what it has in our grammars. The terms singular and plural were not invented till they were wanted, and they were first wanted by the grammarians. Zenodotus, the editor of Homer, was the first to observe the use of the dual in the Homeric poems, and, with the usual zeal of discoverers, he has altered many a plural into a dual when there was no necessity for it.

The scholars of Alexandria, therefore, and of the rival academy of Pergamus, were the first who studied the Greek language critically; that is to say, who analysed the language, arranged it under general categories, distinguished the various parts of speech, invented proper technical terms for the various functions of words, observed the more or less correct usage of certain poets, marked the difference between obsolete and classical forms, and published long and learned treatises on all these subjects. Their works mark a great era in the history of the science of language. But there was still a step to be made before we can expect to meet with a real practical or elementary grammar of the Greek language. The first real Greek grammar was that of Dionysius Thrax. It is still in existence, and though its genuineness has been doubted, these doubts have been completely disposed of.

Dionysius Thrax.

But who was Dionysius Thrax? His father, as we learn from his name, was a Thracian; but Dionysius himself lived at Alexandria, and was a pupil of the famous critic and editor of Homer, Aristarchus.[1] Dionysius afterwards went to Rome, where he taught about the time of Pompey. Now here we see a new feature in the history of mankind. A Greek, a pupil of Aristarchus, settles at Rome, and writes a practical grammar of the Greek language—of course, for the benefit of his young Roman pupils. He was not the inventor of grammatical science. Nearly all the framework of grammar, as we saw, was supplied to him through the labours of his predecessors, from Plato to Aristarchus. But he was the first who applied the results of former philosophers and critics to the practical purpose of teaching Greek; and, what is most important, of teaching Greek, not to Greeks, who knew Greek and only wanted the theory of their language, but to Romans, who had to be taught the declensions and conjugations, regular and irregular. His work thus became one of the principal channels

---

[1] Suidas, s. v. Διονύσιος. Διονύσιος Ἀλεξανδρείας, Θρᾷξ δὲ ἀπὸ πατρὸς τοὔνομα κληθείς, Ἀριστάρχου μαθητής, γραμματικὸς ὃς ἐσοφίστευσεν ἐν Ῥώμῃ ἐπὶ Πομπηίου τοῦ Μεγάλου.

through which the grammatical terminology, which had been carried from Athens to Alexandria, flowed back to Rome, to spread from thence over the whole civilised world.

Teachers of Greek at Rome.

Dionysius, however, though the author of the first practical grammar, was by no means the first '*professeur de langue*' who settled at Rome. At his time Greek was more generally spoken at Rome than French is now spoken in London. The children of gentlemen learnt Greek before they learnt Latin, and though Quintilian in his work on education does not approve of a boy learning nothing but Greek for any length of time,—'as is now the fashion,' he says, 'with most people'—yet he too recommends that a boy should be taught Greek first, and Latin afterwards.[1] This may seem strange, but the fact is, that as long as we know anything of Italy, the Greek language was as much at home there as Latin. Italy owed almost everything to Greece, not only in later days when the setting sun of Greek civilisation mingled its rays with the dawn of Roman greatness; but ever since the first Greek colonists started Westward Ho! in search of new homes. It was from the Greeks that the Italians received their alphabet; it was by them they were taught to read and to write.[2] The names for balance, for measuring-rod, for engines

---

[1] Quintilian, i. 1, 12.

[2] See Mommsen, *Römische Geschichte*, b. i. s. 197. 'The Latin alphabet is the same as the modern alphabet of Sicily; the Etruscan is the same as the old Attic alphabet. *Epistola*, letter, *charta*, paper, and *stilus* (?), are words borrowed from Greek.'—*Mommsen*, b. i. s. 184. M. M., *Biographies of Words*, p. 50.

in general, for coined money,[1] many terms connected with sea-faring.[2] not excepting *nausea* or sea-sickness, are all borrowed from Greek, and show the extent to which the Italians were indebted to the Greeks for the very rudiments of civilisation. The Italians, no doubt, had their own religion; and some of the names of their deities, being the common property of the Aryan nations, are nearly the same in Latin and in Greek. But there are other names in Latin and in Oscan, though not in Umbrian and Sabellian, which were clearly adopted from Greek. Such are *Apollo* (the Oscan 'Απελλοῦν), and *Hercules* (the Oscan *Heraklo*). According to Mommsen there was an Italian god called *Hereclus*, and he was afterwards identified with the Greek *Herakles*. His name was supposed to be derived from *hercere*, and to express the same idea as the Greek ἑρκεῖος, the protector of the boundaries. But this hypothesis is full of difficulties. *Hercere* does not exist in Latin; if it did, it would not come from the same root as ἕρκος; lastly, the diminutive suffix *lus* would give us *herculus* or

---

[1] Mommsen, *Römische Geschichte*, b. i. s. 186. *Statera*, the balance, from the Greek στατήρ, a weight; *machina*, an engine, μηχανή; *nummus*, or *nummus*, a silver coin, νόμος, the Sicilian νοῦμμος; *groma*, measuring-rod, the Greek γνώμων or γνῶμα; *clathri*, a trellis, a grate, the Greek κλῆθρα, the native Italian word for lock being *clanstra*. See also Corssen, *Aussprache*, ii. p. 813. *Libra* cannot be called a Latin corruption of λίτρα, although the two words have the same origin. See Kuhn's *Zeitschrift*, xvi. 119.

[2] *Gubernare*, to steer, from κυβερνᾶν; *anchora*, anchor, from ἄγκυρα; *prora*, the forepart, from πρῶρα. *Navis, remus, velum*, &c., are real Latin words, not borrowed by the Romans from the Greeks, and they show that the Italians were acquainted with navigation before the discovery of Italy by the Phocœans. See Lottner, in Kuhn's *Zeitschrift*, vii. 67.

herclus, but not, in purely Latin words, *hereclus*.¹ *Castor and Pollux*, both of purely Greek origin, were readily believed in as nautical deities by the Italian sailors, and they were the first Greek gods to whom, after the battle on the Lake Regillus (485), a temple was erected at Rome.² In 431 another temple was erected at Rome to Apollo, whose oracle at Delphi had been consulted by Italians ever since Greek colonists had settled on their soil. The oracles of the famous Sibylla of Cumae were written in Greek,³ and the priests (*duoviri sacris faciundis*) were allowed to keep two Greek slaves for the purpose of translating these oracles.⁴

In other cases Greek gods were identified with Italian gods. As *Jupiter* was clearly the same Aryan deity as *Zeus*, *Juno*, his wife, was identified with *Hera*. *Ares* was recognised in *Mars*; *Hephaestos* in *Vulcanus*; *Athene* in *Minerva*, &c.; nay, even *Saturnus* (*Saëturnus*), originally, it would seem, an Italian agricultural deity,⁵ was identified with *Kronos*; and, as

---

¹ See Grassmann in Kuhn's *Zeitschrift*, xvi. p. 103. If *Herculus* were a purely Latin word, it might be identified with *For-culus*.
² Mommsen, i. 408.   ³ Ibid. i. 165.
⁴ In Latin, *Sibulla* may have been taken as a diminutive of *sibus* or *sabius*, words which, though not found in classical writers, must have existed in the Italian dialects. The French *sage* presupposes an Italian *sabius*, for it cannot be derived either from *sapiens* or from *sapius*. — Diez, *Lexicon Etymologicum*, p. 300. *Sapius* has been preserved in *nesapius*, foolish; *sibus* in *persibus*, wise.
⁵ See, however, Schweizer Siedler, in Kuhn's *Zeitschrift*, iv. 68; xvi. 139, who sees in *Saetur-nus* an Italian development of the Vedic Savitar, the Sun, as a generative power. At Rome Saturnus was considered as an agricultural deity, and the sickle in his hand may possibly have recalled the sickle which Kronos used against his father. See Plutarch, *Annot. Roman.* 42: 'Η ὅτι καρπῶν ἀρετῆς ἢ γεωργίας ἡγεμὼν ὁ

Kronos was the son of *Uranos*, a new deity was easily invented, and *Saturnus* fabled to be the son of *Cælus*.

When the Romans, in 454 B.C., wanted to establish a code of laws, the first thing they did was to send commissioners to Greece, to report on the laws of Solon at Athens and the laws of other Greek towns.[1] As Rome rose in political power, Greek manners, Greek art, Greek language and literature found ready admittance.[2] Before the beginning of the Punic wars, many of the Roman statesmen were able to understand, and even to speak Greek. Boys were not only taught the Roman letters by their masters, the *literatores*, but they had to learn at the same time the Greek alphabet. Those who taught Greek at Rome were then called *grammatici*, and they were mostly Greek slaves or *liberti*.

Among the young men whom Cato saw growing up at Rome, to know Greek was the same as to be a gentleman. They read Greek books, they conversed in Greek, they even wrote in Greek. Tiberius Gracchus, consul in 177, made a speech in Greek at Rhodes, which he afterwards published.[3] Flamininus, when addressed by the Greeks in Latin, returned the compliment by writing Greek verses in honour of their gods. The first history of Rome was written at Rome in Greek, by Fabius Pictor,[4] about 200 B.C.; and it was probably in opposition to this work and to those of Lucius Cincius Alimentus, and Publius Scipio,

θεός; ἡ γὰρ ἄρπη τοῦτο σημαίνει· καὶ οὐχ, ὡς γέγραφεν 'Αντίμαχος, 'Ησιόδῳ πειθόμενος.

[1] Mommsen, i. 256. [2] Ibid. i. 425, 444.
[3] Ibid. i. 857. [4] Ibid. i. 902.

that Cato wrote his own history of Rome in Latin. The example of the higher classes was eagerly followed by the lowest. The plays of Plautus are the best proof. The subjects are Greek, and though the language is Latin, yet the affectation of using Greek words is as evident in some of his characters as the foolish display of French in the German writers of the eighteenth century.

Greek influences at Rome.

There was both loss and gain in the inheritance which Rome received from Greece; but what would Rome have been without her Greek masters? The very fathers of Roman literature were Greeks. private teachers, men who made a living by translating school-books and plays. Livius Andronicus. sent as prisoner of war from Tarentum (272 B.C.), established himself at Rome as professor of Greek. His translation of the Odyssey into Latin verse. which marks the beginning of Roman literature, was evidently written by him for the use of his private classes. His style, though clumsy and wooden in the extreme, was looked upon as a model of perfection by the rising poets of the capital. Nævius and Plautus were his contemporaries and immediate successors. All the plays of Plautus were translations and adaptations of Greek originals; and Plautus was not even allowed to transfer the scene from Greece to Rome. The Roman public wanted to see Greek life and Greek depravity; it would have punished the poet who had ventured to bring on the stage a Roman patrician or a Roman matron. Greek tragedies, also, were translated into Latin. Ennius, the contemporary of Naevius and Plautus, though somewhat younger (239–169), was the first to translate Euripides. Ennius, like Andronicus, was an Italian Greek, who settled at Rome as a teacher of languages and translator of Greek. He was patronised by the liberal party, by Publius Scipio, Titus Flamininus, and Marcus Fulvius Nobilior.[1] He became a Roman citizen. But Ennius was more than a poet, more than a teacher of languages. He has been called a neologian, and to a certain extent he deserved that name. Two works written in the most hostile spirit against the religion of Greece, and against the very existence of the Greek gods, were translated by him into Latin.[2] One was the philosophy of Epicharmus (470 B.C., in Megara), who taught that Zeus was nothing but the air, and other gods but names of the powers of nature; the other the work of Euhemerus of Messene (300 B.C.), who proved, in the form of a novel, that the Greek gods had never existed, and that those who were believed in as gods had been men. These two works were not translated without a purpose; and though themselves shallow in the extreme, they proved destructive to the still shallower systems of Roman theology. Greek became synonymous with infidel; and Ennius would hardly have escaped the punishment inflicted on Naevius for his political satires, had he not enjoyed

[1] Mommsen, i. 892.
[2] Ibid. i. 843, 194. It has been doubted whether the work of Ennius was a translation of Epicharmus. See Ennius, ed. Vahlen, p. xciii. On Epicharmus, see Bernays, *Rheinisches Museum*, viii. s. 280 (1853).

the patronage and esteem of the most influential statesmen at Rome. Even Cato, the stubborn enemy of Greek philosophy[1] and rhetoric, was a friend of the dangerous Ennius; and such was the growing influence of Greek at Rome, that Cato himself had to learn it in his old age, in order to teach his boy what he considered, if not useful, at least harmless in Greek literature. It has been the custom to laugh at Cato for his dogged opposition to everything Greek; but there was much truth in his denunciations. We have heard much of young Bengal— young Hindus who read Byron and Voltaire, play at billiards, drive tandems, laugh at their priests, patronise missionaries, and believe nothing. The description which Cato gives of the young idlers at Rome reminds us very much of young Bengal.

When Rome took the torch of knowledge from the dying hands of Greece, that torch was not burning with its brightest light. Plato and Aristotle had been succeeded by Chrysippus and Carneades; Euripides and Menander had taken the place of Æschylus and Aristophanes. In becoming the guardian of the Promethean spark first lighted in Greece, and intended hereafter to illuminate not only Italy, but every country of Europe, Rome lost much of that native virtue to which she owed her greatness. Roman frugality and gravity, Roman citizenship and patriotism, Roman purity and piety, were driven away by Greek luxury and levity, Greek intriguing and self-seeking, Greek vice and infidelity. Restrictions and anathemas were of no avail; and Greek ideas were never so at-

[1] Mommsen, i. 911.

tractive as when they had been reprobated by Cato and his friends. Every new generation became more and more impregnated with Greek. In 131[1] we hear of a consul (Publius Crassus) who, like another Mezzofanti, was able to converse in the various dialects of Greek. Sulla allowed foreign ambassadors to speak in Greek before the Roman senate.[2] The Stoic philosopher Panætius[3] lived in the house of the Scipios, which was for a long time the rendezvous of all the literary celebrities at Rome. Here the Greek historian Polybius, and the philosopher Clitomachus, Lucilius the satirist, Terence, the African poet (196–159), and the improvisatore Archias (102 B.C.), were welcome guests.[4] In this select circle the masterworks of Greek literature were read and criticised; the problems of Greek philosophy were discussed; and the highest interests of human life became the subject of thoughtful conversation. Though no poet of original genius arose from this society, it exercised a most powerful influence on the progress of Roman literature. It formed a tribunal of good taste; and

---

[1] Mommsen, ii. 407.
[2] Ibid. ii. 410. Valerius Maximus, at the time of Tiberius, asks 'Quis ergo huic consuetudini, quâ nunc Graecis actionibus aures curiae exsurdantur, januam patefecit?' (lib. ii. cap. ii. 3). Dio Cassius (lib. lvii. cap. 15) relates that Tiberius heard causes argued, and asked questions himself, in Greek. Πολλὰς μὲν δίκας ἐν τῇ διαλέκτῳ ταύτῃ καὶ ἐκεῖ λεγομένας ἀκούων, πολλὰς δὲ καὶ αὐτὸς ἐπερωτῶν. Cf. Roberts, *Discussions on the Gospels*, p. 29. Suetonius remarks, however, of Tiberius: 'Sermone Graeco, quanquam alias promptus et facilis, non tamen usquequaque usus est, abstinuitque maxime in senatu, adeo quidem, ut "monopolium" nominaturus, prius veniam postulârit, quod sibi verbo peregrino utendum esset.' 'Militem quoque Graeco interrogatum, nisi Latine respondere vetuit.'—Suet. *Tib.* cap. 71.
[3] Mommsen, ii. 408. [4] Ibid. ii. 437, *note*; ii. 430.

much of the correctness, simplicity, and manliness of the classical Latin is due to that 'Cosmopolitan Club,' which met under the hospitable roof of the Scipios. With every succeeding generation the knowledge of Greek became more general at Rome. Cicero spoke Greek in the senate of Syracuse, Augustus in the town of Alexandria. Boys and girls, as Ovid relates, used to read the plays of Menander—'solet pueris virginibusque legi'; and Juvenal (*Sat.* vi. 186 seq.) exclaims:—

> 'Omnia Graece,
> Cum sit turpe magis nostris nescire Latine.
> Hoc sermone pavent, hoc iram, gaudia, curas,
> Hoc cuncta effundunt animi secreta.'

The religious life of the higher Roman society at the close of the Punic wars was more Greek than Roman. All who had learnt to think seriously on religious questions were either Stoics or followers of Epicurus; or they embraced the doctrines of the New Academy, denying the possibility of any knowledge of the Infinite, and putting opinion in the place of truth.[1] Though the doctrines of Epicurus and of the New Academy were always considered dangerous and heretical, the philosophy of the Stoics was tolerated, and a kind of compromise effected between philosophy and religion. There was a state-philosophy as well as a state-religion. The Roman priesthood, though they had succeeded, in 161, in getting all Greek rhetors and philosophers expelled from Rome, perceived that a compromise was necessary. It was openly avowed

---

[1] Zeno died 263; Epicurus died 270; Archesilaus died 241; Carneades died 129.

that in the enlightened classes[1] philosophy must take the place of religion, but that a belief in miracles and oracles was necessary for keeping the large masses in order. Even Cato,[2] the leader of the orthodox, national, and conservative party, expressed his surprise that a haruspex, when meeting a colleague, did not burst out laughing. Men like Scipio Æmilianus and Lælius professed to believe in the popular gods; but with them Jupiter was the soul of the universe, the statues of the gods mere works of art.[3] Their gods, as the people complained, had neither body, parts, nor passions. Peace, however, was preserved between the Stoic philosopher and the orthodox priest. Both parties professed to believe in the same gods, but they claimed the liberty to believe in them in their own way.

I have dwelt at some length on the changes in the intellectual atmosphere of Rome at the end of the Punic wars, and I have endeavoured to show how completely it was impregnated with Greek ideas, in order to explain, what otherwise would seem almost inexplicable, the zeal and earnestness with which the study of Greek grammar was taken up at Rome, not only by a few scholars and philosophers, but by the leading statesmen of the time. To our minds, discussions on nouns and verbs, on cases and gender, on regular and irregular conjugation, retain always something of the tedious character which these sub-

---

[1] Mommsen, ii. 417, 418.
[2] Ibid. i. 845. Cicero, *De Divinatione*, ii. 24: 'Mirari se ajebat (Cato) quod non rideret haruspex haruspicem cum vidisset.'
[3] Ibid. ii. 415, 417.

jects had at school, and we can hardly understand how at Rome, grammar—pure and simple grammar—should have formed a subject of general interest, and a topic of fashionable conversation. Although the grammatical studies of the Romans may have been enlivened by illustrations from the classical authors of Greece, yet their main object was language as such.

Crates of Pergamus.

When one of the first grammarians of the day, Crates of Pergamus, was sent to Rome as ambassador of king Attalus, he was received with the greatest distinction by all the literary statesmen of the capital. He was the pupil of Diogenes Babylonius, who had been the pupil of Chrysippus; and as Chrysippus was a staunch supporter of the theory of 'Anomaly,' the philosophy of language, taught by Crates (αἵρεσις Κρατήτειος), was of the same character.[1] It so happened that when walking one day on the Palatian hill, Crates caught his foot in the grating of a sewer, fell and broke his leg.[2] Being thereby detained at

[1] 'In quo fuit Crates nobilis grammaticus, qui fretus Chrysippo, homine acutissimo, qui reliquit sex libros περὶ ἀνωμαλίας, heis libris contra ἀναλογίαν atque Aristarchum est nixus, sed ita ut scripta indicarent ejus, ut neutrius videatur pervidisse voluntatem; quod et Chrysippus de inaequalitate cum scribit sermonis, propositum habet ostendere similes res dissimilibus verbis et dissimilibus similes esse vocabulis notatas (id quod est verum); et quod Aristarchus, de aequalitate cum scribit et de verborum similitudine, quorundam inclinationes sequi jubet, quoad patiatur consuetudo.'—Varro, *De Linguâ Latinâ*, ed. O. Müller, lib. ix. cap. 1.

[2] 'Primus igitur quantum opinamur studium grammaticae in urbem intulit Crates Mallotes, Aristarchi aequalis, qui missus ad senatum ab Attalo rege inter secundum et tertium Punicum bellum sub ipsam Ennii mortem, cum regione Palatii prolapsus in cloacae foramen crus fregisset, per omne legationis simul et valetudinis tempus plurimas acroasis

Rome longer than he intended, he was persuaded to give some public lectures, or *akroaseis*, on grammar; and from these lectures, says Suetonius, dates the study of grammar at Rome. This took place about 159 B.C., between the second and third Punic wars, shortly after the death of Ennius, and two years after the famous expulsion of the Greek rhetors and philosophers (161).

Carneades.

Four years later Carneades, likewise sent as ambassador to Rome, was prohibited from lecturing by Cato. After these lectures of Crates, grammatical and philological studies became extremely popular at Rome.

Alexander Polyhistor.

His pupil, Alexander Polyhistor, flourished under Sulla. We hear of Lucius Ælius Stilo,[1] who lectured on Latin as Crates had lectured on Greek.

Varro, Lucilius, Cicero.

Among his pupils were Varro, Lucilius, and Cicero. Varro composed twenty-four books on the Latin language, four of which were dedicated to Cicero. Cicero, himself, is quoted as an authority on grammatical questions, though we know of no special work

---

subinde ferit assiduoque disseruit, ac nostris exemplum fuit ad imitandum.'—Suetonius, *De viris inlustribus, De grammaticis et rhetoribus*, cap. 2, ed. Reifferscheid: Lipsiae, 1860. Scioppius, in the introduction to his *Grammatica philosophica* (1628), writes: ' Hæc ergo ut legi, minime jam mirandum mihi visum est, tanti flagitii erroribus inquinatam esse veterem Grammaticam, quae ex cloacae foramine una cum claudo magistro emerserit.'

[1] Mommsen, ii. 413, 426, 445, 457. Lucius Ælius Stilo wrote a work on etymology, and an index to Plautus.—Lersch, *Die Sprachphilosophie der Alten*, ii. 111.

of his on grammar. Lucilius devoted the ninth book of his satires to the reform of spelling.[1]

Cæsar, De Analogiâ.

But nothing shows more clearly the wide interest which grammatical studies had then excited in the foremost ranks of Roman society than Cæsar's work on Latin grammar. It was composed by him during the Gallic war, and dedicated to Cicero, who might well be proud of the compliment thus paid him by the great general and statesman.[2] Most of these works are lost to us, and we can judge of them by means of casual quotations only. Thus we learn from a fragment of Cæsar's work, *De Analogiâ*, that he was the inventor of the term *ablative* in Latin. The word never occurs before, and, of course, could not be borrowed, like the names of the other cases, from Greek grammarians, as no ablative had been admitted in Greek grammar. To think of Cæsar fighting the barbarians of Gaul and Germany, and watching from a distance the political complications at Rome, ready to grasp the sceptre of the world, and at the same time carrying on his philological and grammatical studies together with his secretary, the Greek Didymus,[3] gives us a new view both of that extraordinary man, and of the time in which he lived. After Cæsar had triumphed, one of his favourite plans was to found a Greek and Latin library at Rome, and he offered the librarianship to the best scholar of the day, to Varro, though Varro had fought against him on the side of Pompey.[4]

[1] Lersch, ii. 113, 114, 143.   [2] Cicero, *Brut.* cap. 72.
[3] Lersch, iii. 144.   [4] Mommsen, iii. 557. 48 B.C.

THE EMPIRICAL STAGE. 117

Grammatical Terminology.

We have thus arrived at a time when, as we saw before, Dionysius Thrax published the first elementary grammar of Greek at Rome. Dionysius, as a pupil of Aristarchus, was a believer in 'Analogy,' and therefore opposed to the views propounded by Crates on the anomalous character of language. His influence, however, was chiefly felt as a practical teacher. Through him empirical grammar became transplanted to Rome, the Greek grammatical terminology was translated into Latin, and in this new Latin garb it has travelled for nearly two thousand years over the whole civilised world. Even in India, where a different terminology had grown up in the grammatical schools of the Brahmans, a terminology in some respects more perfect than that of Alexandria and Rome, we may now hear such words as *case*, and *gender*, and *active*, and *passive*, explained by European teachers to their native pupils. The fates of words are curious indeed, and when I looked the other day at some of the examination papers of the government schools in India, such questions as—'What is the genitive case of Siva?' seemed to reduce whole volumes of history into a single sentence. How did these words, genitive case, come to India? They came from England, they had come to England from Rome, to Rome from Alexandria, to Alexandria from Athens. At Athens, the term *case* or *ptôsis* had a philosophical meaning; at Rome, *casus* was merely a literal translation; the original meaning of *fall* was lost, and the word had dwindled down to a mere technical term. At Athens, the philosophy of language was a counterpart of the philosophy of the mind. The terminology of formal logic and formal grammar was the same. The logic of the Stoics was divided into two parts,[1] called *rhetoric* and *dialectic*, and the latter treated first, 'On that which signifies, or language;' secondly, 'On that which is signified, or things.' In their philosophical language *ptōsis*, which the Romans translated by *casus*, really meant fall; that is to say, the inclination or relation of one idea to another, the falling or resting of one word on another. Long and angry discussions were carried on as to whether the name of *ptōsis*, or fall, was applicable to the nominative; and every true Stoic would have scouted the expression of *casus rectus*, because the subject or the nominative, as they argued, did not fall or rest on anything else, but stood erect, the other words of a sentence leaning or depending on it. All this is lost to us when we speak of cases. Cobbett in his English Grammar ventures on his own explanation of the term *case*, stating:—'The word *case*, as applied to the concerns of life, has a variety of meanings, or of different shades of meaning; but its general meaning is, *state of things*, or *state of something*. Thus we say, "*in that case*, I agree with you." Meaning "that being *the state of things*, or that being *the state of the matter*, I agree with you." Lawyers are said, "to make out *their case;* or not to make out *their case:*" meaning the *state of the matter*, which they have undertaken to prove. So, when we say that a horse is *in a good case*, we mean that he is *in a good state*.

---

[1] Lersch, ii. 25. Περὶ σημαινόντων, or περὶ φωνῆς; and περὶ σημαινομένων, or περὶ πραγμάτων.

Nouns may be in different *states*, or *situations*, as to other nouns, or other words. For instance, a noun may be the name of a person who *strikes* a horse, or of a person who *possesses* a horse, or of a person whom a horse *kicks*. And these different situations, or states, are, therefore, called *cases*.'[1]

Genitive Case.

And how are the dark scholars in the government schools of India to guess the meaning of *genitive case*? The Latin *genitivus* is a mere blunder, for the Greek word *genikē* could never mean *genitivus*. *Genitivus*, if it is meant to express the case of origin or birth, would in Greek have been called *gennētikē*, not *genikē*. Nor does the genitive express the relation of son to father. For though we may say, 'the son of the father,' we may likewise say, 'the father of the son.' *Genikē*, in Greek, had a much wider, a much more philosophical meaning.[2] It meant *casus generalis*, the general case, or rather, the case which expresses the genus or kind. This is the real power of the genitive. If I say, 'a bird of the water,' 'of the water' defines the genus to which a certain bird belongs; it refers it to the genus of water-birds. 'Man of the mountains' means a mountaineer. In phrases such as 'son of the father,' or 'father of the son,' the genitives have the same effect. They predicate something of the son or of the father; and if we distinguish

---

[1] William Cobbett, *A Grammar of the English Language*, Letter V. § 44.

[2] Schömann, Was bedeutet γενική πτῶσις, in Höfer's *Zeitschrift für die Wissenschaft der Sprache*, 1846, i. s. 83; ii. s. 126. *Beiträge zur Geschichte der Grammatik*, von Dr. K. E. A. Schmidt, Halle, 1859. Ueber den Begriff der γενική πτῶσις, s. 320.

between the sons of the father, and the sons of the mother, the genitives would mark the class or genus to which the sons respectively belonged. They would answer the same purpose as the adjectives, paternal and maternal. It can be proved etymologically that the termination of the genitive is, in many cases, identical with those derivative suffixes by which substantives are changed into adjectives.[1]

[1] In the Tibetan languages the rule is, 'Adjectives are formed from substantives by the addition of the genitive sign,' which might be inverted into, 'The genitive is formed from the nominative by the addition of the adjective sign.' For instance, *shing*, wood; *shing-gi*, of wood, or wooden: *ser*, gold; *ser-gyi*, of gold, or golden: *mi*, man; *mi-yi*, of man, or human. The same in Garo, where the sign of the genitive is *ni*, we have: *mánde-ni jak*, the hand of man, or the human hand; *ambal-ni kethdli*, a wooden knife, or a knife of wood. In the Dravidian languages adjectives are formed by the same suffixes which occur among the terminations of the genitive; and in Africa the same peculiarity has been pointed out in the Congo language. (Terrien Poncel, *Du Langage*, p. 109; Caldwell, *Dravidian Grammar*, p. 230; see also Boller, *Declination in den Finnischen Sprachen*, p. 167.) In Hindustani, Marâthi, etc., the genitive is so clearly an adjective, that it actually takes the marks of gender according to the words to which it refers. But how is it in Sanskrit and Greek? In Sanskrit we may form adjectives by the addition of tya. (*Turanian Languages*, p. 41 seq.; *Essay on Bengali*, p. 333.) For instance, dakshinâ, south; dakshinâ-tya, southern. This tya is clearly a demonstrative pronoun, the same as the Sanskrit syas, syâ, tyad, this or that. Tya is a pronominal base, and therefore such adjectives as dakshinâ-tya, southern, or âp-tya, aquatic, from âp, water, must have been conceived originally as 'water-there,' or 'south-there.' Followed by the terminations of the nominative singular, which was again an original pronoun, âptyas would mean âp-tya-s, i.e. water-there-he. Now, it makes little difference whether I say an aquatic bird, or a bird of the water. In Sanskrit the genitive of water would be, if we take udaka, udaka-sya. This sya is the same pronominal base as the adjective termination tya, only that the former does not, like the adjective, take any sign for the gender. The genitive udakasya is therefore the same as an adjective without gender. Now let us look to Greek. We there form adjectives by σιος, which is the same as the Sanskrit suffix tyas. For instance, from δῆμος, people, the Greeks formed δημόσιος, belonging to the people. Here ος, α, ον,

THE EMPIRICAL STAGE.

It is hardly necessary to trace the history of what I call the empirical study, or the grammatical analysis of language, beyond Rome. With Dionysius Thrax the framework of grammar was finished. Later writers have improved and completed it, but they have added nothing really new and original. We can follow the stream of grammatical science from Dionysius Thrax to our own time in an almost uninterrupted chain of Greek and Roman writers. We find M. Verrius Flaccus, the tutor of the grandsons of Augustus, and Quintilian in the first century; Scaurus, Apollonius Dyscolus, and his son, Herodianus, in the second; Probus and Donatus, the teacher of St. Jerome,' in the fourth. After Constantine had moved the seat of government from Rome, grammatical science received a new home in the academy of Constantinople. There were no less than twenty Greek and Latin grammarians who held professorships at Constantinople. Under Justinian, in the sixth century, the name of Priscianus gave a new lustro to grammatical studies, and his work remained an authority during the Middle Ages to nearly our own times. We ourselves have been taught grammar

mark the gender. Leave the gender out, and you get δημοσιο. Now, there is a rule in Greek that an s between two vowels, in grammatical terminations, is elided. Thus the genitive of γένος is not γένεσος, but γένεος, or γένους; hence δημοσιο would necessarily become δήμοιο (cf. ἥσιος = ἥοιος). And what is δημοιο but the regular Homeric genitive of δῆμος, which in later Greek was replaced by δήμου ? Thus we see that the same principles which governed the formation of adjectives and genitives in Tibetan, in Garo, and Hindustani, were at work in the primitive stages of Sanskrit and Greek; and we perceive how accurately the real power of the genitive was determined by the ancient Greek grammarians, who called it the general or predicative case, whereas the Romans spoiled the term by wrongly translating it into *genitivus.*

according to the plan which was followed by Dionysius at Rome, by Priscianus at Constantinople, by Alcuin at York; and whatever may be said of the improvements introduced into our system of education, the Greek and Latin grammars used at our public schools are mainly founded on the first empirical analysis of language, prepared by the philosophers of Athens, applied by the scholars of Alexandria, and transferred to the practical purpose of teaching a foreign tongue by the Greek professors at Rome.

CHAPTER IV.

THE CLASSIFICATORY STAGE.

WE traced, in our last chapter, the origin and progress of the empirical study of languages from the time of Plato and Aristotle to our own school-boy days. We saw at what time, and under what circumstances, the first grammatical analysis of language took place; how its component parts, the parts of speech, were named; and how, with the aid of a terminology, half philosophical and half empirical, a system of teaching languages was established, which, whatever we may think of its intrinsic value, has certainly answered that purpose for which it was chiefly intended.

Grammatical Study of Sanskrit.

Considering the process by which this system of grammatical science was elaborated, it could not be expected to give us an insight into the nature of language. The division into nouns and verbs, articles and conjunctions, the schemes of declension and conjugation, were a merely artificial network thrown over the living body of language. We must not look in the grammar of Dionysius Thrax for a correct and well-articulated skeleton of human speech. But it is all the more curious, to observe the striking coincidences between the grammatical terminology of the

Greeks and the Hindus, which would seem to prove that there must be some true and natural foundation for the much-abused grammatical system of the schools. The Hindus are the only nation that cultivated the science of grammar without having received any impulse, directly or indirectly, from the Greeks. Yet we find in Sanskrit too the same system of cases, called vibhakti, or inflections, the active, passive, and middle voices, the tenses, moods, and persons, divided not exactly, but very nearly, in the same manner as in Greek.[1] In Sanskrit, grammar is called Vyâkarana, which means analysis or taking to pieces. As Greek grammar owed its origin to the critical study of Homer, Sanskrit grammar arose from the study of the Vedas, the most ancient poetry of the Brahmans. The differences between the dialect of these sacred hymns and the literary Sanskrit of later ages were noted and preserved with a religious care. We still possess the first essays in the grammatical science of the Brahmans, the so-called Prâtisâkhyas. These works, though they merely profess to give rules on the proper pronunciation of the ancient dialect of the Vedas, furnish us at the same time with observations of a grammatical character, and particularly with those valuable lists of words, irregular or in any other way remarkable, the Ganas. These supplied the solid basis on which successive generations of scholars erected that astounding structure which reached its perfection in the grammar of Pânini. There is no form, regular or irregular, in the whole Sanskrit language, which is not provided

[1] See M. M.'s *History of Ancient Sanskrit Literature*, p. 158.

for in the grammar of Pâṇini and his commentators. It is the perfection of a merely empirical analysis of language, unsurpassed, nay even unapproached, by anything in the grammatical literature of other nations. Yet of the real nature, and natural growth of language, it teaches us nothing.

What then do we know of language after we have learnt the grammar of Greek or Sanskrit, or after we have transferred the network of classical grammar to our own tongue?

The Facts of Grammar.

We know certain forms of language which correspond to certain forms of thought. We know that the subject must assume the form of the nominative, the object that of the accusative. We know that the more remote object may be put in the dative, and that the predicate, in its most general form, may be rendered by the genitive. We are taught that whereas in English the genitive is marked by a final s, or by the preposition *of*, it is in Greek expressed by a final os, in Latin by *is*. But what this os and *is* represent, why they should have the power of changing a nominative into a genitive, a subject into a predicate, remains a riddle. It is self-evident that each language, in order to be a language, must be able to distinguish by some means or other the subject from the object, the nominative from the accusative. But how a mere change of termination should suffice to convey so material a distinction would seem almost incomprehensible. If we look for a moment beyond Greek and Latin, we see that there are in reality but few languages which have distinct forms for these two categories of thought. Even in Greek and Latin there is no outward distinction between the nominative and accusative of neuters. The Chinese language, it is commonly said, has no grammar at all; that is to say, it has no inflections, no declension and conjugation, in our sense of these words; it makes no formal distinction of the various parts of speech, noun, verb, adjective, adverb, &c. Yet there is no shade of thought that cannot be rendered in Chinese. The Chinese have no more difficulty in distinguishing between 'James beats John,' and 'John beats James,' than the Greeks and Romans or we ourselves. They have no termination for the accusative, but they attain the same by always placing the subject before, and the object after the verb, or by employing words, before or after the noun, which clearly indicate that it is to be taken as the object of the verb.

Grammar in Chinese.

The Chinese[1] do not decline their substantives, but they indicate the cases distinctly—

   A. By means of particles.

   B. By means of position.

1. The nominative or the subject of a sentence is always placed at the beginning.

2. The genitive may be marked—

(*a*) By the particle *tchi* placed between the two nouns, of which the first is in the genitive, the second in the nominative. Example, *jin tchi kiun* (hominum princeps, literally, man, sign of the genitive, prince).

---

[1] The statements are made on the authority of Stanislas Julien, the greatest Chinese scholar in Europe (died 1873).

(*b*) By position, placing the word which is in the genitive first, and the word which is in the nominative, second. Ex. *koue* (kingdom) *jin* (man), i.e. a man of the kingdom.

3. The dative may be expressed—

(*a*) By the preposition *yu*, to. Ex. *sse* (to give) *yen* (money) *yu* (to) *jin* (man).

(*b*) By position, placing first the verb, then the word which stands in the dative, lastly, the word which stands in the accusative. Ex. *yu* (to give) *jin* (to a man) *pe* (white) *yu* (jade) *houng* (yellow) *kin* (metal), i.e. gold.

4. The accusative is either left without any mark, for instance, *pao* (to protect) *min* (the people), or it is preceded by certain words which had originally a more tangible meaning, but gradually dwindled away into mere signs of the accusative. These were first discovered and correctly explained by M. Stanislas Julien in his *Vindiciæ Philologicæ in Linguam Sinicam*: Paris, 1830. The particles most frequently used for this purpose by modern writers are *pa* and *tsiang*, to grasp, to take. Ex. *pa* (taking) *tchoung-jin* (crowd of men) *t'eou* (secretly) *k'an* (he looked), i.e. he looked secretly at the crowd of men (hominum turbam furtim aspiciebat). In the more ancient Chinese (*Kou-wen*) the words used for the same purpose are *i* (to employ, &c.), *iu*, *hou*. Ex. *i* (employing) *jin* (humanity) *t'sun* (he preserves) *sin* (in the heart), i.e. humanitatem conservat corde. *I* (taking) *tchi* (right) *wéi* (to make) *k'iŏ* (crooked), i.e. rectum facere curvum. *Pao* (to protect) *hou* (sign of accus.) *min* (the people).

5. The ablative is expressed—

(a) By means of prepositions, such as *thsong, yeou, tseu, hou*. Ex. *thsong* (ex) *thien* (cœlo) *lai* (venire); *te* (obtinere) *hou* (ab) *thien* (cœlo).

(b) By means of position, so that the word in the ablative is placed before the verb. Ex. *thien* (heaven) *hiang-tchi* (descended, *tchi* being the relative particle or sign of the genitive) *tsaï* (calamities), i.e. the calamities which Heaven sends to men.

6. The instrumental is expressed—

(a) By the preposition *yu*, with. Ex. *yu* (with) *kien* (the sword) *cha* (to kill) *jin* (a man).

(b) By position, the substantive which stands in the instrumental case being placed before the verb, which is followed again by the noun in the accusative. Ex. *i* (by hanging) *cha* (he killed) *tchi* (him).

7. The locative may be expressed by simply placing the noun before the verb. Ex. *si* (in the East or East) *yeou* (there is) *suo-tou-po* (a sthúpa); or by prepositions as described in the text.

The adjective is always placed before the substantive to which it belongs. Ex. *meï jin*, a beautiful woman.

The adverb is generally followed by a particle which produces the same effect as *e* in bene, or *ter* in celeriter. Ex. *cho-jen*, in silence, silently; *ngeou-jen*, perchance; *kiu-jen*, with fear.

Sometimes an adjective becomes an adverb through position. Ex. *chen*, good; but *chen ko*, to sing well.

Grammar in Finnish.

But there are other languages also which have more terminations even than Greek and Latin. In Finnish there are fifteen cases, expressive of every possible relation between the subject and the object; but there is no accusative, no purely objective case.[1] In English and French the distinctive terminations of the nominative and accusative have been worn off by phonetic corruption, and these languages are obliged, like Chinese, to mark the subject and object by the collocation of words.

What we learn therefore at school in being taught that *rex* in the nominative becomes *regem* in the accusative, is simply a practical rule. We know when to say *rex*, and when to say *regem*. But why the king as a subject should be called *rex*, and as an object *regem*, remains entirely unexplained. In the same manner we learn that *amo* means I love, *amavi* I loved; but why that tragical change from *love* to *no love* should be represented by the simple change of *o* to *avi*, or, in English, by the addition of a mere *d*, is neither asked nor answered.

The Origin of Grammatical Forms.

Now if there is a science of language, these are the questions which it will have to answer. If they cannot be answered, if we must be content with paradigms and rules, if the terminations of nouns and verbs must be looked upon either as conventional contrivances or as mysterious excrescences, there is no such thing as a science of language, and we must be satisfied

[1] From a similar cause the North-Indians have innumerable verbs to express every shade of action; they have different words for eating as applied to fish, flesh, animal or human, soup, vegetables, &c. But they cannot say either *I am* or *I have*. Cf. Du Ponceau, *Mémoire sur le Système grammatical des langues de quelques nations indiennes de l'Amérique du Nord*, Paris, 1838, pp. 195, 200.

with what has been called the art (τέχνη) of language or grammar.

Historical Study of Languages.

Before we either accept or decline the solution of any problem, it is right to determine what means there are for solving it. Beginning with English we should ask, what means have we for finding out why *I love* should mean I am actually loving, whereas *I loved* indicates that that feeling is past and gone? Or, if we look to languages richer in inflections than English, we should try to discover by what process, and under what circumstances, *amo*, I love, was changed in Latin, through the mere addition of an *r*, into *amor*, expressing no longer, *I love*, but *I am loved*. Did declensions and conjugations bud forth like the blossoms of a tree? Were they imparted to man ready-made by some mysterious power? Or did some wise people invent them, assigning certain letters to certain phases of thought, as mathematicians express unknown quantities by freely chosen algebraic exponents? We are here brought at once face to face with the highest and most difficult problem of our science, the origin of language. But it will be well for the present to turn our eyes away from theories, and fix our attention at first entirely on facts.

Lineal Relationship.

Let us keep to the English perfect, *I loved*, as compared with the present, *I love*. We cannot embrace at once the whole English grammar, but if we can track one form to its true lair, we shall probably have no difficulty in digging out the rest of the brood.

THE CLASSIFICATORY STAGE. 131

Now if we ask how the addition of a final *d* could express the momentous transition from being in love to being indifferent, the first thing we have to do, before attempting any explanation, would be to establish the earliest and most original form of *I loved*. This is a rule which even Plato recognised in his philosophy of language, though, we must confess, he seldom obeyed it. We know what havoc phonetic corruption may make both in the dictionary and the grammar of a language, and it would be a pity to waste our conjectures on formations which a mere reference to the history of language would suffice to explain. Now a very slight acquaintance with the history of the English language teaches us that the grammar of modern English is not the same as the grammar of Wycliffe. Wycliffe's English, again, may be traced back to what, with Sir Frederick Madden, we may call, Middle English, from 1500 to 1330; Middle English to Early English, from 1330 to 1230; Early English to Semi-Saxon, from 1230 to 1100; and Semi-Saxon to Anglo-Saxon.[1] It is evident that if we are to discover the original intention of the syllable which changes *I love* into *I loved*, we must consult the original form of that syllable wherever we can find it. We should never have known that *priest* meant originally *an elder*, unless we had traced it back to its original form *presbyter*, in which a Greek

[1] See some criticisms on this division in Marsh's *Lectures on the English Language*, p. 48. In the *Specimens of Early English* edited by Morris and Skeat, the first volume gives specimens from 1150 to 1300 (Old English Homilies to King Horn); the second from 1298 to 1393 (Robert of Gloucester to John Gower); the third from 1394 to 1579 (Piers the Ploughman to the Shepheardes Calendar, by Edmund Spenser).

K 2

scholar at once recognises the comparative of *presbys*, old.[1] If left to modern English alone, we might attempt to connect *priest* with *praying* or *preaching*, but we should not thus arrive at its true derivation. The modern word *Gospel* conveys no meaning at all. As soon as we trace it back to the original Anglo-Saxon *godspell*, and to *goddspell* in the *Ormulum*, we see that in Anglo-Saxon, if meant for *gôd-spell*, it may be a translation of *Evangelium*, good tidings, while the author of the *Ormulum* took it for God's word, with short, not with long o.[2] *Lord* would be nothing but an empty title in English, unless its original form and meaning had been discovered in the Anglo-Saxon *hláford*, which stands for *hláf-weard*, from *hláf*, a loaf, and *weard*, warden, keeper. In like manner *lady* has to be traced back to Anglo-Saxon *hláf-dige*, supposed to be a contraction of *hláf-wear-dige*, or better, of *hláf*, loaf, and Anglo-Saxon *dége*, kneader.[3]

But even after this is done, after we have traced a

---

[1] In a Greek charter of 1121 we find πρεσβύτερος changed into πρεύτε, from which the modern Italian *prete*. See Trinchera, *Syllabus Græcarum Membranarum*, p. 136.

[2] 'Goddspell onn Ennglissh nemmnedd iss God word, annd god tiþennde, God errnde,' &c.—*Ormulum*, ed. White, Dedication, v. 157. 'And beode þer godes godd-spel.'—*Layamon's Brut*, ed. Sir F. Madden, vol. iii. p. 182, v. 29,507.

[3] See Skeat, *Etymological Dictionary*, s. v. For other etymologies see Grimm, *Deutsche Grammatik*, i. p. 229; ii. pp. 339-405; also *Rechtsalterthümer*, p. 230, *note*.

In Flemish, as I learn from the Rev. Guido Gezelle, children, servants, in fact the *familiares* of a farmer are called *broodaten*, literally bread-eaters. Historically, the giving of bread, as one of the attributes of a sovereign, may be traced back to the *panes palatini* or *gradiles*, the loaves distributed daily from the steps of the imperial palace by Constantine the Great, and even before him, by the Emperor Aurelian,—our daily bread.—See Paulus Cassel, *Der Grál und sein Name*, Berlin, 1865, s. 18.

modern English word back to Anglo-Saxon, it follows by no means that we should there find it in its original form, or that we should succeed in forcing it to disclose its original intention. Anglo-Saxon is not an original or aboriginal language. It points by its very name to the Saxons and Angles of the continent. We have, therefore, to follow our word from Anglo-Saxon through the various Saxon and Low-German dialects, till we arrive at last at the earliest stage of German which is within our reach, the Gothic of the fourth century after Christ. Even here we cannot rest. For, although we cannot trace Gothic back to any earlier Teutonic language, we see at once that Gothic, too, is a modern language, and that it must have passed through numerous phases of growth before it became what it is in the mouth of Bishop Ulfilas.

Collateral Relationship.

What then are we to do?—We must try to do what is done when we have to deal with the modern Romance languages. If we could not trace a French word back to Latin, we should look for its corresponding form in Italian, and endeavour to trace the Italian to its Latin source. If, for instance, we were doubtful about the origin of the French word for fire, *feu*, we have but to look to the Italian *fuoco*, in order to see at once that both *fuoco* and *feu* are derived from the Latin *focus*. We can do this because we know that French and Italian are cognate dialects, and because we have ascertained beforehand the exact degree of relationship in which they stand to each other. Had we, instead of looking to Italian, looked to German for an explanation of the French *feu,* we should have missed the right track; for the German *feuer,* though more like *feu* than the Italian *fuoco,* could never have assumed in French the form *feu.*

Again, in the case of the preposition *hors,* which in French means *without,* we can more easily determine its derivation from the Latin *foris,* outside, after we have found that *hors* corresponds with the Italian *fuora,* the Spanish *fuera.* The French *fromage,* cheese, derives no light from Latin. But as soon as we compare the Italian *formaggio,*[1] we see that *formaggio* and *fromage* are derived from *forma;* cheese being made in Italy by keeping the milk in small baskets or forms. *Feeble,* the French *foible,* is clearly derived from Latin; but it is not till we see the Italian *fievole* that we are reminded of the Latin *flebilis,* tearful. We should never have found the etymology, that is to say the origin, of the French *payer,* the English *to pay,* if we did not consult the dictionary of the cognate dialects, such as Italian and Spanish. Here we find that *to pay* is expressed in Italian by *pagare,* in Spanish by *pagar,* whereas in Provençal we actually find the two forms *pagar* and *payar.* Now *pagar* clearly points back to Latin *pacare,* which means *to pacify, to appease.* Joinville uses *payer* in the sense both of pacifying and of paying.[2] To pacify a creditor meant to pay him; in the

---

[1] Diez, *Lexicon Comparativum.* Columella, vii. 8.

[2] *Joinville,* ed. Nat. de Wailly, p. 34, 'Il s'agenoilla devant l'evesque et se tint bien pour poioz;' p. 256, 'que se les dix mile livres ne sont paiées, que vous les facez paier.'

same manner as *une quittance*, a quittance or receipt, was originally *quietantia*, a quieting, from *quietus*, quiet.[1]

If, therefore, we wish to follow up our researches —if, not satisfied with having traced an English word back to Gothic, we want to know what it was at a still earlier period of its growth—we must determine whether there are any languages that stand to Gothic in the same relation in which Italian and Spanish stand to French—we must restore, as far as possible, the genealogical tree of the various families of human speech. In doing this we enter on the second or classificatory stage of our science; for genealogy, where it is applicable, is the most perfect form of classification.[2]

---

[1] In mediæval Latin *fredum* is ' compositio qua fisco exsoluta reus pacem a principe assequitur.' It is the German *frida*, peace, latinised. From it the French *les frais*, expense, and *défrayer*, to pay. Cf. Scheler, *Dictionnaire d'Étymologie française*, s. v.

[2] ' If we possessed a perfect pedigree of mankind, a genealogical arrangement of the races of men would afford the best classification of the various languages now spoken throughout the world; and if all extinct languages, and all intermediate and slowly-changing dialects had to be included, such an arrangement would, I think, be the only possible one. Yet it might be, that some very ancient language had altered little, and had given rise to few new languages, whilst others (owing to the spreading and subsequent isolation and states of civilisation of the several races descended from a common race) had altered much, and had given rise to many new languages and dialects. The various degrees of difference in the languages from the same stock, would have to be expressed by groups subordinate to groups; but the proper or even only possible arrangement would still be genealogical; and this would be strictly natural, as it would connect together all languages, extinct and modern, by the closest affinities, and would give the filiation and origin of each tongue.'—Darwin, *Origin of Species*, p. 422.

CHAPTER IV.

Classification of Languages.

Before, however, we proceed to examine the results which have been obtained by the combined labours of Schlegel, Humboldt, Pritchard, Bopp, Burnouf, Grimm, Pott, Benfey, Kuhn, Curtius, Schleicher, and others, in this branch of the science of language, it will be well to glance at what had been achieved before their time in the classification of the numberless dialects of mankind.

The Greeks never thought of applying the principle of classification to the varieties of human speech. They only distinguished between Greek on one side, and all other languages on the other, comprehended under the convenient name of 'barbarous.' They succeeded, indeed, in classifying four of their own dialects with tolerable correctness,[1] but they applied the term 'barbarous' so promiscuously to the other more distant relatives of Greek (the dialects of the Pelasgians,[2] Karians, Macedonians, Thracians, and Illyrians), that, for the purposes of scientific classification, it is almost impossible to make any use of the statements of ancient writers about these so-called barbarous idioms.[3]

[1] Strabo, ed. Müller et Dübner, p. 286, l. 10. Τὴν μὲν Ἰάδα τῇ παλαιᾷ Ἀτθίδι τὴν αὐτὴν φαμέν, τὴν δὲ Δωρίδα τῇ Αἰολίδι. The same writer, at the commencement of the Christian era, has the following remark on the numerous spoken dialects of Greece: σχεδὸν δέ τι καὶ νῦν, κατὰ πόλεις, ἄλλοι ἄλλως διαλέγονται· δοκοῦσι δὲ δωρίζειν ἅπαντες διὰ τὴν συμβᾶσαν ἐπικράτειαν (ibid. p. 286, l. 45). See *Romaic and Modern Greek*, by James Clyde, 1855, p. 28.

[2] Über den Namen Pelasgos, see Pischel in Kuhn's *Zeitschrift*, xx. p. 369. He derives it from *paras-ya*, 'going across into a distant country,' which he supports by the name of the עִבְרִים. The phonetic difficulties of this derivation are very serious.

[3] Herodotus (vii. 94 and 95) gives *Pelasgi* as the old name of the

Plato, indeed, in his *Cratylus* (cap. 36), throws out a hint that the Greeks might have received their own Ionians in the Peloponnesus and the islands, and of the Æolians. Nevertheless he argues (i. 57) from the dialect spoken in his time by the Pelasgi of the towns of Kreston, Plakia, and Skylake, that the old Pelasgi spoke a barbarous tongue (βάρβαρον τὴν γλῶσσαν ἱέντες). He has, therefore, to admit that the Attic race, being originally Pelasgic, unlearnt its language (τὸ Ἀττικὸν ἔθνος ἰὸν Πελασγικὸν ἅμα τῇ μεταβολῇ τῇ ἐς Ἕλληνας, καὶ τὴν γλῶσσαν μετέμαθε). See Diefenbach, *Origines Europææ*, p. 59. Dionysius of Halicarnassus (i. 17) avoids this difficulty by declaring the Pelasgi to have been from the beginning a Hellenic race, coming originally from the Peloponnesus, then settled in Thessaly, which was occupied by barbarians, and lastly expelled from Thessaly by Kuretes and Leleges, who are now called Aetolians and Lokrians. Both views, however, are merely individual theories.

The *Karians* are called βαρβαρόφωνοι by Homer (*Il.* v. 867); but Strabo (p. 565, l. 42) takes particular care to show that this was only intended to express the rough sound of their speech, and that Homer did not yet use barbarian as opposed to Hellenes. Strabo himself, however, considers the Karians as originally barbarians. He says that the Karians were formerly called Λέλεγες (p. 267, l. 15; p. 564, l. 20); and these, together with Pelasgians, Kaukones, and others, are reckoned by him (p. 266, l. 47; p. 267, l. 24) as the earlier *barbarous* inhabitants of Hellas. Again, he (p. 267, l. 36), as well as Aristotle and Dionysius of Halicarnassus (i. 17), considers the Lokrians as descendants of the Leleges, though they would hardly call the later Lokrians barbarians.

The *Macedonians* are mentioned by Strabo (p. 395, l. 45) together with 'the other Hellenes.' Demosthenes speaks of Alexander as a barbarian; Isokrates as a Heraclide. To judge from a few extant words, Macedonian might have been a Greek dialect. (Diefenbach, *Origines Europææ*, p. 62.) Justine (vii. 1) says of the Macedonians, 'Populus Pelasgi, regio Paeonia dicebatur.' There was a tradition that the country occupied by the Macedonians belonged formerly to Thracians, whom Strabo treats as barbarians, or Pierians (Thuc. ii. 99; Strabo, p. 267, l. 10); part of it to Thessalians (Strabo, p. 369, l. 44). Livius (31, 29) speaks of Aetolians, Akarnanians, and Macedonians as *ejusdem linguæ homines*.

The *Thracians* are called by Herodotus (v. 3) the greatest people after the Indians. They are distinguished by Strabo from Illyrians (Strabo, p. 260, l. 30; Diefenbach, p. 65), from Celts (Strabo, p. 252, l. 27), and by Thucydides from the Getæ and Scythians (Thuc. ii. 96). What we know of their language rests on a statement of Strabo, that the Thracians

words from the barbarians, the barbarians being older than the Greeks. But he was not able to see the full bearing of this remark. He only points out that some words, such as the names of *fire, water,* and *dog,* were the same in Phrygian and Greek; and he supposes that the Greeks borrowed them from the Phrygians (§ 26). The idea that the Greek language and that of the barbarians could have had a common source never entered his mind. It is strange that even so comprehensive a mind as that of Aristotle should have failed to perceive in languages some of that law and order which he tried to discover in other realms of nature. As Aristotle, however, did not attempt this, we need not wonder that it was not attempted by any one else for the next two thousand years. The Romans, in all scientific matters, were merely the parrots of the Greeks. Having themselves

spoke the same language as the Getæ (Strabo, p. 252, 1. 9), and the Getæ the same as the Dacians (Strabo, p. 253, 1. 15). We possess fragments of Dacian speech in the botanical names collected by Dioskorides, and these, as interpreted by Grimm, are clearly Aryan, though not Greek. The Thracians are called barbarians by Strabo, together with Illyrians and Epirotes (Strabo, p. 267, l. 6).

The *Illyrians* were barbarians in the eyes of the Greeks. They are now considered as an independent branch of the Aryan family. Herodotus refers the Veneti to the Illyrians (i. 196); and the Veneti, according to Polybius (ii. 17), who knew them, spoke a language different from that of the Celts. He adds that they were an old race, and in their manner and dress like the Celts. Hence many writers have mistaken them for Celts, neglecting the criterion of language, on which Polybius lays proper stress. The Illyrians were a widely extended race; the Pannonians, the Dalmatians, and the Dardanians (from whom the Dardanelles were called), are all spoken of as Illyrians (Diefenbach, *Origines Europææ,* pp. 74, 75).

It is lost labour to try to extract anything positive from these statements of the Greeks and Romans on the race and the language of their barbarian neighbours.

been called barbarians, they soon learnt to apply the same name to all other nations, except, of course, to their masters, the Greeks.

Barbarians.

Now *barbarian* is one of those lazy expressions which seem to say everything, but in reality say nothing. It was applied as recklessly as the word *heretic* during the Middle Ages. If the Romans had not received this convenient name of barbarian ready-made for them, they would have treated their neighbours, the Celts and Germans, with more respect and sympathy: they would, at all events, have looked at them with a more discriminating eye. And, if they had done so, they would have discovered, in spite of outward differences, that these barbarians were, after all, not very distant cousins. There was as much similarity between the language of Cæsar and the barbarians against whom he fought in Gaul and Germany as there was between his language and that of Homer. A man of Cæsar's sagacity would have seen this, if he had not been blinded by traditional phraseology. I am not exaggerating. For let us look at one instance only. If we take a verb of such constant occurrence as *to have*, we shall find the paradigms almost identical in sound in Latin and Gothic:—

English	Latin	Gothic[1]
I have	habeo	haba
Thou hast	habes	habais
He has	habet	habaiþ
We have	habemus	habam
You have	habetis	habaiþ
They have	habent	haband.

[1] Leo Meyer, *Die Gothische Sprache*, p. 38.

It surely required a certain amount of blindness, or rather of deafness, not to perceive such similarity, and that blindness or deafness arose, I believe, entirely from the single word *barbarian*. Not till that word barbarian was struck out of the dictionary of mankind, and replaced by brother, not till the right of all nations of the world to be classed as members of one genus or kind was recognised, can we look even for the first beginnings of our science.

Influence of Christianity.

This change was chiefly effected by Christianity. To the Hindu, every man not twice-born was a Mlekkha; to the Greek, every man not speaking Greek was a barbarian; to the Jew, every person not circumcised was a Gentile; to the Mohammedan, every man not believing in the Prophet is a Kâfir, an unbeliever, or a Gaur, a fire-worshipping infidel. It was Christianity which first broke down the barriers between Jew and Gentile, between Greek and Barbarian, between the white and the black. *Humanity* is a word which you look for in vain in Plato or Aristotle[1]; the idea of mankind as one family, as the children of one God, is an idea of Christian growth; and the science of mankind, and of the languages of mankind, is a science which, without Christianity, would never have sprung into life. When people had been taught to look upon all men as brethren, then, and then only, did the variety of human speech present itself as a problem that called

---

[1] See some qualifying remarks by Mr. Higginson, in the *Proceedings of American Philological Associations*, 1874, p. 21.

for a solution in the eyes of thoughtful observers; and from an historical point of view it is not too much to say that the first day of Pentecost marks the real beginning of the science of language. After that day of cloven tongues a new light is spreading over the world, and objects rise into view which had been hidden from the eyes of the nations of antiquity. Old words assume a new meaning, old problems a new interest, old sciences a new purpose. The common origin of mankind, the differences of race and language, the susceptibility of all nations of the highest mental culture—these become, in the new world in which we live, problems of scientific, because of more than scientific, interest. It is no valid objection that so many centuries should have elapsed before the spirit which Christianity infused into every branch of scientific inquiry produced visible results. We see in the oaken fleet which rides the ocean the small acorn which was buried in the ground hundreds of years ago, and we recognise in the philosophy of Albertus Magnus,[1] though nearly 1200 years after the death of Christ, in the aspirations of Kepler,[2]

---

[1] Albert, Count of Bollstädten, or, as he is more generally called, Albertus Magnus, the pioneer of modern physical science, wrote:— 'God has given to man His spirit, and with it also intellect, that man might use it for to know God. And God is known through the soul and by faith from the Bible, through the intellect from nature.' And again: 'It is to the praise and glory of God, and for the benefit of our brethren, that we study the nature of created things. In all of them, not only in the harmonious formation of every single creature, but likewise in the variety of different forms, we can and we ought to admire the majesty and wisdom of God.'

[2] These are the last words in Kepler's *Harmony of the World:*—'Thou who by the light of nature hast kindled in us the longing after the light of Thy grace, in order to raise us to the light of Thy glory, thanks to

and in the researches of the greatest philosophers of our own age, the sound of that key-note of thought which had been struck for the first time by the

Thee, Creator and Lord, that Thou lettest me rejoice in Thy works. Lo, I have done the work of my life with that power of intellect which Thou hast given. I have recorded to men the glory of Thy works, as far as my mind could comprehend their infinite majesty. My senses were awake to search as far as I could, with purity and faithfulness. If I, a worm before Thine eyes, and born in the bonds of sin, have brought forth anything that is unworthy of Thy counsels, inspire me with Thy spirit, that I may correct it. If, by the wonderful beauty of Thy works, I have been led into boldness, if I have sought my own honour among men as I advanced in the work which was destined to Thine honour, pardon me in kindness and charity, and by Thy grace grant that my teaching may be to Thy glory, and the welfare of all men. Praise ye the Lord, ye heavenly Harmonies, and ye that understand the new harmonies, praise the Lord. Praise God, O my soul, as long as I live. From Him, through Him, and in Him is all, the material as well as the spiritual—all that we know and all that we know not yet—for there is much to do that is yet undone.'

These words are all the more remarkable, because written by a man who was persecuted by Christian theologians as a heretic, but who nevertheless was not ashamed to profess himself a Christian.

I end with an extract from one of the most distinguished of living naturalists:—'The antiquarian recognises at once the workings of intelligence in the remains of an ancient civilisation. He may fail to ascertain their age correctly, he may remain doubtful as to the order in which they were successively constructed, but the character of the whole tells him they are works of art, and that men like himself originated these relics of bygone ages. So shall the intelligent naturalist read at once in the pictures which nature presents to him, the works of a higher Intelligence; he shall recognise in the minute perforated cells of the coniferæ, which differ so wonderfully from those of other plants, the hieroglyphics of a peculiar age; in their needle-like leaves, the escutcheon of a peculiar dynasty; in their repeated appearance under most diversified circumstances, a thoughtful and thought-eliciting adaptation. He beholds, indeed, the works of a being *thinking* like himself, but he feels, at the same time, that he stands as much below the Supreme Intelligence, in wisdom, power, and goodness as the works of art are inferior to the wonders of nature. Let naturalists look at the world under such impressions, and evidence will pour in upon us that all creatures are expressions of the thoughts of Him whom we know, love, and adore unseen.'

apostle of the Gentiles:[1] 'For the invisible things of Him from the creation of the world are clearly seen, being understood by the things that are made, even His eternal power and Godhead.'

Work done by Missionaries.

But we shall see that the science of language owes more than its first impulse to Christianity. The pioneers of our science were those very apostles who were commanded 'to go into all the world, and preach the gospel to every creature;' and their true successors, the missionaries of the whole Christian Church. Translations of the Lord's Prayer or of the Bible into every dialect of the world, form even now the most valuable materials for the comparative philologist. As long as the number of known languages was small, the idea of classification hardly suggested itself. The mind must be bewildered by the multiplicity of facts before it has recourse to revision. As long as the only languages studied were Greek, Latin, and Hebrew, the simple division into sacred and profane, or classical and oriental, sufficed.

Semitic Languages.

But when theologians extended their studies to Arabic, Chaldee, and Syriac, a step, and a very important step, was made towards the establishment of a class or family of languages.[2] No one could help

---

[1] Romans i. 20. Locke, *Essay concerning Human Understanding*, iv. 10, 7.

[2] Hervas (*Catalogo*, i. 37) mentions the following works, published during the sixteenth century, bearing on the science of language:—*Introductio in Chaldaicum Linguam, Siriacam, atque Armenicum, et decem alias Linguas*, à Theseo Ambrosio, Papiæ, 1539, 4to. *De Ratione com-*

seeing that these languages were most intimately related to each other, and that they differed from Greek and Latin on all points on which they agreed among themselves. As early as 1606 we find *Guichard*,[1] in his *Harmonie étymologique*, placing Hebrew,

muni omnium Linguarum et Litterarum Commentarius, à Theodoro Bibliandro, Tiguri, 1548, 4to. It contains the Lord's Prayer in fourteen languages. Bibliander derives Welsh and Cornish from Greek, Greek having been carried there from Marseilles, through France. He states that Armenian differs little from Chaldee, and cites Postel, who derived the Turks from the Armenians, because Turkish was spoken in Armenia. He treats the Persians as descendants of Shem, and connects their language with Syriac and Hebrew. Servian and Georgian are, according to him, dialects of Greek.

Other works on language published during the sixteenth century are:—Perion, *Dialogorum de Linguæ Gallicæ Origine ejusque cum Græcâ Cognatione, libri quatuor*, Parisiis, 1554. He says that as French is not mentioned among the seventy-two languages which sprang from the tower of Babel, it must be derived from Greek. He quotes Cæsar (*De Bello Gallico*, vi. 14) to prove that the Druids spoke Greek, and then derives from it the modern French language!

The works of Henri Estienne (1528–1598) stand on a much sounder basis. He has been unjustly accused of having derived French from Greek. See his *Traicté de la Conformité du Langage français avec le grec*, about 1566. It contains chiefly syntactical and grammatical remarks, and its object is to show that modes of expression in Greek, which sound anomalous and difficult, can be rendered easy by a comparison of analogous expressions in French.

The Lord's prayer was published in 1548 in fourteen languages, by Bibliander; in 1591 in twenty-six languages, by Roccha (*Bibliotheca Apostolica Vaticana*, à fratre Angelo Roccha, Romæ, 1591, 4to.); in 1592 in forty languages, by Megiserus (*Specimen XL Linguarum et Dialectorum ab Hieronymo Megisero à diversis auctoribus collectarum quibus Oratio Dominica est expressa*, Francofurti, 1592); in 1593 in fifty languages, by the same author (*Oratio Dominica L diversis linguis*, cura H. Megiseri, Francofurti, 1593, 8vo.).

[1] At the beginning of the seventeenth century was published *Trésor de l'Histoire des Langues de cet Univers*, par Claude Duret, seconde édition, Iverdon, 1619, 4to. Hervas says that Duret repeats the mistakes of Postel, Bibliander, and other writers of the sixteenth century.

Before Duret came Estienne Guichard, *L'Harmonie étymologique*

THE CLASSIFICATORY STAGE.

Chaldee, and Syriac as a class of languages by themselves, and distinguishing besides between the Romance and Teutonic dialects.

Hebrew the Primitive Language.

What prevented however, for a long time, the progress of the science of language was the idea that Hebrew was the primitive language of mankind, and that therefore all languages must be derived from Hebrew. The fathers of the Church never expressed any doubt on this point. St. Jerome, in one of his epistles to Damasus,[1] writes: 'The whole of antiquity (universa antiquitas) affirms that Hebrew, in which the Old Testament is written, was the beginning of all human speech.' Origen, in his eleventh Homily on the book of Numbers, expresses his belief that the Hebrew language, originally given through Adam, remained in that part of the world which was the chosen

---

des Langues hébraïque, chaldaïque, syriaque—grecque—latine, françoise, italienne, espagnole—allemande, flamende, angloise, &c., Paris, 1606.

Hervas only knows the second edition, Paris, 1618, and thinks the first was published in 1608. The title of his book shows that Guichard distinguished between four classes of languages, which we should now call the Semitic, the Hellenic, Italic, and Teutonic: he derives, however, Greek from Hebrew.

I. I. Scaliger, in his *Diatriba de Europaeorum Linguis (Opuscula varia*, Parisiis, 1610), p. 119, distinguishes eleven classes: Latin, Greek, Teutonic, Slavonic, Epirotic or Albanian, Tataric, Hungarian, Finnic, Irish, British in Wales and Brittany, and Bask or Cantabrian.

[1] 'Initium oris et communis eloquii, et hoc omne quod loquimur, Hebraeam esse linguam qua vetus Testamentum scriptum est, universa antiquitas tradidit.' In another place (Isaiah, cap. 7) he writes:—'Omnium enim fere linguarum verbis utuntur Hebraei.' See also *Journal Asiatique*, 1850, juillet, p. 20.

portion of God, not, like the rest, left to one of His angels.[1]

The language of their sacred writings is by many people taken either for the most ancient language, or for the natural language of mankind. With the Brahmans Sanskrit is the language of the gods, and, even with the Buddhists, Pâli or Mâgadhî, the language of Buddha and of their sacred canon, the Tripitaka, a language as clearly derived from Sanskrit as Italian is from Latin, is considered as the root of all languages. The Pâli grammarian Kâtyâyana says: 'There is a language which is the root (of all languages); men and Brahmans spoke it at the commencement of the Kalpa, who never before uttered a human accent, and even the superior Buddha spoke it: it is Mâgadhî.'[2]

---

[1] 'Mansit lingua per Adam primitus data, ut putamus, Hebræa, in ea parte hominum, quae non pars alicujus angeli, sed quae Dei portio permansit.'

[2] See Spence Hardy, *Legends of the Buddhists*, p. 23, quoted from Alwis, *Lectures on Buddhism*, p. 55. The following extract is from the *Wibhanga Atuwawa*:—'Parents place their children when young either on a cot or a chair, and speak different things, or perform different actions. Their words are thus distinctly fixed by their children (on their minds), thinking that such was said by him, and such by the other; and in process of time they learn the entire language. If a child, born of a Damila mother and an Andhaka father, should hear his mother speak first, he would speak the Damila language; but if he should hear his father first, he would speak the Andhaka. If, however, he should not hear either of them, he would speak the Mâgadhî. If, again, a person in an uninhabited forest, in which no speech (is heard), should intuitively attempt to articulate words, he would speak the very Mâgadhî. It predominates in all regions, such as hell, the animal kingdom, the petta (preta) sphere, the human world, and the world of the devas (gods). The remaining eighteen languages, Kirâta, Andhaka, Yonaka, Damila, etc. undergo changes, but not the Mâgadhî, which alone is stationary, as it is said to be the language of Brahman and

When, therefore, the first attempts at a classification of languages were made, the problem, as it presented itself to scholars such as Guichard and Thomassin, was this: 'As Hebrew is undoubtedly the mother of all languages, how are we to explain the process by which Hebrew became split into so many dialects; and how can these numerous dialects, such as Greek and Latin, Coptic, Persian, Turkish, be traced back to their common source, the Hebrew?'

It is astonishing what an amount of real learning and ingenuity was wasted on this question during the seventeenth and eighteenth centuries. It finds, perhaps, but one parallel in the laborious calculations and constructions of early astronomers, who had to account for the movements of the heavenly bodies, always taking it for granted that the earth must be the fixed centre of our planetary system. But, although we know now that the labours of such scholars as Thomassin were and could not be otherwise than fruitless, it would be a most discouraging view to take of the progress of the human race, were we to look upon the exertions of eminent men in former ages, though they may have been in a wrong direction, as mere vanity and vexation of spirit. We must not forget that the very fact of the failure of such men contributed powerfully to a general conviction that there must be something wrong in the problem itself, till at last a bolder genius inverted the problem and thereby solved it. When books after

Aryas. Even Buddha, who rendered his Tepitaka words into doctrines, did so by means of the very Mâgadhî, and why? Because, by doing so, it was easy to acquire their true signification.'

books had been written to show how Greek and Latin and all other languages were derived from Hebrew,[1] and when not one single system proved satisfactory, people asked at last—' Why then *should* all languages be derived from Hebrew?'—and this very question solved the problem. It might have been natural for theologians in the fourth and fifth centuries, many of whom knew neither Hebrew nor any language except their own, to take it for granted that Hebrew was the source of all languages; but there is neither in the Old nor the New Testament a single word to necessitate this view. Of the language of Adam we know nothing; but if theologians hold that Hebrew was one of the languages that sprang from the confusion of tongues at Babel, it could not well have been the language of Adam, or of the whole earth, ' when the whole earth was still of one speech.'[2]

Although, therefore, a certain advance was made towards a classification of languages by the Semitic scholars of the seventeenth century, yet this partial advance became in other respects an impediment. The purely scientific interest in arranging languages according to their characteristic features was lost sight

---

[1] Guichard went so far as to maintain that, as Hebrew was written from right to left, and Greek from left to right, Greek words might be traced back to Hebrew by being simply read from right to left.

[2] Among the different systems of Rabbinical exegesis, there is one according to which every letter in Hebrew is reduced to its numerical value, and the word is explained by another of the same quantity; thus, from the passage, 'And all the inhabitants of the earth were of one language' (Genesis xi. 1), is deduced that they all spoke Hebrew, שָׂפָה being changed for its synonym לָשׁוֹן, and הַקֹּדֶשׁ (5+100+4+300=409) is substituted for its equivalent אֶחָת (1+8+400=409). *Coheleth*, ed. Ginsburg, p. 31. Cf. Quatremère, *Mélanges*, p. 138.

of, and erroneous ideas were propagated, the influence of which has even now not quite subsided.

Leibniz.

The first who really conquered the prejudice that Hebrew was the source of all language was Leibniz,[1] the contemporary and rival of Newton. 'There is as much reason,' he said, 'for supposing Hebrew to have been the primitive language of mankind, as there is for adopting the view of Goropius, who published a work at Antwerp, in 1580, to prove that Dutch was the language spoken in Paradise.'[2] In a letter to

---

[1] As I have repeatedly been taken to task for writing *Leibniz* without a *t*, I may state in self-defence that I did so, neither from negligence, nor from ignorance, nor from affectation, with all of which I have been charged, but for the simple reason that *Leibniz* himself *never*, either in his printed works or in his letters, spelt his name *Leibnitz*. See *Die Werke von Leibniz*, ed. Onno Klopp, Hanover, 1864, vol. i. p. xxiv.

[2] *Hermathena Joannis Goropii Becani:* Antuerpiæ, 1580. *Origines Antwerpianæ*, 1569. André Kempe, in his work on the language of Paradise, maintains that God spoke to Adam in Swedish, Adam answered in Danish, and the serpent spoke to Eve in French.

Chardin relates that the Persians believe three languages to have been spoken in Paradise; Arabic by the Serpent, Persian by Adam and Eve, and Turkish by Gabriel.

J. B. Erro, in his *El Mundo primitivo*, Madrid, 1814, claims Bask as the language spoken by Adam.

A curious discussion took place about two hundred years ago in the Metropolitan chapter of Pampeluna. The decision, as entered in the minutes of the chapter, is as follows:—1. Was Bask the primitive language of mankind? The learned members confess that, in spite of their strong conviction on the subject, they dare not give an affirmative answer. 2. Was Bask the only language spoken by Adam and Eve in Paradise? On this point the chapter declares that no doubt can exist in their minds, and that 'it is impossible to bring forward any serious or rational objection.' See Hennequin, *Essai sur l'Analogie des Langues:* Bordeaux, 1838, p. 60.

I feel bound to add a note from M. Bladé's *Études sur l'Origine des Basques*, Paris, 1859, p. 533:—' Los archivos civiles et réligieuses

Tenzel, Leibniz writes:—'To call Hebrew the primitive language, is like calling branches of a tree primitive branches, or like imagining that in some country hewn trunks could grow instead of trees. Such ideas may be conceived, but they do not agree with the laws of nature, and with the harmony of the universe, that is to say, with the Divine Wisdom.'[1]

Leibniz collects materials.

But Leibniz did more than remove this one great stumbling-block from the threshold of the science of language. He was the first to apply the principle of sound inductive reasoning to a subject which before him had only been treated at random. He pointed out the necessity of collecting, first of all, as large a number of facts as possible.[2] He appealed to missionaries, travellers, ambassadors, princes, and emperors, to help him in a work which he had so much at heart. The Jesuits in China had to work

de Pampelune ont été explorées minutieusement par des savants tels que Garibay, le P. de Moret, Yanguas y Miranda, etc.; et pas un ne confirme, que je sache, le dire de M. Hennequin. J'ai fait moi-même, et j'ai fait faire, sur ce point, des recherches demeurées sans résultat.'

[1] Guhrauer's *Life of Leibniz*, vol. ii. p. 129.

[2] Guhrauer, vol. ii. p. 127. In his *Dissertation on the Origin of Nations*, 1710, Leibniz says:—'The study of languages must not be conducted according to any other principles but those of the exact sciences. Why begin with the unknown instead of the known? It stands to reason that we ought to begin with studying the modern languages which are within our reach, in order to compare them with one another, to discover their differences and affinities, and then to proceed to those which have preceded them in former ages, in order to show their filiation and their origin, and then to ascend step by step to the most ancient tongues, the analysis of which must lead us to the only trustworthy conclusions.'

for him. Witsen,[1] the traveller, sent him a most
precious present, a translation of the Lord's Prayer
into the jargon of the Hottentots. 'My friend,'
writes Leibniz in thanking him, 'remember, I implore
you, and remind your Muscovite friends, to make researches in order to procure specimens of the Scythian
languages, the Samoyedes, Siberians, Bashkirs, Kalmuks, Tungusians, and others.'

Having made the acquaintance of Peter the Great,
Leibniz wrote to him the following letter, dated Vienna,
October the 26th, 1713:—

'I have suggested that the numerous languages,
hitherto almost entirely unknown and unstudied,
which are current in the empire of Your Majesty
and on its frontiers, should be reduced to writing;
also that dictionaries, or at least small vocabularies,
should be collected, and translations be procured in
such languages of the Ten Commandments, the Lord's
Prayer, the Apostolic Symbolum, and other parts of
the Catechism, *ut omnis lingua laudet Dominum*.
This would increase the glory of Your Majesty, who
reigns over so many nations, and is so anxious to
improve them; and it would, likewise, by means of
a comparison of languages, enable us to discover the
origin of those nations who from Scythia, which is
subject to Your Majesty, advanced into other countries.
But principally it would help to plant Christianity
among the nations speaking those dialects, and I have,

---

[1] Nicolaes Witsen, Burgomaster of Amsterdam, travelled in Russia, 1666–1672; published his travels in 1677, dedicated to Peter the Great. Second edition, 1705. It contains many collections of words.

therefore, addressed the Most Rev. Metropolitan on the same subject.'[1]

Leibniz drew up a list of the most simple and necessary terms which should be selected for comparison in various languages. At home, while engaged in historical researches, he collected whatever could throw light on the origin of the German language, and he encouraged others, such as Eccard, to do the same. He pointed out the importance of dialects, and even of provincial and local terms, for elucidating the etymological structure of languages.[2] Leibniz never undertook a systematic classification of the whole realm of language, nor was he successful in classing the dialects with which he had become acquainted. He distinguished between a Japhetic and Aramaic class, the former occupying the north, the latter the south, of the continent of Asia and Europe. He believed in a common origin of languages, and in a migration of the human race from east to west. But he failed to distinguish the exact degrees of relationship in which languages stand to each other, and he mixed up some of the Turanian dialects, such as Finnish and Tataric, with the Japhetic family of speech. If Leibniz had found time to work out all the plans which his fertile and comprehensive genius conceived, or if he had been

[1] *Catherinens der Grossen Verdienste um die vergleichende Sprachkunde*, von F. Adelung: Petersburg, 1815. Another letter of his to the Vice-Chancellor, Baron Schaffiroff, is dated Pirmont, June 22, 1716.
[2] *Collectanea Etymologica*, ii. 255. 'Malim sine discrimine Dialectorum corrogari Germanicas voces. Puto quasdam origines ex superioribus Dialectis melius apparituras; ut ex Ulfilæ Pontogothicis, Otfridi Franciscis.'

understood and supported by contemporary scholars.
the science of language, as one of the inductive
sciences, might have been established a century
earlier. But a man like Leibniz, who was equally
distinguished as a scholar, a theologian, a lawyer,
an historian, and a mathematician, could only throw
out hints as to how language ought to be studied.
Leibniz was not only the discoverer of the differ-
ential calculus. He was one of the first to watch
the geological stratification of the earth. He was
engaged in constructing a calculating machine, the
idea of which he first conceived as a boy. He drew
up an elaborate plan of an expedition to Egypt,
which he submitted to Louis XIV. in order to
avert his attention from the frontiers of Germany.
The same man was engaged in a long correspondence
with Bossuet to bring about a reconciliation between
Protestants and Romanists; and he endeavoured, in
his *Théodicée* and other works, to defend the cause
of truth and religion against the inroads of the
materialistic philosophy of England and France.
It has been said, indeed, that the discoveries of
Leibniz produced but little effect, and that most
of them had to be made again. This is not the case,
however, with regard to the science of language.
The new interest in languages, which Leibniz had
called into life, did not die again. After it had once
been recognised as a desideratum to bring together a
complete *Herbarium* of the languages of mankind,
missionaries and travellers felt it their duty to collect
lists of words and draw up grammars wherever they
came in contact with a new race. The two great

works in which, at the beginning of our century, the results of these researches were summed up— I mean the *Catalogue of Languages* by Hervas, and the *Mithridates* of Adelung—can both be traced back directly to the influence of Leibniz. As to Hervas, he had read Leibniz carefully, and though he differs from him on some points, he fully acknowledges his merits in promoting a truly philosophical study of languages. Of Adelung's *Mithridates* and his obligations to Leibniz we shall have to speak presently.

Hervas lived from 1735 to 1809. He was a Spaniard by birth, and a Jesuit by profession. While working as a missionary among the polyglottous tribes of America, his attention was drawn to a systematic study of languages. After his return, he lived chiefly at Rome in the midst of the numerous Jesuit missionaries who had at that time been recalled from all parts of the world, and who, by their communications on the dialects of the tribes among whom they had been labouring, assisted him greatly in his researches.

Most of his works were written in Italian, and were afterwards translated into Spanish. We cannot enter into the general scope of his literary labours, which are of the most comprehensive character. They were intended to form a kind of Kosmos, for which he chose the title of *Idea del Universo*. What is of interest to us is that portion which treats of man and language as part of the universe; and here, again, chiefly his *Catalogue of Languages*, in six volumes, published in Spanish in the year 1800.

If we compare the work of Hervas with a similar

work which excited much attention towards the end of the last century, and is even now more widely known than that of Hervas, I mean Court de Gebelin's *Monde primitif*,[1] we shall see at once how far superior the Spanish Jesuit is to the French philosopher. Gebelin treats Persian, Armenian, Malay, and Coptic as dialects of Hebrew; he speaks of Bask as a dialect of Celtic, and he tries to discover Hebrew, Greek, English, and French words in the idioms of America. Hervas, on the contrary, though embracing in his catalogue five times the number of languages that were known to Gebelin, is most careful not to allow himself to be carried away by theories not warranted by the evidence before him. It is easy now to point out mistakes and inaccuracies in Hervas, but I think that those who have blamed him most are those who ought most to have acknowledged their obligations to him. To have collected specimens and notices of more than three hundred languages is no small matter. But Hervas did more. He himself composed grammars of more than forty languages.[2] He was one of the first to point out that the true affinity of languages must be determined chiefly by grammatical evidence, not by mere similarity of words.[3] He proved, by a compara-

---

[1] *Monde primitif analysé et comparé avec le monde moderne.* Paris, 1773.

[2] *Catalogo*, i. 63.

[3] 'Mas se deben consultar gramaticas para conocer su caracter proprio por medio de su artificio gramatical.'—*Catalogo*, i. 65. The same principle was expressed by Lord Monboddo, about 1795, in his *Antient Metaphysics*, vol. iv. p. 326: 'My last observation is, that, as the art of a language is less arbitrary and more determined by rule than either the sound or sense of words, it is one of the principal things by which the connection of languages with one another is to be discovered. And, therefore, when we find that two languages practise these great arts of

tive list of declensions and conjugations, that Hebrew, Chaldee, Syriac, Arabic, Ethiopic, and Amharic are all but dialects of one original language, and constitute one family of speech, the Semitic.[1] He scouted the idea of deriving all the languages of mankind from Hebrew. He had perceived clear traces of affinity between Chinese and Indo-Chinese dialects; also between Hungarian, Lapponian, and Finnish, three dialects now classed as members of the Turanian family.[2] He had proved that Bask was not, as was commonly supposed, a Celtic dialect, but an independent language, spoken by the earliest inhabitants of Spain, as proved by the names of the Spanish mountains and rivers.[3] Nay, one of the most brilliant discoveries in the history of the science of language, the establishment of the Malay and Polynesian family of speech, extending from the island of Madagascar east of Africa, over 208 degrees of longitude, to the Easter Islands west of America,[4] was made by

language,—derivation, composition, and flexion,—in the same way, we may conclude, I think, with great certainty, that the one language is the original of the other, or that they are both dialects of the same language.'

[1] *Catalogo*, ii. 468.

[2] *Ibid.* i. 49. Witsen, too, in a letter to Leibniz, dated mai 22, 1698, alludes to the affinity between the Tataric and Mongolic languages. 'On m'a dit que ces deux langues (la langue moegale et tartare) sont différentes à peu près comme l'Allemand l'est du Flamand, et qu'il est de même des Kalmucs et Moegals.'—*Collectanea Etymologica*, ii. p. 363.

[3] Leibniz held the same opinion (see Hervas, *Catalogo*, i. 50), though he considered the Celts in Spain as descendants of the Iberians.

[4] *Catalogo*, i. 30. 'Verá que la lengua llamada *malaya*, la qual se habla en la península de Malaca, es matriz de innumerables dialectos de naciones isleñas, que desde dicha península se extienden por mas de doscientos grados de longitud en los mares Oriental y Pacífico.'

Ibid. ii. 10. 'De esta península de Malaca han salido enjambres de po-

Hervas long before it was worked out and announced to the world by Humboldt.

Hervas was likewise aware of the great grammatical similarity between Sanskrit and Greek, but the imperfect information which he received from his friend, the Carmelite missionary Fra Paolino da S. Bartolommeo, the author of the first Sanskrit grammar, published at Rome in 1790, prevented him from seeing the full meaning of this grammatical similarity. How near Hervas was to the discovery of the truth may be seen from his comparing such words as *Theos*, God, in Greek, with Deva, God, in Sanskrit. He identified the Greek auxiliary verb *eimi, eis, esti*, I am, thou art, he is, with the Sanskrit asmi, asi, asti. He even pointed out that the terminations of the three genders[1] in Greek, os, ē, on, are the same as the Sanskrit, as, à, am.[2] But believing, as he did, that the Greeks derived their philosophy and mythology from India, he supposed that they had likewise borrowed from the

---

bladores de las islas del mar Indiano y Pacífico, en las que, aunque parece haber otra nacion, que es de negros, la *malaya* es generalmente la mas dominante y extendida. La lengua malaya se habla en dicha península, continente del Asia, en las islas Maldivas, en la de Madagascar (perteneciente al Africa), en las de Sonda, en las Molucas, en las Filipinas, en las del archipiélago de San Lazaro, y en muchísimas del mar del Sur desde dicho archipiélago hasta islas, que por su poca distancia de América se creian pobladas por americanos. La isla de Madagascar se pone á 60 grados de longitud, y á los 268 se pone la isla de Pascua ó de Davis, en la que se habla otro dialecto malayo; por lo que la extension de los dialectos malayos es de 208 grados de longitud.'

[1] *Catalogo*, ii. 134.
[2] *Ibid.* ii. 135. From what I had said before of *Guichard, Scaliger, Witsen, Leibniz*, and others, it is quite clear that I did not consider *Hervas* as the first discoverer of those linguistic theories. I only wished to point out his real merits, which other historians had overlooked. See Benfey, *Geschichte der Sprachwissenschaft*, p. 270.

Hindus some of their words, and even the art of distinguishing the gender of words.

Adelung.

The second work which represents the science of language at the beginning of this century, and which is, to a still greater extent, the result of the impulse which Leibniz had given, is the *Mithridates* of Adelung.[1] Adelung's work depends partly on Hervas, partly on the collections of words which had been made under the auspices of the Russian government. Now these collections are clearly due to Leibniz. Although Peter the Great had no time or taste for philological studies, the government kept the idea of collecting all the languages of the Russian empire steadily in view.[2] Still greater luck was in store for the science of language. Having been patronised by Cæsar at Rome, it found a still more devoted patroness in the great Cesarina of the North, Catharine the Great (1762–1796). Even as Grand-duchess, Catharine was engrossed with the idea of a Universal Dictionary, on the plan suggested by Leibniz. She encouraged the chaplain at the British Factory at St. Petersburg, the Rev. Daniel Dumaresq, to undertake the work, and he is said to have published, at

---

[1] The first volume appeared in 1806. He died before the second volume was published, which was brought out by Vater in 1809. The third and fourth volumes followed in 1816 and 1817, edited by Vater and the younger Adelung.

[2] Evidence of this is to be found in Strahlenberg's work on the *North and East of Europe and Asia*, 1730, with tabula polyglotta, &c.; in Messerschmidt's *Travels in Siberia*, from 1729–1730; in Bachmeister, *Idea et desideria de colligendis linguarum speciminibus*, Petropoli, 1773; in Güldenstädt's *Travels in the Caucasus*, &c.

her desire, a *Comparative Vocabulary of Eastern Languages,* in quarto; a work, however, which, if ever published, is now completely lost. The reputed author died in London in 1805, at the advanced age of eighty-four. When Catharine came to the throne, her plans of conquest hardly absorbed more of her time than her philological studies; and she once shut herself up nearly a year, devoting all her time to the compilation of her Comparative Dictionary. A letter of hers to Zimmermann, dated the 9th of May, 1785, may interest some of my readers:—

'Your letter,' she writes, 'has drawn me from the solitude in which I had shut myself up for nearly nine months, and from which I found it hard to stir. You will not guess what I have been about. I will tell you, for such things do not happen every day. I have been making a list of from two to three hundred radical words of the Russian language, and I have had them translated into as many languages and jargons as I could find. Their number exceeds already the second hundred. Every day I took one of these words and wrote it out in all the languages which I could collect. This has taught me that the Celtic is like the Ostiakian: that what means sky in one language means cloud, fog, vault, in others; that the word God in certain dialects means Good, the Highest, in others, sun or fire. [As far as this her letter is written in French; then follows a line of German.] I became tired of my hobby, after I had read your book on Solitude. [Then again in French.] But as I should have been sorry to throw such a mass of paper in the fire,—besides, the room, six fathoms in length, which I use as a boudoir in my hermitage, was pretty well warmed,—I asked Professor Pallas to come to me, and after making an honest confession of my sin, we agreed to publish these collections, and thus make them useful to those who like to occupy themselves with the forsaken toys of others. We are only waiting for some more dialects of Eastern Siberia. Whether the world at large will or will not see in this work bright ideas of different kinds, must depend on the disposition of their minds, and does not concern me in the least.'

If an empress rides a hobby, there are many ready to help her. Not only were all Russian ambassadors instructed to collect materials; not only did German professors[1] supply grammars and dictionaries, but Washington himself, in order to please the empress, sent her list of words to all governors and generals of the United States, enjoining them to supply the equivalents from the American dialects. The first volume of the Imperial Dictionary[2] appeared in 1787, containing a list of 285 words translated into

---

[1] The empress wrote to Nicolai at Berlin to ask him to draw up a catalogue of grammars and dictionaries. The work was sent to her in manuscript from Berlin, in 1785.

[2] *Glossarium comparativum Linguarum totius Orbis.* Petersburg, 1787. A second edition, in which the words are arranged alphabetically, appeared in 1790–91, in 4 vols., edited by Jankiewitsch de Miriewo. It contains 279 (272) languages, i. e. 171 for Asia, 55 for Europe, 30 for Africa, and 23 for America. According to Adelung, as quoted by Pott, *Ungleichheit*, p. 230, it contains 277 languages, 185 for Asia, 52 for Europe, 28 for Africa, 15 for America. This would make 280. The first edition is a very scarce book.

fifty-one European and one hundred and forty-nine Asiatic languages. Though full credit should be given to the empress for this remarkable undertaking, it is but fair to remember that it was the philosopher who, nearly a hundred years before, sowed the seed that fell into good ground.

CHAPTER V.

THE DISCOVERY OF SANSKRIT.

Imperfect Classification.

AS collections, the works of Hervas, of the Empress Catharine, and of Adelung were highly important; though such is the progress made in the science of language during the last fifty years, that few people would now consult them. The principle of classification which is followed in these works can hardly claim to be called scientific. Languages are arranged geographically, as the languages of Europe, Asia, Africa, America, and Polynesia, though, at the same time, natural affinities are admitted which would unite dialects spoken at a distance of 208 degrees. Languages seemed to float about like islands on the ocean of human speech; they did not shoot together to form themselves into larger continents. This is a most critical period in the history of every science, and if it had not been for a happy accident, which, like an electric spark, caused the floating elements to crystallise into regular forms, it is more than doubtful whether the long list of languages and dialects, enumerated and described in the works of Hervas and Adelung, could long have sustained the interest of the student of languages. This electric spark was the discovery of Sanskrit, the ancient language of the Hindus.

The Language of India.

The history of the language and the dialects of India is by no means so simple and clear as was formerly supposed. The more it is studied, the more complicated it becomes. It begins with the Sanskrit of the Vedas, about 1500 B.C., though some scholars are inclined to place its beginning at a much earlier date. To me it seems that the admission of an earlier date would no doubt remove some difficulties, but that direct proof is quite impossible.

Vedic Sanskrit.

We can watch the Vedic language in three stages, that of the hymns, that of the Brâhmanas, and that of the Sûtras. Between the hymns and the Brâhmanas there must have been a complete break, and however carefully the pronunciation of the Vedic hymns may have been preserved by oral tradition, their true meaning had evidently been completely lost between the two periods. There is no such break between the Brâhmanas and the Sûtras, but the language of the Sûtras has preserved but few of the old Vedic peculiarities, and does not differ much from the ordinary Sanskrit, as fixed by the rules of Pâṇini's grammar.

The language of the Vedic hymns must have been at one time a spoken language in the North-West of India, but it should be remembered that we know it in its poetic form only, and mostly as applied to religious subjects. Though we cannot form a clear idea how these hymns were composed, preserved, and finally collected, one thing is quite certain, that they soon assumed a sacred character, and were handed down with the most minute care. It is equally admitted by most Sanskrit scholars who have paid attention to this subject, that they were preserved till about the third century B.C. by means of oral tradition only. When I endeavoured for the first time to establish this fact in my *History of Ancient Sanskrit Literature* (1859),[1] I had to depend to a great extent on circumstantial evidence only. We know now, as a matter of fact, that the alphabets employed in India in the third century B.C. by Asoka, would have been totally inadequate for reducing the Vedic hymns to a written form.[2] But this very ignorance of the art of writing produced a system of oral tradition of which we should have had no idea unless a full account of it had been preserved for us in the Prâtisâkhyas. No written alphabet which we know could ever have rendered the minute shades of pronunciation as detailed by the authors of the Prâtisâkhyas, no copyists could have handed down to us so accurate a representation of the Vedic hymns as we still meet with in the memory of living Srotriyas.[3]

---

[1] *History of Ancient Sanskrit Literature*, pp. 497–524, 'The Introduction of Writing.'

[2] The old alphabet of the North-West has no signs for long vowels. Neither the North-Western nor the Magadha alphabet represents double consonants. The vowel *ri* was at first absent in both. The palatal *s* is absent in the old Magadha alphabet, and develops in later inscriptions. Senart, *Journal Asiatique*, 1886, p. 110.

[3] Our best Vedic MSS. presuppose a knowledge of the rules of pronunciation as laid down in the Prâtisâkhyas, and cannot be read by us without such knowledge. Even in cases where the Devanâgari alphabet could have expressed the more delicate varieties of pronunciation, the writers of the best MSS. are satisfied with indicating them, trusting that the reader will pronounce correctly, according to the rules of Sikshâ phonetics).

It is clear, however, that this scholastic study of the Veda became a retarding element in the growth of the ancient language. Vedic Sanskrit became hieratic and unchangeable, and may thus have imparted even to the spoken language of the higher classes an amount of grammatical fixity which no language possesses in its natural state. We see indeed a small progress between the poetic hymns and the prose Brâhmaṇas, and again between the Brâhmaṇas and the Sûtras, but the grammar of the Sûtras, with the exception of some surviving Vedic forms, remained the grammar of Sanskrit, as fixed once for all by the grammatical rules of Pâṇini, whose probable, though by no means certain, date is the fourth century B.C. All Sanskrit literature after Pâṇini is under the iron sway of that grammarian. The literary language is no longer allowed to grow or to decay, but whatever contravenes his rules is *ipso facto* a blunder.[1] This applies to Kâlidâsa as much as to those who continue to write and speak Sanskrit to the present day.

Asoka's Inscriptions.

So far the history of Sanskrit seems clear and intelligible. But as soon as the real history of India begins, in the third century B.C., all is changed. We then perceive that the Vedic and the Pâṇinean Sanskrit form but one straight channel, and that by its side there run numerous streams of living speech, which are as far removed from Vedic and even from Pâṇinean Sanskrit as the Romanic dialects are from

[1] See M. M., *The Renaissance of Sanskrit Literature*, in 'India, what can it teach us?' pp. 281-360.

Latin. This fact cannot be doubted, for the inscriptions of Asoka are truly historical documents, contemporary witnesses of the language as then spoken in India; and in India, where historical documents are so scarce, their value, not only for chronology and political history, but for the study of the historical growth of the language of the country is immense.

I call the inscriptions of Asoka the only truly historical documents of the growth of the language of India for two reasons; first, because they are contemporary; secondly, because they are not written according to grammatical rules.

Grammatical and Ungrammatical Prâkrits.

If we call all Indian dialects which descend from Sanskrit, Prâkrit, we must distinguish between two classes, the *grammatical* and the *ungrammatical* Prâkrits, which may be called Apabhram̃sas. By grammatical Prâkrits I mean those which, like Sanskrit, are written according to the rules of grammarians, such as Pâli, the Prâkrit of the Buddhist scriptures, the *G*aina Mâgadhî of the *G*aina scriptures, and the Brahmanic Prâkrits, the so-called Mahârâshṭrî, Saurasenî, and Mâgadhî. The last-named Prâkrits were used for popular poetry, such as the Saptasataka of Hâla (467 A. D.), and for academic poetry, such as the Setubandha, the Gau*d*avadha, and, more particularly, for dramatic plays.

Grammatical Prâkrits.

Vararu*k*i, the oldest Prâkrit grammarian, treats of one classical Prâk*r*ita, which in one place he calls

Mahârâshtrî. Whether he meant by this name to assign it to the country commonly called Mahârâshtra, or whether Dr. Hörnle is right in supposing that Mahârâshtrî with him meant the Prâkrit of the great kingdom, i.e. the Doâb and Râjpûtânâ,[1] certain it is that it is the Prâkrita *pur excellence.* Of the other dialects which Vararu*k*i mentions, Saurasenî, if it everwas restricted to the country of the Sûrasenas (about Mathurâ or the Vra*ga*) became for literary purposes the prose dialect, while Mahârâshtrî was reserved for poetry.[2] Saurasenî is in fact a mere subdivision of the Prâk*r*ita (Mahârâsh*t*rî), and hence, after the few special rules for Saurasenî have been given, Vararu*k*i (xii. 32) says, 'the rest is like Mahârâsh*t*rî'; while Hema*k*andra (iv. 286) says, 'the rest is like Prâk*r*ita.'

As to Mâgadhî (Behar), Vararu*k*i (xi. 2) and Hema*k*andra (iv. 302) treat it as a modification of Saurasenî, and therefore indirectly of Mahârâshtrî. Paisâkî, as its very name indicates, is not a dialect properly so called, but Prâkrit as corrupted in the mouths of barbarians or devils.[3] Vararu*k*i (x. 2) and Hema*k*andra (iv. 323) treat it as a corruption of Saurasenî. The Paisâkî in which the popular tales

---

[1] *Comparative Grammar of the Gaudian Languages,* p. xxii; Professor Jacobi takes Mahârâsh*t*rî as the language of Mahârâshtra, the country on the Upper Godâvarî with Pratish*t*hâna as its capital (*Ausgewählte Erzählungen,* p. xiv). Dr. Hörnle maintains that Mahârâsh*t*rî has not one point in common with Marâ*th*î in which the latter differs from Western Hindi.

[2] Sâhitya-Darpa*n*a, vi. § 732.

[3] See Hörnle, *Comparative Grammar of the Gaudian Languages,* p. xix. Lakshmîdhara mentions as Pisâka countries those of the Pâ*n*dya, Kekaya, Vâhlîka, Sahya, Nepâla, Kuntala, Sudesha (sic), Bhota, Gandhâra, Haiva, Kano*y*ana (sic).

168   CHAPTER V.

are said to have been composed, the Brihat-kathâ, is unknown, and was probably a different dialect.

If we call the dialectic peculiarities of the Sauraseṇî x, and those of the Mâgadhî y, those of Paiśâkî z, then

Sauraseṇî is = Prâkrita + x,
Mâgadhî = Prâkrita + x + y,
Paiśâkî = Prâkrita + x + z.

We have therefore, according to Prâkrit grammarians, one general Prâkrita only, that of the great kingdom (Mahârâshtrî), while the other Prâkrits are minor modifications of it, used chiefly for theatrical purposes.

Pâli, the oldest Prâkrit, is naturally ignored by the Prâkrit grammarians, as its use is restricted to Buddhist, that is, to a heretical literature. The Mahârâshtrî was used by the Gainas in their ordinary literature, while the Mahârâshtrî of their sacred canon or Siddhânta, settled at the Council of Valabhî, 454 A.D., has preserved a number of archaic words and forms, and comes nearer in some respects to Pâli.[1]

We must remember that anything written in these grammatical Prâkrits was written, like Sanskrit, in fear and trembling. It is either right or wrong, according as it conforms to the rules of Kâtyâyana for Pâli, of Vararuki, Hemakandra, and other grammarians for the other Prâkrits. The Pâli of the Tipitaka obeys the rules of Kâtyâyana, not *vice versâ*; and the same applies to the language of the Gainas and to the Sauraseṇî and Mâgadhî of the plays. The grammars presuppose, no doubt, a spoken language, but they also regulate it, and we know the spoken language

[1] Jacobi, *S. B. E.*, xxii, p. xli; Kalpasûtra, p. 17.

THE DISCOVERY OF SANSKRIT. 169

only as regulated by them. There are forms in Pâli which may almost be called Vedic, as being no longer allowed for ordinary Sanskrit by Pânini, nor tolerated in the later Prâkrits. This shows that the Pâli of the Tipi*t*aka[1] has an historical foundation, but, as we know it, it has been reduced to strict grammatical regularity. The language spoken by Asoka was certainly not that of the Tipi*t*aka which his son Mahinda is supposed to have taken to Ceylon. In order to account for the grammatical uniformity of the language, both of the Buddhist and the *G*aina Canons, we must, I think, place their final edition later than the date of the earliest Pâli and Prâkrit grammarians. Kâlidâsa wrote his plays in the fear of Vararu*k*i quite as much as of Pâ*n*ini, and to the present day[2] plays are written in Sanskrit and Prâkrit, in which it is as difficult to detect a grammatical blunder as in the works of the great classical poets. It is very significant also, that these so-called grammatical Prâkrits are not used for ancient historical inscriptions.

Ungrammatical Prâkrits. Asoka's Inscriptions.

Quite different from these grammatical Prâkrits are the dialects employed in the inscriptions of Asoka and in some later inscriptions, extending in the North to the first century A. D., in the West to the second. These inscriptions are not written according to the rules of grammarians, but look like more or less successful attempts at representing, for the first time, the vernaculars, such as they were spoken at the time.

[1] See Muir, *Sanskrit Texts*, ii. p. 72.
[2] I have just received a play called the Sâmavatam, by Ambikâdattavyâsa, irreproachable in language and metre.

They represent a degree of corruption half-way between Pâli and the grammatical Prâkrits, but they differ from both by the unsettled state of their phonetic and grammatical character.

The Gâthâ Dialect.

The language used in the sacred writings of the Northern Buddhists, called the *Gâthâ dialect*, or by M. Senart, *Mixed Sanskrit*, belongs to the same category. It has not been written down, nor does it seem to have been remodelled according to the rules of any known grammarian, but it has a more scholastic character, and was probably reduced to writing by men more acquainted with the Sanskrit literature than the scribes of Asoka. It cannot, however, claim the same historical importance as the language of Asoka's inscriptions, because we are unable as yet to fix either its exact date or its locality.

Ancient Apabhramsas.

It seems to me that we must treat the language of the inscriptions as well as the language of the Northern Buddhist Canon as old Apabhramsas. Prâkrit grammarians distinguish between three component elements in Prâkrit, (1) tatsamas, words which are the same in Prâkrit and Sanskrit; (2) tadbhavas, words which are borrowed from Sanskrit and modified according to rule; (3) desî, literally local words, but often of Sanskrit origin, though not easily traced back to it.[1]

In addition to the Prâkrits, however, which comprise these three elements, Hemakandra mentions the

---

[1] See Hemakandra's Desînâmamâlâ, edited by Pischel and Bühler, Bombay, 1880; Prâkrita-lakshanam, ed. Hörnle, p. 1.

THE DISCOVERY OF SANSKRIT. 171

Apabhramsas, the spoken vernaculars of different parts of India. The more important are the Abhirî (Sindhî, Marwârî), the Âvantî (East-Râjpûtànî), the Gaurgarî (Gujarâtî), the Bâhlîkâ (Panjâbî), the Saurasenî (West-Hindî), the Mâgadhî or Prâkyâ (East-Hindî), the Odrî (Orîyâ), the Gaudî (Bangâlî), the Dâkshinâtyâ or Vaidarbhikâ (Marâthî), and the Paippâlî (Naipâlî?).[1]

It is quite clear from this list that these Apabhramsas were local dialects, and as we find a Saurasenî Apabhramsa, and a Mâgadhî Apabhramsa by the side of the Saurasenî and Mâgadhî Prâkrita, it would seem to follow that the Apabhramsas represented the vulgar, the Prâkritas the literary dialects. Dr. Hörnle has called attention to the fact that no Apabhramsa is mentioned for the Mahârâshtrî, and this would no doubt tend to confirm his theory that Mahârâshtrî is not the name of a local Prâkrit, but of the general Prâkrit of the great kingdom.[2]

What chiefly distinguishes Apabhramsas from Prâkrits is their unsettledness. Nearly all the rules applying to them are said to be prâyas, optional,[3] and the same applies to the language of the inscriptions and that of the Gâthâs.

It seems even possible to distinguish two Apabhramsas in the inscriptions which were put up in different parts of Asoka's kingdom.

Two Classes of Asoka's Inscriptions.

One class, the North-Western, comprises the inscriptions of Kapurdigiri and Girnar, the other all the

[1] See Hörnle, *Grammar*, p. xxi. [2] *L. c.* p. xxi.
[3] Hemakandra, iv. 329.

rest, those of Khalsi, Dhauli and Jaugada, Babhra, Sahasarâm, Rûpanâth, Bairat, Kausâmbî, Barâbar, the so-called Edict of the Queen Allahabad, and the inscription on the column of Delhi and similar columns.[1] The first class possesses the lingual n and the palatal ñ, retains the initial y and the r, has the nom. sing. masc. in o and the locative in amhi or e; the second has no lingual n, no palatal ñ, drops initial y, changes r into l, and has the nom. sing. masc. and mostly neuter also in e, the locative in asi.[2] The nominative in e and the change of r into l were formerly considered sufficient for identifying the language of this class of inscriptions with the literary Mâgadhî Prâkrit, but this evidence seems far too meagre.[3] The language spoken in Magadha, the principal portion of his kingdom, may have exercised some influence on the writers of these inscriptions. But we must not forget that these edicts were not meant for Magadha alone, but for the whole kingdom, so that purely dialectic idioms would rather have had to be avoided in composing them.

Introduction of Writing.

And here we must try to realise the difficulties which the ministers of King Asoka had to encounter in trying for the first time to write the language of the people. The whole idea of writing, and of writing a vernacular language, was a novelty to them. They had no standard to follow, and any one who has attempted to write down for the first time a spoken

---

[1] See Map in Hörnle's edition of the Prâkritn-lakshana, p. xx.
[2] See, however, for exceptions, Senart, in *Journal Asiatique*, 1886, p. 102.
[3] Senart, *Journal Asiatique*, 1886, p. 96.

dialect, knows the difficulty of settling what is individual and local or what is general; what is truly dialectic or what is due to literary influences. It is quite possible that the persons employed by King Asoka were not even men of high education or initiated in Vedic lore. This would account for the uncertainty in spelling, in grammar, in expression, sometimes approaching the literary Sanskrit, sometimes running counter to all grammatical rules. We find something analogous in the translations of the Bible by missionaries working independently among savage races. The same language seems hardly the same when reduced for the first time to writing by English or French missionaries. There are many of these irregularities in the inscriptions of Asoka which it is impossible as yet to account for. But for all that, the fact remains that the language in which Asoka addressed his subjects and which his subjects were supposed to understand, is as different from the literary Sanskrit as the Italian *volgare* at the time of Dante was from classical Latin, and as different from Prâkrit as modern Provençal, if written down by ear, would be from French.

This language of the inscriptions of Asoka cannot be treated therefore as the lineal descendent of the Sanskrit of the Vedic hymns, the Brâhmaṇas, and the Sûtras. It rather represents one out of many parallel streams which in the divided kingdoms of that vast country must have developed, unchecked by any literary culture, while the literary Sanskrit remained almost stationary in its phonetic and grammatical organisation.

CHAPTER V.

We know that Buddhism availed itself of the power which the local spoken dialects gave to its teachers. It allowed the doctrines of Buddha to be transferred into any dialect. I see no reason to doubt the belief of the Buddhists that Pâli was the language of Buddha,[1] only reduced to grammatical regularity at a very early time, and probably by the compilers of the Buddhist Canon. It possesses forms decidedly more primitive than the inscriptions of Asoka, and forms that could not have been invented by grammarians. Nor does it follow that it was not a dialect of Magadha, because the later Mâgadhî Prâkrit differs from it. Magadha may have had more than one dialect, and the dialect used by Buddha was fixed centuries before the so-called Mâgadhî Prâkrit. Westergaard[2] and E. Kuhn[3] took Pâli for the dialect of Uggayinî, the birth-place of Mahinda, the son of Asoka, who is believed to have taken the Pâli Tipitaka to Ceylon. Dr. Oldenberg doubts altogether Mahinda's conversion of Ceylon, as related in the Mahâvansa, and thinks that the Pâli text of the Tipitaka reached Ceylon from the country of the Andhras

---

[1] Pâli is sometimes called *Gina-vakana*, i. e. the language of *Gina* or Buddha. It is also called the language of the Mâgadhas (Mahâvansa, pp. 251, 253), because it was from Magadha that Mahinda was believed to have brought the sacred books to Ceylon. The Buddhists call that language the mûlabhâsâ (D'Alwis, *Pâli Grammar*, p. cvii), the root-language, from which all other languages were supposed to be derived, while they use Pâli, not as the name of a language, but in the sense of sacred text or scripture. Tanti also is used in the same sense (D'Alwis, *Pâli Grammar*, p. v). See also Barthélemy St. Hilaire, in his report on Grünblot's *Collection of Buddhist MSS.*, published in the *Journal des Savants*, 1886; p. 26 of the separate edition.

[2] *Über den ältesten Zeitraum der indischen Geschichte*, p. 87.

[3] *Beiträge zur Pâli Grammatik*, p. 7.

and Kalingas in the Dekhan.¹ He lays great stress on the fact that the Sthavira school, which predominated in Ceylon, had its chief seat on the eastern shores of India, beginning at the mouth of the Ganges and extending southward to the kingdom of the Kalingas and the country of the Dravidas; and on the western shores in Bharukakkha and Surâshtra, countries closely connected with Ceylon. In the Malaya kingdom also a monastery is mentioned as having been founded by Mahinda.² Dr. Oldenberg therefore takes Pâli as the old language of the Andhra kingdom, and supposes that the Pâli text of the Tipitaka came to Ceylon from the Dekhan.³

These conclusions seem to me to go far beyond the evidence on which they are based. Even admitting that the language of the inscriptions found in the Andhra and Kalinga country resembled Pâli, this would not prove that Pâli was spoken, but only that, like Sanskrit, it was used there for inscriptions. We are far safer in accepting the view taken by the Buddhists themselves that Pâli was the language of Buddha, only remodelled by later grammarians. As Ceylon (Tambapanni) is mentioned in Asoka's inscriptions, there is no reason to doubt that his son, Mahinda, led a colony to that island and took with him whatever existed then of the Buddhist Canon. If earlier colonies from Magadha had already taken possession of Ceylon, their language would account for the Elu, as the spoken language there, and its difference from the literary

---

¹ Oldenberg, *Vinaya*, vol. i. Introd. p. liv.   ² *L. c.* p. liii.
³ Oldenberg, *Buddha*, English translation, p. 177.

Pâli, just as in India we see the spoken Mâgadhî or the Apabhramsa of the inscriptions quite distinct from the well-regulated language of the Tipitaka.

Difficulty of Writing a Spoken Language.

In judging of the historical inscriptions of Asoka and of their unsettled phonetic and grammatical character, we have always to keep in mind that they represent the first attempt at writing in India. We have absolutely no evidence whatever of writing in India before these inscriptions, and we may be quite certain that the very idea of writing for literary purposes did not touch the Indian mind long before its contact with Alexander the Great, and through him with the West at large. The two alphabets used by Asoka in his inscriptions are both of foreign and Semitic origin: that of Kapurdigiri, written from right to left, is palpably so; that of Girnar, written from left to right, shows evident traces of having been framed systematically out of the same or very similar materials. Neither of these Indian alphabets is, like other alphabets, the result of a natural growth out of ideographic and syllabic elements. It is the work of a committee of learned men who, probably under royal auspices, contrived from foreign sources an alphabet that should somehow or other be adequate to express the sounds of the spoken language. The alphabet used in the North-West (right to left) may have existed before Asoka, but the Magadha alphabet (left to right) was clearly the work of the royal scribes at his court, and varied but slightly when used in different parts of his vast kingdom, and possibly under the influence of different committees of learned men entrusted with the publication of the royal edicts.

If we keep this in view, if we remember that the writers of these inscriptions, though they may have been acquainted with Vedic and even with Pâninean Sanskrit, had no written texts of any kind to guide them in fixing the spelling of the spoken dialects of the country, we shall better understand their hesitation between what may be called phonetic and historical spelling, which is often so perplexing in these inscriptions. We shall also understand, what has been well pointed out by M. Senart, that in the hands of royal scribes the character of these inscriptions approached gradually, as time went on, to a more and more correct system, till at last the idea seems to have arisen that even Sanskrit was not too sacred a language to be reduced to a written form, and to be used for profane purposes, such as royal proclamations, edicts, and all the rest. In the North, according to M. Senart,[1] inscriptions became nearly pure Sanskrit at the time of Kanishka, first century A.D.,[2] in the West, at the time of Rudradâman, second century A.D.[3] At the same time, or a little later, the employment of the historical Prâkrits (without double consonants) ceased, while the grammatical Prâkrits, as we saw, were never used for monumental purposes.

We can thus understand the curious phenomenon that the language of the inscriptions, instead of becoming less regular, becomes more regular, and more

---

[1] *Journal Asiatique*, 1886, p. 331.   [2] Inscription of Mathurâ.
[3] Inscription of Girnar, *S*âka 75 or 80, A.D. 153 or 158.

Sanskrit-like in its historical progress, till at last it is altogether superseded by pure grammatical Sanskrit.

Renaissance of Sanskrit Literature.

About that time, in the third or, at all events, in the fourth century, began in different Brahmanic centres what I have ventured to call the *Renaissance of Sanskrit Literature*, comprising all that we are accustomed to call Sanskrit, with the exception of the ancient Vedic literature. There must have existed, besides the Vedic literature, a considerable amount of poetry, and possibly of prose also, composed in the language which Pâṇini's grammar describes and settles for ever. But that literature, composed in the so-called Bhâshâ, or speech of the country, is lost, though parts of it may survive in certain portions of the Mahâbhârata, even such as we now possess it.

About 400 A.D. the revival of Sanskrit literature begins. Sanskrit and Sanskrit only was now used for public inscriptions. The Apabhraṃsas, i.e. the historical or monumental or ungrammatical Prâkrits, had come to an end, and whatever was written in the dialects of the country, whether the sacred writings of Buddhists and Gainas, or the profane poetry of Hâla, or the conversational portions of the plays, or complete artificial poems such as the Setubandha, had now to submit to the rules of grammarians, such as Kâtyâyana, Vararuki, and in later times Hemakandra, quite as much as Sanskrit writers had to obey the rules of Pâṇini. M. Senart places the origin of the Prâkrit grammars in the third century A.D.,[1] and would there-

---

[1] *Journal Asiatique*, 1881, p. 393. But how can the date of Vararuki be fixed?

fore refer all texts written in grammatical Prâkrits to a period later than the third century. This seems to me quite unobjectionable so long as we admit that the component parts of the Tipi*t*aka existed during preceding centuries, only in a less regulated Prâkrit dialect.

The history of the language spoken in India, so far as we can follow it at present, would therefore fall into two branches:

First Branch, Sanskrit.

(1) The Vedic Sanskrit, Hymns, Brâhma*n*as, Sûtras, 1500–300 B. C.

(2) Pâ*n*inean Sanskrit, from 300 B. C. to the present day, with an interruption from the first to the fourth century A. D.

Second Branch, Prâkrit.

(1) The ungrammatical Prâkrit, Inscriptions from 250 B. C. to 200 A. D.; the Prâkrit of the Northern Buddhist Canon (Apabhra*m*sa).

(2) The grammatical Prâkrits, Pâli, *G*aina-Mâgadhî, Prâk*r*ita (Mahârâsh*t*rî, *S*auraseni, Mâgadhî), from 300 A. D. to present day.

The Modern Vernaculars.

We have now to consider the languages of India, as spoken at the present day. These languages have of late been so carefully studied by scholars such as Hörnle, Beames, Grierson, and others, that we can gain a much clearer view of their origin and spreading than was possible in former years. The spoken languages of India, which have been called Neo-Aryan, Neo-Sanskrit, or Gau*d*ian, seem to me to have a perfect right to the common name of Prâkritic. which would at once distinguish them from the old Prâkrits, and would at the same time indicate their real origin. They are not derived from Sanskrit, but from the old Prâkrits, or, more truly still, from the local Apabhramsas.

These living Prâkritic languages have now been arranged under four heads, as *Western, Northern, Southern,* and *Eastern.*

The Western class comprises Sindhî, Gujarâtî, Panjâbî, and Western Hindî;

The Northern class comprises Garhwâlî, Kumaonî, and Naipâlî;

The Southern class comprises Marâthî;

The Eastern class comprises Bihârî (or Eastern Hindî), Bengâlî, Uriyâ, and Asâmî.

The Northern and Western classes on one side, and the Southern and Eastern on the other, show certain traces of affinity.

All these names are derived from the locality in which each language is spoken. The only exception is Hindî, a name given formerly to the language spoken in the central portion of Northern India. That name, however, has now to be discarded, as it comprises or rather confuses two languages or groups of dialects which are as different from one another as Panjâbî is from Bengâlî. The Eastern group of these dialects is now called Bihârî,[1] the Western still retains the inconvenient name of Western Hindî. The Eastern comprises Baiswârî (Audh) Bhojpurî, Maithilî,

[1] *Seven Grammars of the Dialects and Subdialects of the Bihárí Language,* by G. A. Grierson, 1883.

Mâgadhî, the Western Marwârî, Jaipurî, Braj Bhâshâ, Kanaujî. The dividing line of the two groups is about the 80th degree of E. longitude.

What used to be called Hindî, the literary or High Hindî,[1] is really a modified form of the Braj Bhâshâ, which was first changed into Urdu by being deprived of its wealth of grammatical forms, and mixed with Panjâbî and Marwârî forms. Urdu originated in the twelfth century round Delhi, then the centre of the Mohammedan power, in the camps (urdû) of the soldiers, and its vocabulary was largely recruited from Persian and Arabic. In the sixteenth century, under Akbar, Urdu began to produce a literature and spread over India, but it never became a real vernacular. In the present century Urdu has freed itself more and more of its Persian elements, and under English and Hindu influence has become what is now called High Hindî. Urdu and High Hindî are therefore the same language, identical in grammar, but the former using as many foreign words, the latter as few foreign words as possible.

All these languages and dialects must be considered as the descendants, not of the grammatical Sanskrit, nor of the grammatical Prâkrit, but of the various Apabhra*m*sas, spoken in different parts of India, and reduced to some kind of grammatical order, partly by native schoolmasters, partly by literary cultivation. Hörnle mentions the poet Chand in the twelfth century as representing the Western, Nâmdev and Dnândev in the thirteenth century as representing the Southern, Bidyâpati in the fourteenth or fifteenth century as re-

---

[1] See Hörnle, *Comparative Grammar*, p. vi.

presenting the Eastern Gau*d*ian, as yet undivided into local dialects. Later poets write each in his own dialect; Kabir (fifteenth century) in Western Hindî, Tulsî Dâs (1541-1624) in Eastern Hindî; Kabi Kankan in Bengâlî, Upendro Bhanj in Uriyâ, Tukarâm in Ma*r*âthî, Narsingh Mahta in Gujarâtî.[1]

Dr. Hörnle[2] has collected some evidence to show that the two divisions of the modern vernaculars, are derived from grammatical Prâkrits. The Northern and Western from *S*aurasenî, the Southern and Eastern from Mâgadhî. That evidence is naturally scanty, but it is valuable as showing certain tendencies preserved even in the literary Prâkrits, which appear again in the modern vernaculars. Vernaculars, however, spring from vernaculars, never from literary languages, and it is to the vernaculars or Apabhra*m*sas of the North-West and South-East of India that we must look for the true origin of the dialects now spoken in India, and not to the language of the Vedas, the Tipi*t*aka, *S*akuntalâ, nor to the grammars of Pâ*n*ini, Kâtyâyana, or Vararu*k*i.

Sinhalese.

There is one other vernacular which has now been clearly proved to be Prâkritic, viz. that of Ceylon, the Sinhalese. It is curious that such scholars as Colebrooke, Stevenson and others should have treated that language as a Dravidian dialect. I believe I was the first who in 1854 claimed it as a member of the Aryan family, a view which has since been fully confirmed

---

[1] Hörnle, *Comparative Grammar*, p. xxxv.
[2] Ibid. pp. xxvi-xxx.

by the labours of D'Alwis, Childers, Kuhn, and others. Dr. Goldschmidt tried to prove that the language of Ceylon shares some characteristics in common with the Magadha Prâkrit, but the exact relationship between Sinhalese and any other of the Prâkritic dialects requires still further investigation. Neither Beames nor Hörnle have treated it in their comparative grammars.

In its oldest form the language of Ceylon is called *Elu*, which has been shown by D'Alwis[1] to be a corruption of Sinhala. This language is believed to have been brought to Ceylon by a colony from Lâla, a district of Mâgadhî, at the time of Buddha's death, and this tradition is confirmed by the fact that, according to Childers, Sinhalese agrees with Pâli when Pâli differs from the other Prâkrits. The old Sinhalese or Elu differs from the modern no more than the Anglo-Saxon from English. The modern Sinhalese has, however, evolved many new grammatical forms and admitted a large number of Sanskrit words.

If we may trust the Mahâvansa, Sinhalese must have been distinct from Pâli as early as the third century B. C., for at that time it is said that Mahinda translated the Buddhist Arthakathâs or commentaries, not, as Weber says, the text of the Tipi*t*aka, from Pâli into Sinhalese, while in the fifth century A. D. Buddhaghosha translated Mahinda's Sinhalese translation back into Pâli. From that time, possibly from the date of Mahinda's translation, the changes in the written language of Ceylon seem to have been inconsiderable.[2]

Elu books are said to date from the fifth and sixth

---

[1] *Sidath Sangarawa*, p. xxxii.
[2] See Childers, *Notes on the Sinhalese Language*, 1873.

centuries A.D. By the researches of Dr. P. Goldschmidt and Dr. E. Müller inscriptions have lately been discovered in Ceylon going back to the first and second centuries B. C.[1]

[1] *Report on Inscriptions*, by P. Goldschmidt and Dr. E. Müller; printed by Order of Government, Colombo, 1876-1879.

CHAPTER VI.

SANSKRIT AS KNOWN OUTSIDE INDIA.

WE have seen that the history of the language of India and its various dialects is more complete in its successive periods than that of almost any other language.

Yet such was the surprise created by the discovery of this language and by its startling similarity to the classical languages of Greece and Rome, that some of the most enlightened spirits of the last century declined to believe in its historical reality, and accused the wily Brahmans of having forged it to deceive their conquerors. No one gave stronger expression to that opinion than Dugald Stewart in his *Conjectures concerning the Origin of the Sanskrit*. At present this controversy has no more than an historical interest. Still it may be useful to show how the existence of Sanskrit, as a real language, might have been proved by independent testimony, namely by the accounts left us by the four nations who successively came in contact with India, the Jews, the Greeks, the Chinese, and the Arabs. Besides, though it is true that we do not want their evidence any longer to prove that Sanskrit was a real, not a forged language, that testimony will nevertheless be useful, because in the absence of anything like history or chronology in India, the accounts left us at different periods by Jews, Greeks, Chinese, and Arabs will continue to serve, like broad longitudinal lines, to impart a certain order and regularity to the ill-defined map of Indian language and literature.

I place the Jewish testimonies first because, though the date of the Books of Kings, in which commercial relations between Phenicia, Palestine, and India are alluded to, may be uncertain, it is certainly anterior to that of the Greek testimonies which will follow after.

Jewish Testimonies.

Let it be remembered then that in the hymns of the Veda, which are the oldest literary compositions in Sanskrit, the geographical horizon of the poets is, for the greater part, limited to the north-west of India. There are very few passages in which any allusions to the sea or the sea-coast occur, whereas the Snowy Mountains, and the rivers of the Panjâb, and the scenery of the Upper Ganges valley, are familiar objects to the ancient bards. There is no doubt, in fact, that the people who spoke Sanskrit came into India from the north-west, and gradually extended their sway towards the south-east. Now, at the time of Solomon, it can be proved that Sanskrit was spoken at least as far south as the mouth of the Indus.

The navy-ships which Solomon made at Ezion-geber, which is beside Eloth, on the shore of the Red Sea, in the land of Edom, are well known to Old Testament students. That fleet was manned by the servants of

Solomon and by the servants of Hiram, king of Tyre, and it went to Ophir and fetched from thence gold, and brought it to king Solomon (1 Kings ix. 26–28). From the same Ophir the fleet of Hiram is said to have brought not only gold, but great plenty of algum-trees and precious stones (1 Kings x. 11). The sea-port of the fleet of Solomon is called Ezion-geber, and this Ezion-geber has by most scholars been identified with the modern port of Akaba on the north-east extremity of the Red Sea. It was in the same harbour of Ezion-geber that the ships of Tharshish were broken which Jehoshaphat made to go to Ophir for gold (1 Kings xxii. 48). What is meant by 'ships of Tharshish' is uncertain, but if we read (1 Kings x. 22) that Solomon had at sea a navy of Tharshish with the navy of Hiram, and that the navy of Tharshish came once in three years bringing not only gold, but silver, ivory, apes, and peacocks, the natural conclusion seems to be that Solomon possessed only one sea-port, i.e. that of Ezion-geber, and that his ships started from thence, both in order to fetch gold, algum-trees, and precious stones from Ophir, and gold, silver, ivory, apes, and peacocks from some country not specified.

A great deal has been written[1] to find out where this Ophir was; and though I allow that the question does not admit of a definite answer, yet the evidence seems to me to incline in favour of India, or of a sea-port on the south-east coast of Arabia, carrying on an

---

[1] An excellent account of the whole controversy may be seen in the articles *Ophir* and *Tarshish* in Smith's *Dictionary of the Bible*, contributed by the Hon. E. T. B. Twisleton.

active trade with India. The names for *algum-trees*. as well as for *apes*, *peacocks*, and *ivory*, are foreign words in Hebrew, as much as *gutta-percha* or *tobacco* are in English. Now, if we wished to know from what part of the world *gutta-percha* was first imported into England, we might safely conclude that it came from that country where the name, *gutta-percha*, formed part of the spoken language.[1] If, therefore, we can find a language in which the name for *algum-tree*, which is foreign in Hebrew, is indigenous, we may be certain that the country in which that language was spoken must have been the country from whence Solomon obtained algum-trees, and, therefore, the Ophir of the Bible. It would not yet follow, as Mr. Twisleton has shown, that the other articles. ivory, apes, and peacocks, must likewise have come from Ophir, for the Bible nowhere says that they came from Ophir. But if it should turn out that the names of these articles came from the same language, which can be proved to be the language of Ophir, it would not seem an entirely unfounded conjecture to suppose, in the absence of evidence to the contrary, that these articles too came from the same country. The language in which the names for *algum-trees*, as well as for *ivory*, *apes*, and *peacocks*, find their most plausible etymology is Sanskrit; and if that language was spoken at Ophir and in some other place, it is probable that Ophir as well as that other place were situated in India, and accessible by sea.

---

[1] *Gutta* in Malay means *gum*, *percha* is the name of the tree (Isonandra gutta), or of an island from which the tree was first imported (Pulo-percha).

Now, the *algum-tree*, or, as it is called in other places, the *almug-tree*, is supposed to be the sandal-wood-tree. I feel bound to confess that the evidence on which this identification rests was by no means satisfactory [1] before it was discovered that one of the numerous names for this tree in Sanskrit is **valguka**, sandal-wood. This **valguka**, which points back to a more original form **valgu**, might easily have been corrupted by Phenician and Jewish sailors into *algum*, a form, as we know, still further corrupted, at least in one passage of the Old Testament, into *almug*. Sandal-wood is found indigenous in India only, and there chiefly on the coast of Malabar.

On the evidence, however, of the name *algum* alone, we could hardly say that Ophir was identified with a country in which the spoken language was Sanskrit. But if we examine the names for *peacocks*, *apes*, and *ivory*, and arrive at the same result, viz. that they are foreign in Hebrew, and explicable by Sanskrit, the evidence becomes stronger, and would not only warrant the supposition that Ophir was to be sought for in India, but likewise render it probable that the unknown country which yielded the names of these articles was the same which yielded the articles themselves,—a country within reach of the fleet of Ezion-geber, and probably not far from Ophir.

Now, *apes* are called in Hebrew *koph*, a word without any etymology in the Semitic languages, but nearly identical in sound with the Sanskrit name of

---

[1] See the Hon. E. T. B. Twisleton's article on *Ophir*, in Smith's *Dictionary of the Bible*, vol. ii. p. 640.

ape, **kapi**. Professor Dümichen[1] identifies this word with the hieroglyphic *kafu*, which occurs in inscriptions of the seventeenth century.

Ivory is called either *shen*, tooth, or *karnoth-shen*, horns of tooth; or *shen habbim*. This *habbim* is again without a derivation in Hebrew, but it may be a corruption of the Sanskrit name for elephant, ibha, preceded by the Semitic article.[2]

Lastly, the *peacocks* are called in Hebrew *tukhi-im*, and this finds its explanation in the old classical name of the pea-fowl in Tamil, *tôkei*, dialectically pronounced *tôgei*. In modern Tamil *tôkei* generally signifies only the peacock's tail, but in the old classical Tamil it signifies the peacock itself.[3]

Of these articles, ivory, gold, and apes are indigenous in India, though of course they might have been found in other countries likewise. Not so the *algum-tree*, at least if interpreters are right in taking

---

[1] *Die Flotte einer Aegyptischen Königin*, 1868, tab. ii. p. 17.

[2] See Lassen, *Indische Alterthumskunde*, b. i. s. 537.

[3] Cf. Caldwell, *Dravidian Grammar*, second edition, p. 91. This excellent scholar points out that *tôkei* cannot be a corruption of Sanskrit *sikhin*, crested, as I had supposed, *sikhin* existing in Tamil under the form of *sigi*, peacock. *Tôgei* does not occur either in Canarese, Telugu, or Malayâlim. Dr. Gundert, who has for many years devoted himself to the study of the Dravidian languages, was the first to derive *tôgei* from a root *tô* or *tû*. From this, by the addition of *ngu*, a secondary base, *tongu*, is formed in Tamil, meaning to hang, to be pendent. Hence the Tamil *tongal*, a peacock's tail, ornaments, &c.; in Malayâlim, *tongal*, plumage, ornaments for the ear, drapery, &c. By adding the suffix *kei* or *gei* we get *togei*, what hangs down, tail, &c. If this etymology be right, it would be an important confirmation of the antiquity of the Tamulic languages spoken in India before the advent of the Aryan tribes. Dr. Gundert points to the ordinary name for peacock in Tamil, viz. *may-il* (blue-house), as the probable etymon of the Sanskrit **mayûra**, peacock. Mayûra, however, occurs in the Veda.

algum or *almug* for sandal-wood, nor the peacock. Sandal-wood, as pointed out before, is peculiar to India, and so is the peacock.¹ That the peacock was exported from India to Babylon (Bâberu) is shown by one of Pâli Gâtakas.² The name here used for the peacock is *mora*, Sanskrit *mayûra*.

If then Ophir, i.e. the country of the algum-tree, is to be sought for in India, and if the place from which the fleet of Solomon fetched peacocks, apes, and ivory, must likewise be sought for in a country where Sanskrit was spoken, a most natural place to fix upon is the mouth of the Indus. There gold and precious stones from the north would have been brought down the Indus; and sandal-wood, peacocks, and apes would have been brought from Central and Southern India. In this very locality Ptolemy (vii. 1) gives us the name of *Abiria*, above *Pattalene*. In the same locality Hindu geographers place the people called *Abhira* or *Âbhîra*, who must have been an important people, as their language is always mentioned first among the Apabhram*s*as or ungrammatical vernaculars. In the same neighbourhood MacMurdo, in his account of the province of Cutch, still knows a race of *Ahirs*,³ the descendants, in all probability, of the people who sold to Hiram and Solomon their gold and precious stones, their apes, peacocks, and sandal-wood.⁴

¹ See the article *Tarshish* by E. T. in Smith's *Dictionary of the Bible*, vol. iii. p. 1440. It is strange that, in 2 Chron. ii. 8, algum trees should be mentioned as if growing in Lebanon.
² See Minayeff, in *Mélanges Asiatiques*, vi. p. 593.
³ See also Sir Henry Elliot's *Supplementary Glossary*, s. v. Aheer.
⁴ The arguments brought forward by Quatremère, in his *Mémoire*

This identification of Ophir with some place in India is not a modern conjecture. The Vulgate translates Job xxviii. 16, 'It cannot be valued with the gold of Ophir' (Sophir, LXX), by 'Non conferetur tinctis *Indiæ* coloribus.' In Coptic *Sofir* is the name for India, the same word by which the LXX translated the Hebrew Ophir.

Considering that in the Veda the people who spoke Sanskrit were still settled in the north of India, whereas at the time of Solomon their language had extended to Cutch and even the Malabar coast, we can hardly doubt that Sanskrit was an ancient and historical language, as old as the Books of Kings, or possibly as the book of Job, in which the gold of Ophir is mentioned for the first time.[1]

sur le Pays d'Ophir, against fixing Ophir on the Indian coast, are not conclusive. The arguments derived from the names of the articles exported from Ophir were unknown to him. It is necessary to mention this, because Quatremère's name deservedly carries great weight, and his essay on Ophir has lately been republished in the *Bibliothèque classique des Célébrités contemporaines*, 1861.

[1] Job xxii. 24, xxviii. 16. Some of my critics have demurred to this argument because the Books of Kings are not contemporaneous with Solomon. The articles themselves, however, must have had names at the time of Solomon; and it has never been suggested that at his time they had Semitic names, and that these were replaced by Indian names at a later time, when all maritime commercial intercourse between India and Palestine had ceased. As to the name of sandal-wood, my critics ought to have known that both forms, *algum* as well as *almug*, occur in the Bible. The different opinions on the geographical position of Ophir have lately been most carefully examined and impartially summed up by Mr. Twisleton, in the articles, quoted above, on *Ophir* and *Tarshish* in Dr. Smith's *Biblical Dictionary*. Mr. Twisleton himself leans strongly towards the opinion of those scholars who, like Michaelis, Niebuhr, and Vincent, place Ophir in Arabia; and he argues very ingeniously, that if we consider Ophir simply as an emporium, the principal objection, viz. that gold or any other article brought from Ophir to Palestine was not a natural product of Arabia, falls to the ground. That is true.

Greek Accounts of India.

The next people who possessed a knowledge of India were the Greeks. The earliest information about

But why look for Ophir in Arabia? The only strong argument for fixing Ophir in Arabia is that derived from the genealogical table in the 10th chapter of Genesis, where Ophir appears as the eleventh in order of the sons of Joktan. I accept all the facts brought forward by Mr. Twisleton, but I see no difficulty in admitting commercial intercourse between the south of Arabia and the gulf of Cutch in very ancient times (Renan, *Histoire des Langues sémitiques*, 1858, p. 314); and if Tharshish in Spain can be called a son of Javan, why not Ophir in India a son of Joktan? The expression 'from Mesha, as thou goest unto Sephar a mountain in the East,' on which Mr. Twisleton lays great stress as limiting the geographical position of all the sons of Joktan within the coasts of Arabia, is surely very vague; nor has it been possible to identify the names of all the Joktanide settlements within the sphere thus vaguely indicated by geographical tradition. On the other hand, it must be admitted that on the south-east coast of Arabia, traders between India and Palestine would naturally found commercial emporia. They existed there at the time of Diodorus Siculus, who, after describing the great wealth of Saba in gold, ivory, and precious stones, relates (lib. iii. cap. 47) that there were several islands near, where merchants from all parts of the world landed, and particularly from Potana (Pattana?), which Alexander had founded near the river Indus. Νῆσοι δ' εὐδαίμονες πλησίον ὑπάρχουσιν, ἔχουσαι πόλεις ἀτειχίστους... Εἰς ταύτας δ' ἔμποροι πάντοθεν καταπλέουσι, μάλιστα δ' ἐκ Ποτάνας, ἣν Ἀλέξανδρος ᾤκισε παρὰ τὸν Ἰνδὸν ποταμόν, ναύσταθμον ἔχειν βουλόμενος τῆς παρὰ τὸν Ὠκεανὸν παραλίου. That the same coast was the seat of a very early commerce and a very early civilisation is attested to the present day by magnificent ruins and inscriptions, and by the fragments of a widely spread tradition. See A. von Kremer, *Die Südarabische Sage*, 1866. It is not necessary, however, to discuss here all the controverted points of this question, for even if Ophir should be proved to be in Arabia, the names for *apes* and *peacocks* would still point to Sanskrit, and could have been brought to Ophir from no other country but India. These names, as found in the Old Testament, are foreign words in Hebrew, and they do not receive any light either from the dialects of Arabic, including the Himyaritic inscriptions, or from the languages spoken on the Mozambique coast of Africa, where, according to some authorities, Ophir was situated. These very names have been traced back to Sanskrit and to the languages spoken on the Malabar coast of the Dekhan; and though it must be admitted that, as foreign

CHAPTER VI.

India seems to have reached the Greeks indirectly through Persia and Asia Minor. The name of India was known to the author of the Avesta. It occurs there as Hi*n*du in the singular, and in the plurals as Hapta Hi*n*du, the Seven Rivers, the Vedic Sapta Sindhava*h*, that is, the seven rivers of the Panjâb.[1] It occurs again in the cuneiform inscriptions as Hi*n*du, one of the provinces which paid tribute to Darius, and is mentioned in the inscription of *Nakshi Rustam*, a, 25, by the side of Medians, Parthians, Bactrians, Spartans, and Ionians. This shows through what channel countries so widely separated as India and Greece were first brought into historical contact. It is true that in the Homeric poems the name of India is unknown. But long before Alexander's invasion of India Hekataeos (B. C. 549–486) knew that

words, they have suffered considerable corruption in the mouths of ignorant sailors, yet, allowing the same latitude of phonetic change, it has been impossible to trace them back to any other family of speech. If, therefore, there should seem to exist any stringent evidence that Ophir was a mere *entrepôt*, not in India, but in Arabia, the spreading of Sanskrit names to Arabia before they reached Palestine would only serve to increase the antiquity of Sanskrit as spoken in those parts of India from whence alone the natural products of her language and of her soil could have been exported. And if we consider that there is no other language which can claim these names as her own—that there is no country in which *all* the articles brought by the fleet of Ezion-geber, whether from Ophir or elsewhere, are indigenous, that sandal-wood and peacocks could in ancient times have been exported to Palestine from India only ; if to all these coincidences, all pointing to India, is added the fact pointed out by Lassen, that the names of *cotton*, *nard*, and probably of *bdellium*, have likewise found their way from Sanskrit into Hebrew, we shall, I think, feel justified in admitting, with Lassen and Ritter and others, a very early commercial intercourse between India and Palestine, whatever opinion we may hold on the exact position of Ophir.

[1] See *Biographies of Words*, p. 153.

distant country, and from his mention of the river Indus,[1] we can safely conclude that Sanskrit was then the spoken language of the country.

The Sanskrit name of the river Sindhu must have reached Hekataeos through a Persian channel in which the initial s was regularly changed to h, and afterwards dropt. Indian names mentioned by Herodotus, such as Gandarioi, Sanskrit Gandhára, a name which occurs in the Veda (RV. i, 126, 7), and others, likewise prove the presence of Sanskrit in India at his time. Ktesias (about 400 B.C.), though he did not reach India, but lived at the court of Darius II and Artaxerxes Mnemon, gives us information which, however untrustworthy in other respects, leaves us no doubt that Sanskrit was then the language of the people whom he describes. With Megasthenes we enter into the very life of India. He stayed at Palimbothra, the Pâtaliputra of Sanskrit literature, the modern Patna, the capital of Sandracottus, in Sanskrit *K*andragupta, the King of the Prasii, about 295 B.C. His account of India would probably have made us acquainted not only with the language, but also with the literary works of that period, had not the indifference of the Greeks for barbarous people allowed his work to be lost except the fragments now collected under the name of *Megasthenis Indica*.

The argument that nearly all the names of persons, places, and rivers in India mentioned by Megasthenes and other Greek and Roman writers are pure Sanskrit has been handled so fully and ably by others, more

[1] *Fragmenta Historicorum Graecorum*, ed. C. et T. Müller, vol. i. p. 12, fragm. 174.

particularly by Lassen in his *Indische Alterthumskunde* that nothing remains to be said on that subject.[1]

Chinese Accounts of India.

The next nation after the Greeks that became acquainted with the language and literature of India was the Chinese. Though Buddhism was not recognised as a third state-religion before the year 65 A.D., under the Emperor Ming-ti,[2] Buddhist missionaries had reached China from India as early as the third century, 217 B.C.[3] One Buddhist missionary is mentioned in the Chinese annals in the year 217; and, about the year 120 B.C., a Chinese general, after defeating the barbarous tribes north of the desert of Gobi, brought back as a trophy a golden statue, the statue of Buddha. The very name of Buddha, changed in Chinese into Fo-t'o and Fo,[4] is pure Sanskrit, and so is every word and every thought of that religion. The language which the Chinese pilgrims went to India to study, as the key to the sacred literature of Buddhism, was Sanskrit. They called it Fan; but Fan, as M. Stanislas Julien has shown, is an abbreviation of Fan-lan-mo, and this is the only way in

---

[1] See *Ancient India as described by the Classical Authors*, by J. W. McCrindle. (i) Ancient India as described by Megasthenes (about 295) and Arrian (consul, A.D. 146), 1877. (ii) The Commerce and Navigation of the Erythræan Sea, 1879. (iii) Ancient India as described by Ktesias (about 400 B.C.), 1882. (iv) Ancient India as described by Ptolemy (150 A.D.), 1885.

[2] M. M.'s *Buddhist Pilgrims, Selected Essays*, vol. ii. p. 234.

[3] *Foe Koue Ki*, traduit par Rémusat, Paris, 1836, p. 41.

[4] *Méthode pour déchiffrer et transcrire les noms sanscrits qui se rencontrent dans les livres chinois, inventée et démontrée* par M. Stanislas Julien, Paris, 1861, p. 103.

which the Sanskrit word Brahman could be rendered
in Chinese.¹ We read of the Emperor Ming-ti, of the
dynasty of Han, sending Tsaï-in and other high
officials to India, in order to study there the doctrine
of Buddha. They engaged the services of two learned
Buddhists, Matânga and *K*u-fa-lan, and some of the
most important Buddhist works were translated by
them into Chinese.² The intellectual intercourse
between the Indian peninsula and the northern continent of Asia continued uninterrupted for several
centuries. Missions were sent from China to India
to report on the religious, political, social, and geographical state of the country; and the chief object
of interest which attracted public embassies and
private pilgrims across the Himalayan mountains,
was the religion of Buddha. About three hundred
years after the public recognition of Buddhism by
the Emperor Ming-ti, the great stream of Buddhist
pilgrims began to flow from China to India. The first
account which we possess of these pilgrimages belongs
to the travels of Fa-hian, who visited India towards the
end of the fourth century (A.D. 399-414). These travels
were first translated into French by A. Rémusat.³
After Fa-hian, we have the travels of Hoei-seng and
Song-yun, who were sent to India, in 518, by command

---

[1] 'Fan-chou (brahmâkshara), les caractères de l'écriture indienne, inventée par Fan, c'est-à-dire Fan-lan-mo (brahmâ).'—Stanislas Julien, *Voyages des Pèlerins bouddhistes*, vol. ii. p. 505.

[2] See for a fuller account, M. M. *On Sanskrit Texts discovered in Japan, Selected Essays*, vol. ii. p. 319. *K*u-fa-lan is called Bhârana Pandita in Tibetan; cf. *J. R. A. S.*, 1882, p. 89.

[3] They have been translated into English by the Rev. Samuel Beal, London, 1869; revised 1884; by Mr. Herbert A. Giles, 1877, and by Professor Legge, Oxford, 1886.

of the empress, with the view of collecting sacred books and relics. Then followed Hiouen-thsang, whose life and travels, from 629–645, have been rendered so popular by the excellent translation of M. Stanislas Julien.[1] After Hiouen-thsang, the principal works of Chinese pilgrims are the travels of Itsing[2] (left China in 671, arrived in India in 673, returned to China in 695, died in 713), the Itineraries of the Fifty-six Monks, published in 730, and the travels of Khinie, who visited India in 964, at the head of three hundred pilgrims.

That the language employed for literary purposes in India during all this time was Sanskrit, we learn, not only from the numerous names and religious and philosophical terms mentioned in the travels of the Chinese pilgrims, but from a short paradigm of declension and conjugation in Sanskrit which one of them (Hiouen-thsang) has inserted in his diary. Nay, there is every reason to believe that Hiouen-thsang composed himself a book in Sanskrit.[3]

Persian Accounts of India.

The next evidence of the existence of an ancient literature in India comes to us from Persia. The King of Persia, Khosru Nushirvan, in the middle of the sixth century, had a collection of fables translated from Sanskrit into Pehlevi, a translation which was afterwards turned into Arabic by Abdallah ibn Almokaffa in the middle of the eight century, under the title of *Kalilah and Dimnah*. Though the complete

---
[1] New translation by Rev. S. Beal, 1884.
[2] On Itsing, see M. M., *India, what can it teach us?* p. 210 seq.; Journal Asiat. 1888, p. 411.   [3] M. M., *India*, pp. 305, 310.

SANSKRIT AS KNOWN OUTSIDE INDIA.   199

collection of these fables does no longer exist in Sanskrit, yet the portions of it which have been preserved in the Pañkatantra show clearly that they must have existed in Sanskrit in the sixth century A. D., and that the account given by the Pehlevi translator Barzôi is trustworthy in the main.[1]

Arab Accounts of India.

As soon as the Mohammedans entered India, we hear of translations of Sanskrit works into Persian and Arabic.[2] As early as the reign of the second Abasside Khalif Almansur,[3] in the year 773 A. D., an Indian astronomer, well versed in the science which he professed, visited the court of the Khalif, bringing with him tables of the equations of planets according to the mean motions, with observations relative to both solar and lunar eclipses and the ascension of the signs; taken, as he affirmed, from tables computed by an Indian prince, whose name, as the Arabian author writes it, was Phighar. The Khalif, embracing the opportunity thus happily presented to him, commanded the book to be translated into Arabic, to be published for a guide to the Arabians in matters pertaining to the stars. The task devolved on Mohammed ben Ibrahim Alfazari, whose version is

---

[1] See M. M., *Selected Essays*, vol. i. p. 516. It is curious that Alberuni was so dissatisfied with the Arabic translation of what he calls the Pañkatantra that he wished to translate it anew. See Alberuni's *India*, ed. Sachau, p. xx; also *Fihrist*, ed. Rödiger, vol. i.

[2] Sir Henry Elliot's *Historians of India*, vol. v., appendix, p. 570.

[3] Colebrooke, *Miscellaneous Essays*, ii. p. 504, quotes from the preface to the astronomical tables of Ben al Adami, published by his continuator, Al Casem, in 920 A.D. On Sanskrit figures, see Strachey, *As. Res.* xii. 184; Colebrooke, *Algebra*, p. lii.

200   CHAPTER VI.

known to astronomers by the name of the greater Sind-hind or Hind-sind,[1] for the term occurs written both ways.

About the same time Yacub, the son of Tharek, composed an astronomical work, founded on the Sind-hind.[2] Harun-al-Rashid (786-809) had two Indians, Manka and Saleh, as physicians at his court.[3] Manka translated the classical work on medicine, Susruta,[4] and a treatise on poisons, ascribed to Kânakya, from Sanskrit into Persian.[5] During

---

[1] Sind-hind signifies the revolving ages, according to Ben al Adami; Kasiri translates it perpetuum æternumque. Colebrooke conjectures Siddhânta, and supposes the original to have been Brahmagupta's work, the Brahma-siddhânta. M. Reinaud, in his *Mémoire sur l'Inde*, p. 312, quotes the following passage from the *Taryk-al-Hokama*: 'En l'année 156 de l'hégire (773 de J. C.) il arriva de l'Inde à Bagdad un homme fort instruit dans les doctrines de son pays. Cet homme possédait la méthode du Sindhind, relative aux mouvements des astres et aux équations calculées au moyen de sinus de quart en quart de degré. Il connaissait aussi diverses manières de déterminer les éclipses, ainsi que le lever des signes du zodiaque. Il avait composé un abrégé d'un ouvrage relatif à ces matières qu'on attribuait à un prince nommé Fygar. Dans cet écrit les kardagia (i. e. kramagyâ; see Sûrya-siddhânta, ed. Burgess and Whitney, p. 57 and p. 59) étaient calculés par minutes. Le Khalife ordonna qu'on traduisît le traité indien en arabe, afin d'aider les musulmans à acquérir une connaissance exacte des étoiles. Le soin de la traduction fut confié à Mohammed, fils d'Ibrahim-al-Fazary, le premier entre les musulmans qui s'était livré à une étude approfondie de l'astronomie: on désigne plus tard cette traduction sous le titre de Grand Sindhind.' Alberuni places the translation in the year 771.

[2] Reinaud, *l. c.* p. 314.

[3] Elliot, *Historians of India*, vol. v. p. 572.

[4] Cf. Steinschneider, *Wissenschaftliche Blätter*, vol. i. p. 79.

[5] See Professor Flügel, in *Zeitschrift der D. M. G.*, xi. 148 and 325; Elliot, *Historians of India*, vol. v. p. 572. A Hebrew treatise on poisons, ascribed to the Indian Zanik (Kânakya), is mentioned by Steinschneider, *Wissenschaftliche Blätter*, vol. i. p. 65. Alberuni mentions an Indian Kankah as astrologer of Harun-al-Rashid (Reinaud,

the Khalifate of Al Mamun, a famous treatise on algebra was translated by Mohammed ben Musa from Sanskrit into Arabic (edited by F. Rosen, 1831) and the medical treatises of Mikah and Ibn Dahan, both represented to be Indians, show that Sanskrit was well known then.[1]

Alberuni.

Alberuni (born 973, died 1048) was invited by Mahmud of Ghazni (died 1030) from Khwarizm (the modern Khiva), which the Sultan had conquered in 1017, to accompany him on his Indian campaigns. Avicenna, i.e. Abu' Ali Ibn Sina, declined to accompany him. Alberuni, an astronomer, a large-hearted philosopher, and an acute observer, utilised his stay in India for studying the astronomy, the philosophy and literature of that interesting country. According to his own statement the number of his works exceeded a hundred. The most important among those which have not perished are the 'Chronology of Ancient Nations,' of which a German and an English translation have lately (1878 and 1879) been published by Professor Sachau; a treatise on Astronomy, Al-Kanun Al-Masudi, and his extremely interesting work on India, sometimes called Tarikh-i-Hind (written A.D. 1030), but the full title of which has been translated by its learned editor, Professor Sachau, as 'An accurate de-

---

Mémoire sur l'Inde, p. 315). He is likewise mentioned as a physician. Another Indian physician of Harun-al-Rashid is called Mankba (Reinaud, *l. c.*).

[1] Elliot, *Historians of India*, vol. v. p. 572.

scription of all categories of Hindu thought, as well those which are admissible as those which must be rejected.' The value of Alberuni's *India* was first pointed out by Reinaud in his *Fragments Arabes et Persans inédits relatifs à l'Inde*, 1845, and afterwards in his excellent *Mémoire sur l'Inde*, Paris, 1849. It was then supposed that Alberuni had acquired a complete knowledge of Sanskrit which enabled him not only to translate works on the Sânkhya and Yoga philosophies from Sanskrit into Arabic, but even to translate Arabic texts into Sanskrit. This, however, has been rendered very doubtful by Professor Sachau's researches. He gives Alberuni full credit for having acquired an elementary knowledge of Sanskrit, sufficient for checking to a certain extent the statements of his Pandits, but he shows clearly that his translations from Sanskrit into Arabic and Persian, and still more those from Arabic into Sanskrit could not have been made without the constant help of native scholars.[1] In that respect, therefore, Alberuni was inferior to Hiouen-thsang, who was able to write in Sanskrit and to carry on a public disputation in that language.

About 1150 we hear of Abu Saleh translating a work on the education of kings from Sanskrit into Arabic.[2]

---

[1] Alberuni's *India*, edited in the Arabic original by E. Sachau, London, 1887. *Chronology of Ancient Nations*, by Alberuni, translated by E. Sachau, London, 1879.

[2] In the Persian work *Mujmalu-t-Tawarikh* there are chapters translated from the Arabic of Abu Saleh ben Shib ben Jawn, who had himself abridged them, a hundred years before, from a Sanskrit work called *Instruction of Kings* (Râganîti?). The Persian translator lived about 1150. See Elliot, *l. c.*

Two hundred years later, we are told that Firoz Shah, after the capture of Nagarcote, ordered several Sanskrit works on philosophy to be translated from Sanskrit by Maulana Izzu-d-din Khalid Khani. A work on veterinary medicine ascribed to Sâlotar,[1] said to have been the tutor of Suṣruta, was likewise translated from Sanskrit into Persian in the year 1381. A copy of this, called *Kurrut ul Mulk*, was preserved in the Royal Library of Lucknow. The date is somewhat doubtful, and it is curious that the translator should not have mentioned another work on the same subject, the *Kitab ul Baitarat*, translated from Sanskrit

[1] Sâlotar is not known as the author of such a work. Sâlotarîya occurs instead of Sâlâturîya, in Râga Râdhakânt; but Sâlâturîya is a name of Pânini, and the teacher of Suṣruta is said to have been Divodâsa. Professor Weber, in his *Catalogue of Sanskrit MSS.* (p. 298), has pointed out Sâlihotra, who is mentioned in the Pañkatantra as a teacher of veterinary medicine, and who is quoted by Garga in the Asvâyur-veda. The Professor quotes a translation into Arabic of such a work, made in the year 1361. Such a translation, however, of that date does not exist, and as he refers to Elliot's *Bibliographical Index to the Historians of India*, p. 263, as his authority, the Professor's statement may possibly rest on some misapprehension. Salotrí is the every-day Urdu and Hindi word for a horse-doctor. Professor Aufrecht has discovered a work on medicine by Sâlihotra in the Library of the East India House. A medical work by Sâlinâtha is mentioned in the *Catalogue of Sanskrit MSS. of the College of Fort William*, p. 24. An Arabic translation of a Sanskrit work on veterinary medicine by Kânakya is mentioned by Hâji Chalfa, v. p. 59. A translation of the *Karaka* (Proceedings of As. Soc. Bengal, 1870, Sept.) from Sanskrit into Persian, and from Persian into Arabic, is mentioned in the Fihrist (finished 987 A.D.). It is likewise mentioned by Alberuni (Reinaud, *Mémoire sur l'Inde*, p. 316); the translation is said to have been made for the Barmekides. The names of the persons by whom the doctrines contained in this work were supposed to have been handed down, should be restored in Alberuni as follows: Brahman, Pragâpati, the Asvinau, Indra, the sons of Atri, Agnivesa; cf. *Ashtângahrídaya*, Introduction (MS. Wilson, 298).

into Arabic, at Baghdad. Another translation was made in the reign of Shah Jahán.[1]

Akbar.

Two hundred years more bring us to the reign of Akbar (1556–1605). A more extraordinary man never sat on the throne of India.[2] Brought up as a Mohammedan, he discarded the religion of the Prophet as superstitious,[3] and then devoted himself to a search after the true religion. He called Brahmans and fire-worshippers to his court, and ordered them to discuss in his presence the merits of their religions with the Mohammedan doctors. When he heard of the Jesuits at Goa, he invited them to his capital, and he was for many years looked upon as a secret convert to Christianity. He was, however, a rationalist and deist, and, as he declared himself, never believed anything that he could not understand. The religion which he founded, the so-called Ilâhi religion, was pure Deism, mixed up with the worship of the sun[4] as the purest and highest emblem of the Deity. Though Akbar himself could neither read nor write,[5] his court was the home of literary men of all persuasions. Whatever book, in any language, promised to throw light on the problems nearest to the emperor's heart, he ordered to be translated

---

[1] Elliot's *Historians of India*, vol. v. p. 574.
[2] See M. M., *Introduction to the Science of Religion*, Appendix to Lecture I.
[3] See Vans Kennedy, *Notice respecting the Religion introduced by Akbar*, Transactions of the Literary Society of Bombay, 1820, vol. ii. pp. 242–270.
[4] Elliot's *Historians of India*, p. 249.
[5] Müllbauer, *Geschichte der Katholischen Missionen Ostindiens*, s. 134.

into Persian. The New Testament[1] was thus translated at his command; so were the Mahâbhârata, the Râmâyana, the Amarakosha,[2] and other classical works of Sanskrit literature. But although the emperor set the greatest value on the sacred writings of different nations, he does not seem to have succeeded in extorting from the Brahmans a translation of the Veda. A translation of the Atharva-veda[3] was made for him by Haji Ibrahim Sirhindi; but that Veda never enjoyed the same authority as the other three Vedas, and it is doubtful whether by Atharva-veda is meant more than the Upanishads, some of which may have been composed for the special benefit of

[1] Elliot's *Historians of India*, p. 248.
[2] *Ibid.* pp. 259, 260. The *Tarikh-i-Badauni* or *Muntakhabu-t-Tawarikh*, written by Mulla Abdu-l-Kadir Maluk, Shah of Badaun, and finished in 1595, is a general history of India from the time of the Ghaznevides to the 40th year of Akbar. The author is a bigoted Mohammedan, and judges Akbar severely, though he was himself under great obligations to him. He was employed by Akbar to translate from Arabic and Sanskrit into Persian: he translated the Râmâyana, two out of the eighteen sections of the Mahâbhârata, and abridged a history of Cashmir. It is doubtful, however, by whom and how these translations were made. Abdu-l-Kadir states that learned Brahmans were appointed to translate these books for him (Elliot's *Historians of India*, vol. v. p. 537), and there is no evidence that any of the courtiers of Akbar possessed a real knowledge of Sanskrit, or, as it was then called, Hindî (Alberuni's *India*, ed. Sachau, p. xxii), whether literary or vernacular. As those who are mentioned as translators of Sanskrit texts were probably no more than the patrons of certain Pandits, and responsible only for the Arabic and Persian into which the Sanskrit texts were turned, we can understand why three or four names should be mentioned as translators of the same book. Thus the translation of the Mahâbhârata is ascribed to Abdu-l-Kadir, Nakib Khan, Shaikh Mohammad Sultan Thanesari, and Faizi, the brother of the prime minister, Abu-l-Fazl. Nay, Hervas writes: 'Abulfacel, ministro de Akbar, se valió del Amarasinha y del Mahâbhârata, que traduxo en persiano el año de 1586.'—Hervas, ii. 136.
[3] See M. M.'s *History of Ancient Sanskrit Literature*, p. 327.

Akbar. There is a story which, though evidently of a legendary character, shows how the study of Sanskrit was kept up by the Brahmans during the reign of the Mogul emperors.

'Neither the authority (it is said) nor promises of Akbar could prevail upon the Brahmans to disclose the tenets of their religion: he was therefore obliged to have recourse to artifice. The stratagem he made use of was to cause a boy, of the name of *Feizi*, to be committed to the care of these priests, as a poor orphan of the sacerdotal line, who alone could be initiated into the sacred rights of their theology. Feizi, having received the proper instructions for the part he was to act, was conveyed privately to Benares, the seat of knowledge in Hindostan; he was received into the house of a learned Brahman, who educated him with the same care as if he had been his son. After the youth had spent ten years in study, Akbar was desirous of recalling him; but the boy was struck with the charms of the daughter of his preceptor. The old Brahman laid no restraint on the growing passion of the two lovers. He was fond of Feizi, and offered him his daughter in marriage. The young man, divided between love and gratitude, resolved to conceal the fraud no longer, and falling at the feet of the Brahman, discovered the imposture, and asked pardon for his offences. The priest, without reproaching him, seized a poniard which hung at his girdle, and was going to plunge it in his heart, if Feizi had not prevented him by taking hold of his arm. The young man used every means to pacify him, and declared himself ready to do anything to expiate his treachery. The Brahman, bursting into tears, promised to pardon him on condition that he should swear never to translate the Vedas, or sacred volumes, or to disclose to any person whatever the symbol of the Brahman creed. Feizi readily promised him: how far he kept his word is not known; but the sacred books of the Indians have never been translated.'[1]

[1] *History of the Settlements of the Europeans in the East and West Indies,* translated from the French of the Abbé Bernal by J. Justamond, Dublin, 1776, vol. i. p. 34.

SANSKRIT AS KNOWN OUTSIDE INDIA. 207

We have thus traced the existence of Sanskrit, as the language of literature and religion in India, from the time of Solomon to the reign of Akbar. A hundred years after Akbar the eldest son of Shah Jehan, the unfortunate Dara, manifested the same interest in religious speculations which had distinguished his great grandsire. He became a student of Sanskrit, and translated the Upanishads, philosophical treatises appended to the Vedas, into Persian. This was in the year 1657 or 58,[1] a year before he was put to death by his younger brother, the bigoted Aurengzebe.[2] This prince's translation was translated into French by Anquetil Duperron, in the year 1795, the fourth year of the French Republic; and was for a long time the principal source from which European scholars derived their knowledge of the sacred literature of the Brahmans.

European Accounts of India.

At the time at which we have now arrived, the reign of Aurengzebe (1658–1707), the contemporary and rival of Louis XIV, the existence of Sanskrit and Sanskrit literature was known, if not in Europe generally, at least to Europeans in India, particularly to missionaries. Who was the first European that knew of Sanskrit, or that acquired a knowledge of Sanskrit, it is difficult to say. When Vasco da Gama landed at Calicut, on the 9th of May, 1498, Padre Pedro began at once to preach to the natives, and

[1] See Proceedings of the Asiatic Society of Bengal, 1870, p 252.
[2] See Upanishads, translated by M. M., *Sacred Books of the East*, vol. i. p. lviii.

had suffered a martyr's death before the discoverer of India returned to Lisbon. Every new ship that reached India brought new missionaries; but for a long time we look in vain in their letters and reports for any mention of Sanskrit or Sanskrit literature.

St. Francis Xavier.

Francis, now St. Francis, Xavier was the first to organise the great work of preaching the Gospel in India (1542); and such were his zeal and devotion, such his success in winning the hearts of high and low, that his friends ascribed to him among other miraculous gifts, the gift of tongues [1]—a gift never claimed by St. Francis himself. It is not, however, till the year 1559 that we first hear of the missionaries at Goa studying, with the help of a converted Brahman,[2] the theological and philosophical literature of the country, and challenging the Brahmans to public disputations.

---

[1] Müllbauer, p. 67. He himself speaks of the difficulty he had in learning languages: '*Io non comprendo questo popolo, ed egli non comprende me davantaggio.*' See G. Barone, *Vita del P. Paolino da S. Bartolommeo*, 1888, p. 66.

[2] Müllbauer, p. 80. These Brahmans, according to Robert de Nobili, were of a lower class, not initiated in the sacred literature. They were ignorant, he says, 'of the books Smarta, Apastamba, and Sutra.' —(Ibid. p. 188.) Robert himself quotes from the Âpastamba-Sûtra, in his defence (ibid. p. 192). He also quotes Skanda Purâna, p. 193; Kadambari, p. 193. A work of his is mentioned by Kircher, *China Illustrata*, 1667, p. 152, but it seems to have existed in MS. only. Kircher says, 'legat, qui volet, librum quem de Brahmanum theologia P. Robertus Nobilis Societatis Jesu, missionis Madurensis in Indiâ Malabaricâ fundator, nec non linguae et Brahmanicae genealogiae consultissimus, summâ sane eruditione . . . conscripsit.' This book might still be of great interest.

Filippo Sassetti.

From 1581 to 1588 an Italian scholar of considerable eminence among the literary men of his time, Filippo Sassetti, lived at Goa. His letters have lately been published at Florence, and in one of them he states that the sciences of the Indians are all written in one language, which is called *Sanscruta*. This, he says, means a well-articulated language. The people learn it, as we learn Greek and Latin, and it takes them six or seven years before they master it. No one knows when that language was spoken, but it has many words in common with the spoken vernaculars, nay with Italian, particularly in the numerals 6, 7, 8, and 9, in the names for God, serpent, and many others. And then he adds: 'I ought to have come here at eighteen, in order to return with some knowledge of these beautiful things.'[1]

Roberto de' Nobili.

The first certain instance of a European missionary having mastered the difficulties of the Sanskrit language belongs to a later period — to what may be called the period of Roberto de' Nobili (1577–1656), as distinguished from the first period, which is under the presiding spirit of Francis Xavier. Roberto de' Nobili went to India in 1606. He was himself a man of high family, a nephew of the famous cardinal

---

[1] *Lettere edite e inedite di Filippo Sassetti, raccolte e annotate da Ettore Marcucci*, Firenze, 1855, p. 417. I owe my knowledge of Sassetti to the kindness of Professor Maggi at Milan, who sent me a copy of his letters. See also A. De Gubernatis, *Viaggiatori Italiani*, 1875, p. 321.

CHAPTER VI.

Bellarmino, a man of a refined and cultivated mind. He therefore perceived the more quickly the difficulties which kept the higher castes, and particularly the Brahmans, from joining the Christian communities formed at Madura and other places. These communities consisted chiefly of men of low rank, of no education, and no refinement. He conceived the bold plan of presenting himself as a Brahman, and thus obtaining access to the high and noble, the wise and learned, in the land. He shut himself up for years, acquiring in secret a knowledge, not only of Tamil and Telugu, but of Sanskrit. When, after a patient study of the language and literature of the Brahmans, he felt himself strong enough to grapple with his antagonists, he showed himself in public, dressed in the proper garb of the Brahmans, wearing their cord and their frontal mark, observing their diet, and submitting even to the complicated rules of caste. He was successful, in spite of the persecutions both of the Brahmans, who were afraid of him, and of his own fellow-labourers, who could not understand his policy. His life in India, where he died as an old blind man, is full of interest to the missionary.[1] I can only speak of him here as the first European Sanskrit scholar. A man who could quote from Manu, from the Purânas, nay from works such as the Âpastamba-Sûtras, which are known even at present to only those few Sanskrit scholars who can read Sanskrit

---

[1] In a letter of Burnell's (Tanjore, 27th April, 1876) published in the *Bollettino Italiano*, 1876, p. 16, there are some notices of R. de Nobilibus. 'He died 16th Jan. 1656, in his 80th year, at St. Thomas, near Madras.' The Jesuits had printing offices at Coccino, Ambalakkâdu, and Punikkayal, but none of their books are to be found now.

MSS., must have been far advanced in a knowledge of the sacred language and literature of the Brahmans. The very idea that he came, as he said, to preach a new or a fourth Veda,[1] which had been lost, shows how well he knew the strong and weak points of the theological system which he came to conquer. It is surprising that the reports which he sent to Rome in order to defend himself against the charge of idolatry, and in which he drew a faithful picture of the religion, the customs, and literature of the Brahmans, should not have attracted the attention of scholars. The 'Accommodation Question,' as it was called, occupied cardinals and popes for many years; but not one of them seems to have perceived the extraordinary interest attaching to the existence of an ancient civilisation so perfect and so firmly rooted as to require accommodation even from the missionaries of Rome. At a time when the discovery of one Greek MS. would have been hailed by all the scholars of Europe, the discovery of a complete literature was

[1] The Ezour-veda is not the work of Robert de' Nobili. It was probably written by one of his converts. The translation from Sanskrit is ascribed to '*le grand-prêtre ou archi-brame de la pagode de Cheringham, veillard respecté par vertu incorruptible.*' It is in Sanskrit verse, in the style of the Purâṇas, and contains a wild mixture of Hindu and Christian doctrine. The French translation was sent to Voltaire, and printed by him in 1778: '*L'Ezour Vedam, ou ancien commentaire du Vedam, contenant l'exposition des opinions religieuses et philosophiques des Indous, traduit du Samscretam par un Brame,*' Yverdon, 1778, 2 vols. 8º. Voltaire expressed his belief that the original was four centuries older than Alexander, and that it was the most precious gift for which the West had been ever indebted to the East. Mr. Ellis discovered the Sanskrit original at Pondichery.—(*Asiatic Researches*, vol. xiv.) There is no excuse for ascribing the work to Robert, and it is not mentioned in the list of his works.—(Bertrand, *La Mission du Maduré*, Paris, 1847–50, tom. iii. p. 116; Müllbauer, p. 205, *note*.)

allowed to pass unnoticed. The day of Sanskrit had not yet come.

Heinrich Roth.

There is another Jesuit missionary of the seventeenth century who acquired a knowledge of Sanskrit, Heinrich Roth. While stationed at Agra he succeeded in persuading a Brahman to teach him the elements of Sanskrit, and, after six years of hard study, he had acquired a perfect mastery of this difficult language. He was at Rome in the year 1666, and it was he who drew up the interesting account of the Sanskrit alphabet which Athanasius Kircher published in his *China Illustrata* (1667).

Scholars of the Eighteenth Century.

We now approach the eighteenth century,[1] and there we find that the attention of European scholars begins at last to be attracted to the extraordinary discovery, a discovery that could no longer be doubted, of the existence in India of an immense literature, the age of which was believed to exceed that of every other literature in the world. The French Jesuits whom Louis XIV. sent out to India after the treaty of Ryswick, in 1697, kept up a literary correspondence with members of the French Institute. Questions were addressed to them by members of that learned body, and their answers were printed either in the Memoirs of the Academy, or in the *Lettres édifiantes*. The answers sent by the Père Cœurdoux, in 1767, to the queries addressed to him by the Abbé Barthélemy,

---

[1] In 1677 a Mr. Marshall is said to have been a proficient in Sanskrit.—Elliot's *Historians of India*, vol. v. p. 575.

and his subsequent correspondence with Anquetil
Duperron,[1] are full of interesting materials. Of this
learned missionary we shall have to speak again as
one of the first who saw the real bearing of the similarity between the ancient language of India and the
languages of Europe.

Père Calmette.

One of his colleagues, the Père Calmette, in a
letter dated Vencataguiry, in the kingdom of Car-
natic, the 24th of January, 1733, informs us[2] that
by that time the Jesuits had missionaries who were
not only well grounded in Sanskrit, but able to
read some portions of the Veda. They were forming an Oriental library from which, he says, they
were beginning to derive great advantages for the
advancement of religion. They drew from this ar-
senal of paganism the weapons which wounded the
Brahmans most deeply. They possessed their philosophy, their theology, and particularly the four Vedas
which contain the law of the Brahmans, and which
the Indians from time immemorial regarded as their
sacred books, as books of an irrefragable authority,
and as coming from God himself.

'From the time that missionaries first went to India,' he continues, 'it has always been thought to be impossible to find
this book which is so much respected by the Indians. And,
indeed, we should never have succeeded, if we had not had
Brahmans, who are Christians, hidden among them. For how
would they have communicated this book to Europeans, and
particularly to the enemies of their religion, as they do not

[1] *Mémoires de Littérature de l'Académie Royale des Inscriptions*,
tom. xlix. p. 647.
[2] *Lettres édifiantes* (Paris, 1781), vol. xiii. p. 390.

communicate it even to the Indians, except to those of their own caste? ... The most extraordinary part is that those who are the depositaries of the Veda, do not understand its meaning, for the Veda is written in a very ancient language, and the Samouscroutam, which is as familiar to their learned men as Latin is to us, is not sufficient, without the help of a commentary, to explain the thoughts as well as the words of the Veda. They call it the Maha bachiam, or the great commentary. Those who are given to the study of these books form the first class among their learned men. While the other Brahmans salute, these alone give a blessing.'

And again he says (p. 437):—

'Since the Veda is in our hands we have extracted from it texts which serve to convince them of those fundamental truths that must destroy idolatry; for the unity of God, the qualities of the true God, and a state of blessedness and condemnation, are all in the Veda. But the truths which are to be found in this book are only scattered there like grains of gold in a heap of sand. . . . .'

In another letter, dated 16th Sept. 1737, the same missionary writes:—

'I think like you that it would have been right to consult with greater care the original books of the Indian religion. But hitherto these books were not in our hands, and it was thought for a long time that they could not be found, particularly the most important ones, viz. the four Vedas. It is only five or six years ago that I was allowed to form an Oriental library for the king, and charged to seek for Indian books for that purpose. I then made discoveries of great importance for religion, among which I count that of the four Vedas or sacred books.

'But these books, of which the ablest doctors among them understand hardly half, which a Brahman would not venture to explain to us for fear of getting into trouble with his own caste, and of which a knowledge of Sanskrit does not yet give us the key, because they are written in a more ancient language,—these books, I say, are, in more than one sense, sealed books for us. One finds, however, some of their texts explained in theological works; some become intelligible by means of a knowledge of the ordinary Sanskrit, particularly those that are taken from the last books of the Veda, and which, to judge by the difference of language and style, are more than five centuries later than the rest.'

Père Pons.

A few years after Calmette the Père Pons drew up a comprehensive account of the literary treasures of the Brahmans; and his report, dated Karikal, dans le Maduré, November 23, 1740, and addressed to Father Du Halde, was published in the *Lettres édifiantes*.[1] Father Pons gives in it a most interesting and, in general, a very accurate description of the various branches of Sanskrit literature,—of the four Vedas, the grammatical treatises, the six systems of philosophy, and the astronomy of the Hindus. He anticipated, on several points, the researches of Sir William Jones.

But, although the letters of Father Pons, of Cœurdoux, Calmette, and others excited a deep interest, that interest remained necessarily barren, as long as there were no grammars, dictionaries, or Sanskrit texts to enable scholars in Europe to study Sanskrit in the same spirit in which they studied Greek and Latin. The Abbé Barthélemy, in 1763, had asked the Père Cœurdoux to send him before everything else, a grammar of the Sanskrit language; though it would seem that at that time the Royal Library at Paris

[1] *Lettres édifiantes* (Paris, 1781), vol. xiv. p. 65. See an excellent account of this letter in an article of M. Biot in the *Journal des Savants*, 1861; and in Hervas, *Catalogo de las Lenguas*, ii. p. 125.

possessed a Sanskrit grammar written in Latin, and giving the Sanskrit words in Bengali letters. The only part wanting was the syntax, and this was afterwards supplied by the Père Cœurdoux.

Paolino da S. Bartolommeo.

At Rome also materials for a Sanskrit grammar, from the pen of H. Roth,[1] seem to have existed in the library of the Collegio Romano, and likewise among the valuable papers left by the Jesuit J. Hanxleden, to whom frequent reference is made by Paolino da S. Bartolommeo, Hervas,[2] and others. This Paolino da S. Bartolommeo[3] was the first who succeeded in publishing a Sanskrit grammar in Europe. He was a Carmelite friar, a German of the name of Johann Philip Werdin (not Wesdin), who spent the years from 1776 to 1789 in India, and who published his grammar of Sanskrit at Rome, in 1790.[4] Some years later he printed a more complete grammar; and he likewise wrote several essays on the antiquities, the mythology, and religion of India, availing himself

---

[1] Hervas, *Catalogo de las Lenguas*, ii. p. 133.

[2] *Ibid.* p. 132. 'Este jesuita, segun me ha dicho el referido Fray Paulino, llegó á hablar la lengua malabar, y á entender la samsereda con mayor perfeccion que los Brahmanes, como lo demuestran sus insignes manuscritos en dichas lenguas.' He died in March, 1732; see *Bollettino Italiano*, 1876, p. 46.

[3] An excellent account of the life and literary labours of Paolino is given by Professor Barone in his *Vita, Precursori ed Opere del P. Paolino da S. Bartolommeo* (Filippo Werdin), Napoli, 1888.

[4] *Sidharubam seu Grammatica Samscrdamica*, cui accedit dissertatio historico-critica in linguam Samscrdamicam, vulgo Samscret dictam, in

in all his writings of the papers left by Hanxleden, whose knowledge of Sanskrit, to judge from quotations given by Paolino, must have been very considerable. The grammar of Paolino has been severely criticised, and is now hardly ever consulted; but it is only fair to bear in mind, that the first grammar of any language is a work of infinitely greater difficulty than any later grammar.[1]

The two missionaries whose manuscript materials Paolino was allowed to use were Padre Marco della Tomba, a Capuchin, and Ernestus Hanxleden, a Jesuit.

Marco della Tomba.

The former, Marco della Tomba, arrived in India in 1757, and is said to have returned to Rome from Tibet in 1774. He set himself to study the language and literature of the Brahmans, and tells us that he was able not only to translate Sanskrit texts with the help of the Pandits, but to dispute with them in their own language without embarrassment. This, however, could hardly have been in Sanskrit, for though the account which he gives of the customs, manners, beliefs, and literature of the Brahmans is intelligent, it often betrays an ignorance of the real character of the Sanskrit language. He no doubt handled a large number of Sanskrit MSS., but he admits that he was never allowed to see a MS. of the Vedas, so that he doubts their very existence. He speaks of the wonderful memory of the Brahmans, who seemed to know whole books by heart. His letters must have roused the

---

[1] *Vyacarana seu Locupletissima Samscrdamicæ Linguæ Institutio*, à P. Paulino a S. Bartholomæo: Romæ, 1804.

curiosity of those to whom they were addressed, and they are pleasant to read even now in the extracts published by Count Angelo De Gubernatis,[1] from the MS. preserved in the Museo Borgiano.

E. Hanxleden.

The latter, Joh. Ernestus Hanxleden (died 1732), the Jesuit, seems to have been much more of a real scholar. Count Angelo De Gubernatis gives an account of a MS., now deposited in the Biblioteca Vittorio Emanuele,[2] which formerly belonged to the Jesuit Libraria segreta del Collegio Romano. He supposes that it came from Hanxleden. It contains text and translation of the Vasishtʰasâra on Vedânta subjects, extracts from the Upanishads, the Tarkabhâshâ (logic), the Vedântasâra, and the Ashtâvakragîtâ (published by Carlo Giussani in the *Rivista Orientale*, 1867). This shows a considerable advance, supposing that it was his own work, and though the assertion of Hervas that Hanxleden spoke Sanskrit with greater perfection than the Brahmans, sounds exaggerated, he was probably far in advance of other missionaries returned to Rome from India.[3]

[1] *Gli Scritti del Padre Marco della Tomba*, 1878; *Bollettino Italiano*, 25 July, 1876, p. 43.
[2] *Bollettino Italiano*, July 10, 1876.
[3] Count Ugo Balzani has had the kindness to send me the following titles of MSS. now in the Biblioteca Vittorio Emanuele, formerly in the Convent di Santa Maria della Scala:—

Hanxleden Ernestus.—Dictionarium Malabaricum cui addita multa Vocabula Samscrdamica a P. F. Ernesto Hanxleden, descriptum a P. Franco Carmelita Discalceato Malabariæ Missionario anno 1785. 1 v. in 4°. sec. xviii. chart. S. M. S. 25.

Hanxleden Ernestus.—Vocabularium Malabarico Lusitanum. 1 v. in fol. chart. sec. xviii. S. M. S. 33.

SANSKRIT AS KNOWN OUTSIDE INDIA. 219

We have thus seen how the existence of the
Sanskrit language and literature was known ever
since India had first been discovered by Alexander
and his companions. But what was not known was
that this language, as it was spoken at the time of
Alexander, and, as we saw, even at the time of
Solomon,[1] nay, for centuries before his time, was

Hanxleden Ernestus.—Vita Jesu Christi D. N. Versibus Malabaricis composita a P. F. E. Hanxleden, capita xiv. Dicitur Mishihâde Pâna. Vide Paulinus a S. Bartholomeo, Miscellanea Indica.

Hanxleden Ernestus.—Liber excellens scriptus lingua Samscrit charactere Granthamico, continet poema insigne Brahmanicum Indicum *Yudkishtira vigea* (Yudhish*t*hira-vi*g*aya) inscriptum cum explicatione versuum in lingua.

Paulinus a S. Bartholomæo.—Gramatica Grandonica Regi Travancoridis dicata per F. Paulinum a S. Bartholomæo Carmelitam Discalceatum 1782. S. M. S. 3. Paolino da S. Bartolommeo says: 'Hic (Hanxleden) primus grammaticam Samscrdamicam ex libro grammatico Brahmanico Sidharûbam dicto confecit, atque hæc grammatica Grandonica cum nostra Samscridamica, quam ab Kunhen et Krshna Brahmanibus Angamalensibus accepimus, quoad elementa et regulas una cademque est.' Examen historico-criticum Codicum Indicorum, p. 51; Barone, *Vita*, p. 147. *Grandonica* is not derived from *grantha*, book, as Benfey supposes; but *grantha* is simply the name given to the alphabet in which Sanskrit was written in the South, and therefore to Sanskrit literature. The Grantha MSS. are of great importance for Sanskrit philology. Ziegenbald (vol. iv. p. 381) says, 'Brammhanum linguæ propriæ nomen est *grantham*, neque a Brahmanibus ipsis unquam aliter vocatur.' See Barone, *Vita*, p. 148.

Paulinus a S. Bartholomæo.—Celeberrimum poema Mâga Samscrudanid.—De sex divinis attributis Carmen sermone Malabarico Samscrdamico contra Polytheistas Indos auctore P. Paulino a S. Bartholomæo Carm. Disc.—Vita S. M. Theresiæ a Jesu Versibus Samscrodamico. Malabaricis composita a F. Paulino a S. Barth. C. D. anno 1783. S. M. S. 8. 1 v. in 8°. sec. xviii. chart.

Paulinus a S. Bartholomæo.—Miscellanea Indica a P. Paulino collecta. 1 v. in fol. sec. xviii. chart. S. M. S. 34.

Paulinus a S. Bartholomæo.—Opera Miscellanea. 6 v. in fol. sec. xviii. chart. S. M. S. 38-43.

[1] See before, p. 186.

intimately related to Greek and Latin, in fact, stood to them in the same relation as French to Italian and Spanish.

Asiatic Society of Calcutta.

The history of what may be called European Sanskrit philology dates from the foundation of the Asiatic Society at Calcutta, in 1784.[1] For although some of the early missionaries seem to have possessed a far more considerable knowledge of Sanskrit than was at one time supposed, yet it was through the labours of Sir William Jones, Wilkins, Carey, Forster, Colebrooke, and other members of that illustrious society, that the language and literature of the Brahmans became first accessible to European scholars.

Similarity between Sanskrit, Greek, and Latin.

It would be difficult to say which of the two, the language or the literature, excited the deepest and most lasting interest. It was impossible to look, even in the most cursory manner, at the declensions and conjugations, without being struck by the extraordinary similarity, or, in some cases, by the absolute identity, of the grammatical forms in Sanskrit, Greek, and Latin. We saw that, as early as 1588, Filippo Sassetti was startled by the similarity of the San-

[1] The earliest publications were the Bhagavadgîtâ, translated by Wilkins, 1785; the Hitopadesa, translated by Wilkins, 1787; and the Sakuntalâ, translated by W. Jones, 1789. Original grammars, without mentioning mere compilations, were published by Paolino da S. Bartolommeo, 1790 and 1804; by Colebrooke, 1805; by Carey, 1806; by Wilkins, 1808; by Forster, 1810; by Yates, 1820; by Wilson, 1841. In Germany, Bopp published his grammars in 1827, 1832, 1834; Benfey, in 1852 and 1855.

skrit and Italian numerals, and of the words for God, serpent, and many other things. The same remark must have been made by others, but it was never so distinctly set forth as by the Père Cœurdoux.

Père Cœurdoux.

In the year 1767 that French Jesuit wrote from Pondichery to the Abbé Barthélemy[1] at Paris, who had asked him for a Sanskrit grammar and dictionary and for general information on the history and literature of India, and he enclosed a memoir, which he wished to be laid before the Academy, with the following title:—'*Question proposée à M. l'abbé Barthélemy et aux autres membres de l'Académie de belles-lettres et inscriptions:* "*D'où vient que dans la langue samscroutane il se trouve un grand nombre de mots qui lui sont communs avec le latin et le grec, et surtout avec le latin?*"' The Jesuit missionary first gives his facts, some of which are very interesting. He compares, for instance, deva and *deus*, God; mrityu and *mors*, death; ganitam and *genitum*, produced; gânu and *genu*, knee; vidhavâ, from vi, without, and dhava, man, with *vidua*, widow; na and *non*, not; madhya and *medius*, middle; dattam and *datum*, given; dânam and *donum*, gift; and many more which have since been pointed out afresh by later scholars. Some of his comparisons, no doubt, are untenable, but on the whole his paper deserved more attention than it seems to have received from the Academy. His grammatical comparisons, in particular, are very creditable. He com-

[1] Born 1716, died 1795.

pares the indicative and the subjunctive of the auxiliary verb in Sanskrit and Latin:—

Sanskrit	Latin	Sanskrit	Latin
asmi	sum	syâm	sim
asi	es	syâs	sis
asti	est	syât	sit
smas	sumus	syâma	simus
stha	estis	syâta	sitis
santi	sunt	santu	sint

Among the pronouns he compares aham and *ego*, me and *me*, mahyam and *mihi*, sva and *suus*, tvam and *tu*, tubhyam and *tibi*, kas and *quis*, ke and *qui*, kam and *quem*, &c. He likewise exhibits the striking similarities in the Sanskrit, Greek, and Latin numerals from one to one hundred.

But not satisfied with this, he goes on to examine the different hypotheses that suggest themselves for explaining these facts, and after showing that neither commerce, nor literary intercourse, nor proselytism, nor conquest could account for the common stock of words that is found in Sanskrit, Greek, and Latin, he sums up in favour of viewing these common words as relics of the primitive language of mankind, preserved by different tribes in their migrations north and south, after the great catastrophe of the confusion of tongues at Babel.

Considering that this essay was written a hundred years ago, it is astounding that it should have attracted so little attention, and should, in fact, never have been quoted until M. Michel Bréal disinterred it from the Memoirs of the French Academy, and vindicated for this modest missionary the credit that certainly belongs to him, of having anticipated some of the most important results of Comparative Philology by at least fifty years.

Halhed.

Halhed, in the preface to his Grammar of Bengali,[1] published in 1778, remarked, 'I have been astonished to find this similitude of Sanskrit words with those of Persian and Arabic, and even of Latin and Greek; and these not in technical and metaphorical terms, which the mutation of refined arts and improved manners might have occasionally introduced; but in the main groundwork of language, in monosyllables, in the names of numbers, and the appellations of such things as could be first discriminated on the immediate dawn of civilization.'

Sir William Jones.

Sir William Jones (died 1794), even before he went to India, had been interested in the curious coincidence between words in Persian and in Greek and Latin. In a letter to Prince Adam Czartoryski, dated Febr. 17, 1770, he writes:[2]—'How so many European words crept into the Persian language, I know not with certainty. Procopius, I think, mentions the great intercourse, both in war and peace, between the Persians and the nations in the north of Europe and Asia, whom the ancients knew by the

---

[1] Halhed was a servant of the East-India Company. He was born 1751, and died 1836. Halhed published in 1776 the *Code of Gentoo Laws*, a digest of the most important Sanskrit law-books made by eleven Brahmans, by the order of Warren Hastings. Halhed translated

general name of Scythians. Many learned investigators of antiquity are fully persuaded, that a very old and almost primæval language was in use among these northern nations, from which not only the Celtic dialect but even Greek and Latin, are derived; in fact we find πατήρ and μήτηρ in Persian, nor is θυγάτηρ so far removed from *dockter*, or even ὄνομα and *nomen* from *nâm*, as to make it ridiculous to suppose that they sprang from the same root. We must confess that these researches are very obscure and uncertain; and you will allow, not so agreeable as an ode of Hafez, or an elegy of Amr'alkeis.'

After he had gone to India he declared, after the first glance at Sanskrit, that, whatever its antiquity, it was a language of most wonderful structure, more perfect than the Greek, more copious than the Latin, and more exquisitely refined than either, yet bearing to both of them a strong affinity. 'No philologer,' he writes, 'could examine the Sanskrit, Greek, and Latin, without believing them to have sprung from some common source, which, perhaps, no longer exists. There is a similar reason, though not quite so forcible, for supposing that both the Gothic and Celtic had the same origin with the Sanskrit. The old Persian may be added to the same family.'[1]

But how was that affinity to be explained? People were completely taken by surprise. Theologians shook their heads; classical scholars looked sceptical;

---

[1] It should be remembered that Paolino da S. Bartolommeo, in his *Dissertatio de latini sermonis origine et cum orientalibus linguis connexione*, Romæ, 1802, declared, 'Indos veteres diceres latine loculos

philosophers indulged in the wildest conjectures in order to escape from the only possible conclusion which could be drawn from the facts placed before them, but which threatened to upset their little systems of the history of the world.

Lord Monboddo.

Lord Monboddo had just finished his great work[1] in which he derives all mankind from a couple of apes, and all the dialects of the world from a language originally framed by some Egyptian gods,[2] when the discovery of Sanskrit came on him like a thunderbolt. It must be said, however, to his credit, that he at once perceived the immense importance of the discovery. He could not be expected to sacrifice his primæval monkeys or his Egyptian idols; but, with that reservation, the conclusions which he drew from the new evidence placed before him by his friend Wilkins, the author of one of our first Sanskrit grammars, are highly creditable to the acuteness of the Scotch judge.

'There is a language,' he writes[3] (in 1792), 'still existing, and preserved among the Brahmins of India, which is a richer and in every respect a finer language than even the Greek of Homer. All the other languages of India have a great resem-

---

[1] *Of the Origin and Progress of Language*, second edition, 6 vols. Edinburgh, 1774.

[2] 'I have supposed that language could not be invented without supernatural assistance, and, accordingly, I have maintained that it was the invention of the Dæmon kings of Egypt, who, being more than men, first taught themselves to articulate, and then taught others. But, even among them, I am persuaded there was a progress in the art, and that such a language as the Shanscrit was not at once invented.'— Monboddo, *Antient Metaphysics*, vol. iv. p. 357.

[3] *Of the Origin and Progress of Language*, vol. vi. p. 97.

blance to this language, which is called the Shanscrit. But those languages are dialects of it, and formed from it, not the Shanscrit from them. Of this, and other particulars concerning this language, I have got such certain information from India, that if I live to finish my history of man, which I have begun in my third volume of *Antient Metaphysics*, I shall be able clearly to prove that the Greek is derived from the Shanscrit, which was the antient language of Egypt, and was carried by the Egyptians into India, with their other arts, and into Greece by the colonies which they settled there.'

A few years later (1795) he had arrived at more definite views on the relation of Sanskrit to Greek; and he writes,[1]

'Mr. Wilkins has proved to my conviction such a resemblance betwixt the Greek and the Shanscrit, that the one must be a dialect of the other, or both of some original language. Now the Greek is certainly not a dialect of the Shanscrit, any more than the Shanscrit is of the Greek. They must, therefore, be both dialects of the same language; and that language could be no other than the language of Egypt, brought into India by Osiris, of which, undoubtedly, the Greek was a dialect, as I think I have proved.'

Into these theories of Lord Monboddo's on Egypt and Osiris, we need not inquire at present. But it may be of interest to give one other extract, in order to show how well, apart from his men with, and his monkeys without, tails, Lord Monboddo could sift and handle the evidence that was placed before him:—

'To apply these observations to the similarities which Mr. Wilkins has discovered betwixt the Shanscrit and the Greek; I will begin with these words, which must have been original words in all languages, as the things denoted by them must

[1] *Antient Metaphysics*, vol. iv. p. 322.

have been known in the first ages of civility, and have got
names; so that it is impossible that one language could have
borrowed them from another, unless it was a derivative or
dialect of that language. Of this kind are the names of numbers, of the members of the human body, and of relations, such
as that of father, mother, and brother. And first, as to numbers, the use of which must have been coeval with civil society.
The words in the Shanscrit for the numbers, from one to ten,
are, ek, dwee, tree, chatoor, panch, shat, sapt, augt,
nava, das, which certainly have an affinity to the Greek or
Latin names for those numbers. Then they proceed towards
twenty, saying ten and one, ten and two, and so forth, till they
come to twenty; for their arithmetic is decimal as well as ours.
Twenty they express by the word veensatee. Then they go
on till they come to thirty, which they express by the word
treensat, of which the word expressing three is part of the
composition, as well as it is of the Greek and Latin names for
those numbers. And in like manner they go on expressing
forty, fifty, &c., by a like composition with the words expressing simple numerals, namely, four, five, &c., till they
come to the number one hundred, which they express by *sat*,
a word different from either the Greek or Latin name for that
number. But, in this numeration, there is a very remarkable conformity betwixt the word in Shanscrit expressing
twenty or twice ten, and the words in Greek and Latin expressing the same number; for in none of the three languages has
the word any relation to the number two, which, by multiplying
ten, makes twenty; such as the words expressing the numbers
thirty, forty, &c., have to the words expressing three or four;
for in Greek the word is *eikosi*, which expresses no relation to
the number two; nor does the Latin *viginti*, but which appears
to have more resemblance to the Shanscrit word veensatee.
And thus it appears that in the anomalies of the two languages
of Greek and Latin, there appears to be some conformity with
the Shanscrit.'

Lord Monboddo compares the Sanskrit pada with
the Greek *pous, podos*; the Sanskrit nâsa with the

Latin *nasus*; the Sanskrit de va, god, with the Greek *theos* and Latin *deus*; the Sanskrit ap, water, with the Latin *aqua*; the Sanskrit vidh avâ with the Latin *vidua*, widow. Sanskrit words such as gonia for angle, kentra for centre, hora for hour, he points out as clearly of Greek origin, and imported into Sanskrit. He then proceeds to show the grammatical coincidences between Sanskrit and the classical languages. He dwells on compounds such as tripada, from tri, three, and pada, foot—a tripod; he remarks on the extraordinary fact that Sanskrit, like Greek, changes a positive into a negative adjective by the addition of the *a* privative; and he then produces what he seems to consider as the most valuable present that Mr. Wilkins could have given him, namely, the Sanskrit forms, asmi, I am; asi, thou art; asti, he is; santi, they are; forms clearly of the same origin as the corresponding forms *esmi*, *eis*, *esti*, in Greek, and *sunt* in Latin.

Dugald Stewart.

Another Scotch philosopher, Dugald Stewart, was much less inclined to yield such ready submission. No doubt it must have required a considerable effort for a man brought up in the belief that Greek and Latin were either aboriginal languages, or modifications of Hebrew, to bring himself to acquiesce in the revolutionary doctrine that the classical languages were intimately related to a jargon of mere savages; for such all the subjects of the Great Mogul were then supposed to be. However, if the facts about Sanskrit were true, Dugald Stewart was too wise not to see that the conclusions drawn from them were inevitable. He therefore denied the reality of such a language as Sanskrit altogether, and wrote his famous essay to prove that Sanskrit had been put together after the model of Greek and Latin, by those arch-forgers and liars, the Brahmans, and that the whole of Sanskrit literature was an imposition. I mention this fact, because it shows, better than anything else, how violent a shock was given by the discovery of Sanskrit to prejudices most deeply engrained in the mind of every educated man. The most absurd arguments found favour for a time, if they could only furnish a loophole by which to escape from the unpleasant conclusion that Greek and Latin were of the same kith and kin as the language of the black inhabitants of India. The first who, in the broad daylight of European science, dared boldly to face both the facts and the conclusions of Sanskrit scholarship, was the German poet, Frederick Schlegel.

Frederick Schlegel.

He had been in England during the peace of Amiens (1801–1802), and had acquired a smattering of Sanskrit from Mr. Alexander Hamilton. After carrying on his studies for some time in Paris, he published, in 1808, his work on *The Language and Wisdom of the Indians*. This work became the foundation of the science of language. Though published only two years after the first volume of Adelung's *Mithridates*, it is separated from that work by the same distance which separates the Copernican from the Ptolemæan system. Schlegel was not a great scholar. Many of his statements have proved erroneous; and nothing would be easier than to dissect his essay and hold it up to ridicule. But Schlegel was a man of genius; and when a new science is to be created, the imagination of the poet is wanted, even more than the accuracy of the scholar. It surely required somewhat of poetic vision to embrace with *one* glance the languages of India, Persia, Greece, Italy, and Germany, and to rivet them together by the simple name of Indo-Germanic. This was Schlegel's work; and, in the history of the human intellect, it has been truly called 'the discovery of a new world.'

We shall see how Schlegel's idea was taken up in Germany, and how it led almost immediately to a genealogical classification of the principal languages of mankind.

CHAPTER VII.

GENEALOGICAL CLASSIFICATION OF LANGUAGES.

The Founders of Comparative Philology.

WE traced in a former chapter the history of the various attempts at a classification of languages to the year 1808, the year in which Frederick Schlegel published his little work on *The Language and Wisdom of the Indians*. This work was like the wand of a magician. It pointed out the place where a mine should be opened; and it was not long before some of the most distinguished scholars of the day began to sink their shafts and raise the ore. For a time, everybody who wished to learn Sanskrit had to come to England. Bopp, Schlegel, Lassen, Rosen, Burnouf, all spent some time in this country, copying manuscripts at the East India House, and receiving assistance from Wilkins, Colebrooke, Wilson, and other distinguished members of the old Indian Civil Service. The first minute and scholar-like comparison of the grammar of Sanskrit with that of Greek, Latin, Persian, and German was made by Francis Popp, in 1816.[1] Other essays of his followed; and in 1833 appeared the first volume of his *Comparative Grammar of Sanskrit, Zend, Greek, Latin, Lithuanian,*

---

[1] *Conjugationssystem*, Frankfurt, 1816.

Slavonic, Gothic, and German. This work was not finished till nearly twenty years later, in 1852;[1] but it will form for ever the safe and solid foundation of Comparative Philology.[2] August Wilhelm von Schlegel, the brother of Frederick Schlegel, used the influence which he had acquired as a German poet, to popularise the study of Sanskrit in Germany. His *Indische Bibliothek* was published from 1819 to 1830, and though chiefly intended for Sanskrit literature, it likewise contained several articles on Comparative Philology. This new science soon found a still more powerful patron in Wilhelm von Humboldt, the worthy brother of Alexander von Humboldt, and at that time one of the leading statesmen in Prussia. His essays, chiefly on the philosophy of language, attracted general attention during his lifetime; and he left a lasting monument of his studies in his great work on the Kawi language, which was published after his death, in 1836. Another scholar who must be reckoned among the founders of Comparative Philology is Professor Pott, whose *Etymological Researches* appeared first in 1833 and 1836.[3] More special in its purpose, but based on the same general

---

[1] New edition in 1856, much improved.

[2] This may sound a bold statement in 1888, when Bopp has been relegated to the limbo of the fallen great ones, and his etymologies are only quoted as warning examples of perverse ingenuity. From an historical point of view, however, his work has lost nothing of its greatness. He did what was possible in his time. Let us hope that the same may be said hereafter of those who came after him and carried on his work to higher perfection.

[3] Second edition, 1859 to 1873. Pott's work on *The Language of the Gipsies* appeared in 1846; his work on *Proper Names* in 1856. See obituary notice at the end of this chapter, p. 290.

principles, was Grimm's *Teutonic Grammar*, a work which has truly been called colossal. Its publication occupied nearly twenty years, from 1819 to 1837. We ought, likewise, to mention here the name of an eminent Dane, Erasmus Rask, who devoted himself to the study of the northern languages of Europe. He started, in 1816, for Persia and India, and was the first to acquire a grammatical knowledge of Zend, the language of the Zend-Avesta; but he died before he had time to publish all the results of his learned researches. He had proved, however, that the sacred language of the Parsis was closely connected with the sacred language of the Brahmans, and that, like Sanskrit, it had preserved some of the earliest formations of Indo-European speech. These researches into the ancient Persian language were taken up again by one of the greatest scholars that France ever produced, by Eugène Burnouf. Though the works of Zoroaster had been translated before by Anquetil Duperron, his was only a translation of a modern Persian translation of the original. It was Burnouf who, by means of his knowledge of Sanskrit and Comparative Grammar, deciphered for the first time the very words of the founder of the ancient religion of light. He was, likewise, the first to apply the same key with real success to the cuneiform inscriptions of Darius and Xerxes; and his premature death will long be mourned, not only by those who, like myself, had the privilege of knowing him personally and attending his lectures, but by all who have the interest of oriental literature and of real oriental scholarship at heart.

I cannot give here a list of all the scholars who followed in the track of Bopp, Schlegel, Humboldt, Grimm, and Burnouf. How the science of language has flourished and abounded may best be seen in the library of any comparative philologist. There has been, since the year 1852, a special journal of Comparative Philology in Germany. The Philological Society in London publishes every year a valuable volume of its transactions; and in almost every continental university there is a professor of Sanskrit who lectures likewise on Comparative Grammar and the Science of Language.

The proper place of Sanskrit in the Aryan Family.

But why, it may naturally be asked—why should the discovery of Sanskrit have wrought so complete a change in the classificatory study of languages? If Sanskrit had been the primitive language of mankind, or at least the parent of Greek, Latin, and German, we might understand that it should have led to quite a new classification of these tongues. But Sanskrit does not stand to Greek, Latin, the Teutonic, Celtic, and Slavonic languages, in the relation of Latin to French, Italian, and Spanish. Sanskrit, as we saw before, could not be called their parent, but only their elder sister. It occupies with regard to the classical languages a position analogous to that which Provençal occupies with regard to the modern Romance dialects. This is perfectly true; but it was exactly this necessity of determining distinctly and accurately the mutual relation of Sanskrit and the other members of the same family of speech, which led to such important results, and particularly to the establishment of the laws of phonetic change as the only safe means for measuring the various degrees of relationship of cognate dialects, and thus restoring the genealogical tree of human speech. When Sanskrit had once assumed its right position, when people had once become familiarised with the idea that there must have existed a language more primitive than Greek, Latin, and Sanskrit, and forming the common background of these three, as well as of the Teutonic, Celtic, and Slavonic branches of speech, all languages seemed to fall by themselves into their right position. The key of the puzzle was found, and all the rest was merely a work of patience. The same arguments by which Sanskrit and Greek had been proved to hold co-ordinate rank were perceived to apply with equal strength to Latin and Greek; and after Latin had once been shown to be more primitive on many points than Greek, it was easy to see that the Teutonic, the Celtic, and the Slavonic languages also, contained each a number of formations which it was impossible to derive from Sanskrit, Greek, or Latin. It was perceived that all had to be treated as co-ordinate members of one and the same class.

The first great step in advance, therefore, which was made in the classification of languages, chiefly through the discovery of Sanskrit, was this, that scholars were no longer satisfied with the idea of a general relationship, but began to inquire for the special degrees of relationship in which each member of a class stood to another. Instead of mere *classes*, we hear now for the first time of well-regulated *families* of language.

A second step in advance followed naturally from the first. Whereas, for establishing in a general way the common origin of certain languages, a comparison of numerals, pronouns, prepositions, adverbs, and the most essential nouns and verbs, had been sufficient, it was soon found that a more accurate standard was required for measuring the more minute degrees of relationship. Such a standard was supplied by Comparative Grammar; that is to say, by an intercomparison of the grammatical forms of languages supposed to be related to each other; such intercomparison being carried out according to certain laws which regulate the phonetic changes of letters.

The position of Provençal among the Romanic Languages.

A glance at the modern history of language will make this clearer. There could never be any doubt that the so-called Romance languages, Italian, Roumanian, Provençal, French, Spanish, and Portuguese, were closely related to each other. Everybody could see that they were all derived from Latin. But one of the most distinguished French scholars, Raynouard, who has done more for the history of the Romance languages and literature than any one else, maintained that Provençal only was the daughter of Latin; whereas French, Italian, Spanish, and Portuguese were the daughters of Provençal. He maintained that Latin passed, from the seventh to the ninth century, through an intermediate stage, which he called *Langue Romane*, and which he endeavoured to prove was the same as the Provençal of Southern France, the language of the Troubadours. According to him, it was only after Latin had passed through this uniform metamorphosis, represented by the *Langue Romane* or Provençal, that it became broken up into the various Romance dialects of Italy, France, Spain, and Portugal. This theory, which was vigorously attacked by August Wilhelm von Schlegel, and afterwards minutely criticised by Sir George Cornewall Lewis, can only be refuted by a comparison of the Provençal grammar with that of the other Romance dialects. And here, if you take the auxiliary verb *to be*, and compare its forms in Provençal and French, you will see at once that, on several points, French has really preserved the original Latin forms in a more primitive state than Provençal, and that, therefore, it is impossible to classify French as the daughter of Provençal, and as the granddaughter of Latin. We have in Provençal:—

sem, corresponding to the French *nous sommes*
etz   „   *vous êtes*
son   „   *ils sont*.

And it would be a grammatical miracle if crippled forms, such as *sem*, *etz*, and *son*, had been changed back again into the more healthy, more primitive, more Latin forms, *sommes*, *êtes*, *sont*; *sumus*, *estis*, *sunt*.

Let us apply the same test to Sanskrit, Greek, and Latin; and we shall see how their mutual genealogical position is equally determined by a comparison of their grammatical forms, and that it is as impossible to derive Latin from Greek, or Greek from Sanskrit, as it is to treat French as a modification of Provençal. Keeping to the auxiliary verb *to be*, we find that *I am* is in

Sanskrit	Greek	Lithuanian
asmi	*esmi*	*esmi*.

The Sanskrit root is *as*, the termination *mi*.

Now, the termination of the second person is *si*, which, together with *as*, or *es*, would make

as-si	*es-si*	*es-si*

But here Sanskrit, as far back as its history can be traced, has reduced *assi* to *asi*; and it would be impossible to suppose that the perfect, or, as they are sometimes called, organic, forms in Greek and Lithuanian, *es-si*, could first have passed through the mutilated state of the Sanskrit *asi*.

The third person is the same in Sanskrit, Greek, and Lithuanian, *as-ti* or *es-ti*; and, with the loss of the final *i*, we recognise the Latin *est*, Gothic *ist*, and Russian *est'*.

The same auxiliary verb can be made to furnish sufficient proof that Latin never could have passed through the Greek, or what used to be called the Pelasgic stage, but that both are independent modifications of the same original language. In the singular, Latin is less primitive than Greek; for *sum* could never become ἐσμί, or *es* εἶς, or *est* ἐστί. In the first person plural, too, *sumus* stands for '*s-umus*. the Greek *es-men*, the Sanskrit '*smás*. The second person, *es-tis*, is equal to Greek *es-te*, and more primitive therefore than even the Sanskrit *sthá*. But in the third person plural Latin is more primitive than Greek. The regular form would be '*s-anti*; this, in

Sanskrit, is regularly changed into sánti. In Greek the initial *s* is dropped, and the Æolic *enti* is finally reduced to *eisí*. The Latin, on the contrary, has kept the radical *s*, and it would be perfectly impossible to derive the Latin *sunt* from the Greek *eisí*.

I need hardly say that the modern English, *I am, thou art, he is*, are only secondary modifications of the same primitive verb. We find in Gothic

im	for	*ism*
is	„	*iss*
ist		

In Anglo-Saxon we have

singular:	*eom*	plural:	*sind* for *isind*
„	*eart*	„	*sind*
„	*is*	„	*sind*

By applying this test to all languages, the founders of comparative philology soon reduced the principal dialects of Europe and Asia to certain families, and they were able in each family to distinguish different branches, each consisting again of numerous dialects, both ancient and modern.

Genealogical Classification.

There are many languages, however, which as yet have not been reduced to families, and though there is no reason to doubt that some of them will hereafter be comprehended in a system of genealogical classification, it is right to guard from the beginning against the common but altogether gratuitous supposition, that the principle of genealogical classification must be applicable to all languages. Genealogical classification is no doubt the most perfect of all classifications, but there are but few branches of physical science in which it can be carried out, except very partially. In the science of language, genealogical classification must rest chiefly on the formal or grammatical elements, which, after they have been affected by phonetic change, can be kept up only by a continuous tradition. We know that French, Italian, Spanish, and Portuguese must be derived from a common source, because they share grammatical forms in common, which none of these dialects could have supplied from their own resources, and which have no meaning, or, so to say, no life in any one of them. The termination of the imperfect *ba* in Spanish, *va* in Italian, by which *canto*, I sing, is changed into *cantaba* and *cantava*, has no separate existence, and no independent meaning in either of these modern dialects. It could not have been formed with the materials supplied by Spanish and Italian. It must have been handed down from an earlier generation in which this *ba* had a meaning. We trace it back to Latin *bam*, in *cantabam*, and this *ba-m* to an independent auxiliary verb, the same which exists in Sanskrit bhavâmi, and in the Anglo-Saxon *beom*, I am. Genealogical classification, therefore, applies properly only to decaying languages, to languages in which grammatical growth has been arrested, through the influence of literary cultivation; in which little that is new is added, everything old is retained as long as possible, and where what we call growth or history is nothing but the progress of phonetic corruption. But before languages decay, they have passed through a period of growth; and it seems to have been completely overlooked, that dialects which diverged during that early period, would naturally resist every attempt at genealogical classification. If we remember the manner in which, for instance, the plural was formed in Chinese, and other languages examined by us in a former chapter, we shall easily see that where each dialect may choose its own term expressive of plurality, such as *heap, class, kind, flock, cloud,* &c., it would be unreasonable to expect similarity in grammatical terminations, after these terms have been ground down by phonetic corruption to mere exponents of plurality. But, on the other hand, it would by no means follow that therefore these languages had no common origin. Languages may have a common origin, and yet the words which they originally employed for marking case, number, person, tense, and mood, having been totally different, the grammatical terminations to which these words would gradually dwindle down, could not possibly yield any results, if submitted to the analysis of comparative grammar. A genealogical classification of such languages is, therefore, from the nature of the case, simply impossible, at least if such classification is chiefly to be based on grammatical or formal evidence.

It might be supposed, however, that such languages, though differing in their grammatical articulation, would yet evince their common origin by the identity of their radicals or roots. No doubt they will in many instances. They will probably have retained their numerals in common, some of their pronouns, and some of the commonest words of every-day life. But even here we must not expect too much, nor be surprised if we find even less than we expected. You remember how the names for father varied in the numerous Frisian dialects. Instead of *frater*, the Latin word for brother, you find *hermano* in Spanish. Instead of *ignis*, the Latin word for fire, you have in French *feu*, in Italian *fuoco*. Nobody would doubt the common origin of German and English; yet the English numeral 'the first,' though preserved in *Fürst* (princeps, prince), is quite different from the German 'Der Erste'; 'the second' is quite different from 'Der Zweite'; and there is no connection between the possessive pronoun *its* and the German *sein*. Dialectic freedom works on a much larger scale in ancient and illiterate languages; and those who have most carefully watched the natural growth of dialects will be the least surprised that dialects which had the same origin should differ, not only in their grammatical framework, but likewise in many of those test-words which are very properly used for discovering the relationship of literary languages. How it is possible to say anything about the relationship of such dialects we shall see hereafter. For the present, it is sufficient if I have made it clear why the principle of genealogical classification is not of necessity applicable to all languages; and secondly, why languages, though they cannot be classified genealogically, need not therefore be supposed to have been different from the beginning. The assertion so frequently repeated, that the impossibility of classing all languages genealogically proves the impossibility of a common origin of language, is nothing but a kind of scientific dogmatism which, more than anything else, has impeded the free progress of independent research.

But let us see now how far the genealogical classification of languages has advanced, how many families of human speech have been satisfactorily established. Let us remember what suggested to us the necessity of a genealogical classification. We wished to know the original intention of certain words and grammatical forms in English, and we saw that, before we could attempt to fathom the origin of such words as 'I love,' and 'I loved,' we should have to trace them back to their most primitive state. We likewise found, by a reference to the history of the Romance dialects, that words existing in one dialect had frequently been preserved in a more primitive form in another, and that therefore it was of the highest importance to bring ancient languages into the same genealogical connection by which French, Italian, Spanish, and Portuguese are held together as the members of one and the same family.

English and Anglo-Saxon.

Beginning, therefore, with the living language of England, we traced it, without difficulty, to Anglo-Saxon, divided into four dialects, the Northumbrian and Mercian forming the *Anglian* branch, and the West-Saxon (Saxons) and Kentish (Jutes) forming the *Southern* branch. This carries us back to the seventh century after Christ, for it is to that date that Kemble and Thorpe refer the ancient English epic, the *Beowulf*.¹ Beyond this we cannot follow English literature on English soil.

Continental Saxon, Low-German.

But we know that the Jutes, the Saxons, and the Angles, whose dialects formed the principal tributaries of the so-called Anglo-Saxon, i.e. the ancient English language, came all from the continent. They spoke different dialects of Low-German, that of the Angles in the north being somewhat mixed, it would seem, with High-German elements. Their descendants, along the northern coast of Germany, still speak dialects of Low-German,² or *Nieder-Deutsch*³ which, in the harbours of Antwerp, Bremen, and Hamburg, has been mistaken by many an English sailor for corrupt English. This Low-German lives on in many dialects in the north or the lowlands of Germany, where it is often called *Platt-Deutsch*; but, with few exceptions, these are no longer used for literary purposes. The dialects of the Frisians, who constituted a large portion of the tribes that came to

---

¹ The earliest MS. containing Anglo-Saxon words is a charter, dated A.D. 679.

² 'Het echt engelsch is oud nederduitsch,' 'the genuine English is Old Low-Dutch.'—Bilderdyk. See Delfortrie, *Analogie des Langues*, p. 13.

³ *Nieder-Deutsch*, Low-German, and *Hoch-Deutsch*, High-German, have almost lost their geographical meaning as the German spoken in the highlands and lowlands of Germany. They have come to mean German in the first and in the second stages of the *Lautverschiebung*, and in that sense these technical terms are very useful. (See the Gothic of Ulfilas, by Douse, p. 11.) We must take care, however, not to confound *Low-German* and *High-German*, in their purely grammatical meaning, with *Upper*, *Middle*, and *Low-German*, used in a purely geographical sense. In the latter sense it would perhaps be better to use in English *Southern*, *Central*, and *Northern German*.

settle in England, are Low-German, particularly in their consonantal system; so are the Dutch and the Flemish.

Frisian.

The Frisians of the continent had a literature of their own as early, at least, as the twelfth century, if not earlier.[1] The oldest literary documents now extant date from the thirteenth and fourteenth centuries. From the fifteenth century Frisian became more and more encroached upon by *Platt-Deutsch*, and though there is a certain patriotic feeling among the Frisians that keeps up the language, its approaching fate can hardly be doubted.[2]

Dutch, Flemish, Old Frankish.

The Dutch, the national and literary language of Holland, can be traced back to Middle Dutch and Old Dutch. The oldest specimens of Old Dutch,[3] the

---

[1] Although the old Frisian documents rank, according to their dates, with Middle rather than with Old German, the Frisian language appears there in a much more ancient stage, which very nearly approaches the Old High-German. The political isolation of the Frisians, and their noble attachment to their traditional manners and rights, have imparted to their language also a more conservative spirit. After the fourteenth century the old inflections of the Frisian decay most rapidly. —Grimm, *German Grammar* (first edition), vol. i. p. lxviii.

[2] Nissen, in his *Friske Findling* (Stedesand, 1873), has collected proverbs in seven North-Frisian and in the common West-Frisian dialect. His seven North-Frisian dialects are: the Karrharder, Moringer, Wiedinger, Sylter, Amrumer, Hattstedter, Brecklumer, to which he afterwards adds an eighth, the Ockholmer. He admits, however, that some of these are rapidly disappearing.

[3] Moritz Heyne, *Altniederdeutsche Sprachdenkmäler*, Paderborn, 1877; Cosÿs, *De Oud Nederlandsche Psalmen*, Haarlem, 1873; Gédéon Huet, *Fragments Inédits de la traduction des Cantiques du Psautier en vieux Neerlandais*, re-edited by J. H. Gallée, in *Tÿdschrift van Neederlandsche Letterkunde*, vol. v. p. 274.

Karolingian Psalms, have been referred to the ninth century. They come very near to the Saxon of the Heljand. The Middle Dutch,[1] in various local dialects, which goes on to the sixteenth century, consists chiefly of translations from French. The Flemish was for a time the language of the court of Flanders and Brabant, but has since been considerably infringed on, though by no means extinguished, by the official languages of the kingdoms of Holland and Belgium. Of late years there has been a patriotic revival of Flemish literature.

The oldest literary document of Low-German on the continent is the Christian epic, written in what is old or continental Saxon, the *Heljand* (Heljand = Heiland, the Healer or Saviour). It is preserved to us in two MSS. of the ninth century, and was written at that time for the benefit of the newly-converted Saxons. We have traces of a certain amount of literature in Saxon or Low-German from that time onward through the Middle Ages up to the seventeenth century. But little only of that literature has been preserved; and, after the translation of the Bible by Luther into High-German, the fate of Low-German literature was sealed.

High-German.

The literary language of Germany is, and has been ever since the days of Charlemagne, the High-German. It is spoken in various dialects all over Germany.[2]

---

[1] Franck, *Mittelniederländische Grammatik*, Leipzig, 1885.

[2] The Upper-German dialects in South-Germany, the Alemannic and Bavarian; and the Middle-German dialects, the East-Franconian, Thuringian, Hessian, Upper-Saxon, and Silesian.

Its history may be traced through three periods. The present or New High-German period dates from Luther; the Middle High-German period extends from Luther backwards to the beginning of the twelfth century; the Old High-German period[1] extends from thence to the eighth century.

No Proto-Teutonic Language.

Thus we see that we can follow the High-German as well as the Low-German branch of Teutonic speech back to about the seventh century after Christ. We must not suppose that before that time there was *one* common Teutonic language spoken by all German tribes, and that it afterwards diverged into two streams—the High and Low. There never was a common, uniform Teutonic language; nor is there any evidence to show that there existed at any time a uniform High-German or a uniform Low-German language, from which all High-German and Low-German dialects are respectively derived. We cannot derive Anglo-Saxon, Frisian, Flemish, Dutch, and Platt-Deutsch from the ancient Low-German, which is preserved in the continental Saxon of the ninth century. All we can say is that these various Low-German dialects in England, Holland, Frisia, and Lower Germany passed at different times through the same stages, or, so to say, the same latitudes, of grammatical growth. We may add that, with every century we go back, the convergence of

---

[1] In Old High-German literature three dialects are now distinguished: the *Upper-German* (the Alemannic and Bavarian), the *Upper-Franconian* (East-Franconian and Rhenish-Franconian), the *Middle-Franconian* (from Coblence to Düsseldorf).

these dialects becomes more and more decided; but there is no evidence to justify us in admitting the historical reality of one primitive and uniform Low-German language from which they were all derived. This is a mere creation of grammarians who cannot understand a multiplicity of dialects without a common type. They would likewise demand the admission of a primitive High-German language as the source, not only of the literary Old, Middle, and Modern High-German, but likewise of all the local dialects of Austria, Bavaria, Swabia, Franconia, Thuringia, Hessia, Saxony, and Silesia. And they would wish us to believe that, previous to the separation into High and Low-German, there existed one complete Teutonic language, as yet neither High nor Low, but containing the germs of both. Such a system may be convenient for the purposes of grammatical analysis, but it becomes mischievous as soon as these grammatical abstractions are invested with an historical reality. As there were families, clans, confederacies, and tribes, before there was a nation, so there were dialects before there was one classical language. The grammarian who postulates an historical reality for the one primitive type of Teutonic speech, is no better than the historian who believes in a Francus, the grandson of Hector, and the supposed ancestor of all the Franks, or in a Brutus, the mythical father of all the Britons. When the German races descended, one after the other, from the Danube and from the Baltic, to take possession of Italy and the Roman provinces—when the Goths, the Lombards, the Vandals, the Franks, the Burgundians, each under their own kings, and with their own laws and customs, settled in Italy, Gaul, and Spain, to act their several parts in the last scene of the Roman tragedy—we have no reason to suppose that they all spoke one and the same dialect. If, instead of a few names and glosses, we possessed any literary documents of those ancient German races, we should find them all dialects again, some with the peculiarities of High, others with those of Low, German. Nor is this mere conjecture: for it so happens that, by some fortunate accident, the dialect of one at least of these ancient German races has been preserved to us in the Gothic translation of the Bible by bishop Ulfilas.

Ulfilas.

Ulfilas translated the Bible, but not the Books of Kings. Others may have assisted in the work.[1] For the Old Testament he used the Septuagint; for the New, a Greek text, which comes nearest to Codex Alexandrinus A.[2] Unfortunately, the greater part of his work has been lost, and we have only considerable portions of the four Gospels, all the genuine epistles of St. Paul, though these again not complete; fragments of a Psalm, of Ezra, and Nehemiah.

Though Ulfilas belonged by birth to the Western Goths,[3] his translation was used by all Gothic tribes, when they advanced into Spain and Italy. The

---

[1] See p. 251, l. 20.
[2] Some passages agree with Cod. Sang. Δ, and Cod. Paris. K, while the translation of the Epistles points to the Italian group of MSS. represented by Cod. Claromont. D, and sometimes to the Itala (Cod. Brixianus f). See Piper, *Sprache und Literatur Deutschlands*, p. 10.
[3] See Förstemann, *Geschichte des deutschen Sprachstammes*, vol. ii. p. 4.

Gothic language died out in the ninth century,[1] and after the extinction of the great Gothic empires, the translation of Ulfilas was lost and forgotten. But a MS. of the fifth century had been preserved in the Abbey of Werden, and towards the end of the sixteenth century, a man of the name of Arnold Mercator, who was in the service of William IV. the Landgrave of Hessia, drew attention to this old parchment containing large fragments of the translation of Ulfilas. This MS., now known as the Codex Argenteus, was afterwards transferred to Prague, and when Prague was taken in 1648 by Count Köngismark, he carried this literary relic to Upsala in Sweden, where it is still preserved as one of the greatest treasures. The parchment is purple, the letters in silver, and the MS. bound in solid silver.

In 1818, Cardinal Mai and Count Castiglione discovered some more fragments in the monastery of Bobbio, where they had probably been preserved ever since the Gothic empire of Theodoric the Great in Italy had been destroyed.[2]

Ulfilas must have been a man of extraordinary power to conceive, for the first time, the idea of

---

[1] Gothic was spoken in the ninth century at *Tomi* (now Kustendje) on the Black Sea coast. Crim-Goths (the ancient *Tetraxitæ*) are mentioned by travellers in the Middle Ages, particularly by Rubriquis (1253). The fullest notice of them is given by a Flemish traveller, A. G. von Busbeck, who, when at Constantinople in 1562, met two ambassadors of theirs, and took down some scores of their words and a fragment of verse. See Massmann, *Gothica minora*, in Haupt's *Zeitschrift*, vol. i. p. 354 (1841); Förstemann, *Geschichte des deutschen Sprachstammes*, vol. ii. p. 159; Douse, *Gothic*, p. 5.

[2] These are: the Codices Ambrosiani A, B, C, D; also the Codex

translating the Bible into the vulgar language of his people. At his time there existed in Europe but two languages which a Christian bishop would have thought himself justified in employing, Greek and Latin. All other languages were still considered as barbarous. It required a prophetic sight, a faith in the destinies of these half-savage tribes, and a conviction also of the utter effeteness of the Roman and Byzantine empires, before a bishop could have brought himself to translate the Bible into the vulgar dialect of his barbarous countrymen. Soon after the death of Ulfilas, the number of Christian Goths at Constantinople had so much increased as to induce Chrysostom, the bishop of Constantinople (397–405), to establish a church in the capital, where the service was to be read in Gothic.[1] We have the sermon which he preached on that occasion, and though he treats the Goths as mere barbarians, yet he acknowledges their importance in the Christian church. In 403 St. Jerome received a letter from two Goths, *Sunnia* and *Fretela*, who wished to be enlightened about some differences they had discovered between the Vulgate and the Alexandrian translation of the Psalms. 'Who would have believed,' says St. Jerome, 'that the barbarous tongue of the Getae should inquire after the Hebrew verity, and that, while the Greeks either slay or fight, Germany alone should search for the words of the Holy Ghost.'

Gothic.

The language of Ulfilas, the Gothic, belongs through its phonetic structure, particularly through its con-

[1] Theodoret, *H. E. V.* 30.

sonants, to the Low-German class, but in its grammar it is, with certain exceptions, far more primitive than the Anglo-Saxon of the Beowulf, or the Old High-German of Charlemagne. These exceptions, however, are very important, for they show that it would be grammatically, and therefore, historically, impossible to derive Anglo-Saxon or High-German, or both,[1] from Gothic. It would be impossible, for instance, to treat the first person plural of the indicative present, the Old High-German *nerjamês*, as a corruption of the Gothic *nasjam*; for we know, from the Sanskrit masi, the Greek *mes*, the Latin *mus*, that this was the original termination of the first person plural.

Gothic is but one of the numerous dialects of German speech; other dialects became the feeders of the literary languages of the British Isles, of Holland, Frisia, and of Low and High Germany, others became extinct, and others rolled on from century to century unheeded, and without ever producing any literature at all. It is because Gothic is the only one of these parallel dialects that can be traced back to the fourth century, whereas the others disappear from our sight in the seventh, that it has been mistaken by some for the original source of all Teutonic speech, particularly with regard to the consonantal *Lautverschiebung*. The same arguments, however, which we used against Raynouard, to show that

[1] For instances where Old High-German is more primitive than Gothic, see Bopp, *Vergl. Grammatik*, § 143, 1; 149; Schleicher, *Zeitschrift für V. S.* b. iv. s. 266; Bugge, *ibid.* b. v. s. 59; Pott, *Etym. Forsch.* ii. p. 57, *note*; Piper, *Sprache und Literatur Deutschlands*, p. 12.

Provençal could not be considered as the parent of the six Romance dialects, would tell with equal force against the pretensions of Gothic to be considered as more than the eldest sister of the Teutonic branch of speech.

Scandinavian.

There is, in fact, a third stream of Teutonic speech, which asserts its independence as much as High-German and Low-German, and which it would be impossible to place in any but a co-ordinate position with regard to Gothic, Low and High-German. This is the *Scandinavian* branch. It consists at present of three literary dialects, those of Sweden, Denmark, and Iceland, and of various local dialects, particularly in the secluded valleys and fiords of Norway,[1] where, however, the literary language is Danish.

It is commonly supposed[2] that, as late as the eleventh century, identically the same language was spoken in Sweden, Norway, and Denmark, and that this language was preserved almost intact in Iceland, while in Sweden and Denmark it grew into two new national dialects. Nor is there any doubt that the Icelandic skald recited his poems in Iceland, Norway, Sweden, Denmark, nay, even among his countrymen in England and Gardariki, without fear of not being understood, till, as it is said, William introduced Welsh, i. e. French, into England, and Slavonic tongues grew up in the east.[3] But though one and the same language (then called Danish or Norrænish)

---

[1] See Schleicher, *Deutsche Sprache*, s. 94.
[2] *Ibid.* s. 60.
[3] Weinhold, *Altnordisches Leben*, s. 27; *Gunnlaugssaga*, cap. 7.

was understood, I doubt, in this case also, whether one and the same language was spoken by all Northmen, and whether the first germs of Swedish and Danish did not exist long before the eleventh century, in the dialects of the numerous clans and tribes of the Scandinavian race. That race is clearly divided into two branches, called by Swedish scholars the East and West Scandinavian, by German scholars *West-Nordisch* and *Ost-Nordisch*. The former would be represented by the old language of Norway and Iceland, the latter by Swedish and Danish. This division of the Scandinavian race had taken place before the Northmen settled in Sweden and Norway. The western division migrated westward from Russia, and crossed over from the continent to the Aland Islands, and from thence to the southern coast of the peninsula. The eastern division travelled along the Bothnian Gulf, passing the country occupied by the Fins and Laps, and settled in the northern highlands, spreading towards the south and west.

The Edda.

The earliest fragments of Scandinavian speech are preserved in the two Eddas, the elder or poetical Edda containing old mythic poems, the younger or Snorri's Edda giving an account of the ancient mythology in prose. Both Eddas were collected, not in Norway but in Iceland, an island about as large as Ireland, and which became first known through some Irish monks who settled there in the eighth century.[1] In the ninth century voyages of discovery

---

[1] See Dasent's *Burnt Njal*, Introduction.

were made to Iceland by Naddodd, Gardar, and
Flokki, 860-870, and soon after the remote island,
distant about 750 English miles from Norway, became a kind of America to the Puritans and Re-
publicans of the Scandinavian peninsula. Harald
Haarfagr (850-933) had conquered most of the Norwegian kings, and his despotic sway tended to reduce
the northern freeman to a state of vassalage. Those
who could not resist, and could not bring themselves
to yield to the sceptre of Harald, left their country
and migrated to France, to England, and to Iceland
(874). They were mostly nobles and freemen, and
they soon established in Iceland an aristocratic republic, such as they had had in Norway before the
days of Harald. This northern republic flourished; it
adopted Christianity in the year 1000. Schools were
founded, two bishoprics were established, and classical
literature was studied with the same zeal with which
their own national poems and laws had been collected
and interpreted by native scholars and historians.
The Icelanders were famous travellers, and the names
of Icelandic students are found not only in the chief
cities of Europe, but in the holy places of the East.
At the beginning of the twelfth century Iceland
counted 50,000 inhabitants. Their intellectual and
literary activity lasted to the beginning of the thirteenth century, when the island was conquered by
Hakon VI, king of Norway. In 1380, Norway, together with Iceland, was united with Denmark; and
when, in 1814, Norway was ceded to Sweden, Iceland
remained, as it is still, under Danish sway.

The old poetry which flourished in Norway in the

eighth century, and which was cultivated by the skalds in the ninth, would have been lost in Norway itself, had it not been for the jealous care with which it was preserved by the emigrants of Iceland. The most important branch of their traditional poetry were short songs (*hliod* or *quida*), relating the deeds of their gods and heroes. It is impossible to determine their age, but they existed at least previous to the migration of the Northmen to Iceland, and probably as early as the seventh century, the same century which yields the oldest remnants of Anglo-Saxon or Low-German, and of High-German. Some scholars, particularly Holtzmann, supposed that they were originally composed on German, perhaps on Saxon soil. As they existed in the twelfth century, probably considerably modified in their language, they were collected by Saemund Sigfusson (born 1056, died 1133). In 1643 a similar collection was discovered in MSS. of the fourteenth century, and published under the title of *Edda*, or Great-Grandmother. This collection is called the old or poetic Edda, in order to distinguish it from a later work ascribed to Snorri Sturluson (1179–1241). This, the younger or prose Edda, consists of three parts: the mocking of Gylfi, the speeches of Bragi, and the Skalda, or *Ars poetica*.

Snorri Sturluson has been called the Herodotus of Iceland, his chief work being the *Heimskringla*, the world-ring, which contains the northern history from the mythic times to the time of king Magnus Erlingsson (died 1177). It was probably in preparing this history that, like Cassiodorus, Saxo Grammaticus, Paulus Diaconus, and other historians of the same class, Snorri collected the old songs of the people; for his *Edda*, and still more his *Skalda*, are full of ancient poetic fragments.

The *Skalda*, and the rules which it contains, represent the state of poetry in the thirteenth century; and nothing can be more artificial, nothing more different from the general poetry of the old Edda, than this *Ars poetica* of Snorri Sturluson. One of the chief features of this artificial or skaldic poetry was that nothing should be called by its proper name. A ship was not to be called a ship, but the beast of the sea; blood, not blood, but the dew of pain, or the water of the sword. A warrior was not spoken of as a warrior, but as an armed tree, the tree of battle. A sword was the flame of wounds. In this poetical language, which every skald was bound to speak, there were no less than 115 names for Odin; an island could be called by 120 synonymous titles. The specimens of ancient poetry which Snorri quotes are taken from the skalds, whose names are well known in history, and who lived from the tenth to the thirteenth century. But he never quotes from any song contained in the old Edda,[1] whether it be that those songs were considered by himself as belonging to a different and much more ancient period of literature, or that they could not be used in illustration of the scholastic rules of skaldic poets, rules which were put to shame by the simple style of

---

[1] The name *Edda* is not found before the fourteenth century. Snorri Sturluson does not know the word *Edda*, nor any collection of ancient poems attributed to Saemund; and though Saemund may have made the first collection of national poetry, it is now considered doubtful whether the work which we possess under his name is his.

the national poetry, expressing what it had to express without effort and circumlocution.

We have thus traced the modern Teutonic dialects back to four principal channels—the *High-German*, *Low-German*, *Gothic*, and *Scandinavian*; and we have seen that these four, together with several minor dialects, must be placed in a co-ordinate position from the beginning, as so many varieties of Teutonic speech. This Teutonic speech may, for convenience sake, be spoken of as one—as one branch of that great family of language to which, as we shall see, it belongs; but it should always be borne in mind that this primitive and uniform language never had any real historical existence, and that, like all other languages, German began with dialects, which gradually formed themselves into several distinct national deposits.

Adopting a different principle of classification, Grimm divided the Teutonic class into a *Northern* and *Southern* branch, placing Gothic with German, and not with Scandinavian, while Müllenhoff and Scherer proposed to divide the Teutonic class into an Eastern (Vandilian) and Western (Suevian) branch, the Eastern comprehending Gothic and Scandinavian, the Western, both High and Low-German, that is to say, continental Saxon, Anglo-Saxon, Frisian, Low Franconian (Dutch, Flemish), and High-German. Although there are certain grammatical features [1] which support these two classifications, yet the *Lautverschiebung* seems to me far more characteristic than all the rest, and according to it Gothic and Scandinavian

[1] Piper, *Sprache und Literatur Deutschlands*, p. 3.

belong both grammatically and historically to Low-German, while High-German represents a more independent ramification of the Teutonic stock.

TEUTONIC CLASS.

First Stage of Lautverschiebung.

1. Gothic, 4th cent.
2. Scandinavian—
    Old Scandinavian, 800-1000.
    West-Nordish, Icelandic, Norwegian, 11th cent.
    East-Nordish, Swedish, Danish.
3. Low-German—
    Old Saxon, 9th cent., Platt-Deutsch.
    Anglo-Saxon, 7th cent., English.
    Old Frisian, 13th cent., Modern Frisian.
    Old Dutch, 9th cent. (Old Low Franconian), Middle Dutch, 1600; Modern Dutch (Flemish, Low Franconian).

Second Stage of Lautverschiebung.

4. High-German—
    Old High-German, 700-1100; Middle, 1100-1500; Modern, 1500.

Another division, founded more on geographical position, would be—

TEUTONIC CLASS.

East Teutonic:
1. Gothic.
2. Scandinavian,
    West-Nordish (Icelandic, Norwegian).
    East-Nordish (Swedish, Danish).

West Teutonic:

Low-German
1. Anglo-Saxon, English.
2. Old Frisian, Modern Frisian.
3. Old Saxon (continental), Platt-Deutsch.
4. Old Dutch (Low Franconian), Middle Dutch, Modern Dutch.

High-German 5. Old High-German, Middle, Modern High-German.

Italic Class.

We must now advance more rapidly, and, instead of the minuteness of an Ordnance-map, we must be satisfied with the broad outlines of Wyld's Great Globe in our survey of the languages which, together with the Teutonic, form the Indo-European or Aryan family of speech.

And first the Romanic, or modern Latin languages. Leaving mere local dialects out of sight, we have at present six literary modifications of Latin, or, more correctly, of the ancient language of Italy—the languages of Portugal, of Spain, of France, of Italy, of Roumania,[1] and of the Grisons of Switzerland, called

---

[1] The Roumanians, who used to be called Walachians, call themselves Români, and their language România. This Romanic language is spoken in Walachia and Moldavia, and in parts of Hungary, Transylvania, and Bessarabia. On the right bank of the Danube it occupies some parts of the old Thracia, Macedonia, and even Thessaly. It is divided by the Danube into two branches: the Northern or Daco-romanic, and the Southern or Macedo-romanic. The former is less mixed, and has received a certain literary culture; the latter has borrowed a larger number of Albanian and Greek words, and has not yet been fixed grammatically.

The modern Roumanian is the daughter of the language spoken in the Roman province of Dacia. The original inhabitants of Dacia were called Thracians, and their language Illyrian; but we have hardly any remains of the ancient Illyrian language to enable us to form an opinion as to its relationship with Greek, with Albanian, or any other language.

229 B.C. the Romans conquered Illyria; 30 B.C. they took Mœsia; and 107 A.D. the Emperor Trajan made Dacia a Roman province. At that time the Thracian population had been displaced by the advance of Sarmatian tribes, particularly the Yazyges. Roman colonists introduced the Latin language; and Dacia was maintained as a colony up to 272, when the Emperor Aurelian had to cede it to the Goths. Part of the Roman inhabitants then emigrated and settled south of the Danube. In 489 the Slavonic tribes began their advance into Mœsia and Thracia. They were settled in Mœsia by 678 and eighty years later

the Roumansch or Romanese.[1] The Provençal, which, in the poetry of the Troubadours, attained at a very early time to a high literary excellence, has now sunk down to a mere *patois*. The earliest Provençal poem, the Song of Boëthius, is generally referred to the tenth century; Lebeuf referred it to the eleventh. Of Northern French we possess some specimens of a still earlier date. The text of the oaths of Strassburg, as preserved by Nithart, goes back to A.D. 842, and has been preserved to us in a MS. of the ninth or tenth century. The song of Eulalia has likewise been preserved in a MS. of the ninth century, and in both the traces of Northern French, as distinct from Provençal, have been clearly pointed out by Diez.[2] Nothing can be a better preparation for the study of the comparative grammar of the ancient Aryan languages than a careful perusal of the *Comparative Grammar of the Six Romanic Languages* by Professor Diez.

Though in a general way we trace these six Romanic languages back to Latin, yet it has been

---

[1] The Roumansch or Rumaunsch, the language of the Grisons, is spoken in the valley of the Inn, the Enghadine; and in the valley of the Rhine, the Oberland. The inhabitants of the Enghadine are Protestants; those of the Oberland, Roman Catholics. The dialect of the former is called *Roumansch*, that of the latter *Ladin*. There is a religious literature of the sixteenth century, consisting chiefly of translations of the Bible, catechisms, and hymns in Roumansch. A translation of the New Testament exists in the Bodleian Library: 'L'g Nuof Sainc Testamaint da nos Signer Jesu Christi, prais our dolg Latin et our d'oters launguax et huossa da nœf mis in Arumaunsch très Iachiam Bifrum d'Agnedina. Schquischo ilg an MDLX.' The entire Bible has been published by the Bible Society in both dialects. Some of the dialects of Northern Italy, such as that of Friuli and of the Adige, have been proved by Ascoli to be closely allied to the Roumansch.

[2] *Altromanische Sprachdenkmale*, von F. Diez, Bonn, 1846.

pointed out before that the classical Latin would fail to supply a complete explanation of their origin. Many of the ingredients of the Neo-Latin dialects must be sought for in the ancient dialects of Italy and her provinces. More than one dialect of Latin was spoken there before the rise of Rome, and some important fragments have been preserved to us in inscriptions, of the Umbrian spoken to the north, and of the Oscan spoken to the south of Rome. The Oscan language, spoken by the Samnites, now rendered intelligible by the labours of Mommsen, had produced a literature before the time of Livius Andronicus; and the tables of Iguvium, so elaborately treated by Aufrecht and Kirchhoff, bear witness to a priestly literature among the Umbrians at a very early period. Oscan was still spoken under the Roman emperors, and so were minor local dialects in the south and the north. The Messapian inscriptions in the south are too scanty to count as representatives of an independent Italian dialect, and the few grammatical terminations which they contain point to Greece rather than to Italy. As soon as the literary language of Rome became classical and unchangeable, the first start was made in the future career of those dialects which, even at the time of Dante, are still called *vulgar* or *popular*.[1] A great deal, no doubt, of the corruption of these modern dialects is due to the fact that, in the form in which we know them after the

---

[1] 'E lo primo, che cominciò a dire siccome poeta volgare, si mosse però che volle fare intendere le sue parole a donna, alla quale era malagevole ad intendere versi Latini.'—Dante's *Vita Nuova; Opere Minori di Dante Alighieri*, tom. iii. p. 327; Firenze, 1837.

eighth century, they are really Neo-Latin dialects as adopted by the Teutonic barbarians: full, not only of Teutonic words, but of Teutonic idioms, phrases, and constructions. French is provincial Latin as spoken by the Franks, a Teutonic race; and, to a smaller extent, the same *barbarising* has affected all other Roman dialects. But, from the very beginning, the stock with which the Neo-Latin dialects started was not the classical Latin, but the vulgar, local, provincial dialects of the middle, the lower, and the lowest classes of the Roman empire. Many of the words which give to French and Italian their classical appearance, are really of much later date, and were imported into them by mediæval scholars, lawyers, and divines; thus escaping the rough treatment to which the original vulgar dialects were subjected by the Teutonic conquerors.

ITALIC CLASS.

Oscan, Umbrian, Latin, etc.

Lingua vulgaris.

Langue d'oïl	Langue d'oc					
French	Provençal	Spanish	Portuguese	Italian	Roumanian	Rumansch
9th cent.	10th cent.	12th cent.	12th cent.	12th cent.		

Hellenic Class.

The next branch of the Indo-European family of speech is the *Hellenic*. Its history is well known from the time of Homer to the present day. The only remark which the comparative philologist has to make is that the idea of making Greek the parent of Latin is more preposterous than deriving English from German; the fact being that there are many forms in Latin more primitive than their corresponding forms in Greek. The idea of Pelasgians as the common ancestors of Greeks and Romans is another of those grammatical myths, which fortunately requires no longer any serious refutation.

HELLENIC CLASS.

DORIC, ÆOLIC, ATTIC, IONIC.
Κοινή.
Modern Greek.

Celtic Class.

The fourth branch of our family is the *Celtic*.[1] The Celts are supposed to have been the first of the Aryans to arrive in Europe. Hekataeos knows of them as early as the seventh century, and mentions also a Celtic town (πόλις Κελτική) *Nyrax*, the name of which has been identified with that of *Noricum*. But the pressure of subsequent migrations, particularly of Teutonic tribes, has driven them towards the westernmost parts, and latterly from Ireland across the Atlantic. The Celtic branch may be divided into the *Cymric*[2] and *Goidelic*.[3] The *Cymric* comprises the

---

[1] The name Celt is a Celtic word. Caesar states distinctly that it was so, when saying: '*Qui ipsorum lingua Celtae, nostra Galli appellantur.*' The Greeks used both Κελταί and Κελτοί. The word *Kel-tos* may have meant in the ancient language of Gaul, elevated, upright, proud, like the Latin *celsus* and *excelsus*. See Glück, in Kuhn's *Beiträge*, vol. v. p. 97.

[2] The Welsh call themselves *Cymry*, and their language *Cymraeg*.

[3] The Irish called themselves in Old Irish *Gáidil* or *Góidel*. In modern Irish this name is written *Goidheal*, and with dh muta or omitted, *Gael*. In Welsh *Gwyddel* is the word for an Irishman. Some scholars prefer *Gaelic* instead of *Gaedhelic*.

Welsh; the *Cornish*, extinct in the latter part of the eighteenth century; and the *Armorican*, of Brittany. The *Goidelic* comprises the *Irish* (Erse); the *Gaelic* of the west coast of Scotland; and the dialect of the *Isle of Man*. Sometimes the fragments of the Celtic language preserved in inscriptions, on coins, and in the proper names of Gaul are classed as *Gallic*, while the Cymric branch is designated from its principal habitat as *Britannic*, comprising *Cymric* (i. e. Welsh), *Cornish*, and *Armorican*. The literary documents of the Cymric branch date from the eighth century both for Welsh and Breton, nor is there any more ancient literature in the Goidelic branch, the Irish literature, so far as it is preserved to us, not reaching back beyond the eighth century. The Ogham inscriptions, however, are much older, and are supposed in some instances to go back to the first century A.D. Although these Celtic dialects are still spoken, the Celts themselves can no longer be considered an independent nation, like the Germans or Slaves. In former times, however, they not only enjoyed political autonomy, but asserted it successfully against Germans and Romans. Gaul, Belgium, and Britain were Celtic dominions, and the north of Italy was chiefly inhabited by them. In the time of Herodotus (450 B.C.) we find Celts as the conquerors of Spain; and Switzerland also, the Tyrol, and the country south of the Danube had once been the seats of Celtic tribes. But after repeated inroads into the regions of civilisation, familiarising Latin and Greek writers with the names of their kings, they disappear from the East of Europe. Brennus was supposed to mean king, the Welsh *brenhin*. *Brenhin*, however, points back to an Old Celtic form *brigantinos*, free, noble, and it is doubtful whether this could have sounded like Brennus to Roman ears.[1] A Brennus conquered Rome (390), another Brennus threatened Delphi (280). And about the same time a Celtic colony settled in Asia, and founded Galatia,[2] where the language spoken at the time of St. Jerome is believed to have been the same as that of the Gauls. Celtic words may be found in German, Slavonic, and even in Latin, but only as foreign terms, and their number is much smaller than commonly supposed. A far larger number of Latin and German words have since found their way into the modern Celtic dialects, and these have frequently been mistaken by Celtic enthusiasts for original words, from which German and Latin might, in their turn, be derived. For further information on the Celtic languages I may refer to *Les Celtes*, par H. D'Arbois de Jubainville, 1875, and to Professor John Rhŷs' excellent *Lectures on Welsh Philology*, 1877.

CELTIC CLASS.

Cymric.		Goidelic.		Gallic.
Welsh Cornish Armorican		Irish Gaelic Manx		Inscriptions
8th cent. 8th cent.		8th cent.		in Gaul.

Windic Class.

The fifth branch, which is commonly called *Slavonic*,

---

[1] Rhŷs, *Hibbert Lectures*, pp. 76, 77; *Celtic Britain* (2), p. 282. It should be considered, however, how little of chronological order there is in dialectic corruption; see Senart, Inscription de Piyadasi, *Journ. Asiat.* 1886, pp. 68 seq.

[2] The name *Galatae* occurs first in the third century B.C., as used by Timæos; that of *Galli* is first used by Cato, possibly from the *Annales Maximi* of the fourth century B.C.

I prefer to designate by the name of *Windic*, *Winidæ* being one of the most ancient and comprehensive names by which these tribes were known to the early historians of Europe. We have to divide these tribes into two divisions, the *Lettic* and the *Slavonic*, and we shall have to subdivide the Slavonic again into a *South-East Slavonic* and a *West Slavonic* branch.

The terminology used for the classification of the Slavonic languages has varied and is still varying. I follow chiefly Schaffarik. He, however, though he proves *Winidæ* to have been the oldest authenticated name of the Slaves, does not use it as a general name for the two branches, Lettic and Slavic. Later writers have used Letto-Slavic, or Balto-Slavic.

The *Lettic* division consists of languages hardly known to the student of literature, but of great importance to the student of language. *Lettish* is the language now spoken in Kurland and Livonia. It has a literature going back to the sixteenth century. *Lituanian* is the name given to a language still spoken by about 200,000 people in Eastern Prussia, and by more than a million of people in the conterminous parts of Russia. The earliest literary document of Lituanian is a small catechism of 1547.[1] In this, and even in the language as now spoken by the Lituanian peasant, there are a few grammatical forms more primitive and more like Sanskrit than the corresponding forms in Greek and Latin.

The *Old Prussian*, which is nearly related to Lituanian, became extinct in the seventeenth century, and the entire literature which it has left behind consists

[1] Schleicher, *Beiträge*, b. i. s. 19.

in an old catechism and some other fragments of the fifteenth and sixteenth centuries.

Lettish is the language of Kurland and Livonia, more modern in its grammar than Lituanian, yet not immediately derived from it.

We now come to the *Slavonic* languages, properly so called. The Eastern branch comprehends the *Russian* with various local dialects, the *Bulgarian*, and the *Illyrian*. The most ancient document of this Eastern branch is the so-called Ecclesiastical Slavonic, i.e. the ancient Bulgarian, into which Cyrillus and Methodius translated the Bible, in the middle of the ninth century. This is still the authorised version[1] of the Bible for the whole Slavonic race: and to the student of the Slavonic languages it is what Gothic is to the student of German. The modern Bulgarian, on the contrary, as far as grammatical forms are concerned, is the most reduced among the Slavonic dialects.

Illyrian is a convenient (though historically not quite correct) name to comprehend the *Servian*, *Croatian*, and *Slovenian* dialects.

Servian literature is generally divided into three periods, the first extending to the end of the fourteenth century, the conquest of Servia by Murad I, the second to the middle of the eighteenth century. At that time a national revival took place, which produced not only a new literature, but likewise a warm interest in the ancient literature of the country. What was left

---

[1] Oldest dated MS. of 1056, written for Prince Ostromir. Some older MSS. are written with Glagolitic letters, the alphabet adopted by the Roman Church.—Schleicher, *Beiträge*, b. i. s. 20.

of ancient literary documents has been collected by Miklosich in the *Monumenta Serbica*, 1858. During the second period, under the Turkish sway, it was chiefly at Ragusa and along the Adriatic coast that literature flourished. The third period, beginning in the middle of the last century, may be said to have been inaugurated by Vuk Stephanovitch Karajitch (1787–1864) and his friends. His Servian Grammar (1814) became the foundation of a philological study of the language. Most interesting, however, are the collections of ancient Servian ballads, which form a kind of national epos. They roused the admiration of Goethe, and still form the chief attraction of Servian literature.

The history of the Slovenian language can be traced back to the tenth century.[1] The Codex of Freising, at present at Munich, contains religious compositions, published by Kopitar in his *Glagolita Clozianus*, 1836. At the time of the reformation there was a revival of literature, and as early as 1584 the first grammar was published by Bohorics. Miklosich, the great Slavonic scholar, is a Slovenian by birth.

The Western branch comprehends the language of *Poland, Bohemia,* and *Lusatia.* The oldest specimen of Polish belongs to the fourteenth century, the Psalter of Margarite. The Bohemian language was, till lately, traced back to the ninth century. But most of the old Bohemian poems are now considered spurious; and it is doubtful, even, whether an ancient interlinear translation of the Gospel of St. John can be ascribed to the tenth century.[2]

---

[1] Schleicher, *Beiträge*, b. i. s. 22.   [2] Ibid. *Deutsche Sprache*, s. 77.

The language of Lusatia, divided into two dialects, High and Low, is spoken, probably, by no more than 150,000 people, known in Germany by the name of *Wends* and *Sorbs*. The earliest document we possess is a Roman Catholic prayer-book, printed in 1512.

The Polabian dialect became gradually extinct in the beginning of the last century, and there is nothing left of it besides a few lists of words, a song, and the Lord's Prayer. Schleicher classes it with Polish, the Kashubian being a link between it and Polish.

WINDIC OR LETTO-SLAVIC CLASS.

1. Lettic.

Old Prussian
15th cent.

Lituanian   +   Lettish
16th cent.

2. South-East Slavonic.

Ecclesiastical Slavonic
9th cent.

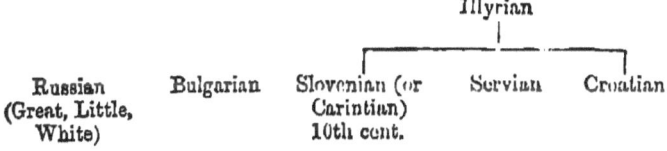

Russian   Bulgarian   Slovenian (or   Servian   Croatian
(Great, Little,   Carintian)
White)   10th cent.

3. West Slavonic.

Polabian   Old Bohemian
Polish   +   Bohemian   Lusatian
14th cent.   10th cent.   (Wends and Sorbs)

Albanian.

We have thus examined all the dialects of our first or Aryan family which are spoken in Europe, with one exception, the *Albanian*. This language is clearly a member of the same family; and as it is sufficiently distinct from Greek or any other recognised language, it has been traced back to one of the neighbouring races of the Greeks, the Illyrians, and is supposed, though without stringent proof, to be the only surviving representative of the various so-called barbarous tongues which surrounded and interpenetrated the dialects of Greece.

South-Eastern Division.

We now pass on from Europe to Asia; and here we begin at once, on the extreme south, with the languages of India.

Indic Class.

As I sketched in a former chapter, pp. 163–184, the history of the Indian language, beginning with the Veda and ending with the spoken vernaculars, I have only to add here the table of the *Indic Class*, and may proceed at once to a survey of the languages spoken in Persia, forming the Iranic Class.

INDIC CLASS.

Vedic Language (*Kḥandas*).	Literary Language (Bhâshâ).	Vulgar Language (Prâkrita).	
		Ungrammatical.	*Grammatical.*
Hymns, 1500 B.C.?			
Brâhmaṇas, 800 B.C.?			
Sûtras, 500 B.C.?	Pâṇini's Grammar, 400–300 B.C.		Pâli, 500 B.C.? — Mâgadhî. Mahârâshṭrî.
Written, 3rd cent. B.C.		Gâthâ Dialect (scholastic).	
		Inscript. of Piyadasi (vernacular) 250 B.C.	
	Inscript. of Kanishka, 1st cent. A.D.		Written 88 B.C. Ceylon.
	Inscript. of Rudradâman, 2nd cent. A.D.		
	Renaissance of Sanskrit Literature, 400 A.D.		
			Written 454 A.D.

Modern Languages.

Sindhî, Gujarâtî, Bihârî, Bengâlî,
Panjâbî, West Uriyâ, Asâmî,
Hindî, Naipâlî, Marâṭhî.

Iranic Class.

Most closely allied to Sanskrit, more particularly to the Sanskrit of the Veda, is the ancient language of the Zend-Avesta,[1] the so-called *Zend*, or sacred

[1] *Zend-Avesta* is the name used by Chaqâni and other Mohammedan writers, and which it seems hopeless now to change. The Parsis themselves use the name '*Aresta* and *Zend*,' taking *Avesta* (Pehlevi, *avastâk*), in the sense of text, and *Zend*, or *Zand*, as the title of the Pehlevi commentary.

Avestâ, or *avastâk*, was, according to J. Müller, derived from the same root which in Sanskrit appears as ava-sthâ, the participle of which, ava-sthita, would mean laid down, settled. According to this etymology *Avestâ* would have been intended as a name for the settled text of the sacred Scriptures. Professor Haug preferred to derive it from *â vid*, taking *âvesta* in the sense of what has been known, knowledge, a title somewhat analogous to the Sanskrit Veda, except that *âvista* or *âvesta* would rather mean notified, proclaimed, than known. Zand is now commonly taken as a corruption of *zainti*, knowledge, the Sanskrit *gñâti*, γνῶσις, which is preserved in Zend *âzainti*, Old Persian *âzanâa*. It would have meant originally an explanation, a commentary, without any reference to the language in which that explanation was conveyed. Afterwards, however, when the Avesta had been translated into Pehlevi, Zand became the name of that translation, and of the Pehlevi language in which the translation was composed. (See Haug, *Pahlavi-Pazend Dictionary*, p. 239.) J. Oppert (*Journal Asiatique*, 1872, p. 293) connected *Avesta* with the Persian *âbashtâ*, law. This word he derived from *â + bakhs*, to attribute, so that *âbashtâ*, instead of *âbakhstâ*, would mean what is determined. He has shown that *âbashtâ* occurs in the Behistun inscription in the sense of law, but hardly as yet as a name of our Avesta. *Zend* he derived from the root *zad* or *zand*, to pray, which occurs in the Behistun tablets, the Zend *zaidhyâmi*; hence *zanda*, prayer. But this cannot be our word Zend, which means commentary, not prayer. See Darmesteter, *Études Iraniennes*, ii. p. 9. Oppert took *Avesta u zend* to mean the Law and the Prayer. We know now, as Dr. West (*Sacred Books of the East*, v. p. x) has shown, that the Pehlevi *avistâk* was derived from *â + vid*, to know, with the meaning of what is announced, while *zand*, the Pehlevi form of *zainti*, comes from the root *zan*, to know, with the meaning of understanding. I have long surrendered my own explanation that Zand was originally the same word as the Sanskrit *Khandas*, metrical language, language of the Veda.

I.   T

language of the Zoroastrians, or worshippers of Ormazd. It was, in fact, chiefly through the Sanskrit, and with the help of comparative philology, that the ancient dialect of the Parsis, or the so-called Fire-worshippers, was first deciphered. The MSS. had been preserved by the Parsi priests at Bombay, where a colony of Zoroastrians had fled in the tenth century,[1] and where it has risen since to considerable wealth and influence. Other settlements of Guebres are to be found in Yezd and parts of Kerman. A Frenchman, Anquetil Duperron,[2] was the first to translate the Zend-Avesta, but his translation was not from the original, but from a modern Persian translation. The first European who attempted to read the original words of Zoroaster was Rask, the Dane; and, after his premature death, Burnouf, in France, achieved one of the greatest triumphs in modern scholarship by deciphering the language of the Zend-Avesta, and establishing its close relationship with Sanskrit. The same doubts which were expressed about the age and the genuineness of the Veda were

[1] 'According to the Kissah-i-Sanján, a tract almost worthless as a record of the early history of the Parsis, the fire-worshippers took refuge in Khorassan forty-nine years before the era of Yezdegerd (632 A.D.), or about 583. Here they stayed a hundred years, to 683, then departed to the city of Hormaz (Ormus, in the Persian Gulf), and after staying fifteen years, proceeded in 698 to Diu, an island on the south-west coast of Katiawar. Here they remained nineteen years, to 717, and then proceeded to Sanján, a town about twenty-four miles south of Damaun. After three hundred years they spread to the neighbouring towns of Guzerat, and established the sacred fire successively at Barsadah, Nausari, near Surat, and Bombay.'—*Bombay Quarterly Review*, 1856, No. viii. p. 67.

[2] Born in Paris, 1731; arrived in Pondichery, 1755; returned to Paris, 1762; died 1805. Translation of *Zendavesta*, 1771; *Oupnekhat*, 1802-1804.

repeated with regard to the Zend-Avesta, by men of high authority as oriental scholars, by Sir W. Jones himself, and even by the late Professor Wilson. But Burnouf's arguments, based at first on grammatical evidence only, were irresistible, and have of late been most signally confirmed by the discovery of the cuneiform inscriptions of Darius and Xerxes. That there was a Zoroaster, an ancient sage, was known long before Burnouf. Plato speaks of a teacher of Zoroaster's Magic (Μαγεία), and calls Zoroaster the son of *Oromazes*.[1]

This name of Oromazes is important; for this Oromazes is clearly meant for *Ormazd*, the god of the Zoroastrians. The name of this god, as read in the inscriptions of Darius and Xerxes, is *Auramazda*, which comes very near to Plato's Oromazes.[2] Thus Darius says, in one passage: 'Through the grace of Auramazda I am king; Auramazda gave me the kingdom.' But what is the meaning of *Auramazda?* We receive a hint from one passage in the Achæmenian inscriptions, where Auramazda is divided into two words, both being declined. The genitive of Auramazda occurs there as *Aurahya mazdáha*. But

---

[1] Alc. i. p. 122, a. Ὁ μὲν μαγείαν διδάσκει τὴν Ζωροάστρου τοῦ 'Ωρομάζου· ἔστι δὲ τοῦτο θεῶν θεραπεία. Aristotle knew not only Oromasdes as the good, but likewise Areimanios as the evil spirit, according to the doctrine of the Magi. See *Diogenes Laertius*, I. 8. Ἀριστοτέλης δ' ἐν πρώτῳ Περὶ φιλοσοφίας καὶ πρεσβυτέρους [τοὺς Μάγους] φησὶν εἶναι τῶν Αἰγυπτίων καὶ δύο κατ' αὐτοὺς εἶναι ἀρχάς, ἀγαθὸν δαίμονα καὶ κακὸν δαίμονα, καὶ τῷ μὲν ὄνομα εἶναι Ζεὺς καὶ 'Ωρομάσδης, τῷ δὲ Ἅιδης καὶ 'Αρειμάνιος. Cf. Bernays, *Die Dialoge des Aristoteles*; Berlin, 1863, p. 95.

[2] In the inscriptions we find—nom. *Auramazdá*, gen. *Auramazdáha*, acc. *Auramazdam*. It should be pronounced A'uramazdá.

even this is unintelligible, and is, in fact, nothing but a phonetic corruption of the name of the supreme Deity as it occurs on every page of the Zend-Avesta, namely, *Ahurô mazdâo* (nom.). Here, too, both words are declined; and instead of *Ahurô mazdâo*, we also find *Mazdâo ahurô*.[1] This *Ahurô mazdâo* is represented in the Zend-Avesta as the creator and ruler of the world; as good, holy, and true; and as doing battle against all that is evil, dark, and false. 'The wicked perish through the wisdom and holiness of the living wise spirit.' In the oldest hymns, the power of darkness which is opposed to *Ahurô mazdâo* has not yet received its proper name, which is *Angrô mainyus*, the later *Ahriman*; but it is spoken of as a power, as the *Drukhs* or deceiver; and the principal doctrine which Zoroaster came to preach was that we must choose between these two powers, that we must be good, and not bad. These are his words:—

'Thus are the primeval spirits who, as a pair and (yet each) independent in his action, have been famed. (They are) a better thing, they two, and a worse, in thought, word, and deed. And between these two let the wise choose aright, not the evil-doers.'[2]

Or again:—

'Yea, I will declare the world's first two spirits, of whom the more bountiful thus spake to the harmful: "Neither our thoughts, nor commands, nor our under-

---

[1] Gen. *Ahurahe mazdâo*, dat. *mazdâi*, acc. *mazdam*.
[2] *Sacred Books of the East*, xxxi. p. 29; translation of the *Gâthas* by Dr. Mills.

standings, nor our beliefs, nor our words, nor our deeds, nor our consciences, nor our souls are at one.'"[1]

Now, if we wanted to prove that Anglo-Saxon was a real language, and more ancient than English, a mere comparison of a few words such as *lord* and *hláford*, *gospel* and *godspell* would be sufficient. *Hláford* has a meaning; *lord* has none; therefore we may safely say that without such a compound as *hláford*, the word *lord* could never have arisen. The same, if we compare the language of the Zend-Avesta with that of the cuneiform inscriptions of Darius. *Auramazdâ* is clearly a corruption of *Ahurô mazdâo*, and if the language of the mountain records of Behistun is genuine, then, *à fortiori*, is the language of the Zend-Avesta genuine, as deciphered by Burnouf, long before he had deciphered the language of Cyrus and Darius. But what is the meaning of *Ahurô mazdâo*? Here Zend does not give us an answer; but we must look to Sanskrit as the more primitive language, just as we looked from French to Italian, in order to discover the original form and meaning of *feu*. According to the rules which govern the changes of words, common to Zend and Sanskrit, *Ahurô mazdâo* would correspond to the Sanskrit *Asura medhas*;[2] and this would mean the 'Wise Spirit,'—neither more nor less.

We have editions, translations, and commentaries

---

[1] *L. c.* p. 125.

[2] This is Benfey's explanation of *mazdâo*. Burnouf took it as a compound of *maz*, great, and *dâo*, knowledge, an opinion supported by Spiegel, *Commentar über das Avesta*, vol. i. p. 3. In RV. viii. 20, 17, we read yáthá rudrásya súnávah diváh visanti ásurasya vedhásah. Could it have been originally ásurasya medhásah?

of the Zend-Avesta by Burnouf, Brockhaus, Spiegel, Westergaard, Darmesteter, Mills, and Geldner.[1] Yet there still remains much to be done. Dr. Haug, who spent some years with the Parsis of Bombay, was the first to point out that the text of the Zend-Avesta, as we have it, comprises fragments of very different antiquity, and that the most ancient only, the so-called Gâthas,[2] may be ascribed to Zarathustra. 'This portion,' he writes in a lecture delivered at Poona in 1861, 'compared with the whole bulk of the Zend fragments is very small; but by the difference of dialect it is easily recognised. The most important pieces written in this peculiar dialect are called Gâthas or songs, arranged in five small collections; they have different metres, which mostly agree with those of the Veda; their language is very near to the Vedic dialect.'[3]

Was Zoroaster a Historical Character?

But even to ascribe to Zarathustra the authorship of the Gâthas is very doubtful so long as it has not been proved who Zarathustra was, and at what time he lived. In the Avesta, Zarathustra appears as a mythological personage,[4] fighting against the powers

---

[1] Geldner's edition of the *Avesta* is still in progress, and promises to be final, unless new MSS. should be discovered, which is not likely.

[2] These have been translated and commented by Dr. Mills in the 31st volume of the *Sacred Books of the East*.

[3] The derivation of the name of Zarathustra from the Vedic word *garadashti*, as proposed by Dr. Haug, is not possible. See on the same subject J. H. C. Kern, *Over het woord Zarathustra en den mythischen persoon von dien naam*; Amsterdam, 1867.

[4] Darmesteter, *Sacred Books of the East*, iv. p. lxxvii; and Kern, *Over het woord Zarathustra*.

of evil, like Verethraghna, Vayu, or Keresâspa; but in the Gâthas he is still a leader of men, and a prophet, not unlikely to have been the author of such songs as the Gâthas. Certainty, however, whether Zarathustra was a man who was changed into a hero, or whether he was from the beginning a mythological being, is unattainable, and we must not try to go beyond what, from the circumstances of the case, is possible. All we can say is that both in the East and in the West the name of Zarathustra, whether as a king or as the founder of a religion, was widely known. Berosus, as preserved in the Armenian translation of Eusebius, mentions a Median dynasty of Babylon, beginning with a king Zoroaster, about 2234 B.C., and anterior therefore to Ninus. Xanthus, the Lydian (470 B.C.), as quoted by Diogenes Laertius, places Zoroaster, the prophet, 600 years before the Trojan war (1800 B.C.), and mentions even his *Logia*. Aristotle and Eudoxus, according to Pliny (*Hist. Nat.* xxx. 1), place Zoroaster 6000 before Plato; Hermippus, Hermodorus, and Theopompus of Chios, 5000 before the Trojan war (Diog. Laert. *procem.*). According to Pliny himself (*Hist. Nat.* xxx. 2), Zoroaster would have lived several thousand years before Moses the Judæan, who founded another kind of Magcia. These dates are startling and possibly exaggerated, nay it is doubtful whether the MSS. of Diogenes Laertius read 500 and 600 or 5000 and 6000.[1] Yet the fact remains that the name of Zoroaster, as a teacher, was known to Plato and Aristotle,

---

[1] See Duncker, *Monatsberichte der Königl. Akad. zu Berlin*, 14 Aug. 1876, p. 518.

and we must admit that, whatever the original purport of the name may have been, it had been accepted as the name of a prophet before the conquest of Persia by Alexander.

Was Zoroaster the Author of the Avesta?

But granting that Zoroaster's name was known at an early time, and certainly before the time of Plato and Aristotle, it still remains to be proved that in the Avesta, as we now have it, we possess his work. Tradition seems unanimous in ascribing to Alexander the Great the complete destruction of the ancient writings of Persia. Pliny tells us indeed (*Hist. Nat.* xxx. 1, 2) that Hermippus, in the third century B.C., had given an analysis of the books of Zoroaster, amounting to 2,000,000 lines, but the Parsis themselves, on the authority of the Dînkart,[1] ascribe the first collection of what remained of their several books, after their destruction by Alexander, to the reign of the last Arsacide, possibly, as M. Darmesteter conjectures, to Vologeses I, the contemporary of Nero. They tell us that the first Sassanian king, Ardeshîr Bâbagân (Artakhshîr i Pâpakân)[2] A.D. 226-240, made the Avesta the sacred book of Iran, and established Mazdeism as the state religion, while they ascribe the last purification or redaction of the Avesta to Âdarbâd Mahraspand under Shapur II (309-380). Our oldest MS., however, of the Avesta (Copenhagen,

---

[1] Darmesteter, *l. c.* p. xxxii. seq.
[2] *Geschichte des Artackshi i Pâpakân,* aus dem Pehlevi übersetzt von Th. Nöldeke; Göttingen, 1879.

GENEALOGICAL CLASSIFICATION OF LANGUAGES. 281

5) is dated A.D. 1323,[1] so that there was ample room for later additions and alterations.

Pehlevi.

One important help for checking the text of the Avesta and to a certain extent establishing its age, is found in the Pehlevi translations made under the Sassanian dynasty. Pehlevi is the name given to the language of Persia after the collapse of the Achæmenian dynasty. The language of the Cuneiform inscriptions of the Achæmenian dynasty does not represent a direct continuation of Zend. In some respects the language of Darius is really more primitive than Zend, in others Zend is more primitive than the language of Darius.[2] This can be accounted for, if we look upon Zend as the sacred language of the Magi, or the priesthood of Media which, though closely allied to the dialect spoken in Persia, was never the spoken language of that country.[3] When after the time of the Achæmenian inscriptions, we meet again with the language of Persia, we find it Pehlevi, the language of the Sassanian dynasty. The interval of five centuries is a blank as far as language is concerned. The first evidence of a new language and a new alphabet are certain Pehlevi inscriptions (third century A.D.),[4] and a literature consisting of (1) translations of Avesta

---

[1] West, in *S. B. E.*, vol. v. p. xxi.
[2] Darmesteter, *Études Iraniennes*, p. 9.
[3] See Darmesteter, in *S. B. E.*, vol. iv. p. xxxvi.
[4] Mr. West (p. 424) mentions a legend on a coin of Abd Zoharâû, satrap of Cilicia (350 B.C.); and Dr. Haug imagined he had discovered a Pehlevi inscription on a tablet of Nineveh.

texts, in which Avesta sentences alternate with a word-for-word Pehlevi translation, more or less interspersed with explanatory glosses, and sometimes interrupted by Pehlevi commentaries of considerable extent. It is difficult to fix their date, though they must have existed before the sixth century A.D.[1] (2) Purely Pehlevi texts on religious subjects, such as the Bundahish, Dînkard, Maînôgî Khirad, mostly of the ninth century A.D., though consisting probably of older materials. (3) Pehlevi texts on miscellaneous subjects, such as social law, legendary history, tales, letters, documents. Most of these works are of small extent. Mr. West, who has taken the trouble to count their words, reckons that the first class consists of 140,160, the second of 404,370, the third of 40,860 words, so that the whole Pehlevi literature would amount to about 585,390 words.[2]

The language which we call Pehlevi has proved a great puzzle to Oriental scholars, and the views advanced by different authorities have often been very contradictory. Some scholars, and among them Dr. Haug, held at first that Pehlevi, though mixed with Iranian words, was a decidedly Semitic dialect, a continuation, it was supposed, of an Aramæan dialect spoken in the ancient Empire of Assyria, though not the dialect of the Assyrian inscriptions. (Haug, Introduction to *Pahlavi Pazand Glossary*, pp. 138–142.) Others considered Pehlevi a dialect that had arisen on the frontiers of Iran and Chaldæa,

---

[1] See West, The Extent, Language, and Age of Pahlavi Literature, in the *Transactions of the Munich Academy*, 1888.
[2] West, *l. c.*, pp. 431, 439.

in the first and second centuries of our era, a dialect, Iranian in grammatical structure, but considerably mixed with Semitic vocables. The mystery has at last been solved, and the results of the latest researches of Haug and West can best be stated in their own words.[1]

All Parsi writers apply the name of Zend or Zand to the Pehlevi translations and explanations of their sacred texts. The texts themselves they call Avesta, and if they speak of both the text and translations and commentaries together they call them Avesta and Zend, but not Zend-Avesta. The Zend or explanation is written in Pehlevi, but there may have been other explanations or Zends, written in the old language of the Avesta, some of them now incorporated in the text, with additional explanations by Pehlevi translators Pehlevi is in fact the general name of the mediæval Persian language. There are legends in Pehlevi on coins, as early as the third century B.C., struck by kings of Persian provinces, subordinate to the Greek successors of Alexander; and later on, some provincial coins of the time of the Arsacide dynasty. But the most important documents in Pehlevi are the inscriptions of Ardeshir, the founder of the Sassanian dynasty, A.D. 226-240, and his immediate successors. Pehlevi continued to be written till about 900 A.D.; any fragments of later date than 1000 must be looked upon as artificial imitations.

The name Pehlevi is supposed to be a corruption of Parthva, which occurs in the Cuneiform inscriptions,

[1] See West, *Bundahis*, Introduction.

in Sanskrit Pahlava.[1] Though Pehlevi was not the language of the Parthian rulers of Persia, the language of Persia became known by that name during the centuries in which Persia was under Parthian sway.

The language of Persia, however, is commonly called Pehlevi only when it is written, neither in Avesta nor in modern Persian, i. e. Arabic letters, but in that peculiar mode of writing which has so long perplexed European scholars. The Persians, during the Parthian times, gave up the Cuneiform alphabet, and borrowed their letters from their Semitic neighbours; but besides the alphabet, they transferred also a number of complete Semitic words to their writings, as representations of corresponding words in their own language. There are about 400 of these Semitic logograms, and they are often followed by Persian terminations, so that there can be little doubt that, though written as Semitic words, they were always pronounced as Persian. They would write, e. g. *malkân malkâ*, king of kings, but pronounce *shâhân shâh*,[2] it being utterly impossible grammatically in any Semitic language to form such a phrase as *malkân malkâ*.[3] The nearest approach to this way of writing is when we write *viz.* but pronounce *namely*; or *e. g.* but pronounce *for instance*. This is the mode in which the Parsis still read their Pehlevi literature. Besides these 400 Semitic, there are about 100 old Persian or Iranian logograms used in Pehlevi, as we

---

[1] Lassen compared *pahlava* with *pakhtu*, the old name of the Afghans, and *bâhlika* with *bâkhdhi*, the Zend name of Bactria.

[2] Ammianus Marcellinus, xix. 2, 11, states that the Persians as early as 350 A.D. called their king *Shahân shâh*.

[3] Darmesteter, *Études Iraniennes*, i. p. 33.

might write y^e for *the*, *Xmas* for *Christmas*. These 500 or more logograms, which were collected in an old glossary for the use of literary men, are sometimes called the *Zvârish*, a term sometimes modified into *Uzvârish*, whence modern Pehlevi *Aúzvárish*, misread *Huzvârish*. Zvârish is supposed to mean obsolete. *Pâzend* is not the name of a language, but is a transliteration of Pehlevi texts in which all Semitic words are replaced by their Iranian equivalents, written either in Avesta or modern Persian characters. Every Pâzend text, therefore, presupposes a Pehlevi original, while some modern Persian texts, written in Avesta characters, have no right to the name of Pâzend.

When the language of Persia is written in Arabic letters, it is called *Pârsî*, a name which has also been applied by European, though not by native, scholars to such Pâzend texts as contain Iranian words only.

Professor Darmesteter in his *Études Iraniennes* uses the technical terms *Zend*, *Pehlevi*, *Huzvârish* or *Zevârish*, *Pâzend*, and *Pârsi* in slightly different senses. There is no difference of opinion about *Zend*. Though it meant originally explanation, commentary, it is to be allowed to continue as the name of the language of the Avesta.

Pehlevi is to remain the name of the language of Persia as spoken under the Sassanians, though the Sassanians would probably have called their language Pârsî.

Huzvârish or *Zevârish* signifies, according to Darmesteter, the mode of writing Pehlevi according to the system described above. Its original meaning is supposed to have been disguisement.

Pazend (below Zend) is explained by the same scholar in the sense of transcript of Pehlevi into ordinary characters, while the language of such transcripts should be called *Pârsî*. These transcripts are not always correct, owing to the difficulty of the Pehlevi alphabet, but they are considered authoritative by the Parsis of the present day.

The language of *Firdusi*, the great epic poet of Persia, the author of the *Shahnâmeh*, about 1000 A.D., is Pârsî or Fârsî, or modern Persian, only much freer from Arabic ingredients than any other Persian poetry of his own and of later times. In one sense it may be called ancient Persian, but the later history of Persian consists chiefly in the gradual increase of Arabic words, which have crept into the language since the conquest of Persia and the conversion of the Persians to the religion of Mohammed.

IRANIC CLASS.

Zend or Median.	Achæmenian Persian. Cuneiform Inscriptions 500 to 336 B.C.
	Sassanian Persian. Pehlevi 226 to 900 A.D.
	Modern Persian 1000 A.D.

Persian is spoken even now in many local dialects. It is said that in the fourteenth century Pehlevi continued to be spoken in Zinjan near Kazwin, and that at Maragah in Adarbaijan the language was a mixture of Pehlevi and Arabic.[1] Sometimes Bokharian is

---

[1] Darmesteter, *Études Iraniennes*, i. p. 43.

mentioned as a separate language, but it is only Persian as spoken at Bokhara.

Kurdish.

The language of the Kurds, the old Karduchi, is an Iranian dialect, but it has assumed a kind of national independence, and is spoken on both sides of the Upper Tigris over a large area. We possess a dictionary and grammar of the language by Justi, 1880.

Balúchi.

The language of Baluchistân is likewise Iranic. It is divided into two dialects, the Northern and Southern, which are separated by people speaking *Brâhuî*, a Dravidian language. Those who speak these two dialects are said to be unable to understand each other.[1]

Language of the Afghans and Dards.

The language of the Afghans, the Pushtu, and the Paktyes of Herodotus, which was formerly classed as an Iranian dialect, has been proved by Trumpp to be more closely related with the vernaculars of India than of Persia.[2] North of Afghanistan the dialects of Dardistan have been examined by Dr. Leitner, and seem to occupy, so far as we may judge at present, the same intermediate position as Pushtu.

Armenian.

Armenian was formerly classed as an Iranian

---

[1] See W. Geiger, *Dialectspaltung im Balûchî*, in *Sitzungsberichte der philos.- philol. und histor. Classe der K. Bayer.-Akad. der Wiss.*, 1889, Heft i.

[2] Trumpp, in the *Journal of the German Oriental Society*, vols. xxi and xxii; also *Grammar of Pushtu*, 1873.

language. This was the opinion of Bopp, Windischmann, F. Müller, and other scholars; nor can it be doubted that on many points it comes very near to the Iranian type of grammar. Pott was the first to express some doubts on the subject, and de Lagarde, in 1866, distinguished in Armenian between an original stratum, an old Iranian alluvium, and a new Iranian stratum. It was reserved, however, for Professor Hübschmann to claim for Armenian an independent position in the Aryan family, distinct in its phonetic structure from Persian, and with peculiarities of grammar which cannot be traced back to any other Aryan language, though on one important point it agrees with Letto-Slavic.[1]

Gipsies.

There remains one more Aryan language which belongs equally to Asia and Europe, the language of the *Gipsies*. Its Indian origin is now fully proved. The Gipsies first appeared in Europe in the twelfth century, and from the words which they carried along with them in their dictionary Miklosich has proved that they must have taken their journey through Persia, Armenia, Greece, Roumania, Hungary, and Bohemia.

South-Eastern, North-Western Branches.

It is possible to divide the whole Aryan family into two divisions: the *South-Eastern*, including the Indic and Iranic classes, and the *North-Western*, comprising

---

[1] Über die Stellung des Armenischen im Kreise der Indo-germanischen Sprachen, Kuhn's *Zeitschrift*, xxiii. 5.

all the rest. Sanskrit and Zend share certain words and grammatical forms in common which do not exist in any of the other Aryan languages; and there can therefore be no doubt that the ancestors of the poets of the Veda and of the worshippers of *Ahurô mazdâo* lived together for some time after they had left the original home of the whole Aryan race. The genealogical classification of languages has in fact an historical meaning. There was a time when out of many possible names for *father, mother, daughter, son, dog, cow, heaven,* and *earth,* those which we find in all the Aryan languages were framed, and obtained a mastery *in the struggle for life* which is carried on among synonymous words as much as among plants and animals. A comparative table of the auxiliary verb AS, to be, in the different Aryan languages teaches the same lesson. The selection of the root AS out of many roots, equally applicable to the idea of being, and the joining of this root with one set of personal terminations, most of them originally personal pronouns, were individual acts, or, if you like, historical events. They took place once, at a certain date and in a certain place; and as we find the same forms preserved by all the members of the Aryan family, it follows that there was once a small clan of Aryas, settled probably somewhere on the highest elevation of Central Asia, speaking a language, not yet Sanskrit or Greek or German, but containing the dialectic germs of all; a clan that had advanced to a state of agricultural civilisation; that had recognised the bonds of blood, and sanctioned the laws of marriage; and that invoked the Giver of light and life in heaven by the same name which may still be heard in the temples of Benares, in the basilicas of Rome, and in our own churches and cathedrals.

After this clan broke up, the ancestors of the Indians and Zoroastrians must have remained together for some time in their migrations or new settlements. Whether, besides this division into a southern and northern branch, it is possible by the same test (the community of particular words and forms) to discover the successive periods when the Germans separated from the Slaves, the Celts from the Italians, or the Italians from the Greeks, seems more than doubtful. The attempts made by different scholars have led to different and by no means satisfactory results;[1] and it seems best, for the present, to trace each of the northern classes back to its own dialect, and to account for the more special coincidences between such languages as, for instance, the Slavonic and Teutonic, by admitting that the ancestors of these races preserved from the beginning certain dialectical peculiarities which existed before, as well as after, the separation of the Aryan family.[2]

---

[1] See Schleicher, *Deutsche Sprache*, s. 81; *Chips from a German Workshop*, vol. iv. pp. 224-227.

[2] *Biographies of Words and the Home of the Aryas*, 1888.

The Origin of the name Ârya.

Ârya is a Sanskrit word, and in the later Sanskrit it means *noble, of a good family.* Teachers are frequently addressed as *Ârya.* It was, however, originally a national name, and we see traces of it as late as the law-book of the Mânavas, where India is still called Ârya-âvarta, the abode of the Âryas.[1] In the old Sanskrit, in the hymns of the Veda, ârya occurs frequently as a national name and as a name of honour, comprising the worshippers of the gods of the Brahmans, as opposed to their enemies, who are called in the Veda Dasyus. Thus one of the gods, Indra, who, in some respects, answers to the Greek Zeus, is invoked in the following words (Rig-veda i. 51, 8): 'Know thou the Âryas, O Indra, and they who are Dasyus; punish the lawless, and deliver them unto thy servant! Be thou the mighty helper of the worshippers, and I will praise all these thy deeds at the festivals.'

In the later dogmatic literature of the Vedic age, the name of Ârya is distinctly appropriated to the first three castes— the Brâhma*n*as, Kshatriyas, Vaisyas—as opposed to the fourth, or the *S*ûdras. In the *S*atapatha-Brâhma*n*a it is laid down distinctly: 'Âryas are only the Brâhma*n*as, the Kshatriyas, and Vaisyas, for they are admitted to the sacrifices. They shall not speak with everybody, but only with the Brâhma*n*a, the Kshatriya, and the Vai*s*ya. If they should fall into a conversation with a *S*ûdra, let them say to another man, "Tell this *S*ûdra so." This is the law.'

In the Atharva-veda (iv. 20, 4 ; xix. 62, 1) expressions occur such as, 'seeing all things, whether *S*ûdra or Ârya,' where *S*ûdra and Ârya are meant to express the whole of mankind.

This word ârya with a long â is derived from arya with a short a, and this name arya is applied in the later Sanskrit

---

[1] Ârya-bhûmi and Ârya-de*s*a are used in the same sense.

to a Vaisya, or a member of the third caste.[1] What is called the third class must originally have constituted the large majority of the Brahmanic society, for all who were not nobles or priests were Vaisyas. We may well understand, therefore, how a name, originally applied to the cultivators of the soil and householders, should in time have become the general name of all Aryas.[2] Why the householders were called arya is a question which would carry us too far at present. I can only state that the etymological signification of Arya seems to be, 'one who ploughs or tills,' and that it is connected with the root of ar-are.[3] The Aryans would seem to have chosen this name for themselves as opposed to the nomadic races, the *Turas*, or quick horsemen, whom we sometimes call *Turanians*.

In India, as we saw, the name of Ârya, as a national name,

---

[1] Pânini, iii. 1, 103. *Encyclopædia Britannica*, s. v. Aryan.

[2] In one of the Vedas, árya, with a short a, is used like á′rya, as opposed to Sûdra. For we read (Vâg-Sanh. xx. 17): 'Whatever sin we have committed in the village, in the forest, in the home, in the open air, against a Sûdra, against an Ârya—thou art our deliverance.'

[3] Bopp derived á′rya from the root ar, to go, or from ark, to venerate. The former etymology would give no adequate sense; the latter is phonetically impossible. Lassen explains árya as *adeundus*, like âkârya, the teacher, which would leave arya unexplained. This arya cannot be a participle fut. pass., because in that case the root would have to take Vriddhi; we could explain ârya, but not arya (Pân. iii. i. 124). I take arya as formed by the taddhita suffix ya, like div-ya, *cœlestis*, i.e. divi-bhava, from div, *cœlum*, or like sit-yam, ploughed, from sitâ, furrow; while ârya, with Vriddhi, would either be derived from arya, or formed like vais-ya, householder, from vis, house. In ar, or arâ, I recognise one of the oldest names of the earth, as the ploughed land, lost in Sanskrit, but preserved in Greek as ἔρ-α (Goth. *air-tha*), so that arya would have conveyed originally the meaning of landholder, cultivator of the land, while vais-ya from vis, meant a householder. Idâ, the daughter of Manu, is another name of the cultivated earth, and probably a modification of arâ. Kern (in his review of Childers' *Pali Dictionary*) derives árya from ari, man, hero; plur. men in general. Ari, in the sense of enemy, he connects with Lat. *alis, alius*, Germ. *ali, alja*, and compares the meanings of para, other, stranger, enemy. See also Lipmann, K. Z. xix. 393; Pischel, K. Z. xx. 376; Arya, if it means Vaisya, has the accent on the first, otherwise on the last syllable.

fell into oblivion in later times, and was preserved in the term Âryâvarta only, the abode of the Aryans.¹ But it was more faithfully preserved by the Zoroastrians who had migrated to the north-west, and whose religion has been preserved to us in the Zend-Avesta, though in fragments only. Now *Airya* in Zend means venerable, and is at the same time the name of the people.² In the first chapter of the Vendidad, where Ahuramazda explains to Zarathustra the order in which he created the earth, sixteen countries are mentioned, each, when created by *Ahuramazda*, being pure and perfect; but each being tainted in turn by *Angro mainyus* or Ahriman. Now the first of these countries is called Airyanem vaêgô, *Arianum semen*, the Aryan seed, and its position is supposed to have been as far east as the western slopes of the Belurtag and Mustag, near the sources of the Oxus and Yaxartes, the highest elevation of Central Asia.³ From this country, which is called their seed, the Aryas, according to their own traditions, advanced towards the south and west, and in the Zend-Avesta the whole extent of country occupied by the Aryans is likewise called *Airyâ*. A line drawn from India along the Paropamisus and Caucasus Indicus in the east, following in the north the direction between the Oxus and Yaxartes,⁴ then running along the Caspian Sea, so as to include Hyrcania and Râgha, then turning south-east on the borders of Nisæa, Aria (i.e. Haria), and the countries washed

---

[1] We are told, however, by the Rev. Dr. Wilson, in his *Notes on the Constituent Elements of the* Marâṭhî *Language*, p. 3, that Aryâr (an Ârya) is the name given to a Marâṭha by his neighbour of the Canarese country, and that Âryûr, too, is the name given to the Marâṭhâs by the degraded tribe of Mangs, located in their own territory. The same distinguished scholar points out that Ariakê is the name given to a great portion of the Marâṭhâ country by the merchant Arrian, the navigator, thought to be the contemporary of Ptolemy.— Vincent's *Periplus*, vol. ii. pp. 397, 428-438.

[2] Lassen, *Ind. Alt.* b. i. s. 6.

[3] *Ibid.* b. i. s. 526.

[4] Ptolemy knows 'Αριάκαι, near the mouth of the Yaxartes. Ptol. vi. 14; Lassen, *l. c.* i. 6. In Plin. vi. 50, Ariacæ ought to be altered into Asiotæ. See Müllenhoff, *Monatsberichte der Berliner Akademie*, 1866, p. 551.

by the Etymandrus and Arachotus, would indicate the general horizon of the Zoroastrian world. It would be what is called in the fourth cardé of the Yasht of Mithra, 'the whole space of Aria,' vîspem airyôsayanem (*totum Ariæ situm*).[1] Opposed to the Aryan (*airyâo dainhâvô*) we find in the *Zend-Avesta* the non-Aryan countries (*anairyâo dainhâvô*),[2] and traces of this name are found in the Άναριάκαι, a people and town on the frontiers of Hyrcania.[3] Greek geographers use the name of Ariana in a wider sense even than the *Zend-Avesta*. All the country between the Indian Ocean in the south and the Indus on the east, the Hindu-kush and Paropamisus in the north, the Caspian gates, Karamania, and the mouth of the Persian gulf in the west, is included by Strabo (xv. 2) under the name of Ariana; and Bactria is called[4] by him 'the ornament of the whole of Ariana.' As the Zoroastrian religion spread westward, Persia, Elymais, and Media all claimed for themselves this Aryan title. Hellanicus, who wrote before Herodotus, knows of Aria as a name of Persia.[5] Herodotus (vii. 62) attests that the Medians were called Arii; and even for Atropatene, the northernmost part of Media, the name of Ariania (not Aria) has been preserved by Stephanus Byzantinus. As to Elymais its name has been derived from *Ailama*, a supposed corruption of *Airyama*.[6] The

---

[1] Burnouf, Yasna, Notes, p. 61. In the same sense the Zend-Avesta uses the expression, Aryan provinces, 'airyanâm daqyunâm' gen. plur., or 'airyâo dainhâvô,' provincias Arianas. Burnouf, Yasna, p. 442; and *Notes*, p. 70.

[2] Burnouf, Yasna, Notes, p. 62.

[3] Strabo, xi. 7, 11; Pliny, *Hist. Nat.* vi. 19; Ptol. vi. 2; De Sacy, *Mémoires sur diverses Antiquités de la Perse*, p. 48; Lassen, *Indische Alterthumskunde*, i. 6.

[4] Strabo, xi. 11; Burnouf, Yasna, Notes, p. 110. 'In another place Eratosthenes is cited as describing the western boundary to be a line separating Parthiene from Media, and Karmania from Paretakene and Persia, thus taking in Yezd and Kerman, but excluding Fars.'—Wilson, *Ariana antiqua*, p. 120.

[5] Hellanicus, fragm. 166, ed. Müller. Άρια Περσική χώρα.

[6] Joseph Müller, *Journal asiatique*, 1839, p. 298. Lassen, *l. c.* i. 6. From this the Elam of Genesis. *Mélanges asiatiques*, i. p. 623. In the cuneiform inscriptions which represent the pronunciation of Persian

Persians, Medians, Bactrians, and Sogdians all spoke, as late as the time of Strabo,[1] nearly the same language, and we may well understand, therefore, that they should have claimed for themselves one common name, in opposition to the hostile tribes of Turan.

That *Aryan* was used as a title of honour in the Persian empire is clearly shown by the cuneiform inscriptions of Darius. He calls himself Ariya and Ariya-kitra, an Aryan and of Aryan descent; and Ahuramazda, or, as he is called by Darius, Auramazda, is rendered in the Turanian translation of the inscription of Behistun, 'the god of the Aryas.' Many historical names of the Persians contain the same element. The great-grandfather of Darius is called in the inscriptions Ariyâramna, the Greek *Ariaramnes* (Herod. vii. 90). Ariobarzanes (i.e. Euergetes), Ariomanes (i.e. Eumenes), Ariomardos, all show the same origin.[2]

About the same time as these inscriptions, Eudemos, a pupil of Aristotle, as quoted by Damascius, speaks of 'the Magi and the whole Arcian race,'[3] evidently using Arcian in the same sense in which the *Zend-Avesta* spoke of 'the whole country of Aria.'

And when after years of foreign invasion and occupation, Persia rose again under the sceptre of the Sassanians to be a national kingdom, we find the new national kings, the worshippers of Mazdanes, calling themselves, in the inscriptions under the Achæmenian dynasty, the letter *l* is wanting altogether. In the names of Babylon and Arbela it is replaced by *r*. The *l* appears, however, in the Sassanian inscriptions, where both Ailân and Airân, Anilân and Anirân occur.

[1] Heeren, *Ideen*, i. p. 337 : ὁμόγλωττοι παρὰ μικρόν. Strabo, p. 1054.
[2] One of the Median classes is called 'Αριζαντοί, which may be âryagantu. Herod. i. 101.
[3] Μάγοι δὲ καὶ πᾶν τὸ Ἄρειον γένος, ὡς καὶ τοῦτο γράφει ὁ Εὔδημος, οἱ μὲν τόπον, οἱ δὲ χρόνον καλοῦσι τὸ νοητὸν ἅπαν καὶ τὸ ἡνωμένον· ἐξ οὗ διακριθῆναι ἢ θεὸν ἀγαθὸν καὶ δαίμονα κακὸν ἢ φῶς καὶ σκότος πρὸ τούτων, ὡς ἐνίους λέγειν. Οὗτοι δὲ οὖν καὶ αὐτοὶ μετὰ τὴν ἀδιάκριτον φύσιν διακρινομένην ποιοῦσι τὴν διττὴν συστοιχὴν τῶν κρειττόνων, τῆς μὲν ἡγεῖσθαι τὸν Ὡρομάσδην, τῆς δὲ τὸν Ἀρειμάνιον.—Damascius, *Quæstiones de primis principiis*, ed. Kopp, 1826, cap. 125, p. 384.

deciphered by De Sacy,[1] 'Kings of the Aryan and un-Aryan races;' in Pehlevi, *Irán va Anirán*; in Greek, Ἀριάνων καὶ Ἀναριάνων.

The modern name of Irán for Persia still keeps up the memory of this ancient title.

In the name of *Armenia* the same element of Arya has been supposed to exist.[2] The name of Armenia, however, does not occur in Zend, and the name *Armina*, which is used for Armenia in the cuneiform inscriptions, is of doubtful etymology.[3] In the language of Armenia, *ari* is used in the widest sense for Aryan or Iranian; it means also brave, and is applied more especially to the Medians.[4] The word *arya*, therefore, though not contained in the name of Armenia, can be proved to have existed in the Armenian language as a national and honourable name.

West of Armenia, on the borders of the Caspian Sea, we find the ancient name of *Albania*. The Armenians call the Albanians *Aghovan*, and as *gh* in Armenian stands for *r* or *l*, it has been conjectured by Boré, that in *Aghovan* also the name of Aria is contained. This seems doubtful. But in the valleys of the Caucasus we meet with an Aryan race speaking an Aryan language, the Os of Ossethi, and these call themselves *Iron*.[5]

---

[1] De Sacy, *Mémoire*, p. 47; Lassen, *Ind. Alt.* i. 8.

[2] Burnouf, Yasna, Notes, p. 107. Spiegel, *Beiträge zur vergl. Sprachf.* i. 31. Anquetil had no authority for taking the Zend *airyaman*, for Armenia.

[3] Bochart shows (*Phaleg.* lib. i. cap. 3, col. 20) that the Chaldee paraphrast renders the Mini of Jeremiah by Har Mini, and as the same country is called Minyas by Nicolaus Damascenus, he infers that the first syllable is the Semitic Har, a mountain (see Rawlinson's *Glossary*, s. v.).

[4] Lassen, *Ind. Alt.* i. 8, note. *Arikh* also is used in Armenian as the name of the Medians, and has been referred by Jos. Müller to Aryaka as a name of Media. *Journ. As.* 1839, p. 298. If, as Quatremère says, *ari* and *anari* are used in Armenian for Medians and Persians, this can only be ascribed to a misunderstanding, and must be a phrase of later date.

[5] Sjögren, *Ossetic Grammar*, p. 396. Scylax and Apollodorus mention Ἄριοι and Ἀριανία, south of the Caucasus. Pictet, *Origines*, p. 67; Scylax, *Perip.* p. 213, ed. Klausen; *Apollodori Biblioth.* p. 437, ed. Heyne.

Along the Caspian, and in the country washed by the Oxus and Yaxartes, Aryan and non-Aryan tribes were mingled together for centuries. Though the relation between Aryas and Turas was hostile, and though there were continual wars between them, as we learn from the great Persian epic, the *Shahnameh*, it does by no means follow that all the nomad races who infested the settlements of the Aryas were of Tatar blood and speech. Turvasa and his descendants, who represent the Turanians, are described in the later epic poems of India as cursed and deprived of their inheritance in India; but in the *Vedas* Turvasa is represented as worshipping Aryan gods. Even in the Shahnameh, Persian heroes go over to the Turanians and lead them against Irán, very much as Coriolanus led the Samnites against Rome. We may thus understand why so many Turanian or Scythian names, mentioned by Greek writers, should show evident traces of Aryan origin. *Aspa* was the Persian name for *horse*, and in the Scythian names *Aspabota*, *Aspakara*, and *Asparatha*[1] we can hardly fail to recognise the same element. Even the name of the Aspasian mountains, placed by Ptolemy in Scythia, indicates a similar origin. Nor is the word Ârya unknown beyond the Oxus. There is a people called *Ariacæ*,[2] another called *Antariani*.[3] A king of the Scythians, at the time of Darius, was called *Ariantes*. A contemporary of Xerxes is known by the name of *Aripithes* (i. e. Sanskrit aryapati; Zend *airyapaiti*); and *Spargapithes* may have had some connection with the Sanskrit svargapati, lord of heaven.

We have thus traced the name of Ârya from India to the west, from Âryâvarta to Ariana, Persia, Media, more doubtfully to Armenia and Albania, to the Iron in the Caucasus, and to some of the nomad tribes in Transoxiana. As we approach Europe the traces of this name grow fainter, yet they are not altogether lost.

[1] Burnouf, Yasna, Notes, p. 105.
[2] Ptolemy, vi. 2, and vi. 14. There are Ἀναριάκαι on the frontiers of Hyrcania. Strabo, xi. 7; Pliny, *Hist. Nat.* vi. 19.
[3] On Arimaspi and Aramæi, see Burnouf, Yasna, Notes, p. 105; Pliny, vi. 9.

CHAPTER VII.

Two roads were opened to the Aryas of Asia in their westward migrations. One through Chorasan¹ to the north, through what is now called Russia, and thence to the shores of the Black Sea and Thrace. Another from Armenia, across the Caucasus or across the Black Sea to Northern Greece, and along the Danube to Germany. Now on the former road the Aryas left a trace of their migrations in the old name of Thrace, which was *Aria*;² on the latter we meet in the eastern part of Germany, near the Vistula, with a German tribe called *Arii*. And as in Persia we found many proper names in which Arya formed an important ingredient, so we find again in German history names such as *Ariovistus*.³

Though we look in vain for any traces of this old national name among the Greeks and Romans, some scholars believe that it may have been preserved in the extreme west of the Aryan migrations, in the very name of *Ireland*. The common etymology of *Erin* is that it means 'island of the west,' *iar-innis*; or land of the west, *iar-in*. But this is clearly wrong,⁴ at least with regard to the second portion of the word. The old name of Ireland is *Ériu* in the nominative, more recently *Éire*. It is only in the oblique cases that the final *n* appears, as in Latin words such as *regio*, *regionis*. *Erin* therefore has been explained as a derivative of *Er* or *Eri*, said to be the ancient name of the Irish Celts as preserved in the Anglo-Saxon name of their country, *Íreland*.⁵ And it is maintained by O'Reilly, though denied by others, that this *er* is used in Irish in the sense of noble, like the Sanskrit ârya.⁶

---

¹ *Qairizam* in the Zend-Avesta, *Uvârazmis* in the inscriptions of Darius.

² Stephanus Byzantinus.

³ Grimm, *Rechtsalterthümer*, s. 292, traces Arii and Ariovistus back to the Gothic *harji*, army. If this etymology be right, this part of our argument must be given up.

⁴ Pictet, *Les Origines indo-européennes*, p. 31. ' *Iar*, l'ouest, ne s'écrit jamais *er* ou *eir*, et la forme *Iarin* ne se rencontre nulle part pour Erin.' Zeuss gives *iar-rend*, insula occidentalis. But *rend* (recte *riud*) makes *rendo* in the gen. sing.

⁵ Old Norse *trar*, Irishmen; Anglo-Saxon *tra*, Irishman.

⁶ Though I state these views on the authority of M. Pictet (Kuhn's

Some of the evidence here collected in tracing the ancient name of the Aryan family, may seem doubtful, and I have pointed out myself some links of the chain uniting the earliest

Beiträge, i. 91), I think it right to add the following note which an eminent Irish scholar has had the kindness to send me :—
The ordinary name of Ireland, in the oldest Irish MSS., is (*h*)*ériu*, gen. (*h*)*érenn*, dat. (*h*)*érinn*. The initial *h* is often omitted. Before etymologising on the word, we must try to fix its Old Celtic form. Of the ancient names of Ireland which are found in Greek and Latin writers, the only one which *hériu* can formally represent is *Hiberio*. The abl. sing. of this form—*Hiberione*—is found in the Book of Armagh, a Latin MS. of the early part of the ninth century. From the same MS. we also learn that a name of the Irish people was *Hyberionaces*, which is obviously a derivative from the stem of *Hiberio*. Now if we remember that the Old Irish scribes often prefixed *h* to words beginning with a vowel (e.g. *h-abunde, h-arundo, h-erimus, h-ostium*), and that they also often wrote *b* for the *v* consonant (e.g. *bobes, fribulas, corbus, fabonius*); if, moreover, we observe that the Welsh and Breton names for Ireland—Y*werddon*, *Iverdon*—point to an Old Celtic name beginning with IVER-, we shall have little difficulty in giving *Hiberio* a correctly Latinised form, viz. *Iverio*. This in Old Celtic would be *Iveriu*, gen. *Iverionos*. So the Old Celtic form of *Fronto* was *Frontú*, as we see from the Gaulish inscription at Vieux Poitiers. As *v* when flanked by vowels is always lost in Irish, *Iveriú* would become *ieriu*, and then, the first two vowels running together, *ériu*. ['Absorbitur *v* in *í* in *íar* (occidens) in formula adverbiali *aníar* (in, ab occidente) Wb. Cr., cui adnumeranda præp. *iarn* (post), adverb. *iarum* (postea), siquidem recte confero nomina Ἰουέρνιοι (n. populi in angulo Hiberniæ verso contra occidentem et meridiem), Ἰοευρνίς (oppid. Hiberniæ), et Ἰουερνία (nomen insulæ) ap. Ptolem. quæ Romani accommodaverint ad vocem suam *hibernus*, i.e. hiemalis.'—Zeuss, *Grammatica Celtica*, i. p. 67.] As regards the double *n* in the oblique cases of *ériu*, the genitive *érenn* (e.g.) is to *Iverionos* as the Old Irish *anmann*, 'names,' is to the Skr. nāmāni, Lat. *nomina*. The doubling of the *n* may perhaps be due to the Old Celtic accent. What then is the etymology of *Iveriú*? I venture to think that it may (like the Lat. *Aver-nus*, Gr. Ἄϝορ-ϝος) be connected with the Skr. avara, 'posterior,' 'western.' So the Irish *des*, Welsh *deheu*, 'right,' 'south,' is the Skr. dakshina, 'dexter'; and the Irish *áir* (in *an-áir*), if it stand for *páir*, 'east,' is the Skr. pûrva, 'anterior.'
M. Pictet regards Ptolemy's Ἰουερνία (Ivernia) as coming nearest to the Old Celtic form of the name in question. He further sees in the first syllable what he calls the Irish *ibh*, 'land,' 'tribe of people,' and he thinks that this *ibh* may be connected not only with the Vedic *ibha*,

name of India with the modern name of Ireland, as weaker than the rest. But the principal links are safe. Names of countries, peoples, rivers, and mountains have an extraordinary vitality, and they will remain while cities, kingdoms, and nations pass away. *Rome* has the same name to-day, and will probably have it for ever, which was given to it by the earliest Latin and Sabine settlers; and wherever we find the name of Rome, whether in Walachia, which by the inhabitants is called Roumania, or in the dialects of the Grisons, the Romansch, in the title of the Romance languages, or in the name of Rouma, given by the Arabs to the Greeks, and in that of Roumelia, we know that some threads would lead us back to the Rome of Romulus and Remus, the stronghold of the earliest warriors of Latium. The ruined city near the mouth of the Upper Zab, now usually known by the name of Nimrud, is called *Athur* by the Arabic geographers, and in Athur we recognise the old name of Assyria, which Dio Cassius writes Atyria, remarking that the barbarians changed the Sigma into Tau. Assyria is called Athurā in the inscriptions of Darius.[1] We hear of battles fought on the *Sutledge*, and we hardly think that the battle-field of the Sikhs was nearly the same where Alexander fought the kings of the Penjâb. But the name of the *Sutledge* is the name of the same river as the *Hesudrus* of Alexander, the *Satadru* of the Indians, and among the oldest hymns of the Veda, about 1500 B.C., we find a war-song referring to a battle fought on the two banks of the same stream.

'family,' but with the Old High-German *eiba*, 'a district.' But, first, according to the Irish phonetic laws, *ibha* would have appeared as *eb* in Old, *cabh* in Modern, Irish. Secondly, the *ci* in *ciba* is a diphthong = Gothic *ái*, Irish *ói, óe*, Skr. *ê*. Consequently, *ibh* and *ibha* cannot be identified with *eiba*. Thirdly, there is no such word as *ibh* in the nom. sing., although it is to be found in O'Reilly's Dictionary, along with his explanation of the intensive prefix *er-*, as 'noble,' and many other blunders and forgeries. The form *ibh* is, no doubt, producible, but it is a very modern dative plural of *úa*, a 'descendant.' Irish districts were often called by the names of the occupying clans. These clans were often called 'descendants (*huí, hí, í*) of such an one.' Hence the blunder of the Irish lexicographer.—W. S.

[1] See Rawlinson's *Glossary*, s. v.

GENEALOGICAL CLASSIFICATION OF LANGUAGES. 301

No doubt, there is danger in trusting to mere similarity of geographical names. Grimm may be right that the Arii of Tacitus were originally Harii, and that their name is not connected with Arya. But in this case, as the evidence on either side is merely conjectural, this must remain an open question. In other cases, however, a strict observation of the phonetic laws peculiar to each language will remove all uncertainty. Grimm, for instance, in his *History of the German Language* (p. 228), imagined that *Hariva*, the name of *Herat* in the cuneiform inscriptions, is connected with Arii, the name which, according to Herodotus, was given to the Medes. This cannot be, for the initial aspiration in *Hariva* points to a word which in Sanskrit begins with s, and not with a vowel, like Ârya. The following remarks will make this clearer.

Herat is called both *Herat* and *Heri*,[1] and the river on which it stands is called *Heri-rud*. This river *Heri* is called by Ptolemy 'Ἀρείας,[2] by other writers *Arius*; and *Aria* is the name given to the country between Parthia (Parthuwa) in the west, Margiana (Marghush) in the north, Bactria (Bakhtrish) and Arachosia (Harauwatish) in the east, and Drangiana (Zaraka) in the south. This, however, though without the initial *h*, is not Ariana, as described by Strabo, but an independent country, forming part of it. It is supposed to be the same as the *Haraiva* (Hariva) of the cuneiform inscriptions, though this is doubtful. But in the *Zend-Avesta* there occurs *Haróyu*,[3] as the name of the sixth

---

[1] W. Ouseley, *Orient. Geog. of Ebn Haukal.* Burnouf, Yasna, Notes, p. 102.   [2] Ptolemy, vi. 17.

[3] It has been supposed that *haróyûm* in the *Zend-Avesta* stands for *haraévem*, and that the nominative was not *Haróyu*, but *Haraévó*. (Oppert, *Journal Asiatique*, 1851, p. 280.) Without denying the correctness of this view, which is partially supported by the accusative *vidóyûm*, from *vidaévo*, enemy of the Divs, there is no reason why *Haróyum* should not be taken for a regular accusative of *Haróyu*, the long *û* in the accusative being due to the final nasal. (Burnouf, Yasna, Notes, p. 103.) This *Haróyu* would be in the nominative as regular a form as Sarayu in Sanskrit, nay even more regular, as *haróyu* would presuppose a Sanskrit sarasyu or saroyu, from saras, water. Sarayû occurs also with a long û; see Wilson, s. v. M. Oppert rightly identifies the people of *Haraiva* with the 'Ἀρεῖοι, not, like Grimm, with the 'Ἄριοι.

CHAPTER VII.

country created by Ormuzd. We can trace this name with the initial *h* even beyond the time of Zoroaster. The Zoroastrians had lived for a time together with the ancestors of the people whose sacred songs have been preserved to us in the Veda. Afterwards the Zoroastrians migrated westward to Arachosia, Media, and Persia, while the Vedic people spread more and more towards the south and west. In their migrations the Zoroastrians did what the Greeks did when they founded new colonies, what the Americans did in founding new cities. They gave to the new cities and to the rivers along which they settled, the names of cities and rivers familiar to them, and reminding them of the localities which they had left. Now, as a Persian *h* points to a Sanskrit *s*, *Harôyu* would be in Sanskrit Saroyu. We do not find Saroyu in the Veda, but we find Sarayu one of the sacred rivers of Vedic India, famous in the epic poems as the River of Ayodhyâ, one of the earliest capitals of India, and still known as the modern *Sarju*, the river of *Awadh* or *Hanumân-garhi*. Saras is a name for water in Sanskrit, derived, like sarit, river, from sar, to go, to run. It was probably this river, the Sarayu, which lent its name to the *Harôyu*, the *Arius* or *Heri-rud*, and this in turn to the country of *Aria* or *Herat*. Anyhow *Aria*, as the name of *Herat*, has no connection with *Aria*, the country of the Âryas.

There is no necessity for restricting Aryan to the language of India and Persia. They can be distinguished as *Indic* and *Iranic*, or as *Perso-Aryan* and *Indo-Aryan*, having Aryan as the shortest and most convenient title of the whole family of Aryan[1] speech.

As Comparative Philology has thus traced the ancient name of Ârya from India to Europe, as the original title assumed by the Aryas, before they left their common home, it is but natural that it should have been chosen as the technical term for the family of languages which was formerly designated as Indo-Germanic, Indo-European, Caucasian, or Japhetic.

[1] For fuller information on the meaning of the word Ârya, see the author's article in the *Encyclopædia Britannica*, s. v. Aryan.

August Friedrich Pott.

The last of the triumvirs who founded the study of comparative philology—Bopp, Grimm, and Pott—has departed. Professor Pott, as the papers inform us, died at Halle on July 5, 1886, in his eighty-fifth year. I have at present no books of reference at hand, and cannot tell where he was born, how he was educated, when he became professor, and what were his titles and orders, and other distinctions. Though I believe I have read or consulted every one of his books, I cannot undertake to give even their titles. And yet I feel anxious to pay my tribute of gratitude and respect to one to whom we all owe so much, who has fought his battle so bravely, and whose whole life was consecrated to what was to him a sacred cause—the conquest of sure and accurate knowledge in the wide realm of human speech. I believe he never left the University of Halle, in which he first began his career. He knew no ambition but that of being in the first rank of hard and honest workers. His salary was small; but it was sufficient to make him independent, and that was all he cared for. Others were appointed over his head to more lucrative posts, but he never grumbled. Others received orders and titles: he knew that there was one order only that he ought to have had long ago—the *Ordre pour le Mérite*, which he received only last year, fortunately before it was too late. He never kept any private trumpeters, nor did he surround himself with what is called a school, so often a misnomer for a clique. His works, he knew, would remain his best monuments, long after the cheap applause of his friends and pupils, or the angry abuse of his envious rivals, had died away. What he cared for was work, work, work. His industry was indefatigable to the end of his life; and to the very last he was pouring out of his note-books streams of curious information which he had gathered during his long life.

A man cannot live to the age of eighty-five, particularly if he be engaged in so new and progressive a science as comparative philology, without having some of his earlier works called antiquated. But we ought to distinguish between books that become antiquated, and books that become historical. Pott's *Etymologische Forschungen*, in their first edition, contain, no doubt, many statements which the merest beginner now knows to be erroneous. But what these beginners are apt to forget is that Pott's mistakes were often inevitable, nay, even creditable. We do not blame the first decipherers of the hieroglyphic inscriptions, because in some of their first interpretations they guessed wrongly. We admire them for what they guessed rightly, and we often find even their mistakes extremely ingenious and instructive. I should advise all those who have been taught to look upon Pott's early works as obsolete to read his *Etymologische Forschungen*, even the first edition; and I promise them they will gain a truer insight into the original purposes of comparative philology than they can gain from any of the more recent manuals. They will be surprised at the numberless discoveries which are due to Pott, though they have been made again and again, quite innocently, by later comers. In Pott's time the most necessary work consisted in the collection of materials. Overwhelming proofs were wanted to establish what seems to us a simple fact, but what was then regarded as a most pestilent heresy, namely, that Greek, Latin, Teutonic, Celtic, Slavonic, and Sanskrit were cognate tongues. It was Pott who brought these overwhelming proofs together, and thus crushed once and for all the opposition of narrow-minded sceptics. It is quite true that his work was always rather massive, but massive work was wanted for laying the foundation of the new science. It is true, also, that his style was very imperfect, was, in fact, no style at all. He simply poured out his knowledge, without any attempt at order and perspicuity. I believe it was Ascoli who once compared his books to what the plain of Shinar might have looked like after the Tower of Babel had come to grief. But, after all, the foundation which he laid has lasted; and, after the rubbish has been cleared away by himself and others, enough remains that will last for ever. Nor should it be forgotten that Pott was really the first who taught respect for phonetic rules. We have almost forgotten the discussion which preceded the establishment of such simple rules as that Sanskrit g may be represented by Greek β, that Sanskrit gaus may be βοῦς, and Sanskrit gam, βαίνω. We can hardly imagine that scholars could have been incredulous as to Sanskrit ksh being represented by Greek κτ, as to an initial s being liable to elision, and certain initial consonants liable to prosthetic vowels. The rules, however, according to which d might or might not be changed into l had to be established by exactly the same careful arguments as those according to which the vowel a is liable to palatal or labial colouring (e and o). And when we look at the second edition of Pott's *Etymologische Forschungen*, we find it a complete storehouse which will supply all our wants, though, no doubt, every student has himself to test the wares which are offered him. The same remark applies to his works on the Gipsies, on Personal Names, and on Numerals; to his numerous essays on Mythology, on African Languages, and on General Grammar. Everywhere there is the same *embarras de richesse*; but, nevertheless, there is *richesse*, and the collection of it implies an amount of devoted labour such as but few scholars have been capable of.

In his earlier years, Professor Pott was very 'fond of fechting'; and when we look at the language which he sometimes allowed himself to use in his controversies with Curtius and others, we cannot help feeling that it was not quite worthy of him. But we must remember what the general tone of scientific wrangling was at that time. Strong language was mistaken for strong argument, and coarseness of expression for honest conviction. In the days of Lachmann and Haupt, no one was considered a real scholar who could not be *grob*. Pott caught the infection; but, with all that, though he dealt hard blows, he never dealt foul blows. He never became the slave of a clique, and never wrote what he did not believe to be true. He must often have felt, like Goethe, that he stumbled over the roots of the trees which he himself had planted; but he remained on pleasant terms with most of the rising generation, and, to the end of his life, was ready to learn from all who had anything to teach. He cared for the science of language with all the devotion of a lover; and he never forgot its highest aims, even when immersed in a perfect whirlpool of details. He had, in his younger days, felt the influence of William von Humboldt; and no one who had ever felt that influence could easily bring himself to believe that language had nothing to teach us but phonetic rules. Pott's name will remain for ever one of the most glorious in the heroic age of comparative philology. Let those who care to know the almost forgotten achievements of that age of heroes study them in Benfey's classical work—*The History of Comparative Philology.*

Ulfilas.

I must say a few words on this remarkable man. The accounts of ecclesiastical historians with regard to the date and the principal events in the life of Ulfilas are very contradictory. This is partly owing to the fact that Ulfilas was an Arian bishop, and that the accounts which we possess of him come from two opposite sides, from Arian and Athanasian writers. Although in forming an estimate of his character it would be necessary to sift this contradictory evidence, it is but fair to suppose that, when dates and simple facts in the life of the bishop have to be settled, his own friends had better means of information than the orthodox historians. It is, therefore, from the writings of his own co-religionists that the chronology and the historical outline of the bishop's life should be determined.

The principal writers to be consulted are Philostorgius, as preserved by Photius, and Auxentius, as preserved by Maximinus in a MS. discovered in 1840 by Professor Waitz[1] in the Library at Paris. (Supplement. Latin. No. 594.) This MS. contains some writings of Hilarius, the first two books of Ambrosius, *De Fide*, and the acts of the Council of Aquileja (381). On the margin of this MS. Maximinus repeated the beginning of the acts of the Council of Aquileja, adding remarks of his own in order to show how unfairly Palladius had been treated in that council by Ambrose. He jotted down his own views on the Arian controversy, and on foll. 282 seq., he copied an account of Ulfilas written by Auxentius, the bishop of Dorostorum (Silistria on the Danube), a pupil of Ulfilas. This is followed again by some dissertations of Maximinus, and on foll. 314-327, a treatise addressed to Ambrose by a Semi-Arian,

---

[1] *Ueber das Leben und die Lehre des Ulfila*, Hanover, 1840; *Ueber das Leben des Ulfila*, von Dr. Bessell, Göttingen, 1860.

a follower of Eusebius, possibly by Prudentius himself, was copied and slightly abbreviated for his own purposes by Maximinus.

It is from Auxentius, as copied by Maximinus, that we learn that Ulfilas died at Constantinople, where he had been invited by the emperor to a disputation. This could not have been later than the year 381, because, according to the same Auxentius, Ulfilas had been bishop for forty years, and, according to Philostorgius, he had been consecrated by Eusebius. Now Eusebius of Nicomedia died 341, and as Philostorgius says that Ulfilas was consecrated by 'Eusebius and the bishops who were with him,' the consecration has been referred with great plausibility to the beginning of the year 341, when Eusebius presided at the Synod of Antioch. As we know that Ulfilas was thirty years old at the time of his consecration, he must have been born in 311, and as he was seventy years of age when he died at Constantinople, his death must have taken place in 381.

Professor Waitz fixed the death of Ulfilas in 388, because it is stated by Auxentius that other Arian bishops had come with Ulfilas on his last journey to Constantinople, and had actually obtained the promise of a new council from the emperor, but that the heretical party, i.e. the Athanasians, succeeded in getting a law published, prohibiting all disputation on the faith, whether in public or private. Maximinus, to whom we owe this notice, has added two laws from the Codex Theodosianus, which he supposed to have reference to this controversy, dated respectively 388 and 386. This shows that Maximinus himself was doubtful as to the exact date. Neither of these laws, however, is applicable to the case, as has been fully shown by Dr. Bessell. They are quotations made by Maximinus at his own risk, from the Codex Theodosianus, and made in error. If the death of Ulfilas were fixed in 388, the important notice of Philostorgius, that Ulfilas was consecrated by Eusebius, would have to be surrendered, and we should have to suppose that as late as 388 Theodosius had been in treaty with the Arians, whereas after the year 383, when the last attempt at a reconciliation had been made by Theodosius, and had failed, no mercy was any longer shown to the party of Ulfilas and his friends.

If, on the contrary, Ulfilas died at Constantinople in 381, he might well have been called there by the Emperor Theodosius, not to a council, but to a disputation (ad disputationem), as Dr. Bessell ingeniously maintains, against the Psathyropolistæ,[1] a new sect of Arians at Constantinople. About the same time, in 380, Sozomen[2] refers to efforts made by the Arians to gain influence with Theodosius. He mentions, like Auxentius, that these efforts were defeated, and a law published to forbid disputations on the nature of God. This law exists in the Codex Theodosianus, and is dated January 10, 381. But what is most important is, that this law actually revokes a rescript that had been obtained fraudulently by the Arian heretics, thus confirming the statement of Auxentius that the emperor had held out to him and his party a promise of a new council.

Ulfilas was born in 310-11. His parents, as Philostorgius tells us, were of Cappadocian origin, and had been carried away by the Goths as captives from a place called Sadagolthina, near the town of Parnassus. It was under Valerian and Gallienus (about 267) that the Goths made this raid from Europe to Asia, Galatia, and Cappadocia, and the Christian captives whom they carried back to the Danube were the first to spread the light of the Gospel among the Goths. Philostorgius was himself a Cappadocian, and there is no reason to doubt this statement of his on the parentage of Ulfilas. Ulfilas was born among the Goths; Gothic was his native language, though he was able in after-life to speak and write both in Latin and Greek. Philostorgius, after speaking of the death of Crispus (326), and before proceeding to the last years of Constantine, says that 'about that time' Ulfilas led his Goths from beyond the Danube into the Roman Empire. They had to leave their country, being persecuted on account of their Christianity. Ulfilas was the leader of the faithful flock, and came to Constantine (not Constantius) as ambassador. This must have been before 337, the year of Constantine's death. It may have been

[1] Bessell, *l. c.* p. 38.   [2] Sozomenus, *H. E.* vii. 6.

in 328, when Constantine had gained a victory over the Goths; and though Ulfilas was then only seventeen years of age, this would be no reason for rejecting the testimony of Philostorgius, who says that Constantine treated Ulfilas with great respect, and called him the Moses of his time. Having led his faithful flock across the Danube into Mœsia, he might well have been compared by the emperor to Moses leading the Israelites from Egypt through the Red Sea. It is true that Auxentius institutes the same comparison between Ulfilas and Moses, after stating that Ulfilas had been received with great honours by Constantius, not by Constantine. But this refers to what took place after Ulfilas had been for seven years bishop among the Goths, in 348, and does not invalidate the statement of Philostorgius as to the earlier intercourse between Ulfilas and Constantine. Sozomen[1] clearly distinguishes between the first crossing of the Danube by the Goths, with Ulfilas as their ambassador, and the later attacks of Athanarich on Fridigern or Fritiger, which led to the settlement of the Goths in the Roman Empire. We must suppose that, after having crossed the Danube, Ulfilas remained for some time with his Goths, or at Constantinople. Auxentius says that he officiated as lector, and it was only when he had reached the requisite age of thirty, that at the synod of Antiochia he was made bishop by Eusebius in 341. He passed the first seven years of his episcopate among the Goths, and the remaining thirty-three of his life 'in solo Romaniæ,' where he had migrated together with Fritiger and the Thervingi. There is some confusion as to the exact date of the Gothic Exodus, but it is not at all unlikely that Ulfilas acted as their leader on more than one occasion.

There is little more to be learnt about Ulfilas from other sources. What is said by ecclesiastical historians about the motives of his adopting the doctrines of Arius, and his changing from one side to the other, deserves no credit. Ulfilas, according to his own confession, was always an Arian (semper sic credidi). Socrates says that Ulfilas was present at the Synod of Constantinople in 360, which may be true, though neither Auxentius nor Philostorgius mentions it. The author of the acts of Nicetas speaks of Ulfilas as present at the Council of Nicæa, in company with Theophilus. Theophilus, it is true, signed his name as a Gothic bishop at that council, but there is nothing to confirm the statement that Ulfilas, then fourteen years of age, was with Theophilus. Auxentius thus speaks of Ulfilas (*Waitz*), p. 19 :—

'Et [ita prædic] ante et per Cristum cum dilectione Deo patri gratias agente, hæc et his similia exsequente, quadraginta annis in episcopatu gloriose florens, apostolica gratia Græcam et Latinam et Goticam linguam sine intermissione in una et sola eclesia Cristi predicavit. . . . Qui et ipsis tribus linguis plures tractatus et multas interpretationes volentibus ad utilitatem et ad ædificationem, sibi ad æternam memoriam et mercedem post se dereliquid. Quem condigne laudare non sufficio et penitus tacere non audeo; cui plus omnium ego sum debitor, quantum et amplius in me laboravit, qui me a prima etate mea a parentibus meis discipulum suscepit et sacras litteras docuit et veritatem manifestavit et per misericordiam Dei et gratiam Cristi et carnaliter et spiritaliter ut filium suum in fide educavit.

'Hic Dei providentia et Cristi misericordia propter multorum salutem in gente Gothorum de lectore triginta annorum episkopus est ordinatus, ut non solum esset heres Dei et coheres Cristi, sed et in hoc per gratiam Cristi imitator Cristi et sanctorum ejus, ut quemadmodum sanctus David triginta annorum rex et profeta est constitutus, ut regeret et doceret populum Dei et filios Hisdrael, ita et iste beatus tamquam profeta est manifestatus et sacerdos Cristi ordinatus, ut regeret et corrigeret et doceret et ædificaret gentem Gothorum; quod et Deo volente et Cristo auxiliante per ministerium ipsius admirabiliter est adinpletum, et sicuti Iosef in Ægypto triginta annorum est manifes[tatus et] quemadmodum dominus et Deus noster Ihesus Cristus filius Dei triginta annorum secundum carnem constitutus et baptizatus, cœpit evangelium predicare et animas hominum pascere: ita et iste sanctus, ipsius Cristi dispositione et ordinatione, et in fame et penuria predicationis indifferenter agentem ipsam gentem Gothorum secundum evangelicam et apostolicam et profeticam regulam emendavit et vibere [Deo] docuit, et cristianos vere cristianos esse, manifestavit et multiplicavit.

'Ubi et ex invidia et operatione inimici thunc ab inreligioso et sacrilego iudice Gothorum tyrannico terrore in varbarico cristianorum persecutio est excitata, ut satanas, qui male facere cupiebat, nolen[s] faceret bene, ut quos desiderabat prevaricatores facere et desertores. Cristo opitulante et propugnante, fierent martyres et confessores, ut persecutor confunderetur, et qui persecutionem patiebantur, coronarentur ut hic qui temtabat vincere, victus erubesceret, et qui temtabantur, victores gauderent. Ubi et post multorum servorum et ancillarum Cristi gloriosum martyrium, imminente vehementer ipsa persecutione, conpletis septem annis tantummodo in episkopatum, supradictus sanctissimus vir beatus Ulfila cum grandi populo confessorum de varbarico pulsus, in solo Romanie a thu[n]c beate memorie Constantio principe honorifice est susceptus, ut sicuti Deus per Moysem de potentia et violentia Faraonis et Egyptorum po[pulum s]uum l[iberav]it [et rubrum] mare transire fecit et sibi servire providit, ita et per sepe dictum Deus confessores sancti filii sui unigeniti de varbarico liberavit et per Danubium transire fecit, et in montibus secundum sanctorum imitationem sibi servire de[crevit] . . . . . eo populo in solo Romaniæ, ubi sine illis septem annis triginta et tribus annis veritatem predicavit, ut et in hoc quorum sanctorum imitator erat [similis esset], quod quadraginta annorum spatium et tempus ut multos . . . . re et . . . . a[nn]orum . . . . e vita.' . . 'Qu[i] c[um] precepto imperiali, conpletis quadraginta annis, ad Constantinopolitanam urbem ad disputationem . . . . . contra p . . . ic . . . [p] . t . stas perrexit, et eundo in . . . . nn . . ne . p . . . ecias sibi ax . . . . . to docerent et contestarent[ur] . . . . abat, et inge . e . . . . supradictam [ci]vitatem, recogitato et in . . . . . de statu concilii, ne arguerentur miseris miserabiliores, proprio judicio damnati et perpetuo supplicio plectendi, statim cœpit infirmari; qua in infirmitate susceptus est ad similitudine Elisei prophete. Considerare modo oportet meritum viri, qui ad hoc duce Domino obiit Constantinopolim, immo vero Cristianopolim, ut sanctus et immaculatus sacerdos Cristi a sanctis et consacerdotibus, a dignis dignus digne [per] tantam multitudinem cristianorum pro meritis [suis] mire et gloriose honoraretur.'—(*Bessell*, p. 37.)

'Unde et cum sancto Hulfila ceterisque consortibus ad alium comitatum Constantinopolim venissent, ibique etiam et imperatores adissent, adque eis promissum fuisset conci[li]um, ut sanctus Aux[en]tius exposuit, [a]gnita promiss[io]ne prefati pr[e]positi heretic[i] omnibus viribu[s] institerunt u[t] lex daretur q[uæ] concilium pro[hi]beret, sed nec p[ri]vatim in domo [nec] in publico, vel i[n] quolibet loco di[s]putatio de fide haberetur, sic[ut] textus indicat [le]gis, etc.'—(*Waitz*, p. 23; *Bessell*, p. 15.)

CHAPTER VIII.

THE SEMITIC FAMILY.

Comparative Study of the Semitic Language.

THE Science of Language owes its origin almost entirely to the study of the Aryan languages, one might almost say, to the study of Sanskrit. The more correct views on the origin and growth of language, on the true nature of grammatical elements, on the possible changes of letters, and on the historical development of the meaning of words, are all the work of the nineteenth century, and may be claimed, in the first instance, as the discoveries of Sanskrit scholars.

But similar discoveries had been attempted by scholars of the sixteenth, seventeenth, and eighteenth centuries, within the narrower sphere of the Semitic languages. That the constituent elements of Hebrew were triliteral roots, that the grammatical terminations were mostly pronominal, that certain consonants were interchangeable, while others were not, all this was known before the rise of Comparative Philology in Europe. Nevertheless, it was the new spirit which animated the schools of Bopp, Pott, and Grimm, which soon began to react powerfully on Semitic students, and in our own time has led to a comparative study of Hebrew, Arabic, and Aramaic, very different from that of former generations.

For the purpose of illustrating the general principles of the Science of Language the Aryan languages may still be considered as the most useful, and I need hardly add that from the nature of my own special studies, I was led to depend mainly on the evidence supplied by them in support of the linguistic theories which I wished to establish. But as it is impossible to avoid reference to the Semitic, if only in order to contrast them with the Aryan languages, and as a certain knowledge of what I called the Turanian languages seems almost indispensable to enable us to understand the only possible antecedents of Aryan grammar, a short survey of the Semitic, and what I called the Turanian languages will be useful, before we proceed further.

Division of the Semitic Family.

The Semitic family has been divided into three branches: the *Aramaic*, the *Hebraic*, and the *Arabic*;[1] or into two, the *Northern*, comprising the *Aramaic* and *Hebraic*, and the Southern the *Arabic*.

Aramaic.

The language of *Aram*, which formerly was represented chiefly by *Syriac* and *Chaldee*, has now received an older representative in the language of Assyria and Babylon, so far as it has been recovered and deciphered in the cuneiform inscriptions. The grammatical structure of this ancient language is clearly Semitic, but it displays no peculiarities which

---

[1] *Histoire générale et Système comparé des Langues sémitiques*, par Ernest Renan.

would connect it more closely with Aramaic than with the other Semitic languages. Geographically, however, the ancient language of Mesopotamia may for the present be called Aramaic. The date also of the most ancient of these inscriptions is still a matter of controversy. If some of them go back, as some scholars maintain, to 4000 B.C., they would represent the very oldest remnants of Semitic speech, and almost any deviations of the later Aramaic dialects might be accounted for by mere growth and decay.

If that ancient Semitic literature was itself preceded, as seems now very generally, though not yet universally, admitted, by another civilisation, not Semitic, and known by the name of *Sumero-Accadian*, this would open to us an insight into a past more distant even than that which is claimed for the oldest Egyptian and Chinese literature. It may be so, but as yet neither the language, nor the ideas conveyed by it, give the impression of so very remote an antiquity.[1] Much, no doubt, has been achieved in deciphering these cuneiform inscriptions, and every year brings new and important results. But this very fact shows how dangerous it would be to look upon every new discovery as final, and to arrange and rearrange the history and chronology of the East in accordance with the latest conjectures, based on the decipherment of the cuneiform inscriptions.[2]

Chaldee and Syriac.

The language spoken in historical times in the

[1] See *Gifford Lectures*, p. 305.
[2] See Sayce, *Hibbert Lectures*, 1887, p. 413.

ancient kingdoms of Babylon and Nineveh is called *Aramaic*. It spread from thence into Syria and Palestine. Owing to the political and literary ascendency of these countries, Aramaic seems for a time to have become a kind of *lingua franca*, asserting its influence over Persia, Syria, Asia Minor, Egypt, and even Arabia.

The language spoken by Abraham and his people, before they emigrated to Canaan, was probably Aramaic. Laban must have spoken the same dialect, and the name which he gave to the heap of stones that was to be a witness between him and Jacob (*Jegar-sahadutha*) is Syriac, whereas *Galeed*, the name by which Jacob called it, is Hebrew.[1]

It has been usual to distinguish between Aramaic as used by the Jews, and Aramaic as used in later times by Christian writers. The former was called *Chaldee*, the latter *Syriac*. It may be true that the name Chaldee owes its origin to the mistaken notion of its having been introduced into Palestine by the Jews returning from the Babylonian captivity. But the name has now been too long in possession to make it advisable to replace it by a new name, such as *Western Aramaic*.

The Jewish *Chaldee*[2] shows itself first in some of the books of the Old Testament, such as the book of Ezra and the book of the Prophet Daniel. Afterwards we find it employed in the *Targums*[3] or Chaldee

---

[1] See Quatremère, *Mémoire sur les Nabatéens*, p. 139.
[2] Renan, pp. 214 seq.: *Le chaldéen biblique serait un dialecte araméen légèrement hébraïsé.*
[3] Arabic, *tarjam*, to explain: *Dragoman*, Arabic, *tarjumân*.

paraphrases of the Pentateuch (Onkelos) and of the Prophets (Jonathan), which were read in the Synagogues[1] long before they were finally collected in about the fourth and fifth centuries A.D. The Jerusalem Targum and the Jerusalem Talmud[2] represent the Chaldee as spoken at that time by the Jews in Jerusalem and Galilee. Christ and his disciples must have employed the same Aramaic dialect, though they used Greek also in addressing the people at large. The few authentic words preserved in the New Testament as spoken by our Lord in his own native language, such as *Talitha kumi, Ephphatha, Abba*, are not Hebrew, but Chaldee.

After the destruction of Jerusalem the literature of the Jews continued to be written in Chaldee. The *Talmud* of Jerusalem of the fourth, and that of Babylon of the fifth century, exhibit the spoken language of the educated Jews, though greatly depraved by an admixture of foreign elements. The conquests of the Arabs and the spreading of their language interfered with the literary cultivation of Chaldee as early as the seventh century; but Chaldee remained the literary idiom of the Jews to the tenth century. The *Masora*[3] and the traditional commentary of the

---

[1] The Targums of Onkelos and Jonathan are referred to the second century A.D. Others are later, later even than the Talmud; see Renan, *l. c.*, p. 220.

[2] *Talmud* (instruction) consists of *Mishna* and *Gemara*. *Mishna* means repetition or teaching, viz. of the Law. It was collected and written down about 218 A D., by Jehuda. *Gemara* is a continuation and commentary of the Mishna. That of Jerusalem was finished toward the end of the fourth, that of Babylon toward the end of the fifth century.

[3] First printed in the Rabbinic Bible, Venice, 1525.

318   CHAPTER VIII.

Old Testament were probably written down about that time. Soon afterwards the Jews adopted Arabic as their literary idiom, and retained it to the thirteenth century. They then returned to a kind of modernised Hebrew, which is still employed by Rabbis in their learned discussions.

The *Samaritan* also may be called an Aramaic dialect. It is used in the Samaritan translation of the Pentateuch, and differs but little from the Chaldee of the Jews.

The *Mandaeans*, sometimes called *Mendaites* and *Nasoreans*, a somewhat mixed Christian sect in Babylonia, chiefly near Bassora, spoke and wrote likewise a corrupt Aramaic dialect. This is preserved in their writings, and in the jargon of a few surviving members of that sect. Best known among their writings is the *Book of Adam*. Though their extant literature cannot claim a date before the tenth century, it was supposed that under a modern crust of wild and senseless hallucinations, it contained some grains of genuine ancient Babylonian thought. These Mandaeans have in fact been identified with the *Nabateans*, who are mentioned as late as the tenth century[1] of our era, as a race purely pagan, and distinct from Jews, Christians, and Mohammedans. In Arabic the name *Nabatean*[2] is used for Babylonians —nay, all the people of Aramaic origin, settled in the earliest times between the Euphrates and Tigris, are referred to by that name.[3] It was supposed that the Nabateans, who are mentioned about the beginning

[1] Renan, p. 241.   [2] Ibid. p. 237.
[3] Quatremère, *Mémoire sur les Nabatéens*, p. 116.

of the Christian era as a race distinguished for their astronomical and general scientific knowledge, were the ancestors of the mediæval Nabateans, and the descendants of the ancient Babylonians and Chaldeans. A work, called *The Nabatean Agriculture*, which exists in an Arabic translation by Ibn-Wahshiyyah, the Chaldean,[1] who lived about 900 years after Christ, was supposed to be a translation of a text written by Kuthami in Aramean, about the beginning of the thirteenth century B.C. Renan, however, has shown that it was really the compilation of a Nabatean who lived about the fourth century after Christ;[2] and though it contains ancient traditions, which may go back to the days of the great Babylonian monarchs, these traditions can hardly be taken as a fair representation of the ancient civilisation of the Aramean race.

Syriac, though spoken long before the rise of Christianity, owes its literary cultivation chiefly to Christian writers. In the second century A.D. the Old and New Testaments were translated into Syriac (the *Peshito*, i.e. simple), and became the recognised text

[1] Ibn-Wahshiyyah was a Mussulman, but his family had been converted for three generations only. He translated a collection of Nabatean books. Three have been preserved: 1. The Nabatean Agriculture; 2. The Book on Poisons; 3. The Book of Tenkelusha (Teucros) the Babylonian; besides fragments of The Book of the Secrets of the Sun and Moon. The Nabatean Agriculture was referred by Quatremère (*Journal asiatique*, 1835) to the period between Belesis who delivered the Babylonians from their Median masters and the taking of Babylon by Cyrus. Professor Chwolson of St. Petersburg, who has examined all the MSS., places Kuthami at the beginning of the thirteenth century B.C.

[2] Renan, *Mémoire sur l'Âge du Livre intitulé Agriculture nabatéenne*, p. 38, Paris, 1860; *Times*, January 31, 1862.

in the school of Edessa and other seats of learning in Syria. A large literature sprang up from the third to the seventh century, and extended its influence to Persia and the Eastern Roman Empire. Ephraem Syrus lived in the middle of the fourth century. During the eighth and ninth centuries the Nestorians of Syria acted as the instructors of the Arabs, but the literary cultivation of their own language began to wane. It was revived for a time in the thirteenth century by Gregorius Barhebraeus (Abulfaraj),[1] and lived on as a learned language to the present day.

The *Neo-Syriac* dialects, still spoken by Nestorian Christians in the neighbourhood of Mossul and in Kurdistan, as far as the lakes of Van and Urmia, also by some Christian tribes in Mesopotamia, are not directly derived from the literary Syriac, but represent remnants of the spoken Aramaic. One of these dialects has lately received some literary cultivation through the exertions of Christian missionaries.[2]

Hebraic.

The second branch of the Semitic family comprises *Phœnician* and *Carthaginian*, as known to us from inscriptions, dating, in the case of Phœnician, from about 600 B.C., and the *Hebrew* of the Old Testament.

The *Moabites* spoke a language almost identical with Hebrew, as may be seen from the inscription of King Mesha, about 900 B.C. The *Philistines* also spoke what may be called a Hebrew dialect. About the time of the Maccabees, Hebrew and its cognate

[1] See Renan, p. 257.
[2] Messrs. Perkins and Stoddard, the latter the author of a grammar, published in the *Journal of the American Oriental Society*, vol. v.

dialects ceased to be spoken by the people at large, though it remained the language of the learned long after the destruction of Jerusalem by Titus. We saw before how, first of all, Aramaic encroached upon Hebrew, owing to the political ascendancy of Babylon, and still more of Syria. Afterwards Greek became for a time the language of civilisation in Palestine as in other parts of the East; and lastly Arabic, after the conquest of Palestine and Syria, in the year 636, monopolised nearly the whole area formerly occupied by the two older branches of the Semitic stock, Aramaic and Hebrew. At present the Jews scattered over Europe and Asia still employ, for their own purposes, a kind of corrupt Hebrew, both for conversation and for literary purposes.

Arabic.

The third branch, the Arabic, has its original home in the Arabian peninsula, where it is still spoken in its greatest purity by the bulk of the inhabitants, and from whence it spread over Asia, Africa, and Europe at the time of the Mohammedan conquests.

The earliest literary documents of Arabic go back beyond Mohammed's time. They are called *Mo'allakât,* literally, suspended poems, because they are said to have been thus publicly exhibited at Mecca. They are old popular poems, descriptive of desert life. Besides these there are the Divans of the six ancient Arabic poets, which likewise are anterior to the rise of Mohammedanism.

Inscriptions have been found in the *Hijâz,* commonly called *Thamudic,* which are supposed to be of an ante-Christian date. Similar Arabic inscriptions continue to be discovered, attesting the use of Arabic, as a cultivated language, long before the age of Mohammed. The trilingual inscription of Zabad (Aramaic, Arabic, Greek) dates from 513 A.D.; a bilingual inscription of Harran (Arabic and Greek) from 568 A.D.

With Mohammed Arabic became the language of a victorious religion and of a victorious literature in Asia, Africa, and, for a time, even in Europe. The language of the Qur'ân became a new type of literary excellence by the side of the ancient Bedouin poetry. In the second century after the Hejra grammatical studies fixed the rules of classical Arabic permanently, and after 1200 years the Qur'ân, representing the language of the seventh century, is still read and understood by all educated Arabs. The spoken Arabic, however, differs dialectically in Egypt, Algeria, Syria, and Arabia. One Arabic dialect continues to be spoken in Malta.

Himyaritic Inscriptions.

There seems to have existed a very ancient civilisation in the south of the Arabian peninsula, sometimes called *Sabaean*, remnants of which have been discovered in colossal monuments and in numerous inscriptions, written in a peculiar alphabet, called *Himyaritic*. Their age is supposed to date from before our era, and to extend to the fourth century A.D. It is possible to distinguish traces of different dialects in these Sabaean inscriptions, but they are all closely allied to Arabic. The Sabaean language was probably spoken in the south of the Arabian peninsula till the advent of Mohammedanism, which made Arabic the language of the whole of Yemen.

Ethiopic.

In very early times a Semitic colony from Arabia, or, more correctly, from Sabaea, crossed over to Africa. Here, south of Egypt and Nubia, a primitive Semitic dialect, closely allied to Sabaean and Arabic, has maintained itself to the present day, called *Ethiopic*, *Abyssinian*, or *Geez*. We have translations of the Bible in Ethiopic, dating from the third and fourth centuries. Other works followed, all of a theological character.

There are inscriptions also in ancient Ethiopic, dating from the days of the kingdom of Axum, which have been referred to 350 and 500 A.D.

The ancient Ethiopic ceased to be spoken in the ninth century, but it remained in use as a literary language for a much longer time.

Beginning with the fifteenth and sixteenth centuries, a new language appears, the modern Ethiopic, or *Amharic*. In it the Semitic type has been intensely modified, probably owing to the fact that the tribes who spoke it were of Hamitic origin. It is still a spreading language, and has given rise in modern times to a new literature.

Other dialects, such as *Tigré*, *Ekhili*, and *Harrari*, so called from the localities in which they are spoken, have not yet been sufficiently explored to enable Semitic scholars to pronounce a decided opinion whether they are varieties of Amharic, or representatives of more ancient independent dialects.[1]

---

[1] The latest and best account of the Semitic languages is given by Nöldeke in the *Cyclopaedia Britannica*.

CHAPTER VIII.

Family likeness of the Semitic Languages.

The family likeness of the Semitic is quite as strong as that of the Aryan languages, nay, even stronger. Their phonetic character is marked by the preponderance of guttural sounds; their etymological character by the triliteral form of most of its roots, and the manner in which these roots are modified by pronominal suffixes and prefixes; their grammatical character by the fixity of the vowels for expressing the principal modifications of meaning, a fixity which made it possible to dispense with writing the vowel signs. These characteristic features are so strongly developed that they render it quite impossible to imagine that a Semitic language could ever have sprung from an Aryan or an Aryan from a Semitic. Whether both could have sprung from a common source is a question that has often been asked, and has generally been answered according to personal predilections. Most scholars, I believe, would admit that it could not be shown that a common origin in far distant times is altogether impossible.[1] But the evidence both for and against is by necessity so intangible and evanescent that it hardly comes within the sphere of practical linguistics.[2]

---

[1] See M. M., *Selected Essays*, i. p. 65, 'Stratification of Language.'

[2] Theologians who still maintain that all languages were derived from Hebrew would do well to read a work by the Abbé Lorenzo Hervas, the dedication of which was accepted by Pope Pius VI, *Saggio Pratico delle Lingue*, 1787, particularly the fourth chapter, which has the title ' La sostanziale diversità degl' idiomi nella sintassi addimostra essere vana l'opinione degli Autori, che li credono derivati dall' Ebreo.'

CHAPTER IX.

ANALYSIS OF LANGUAGE.

BEFORE we proceed to a consideration of the languages which are neither Aryan nor Semitic, languages which in my Letter on the Turanian Languages, published in 1854,[1] I ventured to call *Turanian*, and which Prichard before me had comprehended under the name of *Allophylian*, it will be necessary to discover what are the constituent elements of all human speech, and in how many different ways these elements may be combined. For it is in the combination of these elements that the principle has been discovered according to which languages may be classified, even when it is impossible to discover between them any traces of real genealogical relationship.

Radical and Formal Elements.

The genealogical classification of the Aryan and the Semitic languages was founded, as we saw, on a close comparison of the grammatical characteristics of each. It was the object of such works as Bopp's *Comparative Grammar* to show that the grammatical articulation of Sanskrit, Zend, Greek, Latin, Celtic, Teutonic, and Slavonic was produced once and for

---

[1] Letter to Chevalier Bunsen, 'On the Turanian Languages,' in Bunsen's *Christianity and Mankind*, vol. iii. pp. 263 seq. 1854.

all, and that the apparent differences in the terminations of Sanskrit, Greek, and Latin must be explained by laws of phonetic change, peculiar to each dialect, which modified the original common Aryan type, and transformed it into so many national languages. It might seem, therefore, as if the object of comparative grammar had been fully attained as soon as the exact genealogical relationship of languages had been settled; and those who only look to the higher problems of the science of language have not hesitated to declare that 'there is no longer any painsworthy difficulty nor dispute about declension, number, case, and gender of nouns.' But although it is certainly true that comparative grammar is only a means, and that it has wellnigh taught us all that it has to teach—at least in the Aryan family of speech—it is to be hoped that in the science of language it will always retain that prominent place which has been gained for it through the labours of its founders, Bopp, Grimm, Pott, Benfey, Curtius, Kuhn, and others.

Besides, comparative grammar has more to do than simply to compare. It would be easy enough to place side by side the paradigms of declension and conjugation in Sanskrit, Greek, Latin, and the other Aryan dialects, and to mark both their coincidences and their differences. But after we have done this, and after we have explained the phonetic laws which cause the primitive Aryan type to assume those national varieties which we admire in Sanskrit, Greek, and Latin, new problems arise of a far more interesting nature. It is generally admitted that grammatical terminations, as they are now called, were originally independent words, and had their own purpose and meaning. The question then arises whether it is possible, after comparative grammar has established the original forms of the Aryan terminations, to trace them back to independent words, and to discover their original purpose and meaning? You will remember that this was the point from which we started. We wanted to know why the termination *d* in *I loved* should change a present into a past act, and it was easily seen that, before answering this question, we had to discover, first of all, the most original form of this termination by tracing it from English to Gothic, and afterwards, if necessary, from Gothic to Sanskrit. Having surveyed the genealogical system of the Aryan and Semitic languages, we now return to our original question, namely, What is language that so small and merely formal a change as that of *I love* into *I loved*, should produce so portentous a difference?

Let us clearly see what we mean if we make a distinction between the radical and formal elements of a language. By formal elements I mean not only the terminations of declension and conjugation, but all derivative elements; all, in fact, that is not radical. Our view on the origin of language must chiefly depend on the view which we take of these formal, as opposed to the radical, elements of speech. Those who consider that language is a conventional production, base their arguments principally on these formal elements. The inflections of words, they maintain, are the best proof that language was made by mutual agreement. They look upon them as mere letters or syllables without any meaning by themselves; and if they were asked why the mere addition of a *d* changes *I love* into *I loved*, or why the addition of the syllable *rai* gave to *j'aime*, I love, the power of a future, *j'aimerai*, they would answer, that it was so because, at a very early time in the history of the world, certain persons, or families, or clans, agreed that it should be so.

This view was opposed by another which represents language as an organic and as almost a living being, and explains its formal elements as produced by a principle of growth, inherent in its very nature. 'Languages,'[1] it is maintained, 'are formed by a process, not of crystalline accretion, but of germinal development. Every essential part of language existed as completely (although only implicitly) in the primitive germ, as the petals of a flower exist in the bud, before the mingled influences of the sun and the air caused it to unfold.' This view was first propounded by Frederick Schlegel,[2] and it is still held

[1] Farrar, *Origin of Languages*, p. 35.

[2] 'It has been common among grammarians to regard those terminational changes as evolved by some unknown process from the body of a noun, as the branches of a tree spring from the stem—or as elements, unmeaning in themselves, but employed arbitrarily or conventionally to modify the meanings of words. "Languages with inflections," says Schlegel, "are organic languages, because they include a living principle of development and increase, and alone possess, if I may so express myself, a fruitful and abundant vegetation. The wonderful mechanism of these languages consists in forming an immense variety of words, and in marking the connection of ideas expressed by these words, by the help of an inconsiderable number of syllables, *which, viewed separately, have no signification*, but which determine with precision the sense of the words to which they are attached. By modifying radical letters and by adding derivative syllables to the roots, derivative words of

by many with whom poetical phraseology takes the place of sound and severe reasoning.

The science of language adopts neither of these views. As to imagining a congress for settling the proper exponents of such relations as nominative, genitive, singular, plural, active, and passive, it stands to reason that if such abstruse problems could have been discussed in a language void of inflections, there was no inducement for agreeing on a more perfect means of communication. And as to imagining language, that is to say, nouns and verbs, endowed with an inward principle of growth, all we can say is, that if we only think honestly, we shall find that such a conception is inconceivable. Language may be conceived as a production, but it can never be conceived as a substance that could itself produce.

Nor has the science of language anything to do with mere theories, whether conceivable or not. It collects facts, and its only object is to account for these facts, as far as possible. Instead of looking on inflections in general either as conventional signs or natural excrescences, it takes each termination by itself, establishes its most primitive form by means

---

various sorts are formed, and derivatives from those derivatives. Words are compounded from several roots to express complex ideas. Finally, substantives, adjectives, and pronouns are declined, with gender, number, and case; verbs are conjugated throughout voices, moods, tenses, numbers, and persons, by employing, in like manner, terminations and sometimes augments, which by themselves signify nothing. This method is attended with the advantage of enunciating in a single word the principal idea, frequently greatly modified, and extremely complex already, with its whole array of accessory ideas and mutable relations."¹—*Transactions of the Philological Society*, vol. ii. p. 39.

of comparison, and then treats that primitive syllable as it would treat any other part of language —namely, as something which was originally intended to convey a meaning. Whether we are still able to discover the original intention of every part of language is quite a different question, and it should be admitted at once, that many grammatical forms, after they have been restored to their most primitive type, are still without an explanation. But with every year new discoveries are made by means of careful inductive reasoning. We become more familiar every day with the secret ways of language, and there is no reason to doubt that in the end grammatical analysis will be as successful as chemical analysis. Grammar, though sometimes very bewildering to us in its later stages, is originally a much less formidable undertaking than is commonly supposed. What is Grammar after all but declension and conjugation? Originally declension could not have been anything but the composition of a noun with some other word expressive of number and case. How number could be expressed, we saw in a former chapter. A very similar process led to the formation of cases.

All cases originally local.

In Chinese[1] the locative is formed in various ways; one is by adding such words as *ćung*, the middle, or *néi*, inside. Thus, *kŭŏ-ćung*, in the empire; *i sŭi ćung*, within a year. The instrumental is formed by the preposition *ŷ*, which preposition is an

---
[1] Endlicher, *Chinesische Grammatik*, s. 172.

old root, meaning to *use*. Thus *ỹ ting*, with a stick, where in Latin we should use the ablative, in Greek the dative. Now, however complicated the declensions, regular and irregular, may be in Greek and Latin, we may be certain that originally they were formed by this simple method of composition.

There was originally in all the Aryan languages a most useful case, expressive simply of locality, which grammarians call the *locative*. In Sanskrit every substantive has its locative, as well as its genitive, dative, and accusative. Thus, *heart* in Sanskrit is h r *i* d; in the heart, is h r *i* d-i. Here, therefore, the termination of the locative is simply short *i*. This short *i* may be called a demonstrative root, and there is no reason why the preposition *in* should not be traced back to the same origin. The Sanskrit h r *i* di would thus represent an original compound, as it were, *heart-here*, or *heart-within*, which gradually became settled as one of the recognised cases of nouns ending in consonants. We saw that in Chinese [1] the locative is expressed in the same manner, but with a greater freedom in the choice of the words expressive of locality. 'In the empire,' is expressed by *kŭŏ-ćung*; 'within a year,' is expressed by *i sŭi ćung*. Instead of *ćung*, however, we might have employed other terms, such, for instance, as *nëi*, inside.

It might be said that the formation of so primitive a case as the locative offers little difficulty, but that this process of composition fails to account for the origin of the more abstract cases, the accusative, the

[1] Endlicher, *Chinesische Grammatik*, s. 172.

dative, and the genitive. If we derive our notions of the cases from philosophical grammar, it is true, no doubt, that it would be difficult to realise by simple composition the abstract relations supposed to be expressed by the terminations of the genitive, dative, and accusative. But we should remember that these are only general categories under which philosophers and grammarians have endeavoured to arrange the facts of language. The people with whom language grew up knew nothing of datives and accusatives. Everything that is abstract in language was originally concrete. All relations expressed by the cases, subject, object, predicate, instrument, cause and purpose, were originally conceived as purely local relations.

Before people wanted to say the king of Rome, they really said the king at Rome. The more abstract idea of the genitive had not yet entered into their system of thought. But more than this, it can be proved that the locative has actually taken, in some languages, the place of the genitive. In Accadian the genitive is formed by locative particles, king of the gods being expressed by king among the gods.[1] The *æ* of the Latin genitive was originally *â-i*, that is to say, the old locative in *i*. 'King of Rome,' if rendered by *Rex Romæ*, meant really 'king at Rome.'[2]

And here you will see how the teaching of grammar, which ought to be the most logical of all sciences, is frequently the most illogical. A boy is taught at school, that if he wants to say 'I am staying at

---

[1] Haupt, *Die Sumerisch-Akkadische Sprache*, p. 261.
[2] In Sinhalese the loc. in *e* becomes genitive. Childers, *J.R.A.S.* 1874, p. 41.

Rome,' he must use the genitive to express the locative. How a logician or grammarian can so twist and turn the meaning of the genitive as to make it express rest in a place, it is not for us to inquire; but, if he succeeded, his pupil would at once use the genitive of Carthage (Carthaginis) or of Athens (Athenarum) for the same purpose, and he would then have to be told that these genitives could not be used in the same manner as the genitive of nouns in *a*. How all this is achieved by what is called philosophical grammar, we know not; but comparative grammar at once removes all difficulty. It is only in the first declension that the locative has supplanted the genitive, whereas *Carthaginis* and *Athenarum*, being real genitives, could never be employed to express a locative. A special case, such as the locative, may be generalised into the more general genitive, but not *vice versâ*.

In adopting the opinion of the late Dr. Rosen and of Professor Bopp, who look upon the Latin termination of the genitive singular of feminine nouns in *a* as originally a termination of the locative, I was aware of the objections that had been raised against this view; but I did not feel shaken by them, as little as Professor Bopp, who in the second edition of his *Comparative Grammar* maintains his original explanation of that case. That the relation expressed by the genitive may be rendered by a locative, cannot be disputed, for it is well known that in the dual the locative and genitive cases are in Sanskrit expressed by the same termination. As it could hardly be maintained that an original genitive may be used to convey a local meaning, it would seem to follow that the termination of the locative and genitive dual in *os* conveyed originally a local meaning, and gradually assumed a more general predicative sense. There is no doubt that Latin possessed, like Greek, the regular genitive in *s*. We find ancient forms such as *escas*, *monetas*, *terras*, and *fortunas*, while *familias* has been preserved throughout in *pater familias*. In Oscan, Umbrian, and Sabellian the same genitives occur. (Corssen, i. 769; ii. 722.) It is true also that Latin genitives in *ais* have been established by Ritschl on the evidence of ancient inscriptions, e. g. *Prosepnais*, instead of *Proserpinæ* (see Kuhn's *Zeitschrift*, xii. s. 234, xiii. s. 445); and it has often been pointed out that weakened forms in *aes*, such as *Dianaes*, *Juliaes*, are of more frequent occurrence, and continue in use on inscriptions even under the later emperors. These genitives, however, have now been proved to be Greek rather than Latin forms,[1] and even if it were otherwise, they could never be treated as the original forms from which the ordinary genitive in *di* and *ae* had sprung. The final *s* in Latin is no doubt liable to be dropt; but, as far as I know at present, only after short vowels.[2] Thus we find *ŏ* instead of *us*, *amare* instead of *amaris*, *pote* instead of *potis*; but we never find

---

[1] Corssen, *Aussprache*, 2nd ed. vol. i. p. 686.
[2] I cannot accept the explanation proposed by my learned friend, Professor Kuhn of Berlin, in his essay just published (1866), '*Ueber einige Genetiv und Dativ Bildungen.*' It seems to me to contravene three phonetic rules: 1. that no final *s* in Sanskrit is lost before a surd consonant; 2. that no final *s* in Latin is lost after a long vowel; 3. that no medial *s* in Sanskrit is lost before *y*. The verb *ogāyate* does not invalidate the last rule, for its real base is *oga*, not *ogas*. See also *The Academy*, Jan. 1871, p. 103.

mensî in the dative, or *mensâ* in the accusative plural, instead of *mensîs* and *mensâs*. The only other case where a final *s* is supposed to have been lost after a long vowel is in the nominative plural of the second declension, where forms such as *magistreis* occur in ancient Latin, by the side of *magistrî*. But it has never been proved that *magistrî* was a corruption of *magistris*. On the contrary, *magistrî* belongs to an earlier date than *magistris*,[1] and the latter is probably formed from a secondary base, *magistri*, instead of *magistro*, just as we find the base *acri* by the side of the base *acro*.[2]

We see thus by one instance how what grammarians call a genitive was formed by the same process of composition which we can watch in Chinese, and which we can prove to have taken place in the original language of the Aryas. And the same applies to the dative. If a boy is told that the dative expresses a relation of one object to another, less direct than that of the accusative, he may well wonder how such a flying arch could ever have been built up with the scanty materials which language has at her disposal; but he will be still more surprised if, after having realised this grammatical abstraction, he is told that in Greek, in order to convey the very definite idea of being in a place, he has to use after certain nouns the termination of the dative. 'I am staying at Salamis,' must be expressed by the dative *Salamînî*. If you ask why? comparative grammar again can alone give an answer. The termination of the Greek dative in *î* was likewise a local termination.

[1] Corssen, *Aussprache*, 2nd ed. vol. i. p. 753. [2] Ibid. *l. c.* vol. i. p. 756.

CHAPTER IX.

The locative may well convey the meaning of the dative, but the faded features of the dative can never express the freshness and distinctness of the locative. The dative *Salamîni* was first a locative. 'I live at Salamis,' never conveyed the meaning, 'I live to Salamis.' On the contrary, the dative, in such phrases as 'I give it to the father,' was originally a locative; and after expressing at first the palpable relation of 'I give it unto the father,' or 'I place it on or in the father,' it gradually assumed the more general, and less local, less coloured aspect which logicians and grammarians ascribe to their datives.

If the explanation just given of some of the cases in Greek and Latin should seem too artificial or too forced, we should remember that there are languages which have one case only and that a locative.

The Algonquins, for instance, admit but one case which expresses locality.[1] The Shambalas have one case-termination only, namely, *i*, which expresses in, at, or near.[2] But we can see exactly the same process much nearer home and repeated under our own eyes. The most abstract relations of the genitive, as, for instance, 'the immortality of the soul' (*l'immortalité de l'âme*); or of the dative, as, for instance, 'I trust myself to God' (*je me fie à Dieu*), are expressed by prepositions, such as *de* and *ad*, which in Latin had the distinct local meanings of 'down from' and 'towards.' Nay, the English *of* and *to*, which have taken the place of the German terminations *s* and *m*,

---

[1] *Du Ponceau*, p. 158.
[2] *Collections for a Handbook of the Shambala Language*, p. 3, Zanzibar, 1867.

are likewise prepositions of an originally local character. The only difference between our cases and those of the ancient languages consists in this, that the determining element is now placed before the word, whereas, in the original language of the Aryas, it was placed at the end.

It is generally supposed that the nominative and accusative cases differ from the rest, and it is well known that by the Greeks the nominative was not looked upon as a case at all. Yet, if the nominative has a termination of its own, say the masculine *s*, that too was originally local or demonstrative. It started from the local concept of *here*, or *this*, while the accusative expressed at first the local relation of *thither*. To strike a tree was originally to strike towards a tree, just as to go to Rome, *Romam eo*, was, I move towards Rome.

Verbal Terminations.

What applies to the cases of nouns, applies with equal truth to the terminations of verbs. It may seem difficult to discover in the personal terminations of Greek and Latin the exact pronouns which were added to a verbal base in order to express *I* love, *thou* lovest, *he* loves; but it stands to reason that originally these terminations must have been the same in all languages—namely, personal pronouns. We may be puzzled by the terminations of *thou lovest* and *he loves*, where *st* and *s* can hardly be identified with the modern *thou* and *he*; but we have only to place all the Aryan dialects together, and we shall see at once that they point back to an original set of terminations which can easily be brought to tell their own story.

Yes'r and Yes'm.

Let us begin with quite modern formations, because we have here more daylight for watching the intricate and sometimes wayward movements of language; or better still, let us begin with an imaginary case, or with what may be called the language of the future, in order to see quite clearly how what we should call grammatical forms may arise. Let us suppose that the slaves in America were to rise against their masters, and, after gaining some victories, were to sail back in large numbers to some part of Central Africa, beyond the reach of their white enemies or friends. Let us suppose these men availing themselves of the lessons they had learnt in their captivity, and gradually working out a civilisation of their own. It is quite possible that, some centuries hence, a new Livingstone might find among the descendants of the American slaves, a language, a literature, laws, and manners, bearing a striking similitude to those of his own country. What an interesting problem for any future historian and ethnologist! Yet there are problems in the past history of the world of equal interest, which have been and are still to be solved by the student of language.

I believe that a careful examination of the language of the descendants of those escaped slaves would suffice to determine with perfect certainty their past history, even though no documents and no tradition had preserved the story of their captivity and liberation. At first, no doubt, the threads might seem hopelessly entangled. A missionary might surprise the scholars of Europe by an account of a new African language. He might describe it at first as very imperfect—as a language, for instance, so poor that the same word had to be used to express the most heterogeneous ideas. He might point out how the same sound, without any change of accent, meant *true*, a *ceremony*, a *workman*, and was used also as a verb in the sense of literary composition. All these, he might say, are expressed in that strange dialect by the sound *rait* (right, rite, wright, write). He might likewise observe that this dialect, in this respect, as poor almost as Chinese, had hardly any grammatical inflections, and that it had no genders, except in a few words such as man-of-war and a railway-engine, which were both conceived as feminine beings, and spoken of as *she*. He might then mention an even more extraordinary feature, namely, that although this language had no terminations for the masculine and feminine genders of nouns, it employed a masculine and feminine termination after the affirmative particle, according as it was addressed to a lady or a gentleman. Their affirmative particle being the same as the English *Yes*, they added a final *r* to it, when addressed to a man, and a final *m*, when addressed to a lady: that is to say, instead of simply saying *Yes*, these descendants of the escaped American slaves said *Yesr* to a man, and *Yesm* to a lady.

Absurd as this may sound, I can assure you that the descriptions which are given of the dialects of savage tribes, as explained for the first time by travellers or missionaries, are often even more extraordinary. But let us consider now what the student of language would have to do, if such forms as *Yes'r* and *Yes'm* were, for the first time, brought under his notice. He would first have to trace them back historically, as far as possible, to their more original types, and if he discovered their connection with *Yes Sir* and *Yes Ma'm*, he would point out how such contractions were most likely to spring up in a vulgar dialect. After having traced back the *Yesr* and *Yesm* of the free African negroes to the idiom of their former American masters, the etymologist would next inquire how such phrases as *Yes Sir* and *Yes Madam* came to be used on the American continent.

Finding nothing analogous in the dialects of the aboriginal inhabitants of America, he would be led, by a mere comparison of words, to the languages of Europe, and here again, first to the language of England. Even if no historical documents had been preserved, the documents of language would show that the white masters whose language the ancestors of the free Africans adopted during their servitude, came originally from England, and, within certain limits, it would even be possible to fix the time when the English language was first transplanted to America. That language must have passed at least the age of Chaucer before it migrated to the New World. For Chaucer has two affirmative particles, *Yea* and *Yes*, and he distinguishes between the two. He uses *Yes* only in answer to negative questions. For instance, in answer to 'Does he not go?' he would say *Yes*. In all other cases Chaucer uses *Yea*.

To a question, 'Does he go?' he would answer *Yea*. He observes the same distinction between *No* and *Nay*, the former being used after negative, the latter after all other questions. This distinction became obsolete soon after Sir Thomas More,[1] and it must have become obsolete before phrases such as *Yes Sir* and *Yes Madam* could have assumed their stereotyped character.

But there is still more historical information to be gained from these phrases. The word *Yea* is Anglo-Saxon, the same as the German *Ja*, and it therefore reveals the fact that the white masters of the American slaves who crossed the Atlantic after the time of Chaucer, had crossed the Channel at a still earlier period, after leaving the continental fatherland of the Angles and Saxons. The words *Sir* and *Madam* tell us still more. They are Norman words, and they could only have been imposed on the Anglo-Saxons of Britain by Norman conquerors. They tell us more than this. For these Normans or Northmen spoke originally a Teutonic dialect, closely allied to Anglo-Saxon, and in that dialect words such as *Sir* and *Madam* could never have sprung up. We may conclude, therefore, that, previous to the Norman conquest, the Teutonic Northmen must have made a sufficiently long stay in one of the Roman provinces to forget their own and adopt the language of the Roman provincials.

We may now trace back the Norman *Madam* to the French *Madame*, and we recognise in this a corruption of the Latin *Mea domina*, my mistress.

[1] Marsh, *Lectures*, p. 579.

Domina was changed into *domna, donna*, and *dame*; and the same word *dame* was also used as a masculine in the sense of lord, as a corruption of *domino, domno,* and *donno.* The temporal lord ruling as ecclesiastical seigneur under the bishop, was called a *vidame,* as the vidame of Chartres, &c. The French interjection *Dame!* has no connection with a similar exclamation in English, but it simply means Lord! *Dame-Dieu* in Old French is Lord God.[1] A derivative of *Domina,* mistress, was *dominicella,* which became *Demoiselle* and *Damsel.* The masculine *Dame* for *Domino,* Lord, was afterwards replaced by the Latin *Senior,* a translation possibly of the German *elder.* This word *elder* was a title of honour, as we see in *alderman* and in the Anglo-Saxon *ealdor.* The title *Senior,* meaning originally *elder,* was but rarely [2] applied to ladies as a title of honour. *Senior(em)* was changed into *Seigneur, Seigneur* into *Sieur. Senior* (nom.) was contracted to *sendre,* which is found in the Oath of Strassburg (ninth century) as *Carlos meos sendra.* From this *sendre,* passing through *sindre

---

[1] *Dame-Dieu* :—

'Ja dame Dieus non vuelha Qu'en ma colpa sia'l departimens.' (Que jamais le Seigneur Dieu ne veuille Qu'en ma faute soit la séparation.) (*Anc. Franç.*) 'Grandes miracles fit dames Dex par lui.' (*Roman de Garin,* Du Cange, tom. ii. col. 16, 19.)—Raynouard, *Lexique,* s.v. Don.

Le latin *dominus* était devenu en vieux-français *damne, dan*; mais c'est en catalan que ce mot atteignit les dernières limites de l'ecthlipse, car il se réduisit à deux et même à une seule lettre. On disait tantôt *En,* tantôt *N,* avec un nom propre d'homme : *En Ramon, N Aymes, don Raimon, don Aimes.* On dirait *Ena, Na,* de *domina* avec un nom de femme : *Ena Maria, Na Isabella, dame Marie, dame Isabelle.*— Terrien Poncel, *Du Langage,* p. 791; Chevallet, t. ii. p. 161.

[2] In Old Portuguese, Diez mentions *senhor rainha, mia sennor formosa,* my beautiful mistress.

and *sidre, was derived Sire, unless we prefer, with Bartsch, to derive it direct from se(n)ior.

Thus we see how in two short phrases, such as *Yesr* and *Yesm*, long chapters of history might be read. If a general destruction of books, such as took place in China under the Emperor Thsin-chi-hoang-ti (213 B.C.), should sweep away all historical documents, language, even in its most depraved state, would preserve some of the secrets of the past, and would tell future generations of the home and migrations of their ancestors from the East to the West Indies.

East Indies and West Indies.

It may seem startling at first to find the same name, the *East Indies* and the *West Indies*, at the two extremities of the Aryan migrations; but these very names again are full of historical meaning. They tell us how the Teutonic race, the most vigorous and enterprising of all the members of the Aryan family, gave the name of *West Indies* to the country which, in their world-compassing migrations, they imagined to be India itself; how they discovered their mistake, and then distinguished between the East Indies and West Indies; how they planted new states in the west, and regenerated the effete kingdoms in the east; how they preached Christianity, and at last practised it by abolishing slavery of body and mind among the slaves of West Indian landholders, and the slaves of Brahmanical soulholders, until they greeted at last the very homes from which the Aryan family had started, when setting out on their discovery of the world. All this, and even more, may be read in the vast archives of language. The very name of India has a story to tell, for India is not a native name. We have it from the Romans, the Romans from the Greeks, the Greeks from the Persians. And why from the Persians? Because it is only in Persian that an initial *s* is changed into *h*, which initial *h* was, as usual, dropped in Greek. It is only in Persian that the country of the Sindhu (sindhu is the Sanskrit name for *river*), or of the *seven* sindhus, could have been called *Hindia* or *India*, instead of *Sindia*. Unless the followers of Zoroaster had pronounced every *s* like *h*, we should never have heard of the West Indies!

Grammatical Terminations.

We have thus seen by an imaginary instance what we must be prepared for in the growth of language, and we shall arrive at exactly the same result, if we analyse real grammatical forms such as we find them in ancient languages. The *s*, for instance, of the third person singular, he loves, can be proved to have been the demonstrative pronoun of the third person. The termination of the third person singular of the present is ti in Sanskrit. Thus dâ, to give, becomes dadâti, he gives: dhâ, to place; dadhâti, he places.

In Greek this ti is changed into *si*; just as the Sanskrit tvam, the Latin *tu*, thou, appears in Greek as *sy*. Thus Greek *didōsi* corresponds to Sanskrit dadâti; *tithēsi* to dadhâti. This intervocalic *s*, as it represents an original *t*, ought not to have been elided in Greek. But as there are many words in Greek in which, according to a general rule, an original *s* between two vowels has been elided, the influence of analogy seems to have wrought the same change from *typteti, *typtesi to typtei, as from *genesi to genei. Other scholars, however, admit a different kind of analogy for these new formations. The Latin drops the final *i*, and instead of *ti* has *t*. Thus we get *amat, dicit*.

Now there is a law, commonly called Grimm's Law. According to it every tenuis in Latin is in Gothic represented by its corresponding aspirate. Hence, instead of *t*, we should expect in Gothic *th*; and so we find indeed in Gothic *habaip*, instead of Latin *habet*. This aspirate likewise appears in Anglo-Saxon, where *he loves* is *lufath*. It is preserved in the Biblical *he loveth*, and it is only in modern English that it gradually sank down to *s*. In the *s* of *he loves*, therefore, we have a demonstrative root, added to the predicative root *love*, and this *s* is originally the same as the Sanskrit ti. This ti again must be traced back to the demonstrative root ta, this or there, which exists in the Sanskrit demonstrative pronoun tad, the Greek *to*, the Gothic *thata*, the English *that*; and which in Latin we can trace in *talis, tantus, tunc, tam*, and even in *tamen*, an old locative in *men*.

We have thus seen that what we call the third person singular of the present is in reality a simple compound of a predicative root with a demonstrative root. It is a compound like any other, only that the second part is not predicative, but simply demonstrative. As in pay-master we predicate pay of master, meaning a person whose office it is to pay, so in dadâ-ti, *give-he*, the ancient framers of language simply predicated giving of some third person, and this synthetic proposition, *give-he*, is the same as what we now call the third person singular in the indicative mood of the present tense in the active voice.

We shall now better understand why it must be laid down as a fundamental principle in Comparative Grammar to look upon nothing in language as merely formal, till every attempt has been made to trace the formal elements of language back to their original and substantial prototypes. We are accustomed to the idea of grammatical terminations modifying the meaning of words. But words can be modified by words only; and though in the present state of our science it would be too much to say that all grammatical terminations have been traced back to original independent words, so many of them have, even in cases where only a single letter was left, that we may well lay it down as a rule that all formal elements of language were originally substantial. Suppose English had never been written down before the times of Piers Ploughman. What should we make of such a form as *nadistou*,[1] instead of *ne hadst thou*? *Ne rechi*, instead of *I reck not*? *Al ô'm* in Dorsetshire is *all of them*. *I midden*, is *I may not*; *I cooden*, *I could not*. Yet the changes which Sanskrit had undergone before it was reduced to writing, may have been more considerable by far than what we see in these dialects.[2]

---

[1] Marsh, *Lectures*, p. 387. Barnes, *Poems in Dorsetshire Dialect*.
[2] In Anglo-Saxon we find *nát* for *ne wát*, I do not know; *nist* for he

The Romanic Future.

Let us now look to modern classical languages such as French and Italian. Most of their grammatical terminations are the same as in Latin, only changed by phonetic corruption. Thus *j'aime* is *ego amo*; *tu'aimes, tu amas*; *il aime, ille amat*. There was originally a final *t* in French *il aime*, and it comes out again in such phrases as *aime-t-il?* Thus the French imperfect corresponds to the Latin imperfect, the parfait défini to the Latin perfect. But what about the French future? There is no similarity between *amabo* and *j'aimerai*. Here then we have a new grammatical form, sprung up, as it were, within the recollection of men; or, at least, in the broad daylight of history. Now did the termination *rai* bud forth like a blossom in spring? or did some wise people meet together to invent this new termination, and pledge themselves to use it instead of the old termination *bo*? Certainly not. We see first of all that in all the Romance languages the terminations of the future are identical with the auxiliary verb *to have*.[1] In French you find—

j'ai	and	je chanter-ai	nous avons	and	nous chanterons
tu as	,,	tu chanter-as	vous avez	,,	vous chanterez
il a	,,	il chanter-a	ils ont	,,	ils chanteront.

But besides this, we actually find in Spanish and Provençal the apparent termination of the future used as an independent word and not yet joined to

did not know; *niston* for they did not know; *nolde, noldest,* for I would not, thou wouldst not; *nyle* for I will not; *næbbe* for I have not; *næfth* for he has not; *næron* for they were not, &c.

[1] M. M., *Survey of Languages,* p. 21.

the infinitive. We find in Spanish, instead of '*lo haré*,' I shall do it, the more primitive form *hacer lo he*, i.e. *facere id habeo*. We find in Provençal *dir vos ai* instead of *je vous dirai*; *dir vos em* instead of *nous vous dirons*. There can be no doubt, therefore, that the Romance future was originally a compound of the auxiliary verb *to have* with an infinitive; and *I have to say* easily took the meaning of *I shall say*.[1]

Here, then, we see clearly how grammatical forms arise. An ordinary Frenchman looks upon his futures as merely grammatical forms. He has no idea, unless he is a scholar, that the terminations of his futures are identical with the auxiliary verb *avoir*. The Roman too had no suspicion that *amabo* was a compound; but it can now be proved to contain an auxiliary verb as clearly as the French future. The Latin future was destroyed by means of phonetic corruption. When the final letters lost their distinct pronunciation it became impossible to keep the imperfect *amabam* separate from the future *amabo*. The future was then replaced by dialectical regeneration, for the use of *habeo* with an infinitive is found in Latin, in such expressions as *habeo dicere*, I have to say, which would imperceptibly glide into I shall say.[2] In fact, wherever we look, we see that the future is expressed by means of composition. We

---

[1] The first, as far as I know, who thus explained the origin of the Romance future was *Castelvetro* in his *Correttione* (Basilea, 1577. He says: 'Ciò è con lo 'nfinito del verbo, e col presente del verbo Ho, come Amare Ho, Amare Hai, Amare Ha. Leggere Ho, Leggere Hai, Leggere Ha, e così gli altri.' p. 111.

[2] Fuchs, *Romanische Sprachen*, s. 344.

have in English *I shall* and *thou wilt*, which mean originally *I am bound* and *thou intendest*. In German we use *werden*, the Gothic *vairthan*, which means originally to go, to turn towards. In modern Greek we find *thelō*, I will, in *thelō dōsein*, I shall give. In Roumansch we meet with *vegnir*, to come, forming the future *veng a vegnir*, I shall come; whereas in French *je viens de dire*, I come from saying, is equivalent to 'I have just said.' The French *je vais dire* is almost a future, though originally it is *vado dicere*, I go to say. The Dorsetshire, 'I be gwâin to goo a-pickèn stuones,' is another case in point. Nor is there any doubt that in the Latin *bo* of *amabo* we have the old auxiliary *bhû*, to become; and in the Greek future in σω, the old auxiliary *as*, to be.[1]

[1] The Greek term for the future is ὁ μέλλων, and μέλλω is used as an auxiliary verb to form certain futures in Greek. It has various meanings, but they can all be traced back to the Sanskrit man (manyate), to think. As anya, other, stands by the side of ἄλλος, so manye, I think, by the side of μέλλω. *Il.* ii. 39: θήσειν ἔτ' ἔμελλεν ἐπ' ἀλγεά τε στοναχάς τε Τρωσί τε καὶ Δαναοῖσι, 'he still thought to lay sufferings on Trojans and Greeks.' *Il.* xxiii. 544: μέλλεις ἀφαιρήσεσθαι ἄεθλον, 'thou thinkest thou wouldst have stripped me of the prize.' *Od.* xiii. 293: οὐκ ἄρ' ἔμελλες λήξειν, 'did you not think of stopping?' i.e. were you not going to stop? Or again in such phrases as *Il.* ii. 36, τὰ οὐ τελέεσθαι ἔμελλον, 'these things were not meant to be accomplished,' literally, these things did not mean to be accomplished. Thus μέλλω was used of things that were likely to be, as if these things themselves meant or intended to be or not to be; and, the original meaning being forgotten, μέλλω came to be a mere auxiliary expressing probability. Μέλλω and μέλλομαι, in the sense of 'to hesitate,' are equally explained by the Sanskrit man, to think or consider. In Old Norse the future is likewise formed by muna, to mean. It is perfectly true that *ny* is not changed to *ll*, but that *an* and *al* are parallel pronominal elements, is shown by Sk. anyonya, Gr. ἀλλήλων. On *l* representing *n*, see Curtius, p. 450.

The Teutonic Weak Preterite.

We now go back another step, and ask the question which we asked many times before, How can a mere *d* produce so momentous a change as that from *I love* to *I loved*? As we have learnt in the meantime that English goes back to Anglo-Saxon, and is closely related to continental Saxon and Gothic, we look at once to the Gothic imperfect in order to see whether it has preserved any traces of the original compound; for, after what we have seen in the previous cases, we are no doubt prepared to find here, too, grammatical terminations as mere remnants of independent words.

In Gothic there is a verb *nasjan*, to nourish. Its preterite is as follows:—

Singular	Dual	Plural
nas-i-da	nas-i-dêdu	nas-i-dêdum
nas-i-dês	nas-i-dêduts	nas-i-dêduþ
nas-i-da	——	nas-i-dêdun

The subjunctive of the preterite:

nas-i-dêdjau	nas-i-dêdeiva	nas-i-dêdeima
nas-i-dêdeis	nas-i-dêdeits	nas-i-dêdeiþ
nas-i-dêdi	——	nas-i-dêdeina

This is reduced in Anglo-Saxon to

Singular	Plural
ner-e-de	ner-e-don
ner-e-des(t)	ner-e-don
ner-e-de	ner-e-don

Subjunctive:

ner-e-de	ner-e-den
ner-e-de	ner-e-den

ANALYSIS OF LANGUAGE. 351

Let us now look to the auxiliary verb *to do*, in Anglo-Saxon:

Singular	Plural
dyde	dydon
dydes(t)	dydon
dyde	dydon

If we had only the Anglo-Saxon preterite *nerede* and the Anglo-Saxon *dyde*, the identity of the *de* in *nerede* with *dyde* would not be very apparent. But here you will perceive the advantage which Gothic has over all other Teutonic dialects for the purposes of grammatical comparison and analysis. It is in Gothic, and in Gothic in the plural only, that the full terminations *dêdum*, *dêdup*, *dêdun* have been preserved. In the Gothic singular *nasida*, *nasidês*, *nasida* represent an original, though perhaps never realised, **nasideda*, **nasidedês*, **nasideda*. The same has taken place in Anglo-Saxon, not only in the singular, but in the plural also. Yet such is the similarity between Gothic and Anglo-Saxon that we cannot doubt their preterites having been formed on the same last. If there be any truth in inductive reasoning, there must have been an original Anglo-Saxon preterite:[1]

Singular	Plural
ner-e-dyde	ner-e-dydon
ner-e-dydest	ner-e-dydon
ner-e-dyde	ner-e-dydon

And if *ner-e-dyde* dwindled down to *nerede*, *nerede* could, in modern English, become *nered*. The *d* of the preterite, therefore, which changes *I love* into *I*

[1] Bopp, *Comparative Grammar*, § 620. Grimm, *German Grammar*, ii. 845.

loved is originally the auxiliary verb *to do*, and *I loved* is the same as *I love did,* or *I did love*. In English dialects—as, for instance, in the Dorset dialect—every preterite, if it expresses a lasting or repeated action, is formed by *I did*,[1] and a distinction is thus established between ''e died eesterdae,' and 'the vo'ke did die by scores'; though originally *died* is the same as *die did*. In the spoken Flemish, as Mr. G. Gezelle informs me, the ordinary preterite is *Ik hoorde, Gij hoordet, Hij hoorde, Wij hoorden, Gij hoordet, Zij hoorden*. But the common people frequently use *Ik hoordede* and *Ik hoordege, Wij hoordeden* and *Wij hoordegen, Gij hoordedet* and *Gij hoordegen, Zij hoordeden* and *Zij hoordegen*. *I did* is expressed in the same dialect by *Ik dede* and *Ik dege*.

It might be asked, however, very properly, how *did* itself, or the Anglo-Saxon *dide*, was formed, and how it received the meaning of a preterite. In *dide* the final *de* is not a termination, but it is the root, and the first syllable *di* is the reduplication of the root. All preterites of old, or, as they are called, strong verbs, were formed as in Greek and Sanskrit by means of reduplication, reduplication being one of the principal means by which roots were invested with a verbal character.[2] The root *dô* in Anglo-Saxon is the same as the root *thē* in *tithēmi* in Greek, and the Sanskrit root dhâ in dadhâmi. Anglo-Saxon *dyde* would therefore correspond to Sanskrit dadhe, I placed, I made, I did.

This explanation, which at the time when Bopp

[1] Barnes, *Dorsetshire Dialect*, p. 39.
[2] See M. M.'s *Letter on the Turanian Languages*, pp. 44, 46.

proposed it, seemed so self-evident, has since been called in question, but nothing better has as yet been suggested in its place. I quite admit the difficulty applying to weak preterites such as *mah-ta, kun-tha, wis-sa,* &c., which point to an original *t*, not *dh*. But I do not see the same difficulty with regard to preterites such as *nasida*. It was Begemann who in 1873 (*Das schwache Praeteritum der germanischen Sprachen*) and again in 1874 (*Zur Bedeutung des schwachen Praeteritums*) called attention to this difficulty. Windisch adopted the same view (Kuhn's *Beiträge*, 1876), and Möller defended it more strongly still (Kölbing's *Englische Studien*, 1880). Still, Paul was not convinced by their arguments (Paul und Braune, *Beiträge*, 1880, p. 136), and Möller had once more to defend his position (ibid., p. 457). That position, in its negative character, is no doubt a strong one, but it is weak in its positive suggestions. To derive, as Begemann suggested, the weak preterites from the participle in *t*, such as *mah-t-s* in Gothic, is without any analogy. To take the *t* for a secondary verbal suffix, as in κρύπ-τω, *plec-to*, O. H. G. *fleh-t-an*, is impossible, because that *t* is permanent, and does not mark the preterite. We may leave the question an open one, but it will require stronger arguments than any which have been hitherto produced before we can admit that Gothic forms such as *nas-i-dédum, nas-i-déduþ, nas-i-dédun* have not been produced under the influence of *dédum, *déduþ, *dédun, we did, you did, they did.[1]

[1] The whole question has been fully treated by T. Le Marchant Douse, *Introduction to the Gothic of Ulfilas*, 1886, § 81. He is not

In this manner a considerable portion of the grammatical framework of the Aryan or Indo-European languages has been traced back to original independent words, and even the slightest changes which at first sight seem so mysterious, such as *foot* into *feet*, or *I find* into *I found*, have been fully accounted for. This is what is called comparative grammar, or a scientific analysis of all the formal elements of a language, preceded by a comparison of all the varieties which one and the same form has assumed in the numerous dialects of the Aryan family. The most important dialects for this purpose are Sanskrit, Greek, Latin, and Gothic; but in many cases Zend, or Celtic, or Slavonic dialects come in to throw an unexpected light on forms unintelligible in any of the four principal dialects. The result of such a work as Bopp's *Comparative Grammar* of the Aryan languages may be summed up in a few words. The general framework of grammar, the elements of derivation, declension, and conjugation, had become settled before the separation of the Aryan family. Hence the broad outlines of grammar in Sanskrit, Greek, Latin, Gothic, and the rest, are in reality the same: and the apparent differences can be explained either by dialectic growth, or by phonetic corruption, which is determined by the phonetic peculiarities of each nation. After the grammatical terminations of all these languages have been traced back to their most primitive

prepared to give up the composition theory as recently modified. Collitz, in the *American Journal of Philology*, 1888, vol. ix. No. 1, inclines towards the participial theory. The chief difficulty lies in the terminations of the singular, where *dap, dast, dap* would be expected, representing an original *daidô, daidôst, daidô*. See Douse, pp. 186, 187.

forms, it is possible, in many instances, to determine their original meaning.

We need not say that *mi* and *mas, ti* or *nti*, are directly derived from *mad* or *tad*, but that they are parallel forms of their pronominal stems cannot be doubted. In many cases, no doubt, we can only guess, but the sphere of our guesses is closely limited. The period during which, as in the Provençal *dir vos ai*, the component elements of the old Aryan grammar maintained a separate existence in the language and the mind of the Aryas, had closed long before Sanskrit was Sanskrit or Greek Greek. That, however, there was such a period, we can doubt as little as we can doubt the real existence of fern forests previous to the formation of our coal fields.

Aryan Civilisation.

We can even go a step further. Suppose we had no remnants of Latin; suppose the very existence of Rome and of Latin were unknown to us; we might still prove, on the evidence of the six Romanic dialects, that there must have been a time when these dialects formed the language of a small settlement; nay, by collecting the words which all these dialects share in common, we might to a certain extent reconstruct the original language, and draw a sketch of the state of civilisation, as reflected by these common words. The same can be done if we compare Sanskrit, Greek, Latin, Gothic, Celtic, and Slavonic. The words which have as nearly as possible the same form and meaning in all the languages must have existed before the people, who afterwards formed the prominent nationalities of the Aryan family, separated; and, if carefully interpreted, they, too, will serve as evidence as to the state of civilisation attained by the Aryas before they left their common home. It can be proved by the evidence of language, that before their separation the Aryas led the life of agricultural nomads—a life such as Tacitus describes that of the ancient Germans. They knew the arts of ploughing, of making roads, of building ships, of weaving and sewing, of erecting houses; they had counted at least as far as one hundred. They had domesticated the most important animals, the cow, the horse, the sheep, the dog; they were acquainted with the most useful metals, and armed with hatchets, whether for peaceful or warlike purposes. They had recognised the bonds of blood and the laws of marriage; they followed their leaders and kings, and the distinction between right and wrong was fixed by customs and laws. They were impressed with the idea of a Divine Being, invoked by various names. All this, as I said, can be proved by the evidence of language. For if you find that languages like Greek, Latin, Gothic, Celtic, or Slavonic, which, after their first separation, could have had but little contact with Sanskrit, have the same word, for instance, for metal which exists in Sanskrit, this is proof absolute that some kind of metal was wrought previous to the Aryan separation. Now, metal or ore is *ais* in Gothic, *ár* in Anglo-Saxon, *æs* in Latin, and *áyas* in Sanskrit, a word which, as it could not have been borrowed by the Indians from the Germans or by the Germans from the Indians, must have existed previous to their separation. We could not find the same name for house in Sanskrit, Greek, Latin, Slavonic, and Celtic,[1] unless houses had been known before the separation of these dialects. In this manner a history of Aryan civilisation has been written from the archives of language, stretching back to times far beyond the reach of any documentary history.[2]

Horne Tooke.

It is true, no doubt, that we owe this insight into the true nature of language chiefly to the study of Comparative Philology, such as it has been carried on since the discovery of Sanskrit. But the conviction that all which is now purely formal in language was originally material, that terminations had not always been terminations, but were originally independent words, that the wonderful edifice of language was built up in fact with a limited number of stones—all this had been seen by philosophers who knew nothing of Sanskrit. However wild some of his speculations may appear to us now, the true nature of grammatical elements was clearly perceived by Horne Tooke in his *Diversions of Purley*, first published in 1786. This is what he wrote of terminations:[3]—

'For though I think I have good reasons to believe that all terminations may likewise be traced to their respective origin; and that, however artificial they may now appear to us, they were not originally the effect of premeditated and deliberate *art*, but separate

---

[1] Sansk. dama; Greek, δόμος; Lat. *domus*; Slav. *domŭ*; Celt. *daimh*.
[2] See M. M.'s *Essay on Comparative Mythology*, Oxford Essays, 1856, and *Biographies of Words*, 1888, pp. 128 seq.
[3] *Diversions of Purley*, p. 190.

words by length of time corrupted and coalescing with the words of which they are now considered as the terminations; yet this was less likely to be suspected by others. And if it had been suspected, they would have had much further to travel to their journey's end, and through a road much more embarrassed; as the corruption in those languages is of much longer standing than in ours, and more complex.'

When we have once seen how grammatical terminations are to be traced back in the beginning to independent words, we have learnt at the same time that the component elements of language, which remain in our crucible at the end of a complete grammatical analysis, are of two kinds, namely, *Roots predicative* and *Roots demonstrative*.

We call *root* or *radical* whatever in the words of any language or family of languages cannot be reduced to a simpler or more original form. We assert nothing more about these *residua*, we simply say, they are ultimate, and cannot be traced back to simpler elements. There have been long controversies as to whether these roots ever existed as actual words. The answer is simple enough. From a logical point of view, a root, as soon as it is used as a noun or a verb, can no longer be called a root, though phonetically the root may be identical with the noun. But from a purely historical point of view, there can be no doubt that there are roots which, as far as sound is concerned, remain perfectly unchanged when used as nouns.

There is another controversy, more especially with regard to Sanskrit roots, whether they should be represented as monosyllabic or as dissyllabic, whether in their strong (Guna) or in their weak form. If we keep strictly to our definition that a root is what cannot be reduced to a simpler form, it follows that we must give, for instance, *GAN*, not *GANA*, as the root meaning to beget. We might, no doubt, go a step further, and give GN as the last residue of our analysis, but the objection to this is that GN would be no longer pronounceable. For the same reason it seems preferable to give BUDH (πυθ) as the root, not BEUDH or BHEUDH (πευθ), because the e of Guna can be accounted for and removed, without destroying the character of the root.

Still, these questions are of small moment, and may be settled according to the taste of different scholars. What is of importance is that we should see that these so-called roots, the *residua* of our grammatical analysis, are vital elements, and permeate the whole body of language.

This may be shown, either by tracing back a number of words in Sanskrit, Greek, and Latin to their common root, or by taking a root, after it has once been discovered, and following it through its wanderings from language to language. The latter course is perhaps the more useful, as placing before our eyes the actual growth of an Aryan root.

The Root AR.

This root AR[1] means *to plough*, to stir the soil. From it we have the Latin *ar-are*, the Greek *ar-oun*, the Irish *ar*, the Lithuanian *ar-ti*, the Russian *ora-ti*,

---

[1] AR might be identified with the Sanskrit root **ar**, to go (Pott, *Etymologische Forschungen*, i. 218); but for our present purposes the root AR, to stir, is sufficient.

the Gothic *ar-jan*, the Anglo-Saxon *er-ian*, the modern English *to ear*. Shakespeare says (Richard II. III. 2), 'to ear the land that has some hope to grow.' We read in Deut. xxi. 4, 'a rough valley which is neither eared nor sown.'

From this we have the name of the plough, or the instrument of earing: in Latin, *ara-trum*; in Greek, *aro-tron*; in Bohemian, *ora-dlo*; in Lithuanian, *urkla-s*; in Cornish, *aradar*; in Welsh, *arad*;[1] in Old Norse, *ardhr*. In Old Norse, however, *ardhr*, meaning originally the plough, came to mean earnings or wealth; the plough being, in early times, the most essential possession and means of livelihood. In the same manner the Latin name for money, *pecunia*, was derived from *pecus*, cattle; the word *fee*, which is now restricted to the payment made to a doctor or lawyer, was in Old English *feh*, and in Anglo-Saxon *feoh*, meaning cattle and wealth; for *feoh* and Gothic *faihu* are really the same word as the Latin *pecus*, the modern German *vieh*.

The act of ploughing is called *aratio* in Latin; *arosis* in Greek: and I believe that *arôma*, too, in the sense of perfume, had the same origin. To derive *arôma* from the root *ghrâ*, to smell, is difficult, because there are no parallel cases in which an initial *gh* is dropt in Greek and replaced by *a*. But *arôma* occurs not only in the sense of sweet herbs, but likewise in that of field-fruits in general, such as barley and others. The general meaning, therefore,

---

[1] If, as has been supposed, the Cornish and Welsh words were corruptions of the Latin *arâtrum*, they would have appeared as *areuder*, *arawd*, respectively.

of the word may have become restricted, like that of *spices*, originally *espèces*, and herbs of the field or *arómata*, particularly those offered at sacrifices, may have assumed the sense of sweet herbs.[1]

A more primitive formation of the root ar seems to be the Greek *era*, earth, the Sanskrit irâ and idâ, the Old High-German *ëro*, the Gaelic *ire*, *irionn*. It meant originally the ploughed land, afterwards earth in general. Even the word *earth*, the Gothic *airtha*,[2] the Anglo-Saxon *eorthe*, must have been taken originally in the sense of ploughed or cultivated land. The derivative *ar-mentum*, formed like *ju-mentum*, would naturally have been applied to any animal fit for ploughing and other labour in the field, whether ox or horse.[3]

The Latin *arvus*, ploughed, and *arvum*, field, and the Greek ἄρουρα have been traced back by Benfey to the same root.[4] *Ar-vus* would be formed like pak-va,

---

[1] I retract a guess which I expressed in former editions that *aróma* may have meant originally the smell of a ploughed field. That the smell of a ploughed field was appreciated by the ancients may be seen from the words of Jacob (Genesis xxvii. 27), 'the smell of my son is as the smell of a field which the Lord has blessed.' But *arómata* meant clearly substances first, before it assumed the modern sense of odour. See *Greek Thesaurus* by Stephanus, ed. Didot, s. v.

[2] Grimm remarks justly that *airtha* could not be derived from arjan, on account of the difference in the vowels. But *airtha* is a much more ancient formation, and comes from the root ar, which root, again, was originally rí or ir (Benfey, *Kurze Gr.* p. 27). From this primitive root ri or ir, we must derive both the Sanskrit irâ or idâ, the Greek ἔρα- in ἔραζε, the O. H. G. *ëro* and *ër-da*, and the Gothic *airtha*. The latter would correspond to the Sanskrit *rita*, i.e. arta. The true meaning of the Sanskrit idâ is earth. The Brahmans explain it as prayer, but this is not its original meaning.

[3] Corssen objects to this derivation in his *Kritische Beiträge*, p. 241.

[4] *Augsburger Allgemeine Zeitung*, 27 Juli, 1875.

ripe, from pa*k*, to cook. Another suffix *vara* (as in *pî-vara* by the side of pî-v an) would give us *ar-vará, and this by the change of *va* into *ou*, as in Varu*n*a and Οὐρανός, would give ἄρουρα. The Sanskrit urvarâ, field, shows change of *a* into *u*, as in Varu*n*a for Vara*n*a.

As agriculture was the principal labour in that early state of society when we must suppose most of our Aryan words to have been formed and fixed in their definite meanings, we may well understand how a word which originally meant this special kind of labour was afterwards used to signify labour in general. The most natural tendency in the growth of words and of their meanings is from the special to the general. Thus *regere* and *gubernare*, which originally meant to steer a ship, took the general sense of governing. To *equip*, which originally was to furnish a ship (French *équiper* and *esquif*, from *schifo*, ship), came to mean furnishing in general. Now in modern German, *arbeit* means simply *labour*; *arbeitsam* means industrious. In Gothic, too, *arbaiþs* is only used to express labour and trouble in general. But in Old Norse, *erfidhi* means chiefly *ploughing*, and afterwards labour in general;[1] and the same word in Anglo-Saxon, *earfoth* or *earfethe*, is labour. Of course we might equally suppose that, as *labourer*, from meaning one who labours in general, came to take the special sense of an agricultural labourer, so *arbeit*, from meaning work in general, came to

[1] This statement rests on the authority of Björn Halldórsson's *Dictionary*, Icelandic and Latin, published by Rask, 1814. Dr. Vigfusson, s.v. erfiði, doubts the meaning of ploughing.

be applied, in Old Norse, to the work of ploughing. But as the root of *erfithi* is clearly *ar*, our first explanation is the more plausible. Besides, the simple *ar* in Old Norse means ploughing and labour, and the Old High-German *art* has likewise the sense of ploughing.[1]

And as ploughing was not only one of the earliest kinds of labour, but also one of the most primitive arts, I venture to go a step further, and to derive the Latin *ars* from the same root. Ploughing and cultivating the land was after all the oldest art, and not too mean in the eyes of the Greeks to prevent them from ascribing its invention to the goddess of all wisdom.

In Old High-German *drunti*, in Anglo-Saxon *ærende*, mean simply work; but they, too, must originally have meant the special work of agriculture; and in the English *errand*, and *errand-boy*, the same word is still in existence.

Ar, however, did not only mean to plough, or to cut open the land; it was transferred at a very early time to the ploughing of the sea, or rowing. Thus Shakespeare says:—

> Make the sea serve them, which they *ear* and wound
> With keels:

In Latin such expressions as *perarare aquas, sul-*

---

[1] Grimm derives *arbeit*, Gothic *arbaiths*, Old High-German *arapeit*, Modern High-German *arbeit*, directly from the Gothic *arbja*, heir; but admits a relationship between *arbja* and the root *arjan*, to plough. He identifies *arbja* with the Slavonic *rab*, servant, slave, and *arbeit* with *rabota*, *corvée*, supposing that sons and heirs were the first natural slaves. He supposes even a relationship between *rabota* and the Latin *labor* (*German Dictionary*, s.v. Arbeit). If Gothic *arbi*, inherited

care vada carina, sulcare undas are well known. In French *silloner la mer* and *faucher le grand pré* mean to row or to cut through the green sea.[1] They are expressions especially applied to galley-slaves.[2] In a similar manner we find that Sanskrit derives from ar the substantive **aritra**, not in the sense of a plough, but in the sense of a rudder. In Anglo-Saxon Professor Skeat compares *ár*, the oar, the ploughshare of the water; but this is doubtful. The Greeks, however, had used the root *ar* in the sense of rowing; for *eretēs*[3] in Greek is a rower, and their word *tri-ēr-ēs* meant originally a ship with three oars, or with three rows of oars,[4] a trireme.

This comparison of ploughing and rowing is of frequent occurrence in ancient languages. The English word *plough*, the Slavonic *ploug*, has been compared with the Sanskrit **plava**,[5] a ship, and with the Greek *ploion*, ship. As the Aryas spoke of a ship ploughing the sea, they also spoke of a plough sailing across the field; and thus it was that the same names were applied to both.[6] In English dialects, *plough* or

property, could be derived from a root meaning to plough, its original meaning would have been ploughed land, while *arbja*, the heir, would have been meant for the son to whom the ploughed land descended by inheritance. But this is doubtful.

[1] Pott, *Studien zur Mythologie*, s. 321; Brinkmann, *Metapheren*, p. 188.
[2] *Gil Blas*, ii. 4.
[3] Latin *remus* (Old Irish *rám*) for *resmus*, connected with ἐρετμός. From ἐρέτης comes ἐρέσσω; and ὑπηρέτης, servant, helper; *rostrum* from *rodere*.
[4] Cf. Eur. *Hec.* 455, κώπη ἀλιήρης. Ἀμφήρης means having oars on both sides.
[5] From Sanskrit plu, πλέω: cf. fleet and float.
[6] Other similes: ὕνις and ὕννις, ploughshare, derived by Plutarch from ὗς, boar. *Quæst. Conv.* iv. 5, 2, τὴν δὲ ὗν ἀποχρηστῆσαι καὶ τιμᾶσθαι

plow is still used in the general sense of wagon or conveyance.[1]

We might follow the offshoots of this root *ar* still further, but the number of words which we have examined in various languages will suffice to show what is meant by a root and its ramifications. In all these words *ar* is the radical element, all the rest is merely formative. The root *ar* is called a predicative root, because, in whatever composition it enters, it predicates one and the same conception, whether of the plough, or the rudder, or the ox, or the field. Even in such a word as *artistic*, the predicative power of the root *ar* may still be perceived, though, of course, as it were by means of a powerful telescope only. The Brahmans, who call themselves ârya in India, were no more aware of the real origin of this name

λέγουσι· πρώτη γὰρ σχίσασα τῷ προὔχοντι τῆς ὀρυχῆς, ὥς φασι, τὴν γῆν, ἴχνος ἀρόσεως ἔθηκε, καὶ τὸ τῆς ὕνεως ὑφηγήσατο ἔργον· ὅθεν καὶ τοὔνομα γενέσθαι τῷ ἐργαλείῳ λέγουσι ἀπὸ τῆς ὑός. A plough is said to be called a pig's nose. The Latin *porca*, a ridge between two furrows, is derived from *porcus*, hog; and the German *furicha*, furrow, is connected with *farah*, boar. *Imporcitor* was an Italian deity presiding over the drawing of furrows. Fab. Pictor. *ap. Serv. Virg. G.* i. 21, 'imporcitor qui porcas in agro facit arando.' The Sanskrit vrika, wolf, from vrask, to tear, is used for plough (Rig-veda i. 117,21). The Sanskrit protham and pótram mean both the snout of boar and a ploughshare; see Pân. iii. 2, 183, halasûkarayoh puvah. Godarana, earth-tearer, is another word for plough in Sanskrit. Gothic *hoha*, plough = Sanskrit koka, wolf. See Grimm, *Deutsche Sprache*, and Kuhn, *Indische Studien*, vol. i. p. 321; M. M., *Hibbert Lectures*, p. 192.

[1] In the Vale of Blackmore, a wagon is called *plough* or *plow*; and *zull* (Anglo-Saxon *syl*) is used for *aratrum* (Barnes, *Dorset Dialect*, p. 369). Plough does not occur in Anglo-Saxon writers; and Southern authors of the thirteenth and fourteenth centuries employ it only in compound terms, as plow-land, etc. In the Southern dialects the word for plough is *zuolȝ*, Anglo-Saxon *sulh*. See R. Morris, *Ayenbite of Inwyt*, preface, p. lxxi.

and its connection with agricultural labour, than the artist who now speaks of *his art* as a divine inspiration suspects that the word which he uses was originally applicable only to so primitive an art as that of ploughing.

The Root SPAS.

We shall now examine another family of words, in order to see by what process the radical elements of words were first discovered.

Let us take the word *respectable*. It is a word of Latin, not of Saxon origin. In *respectabilis* we easily distinguish the verb *respecta-re* and the termination *bilis*. We then separate the prefix *re*, which leaves *spectare*, and we trace *spectare* as a participial formation back to the Latin verb *specere* or *spicere*, meaning to see, to look. In *specere*, again, we distinguish between the changeable termination *ere* and the unchangeable remnant *spec*, which we call the root. This root we expect to find in Sanskrit and the other Aryan languages; and so we do. In Sanskrit the more usual form is pas, to see, without the s; but spas also is found in spasa, a spy; in spashta and vi-spashta, clear, manifest; and in the Vedic spas, a guardian. In the Teutonic family we find *spëhôn* in Old High-German, meaning to look, to spy, to contemplate; and *spëha*, the English spy.[1] In Greek, the root *spek* has been changed into *skep*, which exists in *skeptomai*, I look, I examine: from whence *skeptikos*, an examiner or enquirer; in theo-

---

[1] Pott, *Etymologische Forschungen*, s. 267; Benfey, *Griechisches Wurzelwörterbuch*, s. 236.

logical language, a sceptic; and *episkopos*, an overseer, in ecclesiastical language, a bishop.

Let us now examine the various ramifications of this root. Beginning with *respectable*, we found that it originally meant a person who deserves *respect*, *respect* meaning *looking back*. We pass by common objects or persons without noticing them, whereas we turn back to look again at those who deserve our admiration, our regard, our respect. This was the original meaning of *respect* and *respectable*; nor need we be surprised at this if we consider that *noble*, *nobilis* in Latin, conveyed originally no more than the idea of a person that deserves to be known; for *nobilis* stands for *gnobilis*, just as *nomen* stands for *gnomen*, or *natus* for *gnatus*.

'With respect to' has now become almost a mere preposition. For if we say, 'With respect to this point I have no more to say,' this is the same as, 'I have no more to say on this point.'

Again, as in looking back we single out a person, the adjective *respective*, and the adverb *respectively*, are used almost in the same sense as special, or singly.

The English *respite* is the Norman modification of *respectus*, the French *répit*. *Répit* meant originally looking back, reviewing the whole evidence. A criminal received so many days *ad respectum*, to re-examine the case. Afterwards it was said that the prisoner had received a respite, that is to say, had obtained a re-examination; and at last a verb was formed, and it was said that a person had been respited.

As *specere*, to see, with the preposition *re*, came to mean respect, so with the preposition *de*, down, it forms the Latin *despicere*, meaning to look down, the English *despise*. The French *dépit* (Old French *despit*) means no longer contempt, though it is the Latin *despectus*, but rather *anger, vexation*. *Se dépiter* is, to be vexed, to fret. '*En dépit de lui*' is originally 'angry with him,' then 'in spite of him'; and the English *spite, in spite of, spiteful*, are mere abbreviations of *despite, in despite of, despiteful*, and have no more to do with the spitting of cats, than *souris* (sorex), mouse, has with *sourire* (subridere), to laugh.

As *de* means down from above, so *sub* means up from below, and this added to *specere*, to look, gives us *suspicere, suspicari*, to look up, in the sense of to suspect.[1] From it *suspicion, suspicious*; and likewise the French *soupçon*, even in such phrases as 'There is a soupçon of chicory in this coffee,' meaning just a touch, just the smallest atom of chicory.

As *circum* means round about, so *circumspect* means, of course, cautious, careful.

With *in*, meaning into, *specere* forms *inspicere*, to inspect, hence *inspector, inspection*.

With *ad*, towards, *specere* becomes *adspicere*, to look at a thing. Hence *adspectus*, the aspect, the look or appearance of things.

So with *pro*, forward, *specere* became *prospicere*;

---

[1] The Greek ὑπόδρα, askance, is derived from ὑπό, and δρα, which is connected with δέρκομαι, I see; the Sanskrit d*ris*. In Sanskrit, however, the more primitive root d*ri*, or d a r, has likewise been preserved, and is of frequent occurrence, particularly if joined with the preposition â; tad âd*ri*tya, with respect to this.

and gave rise to such words as *prospectus*, as it were a look out, *prospective*, &c. With *con*, with, *spicere* forms *conspicere*, to see together, *conspectus*, *conspicuous*. We saw before in *respectable*, that a new word, *spectare*, is formed from the participle of *spicere*. This, with the preposition *ex*, out, gives us the Latin *expectare*, the English *to expect*, to look out; with its derivatives.

Auspicious is another word which contains our root as the second of its component elements. The Latin *auspicium* stands for *avispicium*, and meant the looking out for certain birds which were considered to be of good or bad omen to the success of any public or private act. Hence *auspicious* in the sense of lucky. *Haru-spex* was the name given to a person who foretold the future from the inspection of the entrails of animals.[1] We also have the feminine *haruspica*, formed like *vestispica*, a wardrobe-keeper.

Again, from *specere, speculum* was formed, in the sense of looking-glass, or any other means of looking at oneself; and from it *speculari*, the English *to speculate, speculative*, &c.

But there are many more offshoots of this one root. Thus, the Latin *speculum*, looking-glass, became *specchio* in Italian; and the same word, though in a roundabout way, came into French as the adjective *espiègle*, waggish. The origin of this French word is curious. There exists in German a famous cycle of stories, mostly tricks played by a half-historical, half-mythical character of the name

[1] See *Chips from a German Workshop*, ii. p. 177.

of *Eulenspiegel*, or *Owl-glass*. These stories were translated into French, and the hero was known at first by the name of *Ulespiègle*, which name, contracted afterwards into *Espiègle*, became a general name for every wag.

As the French borrowed not only from Latin, but likewise from the Teutonic languages, we meet there, side by side with the derivatives of the Latin *specere*, the Old High-German *spëhôn*, slightly disguised as *épier*, to spy, the Italian *spiare*. The German word for a spy was *spëha*, and this appears in Old French as *espie*, in Modern French as *espion*.

One of the most prolific branches of the same root is the Latin *species*. Whether we take species in the sense of a perennial succession of similar individuals in continual generations (Jussieu), or look upon it as existing only as a category of thought (Agassiz), *species* was intended originally as the literal translation of the Greek *eidos*, as opposed to *genos* or *genus*. The Greeks classified things originally according to *kind* and *form*, and though these terms were afterwards technically defined by Aristotle, their etymological meaning is in reality the most appropriate. Things may be classified either because they are of the same *genus* or *kind*, that is to say, because they had the same origin; this gives us a *genealogical* classification: or they can be classified because they have the same appearance, *eidos*, or *form*, without claiming for them a common origin; and this gives us a *morphological* classification. It was, however, in the Aristotelian, and not in its etymological sense, that the Greek *eidos* was rendered in

Latin by *species*, meaning the subdivision of a genus, the class of a family. Hence the French *espèce*, a kind; the English *special*, in the sense of particular as opposed to general. There is a little of the root spa*s*, to see, left in a *special train*, or a *special messenger*; yet the connection, though not apparent, can be restored with perfect certainty. We frequently hear the expression *to specify*. A man specifies his grievances. What does it mean? The mediæval Latin *specificus* is a literal translation of the Greek *eidopoios*. This means what makes or constitutes an *eidos* or species. Now, in classification, what constitutes a species is that particular quality which, superadded to other qualities, shared in common by all the members of a genus, distinguishes one class from all other classes. Thus the specific character which distinguishes man from all other animals is reason or language. Specific, therefore, assumed the sense of *distinguishing* or *distinct*, and the verb *to specify* conveyed the meaning of enumerating distinctly, or one by one.

I finish with the French *épicier*, a respectable grocer, but originally a man who sold drugs. The different kinds of drugs which the apothecary had to sell were spoken of, with a certain learned air, as *species*, not as drugs in general, but as peculiar drugs and special medicines. Hence the chymist or apothecary is still called *speziale* in Italian, his shop *spezieria*.[1] In French *species*, which regularly became *espèce*, assumed a new form to express drugs, namely,

[1] *Generi coloniali*, colonial goods.—Marsh, *Lectures*, p. 253. In Spanish, *generos*, merchandise.

épices; the English *spices*, the German *Spezereien*. Hence the famous *pain d'épices*, gingerbread nuts, and *épicier*, a grocer. If we try for a moment to trace *spicy*, or *a well-spiced* article, back to the simple root *specere*, to look, we shall understand that marvellous power of language which, out of a few simple elements, has created a variety of names hardly surpassed by the unbounded variety of nature herself.[1]

Classes of Roots.

William von Humboldt[2] held that roots are necessarily monosyllabic, and it is certainly true that in the Aryan family of speech roots consisting of more than one syllable can always be proved to be derivative.[3]

We may distinguish between primary, secondary, and tertiary roots.

A. Primary roots are those which consist

(1) of one vowel; for instance, i, to go.
(2) of one vowel and one consonant; for instance, ad, to eat.
(3) of one consonant and one vowel; for instance, dâ, to give.

B. Secondary roots are those which consist

(1) of one consonant, vowel, and consonant; for instance, tud, to strike.

In these roots either the first or the last consonant is modificatory.

---

[1] Many derivatives might have been added, such as *specimen, spectator, le spectacle, spécialité, spectrum, spectacles, specious, specula,* &c.

[2] W. von Humboldt, *Verschiedenheit,* s. 376; Pott, *Etym. Forsch.* ii. s. 216, 311.

[3] See, however, p. 292.

ANALYSIS OF LANGUAGE. 373

C. Tertiary roots are those which consist

(1) of consonant, consonant, and vowel; for instance, plu, to flow.
(2) of vowel, consonant, and consonant; for instance, ard, to hurt.
(3) of consonant, consonant, vowel, and consonant; for instance, spas, to see.
(4) of consonant, consonant, vowel, consonant, and consonant; for instance, spand, to tremble.

In the secondary roots we can frequently observe that one of the consonants, in the Aryan languages generally the final, is liable to modification. The root retains its general meaning, which is slightly modified and determined by the changes of the final consonants. Thus, besides tud (tudati), we have in Sanskrit tup (topati, tupati, and tumpati), meaning to strike; Greek *typ-tō*. We meet likewise with tubh (tubhnâti, tubhyati, tobhate), to strike; and, according to Sanskrit grammarians, also with tuph (tophati, tuphati, tumphati). Then there is a root tug (tuṅgati, togati), to strike, to excite; another root, tur (tutorti), to which the same meaning is ascribed; another, tûr (tûryate), to hurt. Then there is the further derivative turv (tûrvati), to strike, to conquer; there is tuh (tohati), to pain, to vex; and there is tus (tosate), to which Sanskrit grammarians attribute the sense of striking.

In the third class we shall find that one of the two consonants is always a semivowel, nasal, or sibilant, these being more variable than the other consonants. We can almost always point to one consonant as of later origin, and added to a biconsonantal root in order to render its meaning more special. Thus we have, besides spas, the root pas, and even this root has been traced back by Pott to a more primitive as. Thus vand, again, is a mere strengthening of the root vad, like mand of mad, like yu-na-*g* and yu-ñ-*g* of yu*g*. The root yu*g*, to join, and yudh, to fight, both point back to a root yu, to mingle, and this simple root has been preserved in Sanskrit. We may well understand that a root, having the general meaning of mingling or being together, should be employed to express both the friendly joining of hands and the engaging in hostile combat; but we may equally understand that language, in its progress to clearness and definiteness, should have desired a distinction between these two meanings, and should gladly have availed herself of the two derivatives, yu*g* and yudh, to mark this distinction.

The relationship, however, of these three classes of roots is by no means so clear as in the Semitic languages, where triliteral roots have with much greater, though even here with only limited success, been traced back to biliteral forms.[1] All we can say at present is that out of a number of possible parallel developments of the same radical types, certain roots have been preserved in the Aryan languages to express various shades of differentiated meaning. Traces of systematic derivation, however, are very few.[2]

---

[1] Benloew, *Aperçu général*, pp. 28 seq.
[2] This problem has been well worked out by A. Hjalmar Edgren, *On the Verbal Roots of the Sanskrit Language*, 1878.

ANALYSIS OF LANGUAGE.

Number of Roots.

Sanskrit grammarians have reduced the whole growth of their language to 1,706 roots,[1] that is to say, they have admitted so many radicals in order to derive from them, according to their system of grammatical derivation, all nouns, verbs, adjectives, pronouns, prepositions, adverbs, and conjunctions, which occur in Sanskrit. According to our explanation of a root, however, this number of 1,706 would have to be reduced considerably, and though a few new roots would likewise have to be added which Sanskrit grammarians failed to discover, yet the number of primitive sounds, expressive of definite meanings, requisite for the etymological analysis of the whole Sanskrit dictionary does probably not amount to more than 850.[2] Even this number may be still further reduced. In the progress of language many roots disappear, that is to say, their derivatives are no longer wanted, being superseded by derivatives from more familiar roots. Thus Professor Skeat, in his *Etymological Dictionary*, is satisfied with 461 Aryan roots to account for the whole wealth of the English Language. Benloew (*Aperçu général*) estimates the necessary radicals

---

[1] Benfey, *Kurze Grammatik*, § 151:—

  Roots of the 2, 3, 5, 7, 8, 9 classes . . 226
  Roots of the 1, 4, 6, 10 classes . . . 1,480
                                                        1,706
including 143 of the 10th class.

See also § 61; Pott, *Etym. Forsch.* (2 ed.), ii. p. 283; Bopp, *Vergl. Gr.* § 109ª, 3; 109ᵇ, 1, note.

[2] *Science of Thought*, p. 210.

of Gothic at 600, of modern German at only 250 (*l. c.* p. 22). Grimm's list of strong verbs in the Teutonic family amounts to 462 (*Deutsche Grammatik,* i. p. 1030; Pott, *Etym. Forsch.* ii. p. 75). Dobrowsky (*Instit. Ling. Slavicae,* p. 256) gives 1,605 radicals of the Slavonic languages. Hebrew has been reduced to about 500 roots.[1] whereas Chinese, which abstains from composition and derivation, and therefore requires a larger number of radicals, was satisfied with 450.[2] With these 450 sounds, raised to 1,263 by various accents and intonations, the Chinese have produced a dictionary of from 40,000 to 50,000 words.[3]

All this shows a wise spirit of economy on the part of primitive language, for the possibility of forming new roots for every new impression was almost unlimited. Even if we put the number of letters only at twenty-

---

[1] Renan, *Histoire des Langues sémitiques,* p. 138. Leusden counted 5,642 Hebrew and Chaldee words in the Old Testament.

[2] 'Morrison gives 411, Edkins 532, the difference being chiefly occasioned by Morrison not counting aspirated words as distinct from the non-aspirated. The number would be much greater if the final *m* and the soft initials *g, d, b, v,* &c., were still in existence, as under the Mongolian dynasty. There would then be at least 700 radicals. The sounds attached to Chinese characters in the thirteenth century are expressed alphabetically in old Mongolian writings.'—Edkins, *Mandarin Grammar,* pp. 44, 45.

[3] The exact number in the Imperial Dictionary of Khang-hi amounts to 42,718. About one-fourth has become obsolete; and one-half of the rest may be considered of rare occurrence, thus leaving only about 15,000 words in actual use. 'The exact number of the classical characters is 42,718. Many of them are no longer in use in the modern language, but they occur in the canonical and the classical

ANALYSIS OF LANGUAGE. 377

four, the possible number of biliteral and triliteral roots would amount together to 14,400.[1]

Demonstrative Roots.

It is clear, however, that in addition to these predicative roots, we want another class of radical elements to enable us to account for the full growth of language. With the 400 or 500 predicative roots at her disposal, language would not have been at a loss to coin names for all things that come under our cognisance. Language is a thrifty housewife. If we consider the variety of ideas that were expressed by the one root spas, it is easy to see that with 500 such roots a dictionary might have been formed sufficient to satisfy the wants, however extravagant, of her husband—the human mind. If each root yielded fifty derivatives, we should have 25,000 words. Now, we are told by a country clergyman, that some of the labourers in his parish did not use more than 300 words in their daily conversation.[2] The cuneiform inscriptions of Persia contain no more than 379 words, 131 of these being proper names. The vocabulary of the ancient sages of Egypt, at least as far as it is known to us from the hieroglyphic inscriptions, amounts to about 658 words.[3] The *libretto* of an Italian opera

---

[1] Leibniz (*De Arte combinatoria*, Opp. tom. ii. pp. 387, 388, ed. Dutens). 'Quoties situs literarum in alphabeto sit variabilis; 23 literarum linguae Latinae variationes sunt 25,852,016,738,884,976,640,000; 24 literarum Germanicae linguae, 620,448,701,733,239,739,360,000.' Cf. Pott, *Etym. Forsch.* ii. s. 9; Jean Paul, *Leben Fibels*, s. 160. Plut. *Quaest. Convir.* viii. 9, 3. Ξενοκράτης δὲ τὸν τῶν συλλαβῶν ἀριθμὸν ὃν τὰ στοιχεῖα μιγνύμενα πρὸς ἄλληλα παρέχει, μυριάδων ἀπέφηνεν εἰκοσάκις καὶ μυριάκις μυρίων.

[2] *The Study of the English Language*, by A. D'Orsey, p. 15.

[3] This is the number of words in the Vocabulary given by Bunsen,

seldom displays a greater variety.¹ A well-educated person in England, who has been at a public school and at the university, who reads his Bible, his Shakespeare, the *Times*, and all the books of Mudie's Library, seldom uses more than about 3,000 or 4,000

---

in the first volume of his Egypt, pp. 453–491. Several of these words, however, though identical in sound, must be separated etymologically, and later researches have considerably increased the number. The number of hieroglyphic groups in Sharpe's *Egyptian Hieroglyphics*, 1861, amounts to 2,030.

¹ Marsh, *Lectures*, p. 182. M. Thommerel stated the number of words in the dictionaries of Robertson and Webster as 43,566. Todd's edition of Johnson, however, is said to contain 58,000 words, and the later editions of Webster have reached the number of 70,000, counting the participles of the present and perfect as independent vocables. Flügel estimated the number of words in his own dictionary at 94,464, of which 65,085 are simple, 29,379 compound. This was in 1843; and he then expressed a hope that in his next edition the number of words would far exceed 100,000. This is the number fixed upon by Mr. Marsh as the minimum of the *copia vocabulorum* in English. See the *Saturday Review*, Nov. 2, 1861.

'Adamantinos Korais invenit in veteri Academiæ Parisiensis dictionario 29,712 contineri; in Johnsoniano 36,784; in linguæ Armeniacæ vocabulario 50,000; sed in thesauri Stephaniani editione Londinensi, 150,000.' Cf. Pott, *Etym. Forsch.* ii. s. 78.

'The translation of the Scriptures under James I (1611) comprises 773,746 words, of which about 98 per cent. are proper names and repetitions, if it be true that the particle *and* occurs 46,219 times.' See John A. Weisse, 1873.

What we possess of Gothic amounts, according to Loebe, to 3,625 words, exc. 357 proper names, and 120 foreign words. Gaugengigl brings the number to 3,545, Schulze to 3,440; see Gaugengigl, *Einleitung* to 2nd vol.

Varro, L. L. vi. § 35. 'Horum verborum si primigenia sunt ad mille, ut Cosconius scribit, ex eorum declinationibus verborum discrimina quingenta millia esse possunt, ideo quia singulis verbis primigeniis circiter quingentæ species declinationibus fiunt. Primigenia dicuntur verba ut lego, scribo, sto, sedeo et cetera quæ non sunt ab alioquo verbo, sed suas habent radices.' Each verb in Greek, if conjugated through all its voices, tenses, moods, and persons, produces, together with its participles, 1,300 forms.

words in actual conversation. Accurate thinkers and close reasoners, who avoid vague and general expressions, and wait till they find the word that exactly fits their meaning, employ a larger stock; and eloquent speakers may rise to a command of 10,000. The new Oxford Dictionary promises to bring the number of words to 250,000. The Hebrew Testament says all that it has to say with 5,642 words;[1] Milton's poetry is built up with 8,000; and Shakespeare, who probably displayed a greater variety of expression than any writer in any language, produced all his plays with about 15,000 words.

Five hundred roots, therefore, considering their fertility and pliancy, were more than was wanted for the dictionary of our primitive ancestors, nay, with proper management, even for our own times, when there are 245,000 living, and 95,000 fossil species of animals to be named, 100,000 living species, and 2,500 fossil species of plants, to say nothing of crystals, metals, and minerals.

And yet something more was wanted. If our ancestors had a root expressive of light and splendour, that root might have formed the predicate in the names of sun, and moon, and stars, and heaven, dawn, morning, day, spring, joy, beauty, majesty, love, friend, gold, riches, &c. But if they wanted to express *here* and *there, who, what, this, that, thou, he,* they would have found it impossible to discover any predicative root that could be applied to this purpose. Attempts have been made indeed to trace these words back to predicative roots; but if we are told that the demon-

[1] Renan, *Histoire*, p. 138.

strative root *ta*, this or there, may be derived from a predicative root *tan*, to extend, we find that even in our modern languages, the demonstrative pronouns and particles are of too primitive and independent a nature to allow of so artificial an interpretation. The sound *ta* or *sa*, for this or there, is as involuntary, as natural, as independent an expression as any of the predicative roots, and although some of these demonstrative, or pronominal, or local roots, for all these names have been applied to them, may be traced back to a predicative source, we must still admit a small class of independent radicals, not predicative in the usual sense of the word, but simply pointing, simply expressive of existence under certain more or less definite, local or temporal prescriptions.

It will be best to give one illustration at least of a pronominal root and its influence in the formation of words.

In some languages, and particularly in Chinese, a predicative root may by itself be used as a noun, or a verb, or an adjective, or an adverb. Thus the Chinese sound *ta* means, without any change of form, great, greatness, and to be great.[1] If *ta* stands before a substantive, it has the meaning of an adjective. Thus *ta jin* means a great man. If *ta* stands after a substantive, it is a predicate, or, as we should say, a verb. Thus *jin ta* (or *jin ta ye*) would mean the man is great.[2]

[1] Endlicher, *Chinesische Grammatik*, § 128.
[2] If two words are placed like *jin ta*, the first may form the predicate of the second, the second being used as a substantive. Thus *jin ta* might mean the greatness of man, but in this case it is more usual to say *jin thi ta*.
' Another instance: *chen*, virtue; ex. *jin tchi chen*, the virtue of

Or again, *jin ngŏ ye*,¹ *li pŭ ngŏ*, would mean man bad, law not bad. Here we see that there is no outward distinction whatever between a root and a word, and that a noun is distinguished from a verb merely by its collocation in a sentence.

In other languages, however, and particularly in the Aryan languages, no predicative root can by itself form a word. Thus in Latin there is a root *luc*, to shine. In order to have a substantive, such as light, it was necessary to add a pronominal or demonstrative root, this forming the general subject of which the meaning contained in the root is to be predicated. Thus by the addition of the pronominal element *s* we have the Latin noun, *luc-s*, the light, or literally, shining-there. Let us add a personal pronoun to the verbal base *luce*, and we have the verb *luc-e-s*, shining-thou, thou shinest. Let us add other pronominal derivatives, and we get such nouns and adjectives as *lucidus, luculentus, lucerna*, &c.

Composition.

It would be a totally mistaken view, however, were we to suppose that all derivative elements, all that remains of a word after the predicative root has been removed, must be traced back to pronominal roots. We have only to look at some of our own modern derivatives in order to be convinced that many of

man : *chen*, virtuous; ex. *chen jin*, the virtuous man : *chen*, to approve; ex. *chen tchi*, to find it good; *chen*, well; ex. *chen ko*, to sing well.'—Stanislas Julien.

¹ *Ye* is placed at the end to show the verbal character of *ngŏ*; without it we should translate 'the badness of man,' while *jin oŭ li* would mean 'man hates law.'

CHAPTER IX.

them were originally predicative, that they entered into composition with the principal predicative root, and then dwindled down to mere suffixes. Thus *scape* in *landscape*, and the more frequent *ship* in *hardship*, are both derived from the same root which we have in Gothic,[1] *skapa, skôp, skôpum*, to create; in Anglo-Saxon, *scape, scôp, scôpon*. It is the same as the German derivative *schaft*, in *Gesellschaft*, &c. So again *dom* in *wisdom* or *christendom* is derived from the same root which we have in *to do*. It is the same as the German *thum* in *Christenthum*, the Anglo-Saxon *dôm* in *cyning-dôm, Königthum*. *Hood*, the Anglo-Saxon *hâd*, means state or rank; but in *man-hood, child-hood, brother-hood, neighbour-hood*, it becomes a mere abstract suffix.[2]

The same holds good with regard to more ancient languages. Thus in Sanskrit m a y a is used as a secondary suffix to form words such as a s m a m a y a, made of stone, m r i n m a y a, made of earth or loam, and its original meaning is hardly felt. Yet there can be little doubt that m a y a comes from the root mâ, mîyate, to measure, to make, and was originally an independent word, like mita, or vimita, made of. This we see more clearly in gomaya, which means not only *bovinus*, but *cow-dung*. In Greek a trace of

---

[1] Grimm, *Deutsche Grammatik*, b. ii. s. 521.
[2] Spenser, *Shepheard's Calender*, Februarie (ed. Collier, i. p. 25):—
  'Cuddie, I wote thou kenst little good
  So vainly t'advaunce thy headlesse hood;'
(for thy headlessness; *hood*, the German *heit*, is a termination denoting estate, as manhood.—T. Warton.)

In Old High-German *deoheit* and *deomuat* mean the same thing; in modern German we have only *Demuth*, lit. servant-hood, humility. See also *infra*, p. 394, note 3.

the same suffix has been preserved in ἀνδρό-μεος, originally made of men, but used in the sense of human, e.g. Od. ix. 297, ἀνδρόμεα κρέ' ἔδων, eating human flesh; Il. xi. 538, ὅμιλον ἀνδρόμεον, a crowd of men.[1]

We have necessarily confined ourselves in our analysis of language to that family of languages to which our own tongue, and those with which we are best acquainted, belong; but what applies to Sanskrit and the Aryan family applies to the whole realm of human speech. Every language, without a single exception, that has as yet been cast into the crucible of comparative grammar, has been found to contain these two substantial elements, predicative and demonstrative roots. In the Semitic family these two constituent elements are even more palpable than in Sanskrit and Greek. Even before the discovery of Sanskrit, and the rise of comparative philology, Semitic scholars had successfully traced back the whole dictionary of Hebrew and Arabic to a small number of roots, and as every root in these languages consists of three consonants, the Semitic languages have sometimes been called by the name of triliteral.

To a still higher degree the constituent elements are, as it were, on the very surface in the Turanian family of speech. It is one of the characteristic features of that family, that, whatever the number of prefixes and suffixes, the root must always stand out in full relief, and must never be allowed to suffer by its contact with derivative elements.

There is one language, the Chinese, in which no analysis of any kind is required for the discovery of

[1] Pân. v. 4, 21.

its component parts. It is a language in which no coalescence of roots has taken place; every word is a root, and every root is a word. It is, in fact, the most primitive stage in which we can imagine human language to have existed. It is language *comme il faut*; it is what we should naturally have expected all languages to be.

There are, no doubt, numerous dialects in Asia, Africa, America, and Polynesia, which have not yet been dissected by the knife of the grammarian; but we may be satisfied at least with this negative evidence, that, as yet, no language which has passed through the ordeal of grammatical analysis has ever disclosed any but these two constituent elements.

The problem, therefore, of the origin of language, which seemed so perplexing and mysterious to the ancient philosophers, assumes a much simpler aspect with us. We have learnt what language is made of; we have found that everything in language, except the roots, is intelligible, and can be accounted for. There is nothing to surprise us in the combination of the predicative and demonstrative roots which led to the building up of all the languages with which we are acquainted, from Chinese to English. It is not only conceivable, as Professor Pott remarks, 'that the formation of the Sanskrit language, as it is handed down to us, may have been preceded by a state of the greatest simplicity and entire absence of inflections, such as is exhibited to the present day by the Chinese and other monosyllabic languages'; it is absolutely impossible that it should have been otherwise.

CHAPTER X.

MORPHOLOGICAL CLASSIFICATION.

Families and Classes of Languages.

THE analysis of human speech given in the preceding chapter ought to teach us two things: first, that in families of language, held together by genealogical ties, there may be more near and more distant degrees of relationship; secondly, that languages which can claim no genealogical relationship whatever, may still be classified morphologically, that is, according to the manner in which their constituent elements, the predicative and demonstrative roots, have been combined. Both these lessons will be useful to us in treating of the languages which are neither Aryan nor Semitic.

Strictly speaking, the Aryan and Semitic are the only *families* of speech which fully deserve that title. They both presuppose the existence of a finished system of grammar, previous to the first divergence of their dialects. Their history is from the beginning a history of decay rather than of growth, and hence the unmistakeable family-likeness which pervades every one even of their latest descendants. The language of the Sepoy and that of the English soldier are, in one sense, one and the same language. They are both built up of materials which were definitely shaped before the Teutonic and Indic branches separated. No new root has been added to either since their first separation; and the grammatical forms which are of more modern growth in English or Hindustani are, if closely examined, new combinations only of elements which existed from the beginning in all the Aryan dialects. In the termination of the English *he is*, and in the inaudible termination of the French *il est*, we recognise the result of an act performed before the first separation of the Aryan family, the combination of the predicative root as with the demonstrative root ti; an act performed once for all, and continuing to be felt to the present day.

It was the custom of Nebuchadnezzar to have his name stamped on every brick that was used during his reign in erecting his colossal palaces. Those palaces fell to ruins, but from the ruins the ancient materials were carried away for building new cities; and, on examining the bricks in the walls of the modern city of Bagdad on the borders of the Tigris, Sir Henry Rawlinson discovered on each the clear traces of that royal signature. It is the same if we examine the structure of modern languages. They too were built up with the materials taken from the ruins of the ancient languages, and every word, if properly examined, displays the visible stamp impressed upon it from the first by the founders of the Aryan and the Semitic empires of speech.

Distant Relationship.

The relationship of languages, however, is not always so close, and they may nevertheless have to be treated as genealogically akin. The Albanian language, for instance, is clearly Aryan, but the traces of a common descent are so few that it is impossible to decide as yet whether it should be treated as a near relative of Greek, or as an independent branch of the Aryan family. The language of Ceylon was for a long time treated as not Aryan at all, but certain terminations of the verb seemed to me to remove all doubt as to its Sanskritic origin. In these cases the difficulty of proving a common origin is due to the ravages of phonetic decay and dialectic growth. Languages, however, may also diverge before their grammatical system has become fixed and hardened; and in that case they cannot be expected to show the same marked features of a common descent as, for instance, the Neo-Latin dialects, French, Italian, and Spanish. They may have much in common, but they will likewise display an after-growth in words and grammatical forms, peculiar to each dialect. With regard to words we see, for instance, that even languages so intimately related to each other as the six Romance dialects, diverged in some of the commonest expressions. Instead of the Latin *frater*, the French *frère*, we find in Spanish *hermano*. There was a very good reason for this change. The Latin word *frater*, changed into *fray* and *frayle*, had been applied to express a brother or a friar. It was felt inconvenient that the same word should express two ideas which it was sometimes necessary to distinguish, and therefore, by a kind of natural elimination, *frater* was given up as the name of brother in Spanish, and replaced from the dialectical stores of Latin by *germanus*. In the same manner the Latin word for shepherd, *pastor*, was so constantly applied to the shepherd of the people, or the clergyman, *le pasteur*, that a new word was wanted for the real shepherd. Thus *berbicarius*, from *berbex* or *vervex*, a wether, was used instead of *pastor*, and changed into the French *berger*. Instead of the Spanish *enfermo*, ill, we find in French *malade*, in Italian *malato*. Languages so closely related as Greek and Latin have fixed on different expressions for son, daughter, brother, woman, man, sky, earth, moon, hand, mouth, tree, bird, &c.[1] That is to say, out of a large number of synonyms which were supplied by the numerous dialects of the Aryan family, the Greeks perpetuated one, the Romans another. It is clear that when the working of this principle of natural selection is allowed to extend more widely, languages, though proceeding from the same source, may in time acquire a totally different nomenclature for the commonest objects. The number of real synonyms is frequently exaggerated, and if we are told that in Icelandic there are 120 names for island, or in Arabic 500 names for lion,[2] and 1,000 names for sword,[3] or in German sixty names for *Primula elatior*, and about fifty for *Colchicum autumnale*,[4] many of these are no doubt purely poetical or technical. But even where there are in a language four or five names only for the same object,

[1] See *Letter on the Turanian Languages*, p. 62.
[2] Renan, *Histoire des Langues sémitiques*, p. 137.
[3] Pococke, *Notes to Abulfaragius*, p. 153; *Glossology*, p. 352. See *infra*, p. 527.
[4] Behaghel, *Deutsche Sprache*, p. 64.

it is clear that four languages might be derived from it, each in appearance quite distinct from the rest.[1]

The same applies to grammar. When the Romance languages, for instance, formed their new future by placing the auxiliary verb *habere*, to have, after the infinitive, it was quite open to any one of them to fix upon some other expedient for expressing the future. The French might have chosen *je vais dire* or *je dirvais* (I wade to say) instead of *je dirai*, and in this case the future in French would have been totally distinct from the future in Italian. The English *wisdom* is the same word as the German *Weis-heit*, only that in English the derivative element is *dom*, in German *heit*.[2] If such changes are possible in literary languages of such long standing as French and Italian, German and English, we must be prepared for a great deal more in languages which, as I said, diverged before any definite settlement had taken place, either in their grammar or their dictionary. It has been doubted whether Turkish is really related to Finnish, but there are features common to both languages which cannot be the result of accident. Some of the Bántu dialects on the east coast of Africa are mutually unintelligible, but not only their strongly-marked grammatical features, but their common property in certain important words also leaves no doubt of their being descendants of one and the same family. Sometimes, no doubt, we must refrain from pronouncing a decided opinion. That the language of the hieroglyphic inscriptions resembles the Semitic type in its

---

[1] See Terrien Poncel, *Du Langage*, p. 213.
[2] See before, p. 382.

grammatical structure, is generally admitted. But it is not without points of resemblance with Aryan speech too, and it was supposed for a time that Egyptian might represent a most ancient phase of language, which had not yet been differentiated into Semitic and Aryan.

Dr. Lottner in some excellent articles in the Transactions of the Philological Society of 1861, 'On the Sister-families of Languages, especially those connected with the Semitic Family,' tried to prove that the Berber dialects of Northern Africa, spoken formerly on the coast from Egypt to the Atlantic Ocean, but, after the invasion of the Arabs, pushed back towards the interior, were collateral branches of the Semitic family. It is difficult, however, to connect a clear idea with such a term, and the similarities hitherto pointed out between these North-African dialects on one side, and Syriac, Hebrew, and Arabic on the other, are hardly such as to justify the name applied to them as Sub-Semitic.

Morphological Classes.

But while a genealogical classification of languages presupposes always a community of origin, however distant, there is another classification, the purely morphological, which is entirely independent of this consideration. It may happen that languages which are related genealogically, belong to different morphological classes; it constantly happens that languages of the same morphological class have no genealogical relationship whatever.

We saw that all languages can be reduced in the

end to roots, predicative and demonstrative. It is clear, therefore, that, according to the manner in which roots are put together, we may expect to find three kinds of languages, or rather three stages in the gradual formation of speech.

1. Roots may be used as words, each root preserving its full independence.
2. Two roots may be joined together to form words, and in these compounds one root may lose its independence.
3. Two roots may be joined together to form words, and in these compounds both roots may lose their independence.

What applies to two roots, applies to three or four or more. The principle is the same, though it would lead to a more varied subdivision.

Three Stages, Radical, Terminational, Inflectional.

The first stage, in which each root preserves its independence, and in which there is no formal distinction between a root and a word, I call the *Radical Stage*. Languages, while belonging to this first or Radical Stage, have sometimes been called *Monosyllabic* or *Isolating*.

The second stage, in which two or more roots coalesce to form a word, the one retaining its radical independence, the other sinking down to a mere termination, I call the *Terminational Stage*. The languages belonging to it have generally been called *agglutinative*, from *gluten*, glue.

392   CHAPTER X.

The third stage, in which roots coalesce so that neither the one nor the other retains its substantive independence, I call the *Inflectional Stage*. The languages belonging to it have sometimes been distinguished by the name of *amalgamating* or *organic*.

The first stage excludes phonetic corruption altogether.

The second stage excludes phonetic corruption in the principal root, but allows it in the secondary or determinative elements.

The third stage allows phonetic corruption both in the principal root and in the terminations.

Transition from one stage to another.

It is perfectly true that few languages only, if we can trace their history during any length of time, remain stationary in one of these stages. Even Chinese, as has been shown by Dr. Edkins, exhibits in its modern dialects traces of incipient agglutination, if not of inflection. The Ugric languages show the most decided traces of phonetic corruption [1] and in consequence clear tendencies toward inflection, while the modern Aryan languages, such as French and English, avail themselves of agglutinative expedients for contriving new grammatical forms. So far I quite agree with Professor Hunfalvy, who has so strongly protested against substituting a morphological for a genealogical classification of languages. Such a sub-

---

[1] Thus, to quote Professor Hunfalvy, *sydäm*, heart, in Finnish has been changed to *syöm*, in Vogul. to *sim*, in Hungarian to *szüv* and *szű*. The Ostjak. *jôgot*, bow, is *jaut* and *jajt* in Vogul., *jout-se* in Finnish, *ij* and *iv* in Hungarian. The Ostjak. *kauh, kouh,* or *keu*, stone, is *kav* and *käv* in Vogul., *kivi* in Finnish, *kö* in Hungarian.

stitution was never contemplated. The two classifications were both supposed to be useful, each for its own purposes, but the genealogical classification was always considered the more important.

Professor Hunfalvy has proposed a different morphological classification, which is excellent in itself, but liable to the same limitations as my own. He establishes four classes:—

1. *Isolating*, the same as my own.

2. Languages in which the inherent vowels of nominal and verbal bases remain generally unchanged, and determine the vowels of the suffixes; Finnish, Turkish, &c.

3. Languages in which the inherent vowels of the nominal and verbal bases are influenced by the suffixes; Sanskrit, Greek, Latin, Slavonic, German.

4. Languages in which nominal and verbal bases have no inherent vowels, but vowels are used to determine verbal and nominal categories; Hebrew, Arabic, &c.

This division, though ingenious, is liable to the same objection, if objection it can be called, namely that the same language may often share the peculiarities of two or three classes (see p. 399, notes).

To return to our own morphological classification, it may be well to illustrate it by a few instances.

Radical Stage.

In the first stage, which is represented by Chinese, every word is a root, and has its own substantial meaning. There is in Chinese no formal distinction between a noun, a verb, an adjective, an adverb, a preposition. The same root, according to its position in a sentence, may be employed to convey the meaning of great, greatness, greatly, to grow, and to be great. Everything, in fact, depends in Chinese on the proper collocation of words in a sentence. Thus *ngò tà ni* means 'I beat thee'; but *ni tà ngò* would mean 'thou beatest me.' Thus *ngŏ ğin* means 'a bad man'; *ğin ngŏ* would mean 'the man is bad.'

When we say in Latin *baculo*, with a stick, we say in Chinese *ŷ cáng*.[1] Here *ŷ* might be taken for a mere preposition, like the English *with*. But in Chinese this *ŷ* is a root; it is the same word which, if used as a verb, would mean 'to employ.' Therefore in Chinese *ŷ cáng* means literally 'employ stick.' Or again, where we say in English *at home*, or in Latin *domi*, the Chinese say *ŭŏ-li*, *ŭŏ* meaning *house*, and *li* originally *inside*.[2] The name for *day* in modern Chinese is *ği-tse*, which means originally *son of the sun*.[3]

As long as every word, or part of a word, is felt to express its own radical meaning, a language belongs to the first or radical stage. As soon as such words as *tse* in *ği-tse*, day, *li* in *ŭŏ-li*, at home, or *ŷ* in *ŷ-cáng*, with the stick, lose their etymological meaning and become mere signs of derivation or of case, language enters into the second or terminational

---

[1] Endlicher, *Chinesische Grammatik*, s. 223.

[2] *Ibid.* s. 339.

[3] 'In this word *tse* (tseu) does not signify son; it is an addition of frequent occurrence after nouns, adjectives, and verbs. Thus, *lao*, old, + *tseu* is father; *nei*, the interior, + *tseu* is wife; *hiang*, scent, + *tseu* is clove; *hon*, to beg, + *tseu*, a mendicant; *hi*, to act, + *tseu*, an actor.'—Stanislas Julien.

stage. And this transition from one class into another does not, as Professor Hunfalvy imagines, vitiate our division. On the contrary, from an historical point of view, it confirms it.

In some respects the ancient language of Egypt, as recorded to us in the earliest hieroglyphic inscriptions, may be classed with Chinese. The points of similarity, however, are chiefly negative. They arise from the absence of grammatical differentiation and articulation, and from the possibility in consequence of the same word or root being used as a substantive, adjective, verb, or adverb. But there is no trace of any material relationship between the two languages.

Chinese stands by itself as a language which has changed very little since we know it in its most ancient literary records. Some scholars maintain that even in its earliest stage it shows signs of previous phonetic corruption. This may be so, and it seems confirmed by the evidence of local dialects. But we can hardly imagine that its grammatical simplicity, or rather its freedom from all grammar, in our sense of the word, could be due, as in the case of English, to a long-continued process of elimination of useless elements. Here we must wait for the results of further researches. The age claimed for the ancient Chinese literature seems to me as yet unsupported by any such evidence as would carry conviction to a student of Greek, Latin, or Sanskrit literature. Even if we admit that much of the ancient literature which was systematically destroyed by the Emperor Shi Hwang Tî of *Kh*in, B.C. 213, may have been recovered from oral tradition and scattered MSS., we cannot claim for the works of Confucius and Lao-tse an earlier date than that of their compilers. They may contain much older materials, but they give them to us as understood in the sixth century B. C., and they may not altogether have escaped the effects of the burning of books under the Emperor of *Kh*in.

Terminational Stage.

West of China there stretches a cluster of languages which are on the point of leaving or have left the radical stage, which show the development of agglutination in high perfection, and in some instances rise to the level of inflectional grammar. They are called *Ural-Altaic* or *Ugro-Tataric*. In one of my earliest essays, 'A Letter on the Turanian Languages,' 1854, I proposed to comprehend these languages under the name of *Turanian*. I went even further and distinguished them as *North-Turanian*, in opposition to what in my youth I ventured to call the *South-Turanian* languages, namely the *Tamulic*, *Taic*, *Gangetic*, *Lohitic*, and *Malaic*. During the last thirty years, however, the principles of the Science of Language have been worked out with so much greater exactness, and the study of some of these languages has made such rapid progress, that I should not venture at present to suggest such wide generalisations, at all events so far as the *Tamulic*, *Taic*, *Gangetic*, *Lohitic*, and *Malaic* languages are concerned.

It is different, however, with the language I comprehended as North-Turanian. They share not only common morphological features, but they are held together by a real genealogical relationship, though

not a relationship so close as that which holds the
Aryan or Semitic languages together.

Rask's and Prichard's Classification.

Though I am responsible for the name *Turanian*,
and for the first attempt at a classification of the
Turanian languages in the widest sense, similar attempts to comprehend the languages of Asia and
Europe, which are not either Aryan or Semitic, under
a common name had been made long ago by Rask, by
Prichard and others. Rask admitted three families,
the *Thracian* (Aryan), the *Semitic*, and the *Scythian*,
the latter comprising most of what I call the Turanian
languages. During his travels in India, Rask, in a
letter dated 30th July, 1821, claimed for the first time
the Dravidian languages also, Tamil, Telugu, &c., as
decidedly Scythian.[1]

The name *Allophylian*, proposed by Prichard, is in
some respects better than Turanian.

Rask's Scythian and Prichard's Allophylian race
was supposed to have occupied Europe and Asia
before the advent of the Aryan and Semitic races, a
theory which has lately been revived by Westergaard,
Norris, Lenormant, and Oppert, who hold that a
Turanian civilisation preceded likewise the Semitic
civilisation of Babylon and Nineveh, that the cuneiform letters were invented by that Turanian race, and

[1] Professor De Lagarde has stated that F. Rückert lectured at
Berlin in 1843 on the relationship of the Dravidian and Turanian
languages, and that I received the first impulse from him. It may be
so, though I am not aware of it. Anyhow, the first impulse came from
Rask; *Samlede Afhandlinger af R. K. Rask*, Kobenhavn, 1836, pp.
323 seq.

that remnants of its literature have been preserved in the second class of the cuneiform inscriptions, called sometimes Scythian, sometimes Median, and possibly in that large class of inscriptions now called Akkadian or Sumerian.[1]

Whatever may be thought of these far-reaching theories, no one, I believe, doubts any longer a close relationship between Mongolic and Turkic, a wider relationship between these two and Tungusic, and a still wider one between these three and Finnic and Samoyedic. Hence the Mongolic, Turkic, and Tungusic languages have been comprehended under the name of Altaic, the Finnic languages are called Ugric (including Hungarian), while Samoyedic forms, according to some, a more independent *nucleus*. These five groups together constitute a real family of speech, the Ural-Altaic.

Vocalic Harmony.

There is one peculiarity common to many of the Ural-Altaic languages which deserves a short notice, the law of *Vocalic Harmony*. According to this law the vowels of every word must be changed and modulated so as to harmonise with the key-note struck by its chief vowel. This law pervades the Tungusic, Mongolic, Turkic, Samoyedic, and Finnic classes, and even in dialects where it is disappearing, it has often left traces of its former existence behind. The same

---

[1] The affinity of Akkadian and Sumerian with the Finno-Ugric languages has been disproved by Donner. Their affinity with the Altaic languages is maintained by Hommel, 'Die Sumero-Akkaden, ein altaisches Volk,' in *Correspondez-Blatt der deutschen Ges. für Anthropologie*, xv. Jahrg. No. 8, 1884, p. 63.

law has been traced in the Tamulic languages also, particularly in Telugu, and in these languages it is not only the radical vowel that determines the vowels of the suffixes, but the vowel of a suffix also may react on the radical vowel.[1] The vowels in Turkish, for instance, are divided into two classes, *sharp* and *flat*. If a verb contains a sharp vowel in its radical portion, the vowels of the terminations are all sharp, while the same terminations, if following a root with a flat vowel, modulate their vowels into a flat key. Thus we have *sev-mek*, to love, but *bak-mak*, to regard, *mek* or *mak* being the termination of the infinitive. Thus we say *ev-ler*, the houses, but *at-lar*, the horses, *ler* or *lar* being the termination of the plural.

No Aryan or Semitic language has preserved a similar freedom in the harmonic arrangement of its vowels, while traces of it have been found among the most distant members of the Turanian family, as in Hungarian, Mongolian, Turkish, the Yakut, spoken in the north of Siberia, in Telugu, Tulu,[2] and in dialects spoken on the eastern frontier of India.

Nomad Languages.

No doubt, if we expected to find in this immense number of languages the same family likeness which holds the Semitic or Aryan languages together, we should be disappointed. It is the very absence of that family likeness which constitutes one of the distinguishing features of the Turanian dialects. They are

---

[1] Cf. Caldwell, *Dravidian Grammar*, second ed., p. 78.

[2] 'In Tulu final short *u* is left unchanged only after words containing labial vowels (*bududu*, having left); it is changed into *ü* after all other vowels (*pandüdü*, having said).'—Dr. Gundert.

Nomad languages, as contrasted with the Aryan and Semitic languages.[1] In the latter most words and grammatical forms were thrown out but once, and they were not lightly parted with, even though their original distinctness had been blurred by phonetic corruption. To hand down a language in this manner is possible only among people whose history runs on in one main stream, and where religion, law, and poetry supply well-defined borders which hem in on every side the current of language. Among the ancient Turanian nomads no such nucleus of a political, social, or literary character has ever been formed. Empires were no sooner founded than they were scattered again like the sand-clouds of the desert; no laws, no songs, no stories outlived the age of their authors. How quickly language can change, if thus left to itself without any literary standard, we saw when treating of the growth of dialects. The most necessary substantives, such as father, mother, daughter, son, have frequently been lost, and replaced by synonyms in the different dialects of Turanian speech, and the grammatical terminations have been treated with the same freedom. Nevertheless some of the Turanian numerals and pronouns, and several Turanian roots, point to a single original source; and the common words and common roots which have been discovered in the most distant branches of the Turanian stock, warrant, at least provisionally, the admission of a real, though very distant relationship of all Turanian speech.

---

[1] *Letter on the Turanian Languages,* p. 24.

Agglutination and Inflection.

Agglutination,[1] the most characteristic feature of the Turanian languages, means not only that in their grammar pronouns are *glued* to the verbs in order to form the conjugation, or prepositions to substantives in order to form declension. *That* would not be a distinguishing characteristic of the Turanian or nomad languages; for in Hebrew, as well as in Sanskrit, conjugation and declension were originally formed on the same principle, and could hardly have been formed on any other. What distinguishes the Turanian languages is that in them the conjugation and declension can still be taken to pieces; and although the terminations have by no means always retained their significative power as independent words, they are felt as modificatory syllables, and as distinct from the roots to which they are appended.

In the Aryan languages the modifications of words, comprised under declension and conjugation, were likewise originally expressed by agglutination. But the component parts began soon to coalesce, so as to form one integral word, liable in its turn to phonetic corruption to such an extent that it became impossible after a time to decide which was the root and which the modificatory element. The difference between an Aryan and a Turanian language is somewhat the same as between good and bad mosaic. The Aryan words seem made of one piece, the Turanian words clearly show the sutures and fissures where the small stones are cemented together.

[1] *Survey of Languages*, p. 90; De Maistre (died 1821), in his *Soirées de St. Petersburg* (i. 84), uses *agglutination* in a grammatical sense.

There was a very good reason why the Turanian languages should for a long time have remained in this second or agglutinative stage. It was felt essential that the radical portion of each word should stand out in distinct relief, and never be obscured or absorbed, as so often happens in the third or inflectional stage.

The French *âge*, for instance, has lost its whole material body, and is nothing but termination. *Âge* in Old French was *eage* and *edage*. *Edage* is a corruption of the Latin *ætaticum*; *ætaticum* is a derivative of *ætas*; *ætas* an abbreviation of *ævitas*; *ævitas* is derived from *ævum*, and in *ævum*, *æ* only is the radical or predicative element, the Sanskrit â y in â y-us, life, which contains the germ from which these various words derive their life and meaning. From *ævum* the Romans derived *æviternus*, contracted into *æternus*, so that *age* and *eternity* flow from the same source. What trace of *æ* or *ævum*, or even *ævitas* and *ætas*, remains in *âge*? Or, to take a more ancient case, what trace of the root si, to bind, is there left in μάσθλη for ἱμάσθλη, the thong of a whip? Turanian languages cannot afford such words as *âge* in their dictionaries. It is an indispensable requirement in a nomadic language that it should be intelligible to many, though their intercourse be but scanty. It requires tradition, society, and literature to maintain words and forms which can no longer be analysed at once. Such words would seldom spring up in nomadic languages, or if they did, they would die away with each generation.

The Aryan verb contains many forms in which the personal pronoun is no longer felt distinctly. And yet tradition, custom, and law preserve the life of these veterans, and make us feel unwilling to part with them. But in the ever-shifting state of a nomadic society no debased coin can be tolerated in language, no obscure legend accepted on trust. The metal must be pure, and the legend distinct; that the one may be weighed, and the other, if not deciphered, at least recognised as a well-known guarantee. Hence the small proportion of irregular forms in all agglutinative languages.[1]

A Turanian might tolerate the Sanskrit

as-mi,	a-si,	as-ti,	's-mas,	's-tha,	's-anti,
I am,	thou art,	he is,	we are,	you are,	they are;

or even the Latin

| 's-um, | e-s, | es-t, | 'su-mus, | es-tis, | 'sunt. |

In these instances, with a few exceptions, root and affix are as distinguishable as, for instance, in Turkish:

bakar-im,	bakar-sin,	bakar,
I regard,	thou regardest,	he regards.
bakar-iz,	bakar-siniz,	bakar-lar,
we regard,	you regard,	they regard.

But a conjugation like the Hindustani, which is a modern Aryan dialect,

hún, hai, hai, hain, ho, hain,

would not be compatible with the original genius of the Turanian languages, because it would not answer the requirements of a nomadic life. Turanian dialects exhibit either no terminational distinctions at all,

---

[1] The Abbé Molina states that the language of Chili is entirely free from irregular forms (Du Ponceau, *Mémoire*, p. 90).

as in Mandshu, which is a Tungusic dialect; or a complete and intelligible system of affixes, as in the spoken dialect of Nyertchinsk, equally of Tungusic descent. But a state of conjugation in which, through phonetic corruption, the suffix of the first person singular and plural and of the third person plural are the same, where there is no distinction between the second and third persons singular, and between the first and third persons plural, would in a Turanian dialect, which had not yet been fixed by literary cultivation, lead to the adoption of new and more expressive forms. New pronouns would have to be used to mark the persons, or some other expedient be resorted to for the same purpose.

And this will make it clear why the Turanian languages, or in fact all languages in this second or agglutinative stage, though protected against phonetic corruption more than the Aryan and Semitic languages, are so much exposed to the changes produced by dialectical regeneration. A Turanian retains, as it were, the consciousness of his language and grammar. The idea, for instance, which he connects with a plural is that of a noun followed by a syllable indicative of plurality; a passive with him is a verb followed by a syllable expressive of suffering, or eating, or going.[1] Now these determinative ideas may be expressed in various ways, and though in one and the same clan, and during one period of time, a certain number of terminations would become stationary, and be assigned to the expression of certain grammatical categories, such as the plural, the pas-

[1] *Letter on the Turanian Languages,* p. 206.

sive, the genitive, different hordes, as they separated, would still feel themselves at liberty to repeat the process of grammatical composition, and defy the comparative grammarian to prove the identity of the terminations, even in dialects so closely allied as Finnish and Hungarian, or Tamil and Telugu.

It must not be supposed, however, that Turanian or agglutinative languages are for ever passing through this process of grammatical regeneration. Where nomadic tribes approach to a political organisation, their language too, though Turanian or agglutinative, may approach to the system of political or traditional languages, such as Sanskrit or Hebrew. This is particularly the case with the most advanced members of the Turanian family, such as the Turkish, the Hungarian, the Finnish, the Tamil, Telugu, &c. Many of their grammatical terminations have suffered by phonetic corruption, but they have not been replaced by new and more expressive words. The termination of the plural is *lu* in Telugu, and this is supposed to be a mere corruption of *gal*, the termination of the plural in Tamil. The only characteristic Turanian feature which always remains is this,—the root is not obscured.

CHAPTER XI.

URAL-ALTAIC FAMILY.

WE may now proceed to examine the principal languages belonging to the *Ural-Altaic* Family.

This family comprises the *Samoyedic*, *Tungusic*, *Mongolic*, *Turkic* (or Tataric), and *Finnic*, or *Finno-Ugric* classes. Among these we can distinguish three distinct *nuclei*, the *Samoyedic*, the *Altaic*, comprising the Tungusic, Mongolic and Turkic, and the *Finno-Ugric*.

The Samoyedic.

The tribes speaking Samoyedic dialects are spread along the Yenisei and Ob rivers, and were pushed more and more North by their Mongolic successors. They have now dwindled down to about 16,000 souls. Five dialects, however, have been distinguished in their language by Castrén, the *Yurakian*, *Tawgyan*, *Yeniseian*, *Ostjako-Samoyede*, and *Kamassinian*, with several local varieties.

The vocalic harmony is most carefully preserved in the *Kamassinian* dialect, but seems formerly to have existed in all. The Samoyedic has no gender of nouns, but three numbers, singular, dual, and plural, and eight cases. The verb has two tenses, an Aorist (present and future) and a Preterite. Besides the indicative, there is a subjunctive and an imperative.

Altaic Languages.

The name Altaic comprehends the Tungusic, Mongolic, and Turkic languages. Some of the Tungusic and Mongolic dialects represent the lowest phase of agglutination, which in some cases is as yet no more than juxta-position, while in Turkish agglutination has really entered into the inflectional phase. The vocalic harmony prevails throughout.

Tungusic Class.

The *Tungusic* class extends from China northward to Siberia and westward to 113°, where the river Tunguska partly marks its frontier. The Tungusic tribes in Eastern Siberia are under Russian sway. They consist of about 70,000 souls. Some are called *Tchapogires*, others *Orotongs*. Other Tungusic tribes belong to the Chinese empire, and are known by the name of *Mundshu*, a name taken after they had conquered China in 1644, and founded the present imperial dynasty. Their country is called Mandshuria.

Mongolic Class.

The original seats of the people who speak Mongolic dialects lie near the Lake Baikal and in the eastern parts of Siberia, where we find them as early as the ninth century after Christ. They were divided into three classes, the *Mongols* proper, the *Buriäts*, and the *Ölöts* or *Kalmüks*. Chingis-Khan (1227) united them into a nation and founded the Mongolian empire, which included, however, not only Mongolic, but likewise Tungusic and Turkic (commonly, though wrongly, called Tataric) tribes.

The name of Tatar soon became the terror of Asia and Europe, and changed into Tartar, as if derived from *Tartarus*; it was applied promiscuously to all the nomadic warriors whom Asia then poured forth over Europe. Originally Tatar was a name of the Mongolic races, but through their political ascendancy in Asia after Chingis-Khan, it became usual to call all the tribes which were under Mongolian sway by the name of Tatar. In linguistic works Tataric is now used in two several senses. Following the example of writers of the Middle Ages, Tataric, like Scythian in Greek, has been fixed upon as the general term comprising all languages spoken by the nomadic tribes of Asia. Secondly, Tataric, by a strange freak, has become the name of that class of languages of which the Turkish is the most prominent member. While the Mongolic class—that which in fact has the greatest claims to the name of Tataric—is never so called, it has become an almost universal custom to apply this name to the third or Turkic branch of the Ural-Altaic family; and the races belonging to this branch have in many instances themselves adopted the name.

These Turkish, or, as they are more commonly called, Tataric races, were settled on the northern side of the Caspian Sea, and on the Black Sea, and were known as Komanes, Pechenegs, and Bulgars, when conquered by the Mongolic army of the son of Chingis-Khan, who founded the Kapchakian empire, extending from the Dniester to the Yemba and the Kirgisian steppes. Russia for two centuries was under the sway of these Khans, known as the Khans of the Golden Horde.

Their empire was dissolved towards the end of the fifteenth century, and several smaller kingdoms rose out of its ruins. Among these, Krim, Kasan, and Astrachan were the most important. The princes of these kingdoms still gloried in their descent from Chingis-Khan, and had hence a real right to the name of Mongols or Tatars. But their armies and subjects also, who were not of Mongol, but of Turkish blood, received the name of their princes; and their languages continued to be called Tataric, even after the Turkish tribes by whom they were spoken had been brought under the Russian sceptre, and were no longer governed by Khans of Mongolic or Tataric origin. It would therefore be desirable to use Turkic instead of Tataric, when speaking of the third branch of the northern division of the Ural-Altaic family, did not a change of terminology generally produce as much confusion as it remedies. The recollection of their non-Tataric, i.e. non-Mongolic, origin remains, it appears, among the so-called Tatars of Kasan and Astrachan. If asked whether they are Tatars, they reply No; and they call their language Turki or Turuk, but not Tatari. Nay, they consider Tatar as a term of reproach, synonymous with robber, evidently from a recollection that their ancestors had once been conquered and enslaved by Mongolic, that is, Tataric, tribes. All this rests on the authority of Klaproth, who during his stay in Russia had great opportunities of studying the languages spoken on the frontiers of this half-Asiatic empire.

The conquests of the Mongols, or the descendants of Chingis-Khan, were not confined, however, to these

Turkish tribes. They conquered China in the East, where they founded the Mongolic dynasty of Yuan, and in the West, after subduing the Khalifs of Bagdad and the Sultans of Iconium, they conquered Moscow, and devastated the greater part of Russia. In 1240 they invaded Poland, in 1241 Silesia. Here they recoiled before the united armies of Germany, Poland, and Silesia. They retired into Moravia, and, having exhausted that country, occupied Hungary.

At that time they had to choose a new Khan, which could only be done at Karakorum, the old capital of their empire. Thither they withdrew to elect an emperor to govern an empire which then extended from China to Poland, from India to Siberia. But a realm of such vast proportions could not be long held together, and towards the end of the thirteenth century it broke up into several independent states, all under Mongolian princes, but no longer under one Khan of Khans. Thus new independent Mongolic empires arose in China, Turkestan, Siberia, Southern Russia, and Persia. In 1360 the Mongolian dynasty was driven out of China; in the fifteenth century they lost their hold on Russia. In Central Asia they rallied once more under Timur (1369), whose sway was again acknowledged from Karakorum to Persia and Anatolia. But, in 1468, this empire also fell by its own weight, and for want of powerful rulers like Chingis-Khan or Timur. In Jagatai alone—the country extending from the Aral lake to the Hindu-kush between the rivers Oxus and Yaxartes (Jihon and Sihon), and once governed by Jagatai, the son of Chingis-Khan—the Mongolian dynasty maintained itself, and thence it was that Baber, a descendant of Timur, conquered India, and founded there a Mongolian dynasty, surviving up to our own times in the Great Moguls of Delhi. Most Mongolic tribes are now under the sway of the nations whom they once had conquered, the Tungusic sovereigns of China, the Russian Czars, and the Turkish Sultans.

The Mongolic language, although spoken (but not continuously) from China as far as the Volga, has given rise to but few dialects. Next to Tungusic, the Mongolic is the poorest language of the Ural-Altaic family, and the scantiness of grammatical terminations accounts for the fact that, as a language, it has remained very much unchanged. There is, however, a distinction between the language as spoken by the Eastern, Western, and Northern tribes; and incipient traces of grammatical life have lately been discovered by Castrén, the great Swedish traveller and Turanian philologist, in the spoken dialects of the Buriäts. In it the persons of the verb are distinguished by affixes, while, according to the rules of Mongolic grammar, no other dialect distinguishes in the verb between amo, am*as*, am*at*.

The Mongols who live in Europe have fixed their tents on each side of the Volga and along the coast of the Caspian Sea near Astrachan. Another colony is found south-east of Sembirsk. They belong to the Western branch, and are Ölöts or Kalmüks, who left their seats on the Koko-nur, and entered Europe in 1662. They proceeded from the clans Dürbet and Torgod, but most of the Torgods returned again in

1770, and their descendants are now scattered over the Kirgisian steppes.

Some Mongolic tribes, called Aimak and Hazara, live between Herat and Cabul, on the frontier of the North-Western Provinces of India.

Turkic Class.

Much more important are the Turkic languages, most prominent among which is the Turkish itself, or the Osmanli of Constantinople. The number of the Turkish inhabitants of European Turkey is indeed small. It is generally stated at 2,000.000; but Shafarik estimates the number of genuine Turks at not more than 700,000, who rule over fifteen millions of people. The different Turkic dialects of which the Osmanli is one, occupy one of the largest linguistic areas, extending from the Lena and the Polar Sea down to the Adriatic.

The most ancient name by which the Turkic tribes of Central Asia were known to the Chinese was *Hiung-nu*. These Hiung-nu founded an empire (206 B. C.) comprising a large portion of Asia, west of China. Engaged in frequent wars with the Chinese, they were defeated at last in the middle of the first century after Christ. Thereupon they divided into a northern and southern empire; and, after the southern Hiung-nu had become subjects of China, they attacked the northern Hiung-nu, together with the Chinese, and, driving them out of their seats between the rivers Amur and Selenga and the Altai mountains, westward, they are supposed to have given the first impulse to the inroads of the barbarians into

Europe. In the beginning of the third century, the Mongolic and Tungusic tribes, who had filled the seats of the northern Hiung-nu, had grown so powerful as to attack the southern Hiung-nu and drive them from their territories. This occasioned a second migration of Asiatic tribes towards the west, which culminated under Attila (died 453).

Another name by which the Chinese designate these Hiung-nu or Turkish tribes is *Tu-kiu*. This Tu-kiu is supposed to be identical with Turk. Although the tribe to which this name was given was originally but small, it began to spread in the sixth century from the Altai to the Caspian, and it was probably to them that in 569 the Emperor Justinian sent an ambassador in the person of Semarchos. The empire of the Tu-kiu was destroyed in the eighth century, by the 'Hui-'he (Chinese Kao-che), a branch of the Uigurs. This tribe, equally of Turkish origin, maintained itself for about a century, and was then conquered by the Chinese and driven back from the northern borders of China. Part of the 'Hui-'he occupied Tangut, and, after a second defeat by the Mongolians in 1257, the remnant proceeded still farther west, and joined the Uigurs, whose tents were pitched near the towns of Turfan, Kashgar, Khamil, and Aksu.

The *Yueh-chi* also, the so-called Indo-Scythian conquerors of India, belonged to the same race, and are often called the White Huns. Pressed by the Hiung-nu, they invaded Bactria (about 128 B.C.), then held by the Tochâri, and mixed with the Tochâri, they conquered the North of India about the beginning of our era. They are the Ἐφθαλῖται of the Greek, the Hayathalah or Haithal (i. e. Habathilah) of the Persian writers.[1]

These facts, gleaned chiefly from Chinese historians, show from the very earliest times the westward tendency of the Turkish nations. In 568 A. D. Turkish tribes occupied the country between the Volga and the sea of Azov, and numerous reinforcements have since strengthened their position in those parts.

The northern part of Persia, west of the Caspian Sea, Armenia, the south of Georgia, Shirwan, and Dagestan, harbour a Turkish population, known by the general name of *Turkman* or *Kisil-bash* (Quazalbáshí, i. e. Red-caps). They are nomadic robbers, and their arrival in these countries dates from the eleventh and twelfth centuries.

East of the Caspian Sea the Turkman tribes are under command of the Usbek-Khans of Khiva, Fergana, and Bokhara. They call themselves, however, not subjects, but guests of these Khans. Still more to the east the Turkmans are under Chinese sovereignty, and in the south-west they reach as far as Khorasan and other provinces of Persia.

The *Usbeks*, descendants of the 'Hui-'he and Uigurs, and originally settled in the neighbourhood of the towns of Khoten, Kashgar, Turfan, and Khamil, crossed the Yaxartes in the sixteenth century, and, after several successful campaigns, gained possession of Balkh, Kharism (Khiva), Bokhara, and Fergana. In the latter country and in Balkh they have become

[1] See M. M., *India, what can it teach us?* pp. 274-277.

agricultural; but generally their life is nomadic, and too warlike to be called pastoral.

Another Turkish tribe are the *Nogái*, west of the Caspian, and also north of the Black Sea. To the beginning of the seventeenth century they lived north-east of the Caspian, and the steppes on the left of the Irtish bore their name. Pressed by the Kalmüks, a Mongolic tribe, the Nogáis advanced westward as far as Astrachan. Peter I. transferred them thence to the north of the Caucasian mountains, where they grazed their flocks on the shores of the Kuban and the Kuma. One horde, that of Kundur, remained on the Volga, subject to the Kalmüks.

Another tribe of Turkish origin in the Caucasus are the *Buzianes*. They now live near the sources of the Kuban, but before the fifteenth century within the town Majari, on the Kuma.

A third Turkish tribe in the Caucasus are the *Kumüks*, on the rivers Sunja, Aksai, and Koisu: subjects of Russia, though under native princes.

The southern portion of the Ural mountains has long been inhabited by the *Bashkirs*, a race considerably mixed with Mongolic blood, savage and ignorant, subjects of Russia and Mohammedans by faith.[1] Their

[1] With regard to the Bashkirs as well as other Ugro-Altaic tribes, I am afraid that my information was chiefly derived from works which were considered authoritative thirty years ago, and would require occasional correction after what has happened since my Lectures were first delivered. I received from time to time most useful notes from my readers, which I have tried to incorporate in my book. Mr. M. A. Morrison, Agent to the British and Foreign Bible Society for South Russia, the Caucasus and Turkestan, wrote to me last April (1889), that he found the Bashkirs by no means savage and ignorant,

land is divided into four Roads, called the Roads of Siberia, of Kasan, of Nogái, and of Osa, a place on the Kama. Among the Bashkirs, and in villages near Ufa, is now settled a Turkish tribe, the *Meshcheräks*, who formerly lived near the Volga.

The tribes near the Lake of Aral are called *Kara-Kalpak*. They are subject partly to Russia, partly to the Khans of Khiva.

The *Turks of Siberia*, commonly called Tatars, are partly original settlers, who crossed the Ural and founded the Khanat of Sibir, partly later colonists. Their chief towns are Tobolsk, Yeniseisk, and Tomsk. Separate tribes are the Uran'hat on the Chulym, and the Barabas in the steppes between the Irtish and the Ob.

The dialects of these Siberian Turks are considerably intermingled with foreign words, taken from Mongolic, Samoyedic, or Russian sources. Still they resemble one another closely in all that belongs to the original stock of the language.

In the north-east of Asia, on both sides of the river Lena, the *Yakuts* form the most remote link in the Turkic chain of languages. Their male population has lately risen to 100,000, while in 1795 it amounted only to 50,066. The Russians became first acquainted with them in 1620. They call themselves Sakha, and are mostly heathen, though Christianity is gaining

but rather mild and inoffensive, and mostly occupied with agriculture. This shows the danger of all generalisation with regard to national character, for the description of the Bashkirs by German officers who had known them during the Napoleonic wars, did certainly not represent them as mild and inoffensive. Their seats are at present on the Ural, not in the Altaic mountains.

ground among them. According to their traditions, their ancestors lived for a long time in company with Mongolic tribes, and traces of this intercourse can still be discovered in their language. Attacked by their neighbours, they built rafts and floated down the river Lena, where they settled in the neighbourhood of what is now Yakutzk. Their original seats seem to have been north-west of Lake Baikal. Their language has preserved the Turkic type more completely than any other Turco-Tataric dialect. Separated from the common stock at an early time, and removed from the disturbing influences to which the other dialects were exposed, whether in war or in peace, the Yakutian has preserved so many primitive features of Tataric grammar, that even now it may be used as a key to the grammatical forms of the Osmanli and other more cultivated Turkic dialects.

Southern Siberia is the mother-country of the *Kirgis*, one of the most numerous tribes of Turco-Tataric origin. The Kirgis lived originally between the Ob and Yenisei, where Mongolic tribes settled among them. At the beginning of the seventeenth century the Russians became acquainted with the Eastern Kirgis, then living along the Yenisei. In 1606 they had become tributary to Russia, and after several wars with two neighbouring tribes, they were driven more and more south-westward, till they left Siberia altogether at the beginning of the eighteenth century. They now live at Burut, in Chinese Turkestan, together with the Kirgis of the 'Great Horde,' near the town of Kashgar, and north as far as the Irtish.

Another tribe is that of the *Western Kirgis*, or *Kirgis-Kasak*, who are partly independent, partly tributary to Russia and China.

Of what are called the three Kirgis Hordes, from the Caspian Sea east as far as Lake Tenghiz, the Small Horde is fixed in the west, between the rivers Yemba and Ural; the Great Horde in the east; while the most powerful occupies the centre between the Sarasu and Yemba, and is called the Middle Horde. Since 1819, the Great Horde has been subject to Russia. Other Kirgis tribes, though nominally subject to Russia, have often been her most dangerous enemies.

The *Turks of Asia Minor and Syria* came from Khorasan and Eastern Persia, and are *Turkmans*, or remnants of the Seljuks, the rulers of Persia during the Middle Ages. It was here that Turkish received its strong admixture of Persian words and idioms. The Osmanli, whom we are accustomed to call Turks *par excellence*, and who form the ruling portion of the Turkish empire, must be traced to the same source. They are Seljuks, and the Seljuks were a branch of the Uigurs. They are now scattered over the whole Turkish empire in Europe, Asia, and Africa, and their number amounts to between 11,000,000 and 12,000,000. They form the landed gentry, the aristocracy, and the bureaucracy of Turkey; and their language, the Osmanli, is spoken by persons of rank and education, and by all government authorities in Syria, in Egypt, at Tunis, and at Tripoli. It is heard even at the court of Teheran, and is understood by official personages in Persia. Osmanli is spoken in the neighbourhood of Kars, Batoum, and generally by the Turks of Lazistan, but further east, commencing at Alexandropol (the Turkish Gumri), and right into Mazandaran, Ghilan, and Azerbijan, the dialect of Azerbijan prevails, which has its own literature and even its own newspaper, and differs considerably from the pure Osmanli.[1]

The rise of this powerful tribe of Osman, and the spreading of the Turkish dialect which is now emphatically called the Turkish, are matters of historical notoriety. We need not search for evidence in Chinese annals, or try to discover analogies between names that a Greek or an Arabic writer may by chance have heard and handed down to us, and which some of these tribes have preserved to the present day. The ancestors of the Osman Turks are men as well known to European historians as Charlemagne or Alfred. It was in the year 1224 that Soliman-shah and his tribe, pressed by Mongolians, left Khorasan and pushed westward into Syria, Armenia, and Asia Minor. Soliman's son, Ertoghrul, took service under Aladdin, the Seljuk Sultan of Iconium (Konieh), and, after several successful campaigns against Greeks and Mongolians, received part of Phrygia as his own. There he founded what was afterwards to become the basis of the Osman empire. During the last years of the thirteenth century the Sultans of Iconium lost their power, and their former vassals became independent sovereigns. Osman, after taking his share of the spoil in Asia, advanced through the Olympic passes into Bithynia, and was successful against the

[1] Letter from M. A. Morrison, see p. 415, note.

armies of the Emperors of Byzantium. Osman became henceforth the national name of his people. His son, Orkhan, whose capital was Prusa (Bursa), after conquering Nicomedia (1327) and Nicæa (1330), threatened the Hellespont. He took the title of Padishah, and his court was called the 'High Porte.' His son, Soliman, crossed the Hellespont (1357), and took possession of Gallipoli and Sestos. He thus became master of the Dardanelles. Murad I. took Adrianople (1362), made it his capital, conquered Macedonia, and, after a severe struggle, overthrew the united forces of the Slavonic races south of the Danube, the Bulgarians, Servians, and Croatians, in the battle of Kossova-polye (1389). He fell himself, but his successor Bayazeth followed his course, took Thessaly, passed Thermopylæ, and devastated the Peloponnesus. The Emperor of Germany, Sigismund, who advanced at the head of an army composed of French, German, and Slavonic soldiers, was defeated by Bayazeth on the Danube in the battle of Nicopolis, 1399. Bayazeth took Bosnia, and would have taken Constantinople, had not the same Mongolians, who in 1244 drove the first Turkish tribes westward into Persia, threatened again their newly-acquired possessions. Timur had grasped the reins fallen from the hands of Chingis-Khan: Bayazeth was compelled to meet him, and suffered defeat (1402) in the battle of Angora (Ankyra) in Galatia.

Europe now had respite, but not long. Timur died, and with him his empire fell to pieces, while the Osman army rallied again under Mahomet I. (1413), and re-gained its former power under Murad II.

(1421). Successful in Asia, Murad sent his armies back to the Danube, and after long-continued campaigns, and powerful resistance from the Hungarians and Slaves under Hunyad, he at last gained two decisive victories; Varna in 1444, and Kossova in 1448. Constantinople could no longer be held, and the Pope endeavoured in vain to rouse the chivalry of Western Europe to a crusade against the Turks. Mahomet II. succeeded in 1451, and on the 26th of May, 1453, Constantinople, after a valiant resistance, fell, and became the capital of the Turkish empire.

Turkish Grammar.

It is a real pleasure to read a Turkish grammar, even though one may have no wish to acquire it practically. The ingenious manner in which the numerous grammatical forms are brought out, the regularity which pervades the system of declension and conjugation, the transparency and intelligibility of the whole structure, must strike all who have a sense for that wonderful power of the human mind which is displayed in language. Given so small a number of predicative and demonstrative roots as would hardly suffice to express the commonest wants of human beings, to produce an instrument that shall render the faintest shades of feeling and thought; given a vague infinitive or a stern imperative, to derive from it such moods as an optative or subjunctive, and tenses as an aorist or paulo-post future; given incoherent utterances, to arrange them into a system where all is uniform and regular, all combined and harmonious; such is the work of the human mind which we see realised in language. But in most languages nothing of this early process remains visible. They stand before us like solid rocks, and the microscope of the philologist alone can reveal the remains of organic life with which they are built up.

In the grammar of the Turkic languages, on the contrary, we have before us a language of perfectly transparent structure, and a grammar the inner workings of which we can study, as if watching the building of cells in a crystal beehive. An eminent orientalist remarked, 'We might imagine Turkish to be the result of the deliberations of some eminent society of learned men.' But no such society could have devised what the mind of man produced, left to itself in the steppes of Tartary, and guided only by its innate laws, or by an instinctive power as wonderful as any within the realm of nature.

Let us examine a few forms. 'To love,' in the most general sense of the word, or 'love,' as a root, is in Turkish *sev*. This does not yet mean 'to love,' which is *sevmek*, or 'love' as a substantive, which is *sevgu* or *sevi* ; it only expresses the general idea of loving in the abstract. This root, as we remarked before, can never be touched. Whatever syllables may be added for the modification of its meaning, the root itself must stand out in full prominence like a pearl set in diamonds. It must never be changed or broken, assimilated or modified, as in the English I fall, I fell, I take, I took, I think, I thought, and similar forms. With this one restriction, however, we are free to treat it at pleasure.

Let us suppose we possessed nothing like our conjugation, but had to express such ideas as I love, thou lovest, and the rest, for the first time. Nothing would seem more natural now than to form an adjective or a participle, meaning 'loving,' and then add the different pronouns, as I loving, thou loving, &c. Exactly this the Turks have done. We need not inquire at present how they produced what we call a participle. It was a task, however, by no means so facile as we now conceive it. In Turkish, one participle is formed by *er*. *Sev + er* would, therefore, mean lov + er or lov + ing. *Thou* in Turkish is *sen*, and as all modificatory syllables are placed at the end of the root, we get *sev-er-sen*, thou lovest. *You* in Turkish is *siz*; hence *sev-er-siz*, you love. In these cases the pronouns and the terminations of the verb coincide exactly. In other persons the coincidences are less complete, because the pronominal terminations have sometimes been modified, or, as in the third person singular, *sever*, dropt altogether as unnecessary. A reference to other cognate languages, however, where either the terminations or the pronouns themselves have maintained a more primitive form, enables us to say that, in the original Turkish verb, all persons of the present were formed by means of pronouns appended to this participle *sever*. Instead of 'I love, thou lovest, he loves,' the Turkish grammarian says, 'lover-I, lover-thou, lover.'

But these personal terminations are not the same in the imperfect as in the present.

CHAPTER XI.

Present	Imperfect
Sever-im, I love	sever-di-m, I loved
Sever-sen	sever-di-ñ
Sever	sever-di
Sever-iz	sever-di-k (miz)
Sever-siz	sever-di-ñiz
Sever-ler	sever-di-ler

We need not inquire as yet into the origin of the *di*, added to form the imperfect; but it should be stated that in the first person plural of the imperfect a various reading occurs in other Tataric dialects, and that *miz* is used there instead of *k*. Now, looking at these terminations, *m*, *ñ*, *i*, *miz*, *ñiz*, and *ler*, we find that they are exactly the same as the possessive pronouns used after nouns. As the Italian says *fratel-mo*, my brother, as in Hebrew we say *El-i*, God (of) I, i.e. my God, the Tataric languages form the phrases 'my house, thy house, his house,' by possessive pronouns appended to substantives. A Turk says

Bâbâ	father	bâbâ-m	my father
Aghâ	lord	aghâ-ñ	thy lord
El	hand	el-i	his hand
Oghlu	son	oghlu-muz	our son
Anâ	mother	anâ-niz	your mother
Kitâb	book	kitâb-leri	their book.

We may hence infer that in the imperfect these pronominal terminations were originally taken in a possessive sense, and that, therefore, what remains after the personal terminations are removed, *sever-di*, was never an adjective or a participle, but must have been originally a substantive capable of receiving terminal possessive pronouns; that is, the idea originally expressed by the imperfect could not have been 'loving-I,' but 'love of me.'

How, then, could this convey the idea of a past tense as contrasted with the present? Let us look to our own language. If desirous to express the perfect, we say, I have loved, *j'ai aimé*. This 'I have' meant originally, 'I possess,' and in Latin 'amicus quem amatum habeo' signified in fact a friend whom I hold dear—not, as yet, whom I *have* loved. In the course of time, however, these phrases 'I have said, I have loved,' took the sense of the perfect, and of time past—and not unnaturally, inasmuch as what I *hold*, or *have* done, *is* done—done, as we say, and past. In place of an auxiliary possessive verb, the Turkish language uses an auxiliary possessive pronoun to the same effect. 'Paying belonging to me,' equals 'I have paid'; in either case, a phrase originally possessive took a temporal signification, and became a past or perfect tense. This, however, is the very anatomy of grammar, and when a Turk says 'severdim,' he is, of course, as unconscious of its literal force, 'loving belonging to me,' as of the circulation of his blood.

The most ingenious part of Turkish is undoubtedly the verb. Like Greek and Sanskrit, it exhibits a variety of moods and tenses, sufficient to express the nicest shades of doubt, of surmise, of hope, and supposition. In all these forms the root remains intact, and sounds like the key-note through all the various modulations produced by the changes of person, number, mood, and time. But there is one feature peculiar to the Turkish verb, of which but scant analogies can be discovered in other languages—the power of producing new verbal bases by the mere addition of certain letters, which give, to every verb a negative, or causative, or reflexive, or reciprocal meaning.

Sev-mek, for instance, as a simple root, means to love. By adding *in*, we obtain a reflexive verb, *sev-in-mek*, which means to love oneself, or rather, to rejoice, to be happy. This may now be conjugated through all moods and tenses, *sevin* being in every respect equal to a new root. By adding *ish* we form a reciprocal verb, *sev-ish-mek*, to love one another.

To each of these three forms a causative sense may be imparted by the addition of the syllable *dir*. Thus

I. *sev-mek*, to love, becomes IV. *sev-dir-mek*, to cause to love.
II. *sev-in-mek*, to rejoice, becomes V. *sev-in-dir-mek*, to cause to rejoice.
III. *sev-ish-mek*, to love one another, becomes VI. *sev-ish-dir-mek*, to cause one to love one another.

Each of these six forms may again be turned into a passive by the addition of *il*. Thus

I. *sev-mek*, to love, becomes VII. *sev-il-mek*, to be loved.
II. *sev-in-mek*, to rejoice, becomes VIII. *sev-in-il-mek*, to be rejoiced at.
III. *sev-ish-mek*, to love one another, becomes IX. *sev-ish-il-mek*, not translatable.
IV. *sev-dir-mek*, to cause one to love, becomes X. *sev-dir-il-mek*, to be brought to love.
V. *sev-in-dir-mek*, to cause to rejoice, becomes XI. *sev-in-dir-il-mek*, to be made to rejoice.
VI. *sev-ish-dir-mek*, to cause them to love one another, becomes XII. *sev-ish-dir-il-mek*, to be brought to love one another.

This, however, is by no means the whole verbal contingent at the command of a Turkish grammarian. Every one of these twelve secondary or tertiary roots may again be turned into a negative by the mere addition of *me*. Thus, *sev-mek*, to love, becomes *sev-me-mek*, not to love. And if it is necessary to express the impossibility of loving, the Turk has a new root at hand to convey even that idea. Thus while *sev-me-mek* denies only the fact of loving, *sev-eme-mek*, denies its possibility, and means not to be able to love. By the addition of these two modificatory syllables, the number of derivative roots is at once raised to thirty-six. Thus

I. *sev-mek*, to love, becomes XIII. *sev-me-mek*, not to love.
II. *sev-in-mek*, to rejoice, becomes XIV. *sev-in-me-mek*, not to rejoice.
III. *sev-ish-mek*, to love one another, becomes XV. *sev-ish-me-mek*, not to love one another.
IV. *sev-dir-mek*, to cause to love, becomes XVI. *sev-dir-me-mek*, not to cause one to love.
V. *sev-in-dir-mek*, to cause to rejoice, becomes XVII. *sev-in-dir-me-mek*, not to cause one to rejoice.
VI. *sev-ish-dir-mek*, to cause them to love one another, becomes XVIII. *sev-ish-der-me-mek*, not to cause them to love one another.
VII. *sev-il-mek*, to be loved, becomes XIX. *sev-il-me-mek*, not to be loved.
VIII. *sev-in-il-mek*, to be rejoiced at, becomes XX. *sev-in-il-me-mek*, not to be the object of rejoicing.
IX. *sev-ish-il-mek*, if it were used, would become XXI. *sev-ish-il-me-mek*, neither form being translatable.
X. *sev-dir-il-mek*, to be brought to love, becomes XXII. *sev-dir-il-me-mek*, not to be brought to love.
XI. *sev-in-dir-il-mek*, to be made to rejoice, becomes XXIII. *sev-in-dir-il-me-mek*, not to be made to rejoice.

xii. *sev-ish-dir-il-mek*, to be brought to love one another, becomes xxiv. *sev-ish-dir-il-me-mek*, not to be brought to love one another.[1]

Some of these forms are of course of rare occurrence, and with many verbs these derivative roots, though possible grammatically, would be logically impossible. Even a verb like 'to love,' perhaps the most pliant of all, resists some of the modifications to which a Turkish grammarian is fain to subject it. It is clear, however, that wherever a negation can be formed, the idea of impossibility also can be superadded, so that by substituting *eme* for *me*, we should raise the number of derivative roots to thirty-six. The very last of these, xxxvi. *sev-ish-dir-il-eme-mek*, would be perfectly intelligible, and might be used, for instance, if, in speaking of the Sultan and the Czar, we wished to say, that it was impossible that they should be brought to love one another.

Finno-Ugric Class.

We now proceed to consider the Finnic or Finno-Ugric class of languages.

It is generally supposed that the original seat of the Fin tribes was in the Ural mountains, and their languages have sometimes been called *Uralic*. From this centre they spread east and west, and southward

---

[1] Professor Pott, in the second edition of his *Etymologische Forschungen*, ii. s. 118, refers to similar verbal formations in Arabic, in the language of the Gallas, &c. Analogous forms, according to Dr. Gundert, exist also in Tulu, but they have not yet been analysed as successfully as in Turkish. Thus *malpuwe* is I do; *malpâwe*, I do habitually; *maltürüwe*, I do all at once; *malpâwe*, I cause to do; *malpawdye*, I cause not to do.

in ancient times, as far as the Black Sea, where Finnic tribes, together with Mongolic and Turkic, are supposed to have been known to the Greeks under the comprehensive and convenient name of Scythians. As we possess no literary documents of any of these nomadic nations, it is impossible to say, even where Greek writers have preserved their barbarous names, to what branch of the vast North-Turanian class they belonged. Their habits were probably identical before the Christian era, during the Middle Ages, and at the present day. One tribe takes possession of a tract and retains it for several generations, and gives its name to the meadows where it tends its flocks, and to the rivers where the horses are watered. If the country be fertile, it will attract the eye of other tribes; wars begin, and if resistance be hopeless, hundreds of families fly from their paternal pastures, to migrate perhaps for generations, for migration they find a more natural life than permanent habitation; and after a time we may rediscover their names a thousand miles distant. Or two tribes will carry on their warfare for ages, till with reduced numbers both have perhaps to make common cause against some new enemy.

During these continued struggles their languages lose as many words as men are killed on the field of battle. Some words, we might say, go over, others are made prisoners, and exchanged again during times of peace. Besides, there are parleys and challenges, and at last a dialect is produced which may very properly be called a language of the camp (Urdu-zabân, camp-language, is the proper name of

Hindustani, formed in the armies of the Mogul emperors), but where it is difficult for the philologist to arrange the living and to number the slain, unless some salient points of grammar have been preserved throughout the medley. We saw how a number of tribes may be at times suddenly gathered by the command of a Chingis-Khan or Timur, like billows heaving and swelling at the call of a thunder-storm. One such wave rolling on from Karakorum to Liegnitz may sweep away all the sheepfolds and landmarks of centuries, and when the storm is over, a thin crust will, as after a flood, remain, concealing the underlying stratum of people and languages.

Castrén's Classification.

On the evidence of language, the Finno-Ugric family has been divided by Castrén into four branches,

(1) The *Ugric*, comprising Ostjakian, Vogulian, and Hungarian.

(2) The *Bulgaric*,[1] comprising Tcheremissian and Mordvinian.

(3) The *Permic*, comprising Syrjänian, Permian, and Votjakian.

(4) The *Finnic* (or *Chudic*), comprising Finnish, Estonian, Lapponian, Livonian, and Votian.

[1] The name Bulgaric is not borrowed from Bulgaria, on the Danube; Bulgaria, on the contrary, received its name (replacing Mœsia) from Bulgaric armies by whom it was conquered in the seventh century. Bulgarian tribes marched from the Volga to the Don, and after remaining for a time under the sovereignty of the Avars on the Don and Dnieper, they advanced to the Danube in 635, and founded there the Bulgarian kingdom. This has retained its name to the present day, though the original Bulgarians have long been absorbed and replaced by Slavonic inhabitants, and both brought under Turkish sway since 1392.

Hunfalvy's Classification.

Later researches induced P. Hunfalvy to modify this classification, first proposed by Castrén, and to divide the whole stock into two branches,

(1) The *Western or Finnic*, comprising the Finnish and the Lapponian.

(2) The *Eastern or Ugrian*, comprising the other three branches.

Later on he classed Finnish, Estonian, Karelian, Votian, Vepsian, and Livonian as true *Finnic*; while Permian, Syrjänian, Votjakian, Vogulian, Ostjakian, Magyar, Tcheremissian and Mordvinian were classed as *Ugric*, less closely held together. Lapponian was then supposed to hold an intermediate position between the two.

Budenz's Classification.

Still more recently a new division was advocated by Budenz in his essay, *Über die Verzweigung der Ugrischen Sprachen*, Göttingen, 1879. He proposed to divide these languages into

(1) a North-Ugrian branch, i. e. Lapponian, Syrjänian, Votjakian, Vogul-Ostjakian, and Magyar;

(2) a South-Ugrian branch, i. e, Finnish, Mordvinian, and Tcheremissian.

The chief distinction between these two branches would seem to consist in the initial n, which is palatal in the Northern, dental in the Southern branch.

In the further progress of phonetic change, the Lapponian was separated from the rest of the North-Ugrian branch; Mordvinian and Tcheremissian from the South-Ugrian branch.

Donner's Classification.

After an examination of the classification of his predecessors, Professor Donner in his essay on *Die gegenseitige Verwandtschaft der Finnisch-Ugrischen Sprachen*, published at Helsingfors, 1879, has proposed still another classification, based on a careful intercomparison of the phonetic and grammatical structure of the principal Finno-Ugric languages. He accepts the division into two branches, the *Finnic* and the *Ugric*, the later comprising Ostjakian, Vogulian, and Magyar, the former all the rest. He then proceeds to trace the ramifications of each branch according to certain peculiarities which different languages do or do not share in common, and arrives in the end at the following result.

Finno-Ugric Family.

I. Ugric Branch, represented by—
    (1) Irtish- and Surgut-Ostjakes, and North-Ostjakes.
    (2) Sosva- or North-Voguls, and Konda-Voguls.
    (3) Magyars.

II. Finnic Branch—
  (*a*) Permian division,
    (1) Syrjänes, Permians.
    (2) Votjakes.
  (*b*) Volga-Baltic division,
  (α) Volga group,
    (1) Tcheremissians.
    (2) Ersa- and Moksha-Mordvines.
  (β) West-Finnic group,
    (1) Russian, Norwegian, and Swedish Laps.
    (2) Lives.
    (3) Vepses.
    (4) Ests.
    (5) Votes.
    (6) Fins.

URAL-ALTAIC FAMILY.

The successive spreading of this family may be represented by the following outline:—

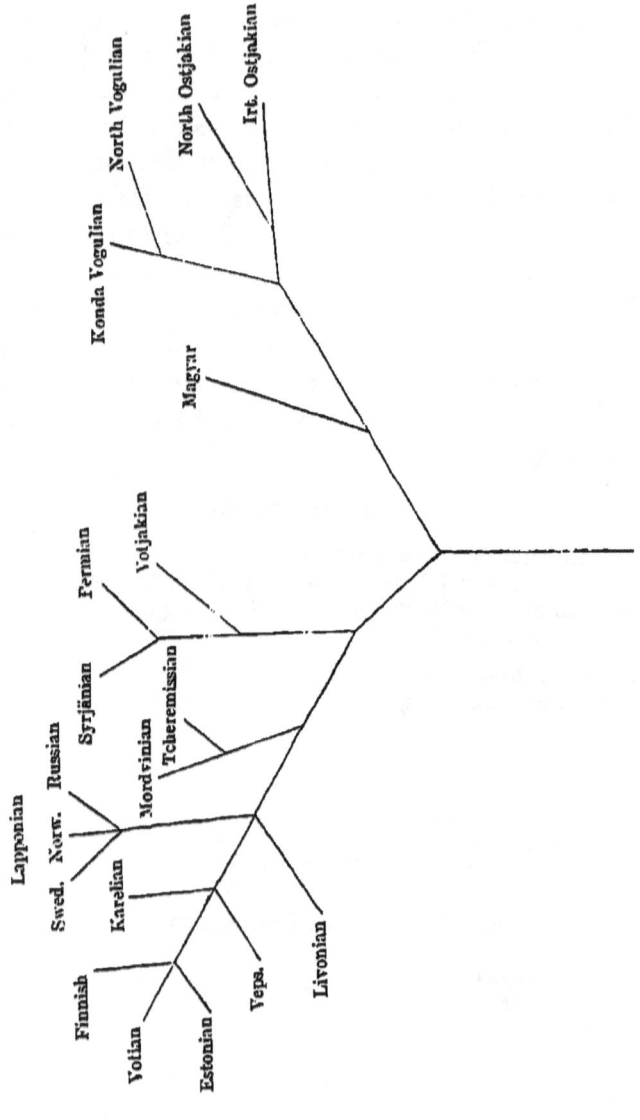

Spreading of the Finno-Ugric Languages.

Trusting to linguistic evidence alone, Professor Donner makes out the following history of the gradual spreading of the Finno-Ugric languages.

The Finnic branch must have started, he thinks, from its original home towards Europe, leaving successive settlements behind on its way towards the West. We do not know what caused the separation between the Volga-Baltic division and the Permic divisions. Possibly the pressure of Tatar tribes drove the Permians to move towards the north. The formation of the Permian numerals seems to have taken place under Tatar influences. The Volga-Baltic tribes remained together for some time, in contact with German tribes from whom they received the decimal method of counting, and a few words connected with higher culture. New historical convulsions drove the West-Finnic people more towards the west and the north, and during this period the German influence became considerable. To judge from the phonetic character of the words borrowed from German, which is more primitive than the Old Norse and Gothic, this period is supposed to have been anterior to the third century.

During the same time the Laps must have had their seats on the Eastern frontiers of the common group, which would explain their closer relation with the Tcheremissians. At this time a Lituanian influence begins to show itself. In Lapponian the number of Lituanian words is small. But after the Laps had migrated more northward, the Baltic

Fins, properly so-called, came into closer contact both with Lituanians and Scandinavians.

About the same time the Magyars began their migrations. It was after the dismemberment of Attila's Hunnic Empire that the Ugrian tribes approached Europe. They were then called Onagurs, Saragurs, and Urogs; and in later times they appear in Russian chronicles as Ugry, the ancestors of the Hungarians.

These conclusions drawn from linguistic evidence alone, are confirmed by what history teaches us, and thus gain even greater probability.[1]

Geographical Distribution.

I. Ugric Branch:
- (1) The Ostjakes live in the districts of Tobolsk and Tomsk, about 28,000 people.
- (2) The Voguls, about 7,000 people, are scattered on the Northern Ural, along the Konda and Sosva rivers.
- (3) The Magyars inhabit Hungary and parts of Siebenbürgen.

II. Finnic Branch:
- (a) Permian division,
    - (1) The Syrjänes, about 90,000 people, live in the districts of Archangel and Vologda.

Their southern neighbours, the Permians, about 60,000, inhabit the districts of Perm and Vjatka. Their country was known to the Scandinavians under the name of Bjarma-land, then peopled by Karelian Fins.

[1] See Donner, *Die gegenseitige Verwandtschaft* (1879), pp. 146-158.

(2) The Votjakes, about 230,000, are found in the district of Vjatka, and scattered in those of Kasan, Ufa, and Orenburg.

(b) Volga-Baltic division,
 (a) Volga group,
  (1) The Tcheremissians, about 200,000, are settled in the districts of Kasan and Vjatka, on the left side of the Volga.
  (2) The Mordvines, about 700,000, in the districts of Novgorod, Tambow, Pensa, Simbirsk, Saratow, and Samara, stretching as far as Orenburg and Astrachan.

The Fins and their Literature.

The most interesting among the Finno-Ugric tribes are, no doubt, the Fins, or, as they call themselves, *Suomalaiset*, i.e. inhabitants of fens. Their number is estimated at 1,521,515. They are divided into *Karelians* and *Tavastians*. The Karelians dwell in Eastern Finland, and in the western part of the district of Archangel, also in the north-western part of the districts of Olonetz and in Ingermanland. The old *Bjarmar*, known to the Scandinavians, were Karelians.

The Tavastians live in Finland, west of the Karelians. The *Vepses* or *North-Tchudes* and the *Votes* or *South-Tchudes* are Tavastians. Their literature and, above all, their popular poetry bear witness to a high intellectual development in times which we may call almost mythical, and in places more favourable to the glow of poetical feelings than their present abode, the last refuge Europe could afford them. Their epic songs still live among the poorest, recorded by oral tradition alone, and preserving all the features of a perfect metre and of a more ancient language. A national feeling has arisen amongst the Fins, despite of Russian supremacy; and the labours of Sjögern, Lönnrot, Castrén, Kellgren, Krohne, and Donner, receiving hence a powerful impulse, have produced results truly surprising. From the mouths of the aged an epic poem has been collected equalling the *Iliad* in length and completeness—nay, if we can forget for a moment all that we in our youth learned to call beautiful, not less beautiful. A Fin is not a Greek, and Wainamoïnen was not a Homeric rhapsôdos. But if the poet may take his colours from that nature by which he is surrounded, if he may depict the men with whom he lives, the *Kalevala* possesses merits not dissimilar from those of the *Iliad*, and will claim its place as the fifth national epic of the world, side by side with the Ionian songs, with the *Mahâbhârata*, the *Shâhnâmeh*, and the *Nibelunge*. If we want to study the circumstances under which short ballads may grow up and become amalgamated after a time into a real epic poem, nothing can be more instructive than the history of the collection of the Kalevala. We have here facts before us, not mere surmises, as in the case of the Homeric poems and the Nibelunge. We can still see how some poems were lost, others were modified; how certain heroes and episodes became popular, and attracted and absorbed what had been originally told of other heroes and other episodes. Lönnrot could watch the effect of a good and of a bad memory among the people who repeated the songs to him, and he makes no secret of having himself used the same freedom in the final arrangement of these poems which the people used from whom he learnt them.

This early literary cultivation has not been without a powerful influence on the language. It has imparted permanence to its forms and a traditional character to its words, so that at first sight we might almost doubt whether the grammar of this language had not left the agglutinative stage altogether. The agglutinative type, however, yet remains, and its grammar shows a luxuriance of grammatical combination second only to Turkish and Hungarian. Like Turkish it observes the 'harmony of vowels,' a feature which lends a peculiar charm to its poetry.

Karelian and Tavastian are dialectical varieties of Finnish.

The Ests and their Literature.

The *Ests*, the neighbours of the Fins, and speaking a language closely allied to the Finnish, inhabit Estonia and Livonia. Their number is said to be about 100,000. They possess, like the Fins, large fragments of ancient national poetry. Dr. Kreutzwald has been able to put together a kind of epic poem, called *Kalewipoeg*, the Son of Kalew, not so grand and perfect as the Kalevala, yet interesting as a parallel. There are two dialects of Estonian, that of Dorpat in Livonia, and that of Revel.

The *Lives* have dwindled down to about 2,000. They live on the coast of Kurland, from Lyserort to the gulf of Riga.

Estonia, Livonia, and Kurland form the three

Baltic provinces of Russia. The population on the islands of the Gulf of Finland is mostly Estonian. In the higher ranks of society, however, Estonian is hardly understood, and never spoken.

Finno-Ugric Philology.

The similarity between the Hungarian language and the dialects of Finnic origin, spoken East of the Volga, is not a new discovery. In 1253, Wilhelm Ruysbroeck, a priest who travelled beyond the Volga, remarked that a race called Pascatir, who lived on the Yaïk, spoke the same language as the Hungarians. They were then still settled east of the old Bulgarian kingdom, the capital of which, the ancient Bolgari on the left of the Volga, may still be traced in the ruins of Spask. The affinity of the Hungarians with the Ugro-Finnic dialects was first proved philologically by Gyarmathi in 1799, before the rise of Aryan Comparative Philology. It is still a subject of patriotic controversy, and Vambéry in 1882 tried to establish a closer affinity between Hungarian and Turkish. His theory, however, has not been accepted.

A few paradigms may suffice to show how close this affinity really is:—

Hungarian	Tcheremissian	English
Atyá-m	ätyä-m	my father
Atyú-d	ätyä-t	thy father
Aty-ja	ätyä-że	his father
Atyú-nk	ätyä-nä	our father
Atyú-tok	ätyä-dä	your father
Aty-jok	ätyä-ńt	their father.

CHAPTER XI.

DECLENSION.

Hungarian	Estonian	English
Nom. vér	werri	blood
Gen. véré	werre	of blood
Dat. vérnek	werrele	to blood
Acc. vért	werd	blood
Abl. vérestöl	werrist	from blood.

CONJUGATION.

Hungarian	Estonian	English
Lelek	leian	I find
Lelsz	leiad	thou findest
Lel	leiab	he finds
Leljük	leiame	we find
Lelitek	leiate	you find
Lelik	leiawad	they find.

A COMPARATIVE TABLE[1]
OF THE
NUMERALS OF THE FINNO-UGRIC CLASS.

	1	2	3	4	5	6	7	8	9	10
I. Ugric Branch—										
(1) Irtish-Ostjakian	it, i, ja	kāt, kātn / kāden, kādn	x̄uden	{ iitcta. het / nicda, nicdn	wēt	x̄ut	tūbet	nida, nit	ūr joń	joń, jań
(2) North Vogulian	ákwe	kit, kiti, hét	koroun	ńile	ät	kat	sāt, sout	ńalo-lu	antel-lu	lau
(3) Magyar	ádj	kēt, kåtō	hārom	nēdj	ōt	hat	hét	ńol-ts	kilän-ts	tíz
II. Finnic Branch—										
(a) Permian Division—										
(1) Syrjänian	ötik, öti	kik	kuim, kujim	ńolj	vit	kvait	sizim	kökjamis	ökmis	das
(2) Votjakian	odig, og	kik	kūiń	ńiľ	vit́	kvat́	sizim	tamis	ukmis	das
(b) Volga-Baltic Division—										
(α) Volga group										
(1) Tcheremissian	iktɛ, ik	kok	kum	nil	vit́, viz	kut	šem, šim	{ kande-kš / kāndåx̄še	{ inde-kš / endeɣše	lu, luo
(2) Mordvinian	veike, ve	kavko	kolmo	nile	vät́o	koko	sisem	kavkso	veikso	kämen
(β) West-Finnic group										
(1) Swedish Lapponian	akt	kuakt	kolm	nelje	vit	kot	čieča, ӡeӡe	loktse	oktse	lokke
(2) Livonian	ūt	kād	kuolm	nēļa	vit́	kūt	seis	kodōke	tüdōks	kūm
(3) Estonian	üks	kaks	kohm	neli	viž	kūž	seitse	kaheksa	üheksa	kümme
(4) Votian	ūhsi	kahsi	kölme	nellā	visi	kūsi	seitsē	kahehsē	ūhehsē	čümmē
(5) Finnish	ūhte	kahte	kolme	neljā	vīto	kūte	seitsemān	kahdeksan	ūhdeksan	kümmenen

[1] See Donner, *Die gegenseitige Verwandtschaft der Finno-Ugrischen Sprachen*, 1879; pp. 118-119.

CHAPTER XII.

SURVEY OF LANGUAGES.

The Northern and Southern Divisions of the Turanian Class.

WE have now examined the five classes of the Ural-Altaic family, the Samoyedic, Tungusic, Mongolic, Turkic, and Finnic. The Tungusic branch stands lowest; its grammar is not much richer than Chinese, and in its structure there is an absence of that architectonic order which in Chinese makes the Cyclopean stones of language hold together without cement. This applies, however, principally to the Mandshu; other Tungusic dialects spoken, not in China, but in the original seats of the Mandshus, are even now beginning to develop grammatical forms.

The Mongolic dialects excel the Tungusic, but in their grammar can hardly distinguish between the different parts of speech. The spoken idioms of the Mongolians, as of the Tungusians, are evidently struggling towards a more organic life, and Castrén has brought home evidence of incipient verbal growth in the language of the Buriäts and of a Tungusic dialect spoken near Nyertchinsk.

This is, however, only a small beginning, if compared with the profusion of grammatical resources displayed by the Turkic languages. In their system of conjugation, the Turkic dialects can hardly be surpassed. Their verbs are like branches which break down under the heavy burden of fruit and blossom. The excellence of the Finnic languages consists rather in a diminution than increase of verbal forms. The Tcheremissian and Mordvinian languages, however, are extremely artificial in their grammar, and allow an accumulation of pronominal suffixes at the end of verbs, surpassed only by the Bask, the Caucasian, and those American dialects that have been called *polysynthetic*. In declension also Finnish is richer even than Turkish.

These five classes constitute the northern or Ural-Altaic division of the Turanian class.

South-Turanian Languages.

The languages which I formerly comprehended under the general name of *South-Turanian*, should, for the present at least, be treated as independent branches of speech. My work, thirty-five years ago, was that of a bold, perhaps a too bold pioneer. The materials then accessible were extremely scanty, rough-hewn, and often untrustworthy. We have learnt more caution since, and know that we have to account, not only for points of similarity, but for dissimilarities also, before we can speak with authority on the genealogical relationship of languages. I do not mean to say that my rough classification of these South-Turanian languages has been proved to be altogether wrong, but I am quite ready to admit that what is 'not proven' in linguistic science should be treated, for the present at least, as non-existent. Otherwise there is considerable danger of hasty conclusions impeding the free and untrammelled progress of scientific inquiry. I still hold, for instance, that *Tibetan* and *Burmese*, or what I called the *Gangetic* and *Lohitic* languages, show traces of relationship which have to be accounted for, and which induced me to comprehend them under the common name of *Bhotîya* languages. I likewise hold that *Siamese* and what I called the *Taic* languages are closely connected with Chinese, and that both the *Bhotîya* and *Taic* groups point to a common origin with Chinese, though at a more distant period. The future will show whether I have guessed rightly or wrongly, for I cannot claim for my classification of these languages more than a hypothetical character. In the presence of scholars who have since made a special study of Chinese, Siamese, Tibetan, and Burmese, it would be unbecoming on my part to offer any opinion on the ultimate issues of these great linguistic problems which still await their final solution, and I gladly leave these matters to younger and stronger hands.[1]

For our own immediate purposes there is no necessity why we should extend our survey of languages beyond Europe and Asia. The principles of the Science of Language, with which alone we are concerned, have hitherto been elucidated almost exclusively by students of the Aryan, Semitic, the Chinese, and the Ural-Altaic, and the Malayo-Polynesian languages. This is, no doubt, an imperfection, but such imperfections exist in all sciences. Science can only advance step by step, and nowhere is this more true than

---

[1] I give at the end a tabular survey of these North and South Turanian Languages, referring for further particulars to my 'Letter on the Turanian Languages,' published in 1854.

in the Science of Language. Even after new clusters of languages have been explored and arranged into families, it will always remain extremely difficult, if not impossible, for one scholar to control the whole of the ever widening field of linguistic knowledge. There are, however, some excellent books in which the researches of scholars in different fields of human speech have been catalogued; and I can strongly recommend two works by Frederick Müller to those who wish to make themselves acquainted with the latest advances in linguistic and ethnological science, *Grundriss der Sprachwissenschaft*, Wien, 1876–1888, 4 vols.; and *Allgemeine Ethnographic*, Wien, 1879, 1 vol.

It may be useful, however, for our own purposes to add a short list of such languages and families of languages as have by this time been reduced to some kind of order, because some of them have to be used by ourselves from time to time in order to illustrate important features in the growth and decay of human speech.

Tamulic Languages.

Tamil, Telugu, Canarese, and *Malayalam*, constitute a well-defined family, with its smaller dialects, such as *Tulu,* and the vernaculars spoken by the *Todas, Gonds, Uraon-Kols, Râjmahals,* and, we may safely add, by the *Brahuis.* They occupy nearly the whole of the Indian peninsula, while dialects such as those of the Gonds, Uraon-Kols, Râjmahals, and Brahuis, scattered in less accessible places in the North, indicate the former more extended seats of the Tamulic or Dravidian race, before it had to make room before the advance of the Aryan conquerors of India. These languages have been carefully analysed by Caldwell in his *Comparative Grammar of the Dravidian or South-Indian Family of Languages,* Second Edition, 1875.

Munda Languages.

The dialects spoken by the *Santhals, Kols, Hos,* and *Bhumij,* which were formerly classed as Tamulic, must be recognised, as I tried to show in 1854, as an independent family. For reasons which I explained, I called these languages by the general name of *Munda.* Sir G. Campbell, who accepted my discovery, suggested the name *Kolarian.* This name, however, seems too restricted, if it refers to the Koles only, while the termination *arian* has either no meaning at all, or is misleading by its similarity to Arian.

Taic Languages.

The Taic family is represented by *Siamese* and its congeners, such as *Laos, Shan, Ahom, Khamti,* and *Kassia.* Its close connection with Chinese seems now admitted.

Bhotîya Languages.

The *Gangetic* and *Lohitic* languages, the former represented chiefly by *Tibetan,* the latter by *Burmese,* show traces of close relationship. With Tibetan we have to class such dialects as *Lepcha, Murmi, Magar, Gurnuug;* with Burmese *Bodo, Garo, Nâga, Singpho,* and similar dialects.

Whether the Bhotîya and Taic languages can both claim a distant relationship with Chinese, is as yet an open question, but several competent scholars seem inclined to answer it in the affirmative.

Languages of Farther India.

The languages spoken in *Annam*, *Pegu*, and *Cambodja* formed till lately an undistinguishable agglomerate. Some light, however, begins to dawn even here, and instead of purely isolated languages, certain groups of dialects become discernible.[1] The supposition of a relationship between the Munda dialects and the *Môn* or *Talaing*, first started by Mason, has received no support from further researches, and several languages, such as the *Khasi* (or Kassia) and *Tjam*, for instance, must for the present remain unclassed.

Languages of the Caucasus.

The same remark applies to the numerous dialects spoken in the Caucasus, such as the *Georgian, Lazian, Suanian, Mingrelian; Abchasian, Circassian; Thush* and *Tchetchenzian; Lesghian, Awarian, Kasikumükian*, &c. Some of these languages have been studied carefully, and attempts have been made to trace them back to a common type, but as yet without complete success.

The *Ossetian*, spoken in the Caucasus, is an Aryan language.

Egypt.

The ancient language of Egypt stands by itself. It has been mentioned already that some scholars recognise in it the most ancient phase of a language, as yet neither Semitic nor Aryan, but containing the germs of both families. Such a theory, however, if it

---

[1] See E. Kuhn, *Beiträge zur Sprachenkunde Hinterindiens*, in the *Sitzungsberichte* der philos.-philol. Classe der Bayer. Akad. der Wissenschaften, 1889, Heft II.

SURVEY OF LANGUAGES. 449

ever can be proved, requires much stronger support than it has hitherto received.

Sub-semitic Languages.

The same applies to the so-called *Sub-semitic* languages, the *Berber* or *Libyan* (*Kabyl, Shilhe, Tuareg* or *Tamasheg*), and to some of the native dialects of Abyssinia or Ethiopia (*Somáli, Galla, Beja* or *Bihári, Agau, Dankali*, etc.). Some scholars treat them as Semitic, modified by people who spoke originally a Hamitic language, others as Hamitic, modified by Semitic influences. These questions may be solved hereafter, though it is difficult to see how the evidence can ever acquire sufficient strength to support such far-reaching theories.

Languages of Africa.

Some of the languages of Africa have lately been studied with a truly scholarlike accuracy, and the work of classification has made considerable progress.

(1) The languages spoken by *Hottentots* and *Bushmen* in the South, may now safely be treated as related, though their more distant relationship with ancient Egyptian can for the present be looked upon as a suggestion only. The fully developed system of clicks in these languages constitutes a very characteristic feature, though the Bántu tribes, nearest to the Hottentot, have adopted the same.[1]

(2) The *Bántu* races or *Kafirs*, extending in an unbroken line on the East coast of Africa, from

---
[1] Some scholars speak of clicks in the Galla dialect, north of the equator, in the Circassian of the Caucasus, and even in the Kechua as spoken in Guatemala; see Bleek, *Compar. Gr.* § 67; Hahn, *Sprache der Nama*, pp. 15 seq.

I. G g

North of the Equator down to the Hottentots, and from East to West across the whole continent, speak languages both radically and formally most closely related to each other.

(3) The dialects spoken by the Negro-races, extending from the Western coast of Africa towards the interior, are as yet classed as one mass, though recent researches tend more and more to the discovery of separate classes among them.

When so much remains to be done even for a preliminary survey of the languages of Africa, it seems rather premature to attempt to trace them all back to three sources, as Lepsius has done in his last great work, the 'Nubische Grammatik.' He there tries to reduce the inhabitants of Africa to three types, (1) the Northern negroes, (2) the Southern or Bântu negroes, (3) the Cape negroes.

In accordance with this ethnological system, he arranges the languages also into three zones:—

(1) The Southern, south of the equator, the Bântu dialects, explored chiefly on the west and east coasts, but probably stretching across the whole continent, comprising the Herero, Pongue, Fernando Po, Kafir ('Osa and Zulu), Tshuana (Soto and Rolon), Suahili, etc.

(2) The Northern zone, between the equator and the Sahara, and east as far as the Nile, comprising Efik, Ibo, Yoruba, Ewe, Akra or Ga, Otyi, Kru, Vei (Mande), Temne, Bullom, Wolof, Fula, Sonrhai, Kanuri, Teda (Tibu), Logone, Wandala, Bagirmi, Mâba, Konjâra, Umâle, Dinka, Shilluk, Bongo, Bari, Oigob, Nuba, and Barea.

(3) The Hamitic zone, including the extinct Egyp-

tian and Coptic, the Libyan dialects, such as Tuareg (Kabyl and Tamasheg), Hausa, the Kushitic or Ethiopian languages, including the Beja dialects, the Soho, Falasha, Agau, Galla, Dankali, and Somâli. Even the Hottentot and Bushman languages are referred by Lepsius to the same zone.

The languages of the third zone are considered by Lepsius as alien, and as having reached Africa from the East at different times and by different roads. He looks upon the Bântu languages as the true aboriginal nucleus of African speech, and he attempts to show that the languages of the Northern zone are modifications of Bântu speech, produced by contact and more or less violent friction with the languages of the Hamitic zone and with Semitic languages also.

This would considerably simplify the linguistic map of Africa; the question is whether this bold attempt will stand the test of further inquiry.

America.

The greatest diversity of opinion prevails with regard to the languages of America. Some scholars see nothing but diversity, others discover everywhere traces of uniformity, if not in the radical elements, at least in the formal structure of these languages. Without trying to anticipate the results of further research, which is now actively pushed forward by some of the most eminent scholars in America, we may safely accept at least four centres of language clearly defined and separated from the rest.

(i) The languages of the Red Indians in the North, with numerous subdivisions;

(ii) The languages of Mexico;
(iii) The languages of Central America;
(iv) The languages of Peru.

These four centres of speech represent, however, four islands only in the vast ocean of American speech. They are surrounded by other islands which may formerly have belonged to larger continents of speech, but which for the present remain isolated. Such are the dialects of the *Arctic* or *Hyperborean* tribes, of the *Eskimos* and *Greenlanders* in the extreme North, the *Arowakes* and the once famous *Caribes*, in the north of South America and in the islands of the Antilles, of the aboriginal inhabitants of Brazil, of the *Abipones*, the *Patagonians*, and the inhabitants of Tierra del Fuego.

It will require much time and labour before this abundant linguistic flora of America can be reduced to something like scientific order. To attempt at present to trace back the inhabitants of America to a Jewish, Phenician, Chinese, or Celtic source is simply labour lost, and outside the pale of real science.

Oceanic Languages.

Much more progress has been made in classifying the languages which extend from Madagascar on the East coast of Africa to the Sandwich Islands west of America.

There is an original, though very distant, relationship between the *Malay*, the *Polynesian*, and the *Melanesian* (and *Micronesian*) languages. They are independent branches of a common stem. The dialects of Australia, however, divided into three groups, and those spoken by the Papuas of New Guinea, stand apart and have not yet been properly classified, though some dialects spoken in New Guinea, such as Motu, are clearly Melanesian.

This short survey of the work of linguistic classification, so far as it has been carried on at present, gives but a very imperfect idea of the labours bestowed on the study of languages all over the world. My object was only to point out the centres of linguistic life which have been discovered, and the ramifications from which have been determined with some amount of scientific accuracy. In some cases that ramification is perfectly clear, in others it is as yet vague and obscure. Many languages in Europe and Asia stand still completely isolated, such as Etruscan, Bask, Lycian, Japanese, Corean, the dialects of the Andaman and Nicobar islands, to say nothing of dialects spoken in other parts of the world. Future generations will probably smile at our linguistic maps of the world as we smile at the *Orbis terrarum veteribus notus*. Still, considering the difficulties in the way of studying unwritten languages, and the shortness of time that has elapsed since the genius of Leibniz, Humboldt, Bopp, Grimm, and Pott first gave the proper direction to these studies, the record of the Science of Language can well bear comparison with that of other sciences.

Inflectional Stage.

It must not be supposed, because this survey of languages has been inserted here as part of our discussion of the Terminational or Agglutinative Stage, that therefore all these languages, or even most of them, are purely agglutinative. All we can say of them in general is that they have left the radical stage, and that they have not entered completely into the inflectional stage. But we must remember that these three stages are natural to all languages, that inflection invariably presupposes agglutination, and agglutination juxtaposition. The chief distinction between an inflectional and an agglutinative language consists in the fact that the speakers of agglutinative languages retain the consciousness of their roots, and therefore do but seldom allow them to be affected by phonetic corruption. Even when they have lost the consciousness of the original meaning of terminations, they feel distinctly the difference between the significative root and the modifying elements. Not so in the inflectional languages. There the various elements which enter into the composition of words, may become so welded together, and suffer so much from phonetic corruption, that none but the scholar would be aware of an original distinction between root and termination, and none but the comparative grammarian able to discover the seams that separate the component parts.

CHAPTER XIII.

THE QUESTION OF THE COMMON ORIGIN OF LANGUAGES.

The Exhaustive Character of the Morphological Classification.

IF you consider the character of our morphological classification, you will see that this classification, differing thereby from the genealogical, must be applicable to all languages. Our classification exhausts all possibilities. If the component elements of language are roots, predicative and demonstrative, we cannot have more than three combinations. Roots may either become words without any outward modification; or, secondly, they may be joined so that one determines the other and loses its independent existence; or, thirdly, they may be joined and be allowed to coalesce, so that both lose their independent character.

The number of roots which enter into the composition of a word makes no difference, and it is unnecessary, therefore, to admit a fourth class, sometimes called *polysynthetic*, or *incorporating*, including most of the American languages. As long as in these sesquipedalian compounds the significative root remains distinct, they belong to the agglutinative stage; as soon as it is absorbed by the terminations, they belong to the inflectional stage.

We must guard, however, against a very common mistake. It often happens that in polysynthetic languages words appear in a fuller form when standing by themselves, and in a shorter form when incorporated in a compound. Scholars are generally inclined in such cases to look upon the shorter form as shortened, while it is far more likely that the short is the original form, which has been more fully developed when used as an independent noun or verb.

Nor is it necessary to distinguish between *synthetic* and *analytical* languages, including under the former name the ancient, and under the latter the modern, languages of the inflectional class. The formation of such phrases as the French *j'aimerai*, for *j'ai à aimer*, or the English, *I shall do, thou wilt do*, may be called *analytical* or *metaphrastic*. But in their morphological nature these phrases are still inflectional. If we analyse such a phrase as *je vivrai*, we find it was originally *ego* (Sanskrit aham) *vivere* (Sanskrit gîv-as-e, dat. neutr.) *habeo* (Sanskrit *ghâbh-ayâ-mi); that is to say, we have a number of words in which grammatical articulation has been almost entirely destroyed, but has not been cast off; whereas in Turanian languages grammatical forms are produced by the combination of integral roots, and the old and useless terminations are first discarded before any new combination takes place.[1]

Common Origin of Languages.

At the end of our morphological classification a problem presents itself, which we might have declined to enter upon if we had confined ourselves to a genea-

[1] *Letter on the Turanian Languages*, p. 75.

logical classification of languages. At the end of our genealogical classification we had to confess that only a certain number of languages had as yet been arranged genealogically, and that therefore the time for approaching the problem of the common origin of all had not yet come. In languages which have been proved to constitute one family, the constituent elements or roots are, no doubt, accessible, but all attempts at comparing the roots of different families of speech have hitherto proved useless. It may be true that there are roots in the Aryan languages which are identical, both in form and meaning, with roots of the Semitic, the Ural-Altaic, the Bântu, and Oceanic languages. But let us consider what this means, and what stringency of proof it would possess in support of a real common origin of these families. These roots, say about 1000 for each family, consist of one vowel and one or two consonants, and their meaning is of the most general character. Suppose a root like SAR expressed some kind of movement in all these families of speech, would that prove a real genealogical relationship? Only if all, or if at least a majority of roots in all these families, could be proved to run parallel, would there be any nerve in such an argument, and such a result can hardly be anticipated in the present state of our knowledge.

But the case is very different at the end of our morphological classification. Though we have not yet examined all languages which belong to the radical, the terminational, and inflectional classes, we have arrived at the conclusion that all languages must fall under one or the other of these three categories of human speech. It would not be consistent, therefore, to shrink from the consideration of a problem which, though beset with many difficulties, cannot be excluded altogether from the science of language.

Language and Race.

Let us first see our problem clearly and distinctly. The problem of the common origin of languages has no necessary connection with the problem of the common origin of mankind. If it could be proved that languages had had different beginnings, this would in no wise necessitate the admission of different beginnings of the human race. For if we look upon language as natural to man, it might have broken out at different times and in different countries among the scattered descendants of one original pair; if, on the contrary, language is to be treated as an invention, there is still less reason why each succeeding generation should not have invented its own idiom.

Nor would it follow, if it could be proved that all the dialects of mankind point to one common source, that therefore the human race must descend from one pair. For language might have been the property of one favoured race, and have been communicated to the other races in the progress of history.

Comparative Philology.

The science of language and the science of ethnology have both suffered most seriously from being mixed up together.[1] The classification of races and lan-

[1] See an excellent article of Professor Huxley, in the *Fortnightly Review*, 1866; and my *Letter on the Turanian Languages*, 1856, pp. 89-92.

guages should be quite independent of each other. Races may change their languages, and history supplies us with several instances where one race adopted the language of another. Different languages, therefore, may be spoken by one race, or the same language may be spoken by different races; so that any attempt at squaring the classification of races and tongues must necessarily fail.[1]

Biblical Genealogies.

Secondly, the problem of the common origin of languages has no connection with the statements contained in the Old Testament regarding the creation of man and the genealogies of the patriarchs. Those statements are interesting from a purely historical point of view, though no higher authority can be claimed for them than for the statements contained in ancient hieroglyphic or cuneiform inscriptions. But what even those who believe in a higher authority of the Bible as an historical document should consider, is that if our researches lead us to the admission of different beginnings for the languages of mankind, there is nothing in the Old Testament opposed to this view. For although the Jews believed that for a time the whole earth was of one language and of one speech, it has long been pointed out by eminent divines, with particular reference to the dialects of America, that new languages might have arisen at later times. If,

[1] The opposite view, namely, that a genealogical arrangement of the races of man would afford the best classification of the various languages now spoken throughout the world, is maintained by Darwin, *Origin of Species*, p. 422, though without sufficient proof.

on the contrary, we arrive at the conviction that all languages can be traced back to one common source, we should never think of transferring the genealogies of the Old Testament to the genealogical classification of languages. The genealogies of the Old Testament refer to blood, not to language, and as we know that people, without changing their name, did frequently change their language, it is clearly impossible that the genealogies of the Old Testament should coincide with the genealogical classification of languages. In order to avoid a confusion of ideas, it would be preferable to abstain altogether from using the same names to express relationship of language which in the Bible are used to express relationship of blood. It was usual formerly to speak of *Japhetic*, *Hamitic*, and *Semitic* languages. The first name has now been replaced by *Aryan*, the second by *African*; and though the third is still retained, it has received a scientific definition quite different from the meaning which it would have in the Bible. It is well to bear this in mind, in order to prevent not only those who are for ever attacking the Bible with arrows that cannot reach it, but likewise those who defend it with weapons they know not how to wield, from disturbing in any way the quiet progress of the science of language.

Formal Relationship of Languages.

Let us now look dispassionately at our problem. The problem of the possibility of a common origin of all languages naturally divides itself into two parts, the *material* and the *formal*. We are here concerned with the formal part only. We have examined all

COMMON ORIGIN OF LANGUAGES. 461

possible forms which language can assume, and we have now to ask, Can we reconcile with these three distinct forms, the radical, the terminational, and the inflectional, the admission of one common origin of human speech?—I answer decidedly, Yes.

The chief argument that has been brought forward against the common origin of language is this, that no monosyllabic or radical language has ever entered into an agglutinative or terminational stage, and that no agglutinative or terminational language has ever risen to the inflectional stage. Chinese, it is said, is still what it has been from the beginning; it has never produced agglutinative or inflectional forms; nor has any agglutinative language ever given up the distinctive feature of the terminational stage, namely, the integrity of its roots.

In answer to this, it should be pointed out that though each language, as soon as it once becomes settled, is apt to retain that morphological character which it had when it first assumed its individual or national existence, it does not lose altogether the power of producing grammatical forms that belong to a higher stage. In Chinese, and particularly in Chinese dialects, we find rudimentary traces of agglutination. The *li* which I mentioned before as the sign of the locative, has dwindled down to a mere postposition, and a modern Chinese is no more aware that *li* originally meant interior, than the Turanian is of the origin of his case terminations.[1] In the spoken dialects of

[1] M. Stanislas Julien remarks that the numerous compounds which occur in Chinese prove the wide-spread influence of the principle of agglutination in that language. The fact is, that in Chinese every sound

Chinese, agglutinative forms are of more frequent occurrence. Thus, in the Shanghai dialect, *wo* is to speak, as a verb; *woda*, a word. Of *woda* a genitive is formed, *woda-ka*, a dative *pela woda*, an accusative *tang woda*.[1] In agglutinative languages, again, we meet with rudimentary traces of inflection. Thus in Tamil the verb *tûngu*, to sleep, has not retained its full integrity in the derivative *tûkkam*, sleep; and *tûngu* itself might probably be traced back to a simpler root, such as *tu*, to recline, to be suspended, to sleep.

I mention these instances, which might be greatly multiplied, in order to show that there is nothing mysterious in the tenacity with which each language clings in general to that stage of grammar which it had attained at the time of its first settlement. If a family, or a tribe, or a nation, has once accustomed itself to express its ideas according to one system of grammar, that first mould becomes stronger with each generation. But, while Chinese was arrested and be-

---

has numerous meanings; and in order to avoid ambiguity, one word is frequently followed by another which agrees with it in the one particular meaning which is intended by the speaker. Thus

chi-youen	(beginning-origin)	signifies	beginning
ken-youen	(root-origin)	,,	beginning
youen-chi	(origin-beginning)	,,	beginning
meï-miai	(beautiful-remarkable)	,,	beautiful
meï-li	(beautiful-elegant)	,,	beautiful
chen-youen	(charming-lovely)	,,	beautiful
yong-i	(easy-facile)	,,	easily
tsong-yong	(to obey, easy)	,,	easily

In order to express 'to boast,' the Chinese say *king-koua*, *king-fa*, etc., both words having one and the same meaning.

This peculiar system of *juxtaposition*, however, cannot be considered as agglutination in the strict sense of the word.

[1] M. M., *Letter on the Turanian Languages*, p. 24.

came traditional in this very early stage, the radical, other dialects passed on through that stage, retaining their pliancy. They were not arrested, and did not become traditional or national, before those who spoke them had learnt to appreciate the advantage of agglutination. That advantage being once perceived, a few single forms in which agglutination first showed itself, would soon, by that sense of analogy which is inherent in language, extend their influence irresistibly. Languages arrested in that stage would cling with equal tenacity to the system of agglutination. A Chinese can hardly understand how language is possible unless every syllable is significative; a Turanian would despise every idiom in which each word does not display distinctly its radical and significative element; whereas we, who are accustomed to the use of inflectional languages, are proud of the very grammar which a Chinese and Turanian would treat with contempt.

The fact, therefore, that languages, if once settled, do not change their grammatical constitution, is no argument against our theory, that every inflectional language was once agglutinative, and every agglutinative language was once monosyllabic. I call it a theory, but it is more than a theory, for it is the only possible way in which the realities of Sanskrit or any other inflectional language can be explained. As far as the formal part of language is concerned, we cannot resist the conclusion that what is now *inflectional* was formerly *agglutinative*, and what is now *agglutinative* was at first *radical*. The great stream of language rolled on in numberless dialects, and changed its grammatical colouring as it passed from time to time through new deposits. The different channels which left the main current and became stationary and stagnant, or, if you like, literary and traditional, retained for ever that colouring which the main current displayed at the stage of their separation. If we call the radical stage *white*, the agglutinative *red*, and the inflectional *blue*, then we may well understand why the white channels should show hardly a drop of red or blue, or why the red channels should hardly betray a shadow of blue; and we shall be prepared to find what we do find, namely, white tints in the red, and white and red tints in the blue channels of speech.

True Meaning of the Problem of the Common Origin of Languages.

In all this, however, I only argue for the possibility, not for the necessity, of a common origin of language.

I look upon the problem of the common origin of language, which I have shown to be quite independent of the problem of the common origin of mankind, as a question which ought to be kept open as long as possible. It is not, I believe, a problem quite as hopeless as that of the plurality of worlds, on which so much has been written, but it should be treated very much in the same manner. As it is impossible to demonstrate by the evidence of the senses that the planets are inhabited, the only way to prove that they are, is to prove that it is impossible that they should not be. Thus, on the other hand, in order to prove that the planets are not inhabited, you must prove that it is impossible that they should be. As soon as the one or the other has been proved, the question will be set at rest; till then it must remain an open question, whatever our own predilections on the subject may be.

I do not take quite as desponding a view of the problem of the common origin of language, but I insist on this, that we ought not to allow this problem to be in any way prejudged. Now it has been the tendency of the most distinguished writers on comparative philology to take it almost for granted, that after the discovery of the two families of language, the Aryan and Semitic, and after the establishment of the close ties of relationship which unite the members of each, it would be impossible to admit any longer a common origin of language. After the criteria by which the unity of the Aryan as well as the Semitic dialects can be proved, had been so successfully defined, it was but natural that the absence of similar coincidences between any Semitic and Aryan language, or between these and any other branch of speech, should have led to a belief that no connection was admissible between them. A Linnæan botanist, who has his definite marks by which to recognise an anemone, would reject with equal confidence any connection between the species anemone and other flowers which have since been classed under the same head, though deficient in the Linnæan marks of the anemone.

But there are surely different degrees of affinity in languages as well as in all other productions of nature, and the different families of speech, though they cannot show the same signs of relationship by which their members are held together, need not of necessity have been perfect strangers to each other from the beginning.

Now I confess that when I found the argument used over and over again, that it is impossible any longer to speak of a common origin of language, because comparative philology had proved that there existed various families of speech, I felt that this was not true, that at all events it was an exaggeration.

The problem, if properly viewed, bears the following aspect:—'*If you wish to assert that language had various beginnings, you must prove it impossible that language could have had a common origin.*'

No such impossibility has ever been established with regard to a common origin of the Aryan and Semitic dialects; while, on the contrary, the analysis of the grammatical forms in either family has removed many difficulties, and made it at least intelligible how, with materials identical or very similar, two individuals, or two families, or two nations, could in the course of time have produced languages so different in form as Hebrew and Sanskrit.

But still greater light was thrown on the formative and metamorphic process of language by the study of other dialects unconnected with Sanskrit or Hebrew, and exhibiting before our eyes the growth of those grammatical forms (grammatical in the widest sense of the word) which in the Aryan and Semitic families we know only as formed, not as forming; as decaying, not as living; as traditional, not as understood and intentional: I mean the Ural-Altaic, the Bântu, the Oceanic, and other languages. The traces by which these languages attest their original relationship are much fainter than in the Semitic and Aryan families, but they are so of necessity. In the Aryan and Semitic families the agglutinative process by which alone grammatical forms can be obtained, has been arrested at some time, and this could only have been through social, religious, or political influences. By the same power through which an advancing civilisation absorbs the manifold dialects in which every spoken idiom naturally represents itself, the first political or religious centralisation must necessarily have put a check on the exuberance of an agglutinative speech. Out of many possible forms one became popular, fixed, and technical for each word, for each grammatical category; and by means of poetry, law, and religion, a literary or political language was produced to which thenceforth nothing had to be added; which in a short time, after becoming unintelligible in its formal elements, was liable to phonetic corruption only, but incapable of internal resuscitation. It is necessary to admit a primitive concentration of this kind for the Aryan and Semitic families, for it is thus only that we can account for coincidences between Sanskrit and Greek terminations, which were formed neither from Greek nor from Sanskrit materials, but which are still identically the same in both. It is in this sense that I call these languages political or state languages, and it has been truly said that languages belonging to these families must be able to prove their relationship by sharing in common not only what is regular and intelligible, but what is anomalous, unintelligible, and dead.

If no such concentration takes place, languages, though formed of the same materials and originally identical, must necessarily diverge in what we may call dialects, but in a very different sense from the dialects such as we find in the later periods of political languages. The process of agglutination will continue in each clan, and forms becoming unintelligible will be easily replaced by new and more intelligible compounds. If the cases are formed by postpositions, new postpositions can be used as soon as the old ones become obsolete. If the conjugation is formed by pronouns, new pronouns can be used if the old ones are no longer sufficiently distinct.

Let us ask, then, what coincidences we are likely to find in agglutinative dialects which have become separated, and which gradually approach to a more settled state? It seems to me that we can only expect to find in them such coincidences as Castrén and Schott have succeeded in discovering in the Samoyedic, Tungusic, Mongolic, Turkic, and Finno-Ugric languages; and such as Hodgson, Caldwell, Logan, and myself have pointed out in the Tamulic, Taic, Gangetic, Lohitic, and Malaic languages. They must refer chiefly to those parts of speech which it is most difficult to reproduce—I mean pronouns, numerals, and prepositions. These languages will hardly ever agree in what is anomalous or inorganic, because their organism repels continually what begins to be formal and unintelligible. It is astonishing rather that any words of a conventional meaning should have been discovered as the common property of such languages, than that most of their words and forms should be peculiar to each. These coincidences must, however, be accounted for by those who deny the possibility of their common origin; they must be accounted for, either as the result of accident, or of an imitative instinct which led the human mind everywhere to the same purely onomatopoetic formations. This has never been done, and it will require great efforts to achieve it.

To myself the study of the languages, neither Aryan nor Semitic, was interesting particularly because it offered an opportunity of learning how far languages, supposed to be of a common origin, might diverge and become dissimilar by the unrestrained operation of dialectic regeneration.

In a letter which in 1854 I addressed to my friend, the late Baron Bunsen, and which was published by him in his *Outlines of the Philosophy of Universal History*[1] (vol. i. pp. 263-521), it had been my object to trace, as far as I was able, the principles which guided the formation of agglutinative languages, and to show how far languages may become dissimilar in their grammar and dictionary, and yet allow us to treat them as cognate dialects. In answer to the assertion that it was impossible, I tried, in the fourth, fifth, and sixth sections of that Essay, to show *how* it was possible that, starting from a common ground, languages as different as Mandshu

[1] These *Outlines* form vols. iii. and iv. of Bunsen's work, *Christianity and Mankind*, in 7 vols. (London, 1854: Longman), and are sold separately.

and Finnish, Chinese and Siamese, should have arrived at their present state, and might still be treated as cognate tongues. And as I look upon this process of agglutination as the only intelligible means by which language can acquire a grammatical organisation, and clear the barrier which has arrested the growth of the Chinese idiom, I felt justified in applying the principles derived from the formation of agglutinative languages to the Aryan and Semitic families likewise. They also must have passed through an agglutinative stage, and it is during that period alone that we can account for the gradual divergence and individualisation of what we afterwards call the Aryan and Semitic forms of speech. If we can account for the different appearance of Mandshu and Finnish, we can also account for the distance between Hebrew and Sanskrit. It is true that we do not know the Aryan speech during its purely agglutinative period, but we can infer what it was, when we see languages like Finnish and Turkish approaching more and more towards an Aryan type. Such has been the advance which Turkish has made towards inflectional forms, that Professor Ewald claimed for it the title of a synthetic language, a title which he gives to the Aryan and Semitic dialects, after they have left the agglutinative stage, and entered into a process of phonetic corruption and dissolution. 'Many of its component parts,' he says, 'though they were no doubt originally, as in every language, independent words, have been reduced to mere vowels, or have been lost altogether, so that we must infer their former presence by the changes which they have wrought in the body of the word. *Göz* means eye, and *gör*, to see; *ish*, deed, and *it*, to do; *ĭch*, the interior, and *gîr*, to enter.'[1] Nay, he goes so far as to admit some formal elements which Turkish shares in common with the Aryan family, and which therefore could only date from a period when both were still in their agglutinative infancy. For instance, *di*, as exponent of a past action; *ta*, as the sign of the past participle of the passive; *lu*, as a suffix to form adjectives, &c.[2] This is more than I should venture to assert.

Taking this view of the gradual formation of language by agglutination, as opposed to internal development, it is hardly necessary to say that, when I spoke of a Turanian family of speech, I used the word family in a different sense from that which it has with regard to the Aryan and Semitic languages. In my *Letter on the Turanian Languages*, which has been the subject of so many random attacks on the part of those who believe in different beginnings of language and mankind, I had explained this repeatedly, and I had preferred the term of *group* for the Turanian languages, in order to express as clearly as possible that the relation between Turkish and Mandshu, between Tamil and Finnish, was a different one, not in degree only but in kind, from that between Sanskrit and Greek. 'These Turanian languages,' I said (p. 216), 'cannot be considered as standing to each other in the same relation as He-

[1] *Götlingische Gelehrte Anzeigen*, 1855, s. 298; see Hunfalvy's remarks, on p. 392.
[2] Ewald, *l. c.* s. 302, *note*.

brew to Arabic, Sanskrit and Greek.' 'They are radii diverging from a common centre, not children of a common parent.' And still they are not so widely distant as Hebrew and Sanskrit, because none of them has fully entered into that new phase of growth or decay through which the Semitic and Aryan languages passed after they had been settled, individualised and nationalised.

The real object of my Essay was therefore a defensive one. It was intended to show how rash it was to speak of different independent beginnings in the history of human speech, before a single argument had been brought forward to establish the necessity of such an admission. The impossibility of a common origin of language has never been proved, but, in order to remove what were considered difficulties affecting the theory of a common origin, I felt it my duty to show practically, and by the very history of the Turanian languages, how such a theory was possible, or, as I say in one instance only, probable. I endeavoured to show how even the most distant members of the Turanian family, the one spoken in the north, the other in the south of Asia, the *Finnic* and the *Tamulic*, have preserved in their grammatical organisation traces of a former unity; and, if some of my most determined opponents admit that I have proved the ante-Brahmanic or Tamulic inhabitants of India to belong to the Turanian family, and that these proofs have been considerably strengthened by Caldwell's Comparative Grammar of the Dravidian Languages, they can hardly fail to see that if this, the most extreme point of my argument, be conceded, everything else is conceded, and must follow by necessity.

Yet I did not call the last chapter of my Essay, 'On the Necessity of a Common Origin of Language,' but 'On the Possibility'; and, in answer to the opinions advanced by the opposite party, I summed up my defence in these two paragraphs:—

I.

'Nothing necessitates the admission of different independent beginnings for the *material* elements of the Turanian, Semitic, and Aryan branches of speech: nay, it is possible even now to point out radicals which, under various changes and disguises, have been current in these three branches ever since their first separation.'

II.

'Nothing necessitates the admission of different beginnings for the formal elements of the Turanian, Semitic, and Aryan branches of speech; and though it is impossible to derive the Aryan system of grammar from the Semitic, or the Semitic from the Aryan, we can perfectly understand how, either through individual influences, or by the wear and tear of speech in its own continuous working, the different systems of grammar of Asia and Europe may have been produced.'

It will be seen, from the very wording of these two paragraphs, that my object was to deny the necessity of independent beginnings, and to assert the possibility of a common origin of language. I have been accused of having been biassed in my researches by an implicit belief in the common origin of mankind. I do not deny that I hold this belief, and, if it wanted confirmation, that confirmation has been supplied by Darwin's book, *On the Origin of Species*.[1] But I defy my adversaries to point out one single passage where I have mixed up scientific with theological arguments. Only, if I am told that no 'quiet observer would ever have conceived the idea of deriving all mankind from one pair, unless the Mosaic records had taught it,' I must be allowed to say in reply, that this idea, on the contrary, is so natural, so consistent with all human laws of reasoning, that, as far as I know, there has been no nation on earth which, if it possessed any traditions on the origin of mankind, did not derive the human race from one pair, if not from one person. The author of the Mosaic records, therefore, though rightly stripped, before the tribunal of Physical Science, of his claims as an inspired writer, may at least claim the modest title of a quiet

---

[1] 'Here the lines converge as they recede into the geological ages, and point to conclusions which, upon Darwin's theory, are inevitable, but hardly welcome. The very first step backward makes the Negro and the Hottentot our blood-relations; not that reason or Scripture objects to that, though pride may.'—Asa Grey, *Natural Selection not inconsistent with Natural Theology*, 1861, p. 5.

'One good effect is already manifest, its enabling the advocates of the hypothesis of a multiplicity of human species to perceive the double insecurity of their ground. When the races of men are admitted to be of one species, the corollary, that they are of one origin, may be expected to follow. Those who allow them to be of one species must admit an actual diversification into strongly marked and persistent varieties; while those, on the other hand, who recognise several or numerous human species, will hardly be able to maintain that such species were primordial and supernatural in the ordinary sense of the word.'—*Ibid.* p. 54.

observer; and if his conception of the physical unity of the human race can be proved to be an error, it is an error which he shares in common with other quiet observers, such as Humboldt, Bunsen, Prichard, Owen, and, I may now add, Darwin.[1]

[1] Professor Pott, the most distinguished advocate of the polygenetic dogma, has pleaded the necessity of admitting more than one beginning for the human race and for language in an article in the *Journal of the German Oriental Society*, ix. 405; *Max Müller und die Kennzeichen der Sprachverwandtschaft*, 1855; in a treatise *Die Ungleichheit menschlicher Rassen*, 1856; and in the new edition of his *Etymologische Forschungen*, 1861.

On the other hand, the researches carried on independently by different scholars tend more and more to confirm, not only the close relationship of the languages belonging respectively to the northern and southern branches of the Turanian class, but likewise the relationship of these two branches themselves, and their ultimate dependence on Chinese. Nor is the evidence on which this relationship rests purely formal or grammatical, but it is likewise supported by evidence taken from the dictionary. The following letter from Mr. Edkins, the author of *A Grammar of the Chinese Colloquial Language* (second edition, Shanghai, 1864), will show how his inquiries into the primitive state of the Chinese language have brought to light the convergence of the Mongolic and the Tibetan languages toward a common centre, viz. the ancient language of China, not deprived as yet of its various final consonants, most of which have disappeared in the Mandarin language:—

'*Peking*, Oct. 12, 1864.

'I am now seeking to compare the Mongolian and Tibetan with Chinese, and have already obtained some interesting results.

'I. A large proportion of Mongol words are Chinese. Perhaps a fifth are so. The identity is in the first syllable of the Mongol words; that being the root. The correspondence is most striking in the adjectives, of which, perhaps, one-half of the most common are the same radically as in Chinese: e.g. *sain*, good; *begen*, low; *icki*, right; *sologai*, left; *chille*, straight; *gadan*, outside; *ckohon*, few; *logon*, green; *hunggun*, light (not heavy). But the identity is also extensive in all parts of speech. This identity in common roots seems to extend into the Turkish Tartar: e.g. *su*, water; *tenri*, heaven.

'II. To compare Mongol with Chinese it is necessary to go back at least six centuries in the development of the Chinese language. For we find in common roots final letters peculiar to the old Chinese, e.g. final *m*. The initial letters also need to be considered from an older stand-

The only question which remains to be answered is this, Was it one and the same volume of water which supplied all the lateral channels of speech? or, to drop all metaphor, are the roots which were joined together according to the radical, the terminational, and inflectional systems, identically the same? The only way to answer, or at least to dispose of, this question is to consider the nature and origin of roots; and we shall then have reached the extreme limits to which inductive reasoning can carry us in our researches into the mysteries of human speech.

point than the Mandarin pronunciation. If a large number of words are common to Chinese, Mongol, and Tartar, we must go back at least twelve centuries to obtain a convenient epoch of comparison.

'III. While Mongol has no traces of tones, they are very distinctly developed in Tibetan. Csoma de Körös and Schmidt do not mention the existence of tones. But they plainly occur in the pronunciation of native Tibetans resident in Peking.

'IV. As in the case of the comparison with Mongol, it is necessary in examining the connection of Tibetan with Chinese to adopt the old form of the Chinese, with its more numerous final consonants, and its full system of soft and aspirated initials. The Tibetan numerals exemplify this with sufficient clearness.

'V. While the Mongol is near the Chinese in the extensive prevalence of words common to the two languages, the Tibetan is nearer in phonal structure as being tonic and monosyllabic. This being so, it is not so remarkable that there are many words common to the Chinese and the Tibetan (for they are to be expected). But that there should be, perhaps, as many in the Mongol with its long untoned polysyllables, is a curious circumstance.'

An Essay by Mr. Edkins on the same subject, 'On the Common Origin of the Chinese and Mongol Languages,' has just been published in the *Revue orientale*, No. 56, p. 75. Paris, 1865.

See also M. M., *On the Stratification of Language*, 1868.

CHAPTER XIV.

THE THEORETICAL STAGE.

The Problem of the Origin of Language.

'IN examining the history of mankind, as well as in examining the phenomena of the material world, when we cannot trace the process by which an event *has been* produced, it is often of importance to be able to show how it *may have been* produced by natural causes. Thus, although it is impossible to determine with certainty what the steps were by which any particular language was formed, yet, if we can show, from the known principles of human nature, how all its various parts *might* gradually have arisen, the mind is not only to a certain degree satisfied, but a check is given to that indolent philosophy which refers to a miracle whatever appearances, both in the natural and moral worlds, it is unable to explain.'[1]

This quotation from an eminent Scotch philosopher contains the best advice that could be given to the student of the science of language, when he approaches the problem of the origin of language. Though we have stripped that problem of the perplexing and mysterious aspect which it presented to the philo-

[1] Dugald Stewart, *Works,* vol. iii. p. 35.

sophers of old, yet, even in its simplest form, it seems to be almost beyond the reach of the human understanding.

Herder has truly remarked that if we were asked the riddle how images of the eye and all the sensations of our senses could be represented by sounds, nay, could be so embodied in sounds as to express thought and excite thought, we should probably give it up as the question of a madman, who, mixing up the most heterogeneous subjects, attempted to change colour into sound and sound into thought.[1] Yet this is the riddle which we have now to solve.

It is quite clear that we have no means of solving the problem of the origin of language *historically*, or of explaining it as a matter of fact which happened once in a certain locality and at a certain time. History does not begin till long after mankind had acquired the power of language, and even the most ancient traditions are silent as to the manner in which man came in possession of his earliest thoughts and words. Nothing, no doubt, would be more interesting than to know from historical documents the exact process by which the first man began to lisp his first words, and thus to be rid for ever of all the theories on the origin of speech. But this knowledge is denied us; and, if it had been otherwise, we should probably be quite unable to understand those primitive events in the history of the human mind.[2] We are

---

[1] Herder, as quoted by Steinthal, *Ursprung der Sprache*, s. 39.

[2] 'In all these paths of research, when we travel far backwards, the aspect of the earlier portions becomes very different from that of the advanced part on which we now stand; but in all cases the path is lost in obscurity as it is traced backwards towards its starting-point:—it

told that the first man was the son of God, that God created him in His own image, formed him of the dust of the ground, and breathed into his nostrils the breath of life. These are simple natural thoughts, and to be accepted as such. If we begin to reason on them, the edge of the human understanding glances off. Our mind is so constituted that it cannot apprehend the absolute beginning or the absolute end of anything. If we tried to conceive the first man created as a child, and gradually unfolding his physical and mental powers, we could not understand his living for one day, without supernatural aid. If, on the contrary, we tried to conceive the first man created full-grown in body and mind, the conception of an effect without a cause would equally transcend our reasoning powers. Nor should we gain anything by imagining a number of intermediate stages between lower animals and man. We should only disguise the real difficulty, we should not solve it.

It is the same with the first beginnings of language. Theologians who claim for language a divine origin drift into the most dangerous anthropomorphism when they enter into any details as to the manner in which they suppose the Deity to have compiled a dictionary and grammar in order to teach them to the first man, as a schoolmaster teaches the deaf and dumb. And they do not see that, even if all their premisses were granted, they would have explained no more than how the first man might have learnt a language, if

becomes not only invisible, but unimaginable; it is not only an interruption, but an abyss, which interposes itself between us and any intelligible beginning of things.'—Whewell, *Indications*, p. 166.

there was a language ready-made for him. How that language was made, would remain as great a mystery as ever. Philosophers, on the contrary, who imagine that the first man, though left to himself, would gradually have emerged from a state of mutism and have invented words for every new conception that arose in his mind, forget that man could not by his own power have acquired the faculty of speech which, so far as our experience goes, is the distinctive character of man,[1] unattainable, or, at all events, unattained by the brute and mute creation. It shows a want of appreciation as to the real bearings of our problem, if philosophers appeal to the fact that children are born without language, and gradually emerge from mutism to the full command of articulate speech. We want no explanation how birds learn to fly, created as they are with organs adapted to that purpose. Nor do we wish to inquire here how children learn to use the various faculties with which the human body and soul are endowed. We want to gain, if possible, an insight into the original faculty of speech; and for that purpose I fear it is as useless to watch the first stammerings of children, as it would be to repeat the experiment of the Egyptian king Psammetichus, who entrusted two new-born infants to a shepherd, with the injunction to let them suck goat's milk, to speak no word in their presence,

---

[1] 'Der Mensch ist nur Mensch durch Sprache; um aber die Sprache zu erfinden, müsste er schon Mensch sein.'—W. von Humboldt, *Sämmtliche Werke*, b. iii. s. 252. The same argument is ridden to death by Süssmilch, *Versuch eines Beweises, dass die erste Sprache ihren Ursprung nicht vom Menschen, sondern allein vom Schöpfer erhalten habe*, Berlin, 1766.

and to observe what word they would first utter.[1] The same experiment is said to have been repeated by the Swabian emperor, Frederic II., by James IV. of Scotland, and by Akbar, the emperor of India.[2] But, whether for the purpose of finding out which was the primitive language of mankind, or of discovering how far language was natural to man, the experiments have failed to throw any light on the problem before us. Children, in learning to speak, do not invent language. Language is there ready-made for them. It has been there for thousands of years. They acquire the use of a language, and, as they grow up, they may acquire the use of a second and a third. It is useless to inquire whether infants, left to themselves, would

---

[1] Farrar, *Origin of Language*, p. 10; Grimm, *Ursprung der Sprache*, s. 32. The word βεκός, which these children are reported to have uttered, and which, in the Phrygian language, meant bread—thus proving, it was supposed, that the Phrygian was the primitive language of mankind—is probably derived from the same Aryan root which exists in the English, to bake. How these unfortunate children came by the idea of baked bread, involving the ideas of corn, mill, oven, fire, &c., seems never to have struck the ancient sages of Egypt. Quintilian distinguishes very properly between the power of uttering a few words and the faculty of speaking: 'Propter quod infantes a mutis nutricibus jussu regum in solitudine educati, etiamsi verba quaedam emisisse traduntur, tamen loquendi facultate caruerunt.'—*Instit. Orat.* x. 1, 10.

[2] Hervas, *Origine degl' idiomi* (1785), pp. 147 seq. Akbar told Jerome Xavier that he had thirty children shut up before they could speak, and put guards over them, so that the nurses might not teach them their language. His object was to see what language they would talk when they grew older, and he was resolved to follow the laws and customs of the country whose language was that spoken by the children. None of the children, however, came to speak distinctly, wherefore he allowed no law but his own. See H. Beveridge, in *Journal of the Asiat. Soc. of Bengal*, 1888, p. 38. Badaoni relates the same story, and states that the experiment was made in 1580. He says that after three or four years all the children who survived were found to be dumb.

invent a language. It would be impossible, unnatural,[1] and illegal to try the experiment, and, without repeated experiments, the assertions of those who believe and those who disbelieve the possibility of children inventing a language of their own are equally valueless. All we know for certain is, that an English child, if left to itself, would never begin to speak English, and that history supplies no instance of any language having thus been invented.[2]

Man and Brute.

If we want to gain an insight into the faculty of flying, which is a characteristic feature of birds, all we can do is, first, to compare the structure of birds with that of other animals which are devoid of that faculty, and secondly, to examine the conditions under which the act of flying becomes possible. It is the same with speech. Speech, so far as we know, is a specific faculty of man. It distinguishes man from all other creatures; and if we wish to acquire more definite ideas as to the real nature of human speech, all we can do is to compare man with those animals that seem to come nearest to him, and thus to try to discover what he shares in common with these animals, and what is peculiar to him, and to him alone. After we have discovered this, we may proceed to inquire

---

[1] 'Cioè a dire, si voleva porlo nella condizione più contraria alla natura, per sapere ciò che naturalmente avrebbe fatto.'—Villari, *Il Politecnico*, vol. i. p. 22. See also the extract from the *Wibhanga Atuwawa*, p. 146.

[2] How children brought up among people speaking a real language, may invent an artificial language of their own has been well shown by Mr. Horatio Hale, *The Origin of Languages*, 1888.

into the conditions under which speech becomes possible, and we shall then have done all that we can do, considering that our instruments of knowledge, wonderful as they are, are yet far too weak to carry us through all the regions to which we may soar on the wings of our imagination!

In comparing man with the other animals, we need not enter here into the physiological question whether the difference between the body of an ape and the body of a man is one of degree or of kind. However that question is settled by physiologists, we need not be afraid. If the structure of a mere worm is such as to fill the human mind with awe, if a single glimpse which we catch of the infinite wisdom displayed in the organs of the lowest creature gives us an intimation of a wisdom far transcending the powers of our conception, how are we to criticise or disparage the most highly organised creatures, creatures as wonderfully made as we ourselves? Are there not many animals in many points more perfect even than man! Do we not envy the lion's strength, the eagle's eye, the wings of every bird? If there existed animals altogether as perfect as man in their physical structure, nay, even more perfect, no thoughtful man would ever be uneasy. The true superiority of man rests on very different grounds. 'I confess,' Sydney Smith writes, 'I feel myself so much at ease about the superiority of mankind—I have such a marked and decided contempt for the understanding of every baboon I have ever seen—I feel so sure that the blue ape without a tail will never rival us in poetry, painting, and music, that I see no reason whatever that justice may not be done to the few fragments of soul and tatters of understanding which they may really possess.' The playfulness of Sydney Smith in handling serious and sacred subjects has of late been found fault with by many; but humour is often a safer sign of strong convictions and perfect safety than guarded solemnity.

With regard to our own problem, no one can doubt that certain animals possess all the physical requirements for articulate speech. There is no letter of the alphabet which a parrot will not learn to pronounce.[1] The fact, therefore, that the parrot is without a language of his own, a Parrotese dialect, must be explained by a difference between the *mental*, not between the *physical*, faculties of the animal and man; and it is by a comparison of the mental faculties alone, such as we find them in man and brutes, that we may hope to discover what constitutes the indispensable qualification for language, a qualification to be found in man alone, and in no other creature on earth.

I say *mental faculties*, and I mean to claim a large

---

[1] 'L'usage de la main, la marche à deux pieds, la ressemblance, quoique grossière, de la face, tous les actes qui peuvent résulter de cette conformité d'organisation, ont fait donner au singe le nom d'*homme sauvage* par des hommes à la vérité qui l'étaient à demi, et qui ne savaient comparer que les rapports extérieurs. Que serait-ce, si, par une combinaison de nature aussi possible que toute autre, le singe eût eu la voix du perroquet, et, comme lui, la faculté de la parole ? Le singe parlant eût rendu muette d'étonnement l'espèce humaine entière, et l'aurait séduite au point que le philosophe aurait eu grand'peine à démontrer qu'avec tous ces beaux attributs humains le singe n'en était pas moins une bête. Il est donc heureux, pour notre intelligence, que la Nature ait séparé et placé, dans deux espèces très-différentes, l'imitation de la parole et celle de nos gestes.'—Buffon, as quoted by Flourens, p. 77.

share of what we call our mental faculties for the higher animals. These animals have *sensation, perception, memory, will,* and *intellect* ; only we must restrict intellect to the comparing or interlacing of single perceptions. All these points can be proved by irrefragable evidence, and that evidence has never, I believe, been summed up with greater lucidity and power than by Flourens, in one of his most instructive works, *De la Raison, du Génie, et de la Folie* ; Paris, 1861. There are no doubt many people who are as much frightened at the idea that brutes have souls and are able to think, as by ' the blue ape without a tail.' But their fright is entirely of their own making. If people will use such words as soul or thought without making it clear to themselves and others what they mean by them, these words will slip away under their feet, and the result must be painful. If we once ask the question, Have brutes a soul ? we shall never arrive at any conclusion ; for *soul* has been so many times defined by philosophers, from Aristotle down to Hegel, that it means everything and nothing. Such has been the confusion caused by the promiscuous employment of the ill-defined terms of mental philosophy that we find Descartes representing brutes as living machines, whereas Leibniz claims for them not only souls, but immortal souls. 'Next to the error of those who deny the existence of God,' says Descartes, 'there is none so apt to lead weak minds from the right path of virtue, as to think that the soul of brutes is of the same nature as our own, and, consequently, that we have nothing to fear or to hope after this life, any more than flies or ants; whereas, if we know how much they differ, we understand much better that *our* soul is quite independent of the body, and consequently not subject to die with the body.'

The spirit of these remarks is excellent, but the argument is extremely weak. It does not follow that brutes have no souls because they have no human souls. It does not follow that the souls of men are not immortal, because the souls of brutes are not immortal; nor has it ever been proved by any philosopher that the souls of brutes must necessarily be destroyed and annihilated by death. Leibniz, who has defended the immortality of the human soul with stronger arguments than even Descartes, writes,—'I found at last how the souls of brutes and their sensations do not at all interfere with the immortality of human souls; on the contrary, nothing serves better to establish our natural immortality than to believe that all souls are imperishable.'

Instead of entering into these perplexities, which are chiefly due to the loose employment of ill-defined terms, let us simply look at the facts. Every unprejudiced observer will admit that—

1. Brutes see, hear, taste, smell, and feel; that is to say, they have five senses, just like ourselves, neither more nor less. They have both sensation and perception—a point which has been illustrated by M. Flourens by the most interesting experiments. If the roots of the optic nerve are removed, the retina in the eye of a bird ceases to be excitable, the iris is no longer movable; the animal is blind, because it has lost the organ of *sensation*. If, on the contrary, the cerebral lobes are removed, the eye remains pure and

sound, the retina excitable, the iris movable. The eye is preserved, yet the animal cannot see, because it has lost the organs of perception.

2. Brutes have sensations of pleasure and pain. A dog that is beaten behaves exactly like a child that is chastised, and a dog that is fed and fondled exhibits the same signs of satisfaction as a boy under the same circumstances. We can judge from signs only, and if they are to be trusted in the case of children, they must be trusted likewise in the case of brutes.

3. Brutes do not forget, or, as philosophers would say, brutes have memory. They know their masters, they know their home; they evince joy on recognising those who have been kind to them, and they bear malice for years to those by whom they have been insulted or ill-treated. Who does not recollect the dog Argos in the *Odyssey*, who, after so many years' absence, was the first to recognise Ulysses?[1]

4. Brutes are able to compare and to distinguish. A parrot will take up a nut, and throw it down again without attempting to crack it. He has found that it is light. This he could discover only by comparing the weight of the good nuts with that of the bad. And he has found that it has no kernel. This he could discover only by what philosophers would dignify with the grand title of syllogism, namely, 'All light nuts are hollow; this is a light nut, therefore this nut is hollow.'

5. Brutes have a will of their own. I appeal to any one who has ever ridden a restive horse.

[1] *Odyssey*, xvii. 300.

6. Brutes show signs of shame and pride. Here again any one who has to deal with dogs, who has watched a retriever with sparkling eyes placing a partridge at his master's feet, or a hound slinking away with his tail between his legs from the huntsman's call, will agree that these signs admit of but one interpretation. The difficulty begins when we use philosophical language, when we claim for brutes a moral sense, a conscience, a power of distinguishing good and evil; and, as we gain nothing by these scholastic terms, it is better to avoid them altogether.

7. Brutes show signs of love and hatred. There are well-authenticated stories of dogs following their master to the grave, and refusing food from any one. Nor is there any doubt that brutes will watch their opportunity till they revenge themselves on those whom they dislike.

If, with all these facts before us, we deny that brutes have sensation, perception, memory, will, and intellect, we ought to bring forward powerful arguments for interpreting the signs which we observe in brutes so differently from those which we observe in men.[1]

Some philosophers imagine they have explained everything if they ascribe to brutes instinct instead of intellect. But, if we take these two words in their usual acceptations, they surely do not exclude each other.[2] There are instincts in man as well as in

---

[1] See the whole of these questions admirably argued by Porphyry, in his four books on 'Abstinence from Animal Food,' book 3.

[2] 'The evident marks of reasoning in the other animals—of reasoning which I cannot but think as unquestionable as the instincts that mingle with it.'—Brown, *Works*, vol. i. p. 446.

brutes. A child takes his mother's breast by instinct; the spider weaves his net by instinct; the bee builds her cell by instinct. No one would ascribe to the child a knowledge of physiology because it employs the exact muscles which are required for sucking; nor can we claim for the spider a knowledge of mechanics, or for the bee an acquaintance with geometry, because *we* could not do what they do without a study of these sciences. But what if we tear a spider's web, and see the spider examining the mischief that is done, and either giving up his work in despair, or endeavouring to mend it as well as may be?[1] Surely here we have the instinct of weaving controlled by observation, by comparison, by reflection, by judgment. Instinct, whether mechanical or moral, is more prominent in brutes than in man; but it exists in both, as much as intellect is shared by both.

Where, then, is the difference between brute and man?[2] What is it that man can do, and of which we find no signs, no rudiments, in the whole brute world? I answer without hesitation: the one great barrier between the brute and man is *Language*. Man

[1] Flourens, *De la Raison*, p. 51.
[2] To allow that 'brutes have certain mental endowments in common with men, ... desires, affections, memory, simple imagination, or the power of reproducing the sensible past in mental pictures, and even judgment of the simple or intuitive kind;'—that 'they compare and judge' (*Mem. Amer. Acad.* 8, p. 118), is to concede that the intellect of brutes really acts, so far as we know, like human intellect, as far as it goes; for the philosophical logicians tell us that all reasoning is reducible to a series of simple judgments. And Aristotle declares that even reminiscence—which is, we suppose, 'reproducing the sensible past in mental pictures'—is a sort of reasoning (τὸ ἀναμιμνήσκεσθαί ἐστι οἷον συλλογισμός τις).—Asa Grey, *Natural Selection, &c.* p. 58, *note.*

speaks, and no brute has ever uttered a word. Language is our Rubicon, and no brute will dare to cross it. This is our matter-of-fact answer to those who speak of development, who think they discover the rudiments at least of all human faculties in apes, and who would fain keep open the possibility that man is only a more favoured beast, the triumphant conqueror in the primeval struggle for life. Language is something more palpable than a fold of the brain or an angle of the skull. It admits of no cavilling, and no process of natural selection will ever distil significant words out of the notes of birds or the cries of beasts.

Language the Barrier between Man and Brute.

Language, however, is only the outward sign. We may point to it in our arguments, we may challenge our opponent to produce anything approaching to it from the whole brute world. But if this were all, if the art of employing articulate sounds for the purpose of communicating our impressions were the only thing by which we could assert our superiority over the brute creation, we might not unreasonably feel somewhat uneasy at having the gorilla so close on our heels.

It cannot be denied that brutes, though they do not use articulate sounds for that purpose, have nevertheless means of their own for communicating with each other. When a whale is struck, the whole shoal, though widely dispersed, are instantly made aware of the presence of an enemy; and when the grave-digger beetle finds the carcase of a mole, he hastens to communicate the discovery to his fellows, and soon returns with his *four* confederates.[1] It is evident, too, that dogs, though they do not speak, possess the power of understanding much that is said to them, their names and the calls of their master; and other animals, such as the parrot, can pronounce almost any articulate sound. Hence, although, for the purpose of philosophical warfare, articulate language would still form an impregnable position, yet it is but natural that for our own satisfaction we should try to find out in what the strength of our position really consists; or, in other words, that we should try to discover that inward power of which language is the outward sign and manifestation.

For this purpose it will be best to examine the opinions of those who approached our problem from another point; who, instead of looking for outward and palpable signs of difference between brute and man, inquired into the inward mental faculties, and tried to determine the point where man transcends the barriers of the brute intellect. That point, if truly determined, ought to coincide with the starting-point of language; and, if so, that coincidence ought to explain the problem which occupies us at present.

I shall begin with an extract from Locke's *Essay concerning Human Understanding*.

After having explained how he thinks that universal ideas are produced,—how the mind, having observed the same colour in chalk, and snow, and milk, comprehends these single perceptions under the

---

[1] Conscience, *Boek der Natuer*, vi., quoted by Marsh, p. 32. See also some curious instances collected by Porphyry, in the third book on 'Abstinence from Animal Food.'

general conception of whiteness, Locke continues:[1] 'If it may be doubted, whether beasts compound and enlarge their ideas that way to any degree: this, I think, I may be positive in, that the power of abstracting is not at all in them; and that the having of general ideas is that which puts a perfect distinction betwixt man and brutes, and is an excellency which the faculties of brutes do by no means attain to.'

If Locke is right in considering the having of general ideas as the distinguishing feature between man and brutes, and if we ourselves are right in pointing to language as the one palpable distinction between the two, it would seem to follow that language is the outward sign and realisation of that inward faculty which is called the faculty of abstraction, but which is better known to us by the homely name of Reason.

Roots.

Let us now look back to the result of our former discussions. It was this. After we had explained everything in the growth of language that can be explained, there remained in the end, as the only inexplicable residuum, what we called *roots*. These roots formed the constituent elements of all languages. This discovery has simplified the problem of the origin of language immensely. It has taken away all excuse for those rapturous descriptions of language which invariably precede the argument that language must have a divine origin. We shall hear no more of that wonderful instrument which can

[1] Book ii. chap. xi. § 10.

express all we see, and hear, and taste, and touch, and smell; which is the breathing image of the whole world; which gives form to the airy feelings of our souls, and body to the loftiest dreams of our imagination; which can arrange in accurate perspective the past, the present, and the future, and throw over everything the varying hues of certainty, of doubt, of contingency. All this is perfectly true, but it is no longer wonderful, at least not in the Arabian Nights' sense of that word. 'The speculative mind,' as Dr. Ferguson says, 'in comparing the first and last steps of the progress of language, feels the same sort of amazement with a traveller, who, after rising insensibly on the slope of a hill, comes to look from a precipice of an almost unfathomable depth, to the summit of which he scarcely believes himself to have ascended without supernatural aid.' To certain minds it is a disappointment to be led down again by the hand of history from that high summit. They prefer the unintelligible which they can admire, to the intelligible which they can only understand. But to a mature mind reality is more attractive than fiction, and simplicity more wonderful than complication. Roots may seem dry things as compared with the poetry of Goethe; yet there is something more truly wonderful in a root than in all the lyrics of the world.

What, then, are these roots? In our modern languages roots can only be discovered by scientific analysis, and, even as far back as Sanskrit, there are but few instances where a word is not distinguished by the addition of formal elements from a root. In

Chinese, however, there is as yet no outward distinction between roots and words, and it is but natural to suppose that this was the case everywhere during the earliest periods of human speech. The Aryan root *DÂ*, to give, appears in Sanskrit dâ-nam, Latin *do-num*, gift, as a substantive; in Latin *do*, Sanskrit da-dâ-mi, Greek *di-dō-mi*, I give, as a verb. But the root *DÂ* is never used by itself. In Chinese, on the contrary, the root *TA* is used in the sense of a noun, greatness; of a verb, to be great; of an adverb, greatly or much. Roots, therefore, are not, as is commonly maintained, merely scientific abstractions, but they were, outwardly at least, identical with the real words of a language. What we now want to find out is this, What inward mental phase is it that corresponds to these roots, as the germs of human speech?

The Bow-wow and Pooh-pooh Theories.

Two theories have been started to solve this problem, which, for shortness sake, I shall call the *Bow-wow* theory and the *Pooh-pooh* theory.[1]

According to the first, roots are imitations of sounds; according to the second, they are involuntary interjections. The first theory was very popular among the philosophers of the eighteenth century, and, as it has been held by many distinguished scholars

---

[1] I regret to find that the expressions here used have given offence to several of my reviewers. They were used simply and solely because the names Onomatopoetic and Interjectional are awkward and not very clear. They were not intended to be disrespectful to those who hold the one or the other theory—some of them scholars for whose achievements in comparative philology I entertain the most sincere respect.

and philosophers, we must examine it more carefully. It is supposed, then, that man, being as yet mute, heard the voices of birds and dogs and cows, the thunder of the clouds, the roaring of the sea, the rustling of the forest, the murmurs of the brook, and the whisper of the breeze. He tried to imitate these sounds, and finding his mimicking cries useful as signs of the objects from which they proceeded, he followed up the idea and elaborated language. This view was most ably defended by Herder.[1] 'Man,' he says, 'shows conscious reflection when his soul acts so freely that it may separate in the ocean of sensations which rush into it through the senses, one single wave, arrest it, regard it, being conscious all the time of regarding this one single wave. Man proves his conscious reflection when, out of the dream of images that float past his senses, he can gather himself up and wake for a moment, dwelling intently on one image, fixing it with a bright and tranquil glance, and discovering for himself those signs by which he knows that *this* is *this* image and no other. Man proves his conscious reflection when he not only perceives vividly and distinctly all the features of an object, but is able to separate and recognise one or more of them as its distinguishing features.' For instance, 'Man sees a lamb. He does not see it like the ravenous wolf. He is not disturbed by any uncontrollable instinct. He wants to know it, but he is neither drawn towards it nor repelled from it by his

---

[1] A fuller account of the views of Herder and other philosophers on the origin of language may be found in Steinthal's useful little work, *Der Ursprung der Sprache*, first published in 1858.

senses. The lamb stands before him, as represented by his senses, white, soft, woolly. The conscious and reflecting soul of man looks for a distinguishing mark;—the lamb bleats!—the mark is found. The bleating, which made the strongest impression, which stood apart from all other impressions of sight or touch, remains in the soul. The lamb returns— white, soft, woolly. The soul sees, touches, reflects, looks for a mark. The lamb bleats, and now the soul has recognised it. "Ah, thou art the bleating animal," the soul says within herself; and the sound of bleating, perceived as the distinguishing mark of the lamb, becomes the name of the lamb. It was the comprehended mark, the word. And what is the whole of our language but a collection of such words?'

Our answer is, that though there are names in every language formed by mere imitation of sound, yet these constitute a very small proportion of our dictionary. Scholars may differ as to the exact number of such words in different languages, but whatever their number, they offer no difficulty, and require no explanation. They are the playthings, not the tools, of language, and any attempt to reduce the most common and necessary words to imitative roots ends in complete failure. Herder himself, after having most strenuously defended this theory of Onomatopoieia, as it is called, and having gained a prize which the Berlin Academy had offered for the best essay on the origin of language, renounced it openly towards the latter years of his life, and threw himself in despair into the arms of those who looked upon languages as miraculously revealed. We cannot deny the possibility that *a* language might have been formed on the principle of imitation; all we say is, that as yet no language has been discovered that was so formed. An Englishman in China,[1] seeing a dish placed before him about which he felt suspicious, and wishing to know whether it was a duck, said, with an interrogative accent,

Quack-Quack?

He received the clear and straightforward answer,

Bow-wow!

This, no doubt, was as good as the most eloquent conversation on the same subject between an Englishman and a French waiter. But I doubt whether it deserves the name of language. We do not speak of a *bow-wow*, but of a dog. We speak of a cow, not of a *moo*; of a lamb, not of a *baa*. It is the same in more ancient languages, such as Greek, Latin, and Sanskrit. If this principle of Onomatopoieia is applicable anywhere, it would be in the formation of the names of animals. Yet we listen in vain for any similarity between goose and cackling, hen and clucking, duck and quacking, sparrow and chirping, dove and cooing, hog and grunting, cat and mewing, between dog and barking, yelping, snarling, or growling.

There are of course some names, such as *cuckoo*, or the American *whip-poor-will*, which are clearly formed by an imitation of sound. But words of this kind are, like artificial flowers, without a root. They are sterile, and unfit to express anything beyond the

[1] Farrar, *Essay on the Origin of Language*, p. 74.

one object which they imitate. If you remember the variety of derivatives that could be formed from the single root SPAS, to see, you will at once perceive the difference between the fabrication of such a word as *cuckoo*, and the true natural growth of predicative words.

Let us compare two words such as *cuckoo* and *raven*. *Cuckoo* in English is clearly a mere imitation of the cry of that bird, even more so than the corresponding terms in Greek, Sanskrit, and Latin. In these languages the imitative element has received the support of a derivative suffix; we have kokila in Sanskrit, and *kokkyx* in Greek, *cucŭlus* in Latin.[1] *Cuckoo* is, in fact, a modern word, which has taken the place of the Anglo-Saxon *geac*, the German *gauch*, and being purely onomatopoetic, it is of course not liable to the changes of Grimm's Law. As the word *cuckoo* predicates nothing but the sound of a particular bird, it could never be applied for expressing any general quality in which other animals might share; and the only derivatives to which it might give rise are words expressive of a metaphorical likeness to the bird. The same applies to *cock*, the Sanskrit kukkuta. Here, too, Grimm's Law does not apply, for both words were intended to convey merely the cackling sound of the bird; and, as this intention continued to be felt, phonetic change was less likely to set in. The Sanskrit kukkuta is not derived from any root; it simply repeats the cry of the bird, and the only derivatives to which it gives

---

[1] Pott, *Etymologische Forschungen*, i. s. 87; Kuhn's *Zeitschrift*, iii. s. 43.

rise are metaphorical expressions, such as the French *coquet*, originally strutting about like a cock; *coquetterie*; *cocart*, conceited; *cocarde*, a cockade; *coquelicot*, originally a cock's comb, then the wild red poppy, likewise so called from its similarity to a cock's comb.

Let us now examine the word *raven*. It might seem at first as if this also was merely onomatopoetic. Some people imagine they perceive a kind of similarity between the word *raven* and the cry of that bird. This seems still more so if we compare the Anglo-Saxon *hræfn*, the German *rabe*, Old High-German *hraban*. The Sanskrit kârava also, the Latin *corvus*, the English *crow*, and the Greek *korōnē*, all are supposed to show some similarity to the unmelodious sound of *Maître Corbeau*. But if we look more closely we find that these words, though so similar in sound, spring from different sources. The English *crow*, for instance, can claim no relationship whatever with *corvus*, for the simple reason that, according to Grimm's Law, an English c cannot correspond to a Latin c. *Raven*, on the contrary, which in outward appearance differs from *corvus* much more than *crow*, offers much less real difficulty in being traced back to the same source from which sprang the Latin *corvus*. For *raven* is the Anglo-Saxon *hræfen* or *hræfn*, and its first syllable *hræ* would be a legitimate substitute for the Latin *cor*. Opinions differ widely as to the root or roots from which the various names of the crow, the raven, and the rook in the Aryan dialects are derived. Those who look on Sanskrit as the most primitive form of Aryan speech, are disposed to admit the Sanskrit kârava as the original type; and as kârava is by native etymologists derived from kâ+rava, making a harsh noise,¹ ru, to make a noise, the root of rava, noise, was readily fixed upon as the etymon for the corresponding words in Latin, Greek, and German. I cannot enter here into the question whether such compounds as kâ+rava, in which the initial interrogative or exclamatory element kâ or ku is supposed to fill the office of the Greek *dys* or the English *mis*, are so numerous as they are supposed to be in Sanskrit. The question has been discussed again and again, and though it is impossible to deny the existence of such compounds in Sanskrit, particularly in the later Sanskrit, I know of no well-established instance where such formations have found their way into Greek, Latin, or German. If, therefore, kârava *corvus*, *korōnē*, and *hrafen* are cognate words, it would be more advisable to look upon the k as part of the radical, and thus to derive all these words from a root kru, a secondary form, it may be, of the root ru. This root kru, or, in its more primitive form, ru (rauti and ravîti), is not a mere imitation of the cry of the raven; it embraces many cries, from the harshest to the softest, and it might have been applied to the note of the nightingale as well as to the cry of the raven. In Sanskrit the root ru is applied in its verbal and nominal derivatives to the murmuring sound of birds, bees, and trees, to the barking of dogs, the lowing of cows, and the whispering of men.² In

---

[1] See Boehtlingk and Roth, *Sanskrit Dictionary*, s. v.

[2] Cf. Hitopadesa, i. 76, where rauti is used both of the humming of the gnat and the flatteries whispered into the ear by an enemy.

THE THEORETICAL STAGE. 501

Latin we have from it both *raucus*, hoarse, and *rumor*, a whisper; in German *rûnen*, to speak low, and *rûna*, mystery. The Latin *lamentum* stands for a more original *lavimentum* or *ravimentum*, for there is no necessity for deriving this noun from the secondary root kru, krav, krâv, and for admitting the loss of the initial guttural in *cravimentum*, particularly as in *clamare* the same guttural is preserved. It is true, however, that this root ru appears under many secondary forms. I call *kru* and *klu*, for instance, a secondary or parallel form, well known by its numerous offshoots, such as the Greek *klyo*, *klytos*, the Latin *cluo*, *inclitus*, *cliens*, the English *loud*, the Slavonic *slava*, glory.[1] The Sanskrit rud, to cry, the Latin *rug* in *rugire*, to howl, nay even the Sanskrit krus, to shout, the Greek *kraugē*, cry, and the Gothic *hrukjan*,[2] to crow, all may be traced back to the same cluster of roots. The Sanskrit sru and the Greek *klyo* have been used to convey the sense of hearing; naturally, because, when a noise was to be heard from a far distance, the man who first perceived it might well have said 'I ring,' for his ears were sounding or ringing; and the same verb, if once used as a transitive, would well come in in such forms as the Homeric *klythi*, hear, or the Sanskrit srudhi, hear!

[1] The causative of *sru*, to hear, would be *srâvayâmi*, I cause to hear; but this would not explain the Old High-German *hruofan*, the modern German *rufen*. See Grimm, *Deutsche Grammatik*, vol. i. second edition, s. 1023. Heyse, *Handwörterbuch der Deutschen Sprache*, s. v. *rufen*. Heyse compares the Latin *crepare*, which in *increpare*, to blame, has the same meaning as the Old Icelandic *hrópa*.

[2] See Curtius, *Grundzüge der Griechischen Etymologie*, zweite Ausgabe, s. 468.

But although, as far as the meaning of kârava, *corvus*, *korōnē*, and *hræfn* is concerned, there would seem to be no difficulty in deriving them from a root kru, to sound, no satisfactory explanation has yet been suggested of the exact etymological process by which the Sanskrit kârava could be formed from kru. Kru, no doubt, might yield krava, but to admit a dialectic corruption of krava into karva, and of karva into kârava, is tantamount to giving up all rules of analogy. Are we therefore forced to be satisfied with the assertion that kârava is no grammatical derivative at all, but a mere imitation of the sound *cor cor*, uttered by the raven? I believe not. We may, as I hinted at before, treat kârava as a regular derivative of the Sanskrit kâru. This kâru is a Vedic word, and means one who sings praises to the gods, literally one that shouts. It comes from a root kar, to shout, to praise, to record; from which the Vedic word kîri, a poet, and the well-known kîrti, glory, kîrtayati, he praises.[1] Kâru from kar meant originally a shouter (like the Greek *kēryx*, a herald);[2] and its derivative kârava was therefore applied to the raven in the general sense of the shouter. All the other names of the raven can easily be traced back to the same root kar:—*cor-vus* from kar, like *tor-vus* from tar;[3] *kor-ōnē* from kar, like *chelōnē* from har;[4] *kor-ax* from kar, like *phylax*,

---

[1] See Boehtlingk and Roth, *Sanskrit Dictionary*, s. v. Kar, 2; Lassen, *Anthol.* p. 203.

[2] Cf. Bopp, *Vergleichende Grammatik*, § 949.

[3] *Ibid.* § 943.

[4] Bopp, *l. c.* § 837; Curtius, *Grundzüge*, i. s. 167; Hugo Weber, in Kuhn's *Zeitschrift*, x. s. 257.

&c. The Anglo-Saxon *hræfen*, as well as the Old High-German *hraban*, might be represented in Sanskrit by such forms as kar-van or kar-va*n*-a; while the English *rook*, the Anglo-Saxon *hrôc*, the Old High-German *hruoh*, would seem to derive their origin from a different root altogether, viz. from the Sanskrit krus.

The English *crow*, the Anglo-Saxon *crâwe*, cannot, as was pointed out before, be derived from the same root kar. Beginning with a guttural tenuis in Anglo-Saxon, its corresponding forms in Sanskrit would there begin with the guttural media. There exists in Sanskrit a root gar, meaning to sound, to praise; from which the Sanskrit gir, voice, the Greek *gērys*, voice, the Latin *garrulus*. From it was framed the name of the crane, *geranos* in Greek, *cran* in Anglo-Saxon, and likewise the Latin name for cock, *gallus* instead of *garrus*. The name of the nightingale, Old High-German *nahti-gal*, has been referred to the same root, but in violation of Grimm's Law.[1] From this root gar or gal, *crow* might have been derived, but again not from the root kar, which yielded *corvus*, *korax*, or kârava, still less from *cor cor*, the supposed cry of the bird.

It will be clear from these remarks that the process which led to the formation of the word *raven* is quite distinct from that which produced *cuckoo*. *Raven* means a shouter, a caller, a crier. It might have been applied to many birds; and it became the traditional and recognised name of one, and of one only. Cuckoo could never mean anything but the

[1] Curtius, *Grundzüge*, i. s. 145, 147.

cuckoo, and while a word like *raven* has ever so many relations, cuckoo stands by itself like a stick in a living hedge.[1]

It is curious to observe how apt we are to deceive ourselves when we once adopt this system of Onomatopoieia. Who does not imagine that he hears in the word 'thunder' an imitation of the rolling and rumbling noise which the old Germans ascribed to their god Thor playing at nine-pins? Yet *thunder*, Anglo-Saxon *thunor*, has clearly the same origin as the Latin *tonitru*. The root is *tan*, to stretch. From this root *tan* we have in Greek *tonos*, our tone, *tone* being produced by the stretching and vibrating of cords; Latin *tonare*.[2] In Sanskrit the sound thunder is expressed by the same root tan, but in the derivatives tanyu, tanyatu, and tanayitnu, thundering, we perceive no trace of the rumbling noise which we imagined we perceived in the Latin *tonitru* and the English *thunder*.[3] The very same root, tan, to

---

[1] The following remarks on the interjectional theory, from Yâska's Nirukta (iii. 18), a work anterior to Pânini, and therefore belonging at least to the fourth century B.C., may be of interest.

After mentioning that words like lion and tiger, or dog and crow, may be applied to men to express either admiration or contempt, Yâska continues: 'kâka, crow, is an imitation of the sound (kâku kâku, according to Durga), and this is very common with regard to birds. Aupamanyava, however, maintains that imitation of sound does never take place. He therefore derives kâka, crow, from apakâlayitavya, i.e. a bird that is to be driven away; tittiri, partridge, from tar, to jump, or from tilamâtraḱitra, with small spots, etc.'

[2] Hom. *Il.* xvi. 365: ὅτε τε Ζεὺς λαίλαπα τείνῃ. Cf. Grimm, *Namen des Donners*, p. 8.

[3] A secondary root is stan, to sound; from which stanitam, the rattling of thunder; stanayitnu, thunder, lightning, cloud (see Wilson's *Dict.*); Greek στένω, I groan, and its numerous derivatives; also Στέντωρ, the shouter; Bopp, *Vergl. Gr.* s. 914, *note*. Professor Bopp (*Vergleichende*

stretch, yields some derivatives which are anything but rough and noisy. The English *tender*, the French *tendre*, the Latin *tener*, are derived from it. Like *tenuis*, the Sanskrit tanu, the English *thin*, *tener* meant originally what was extended over a larger surface, then *thin*, then *delicate*. The relationship betwixt *tender*, *thin*, and *thunder* would be hard to establish, if the original conception of thunder had really been its rumbling noise.

Who does not imagine that he hears something sweet in the French *sucre*, *sucré*? Yet sugar came from India, and it is there called sarkhara, which is anything but sweet-sounding. This sarkhara is the same word as *sugar*; it was called in Latin *saccharum*, and we still speak of *saccharine* juice, which is sugar juice.[1] Who does not think that there is something stirring in *stirrup*; yet in its earliest Anglo-Saxon form *stirrup* is *stîg-râp*, i.e. a stepping-rope, the German *steig-riemen*.

In *squirrel*, again, some people imagine they hear something of the rustling and whirling of the little animal. But we have only to trace the name back to Greek, and there we find that *skiouros* is composed of two distinct words, the one meaning shade, the other tail; the animal being called shade-tail by the Greeks.

Grammatik, § 3) and Professor Kuhn (*Zeitschrift*, iv. s. 7) consider stan as the primitive form; Professor Pott (*Etym. Forsch.* ii. s. 293) treats stan as formed from tan.

[1] 'Lo nome d' Amore è sì dolce a udire, che impossibile mi pare, che la sua operazione sia nelle più cose altro che dolce, conciossiacosachè i nomi seguitino le nominate cose, siccome è scritto: Nomina sunt consequentia rerum.'—Dante, *Vita Nuova Opere Minori:* Firenze, 1837, tom. iii. p. 289.

Thus the German *katze*, cat, is supposed to be an imitation of the sound made by a cat spitting. But if the spitting were expressed by the sibilant, that sibilant does not exist in the Latin *catus*, nor in *cat* or *kitten*, nor in the German *kater*.[1] The Sanskrit mârgâra, cat, might seem to imitate the purring of the cat; but it is derived from the root mrig, to clean, mârgâra meaning the animal that always cleans itself.

Many more instances might be given to show how easily we are deceived by the constant connection of certain sounds and certain meanings in the words of our own language, and how readily we imagine that there is something in the sound to tell us the meaning of the words. 'The sound must seem an echo to the sense.'

Most of these onomatopoieias vanish as soon as we trace our own words back to Anglo-Saxon and Gothic, or compare them with their cognates in Greek, Latin, or Sanskrit. The number of names which are really formed by an imitation of sound dwindle down to a very small quotum, if cross-examined by the comparative philologist; and we are left in the end with the conviction that though some kind of language might have been made out of the roaring, fizzing, hissing, gobbling, twittering, cracking, banging, slamming, and rattling sounds of nature, the tongues with which *we* are acquainted point to a different origin.[2]

---

[1] See Pictet, *Aryas primitifs*, p. 381.

[2] In Chinese the number of imitative sounds is very considerable. They are mostly written phonetically, and followed by the determinative

THE THEORETICAL STAGE.

There is another class of philosophers, and among them Condillac, who protest against a theory which would place men even below the animal. Why should man be supposed, they say, to have taken a lesson from birds and beasts? Does he not utter cries, and sobs, and shouts himself, according as he is affected by fear, pain, or joy? These cries or interjections are represented as the natural and real beginnings of human speech, and everything else was supposed to have been elaborated after their model. This theory may be called the Interjectional, or the Pooh-pooh, Theory.

Our answer to this theory is the same as that which we gave to the Bow-wow theory. There are no doubt in every language interjections, and some of them may become traditional, and enter into the composition of words. But these interjections are only the outskirts of real language. Language begins where interjections end. There is as much difference between a real word, such as 'to laugh,' and the interjection ha, ha! between 'I suffer,' and oh! as there is between the involuntary act and noise of sneezing, and the verb 'to sneeze.' We sneeze, and cough, and sign 'mouth.' We give a few, together with the corresponding sounds in Mandshu. The difference between the two will show how differently the same sounds strike different ears, and how differently they are rendered into articulate language:—

The cock crows	kiao kiao	in Chinese	dchor dchor	in Mandshu
The wild goose cries	kao kao	,,	kôr kôr	,,
The wind and rain sound	siao siao	,,	chor chor	,,
Wagons sound	lin lin	,,	koungour koungour	,,
Dogs coupled together	ling-ling	,,	kalang kalang	,,
Chains	tsiang-tsiang	,,	kiling kiling	,,
Bells	tsiang-tsiang	,,	tang tang	,,
Drums	kan kan	,,	tung tung	,,

scream, and laugh in the same manner as animals; but if Epicurus tells us that we speak in the same manner as dogs bark, moved by nature,[1] our own experience will tell us that this is not the case.

An excellent answer to the interjectional theory has been given by Horne Tooke.

'The dominion of speech,' he says,[2] 'is erected upon the downfal of interjections. Without the artful contrivances of language, mankind would have had nothing but interjections with which to communicate, orally, any of their feelings. The neighing of a horse, the lowing of a cow, the barking of a dog, the purring of a cat, sneezing, coughing, groaning, shrieking, and every other involuntary convulsion with oral sound, have almost as good a title to be called parts of speech, as interjections have. Voluntary interjections are only employed where the suddenness and vehemence of some affection or passion returns men to their natural state, and makes them for a moment forget the use of speech; or when, from some circumstance, the shortness of time will not permit them to exercise it.'

As in the case of onomatopoieia, it cannot be denied that with interjections, too, some kind of language might have been formed; but not a language like that which we find in numerous varieties among all the races of men. One short interjection may be

---

[1] Ὁ γὰρ Ἐπίκουρος ἔλεγεν, ὅτι οὐχὶ ἐπιστημόνως οὗτοι ἔθεντο τὰ ὀνόματα, ἀλλὰ φυσικῶς κινούμενοι, ὡς οἱ βήσσοντες καὶ πταίροντες καὶ μυκώμενοι καὶ ὑλακτοῦντες καὶ στενάζοντες.—Lersch, *Sprachphilosophie der Alten*, i. 40. Cf. *Diog. Laert.* x. § 75. The statement is taken from Proclus, and I doubt whether he represented Epicurus fairly.

[2] *Diversions of Purley*, p. 32.

more powerful, more intelligible, more eloquent than a long speech. In fact, interjections, together with gestures, the movements of the muscles of the mouth, and the eye, would be quite sufficient for all purposes which language answers with the majority of mankind.

> Sæpe tacens vocem verbaque vultus habet:
> Me specta, nutusque meos, vultumque loquacem,
> Excipe, furtivas et refer ipse notas.
> Verba superciliis sine voce loquentia dicam:
> Verba legam digitis, verba notata mero.
> *Ovid.*

Lucian, in his treatise on dancing, mentions a king whose dominions bordered on the Euxine. He happened to be at Rome in the reign of Nero, and, having seen a pantomime perform, he begged him of the emperor as a present, in order that he might employ him as an interpreter among the nations in his neighbourhood with whom he could hold no intercourse on account of the diversity of language. A pantomime meant a person who could mimic everything, and there is hardly anything which cannot be thus expressed. We, having language at our command, have neglected the art of speaking without words; but in the south of Europe that art is still preserved. If it be true that one look may speak volumes, it is clear that we might save ourselves much of the trouble entailed by the use of discursive speech. Yet we must not forget that *hum!* *ugh! tut! pooh!* are as little to be called words as the expressive gestures which usually accompany these exclamations.

CHAPTER XIV.

The attempts at deriving some of our words etymologically from mere interjections are apt to fail from the same kind of misconception which leads us to imagine that there is something expressive in the sounds of words. Thus it is said 'that the idea of disgust takes its rise in the senses of smell and taste, in the first instance probably in smell alone ; that in defending ourselves from a bad smell we are instinctively impelled to screw up the nose, and to expire strongly through the compressed and protruded lips, giving rise to a sound represented by the interjections faugh! foh! fie! From this interjection it is proposed to derive not only such words as *foul* and *filth*, but, by transferring it from natural to moral aversion, the English *fiend*, the German *Feind*. If this were true, we should suppose that the expression of contempt was chiefly conveyed by the *f*, that is, by the strong emission of the breathing with half-opened lips. But *fiend* is a participle from a root *fian*, to hate ; in Gothic *fijan*; and as a Gothic *f* always corresponds to a labial tenuis in Sanskrit, the same root in Sanskrit would at once lose its expressive power. It exists in fact in Sanskrit as pîy, to hate, to destroy ; just as *friend* is derived from a root which in Sanskrit is prî, to delight.[1]

[1] The following list of Chinese interjections may be of interest:—
    hu, to express surprise.
    fu, the same.
    tsai, to express admiration and approbation.
    i, to express distress.

There is one more remark which I have to make about the interjectional and the onomatopoetic theories, namely this: If the constituent elements of human speech were either mere cries, or the mimicking of the sounds of nature, it would indeed be difficult to understand why brutes should be without language. There is not only the parrot, but the mocking-bird and others, which can imitate most successfully both articulate and inarticulate sounds; and there is hardly an animal without the faculty of uttering interjections, such as huff, hiss, baa, &c. What then is the difference between these interjections, which never led to a language among animals, and the roots, which are the living germs of human speech? Surely, if what puts a perfect distinction betwixt man and brutes is the having of general ideas, a language which arises from interjections and from the imitation of the cries of animals could not claim to be the outward sign of that distinctive faculty of man. I may quote from Professor Rosenkranz: 'If speaking,' he says, 'is considered merely as a sensuous imitation of objects received through the senses, if in its definition the logical articulation, which alone (being inherent) makes the sounds into heralds of thought, is forgotten, then speech would be the most striking and complete example for the supposition that knowledge is the result of the

shin-i, ah! indeed.
pŭ sin, alas.
ngo, stop!

In many cases interjections were originally words, just as the French *hélas* is derived from *lassus*, tired, miserable.—Diez, *Lexicon Etymologicum*, s. v. lasso.

mechanical co-operation of sensation and reflection.'[1]

The theory which is suggested to us by an analysis of language carried out according to the principles of comparative philology, is the very opposite. We arrive in the end at roots, and every one of these expresses a general, not a particular, idea. Every name, if we analyse it, contains a predicate by which the object to which the name is applied was known.

The Primum Cognitum.

There is an old controversy among philosophers, whether language originated in general appellatives, or in proper names.[2] It is the question of the *primum cognitum*, and its consideration may help us perhaps in discovering the true nature of the root, or the *primum appellatum*.

Adam Smith.

Some philosophers, among whom I may mention Locke, Condillac, Adam Smith, Dr. Brown, and with some qualification Dugald Stewart, maintain that all terms, as at first employed, are expressive of individual objects. I quote from Adam Smith: 'The assignation,' he says, 'of particular names to denote particular objects, that is, the institution of nouns substantive, would probably be one of the first steps towards the formation of language. Two savages who had never been taught to speak, but had been bred up remote from the societies of men, would naturally

---

[1] Kant's *Werke*, vol. xii. p. 20.
[2] Sir W. Hamilton's Lectures, ii. p. 319.

THE THEORETICAL STAGE.

begin to form that language by which they would endeavour to make their mutual wants intelligible to each other by uttering certain sounds, whenever they meant to denote certain objects. Those objects only which were most familiar to them, and which they had most frequent occasion to mention, would have particular names assigned to them. The particular cave whose covering sheltered them from the weather, the particular tree whose fruit relieved their hunger, the particular fountain whose water allayed their thirst, would first be denominated by the words *cave, tree, fountain,* or by whatever other appellations they might think proper, in that primitive jargon, to mark them. Afterwards, when the more enlarged experience of these savages had led them to observe, and their necessary occasions obliged them to make mention of, other caves, and other trees, and other fountains, they would naturally bestow upon each of those new objects the same name by which they had been accustomed to express the similar object they were first acquainted with. The new objects had none of them any name of their own, but each of them exactly resembled another object which had such an appellation. It was impossible that those savages could behold the new objects without recollecting the old ones, and the name of the old ones, to which the new bore so close a resemblance. When they had occasion, therefore, to mention, or to point out to each other many of the new objects, they would naturally utter the name of the correspondent old one, of which the idea could not fail, at that instant, to present itself to their memory in the strongest and liveliest manner. And thus those words, which were originally the proper names of individuals, became the common name of a multitude. A child that is just learning to speak calls every person who comes to the house its papa or its mamma; and thus bestows upon the whole species those names which it had been taught to apply to two individuals. I have known a clown who did not know the proper name of the river which ran by his own door. It was *the river*, he said, and he never heard any other name for it. His experience, it seems, had not led him to observe any other river. The general word *river*, therefore, was, it is evident, in his acceptance of it, a proper name signifying an individual object. If this person had been carried to another river, would he not readily have called it *a river*? Could we suppose any person living on the banks of the Thames so ignorant as not to know the general word *river*, but to be acquainted only with the particular word *Thames*, if he were brought to any other river, would he not readily call it a *Thames*? This, in reality, is no more than what they who are well acquainted with the general word are very apt to do. An Englishman, describing any great river which he may have seen in some foreign country, naturally says that it is another Thames. . . . . It is this application of the name of an individual to a great multitude of objects, whose resemblance naturally recalls the idea of that individual, and of the name which expresses it, that seems originally to have given occasion to the formation of those classes and assortments which, in the schools, are called *genera* and *species*.'

Leibniz.

This extract from Adam Smith will give a clear idea of one view of the formation of thought and language. I shall now read another extract, representing the diametrically opposite view. It is taken from Leibniz,[1] who maintains that general terms are necessary for the essential constitution of languages. He likewise appeals to children. 'Children,' he says, 'and those who know but little of the language which they attempt to speak, or little of the subject on which they would employ it, make use of general terms, as *thing, plant, animal,* instead of using proper names, of which they are destitute. And it is certain that all proper or individual names have been originally appellative or general.' And again: 'Thus, I would make bold to affirm that almost all words have been originally general terms, because it would happen very rarely that man would invent a name, expressly and without a reason, to denote this or that individual. We may, therefore, assert that the names of individual things were names of species, which were given *par excellence,* or otherwise, to some individual; as the name *Great Head* to him of the whole town who had the largest, or who was the man of the most consideration of the great heads known.'

It might seem presumptuous to attempt to arbitrate between such men as Leibniz and Adam Smith, particularly when both speak so positively as they do on this subject. But there are two ways of judging

---

[1] *Nouveaux Essais,* lib. iii. cap. i. p. 297 (Erdmann); Sir W. Hamilton, *Lectures,* ii. p. 324.

of former philosophers. One is to put aside their opinions as simply erroneous where they differ from our own. This is the least satisfactory way of studying ancient philosophy. Another way is to try to enter fully into the opinions of those from whom we differ, to make them, for a time at least, our own, till at last we discover the point of view from which each philosopher looked at the facts before him, and catch the light in which they struck his mental vision. We shall then find that there is much less of downright error in the history of philosophy than is commonly supposed; nay, we shall find nothing so conducive to a right appreciation of truth as a right appreciation of the errors by which it is surrounded.

Primum Appellatum.

Now, in the case before us, Adam Smith is no doubt right, when he says that the first individual cave which is called cave gave the name to all other caves. In the same manner the first town, though a mere enclosure, gave the name to all other towns; the first imperial residence on the Palatine hill gave the name to all palaces. Slight differences between caves, towns, or palaces are readily passed by, and the first name becomes more and more general with every new individual to which it is applied. So far Adam Smith is right, and the history of almost every substantive might be cited in support of his view. But Leibniz is equally right when, in looking beyond the first emergence of such names as cave or town or palace, he asks how such names could have arisen. Let us take the Latin names of cave. A cave in Latin is called *antrum, cavea, spelunca.* Now *antrum* means really the same as *internum.* Antar in Sanskrit means *between* and *within.*[1] *Antrum,* therefore, meant originally what is within or inside the earth or anything else. It is clear, therefore, that such a name could not have been given to any individual cave, unless the general idea of being within, or inwardness, had been present in the mind. This general idea once formed, and once expressed by the pronominal root an or antar, the process of naming is clear and intelligible. The place where the savage could live safe from rain and from the sudden attacks of wild beasts, a natural hollow in the rock, he would call his *within*, his *antrum*; and afterwards similar places, whether dug in the earth or cut in a tree, would be designated by the same name. The same general idea, however, would likewise supply other names, and thus we find that the *entrails* (*intrania* in lex Salica) were called antra (neuter) in Sanskrit, *entera* in Greek, originally things within.

Let us take another word for cave, which is *căvea* or *căverna.* Here again Adam Smith would be perfectly right in maintaining that this name, when first given, was applied to one particular cave, and was afterwards extended to other caves. But Leibniz would be equally right in maintaining that in order to call even the first hollow *cavea*, it was necessary that the general idea of *hollow* should have been formed in the mind, and should have received its vocal expression *cav.* Nay, we may go a step beyond, for *cavus*, or hollow, is a secondary, not a primary,

[1] Pott, *Etymologische Forschungen,* s. 324 seq.

CHAPTER XIV.

idea. Before a cave was called *cavea*, a hollow thing, many things hollow had passed before the eyes of men. Why then was a hollow thing, or a hole, called by the root *cav*? Because what had been hollowed out was intended at first as a place of safety and protection, as a cover; and it was called therefore by the root ku or sku, which conveyed the idea of to cover.[1] Hence the general idea of covering existed in the mind before it was applied to hiding-places in rocks or trees, and it was not till an expression had thus been framed for things hollow or safe in general, that caves in particular could be designated by the name of *cavea* or hollows.

Another form for *cavus* was *koilos*, hollow. The conception was originally the same; a hole was called *koilon* because it served as a cover. But once so used, *koilon* came to mean a cave, a vaulted cave, a vault; and thus the heaven was called *cœlum*, the modern *ciel*, because it was looked upon as a vault or cover for the earth.

It is the same with all nouns. They all express originally one out of the many attributes of a thing, and that attribute, whether it be an action or a quality, is necessarily a general idea. The word thus formed was in the first instance intended for one object only, though of course it was almost immediately extended to the whole class to which this object seemed to belong. When a word such as *rivus*, river, was first formed, no doubt it was intended for a certain river, and that river was called *rivus*, from a root ru or

---

[1] Benfey, *Griech. Wurzel-Lex.* s. 611. From sku or ku, σκῦτος, skin; *cŭtis*, hide.

sru, to run, because of its running water. In many instances, a word meaning river or runner remained the proper name of one river, without ever rising to the dignity of an appellative. Thus *Rhenus*, the Rhine, means river or runner, but it clung to one river, and could not well be used as an appellative for others.[1] The Ganges is the Sanskrit Gangâ, literally the Go-go;[2] a name applied to the sacred river, and to several minor rivers in India. The Indus again is the Sanskrit Sindhu, and means the protector, from sidh, to keep off. In this case, however, the proper name was not checked in its growth, but was used likewise as an appellative for any great stream.

We have thus seen how the controversy about the *primum cognitum* assumes a new and perfectly clear aspect. The first thing really known is the general. It is through it that we know and name afterwards individual objects of which any general idea can be predicated; and it is only in the third stage that these individual objects, thus known and named, become again the representatives of whole classes, and their names or proper names are raised into appellatives.[3]

[1] In Somersetshire the large drains which carry off the abundant water from the Sedgemoor district are locally termed *rhines*, the German *Rinne*.

[2] The following notice was sent me from Scotland:—'At the village of Largs, on the Ayrshire coast, there is a small river or burn which is called *Gogo*. The local tradition is that the name originated in the expression of the Scots when driving the soldiers of Haco into the sea at the battle of Largs.'

[3] Sir William Hamilton (*Lectures on Metaphysics*, ii. p. 327) holds a view intermediate between those of Adam Smith and Leibniz. 'As our knowledge,' he says, 'proceeds from the confused to the distinct, from the vague to the determinate, so, in the mouths of children, language at

There is a petrified philosophy in language, and if we examine the most ancient word for *name*, we find it is nâman in Sanskrit, *nomen* in Latin, *namô* in Gothic. This nâman stands for gnâman, which is preserved in the Latin *co-gnomen*. The *g* is dropped as in *notus*, son, for *gnatus*. Nâman, therefore, and *name* are derived from the root gnâ, to know, and meant originally that by which we know a thing.

And how do we know things? We perceive things by our senses. These, however, convey to us information about single things only. But to *know* is more than to feel, than to perceive, more than to remember, more than to compare. No doubt words are much abused. We speak of a dog *knowing* his master, of an infant *knowing* his mother. In such expressions, to know means to recognise. But to know a thing means more than to recognise it. We know a thing if we are able to bring it, or any part of it, under more general ideas. We then say that we have not only a perception, but a conception, or that we have a general idea of a thing. The facts of nature are perceived by our senses; the thoughts of nature, to borrow an expression of Oersted's, can be conceived by our reason only.[1] Now the first step towards this

---

first expresses neither the precisely general nor the determinately individual, but the vague and confused, and out of this the universal is elaborated by generification, the particular and singular by specification and individualisation.' See some further remarks on this point in the *Literary Gazette*, 1861, p. 173.

[1] 'We receive the impression of the falling of a large mass of water, descending always from the same height and with the same difficulty. The scattering of the drops of water, the formation of froth, the sound of the fall by the roaring and by the froth, are constantly produced by the same causes, and, consequently, are always the same. The impres-

THE THEORETICAL STAGE.

real knowledge, a step which, however small in appearance, separates man for ever from all other animals, is *the naming of a thing*, or the making a thing knowable. All naming is classification, bringing the individual under the general; and whatever we know, whether empirically or scientifically, we know it by means of our general ideas only. Other animals have sensation, perception, memory, and, in a certain sense, intellect; but all these, in the animal, are conversant with single objects only. Man has sensation, perception, memory, intellect, and reason, and it is his reason which is conversant with general ideas.[1]

Through reason we not only stand a step above the brute creation; we belong to a different world. We look down on our merely animal experience, on our sensations, perceptions, our memory, and our intellect, as something belonging to us, but not as constituting our most inward and eternal self. Our senses, our memory, our intellect, are like the lenses of a telescope. But there is an eye that looks through them at the realities of the outer world, our own rational and self-conscious self; a power as distinct from our perceptive faculties as the sun is

---

sion which all this produces on us is no doubt at first felt as multiform, but it soon forms a whole, or, in other terms, we feel all the diversity of the isolated impressions as the work of a great physical activity which results from the particular nature of the spot. We may, perhaps, till we are better informed, call all that is fixed in the phenomenon, *the thoughts of nature.*'—Oersted, *Esprit dans la Nature*, p. 152.

[1] 'Ce qui trompe l'homme, c'est qu'il voit faire aux bêtes plusieurs des choses qu'il fait, et qu'il ne voit pas que, dans ces choses-là même, les bêtes ne mettent qu'une intelligence grossière, bornée, et qu'il met, lui, une intelligence *doublée d'esprit.*'—Flourens, *De la Raison*, p. 73.

from the earth which it fills with light, and warmth, and life.

Reason and Language.

At the very point where man parts company with the brute world, at the first flash of reason as the manifestation of the light within us, there we see the true genesis of language. Analyse any word you like, and you will find that it expresses a general idea peculiar to the individual to whom the name belongs. What is the meaning of moon ?—the measurer. What is the meaning of sun ?—the begetter. What is the meaning of earth ?—the ploughed. The old name given to animals, such as cows and sheep, was pasu, the Latin *pecus*, which means *tethered*. *Animal* itself is a later name, and derived from *anima*, soul. This *anima* again meant originally blowing or breathing, like spirit from *spirare*, and was derived from a root an, to blow, which gives us anila, wind, in Sanskrit, and *anemos*, wind, in Greek. *Ghost*, A.S. *gâst*, the German *Geist*, seems to be based on a similar conception, if it is connected, as Wackernagel thinks, with *yeast*. Certainly *Geist* is used in German both for spirit and for yeast (Hefe). The boiling *Geyser* of Iceland also may be remotely related.[1] *Soul*, A.S. *sâwol*, is the Gothic *saivala*, and this is clearly related to another Gothic word, *saivs*,[2] which means the sea. The sea, A.S. *sœ*, was called *saivs*, from a root *si* or *siv*, the Greek *seio*, to shake ; it meant the tossed-about water, in contradistinction to stagnant or running water. The

---

[1] See *Biographies of Words*, p. 27; Curtius, p. 352; Kuhn's *Zeitschrift*, ii. 137, xx. 305.
[2] See Heyse, *System der Sprachwissenschaft*, s. 97.

soul being called *saivala*, we see that it was originally conceived by the Teutonic nations as a sea within, heaving up and down with every breath, and reflecting heaven and earth on the mirror of the deep.

The Sanskrit name for love is **smara**; it is derived from **smar**, to recollect; and the same root may have supplied the German *schmerz*, pain, and the English *smart*.[1]

If the serpent is called in Sanskrit **sarpa**, it is because it was conceived under the general idea of creeping, an idea expressed by the root *srip*. But the serpent was also called **ahi** in Sanskrit, in Greek *echis* or *echidna*, in Latin *anguis*. This name is derived from quite a different root and idea. The root is **ah** in Sanskrit, or **amh**, which means to press together, to choke, to throttle. Here the distinguishing mark from which the serpent was named was his throttling, and ahi meant serpent, as expressing the general idea of throttler. It is a curious root this amh, and it still lives in several modern words. In Latin it appears as *ango, anxi, anctum*, to strangle; in *angina*, quinsy;[2] in *angor*, suffocation. But *angor* meant not only quinsy or compression of the throat: it assumed a moral import and signifies anguish or anxiety. The two adjectives *angustus*, narrow, and *anxius*, uneasy, both come from the same source. In Sanskrit the same root was chosen with great truth

---

[1] Cf. Pott, *Etymologische Forschungen,* ii. s. 290.

[2] The word *quinsy*, as was pointed out to me, offers a striking illustration of the ravages produced by phonetic decay. The root a m h has here completely vanished. But it was there originally, for *quinsy* is the Greek κυνάγχη, dog-throttling. See Richardson's *Dictionary*, s. v. Quinancy.

as the proper name of sin. Evil no doubt presented itself under various aspects to the human mind, and its names are many; but none so expressive as those derived from our root *amh*, to throttle. *Amhas* in Sanskrit means sin, but it does so only because it meant originally throttling—the consciousness of sin being like the grasp of the assassin on the throat of his victim. All who have seen and contemplated the statue of Laokoon and his sons, with the serpent coiled round them from head to foot, may realise what those ancients saw and felt when they called sin *amhas*, or the throttler. This *amhas* is the same word as the Greek *áchos*, fear. In Gothic the same root has produced *ag-is*, in the sense of *fear*, and from this source we have *awe*, in awful, i.e. fearful, and *ug*, in *ugly*. The English *anguish* is from the French *angoisse*, the Italian *angoscia*, a corruption of the Latin *angustiæ*, a strait.[1]

And how did those early thinkers and framers of language distinguish between man and the other animals? What general idea did they connect with the first conception of themselves? The Latin word *homo*, the French *l'homme*, which has been reduced to *on* in *on dit*, is derived from the same root which we have in *humus*, the soil, *humilis*, humble. *Homo*, therefore, would express the idea of a being made of the dust of the earth.[2]

Another ancient word for man was the Sanskrit marta,[3] the Greek *brotos*, the Latin *mortalis* (a

[1] Kuhn, *Zeitschrift*, i. s. 152, 355; Curtius, p. 190.
[2] Greek χαμαί, Zend *zem*, Lithuanian *żeme* and *żmenes, homines*. See Bopp, *Glossarium Sanscritum*, s. v.
[3] See Windischmann, *Fortschritt der Sprachenkunde*, s. 23.

secondary derivative), our own *mortal.* Marta means
'he who dies,' and it is remarkable that, where everything else was changing, fading, and dying, this should have been chosen as the distinguishing name for man. Those early poets would hardly have called themselves mortals, unless they had believed in other beings as immortal.

There is a third name for man which means simply the thinker, and this, the true title of our race, still lives in the name of *man.* Mâ in Sanskrit means to measure, from which, as pointed out before, we had the name of moon. *Man,* a derivative root, means to think. From this we have the Sanskrit manu, originally thinker, then man. In the later Sanskrit we find derivatives, such as mânava, mânusha, manushya, all expressing man or son of man. In Gothic we find both *man* and *mannisks,* the modern German *mann* and *mensch.*

There were many more names for man, as there were many names for all things in ancient languages. Any feature that struck the observing mind as peculiarly characteristic could be made to furnish a new name. In common Sanskrit dictionaries we find 5 words for hand, 11 for light, 15 for cloud, 20 for moon, 26 for snake, 33 for slaughter, 35 for fire, 37 for sun.[1] The sun might be called the bright, the warm, the golden, the preserver, the destroyer, the wolf, the lion, the heavenly eye, the father of light and life. Hence that superabundance of synonyms in ancient dialects, and hence that *struggle for life* carried on among these words, which led to the destruction of

[1] Cf. Yates, *Sanskrit Grammar,* p. xviii.

the less strong, the less fertile, the less happy words, and ended in the triumph of *one*, as the recognised and proper name for every object in every language. On a very small scale this process of *natural selection*, or, as it would better be called, *elimination*, may still be watched even in modern languages, that is to say, even in languages so old and stricken in years as English and French. What it was at the first burst of dialects we can only gather from such isolated cases as when Von Hammer counts 5,744 words all relating to the camel.[1]

The fact that every word is originally a predicate —that names, though signs of individual conceptions, are all, without exception, derived from general ideas —is one of the most important discoveries in the science of language. It was known before that language is the distinguishing characteristic of man; it was known also that the having of general ideas is that which puts a perfect distinction betwixt man and brutes; but that these two were only different expressions of the same fact was not known till the theory of roots had been established as preferable to the theories both of Onomatopoieia and of Interjec-

---

[1] Farrar, *Origin of Language*, p. 85. 'Das Kamel,' *Extrait des Mém. de l'Acad. de Vienne, classe de phil. et d'hist.* tom. vii. In Arabic a work is mentioned on the 500 names of the lion; another on the 200 names of the serpent. Firuzabadi, the author of the *Kamus*, says he wrote a work on the names of honey, and that he counted 80 without exhausting the subject. The same author maintains that in Arabic there are at least 1,000 words for sword; others maintain that there are 400 to signify misfortune. Hervas (*Dell' Origine delle Lingue*, § 233) states that the Mandshu Tatars have more than 100 words to express the different ages and qualities of the horse. See supra, p. 329. There is, however, much exaggeration in these statements. See Renan, *Histoire des Langues sémitiques*, p. 377; Sayce, *Principles*, p. 208.

tions. But, though our modern philosophy did not know it, the ancient poets and framers of language must have known it. For in Greek, language is *logos*, but *logos* means also reason, and *alogon* was chosen as the name, and the most proper name, for brute. No animal, so far as we know, thinks and speaks, except man. Language and thought are inseparable. Words without thought are dead sounds; thoughts without words are nothing. To think is to speak low; to speak is to think aloud. The word is the thought incarnate.

We may still go a step further back and ask the question, How can sound express thought? How did roots become the signs of general ideas? How was the abstract idea of measuring expressed by mâ, the idea of thinking by *man*? How did gâ come to mean going; sthâ, standing; sad, sitting; dâ, giving; mar, dying; kar, walking; kar, doing?

Roots as Phonetic Types.

Though this question belongs to the Science of Thought rather than to the Science of Language, I shall try to answer it, at least negatively, by showing what roots are not. If we know this, it may help us hereafter in finding out what roots are.

The roots, whether 400 or 1000, which remain as the residue of a scientific analysis in different families of language, and which we are justified in regarding as the constituent elements of human speech, are not mere interjections, nor are they mere imitations. They may be called *phonetic types*, and whatever explanation the psychologist or the metaphysician may propose, to the student of language these roots are simply ultimate facts. We might say with Plato, that they exist by nature; though with Plato we should have to add that, when we say by nature, we mean by the hand of God.[1] If we must look for analogies, however imperfect, they have been pointed out by others. There is a law, it has been said, which runs through nearly the whole of nature, that everything which is struck rings. Each substance has its peculiar ring. We can tell the more or less perfect structure of metals by their vibrations, by the answer which they give. Gold rings differently from tin, wood rings differently from stone; and different sounds are produced according to the nature of each percussion. It is the same, we are told, with man, the most highly organised of nature's work.[2] Man responds. Man rings. Man, in his primitive and perfect state, was not only endowed, like the brute, with the power of expressing his sensations by interjections, and his perceptions by onomatopoieia. He possessed likewise the faculty of giving more articulate expression to the general conceptions of his mind. That faculty was

---

[1] Θήσω τὰ μὲν φύσει λεγόμενα ποιεῖσθαι θείᾳ τέχνῃ.

[2] This view was propounded many years ago by Professor Heyse in the lectures which he gave at Berlin, and which have been very carefully published since his death by one of his pupils, Dr. Steinthal. The fact that wood, metals, cords, &c., if struck, vibrate and ring, can, of course, be used as an illustration only, and not as an explanation. The faculty peculiar to man, in his primitive state, by which every impression from without received its vocal expression from within, must be accepted as an ultimate fact, while the formation of roots, as the exponents of general conceptions, will always be viewed differently by different schools of philosophy. Much new light has been thrown on the origin of roots by Professor Noiré, and the whole subject has now been fully treated by myself in the *Science of Thought*, 1887.

not of his own making. It was an instinct, an instinct of the mind as irresistible as any other instinct. Man loses his instincts as he ceases to want them. His senses become fainter when, as in the case of scent, they become useless. Thus the creative faculty which gave to each general conception, as it thrilled for the first time through the brain, a phonetic expression, became extinct when its object was fulfilled.

There may be some value in speculations of this kind, but I should not like to endorse them, for we have no right to imagine that a vague analogy can ever become an explanation of the problem of the origin of roots. If there is any truth in the results at which we have arrived after a careful and unprejudiced analysis of all the facts before us, all that we have a right to assert is that language begins with roots, and that these roots are neither more nor less than phonetic types, or typical sounds. What lies beyond them is no longer, or, if we speak historically, is not yet language, however interesting it may be for psychological researches. But whatever exists in real language is the upshot of these roots. Words are various impressions taken from those phonetic moulds, or, if you like, varieties and modifications, perfectly intelligible in their structure, of those typical sounds which, by means of unerring tests, have been discovered as the residuum of all human speech.

The number of these *phonetic types* must have been almost infinite in the beginning, and it was only through the same process of *natural elimination* which we observed in the early history of words that clusters of roots, more or less synonymous, were gradually reduced to one definite type. Instead of deriving language from nine roots, like Dr. Murray,[1] or from *one* root, a feat actually accomplished by a Dr. Schmidt,[2] we must suppose that the first settlement of the radical elements of language was preceded by a period of unrestrained growth—the spring of speech—to be followed by many an autumn.

With the process of elimination, or natural selection, the historical element enters into the science of language. However primitive the Chinese may be as compared with terminational and inflectional languages, its roots or words have clearly passed through a long process of mutual attrition. There are many things of a merely traditional character even in Chinese. The rule that in a simple sentence the first word is the subject, the second the verb, the third the object, is a traditional rule. It is by tradition only that *ngŏ ǵin*, in Chinese, means a bad man, whereas *ǵin ngŏ* signifies man is bad. The Chinese themselves distinguish between *full* and *empty* roots,[3] the former being predicative, the latter corresponding to our particles, which modify the meaning of full roots and determine their relation to each other. Now it is only by tradition that roots became empty. All roots were originally full, whether predicative or demonstrative, and the fact that empty roots in

---

[1] Dr. Murray's primitive roots were *ag, bag, dwag, cwag, lag, mag, nag, rag, swag*. See Pott, *Etymologische Forschungen*, 2nd ed., 1861, p. 75.

[2] Curtius, *Griechische Etymologie*, s. 13. Dr. Schmidt derives all Greek words from the root *e*, and all Latin words from the arch-radical *hi*.

[3] Endlicher, *Chinesische Grammatik*, s. 163.

Chinese cannot always be traced back to their full prototypes shows that even the most ancient Chinese had passed through successive periods of growth. Chinese commentators admit that all empty words were originally full words, just as Sanskrit grammarians maintain that all that is formal in grammar was originally substantial. But we must be satisfied with but partial proofs of this general principle, and must be prepared to find as many fanciful derivations in Chinese as in Sanskrit. The fact again that not all roots in Chinese are capable of being employed at pleasure, either as substantives, or verbs, or adjectives, is another proof that, even in this most primitive stage, language points back to a previous growth. *Fu* is father, *mu* is mother, *fu mu* parents; but neither *fu* nor *mu* is used as a root in its original predicative sense. The amplest proof, however, of the various stages through which even so simple a language as Chinese must have passed, is to be found in the comparatively small number of roots, and in the number of definite meanings attached to each—a result which could only have been obtained by that constant struggle which has been so well described in natural history as the struggle for life.

But although this sifting of roots, and still more the subsequent combination of roots, cannot be ascribed to the mere working of nature or natural instincts, it is still less, as we saw in a former lecture, the effect of deliberate or premeditated art, in the sense in which, for instance, a picture of Raphael or a symphony of Beethoven is. Given a root to express flying, or bird, and another to express heap, then the joining together of the two to express many birds, or birds in the plural, is the natural effect of the synthetic power of the human mind, or, to use more homely language, of the power of putting two and two together. Some philosophers maintain that this explains nothing, and that the real mystery is how the mind can form any synthesis, and conceive many things as one. This is quite true, but we must not enter into these depths. Other philosophers imagine that the combination of roots to form agglutinative and inflectional language is, like the first formation of roots, the result of a natural instinct. Thus Professor Heyse [1] maintained that 'the various forms of development in language must be explained by philosophers as *necessary* evolutions, founded in the very essence of human speech.' This is not the case. We can watch the growth of language, and we can understand and explain all that is the result of that growth. But we cannot undertake to prove that all that is in language is so by necessity, and could not have been otherwise. When we have, as in Chinese, two such words as *kiai* and *tu*, both expressing a heap, an assembly, a quantity, then we may perfectly understand why either the one or the other should have been used to form the plural. But if one of the two becomes fixed and traditional while the other becomes obsolete, then we can only register the fact as historical, but no philosophy on earth will explain its absolute necessity. We can perfectly understand how, with two such roots as *kŭŏ*, empire, and *cung*, middle, the Chinese should have formed what

[1] *System der Sprachwissenschaft*, s. 61.

we call a locative *kŭŏ ćung*, in the empire. But to say that this was the only way to express this conception is an assertion contradicted both by fact and reason. We saw the various ways in which the future can be formed. They are all equally intelligible and equally possible, but not one of them can be called inevitable. In Chinese *ẏaó* means to will, *ngò* is I; hence *ngò ẏaó*, I will. The same root *ẏaó*, added to *kiú*, to go, gives us *ngò ẏaó kiú*, I will go, the first germ of our futures. To say that *ngò ẏaó kiú* was the necessary form of the future in Chinese would introduce a fatalism into language which rests on no authority whatever. The building up of language is not like the building of the cells in a beehive, nor is it like the building of St. Peter's by Michael Angelo. It is the result of innumerable agencies, working each according to certain laws, and leaving, in the end, the result of their combined efforts freed from all that proved superfluous or useless. From the first combination of two such words as *g̈in*, man, *kiai*, many, forming the plural *g̈in kiai*, to such inflectional forms as Sanskrit n a r - a s, from n r*i*, Greek ἄνδρες from ἀνήρ, English *men* from *man*, everything is intelligible as the result of the two principles of development in language, phonetic decay and dialectic growth. What is antecedent to the production of roots is the work of nature; what follows after is the work of man, not in his individual and free, but in his collective and moderating, capacity.

I do not say that every form in Greek or Sanskrit has as yet been analysed and explained. There are formations in Greek and Latin and English which have hitherto baffled all tests; and there are certain contrivances, such as the augment in Greek, the change of vowels in Hebrew, the Umlaut and Ablaut in the Teutonic dialects, where we might feel inclined to suppose that language admitted distinctions purely musical or phonetic, corresponding to very palpable and material distinctions of thought. Such a supposition, however, is not founded on any safe induction. It may seem inexplicable to us why *bruder* in German should form its plural as *brüder*; or *brother*, *brethren*. But what is inexplicable and apparently artificial in our modern languages becomes intelligible in their more ancient phases. The change of *u* into *ü*, as in *bruder*, *brüder*, was not intentional; least of all was it introduced to express plurality. The change was purely phonetic, and due originally to the influence of an *i* or *j*[1] in the next syllable, which reacted regularly on the vowel of the preceding syllable —nay, which left its effect behind, even after it has itself disappeared. By a false analogy such a change, justifiable in a small class of words only, was applied to other words also where no such change was called for; and it may then appear as if an arbitrary change of vowels was intended to convey a change of meaning. But into these recesses also the comparative philologist can follow language, thus discovering a reason even for what in reality was irrational and wrong. It seems difficult to believe that the augment in Greek should originally have had an independent

[1] See Schleicher, *Deutsche Sprache*, s. 146; J. Wright, *High-German Primer*, p. 11.

substantial existence, yet all analogy is in favour of such a view. Suppose English had never been written down before Wycliffe's time, we should then find that in some instances the perfect was formed by the mere addition of a short *a*. Wycliffe spoke and wrote,[1] *I knowlech to a felid and seid þus*, i.e. I acknowledge to have felt and said thus. In a similar way we read *it should a fallen*, instead of 'it should have fallen'; and in some parts of England common people still say very much the same: *I should a done it*. Now in some old English books this *a* actually coalesces with the verb—at least they are printed together—so that a grammar founded on them would give us 'to fall' as the infinitive of the present, *to afallen* as the infinitive of the past. I do not wish for one moment to be understood as if there was any connection between this *a*, a contraction of *have* in English, and the Greek augment which is placed before past tenses. All I mean is, that, if the origin of the augment has not yet been satisfactorily explained, we are not therefore to despair, or to admit an arbitrary addition of a consonant or vowel, used as it were algebraically or by mutual agreement, to distinguish a past from a present tense.

Origin and Confusion of Tongues.

If inductive reasoning is worth anything, we are justified in believing that what has been proved to be true on so large a scale, and in cases where it was least expected, is true with regard to language in general. We require no supernatural interference, nor any conclave of ancient sages, to explain the realities

[1] Marsh, *Lectures*, p. 388.

of human speech. All that is formal in language is the result of rational combination; all that is material is the result of a mental instinct, call it interjectional, onomatopoetic, or mimetic. The first natural and instinctive utterances, if sifted differently by different clans, would fully account both for the first origin and for the first divergence of human speech. We can understand not only the origin of language, but likewise the necessary breaking up of one language into many; and we perceive that no amount of variety in the material or the formal elements of speech is incompatible with the admission of one common source.

The Science of Language thus leads us up to that highest summit from whence we see into the very dawn of man's life on earth, and where the words which we have heard so often from the days of our childhood—'And the whole earth was of one language and of one speech'—assume a meaning more natural, more intelligible, more convincing, than they ever had before.

GENEALOGICAL TABLE OF THE ARYAN FAMILY OF LANGUAGES.

Division	Classes	Branches	Dead Languages	Living Languages / Spoken Dialects of:
South-Eastern	Indic		Modern Sanskrit—Prākrit and Pali, Vedic Sanskrit	India, Afghanistan, Pushtu, the Gipsies
South-Eastern	Iranic		Parsi, Pehlevi, Achaemenian Inscriptions, Zend	Persia, Kurdistan, Baluchistan, Ossethi, Armenia
North-Western	Celtic		Old Armenian	
North-Western	Celtic	Cymric	Old Welsh, Old Armorican, Cornish	Wales, Brittany
North-Western	Celtic	Gadelic	Old Irish	Scotland, Ireland, Isle of Man
North-Western	Celtic	Gallic	Inscriptions in Gaul	†
North-Western	Italic		Langue d'Oc, Langue d'Oïl } Lingua vulgaris { Oscan, Latin, Umbrian }	Portugal, Spain, Provence, France, Italy, Rumania, Grisons
North-Western	Illyric Hellenic		Κοινή { Doric, Aeolic, Attic, Ionic }	Albania, Greece
North-Western	Windic or Letto-Slavic	Lettic	Old Prussian	Lituania, Kurland and Livonia (Lettish) †
North-Western	Windic or Letto-Slavic	South-East Slavonic	Ecclesiastical Slavonic	Bulgaria, Russia (Great, Little, White Russian), Illyria (Slovenian or Carinthian, Servian, Croatian)
North-Western	Windic or Letto-Slavic	West Slavonic	Old Bohemian	Poland, Bohemia (Slovakian), Lusatia (Wends and Sorbs) †
North-Western	Windic or Letto-Slavic	West Slavonic	Polabian	West
North-Western	Teutonic	High-German	Middle and Old High-German, Anglo-Saxon, Middle and Old Dutch (Low-Franconian), Old Frisian, Old Saxon, Gothic	Germany, England, Holland, Frisland, North of Germany (Platt-Deutsch) †
North-Western	Teutonic	Low-German		

No. II.—Genealogical Table of the Semitic Family of Languages.

Living Languages	Dead Languages	Classes	
Dialects of:—			
†	Chaldee (Masora, Talmud, Targum, Biblical Chaldee)		
†	Samaritan	Aramaic	Northern
†	Mandaean		
Syria	Syriac (Peshito)		
the Jews . . .	Biblical Hebrew		
†	Phenician and Carthaginian Inscriptions	Hebraic	
†	Moabites		
Arabia . . .	Thamudic Inscriptions, Himyaritic Inscriptions	Arabic	Southern
Abyssinia (Amharic, Tigre, Ekhili)	Ethiopic or Geez		

No. III.

GENEALOGICAL TABLE OF THE TURANIAN FAMILY OF LANGUAGES.—NORTHERN DIVISION.

Living Languages	Dead Languages	Branches	Classes	
Dialects of the—				
Yurakians	.	} Northern	} Samoyedic	
Tawgyans	.			
Yeniseians	.			
Ostiako-Samoyedes	.	} Eastern		
Kamassinians	.			
Chapogires (Upper Tunguska)	.	} Western	} Tungusic (Altaic)	
Orotongs (Lower Tunguska)	.			
People of Nyertchinsk	.			
Lamutes (Coast of O'hotsk)	.	} Eastern		
Mandshu (China)	.			
Sharra-Mongols (South of Gobi)	.	} Eastern or Mongols Proper	} Mongolic (Altaic)	TURANIAN FAMILY. Northern Division.
Khalkhas (North of Gobi)	.			
Sharaigol (Tibet and Tangut)	.			
Choshot (Kokonúr)	.	} Ölöt or Kalmüks	} Western Mongols	
Dsungur	.			
Torgod	.			
Dürbet	.			
Aimaks (i.e. Tribes of Persia)	.			
Sokpas (Tibet)	.		Northern Mongols	
Buriäts (Lake Baikal)	.			
Uigurs	.	} Chagataic, S.E.	} Turkic (Altaic)	
Komanes	.			
Chagatais	.			
Usbeks	.			
Turkmans	.			
People of Kasan	.	} Turkic, N.		
Kirgis	.			
Bashkirs	.			
Nogais	.			
Kumians	.			
Karachais	.			
Karakalpaks	.			
Meshcheräks	.			
People of Siberia	.			
Yakuts	.			
People of Durbend	.	} Turkic, W.		
,, Aderbijan	.			
,, Krimea	.			
,, Anatolia	.			
,, Rumelia	.			
Hungarians	.	} Ugric	} Finnic (Uralic)	
Voguls	.			
Ugro-Ostiakes	.			
Tcheremissians	.	} Bulgaric		
Mordvins	.			
Permians	.	} Permic		
Syrjänes	.			
Votiaks	.			
Laps	.	} Chudic		
Fins	.			
Esths	.			
Lives	.			
Votes	.			

No. IV.

GENEALOGICAL TABLE OF THE TURANIAN FAMILY OF LANGUAGES.—SOUTHERN DIVISION.

LIVING LANGUAGES	DEAD LANGUAGES	BRANCHES	CLASSES
Dialects of :— Chinese.			
Siamese			
Ahom			
Laos		Taic	
Khamti			
Shan (Tenasserim)			
Malay and Polynesian Islands (See Humboldt, Kawi Sprache)		Malaic	
Tibetan			
Horpa (NW. Tibet, Bucharia)			
Thochu-Sifan (NE. Tibet, China)		Trans-Himalayan	
Gyarung-Sifan (NE. Tibet, China)			
Manyak-Sifan (NE. Tibet, China)			
Takpa (West of Kwombo)			Gangetic
Kenaveri (Setlej basin)			
Sarpa (West of Gandakéan basin)			
Sunwár (Gandakéan basin)			
Gurung (Gandakéan basin)			
Magar (Gandakéan basin)		Sub-Himalayan	
Newár (between Gandakéan and Koséan basins)			
Murmi (between Gandakéan and Koséan basins)			
Limbu (Koséan basin)			
Kiranti (Koséan basin)			
Lepcha (Tishtéan basin)			Bhotiya
Bhutanese (Manaséan basin)			
Chepang (Nepal-Terai)			
Burmese (Burmah and Arakan)			
Dhimal (between Konki and Dhorla)			
Kachari-Bodo (Migrat. 80°–93½°, and 25°–27°)			
Garo (90°–91° E. long.; 25°–26° N. lat.)			
Changlo (91°–92° E. long.)			
Mikir (Nowgong)			
Dophla (92° 50'–97° N. lat.)			
Miri (94°–97° E. long. ?)			
Abor-Miri			
Abor (97°–99° E. long.)			
Sibsagor-Miri			
Singpho (27°–28° N. lat.)			
Naga tribes (93°–97° E. long.; 23° N. lat. [Mithan] East of Sibsagor)		Lohitic	TURANIAN FAMILY, Southern Division.
Naga tribes (Namsang)			
Naga tribes (Nowgong)			
Naga tribes (Tengsa)			
Naga tribes (Tablung, North of Sibsagor)			
Naga tribes (Khati, Jorhat)			
Naga tribes (Angami, South)			
Kuki (NE. of Chittagong)			
Khyeng (Shyu) 19°–21° N. lat. Arakan)			
Kami (Kuladan R. Arakan)			
Kumi (Kuladan R. Arakan)			
Shendus (22°–23° and 93–94°)			
Mru (Arakan, Chittagong)			
Sak (Nauf River, East)			
Tunglhu (Tenasserim)			
Ho (Kolehan)			Munda (See Turanian Languages, p. 175)
Sinhbhum Kol (Chyebossa)			
Sontal (Chyebossa)			
Bhumij (Chyebossa)			
Mundala (Chota Nagpur)			
Canarese			
Tamil			
Telugu			
Malayalam			
Gond		Tamulic	
Brahvi			
Tuluva			
Toduva			
Uraon-kol			

INDEX.

A, as a contraction of have in English, 535.
À, real meaning of, 336.
Abba, father in the N.T., 317.
Abchasian, 448.
Abdu-l-Kadir Maluk, Shah of Badâun, his history of India, &c., 205 n.
Abhíra, or Âbhíra, 191.
Abin for abisne, 75 n.
Abipones, 452.
Abiria, the, of Ptolemy, 191.
Ablative in Latin, Cæsar the inventor of the term, 116.
— the, in Chinese, 128.
Ablaut, 534.
Able, 86.
Abraham, language of, 316.
Abul Fazl, the minister, 205 n.
Abul Walid, or Rabbi Jonâ, author of the first Hebrew grammar, 89 n.
Abu Rihan al Birûni, his work on Hindu literature and sciences, 201, 202 n. *See* Albirûni.
Abu Saleh, his translations from Sanskrit into Arabic, 202.
Abu Zacariyya 'Hayyudj, on Hebrew roots, 89 n.
Abyssinian language, ancient and modern, 323, 449.
Academy, New, doctrines of the, embraced in Rome, 112.
Accadian views on the Sun and Moon, 5. *See* Akkadian.
Accommodation Question, 211.
Accusative, formation of the, in Chinese, 127.
Achæmenian dynasty, inscriptions of the, 275, 277, 281.
Achos, 524.
Active, 117.
Adam, book of, 318.
Adelung's Mithridates, 154, 158, 229.
Adjectives, formation of, in Tibetan, Dravidian, Sanskrit, Greek, &c., 120 n.
— — in Chinese, 128.
Adverb, formation of, in Chinese, 128.
— — French, 52.
Ælius Stilo, his lectures in Rome on Latin grammar, 115, 115 n.
Ærend, 363.
Æternus, 402.
Affinity, indications of true, in the animal and vegetable worlds, 16, 17.
Affixes in Turanian languages, 404.
Afghanistan, language of, 287.
Africa, South, dialects of, 69, 449.
— Lepsius, on the languages of, 450.
African language, an imaginary, 339.
Agau dialect, 449, 451.
Âge, history of the French word, 402.
Agglutination in Turanian languages, 401.
— rudimentary traces of, in Chinese, 392, 461, 462.
— the only intelligible means by which language acquires grammatical organisation, 470.
Agglutinative languages, 47, 51, 391, 402, 453, 469.
— — rudimentary traces of inflection in, 462.

Agglutinative stage, 455-461.
— dialects, coincidences in, 468.
Aghovan, 296.
Agis, fear, 524.
Aglossoi, the, of the Greeks, 93.
Agnivesa, 203 *n.*
Agnone, Oscan inscriptions of, 6 *n.*
Agriculture of the Chaldeans, work on the, 319.
— Punic work of Mago on, 97 *n.*
Ahi, 523.
Ahirs, the, of Cutch, 191.
Ahom, the, 447.
Ahurô-mazdão, 277.
Aime, 347.
Airtha, 361.
Airyâ, 293.
Ais, 556.
Akbar, rise of Urdu literature under, 181.
— his search for the true religion, 204.
— his founding of the Ilâhi religion, 204.
— works translated into Persian for, 205.
— not able to obtain a translation of the Veda, 205, 206.
— his experiments on the origin of speech, 481 *n.*
Akkadian inscriptions, 398.
Akra, or Ga language, 450.
À la, 86.
Aladdin, Siljuk, Sultan of Iconium, 419.
Albania, origin of the name, 296.
Albanian language, 270, 387.
Albans, St., book of, 72.
Albertus Magnus, on the influence of Christianity, 141 *n.*
Albirûni, 199 *n,* 200 *n,* 201, 202 *n,* 203 *n.*
— his Tarîkhu-l-Hind, 201.
— his knowledge of Sanskrit, 202.
Alchemy, extinction of, 9.
Alcuin, 122.
Alderman, 342.
Alemannic, 246 *n,* 248.
Alexander the Great, influence of his expedition in giving the Greeks a knowledge of other nations, 95.
Alexander the Great, his difficulty in conversing with the Brahmans, 95.
— called a barbarian by Demosthenes, 137 *n.*
— destroyed the old Persian writings, 280.
Alexander Polyhistor, 95 *n,* 115.
Alexandria, influence of, on the study of foreign languages, 92, 98.
— discussions on antiquity at, 98.
— scholars at, 99.
— critical study of ancient Greek at, 99, 102.
— scholars of, the first students of the forms of language, 100.
Algebra, Sanskrit work on, translated into Arabic, 201.
Algonquins, the one case of the, 336.
Algum trees, 189, 191 *n.*
Alimentus, L. C., his history of Rome in Greek, 107.
Alkmæon, 7 *n.*
Allahabad, edict of Queen, 172.
Allemannic, 246 *n,* 247 *n.*
Allophyllian languages, 325, 397.
Al Mâmum, Kalif, 201.
Almansur, caused a Sanskrit astronomical work to be translated into Arabic, 199.
Alogon, 527.
Alphabet, Latin, from Sicily, 104 *n.*
— Etruscan, from Attica, 104 *n.*
— Grantha, 219 *n.*
Alphabets, early ones in India, 164, 164 *n.*
— — derived from the West, 176.
Altaic languages, 398, 407.
Alwis, 146 *n.*
Amalgamating languages, 392.
Amarakosha, translated for Akbar, 205.
Ambrosio, Theseo, 143 *n.*
America, Central, rapid changes in the languages of the tribes of, 65, 452.
— great number of languages spoken by the natives of, 66, 66 *n.*

INDEX. 543

America, different views of scholars on the languages of, 451.
American dialects, 64, 451.
— — influence of Bible on, 64.
— — Hervas reduced them to eleven families, 66.
— — Dr. Brinton on, 67.
— — Leland on, 67.
— languages, mostly polysynthetic, 455.
Amharic, or modern Abyssinian, 323.
Amhas, 524.
Ammianus Marcellinus, on Shahan shâb, 284 n.
Amo, amavi, 129.
Amor, 130.
Amore, 505 n.
Analogy, 117.
Analytical languages, 456.
Anatomy, comparative, 17.
Anaximenes, 7 n.
Anchora, 105 n.
Andaman islands, dialect of, 453.
Andhaka and Damila parents, language of child of, 146 n.
Andhra country, 175.
Ἀνδρόμεος, 383.
Andronicus, Livius, teacher of Greek at Rome, 74, 108.
Angina, 523.
Anglo-Saxon, 243, 247.
— and Semi-Saxon, 131.
— not an original language, 133.
— four branches of, 243.
— the most ancient epic in, 244.
— the earliest MS. in, 244 n.
— cannot be derived from Gothic, 252.
Ango, 523.
Angor, 523.
Angora in Galatia, battle of, 420.
Anguis, 523.
Anguish, 524.
Angustus, 523.
Anima, Animal, 522.
Annam, language of, 448.
Anomaly, theory of, 114.
Anquetil Duperron, his translation of the Upanishads, 207.

Anquetil Duperron, his correspondence with the Père Cœurdoux, 213.
— — his translation of Zoroaster's works, 233, 274, 296 n.
Antōnymíai, personal pronouns, 101.
Antra, 517.
Antrum, 517.
Anxius, 523.
Apabhramsas, 166, 170, 171, 178, 179, 180, 181.
— or vulgar dialects, 171, 182.
— as distinguished from Prâkrits, 171.
Âpastamba-Sûtra, 208 n.
Apes, Hebrew Koph, 189.
— a Sanskrit word, 189, 193 n.
Apollo, name adopted from Greek, 105.
— temple to, in Rome, 106.
Apollonius Dyscolus, the grammarian, 121.
Aquilia, Council of, 307.
AR, the root, 359, 359 n.
Âr, in Anglo-Saxon, 356.
Arabe vulgaire, 58 n.
Arabia, Ophir in, 192 n.
Arabic, influencing Persian and influenced by it, 82, 286.
— adopted by the Jews, 318.
— ascendancy of, in Syria and Palestine, 321.
— original seat of, 321.
— earliest literary documents in, 321.
— ancient Himyaritic inscriptions, 322.
— classical, 322.
— spoken dialects of, 322.
— verbal formations in, 428 n.
Arabs, their learned men mostly of Persian origin, 83.
Aramaic division of Semitic languages, 314.
— of the Cuneiform inscriptions, 314.
— two dialects of, 316.
— of Babylon and Nineveh, 316.
— spoken by Christ, 317.

Aramaic, the modern Mendaïtes or Nasoreans, 318.
Aratrum, 360, 360 n.
Araucans, language of the, 85.
Arbeit, 362, 363 n.
Archias in Scipio's house, 111.
Arctic tribes, their languages, 452.
Ardeshir, inscriptions of, 283.
Areimanios, 275 n.
Ares, 106.
Argi-izari, Bask for moon, 4 n.
Argonautic expeditions, want of interpreters, 94.
Aria, 301.
'Αριάκαι, 293 n.
Ariaké, 293.
Arian, Ulfilas an, 307.
Ariana, the, of Greek geographers, 294, 301.
Ariaramnes, great grandfather of Darius, 295.
Arii, 298.
Arikh, 296 n.
"Αριοι, 296 n.
Ariovistus, 298.
Aristarchus, 100, 103, 117.
Aristeas, the Jew, 99 n.
Aristocrates, 96.
Aristotle and the fixed stars, 7 n.
— on grammatical categories, 91, 100, 102.
— first used the word article, 101.
— on the Lokrians, 137 n.
— failed to see any order in languages, 138.
— on Oromasdes, 275 n, 279.
Aritra, 364.
Armenia, 296.
Armenian language, 287, 288.
Armentum, 361.
Armorican, 265.
Arôma, 360.
Aroura, 361.
Arowakes, 452.
Arpinum, provincial Latin of, 75.
Ars, 363.
Art, 363, 366.
Artali, name for moon in the Edda, 4 n.
Arthakathâs, translated from Pâli into Sinhalese, 183.
Arthron, article derived from, 101.
Article, added by Aristotle, 100.
— original meaning of, 101.
— the Greek, restored by Zenodotus, 101.
Artistic, 365.
Arvum, 361.
Ârya, 365.
— as a national name, 291, 296.
— origin and gradual spreading of the word, 291.
— etymology of, 292 n, 302.
— modern use of the word, 293 n.
Ârya-âvarta, India so-called, 291, 293.
Aryan, or Indo-European family of languages, 33, 45.
— north-western and south-eastern divisions, 288.
— original clan of Central Asia, 289.
— period when this clan broke up, 289, 290.
— civilisation proved from language, 289, 356.
— a title of honour, 295.
— formation of the locative, 331.
— grammar, 354.
— and Semitic, the only families of speech deserving that title, 385.
— grammar, finished before the divergence of their branches, 385.
— or Thracian, 397.
— and Turanian languages, difference between, 401.
— instead of Japhetic, 460.
— and Semitic languages were passed through an agglutinative stage, 470.
— genealogical table, 537.
Aryans, original seat of the, 293.
— their westward path, 298.
Aryâr or Marâtha, 293 n.
Aryas, the three first castes, 291.
AS, the root, 289.
Asâmi, 180.
Ascoli, 261 n.

INDEX.

Asia Minor, origin of the Turks of, 418.
Asiatic Society, founded at Calcutta, 220.
—— earliest publications, 220 *n*.
Asoka, king, inscriptions of, 164, 165, 169, 171.
— his language, 169, 170, 173.
— two classes of his inscriptions, 171.
— alphabets of, 176.
Aspasian mountains, name of, 297.
Aspect, 368.
Assyria, various forms of the name, 300.
Astrology, causes of the extinction of, 9.
— not quite extinct, 9 *n*.
Astronomy, the Ptolemæic system, though wrong, important to science, 17.
Asvinau, the, 203 *n*.
Atharva-Veda, translated for Akbar, 205.
Athene, 206.
Athur, Nimroud, 300.
Atri, the sons of, 203 *n*.
Attila, 413, 435.
Aufrecht, Prof., 203 *n*.
Augment, the, in Greek, 534.
Augustus spoke Greek, 112.
Aujourd'hui, 54.
Auramazda, of the Cuneiform inscriptions, 275, 275 *n*. See Ormazd.
Aurengzebe, 207.
Auspicium, 369.
Australia, dialects of, 452.
Austrian dialects, 204 *n*.
Autrement, 52.
Auxentius on Ulfilas, 307, 308, 310.
Aûzvârish, 285.
Avesta, 194 *n*, 273, 280, 283.
— oldest MS. of, 281.
— Pehlevi translations of, 281.
Avicenna, 201.
Awadh, 302.
Awarian, 448.
Awe, 524.

Ayas, 356.
Ayodhyâ, 302.

BABER, foundation of his empire, 411.
Babylonia, language of, 314.
— date of the inscriptions of, 315.
Bachmeister, 158 *n*.
Bacon on Science, 8.
— on Astrology, 9.
Bactria, 294.
Bagirmi, 450.
Balance, 104.
Balbi's Atlas, 25 *n*.
Balcony, 36.
Balto-Sclavic, 267.
Balzani, Count Ugo, 218 *n*.
Bam, 240.
Bântu dialects, 389, 449, 450, 451.
Barabas tribe, 416.
Barbarians, of the Greeks and Romans, 93, 139, 140.
— possessed greater facility for acquiring languages than the Greeks and Romans, 96.
— after Alexander's time studied Greek, 98.
— unfortunate influence of the term, 140.
Barbarous, all languages but their own, called so by the Greeks, 136.
Barea, 450.
Bari, 450.
Barone, G., 238 *n*, 216 *n*.
Barthélemy, the Abbé, 212, 215, 221.
Bashkirs, race of the, 415, 415 *n*.
Basil, St., denied that God created the names of all things, 30 *n*.
Bask name for moon, 4 *n*.
— the language of Paradise, 149 *n*.
— language, 453.
Bavaria, dialects of, 246, 248.
Bayazeth defeats Sigismund, 420.
Baziane tribe, 415.
Bdellium, 194 *n*.
Be, to, the verb in Latin, Provençal, and French, 237.
—— Sanskrit, Greek, and Latin, 238.

I. N n

Be, to, in Gothic, Saxon, and English, 239.
Beal, Rev. S., 197 n.
Beames, 179.
Beaver, sagacity of the, 13.
Begemann, 353.
Behistún, inscription of, 273 n.
Beja, or Bihâri, 449, 451.
Bekos, 481 n.
Beluch, same as Mlekkha, 93 n.
Benfey, 157 n, 219 n.
Bengal, young, 110.
Bengali, 171, 180, 182.
Benloew, 374 n, 375.
Beowulf, the, 243, 252.
Berber dialects, 390, 449.
Berbicarius, 388.
Berger, 388.
Bernays, 275 n.
Berners, Juliana, 72.
Berosus, his study of Greek, 97.
— his history of Babylon, 97.
— his knowledge of the Cuneiform inscriptions, 97.
— his mention of Zoroaster, 279.
Bertrand, 211 n.
Bessell, Dr., 307 n, 308.
Bhagavadgîtâ, translated by Wilkins, 220 n.
Bhâshâ literature, 178.
Bhotiya languages, 445, 447.
Bhumija, 447.
Bible, obsolete words in the English version of 1611, 36.
— Word Books, Eastwood and Aldis Wright, 36 n.
— first complete grammar and dictionary of, 89.
— translated into Gothic, 249.
— authorised Slavonic version, 268, 268 n.
— in Ethiopic, 323.
— number of words in the authorised version, 378 n.
Bibliander, his work on language, 144 n.
— his translations of the Lord's Prayer, 144 n.
Biblical genealogies, 459.
Bidyâpati, the poet, 181.

Bihârî, or Eastern Hindî, 180.
— its subdivisions, 180, 181.
Bilderdyk, 244 n.
Biot, M., 215 n.
Bis, 49.
Bishop and sceptic have the same root, 367.
Bjarma-land, 435.
Bjarmar, the, 436.
'Black legs begin to swing,' 72 n.
Bladé, on the Pampeluna conference, 149 n.
Bleek, Dr., 449 n.
Bochart, 296 n.
Bodo, 447.
Boehtlingk, 500 n.
Boethius, Song of, 261.
Bohemian, oldest specimens of, 269.
Bokhara, language of, 287.
Bona mente, 52.
Bonaparte, Prince L., his collection of English dialects, 77.
Bongo, 450.
Book of St. Albans, 72.
Booker's Scripture and Prayer Book Glossary, 36 n.
Books, destruction of, in China in 213 B.C., 343.
Bopp, Francis, his Grammar, 220 n, 252 n.
— his great work, 230, 288.
— results of his 'Comparative Grammar,' 325, 354.
— on the locative, 333.
— Glossarium Sanscritum, 524 n.
Botany, 3.
— study of, 20.
Bow-wow theory, 494.
Brahman, the highest being, known through speech, 89, 89 n, 203 n.
Brahmans, their deification of language, 88.
— their early achievements in grammar, 89.
— difficulties of Alexander in conversing with, 95.
Brâhmaṇas, the, on language, 88.
— Sanskrit of the, 163, 165, 179.
Brahmanic Prâkrits, 166.
Brâhuis, 287, 446.

INDEX.

Braj Bhâshâ, 181.
Brazil, aboriginal dialects of, 452.
Bréal, Michel, on Père Cœurdoux's essay on Sanskrit, 222.
Brennus, 265.
Brewster, Sir D., on imagination, 19.
Brih, 89 n.
Brinkmann, 364 n.
Brinton, Dr., on American dialects, 67.
Britannic or Cymric, 265.
Brockhaus, Prof., 278.
Brogue, 55.
Broodaten, in Flemish, 132 n.
Brown, Rev. N., on Burmese dialects, 68.
Bruder, brüder, 534.
Brutes, faculties of, 485-488.
— instinct and intellect, 489, 521.
— language, the difference between man and, 489.
— can communicate, 490.
— the old name given to, 527.
Brutus, 248.
Buddhaghosha, 163.
Buddhism introduced into China, 196.
Buddhist canon, language of, 169.
— use of dialects, 174.
Budenz on Ugric languages, 431.
Buffon on the ape, 484 n.
Bugge, 252 n.
Bühler, 170 n.
Bulgarian language and literature, 268.
— ancient, 268.
— kingdom on the Danube, 430 n.
— — on the Volga, 439.
Bulgaric branch of the Finnic class, 430.
— derivation of the name, 430 n.
Bullom dialect, 450.
Bundalesh, the, 282.
Buriäts, new phase in the grammatical life of the dialects of the, 69, 411, 443.
Burmese language and literature, 68.
— dialects, 68, 447.
— Captain Gordon on, 68.

Burnell, 210 n.
Burnouf, Eugène, 231, 277 n, 278.
— his Zend studies, 233, 274.
— his studies on the Cuneiform inscriptions, 233.
Bushmen, language of the, 449, 451.
Buss, 37.

CAB, 37.
Cæsar, Julius, his work on 'De Analogia,' 116.
— invented the term ablative, 116.
— on the Celts, 264 n.
Caldwell, 190 n.
— on the Dravidian languages, 447.
Callimachus, 99.
Calmette, le Père, 213, 215.
Cambodja, language of, 448.
Camel, many words for the, 526.
Campbell, Sir G., 447.
Canada, French of, 78.
Canarese, 446.
Capito, the grammarian, 39.
Carey, 220, 220 n.
Carneades, 110.
— forbidden to lecture at Rome by Cato, 115.
Carthaginian language, allied to Hebrew, 320.
Case, 91, 117, 118.
— how used by Aristotle, 102.
— Cobbett on, 118.
Cases, formation of in the Aryan languages, 330, 336.
Cashmere, early history of, 205 n.
Cassel, P., 132 n.
Cassia, 447.
Cassius, Dionysius of Utica, his translation of Mago's work on agriculture, 97 n.
Castelvetro on verbal terminations, 46 n, 348 n.
Castor and Pollux, worship of in Italy, 106.
Castrén on Mongolian dialects, 68, 411, 443, 468.
— on the Finno-Ugric family, 430.
Casus generalis, 119.
— rectus, 118.
Cat, 506.

INDEX.

Catherine the Great, her Comparative Dictionary, 159.
Cato, 74.
— his history of Rome in Latin, 108.
— learnt Greek in his old age, 110.
— reasons for his opposition to everything Greek, 110.
— his contempt for the haruspices, 113.
Caucasian Isthmus, 'The Mountain of Languages,' 62, 94, 448.
— — Turkish tribes of the, 62, 94, 415.
Cave, 516.
Cavea, 517.
Celt, a Celtic word, 264 n.
Celtic language, substantive existence of, 44, 266.
— — a branch of the Aryan family, 264.
Celts, their former political autonomy, 265.
Ceylon, conversion of, 174, 175.
— mentioned in Asoka's inscriptions, 175.
— dialect of, 182, 387.
— inscriptions in, 184.
Chaldee, origin of name, 316.
— fragments in Ezra, 316.
— language of the Targums, 317.
— literature of Babylon and Nineveh, 317-319.
Chand, the poet, 181.
Change in language, not in the power of man to produce or prevent, 39.
Changes, historical, affecting every variety of language, 35.
— rapid, in the languages of savage tribes, 35.
— in words or meanings in English since 1611, 36.
— smaller, 36.
— grammatical, 37.
Chardin, on the languages used in Paradise, 149 n.
Charta, 104.
Chaucer makes the sun feminine, 5.
Chiaramente, 52.
Childers, 183.

Children, linguistic experiments on, 480, 481 n.
— invent a language of their own, 482 n.
Chili, language of, 403 n.
China, 36.
— introduction of Buddhism, 196.
— conquered by the Mongols, 410.
Chinese, plural in, 51, 241.
— no trace of grammar in ancient, 87, 126.
— M. Stanislas Julien on substantives and adjectives in, 126.
— the accusative in, 127.
— the ablative in, 128.
— the locative in, 128, 330, 533.
— the adjective and adverb in, 128.
— Buddhist pilgrims sent to India, 197.
— translations of Buddhist Books, 197.
— formation of the instrumental in, 330.
— number of roots in, 376.
— number of words rare, obsolete, and in use in, 376 n.
— mode of using a predicative root in, 380.
— no analysis required to discover the component parts of, 383.
— rudimentary traces of agglutination in, 392, 461, 461 n, 462.
— roots in, 394.
— the parts of speech determined by their position in a sentence, 394.
— literature, age of, 395.
— juxtaposition of words in, 462 n.
— convergence of Mongolian and Tibetan towards ancient, 475 n.
— imitative sounds in, 506 n.
— list of interjections, 510 n.
— natural selection of roots in, 531.
— has passed through various stages, 531.
— the future in, 533.
Chingis-Khan founds the Mongolian or Kapchakian empire, 407, 408.
Cho, Ossetian for sister, 54.

INDEX.

'Choking a parrot,' 72 *n.*
Christ, language of, 317.
Christendom, 51.
Christianity, humanising influence of, 140.
Chrysippos, 110, 114.
Chrysostom, his church for Gothic Christians, 251.
Chudic branch of the Finnic languages, 430.
Cicero, his provincial Latin, 75.
— speaks Greek, 112.
— quoted as an authority on grammar, 115.
— Cæsar's 'De Analogia' dedicated to, 116.
Circassian, 448.
Circumspect, 368.
Clamare, 501.
Class dialects, 71.
Classes of languages different from families, 195, 199, 328, 333, 385.
Classical or literary languages, origin of, 70.
— — stagnation and certain decay of, 75, 76.
Classification in the physical sciences, 15.
— of languages, Darwin on, 135 *n.*
— naming is, 521.
Classificatory stage, 14, 87.
Clathri, 105 *n.*
Claustra, 105 *n.*
Clergy, 51.
Clicks of the Hottentots, 449.
— in other languages, 449 *n.*
Clitomachus in Scipio's house, 111.
Cluo, 501.
Clyde, 736 *n.*
Cobbett on Case, 118.
Cocarde, 499.
Cocart, 499.
Cock, 498.
Codex Alexandrinus, 249.
— Argenteus, 250.
— Ambrosianus, 250 *n.*
— Carolinus, 250 *n.*
Cœlum, 518.
Cœlus, 107.

Cœurdoux, le Père, 212, 215.
— his comparison of Latin and Sanskrit, 221, 222.
Cognomen, 530.
Colchis, Pliny and Strabo on the dialects of, 62.
Colebrooke, 182, 199 *n*, 200 *n*, 220, 230 *n*, 231.
Collitz, 354 *n.*
Conabere, for conaberis, 75 *n.*
Condillac, 507, 512.
Confucius, works of, 396.
Congo language, adjectives in the, 120 *n.*
Conjugation in Aryan and Turanian languages, 403.
Conjunctions, added by Aristotle, 100.
Conscience, 491 *n.*
Conspicuous, 369.
Constantinople, grammar studied at, 121.
— taking of, 421.
Contemplate, 36.
Copernicus, causes which led to the discovery of his system, 18.
Coptic, 451.
— name for India, 192.
Coquelicot, 499.
Coquet, 499.
Corean, 453.
Cornish, last person who spoke, 44.
— a branch of the Celtic family, 265.
Corssen, 361 *n.*
Corvée, 363 *n.*
Corvus, 499.
Cosmopolitan Club, 112.
Cosys, 245 *n.*
Cotton, 194 *n.*
Crane, 503.
Crassus, Publius, his knowledge of Greek dialects, 111.
Crates of Pergamus, his visit to Rome, 114.
— — his views on language, 114, 117.
— — his public lectures on grammar at Rome, 115.
Crepare, 501 *n.*
Crim-Goths, 250 *n.*

550 INDEX.

Crimea, want of interpreters in the English army in the, 94.
Croatian dialect, 268.
Crow, 499, 503.
Cuckoo, 497, 498.
Cuculus, 498.
Cumæan Sybil, her oracles written in Greek, 106.
Cuneiform inscriptions, deciphered by Burnouf, 233.
—— of Darius and Xerxes, importance of the discovery of, 275, 277.
—— number of words in the, 377.
—— progress in deciphering, 315.
Curtius on labialism and dentalism, 60 n.
Cutch, the Ahirs of, 191.
— the seat of Ophir, 193 n.
Cutis, 418 n.
Cyaxares, forms interpreters, 94.
Cymric, 264, 265.
Cyrillus, 268.

D, origin of the letter in forming the past tense in English, 131, 350.
Dacian language, the ancient, 138 n, 260 n.
Daco-Romanic, 260 n.
Dalmatians, 138 n.
D'Alwis, 174 n, 183.
Damasus, St. Jerome's epistles to, 145.
Dame, 342.
Damila and Andhaka parents, 146 n.
Damne, 342 n.
Damsel, 342.
Dan, 342 n.
Danaë, 11.
Danish language, growth of, 78, 253, 254.
Dante, language of, 173.
— on dialects, 262 n.
Dara, son of Shah Jehan, 207.
D'Arbois de Jubainville, 266.
Dardanelles, 138 n.
Dardistan, dialects of, 287.
Darius, claimed for himself an Aryan descent, 295.

Darmesteter, 273 n, 278, 278 n, 280, 281 n, 284 n.
— his use of the words Zend, Pehlevi, &c., 285.
Darwin on classification of languages, 135 n, 459 n.
Dasati, Sanskrit ten, 49, 53.
Dasent, Sir G., 254 n.
Dasyu, 291.
Dative case in Chinese, 127.
—— Greek, 335.
— and locative, 336.
Daughter, 54.
Dci, Bohemian for daughter, 54.
De, 336.
De Analogia, 116.
Decay, phonetic, one of the two causes of the changes in language, 47.
—— instances of, 50-54.
Declension, most of the terminations of, demonstrative roots, 345.
Défrayer, 135 n.
Dekhan, Buddhism spread to Ceylon from the, 175.
De Lagarde, 288.
Delaware tribes, 65 n.
Delhi, column of, 172.
De Maistre, his definition of agglutination, 401.
Demetrius Phalereus, 99 n.
Democritus, his travels, 96.
Demosthenes, 137 n.
Demuth, 382 n.
Déoheit, 382 n.
Deomuot, 382 n.
Dépit, 368.
Descartes, his view of brutes, 485.
Despise, 168.
Deux, 50, 53.
Deva and deus, 221.
Devanâgarî alphabet, 164 n.
Dialect, what is meant by, 54.
Dialectic, 118.
— regeneration, 54, 469.
— growth, beyond the control of individuals, 79.
— freedom, 241.
Dialects, importance of, 23, 55.

INDEX.

Dialects, Italian, 55, 77.
— French, 55.
— Norse, 55.
— Modern Greek, 56.
— Frisian, 56.
— English, 58, 58 n, 77.
— the feeders, rather than the channels of a literary language, 59, 77.
— two kinds of, 59.
— of Märchen, 59 n.
— difficulty in tracing the history of, 61.
— in Colchis, 62.
Mr. W. W. Gill, on Polynesian, 63.
— American, 64-67.
— Burmese, 68.
— of the Ostiakes, 68.
— of Southern Africa, 69.
— wealth of, 69.
— Lithuanian, 69 n.
— class dialects, 71.
— unbounded resources of, 71.
— popular, come to the front in revolutions, 76.
— of India, 170, 171, 179.
— exist before the literary language, 248.
— how they arise, 467.
Dictionary, Oxford, 85 n.
— Comparative, of Catherine the Great, 158, 160 n.
Chinese, 40,000 to 50,000 words in the, 376.
— 300 words in a village labourer's, 377.
— 379 words in the Cuneiform inscriptions, 377.
— 658 words in the Egyptian hieroglyphics, 377.
— many not yet examined, 384.
Dictionaries, 84 n.
— number of words in various, 378 n.
Did, origin of, as a preterite, 352.
Didymus, Cæsar's secretary, 116.
Diez, Professor, his 'Comparative Grammar of the Six Romanic Dialects,' 134 n, 161, 342 n.

Dig, plural in Bengali, 51, 51 n.
Dilettante, 15.
Din, faith, 82.
Dinka, 450.
Dinkart, the, 280, 282.
Diodorus Siculus, on Saba in Arabia, 193 n.
Diogenes Laertius, 279.
Dionysius Thrax, author of the first practical Greek Grammar, 103, 117, 121, 123.
— of Halicarnassus on the Pelasgi and Lokrians, 137 n.
Dioskurias, mentioned by Strabo, 62 n.
Discussion, 49.
Divans, the Arabic, 321.
Dix, 50, 53.
Dnândev, the poet, 181.
Do, to, 351.
Dom, 382.
Donatus, the grammarian, 121.
Donner, 398 n, 432, 434, 435 n.
Dorpat dialect, 438.
D'Orsay, 377 n.
Dorset dialect, 58 n, 346.
Douse, 250 n, 353 n.
Douze, 53.
Dowal, to dovetail, 54.
Dragoman, 316 n.
Drave, obsolete, 37.
Dravidian races, 446.
— languages, adjectives in, 120.
— Sinhalese not one of the, 182.
Dual, the, first recognised by Zenodotus, 102.
Duhitar, daughter, in Sanskrit, 54.
Dumaresq, Rev. D., 'Comparative Vocabulary of Eastern Languages,' 158.
Dümichen, Professor, on kafu = kapi, 190.
Duncker, 279 n.
Duperron, Anquetil, his translation of Dârâ's Persian edition of the Upanishads, 207.
— correspondence with le Père Cœurdoux, 213.
Du Ponceau, 129 n, 336 n.

INDEX.

Duret, Claude, his work on language, 144 n.
Dutch, proved by Goropius to be the language of Paradise, 149.
— age of, 245,
— is Low German, 45, 246, 247.
Dvi, 48, 49, 53.
Dvořák, on the foreign words in the Koran, 82 n.

EAR, to, 360.
Early English, 131, 131 n.
Earth, guess of Philolaos as to its motion round the sun, 19.
Earth, 361, 522.
East Teutonic, 258, 259.
Eastern Hindi, 171, 180, 182.
Echis, 523.
Edda, name for moon in the, 4 n.
— the name, 256, 257.
Eddas, the two, 254.
Edgren, on Sanskrit roots, 374 n.
Edkins, on the relationship of Chinese, Tibetan, and Mongolian, 475 n.
Efik, 450.
Egypt, number of words in the ancient vocabulary of, 377.
Egyptian language, treated by Lord Monboddo as the origin of Sanskrit, 226.
— — family to which it belongs, 389, 395, 448, 451.
Eidos, 370.
Eimi and asmi, 157.
Ekhili language, 323.
Elam of Genesis, 294 n.
Elder, 131, 342.
Elements, component, of language, 358.
Elimination, process of, 526.
Elliot, Sir H., 191 n, 199 n, 200 n, 202 n, 203 n, 204 n, 212 n.
Ellis, 211 n.
Elu, spoken in Ceylon, 175, 183.
— brought to Ceylon from Magadha, 183.
— books, 183.
— inscriptions, 184.
Empirical stage, 3, 87, 88, 90.

En, 242 n.
Endlicher on Chinese, 394 n.
Engines, 105 n.
England, language of, 44.
English, changes in, since the translation of the Bible in 1611, 36.
— pronunciations in Pope and Johnson's times, 37 n.
— history of, 44.
— a Teutonic language, 45.
— is Low German, 45.
— grammar purely Teutonic, 46.
— richness of the dialects of, 59.
— real sources of, 77.
— dialects, Prince L. Bonaparte's collection of, 77.
— of the United States, 78 n.
— full of words derived from the most distant sources, 83.
— proportion of Saxon to Norman words in, 83.
— tests proving the Teutonic origin of, 86.
— grammar, 86.
— genitives, 119, 125.
— nominatives and accusatives, 125, 129.
— early, 131.
— middle, 131.
— origin of grammatical forms in, 130.
— number of words used by a labourer, 377.
— number of words in, 378 n, 379.
— number of words used by a well-educated man, 378.
— Dictionary, New Oxford, 378.
— number of words in Milton, Shakespeare, and the Old Testament, 379.
Englishman in China, 497.
Ennius, 74, 109, 115.
— his translations from Greek into Latin, 109.
Entrails, 517.
Eorthe, 361.
Eos, 11.
Ephphatha, 317.
Epices, 372.
Epicharmus, Latin translation of

his philosophy by Ennius, 109, 109 n.
Epicier, 371.
Epicurus, doctrines of, embraced in Rome, 112.
Epier, 370.
Epirotes, 138 n.
Episkopos, 367.
Epistola, 104 n.
Equip, 362.
Équiper, 362.
Era, 361.
Eratosthenes, 294 n.
Erin, Pictet's derivation of, 298 n.
— Mr. Whitley Stokes on, 299 n.
Ero, 361.
Errand, 363.
Erro, 149 n.
Erse, 265.
Erste, der, 242.
Ertoghrul, son of Soliman-Shah, 419.
Eskimo language, 452.
Espèce, 371.
Espiègle, 369.
Esquif, 362.
Estienne, Henri, his grammatical labours anticipated by the Brahmans 500 B.C., 89.
— his work on language, 144 n.
Ests, or Estonians, language of the, 430, 431, 438.
— — dialects of, 438.
— — poetry of the, 438.
Ethiopic or Abyssinian, 449, 451.
Ethnology, distinct from the science of language, 43, 458.
Etruscan, 453.
Eudemos on the Aryan race, 295.
Eudoxus, 279.
Euhemerus of Messene, his work translated into Latin by Ennius, 109.
Eulalia, song of, age of the, 261.
Eulenspiegel, 370.
Eul-shi, Chinese, two-ten, 48, 49, 53.
Eunomius, 30 n.
Euripides first translated into Latin by Ennius, 109.

Eusebius, Armenian translation of, 279.
Ewald, on the relation of the Turanian to the Aryan languages, 470.
Ewe language, 450.
Expect, 369.
Eziongeber, or Akaba, 187.
Ezour-veda, 211 n.
Ezra, Chaldee fragments in the Book of, 316.

FABIUS PICTOR, his history of Rome in Greek, 107.
Faculties of man and brutes, 483.
Fahian, the Chinese pilgrim to India, 197.
Faizi, superintended the translations made for Akbar, 205 n.
Falasha, 451.
Families of languages, tests for reducing the principal dialects of Europe and Asia to certain, 236.
— — how many are there, 243.
Fan, or Fan-lan-mo, Chinese rendering of the Sanskrit Brahman, 196, 197 n.
Farah, 365 n.
Farrar, 328 n, 481 n, 497 n.
Fatum, 11.
Faucher le grand pré, 364.
Fee, 360.
Feeble, 134.
Feizi and the Brahman, 206.
Ferguson, Dr., on language, 493.
Fernando Po, 450.
Feu, 133, 242.
Feuer, 134.
Fiend, 510.
Filth, 510.
Finnic, or Finno-Ugric languages, 398, 428, 435, 472.
— likeness to Turkish, 389.
— tribes, original seat of the, 428.
— branches of, 430–432.
— spread of, 434.
— language and literature, 436–444.

Finnic, the Kalewala, the Iliad of the Finns, 437.
— national feeling lately arisen, 437.
— philology, 439.
— likeness to Hungarian, 439.
Finnish grammar, 128.
Firdusi, language in which he wrote his 'Shahnameh,' 286.
Fire-worshippers. *See* Parsis.
Firoz-Shah, translations made by his order from Sanskrit into Persian, 203.
First, 242.
Fixed stars, 7.
Flaccus, M. Verrius, the grammarian, 121.
Flamininus, his knowledge of Greek, 107.
Flemish language and literature, 245–247, 352.
Flourens, on souls, animal and human, 485, 521 *n*.
Flügel, Professor, 200 *n*.
Flügel's Dictionary, words in, 378 *n*.
Fo, Chinese name for Buddha, 196.
Foerstemann, 249 *n*.
Force, 37.
Forculus, 106 *n*.
Form, 370.
Formal elements, 327, 328.
Forster, 220, 220 *n*.
Foul, 510.
Fra Paolino da S. Bartolommeo, 157.
Frais, 135.
Franck, 246 *n*.
Franconia, dialects of, are High German, 246, 247 *n*, 248.
Francus, 248.
Frankish, Old, 245.
Frater, 248, 387.
Fray, 387.
Frayle, 387.
Frederic II, his experiments on the origin of language, 481.
Fredum, friede, frais, and défrayer, 135 *n*.
Freising, Codex of, 269.
French, dialects, number of, 55.

French, of Canada, 78.
— nominatives and accusatives, 129.
— in some points more primitive than Provençal, 237.
— a Romanic language, 260.
— Northern, 261.
— origin of grammatical terminations in, 347.
— origin of the future in -rai, 347.
Frère, 387.
Fretela, 251.
Friend, 510.
Frisian is Low German, 45.
— multitude of dialects, 56, 242, 245 *n*.
— Klaus Groth on, 57.
— language and literature, 245, 247.
Friska Findling, Nissen's, 245 *n*.
Fromage, 134.
Fuchs, 348 *n*.
Fula, 450.
Fuoco, 133, 242.
Furicha, 365 *n*.
Fürst, 241.
Further India, languages of, 448.
Future, the, in French, 347.
— in Latin, 348.
— in Spanish, 348.
— in Greek, 349, 349 *n*.
— in Old Norse, 349 *n*.
— in Romanic languages, 389.
— in Chinese, 533.
Fygar, astronomical tables of, 200.

G in Sanskrit, represented in Greek by β, 293.
Gaedhelic, 264 *n*.
Gaelic, 264 *n*, 265.
Gaina Mâgadhi, 168, 178, 179.
— Canon, language of the, 169.
Galatia, foundation and language of, 266.
Galatæ, 266 *n*.
Galla language of Africa, 449, 451.
Gallée, J. H., 245 *n*.
Galli, 266 *n*.
Gallic, 265.
Gallus, Alexander, quoted against the Emperor Sigismund, 40.

INDEX.   555

Ganas, lists of remarkable Sanskrit words, 124.
Gandhâra, 195.
Gangâ, Ganges, 519.
Gangetic class of languages, 445, 447.
Gardariki, 253.
Garhwâli, 180.
Garo, 447.
— formation of adjectives in, 120 n.
Gâthâ dialect, 170, 171.
Gâthâs, or songs of Zoroaster, 278, 279.
Gauch, 498.
Gaudian languages, 167 n, 179, 182.
Gaugengigl, 378 n.
Gaur, an infidel, 82, 140.
Gaus, Sanskrit, may be βοῦς, 293.
Geac, 498.
Gebelin, Court de, his 'Monde primitif,' 155.
— — compared with Hervas, 155.
Goez language, 323.
Geiger, 287 n.
Geist, 522
Geldner, 278, 278 n.
Gemara, 317 n.
Gonder, 91, 117.
Genealogy, best form of classification, 136, 240.
Genealogical classification, 239, 240, 370, 385.
— — not possible for all languages, 241.
Genera and species, 514.
General ideas, 511, 521, 526.
Generi coloniali, 371 n.
Generis neutrius, 40 n.
Generos, 371 n.
Genike, 119, 119 n.
Genitive case, the term used in India, 119.
— terminations of the, generally identical with the suffixes which change substantives into adjectives, 120.
— how formed in Chinese, 126.
— — in Latin, 332-334.

Genitive, when supplied by the locative, 333.
— in Oscan, &c., 334.
— formation of, in Sanskrit and Greek, 120 n.
— — in Latin, English, and Greek, 125.
Genos, 370.
Gentile, 140.
Geographical arrangement of languages, 162.
Geometry, 3.
Georgian, 448.
Geranos, 503.
German, history of, 246.
— High and Low, Middle and Upper, 244 n, 246 n.
— number of dialects in Old, 249, 252.
— number of roots in Modern, 376.
Germanus, 388.
Getae, 138 n.
Geyser, 522.
Gezelle, M., 352.
Ghost, 522.
Giles, Herbert, 197 n.
Gill, Rev. W. W., on Polynesian dialects, 63, 64.
Gill, 37.
Ginsburg, Dr., 148 n.
Gipsy language, 288, 293.
Glass, painted, before and since the Reformation, 10.
Glossology, a name for the science of language, 1.
Glottic, 28 n.
Glück, 264 n.
Godarana, 365 n.
Go-go, the, 519, 519 n.
Goidelic, 264, 265.
Goldschmidt, 183, 184.
Gonds, 446.
Goold, 36.
Gordon, Captain, on Burmese dialects, 68.
Goropius, proved Dutch to be the language of Paradise, 149.
Gospel, 132, 277.
Gothic, a modern language, 133.
— similarity with Latin, 139.

INDEX.

Gothic, when extinct, 250.
— class of languages to which it belongs, 251, 258, 259.
— the eldest sister only of the Teutonic branch, 253.
— number of roots in, 376 n.
— number of words in, 378 n.
Goths, the, and Bishop Ulfilas, 249, 297.
Gracchus, T., spoke Greek, 107.
Grammar, the criterion of relationship in almost all languages, 45, 85.
— English, unmistakably Teutonic, 45.
— the most essential element in language, 81.
— no trace of, in ancient Chinese, 87, 126.
— early achievements of the Brahmans in, 89.
— and the Greeks, 91.
— terms of, borrowed from philosophy, 91, 100.
— Greek, why studied at Rome, 113.
— Latin, Cæsar's work on, 116.
— Hindu, science of, 124.
— Sanskrit, origin and history of, 124.
— the facts of, 125.
— in Chinese, 126.
— in Finnish, 128.
— historical evidence, 130.
— collateral relationship, 133.
— genealogical classification, 135.
— original Sanskrit, 220.
— Bopp's 'Comparative Grammar,' 232, 232 n, 254, 325.
— comparative, value of, in the classification of languages, 236, 326, 354.
— Aryan, 255.
— Turkish, 421.
Grammarian, the first, 89 n.
Grammarians, the early, 92.
Grammatical changes since 1611, 37.
— or formal elements in language, 50.

Grammatical forms produced by phonetic decay, 50.
— forms, origin of, 129, 330.
— framework of the Aryan languages, can be traced back to independent words, 350, 354.
Grammatici at Rome, 107.
Grantha and grandonica, 219 n.
— MSS., 219 n.
Grassmann, 106 n.
Greek dialects, modern, Tzaconic, &c., 56.
— classical, local dialects, 60, 136, 136 n.
— enquiries into language, 91.
— travellers, 96.
— language, studied by the barbarians, Berosus, Menander, Manetho, 97, 98.
— translations of the Old Testament and Zend-Avesta, 98, 99.
— critical study of, at Alexandria, 99, 102.
— article, 101.
— grammar, first practical, 103.
— taught at Rome, 103.
— generally spoken at Rome, 104, 107.
— gods identified with Italian, 106.
— laws, manners and language, influence of, at Rome, 107.
— plays in Rome, 108.
— rhetors expelled from Rome, 112.
— grammar taken up at Rome, 113, 117.
— adjectives and genitives, 121, 125, 334.
— grammar, spread of, 122.
— use of the term Barbarian, 136.
— Plato's notion of the origin of, 137.
— French derived from, 144 n.
— and Hebrew, Guichard on, 148 n.
— and Sanskrit, similarity between, 157.
— accounts of India, 193.
— Latin and Sanskrit, affinity between, 227, 228, 237.
— dative in, 335.
— s between two vowels, 345.
— future, 349, 349 n.

Greek verb, number of forms in, if conjugated through all its voices, tenses, &c., 378 n.
— and Sanskrit, coincidences between accounted for the augment, 534.
Greeks, their speculations on language, 90.
— ancient, never thought of learning a foreign language, 93.
— first encouraged interpreters for the sake of trade, 95.
— philosophers, imaginary travels of, 96 n.
— and Barbarians, 98, 136, 140.
— — no intellectual intercourse between, before Alexander the Great, 98.
— never applied the principle of classification to speech, 136.
Greenlanders, language of, 452.
Groet for great, 37 n.
Gregory of Nyssa, his defence of St. Basil, 30 n.
Grey, Asa, on the descent of man from one pair, 474 n.
— on the intellect of brutes, 489 n.
Grierson, 179, 180 n.
Grimm on the origin of dialects, 59.
— on the idiom of nomads, 72.
— on etymologies, 132 n.
— his 'Teutonic Grammar,' 233, 245 n.
— his division of the Teutonic class, 258.
— his Deutsche Sprache, 365 n.
Grimm's Law, 345.
Grisons, language of the, 260.
Groma, 105 n.
Groth, Klaus, on Frisian dialects, 57.
Growth of language, 39, 73.
— — independent of man, 40.
Gubernare, 105 n, 362.
Gubernatis, A. De, 209 n, 218.
Guebres, 274.
Guhrauer, 150 n.
Guichard, Estienne, his work on language, 144, 144 n, 147, 148 n, 157 n.
Gujarati, 171, 180, 182.

Güldenstädt's Travels in the Caucasus, 158 n.
Gundert, Dr., 190 n, 428 n.
Gurmug language, 447.
Gutta-percha, 188 n.
Gyarmathi, on Hungarian, 439.

H, initial in Armenian, 54.
Habbim, 190.
Hahn, Dr., 449 n.
Hakon VI, conquers Iceland, 255.
Hâla, poetry of, 178.
Hale, H., on the Hurons, 65 n.
Halhed, on the affinity between Greek and Sanskrit, 223.
— his Code of Gentoo Laws, 223 n.
Hamilton, Alexander, taught Schlegel the rudiments of Sanskrit, 229.
— Sir W., on the general and particular in language, 519 n.
Hammer, von, 526.
Handbook, 37.
Hanxleden, J., 216, 217, 218, 218 n.
Harald Haarfagr, King of Norway, 255.
Haröyu, 301, 301 n.
Harran, inscription of, 322.
Harrari language, 323.
Harun-al-Raschid, translations made at his court from Sanskrit, 200.
— Indian physicians at the court of, 200.
Haruspex, Cato's contempt for the, 113.
— origin of name, 369.
Haug, his labours in Zend, 273 n, 278, 282.
— on a Pehlevi inscription at Nineveh, 281 n.
Haupt, 293.
Haussa language, 451.
Have, to, paradigms almost identical in Latin and Gothic, 139.
Hayr, father in Armenian, 54.
Hebraic, 314, 320.
Hebrew, first Grammar and Dictionary of the Bible, 89 n.
— roots first explained, 89 n.
— Bible, translated into Greek, 99 n.

Hebrew, according to the Fathers, the primitive language of mankind, 145.
— amount of learning wasted on this question, 147.
— letters, numerical value, 148 n.
— Leibniz, the first to deny Hebrew being the primitive language, 149.
— modernised, 318–321.
— ancient form of, 320.
— Aramean modifications of, 321.
— swept away by Arabic, 321.
— number of roots in, 376.
— change of vowels in, 534.
Heimskringla, the, 256.
He is, 386.
Hekatæos, 194, 195, 264.
Hekate, old name of the moon, 11.
Hekatebolos, 11.
Hélas, 511 n.
Heljand, the, of the Low Germans, 246.
Hellanicus, 294.
Hellenic branch of languages, 263.
Helvetius, on man's faculties, 13 n.
Hemakandra, 167, 168, 170 n, 178.
Hennequin, 149 n.
Hephaestos, 106.
Hephthalitae, 414.
Hera, 106.
Herakles, 105.
Herat, 301, 302.
Hercere, 105.
Hercules, 105.
Herculus, 106 n.
Herder, on the origin of language, 478, 495, 495 n.
Hereclus, 105.
Herero, 450.
Heretic, 139.
Hermano, 242, 387.
Hermippus, his Greek translation of Zoroaster's works, 99, 279, 280.
Herodianus, the grammarian, 121.
Herodotus, mentions Greek merchants on the Volga, 95.
— his travels, 96.
— on the Pelasgi, 137 n.
— mention of Indian names, 195.

Herodotus, Celts in the time of, 265.
Hervas, reduces American dialects to eleven families, 66.
— his works on the Science of Language, 143 n.
— accounts of his life and works, 154, 215 n, 216 n.
— compared with Gebelin, 155.
— his views on Bask, 156.
— — on the Malay and Polynesian family, 156.
— his view of Greek and Sanskrit, 157.
— his account of Abu-l-Fazl, 205 n.
— his opinion of Hebrew, 324.
Hessian dialects, 246 n, 248.
Heyne, Moritz, 245 n.
Heyse, on the origin of language, 501 n, 528, 532.
Hickes, on the proportion of Saxon to Norman words in English, 84.
Hieroglyphic words, number of, 377.
— groups, 2030, 378 n.
Higginson, 140 n.
High German, 244, 244 n, 246, 248, 258, 259.
— — New, Middle, and Old, 247, 248, 259.
— — cannot be derived from Gothic, 252.
Himyaritic inscriptions, 193 n, 322.
Hindi, 171, 180, 181, 205 n.
— High, or Urdu, 181.
Hind-sind, 200.
Hindu. Hapta Hindu, 194.
Hindustani, real origin of, 77.
— genitive and adjective in, 120 n.
— Urdu-zabân, the proper name of, 429.
Hiouen-thsang, the Chinese pilgrim, his travels in India, 198.
— wrote a book in Sanskrit, 202.
Hiram, fleet of, 187.
History and growth, difference between, 42.
— and language, connection between, 42.
Historical science, 22.

Hitopadesa, translated by Wilkins, 220 n.
Hiung-nu, 412.
Hlaford, 132, 277.
Hliod or Quida, of Norway, 256.
— Saemund's collection of, 256.
Hodgson, 468.
Hoei-seng, the Chinese pilgrim to India, 197.
Hoha, 365 n.
Holden, 37.
Holpen, 37.
Holtzmann, 256.
Homer, critical study of, at Alexandria, 91, 100, 102.
— influence of the study of, on grammatical terminology, 101, 102, 124.
— did he use the article, 101.
— on the Karians and Lokrians, 137 n.
Hommel, 292 n.
Homo, 524.
Honey, many names for, 526 n.
Hood, 382, 382 n.
Horace, on the changes of Latin in his time, 74.
Hörnle, Dr., 167, 167 n, 171, 179, 183.
— on Indian poets, 181, 182 n.
Hors, 134.
Horse, many names for, among the Mandshu Tatars, 526 n.
Hortensius, 74.
Hos tribe, 447.
Hottentot language, 449, 451.
House, same name for, in Sanskrit and other Aryan languages, 357.
Hruofan, 501 n.
Hübschmann, his Armenian studies, 288.
Huet, Gédéon, 245 n.
Human knowledge, physical or historical, 22.
Humanity, a word not found in Plato or Aristotle, 140.
Humboldt, A. von, on the limits of exact knowledge, 19.
Humboldt, W. von, his patronage of Comparative Philology, 232, 294.
Humilis, 524.
Humus, 524.
Hunfalvy on Ugric languages, 392 n, 431, 471 n.
Hungarian, its affinity with the Finno-Ugric dialects, 398, 430, 439.
— language, 430.
— its affinity with Turkish, 439.
Hungarians, ancestors of the, 435.
Hungary, Mongols in, 410.
Hunyad, long opposed the Turks, 421.
Huron Indians, rapid changes in their dialects, 65.
Huzvârish, 285.
— its proper meaning, 285.
Hyádes or Pluviæ, 7.
Hymns of the Veda, 163, 179.

IBN EZRA, 89.
Ibn-Wahshiyyah, his Arabic translation of the Nabatean Agriculture, 319.
— account of him and his works, 319 n.
Ibo, 450.
Ic, names in, 34 n.
Iceland, language of, 78, 253, 256.
— first known, 254.
— foundation of aristocratic republic in, 255.
— intellectual and literary activity in, 255, 256.
— later history of, 255.
Icelandic Skalds, 253, 256.
Iconium, Turkish Sultans of, 419.
Idâ, 292 n, 361.
Ignis, 242.
Iguvium, tables of, 262.
Ilâhi religion of Akbar, 204.
'Il est,' 386.
Illumination of MSS. a lost art, 10.
Illyria, Roman conquest of, 260 n.
Illyrian language, the ancient, 138 n, 260 n.
— languages, 268, 269.

INDEX.

Illyrians, Greek and Roman writers on the, 138 n, 271.
Imagination, value of, 19.
Imperfect, new forms of the, 37.
Imperial Dictionary, 160, 160 n.
Importitor, 365 n.
Incorporating class of languages, 455.
India, Jewish accounts of, 186–192.
— Greek accounts of, 192–195.
— known to the Persians, 194–198, 199.
— Chinese accounts of, 196-198.
— Arab accounts of, 199–203.
— the Mulla Abdu-l-Kádir Maluk's history of, 205 n.
— origin of the name, 344.
Indian philosophers, difficulty of admitting their influence on Greek philosophy, 95 n.
— Gymnosophists and Lycurgus, 96.
Indians at the Court of Harun al Raschid, 200, 200 n.
Indicative and subjunctive in Greek and Sanskrit, 222.
Indies, East and West, historical meanings of the names, 243.
Indo-European family. *See* Aryan.
Indus, mentioned by Hekataeos, 195.
— meaning of, 519.
Inflectional stage of language, 47, 51, 392, 453, 461.
Inflections and terminations, 327–330.
Inspector, 368.
Instinct, always remains the same, 33.
— exists in man and brutes, 488.
Instincts, lost by man as he ceases to use them, 529.
Instrumental, formation of the, in Chinese, 252.
Interjectional theory of roots, 128, 507.
Internum, 517.
Interpreters, first encouraged for trade, 95.
Irâ, 361, 361 n.
Irân, modern name of Persia, 296.

Iranian logograms in Pehlevi, 284.
Iranic class, 273, 286.
Ire, 361.
Ireland, 298.
Irionn, 361.
Irish language, 264 n, 265.
Iron, name for the Os of the Caucasus, 296.
Iroquois language, 65 n.
Isilimela, Zulu name for the Pleiades, 6 n.
Island, many Icelandic names for, 388.
Isle of Man, dialect, 265.
Isokrates, 137 n.
Isolating languages, 47, 51, 391.
It, used in the Bible, 38 n.
Italian dialects, number of, 55.
— — natural growth of, 74.
— real sources of, 77, 260.
— northern dialects, 261 n.
— dialects are Neo-Latin, adopted by Teutons, 263.
— origin of grammatical terminations in, 347.
Italians, indebted to the Greeks for civilisation, 105.
— had their own religion, 105.
Italic class, 260, 263.
Italy, its debt to Greece, 104.
— dialects spoken in, before the rise of Rome, 262.
Its, as a possessive pronoun, 38.
Itsing, travels of, 198.
Ivernia, 299 n.
Ivory, 190.

JACOBI, Professor, 167 n, 168 n.
James IV of Scotland, his experiments on the origin of language, 481.
Japanese, 453.
Japhetic languages, 460.
Jargon, 55.
Jean Paul, 377 n.
Jerome, St., on Hebrew as the primitive language, 145.
— his correspondence with Sunnia and Fretela, 251.

Jesuits, their work for Leibniz, 150.
— their printing offices in India, 210 n.
— their letters to France, 212.
— their knowledge of Sanskrit, 213.
Jewish accounts of India, 186.
Jews, literary idiom of the, in the first centuries B.C. and A.D., 316, 317.
— — and from the fourth to the tenth centuries, 317.
— adopted Arabic, 318.
— returned to a modernised Hebrew, 318.
Job, mention of Ophir in the book of, 192.
Joinville, 134 n.
Joktan, sons of, 193 n.
Jonathan, Targum of, 317.
Jones, Sir William, his translation of the Sakuntalâ, 220 n.
— on the affinity between Sanskrit, Persian, and Greek, 223, 224.
— his doubts as to the Zend-Avesta, 275.
Jonson, Ben, does not recognise *its* as a possessive pronoun, 38.
Jour, 54 n.
Julien, Stanislas, notes on Chinese, 126, 127, 196, 380 n.
— — his translations from Chinese, 197 n, 198.
Jumentum, 361.
Juno, 106.
Jupiter Virgarius or Viminius, 6 n.
— same as Zeus, 106.
— soul of the universe, 113.
Justamond, translation of Bernal's East and West Indies, 206 n.
Justinian, the Emperor, his embassy to the Turks, 413.
Jutes, Saxons, and Angles, 244.

KABI KANKAN, the poet, 182.
Kabir, the poet, 182.
Kabyl, 449.
Kadambarî, 208 n.
Kafir, 140, 449, 450.
Kalew, the son of, 438.

'Kalewala,' the Iliad of the Finns, 437.
'Kalewipoeg,' the Esthonian epic, 438.
Kôlidâsa, 165, 169.
Kalilah and Dimnah, 198.
Kalmüks, 407, 411.
Kamassinian dialect, 406.
Kânakya, his Sanskrit work on poisons translated into Persian, 200, 203 n.
Kanishka, 177.
Kankah, astrologer to Harun-al-Raschid, 200 n.
Kanuri, 450.
Kapchakian empire, 408.
KAR, 502.
Karaka, translated from Sanskrit into Persian, 203 n.
Kara-Kalpak tribes near Lake Aral, 416.
Kûrava, 499, 500, 502.
Kardagia, 200 n.
Karelian dialect of Finnic, 431, 436.
Karians, Greek authors on the, 137 n.
Karolingian psalms, 246.
Kâru, 502.
Kasan, 409.
Kashubian dialect, 270.
Kasikumükian, 448.
Katyâyana, 178, 182.
— on Mâgadhî, as the root of all languages, 146.
Katze, 506.
Kaukones, the, 137 n.
Kawi language, 232.
Kechua of Guatemala, 449 n.
Keltos, 264 n.
Kemble, 243.
Kempe, André, on the languages spoken in Paradise, 149 n.
Kepler, 19, 141 n.
Kerman, 274.
Kern, Dr., 278 n, 292 n.
Khamti, 447.
Khasi, or Kassia, 448.
Khi-nie, the Chinese pilgrim in India, 198.

INDEX.

Khosru Nushirvan, his translations from Sanskrit, 198.
Kind, 370.
Kings, Jewish books of, 186, 192 n.
Kirâta language, 146 n.
Kircher, A., 208 n, 212.
Kirchhoff, 262.
Kirgis tribe, the, 417.
— Hordes, the three, 418.
— Kasak, tribe of the, 418.
Kitab al Baitarat, 203.
Klaproth, 409.
Klu and Kru, 501.
Klyo, hearing, 501.
Know, to, 520.
Knowledge, human, two divisions of, 22.
Kohl, on Frisian dialects, 56.
Koilos, 518.
Koka, 365 n.
Kokila, 498.
Kokkyx, 498.
Kolarian language, 447.
Kols, 447.
Konjâra, 450.
Koph, 189.
Kopitar, 269.
Koran, Persian expressions in, 82.
Korone, 499.
Kremer, A. von., 193 n.
Kreuzwald, Dr., his restoration of the 'Kalewipoeg,' 438.
Krim, 409.
Kronos, 106.
Kru, 450.
Krukjan, 501.
Ktesias, 195.
Kuenen, 99 n.
Kuhn, 174, 183, 365 n, 448 n.
— on genitives and datives, 334 n.
Ku-fa-lan, a learned Buddhist, 197.
Kukkuta, 498.
Kumaoni, 180.
Kumüks in the Caucasus, 415.
Kurds, language of the, 287.
Kurland, 267.
Kurrut Al Mulk, 203.
Kushitic languages, 451.
Kuthami, his work on Nabatean Agriculture, 319.

Kuthami, period when he lived, 319 n.

L, wanting in the Cuneiform inscriptions, 294 n.
Laban, language of, 316.
Lahor, 363 n.
Lachmann, 293.
Ladin, dialect of the Oberland, 261 n.
Lady with 1258 descendants, 70 n.
Lady, 132.
Lakshmidhara, 167 n.
Laloc, 36.
Lamentum, 501.
Language, the barrier between man and beast, 12, 480, 489, 511.
— first examined in the last fifty years, 27.
— growth of, in contradistinction to the history of, 28, 43, 80.
— considered as an invention of man, 29.
— the beginning of, 31.
— has a history, 32.
— changes in, 34, 35.
— almost stationary in civilised nations, 35.
— changes rapidly among savages, 35.
— cannot be changed or improved by man, 42, 79, 80, 328.
— connection between history and, 42.
— independent of historical events, 43.
— of England, 44.
— of the English, 44.
— causes of the growth of, 46.
— processes of the growth of—
  (1) phonetic decay, 47.
  (2) dialectic regeneration, 54.
— written, an accident, 54.
— existed in the form of dialects from its very beginning, 62.
— history of, 79.
— no possibility of a mixed, 81, 86.
— grammar the most essential element in, 81.
— speculations of the Brahmans and Greeks on, 88, 89, 90.

INDEX. 563

Language, study of, at Alexandria, 100.
— empirical or formal grammar of, 125.
— Leibniz on, 149 et seq.
— Hervas, 154.
— Adelung, 158.
— Catherine the Great, 158.
— glance at the modern history of, 236.
— constituent elements of, 324.
— distinction between the radical and formal elements of, 324, 327.
— nothing merely formal in, 346.
— what it is made of, 384.
— radical stage of, 393.
— terminational stage of, 396.
— difference between an inflectional and agglutinative, 454.
— agglutinative stage of, 455.
— the origin of, 478 et seq.
— the outward sign of an inward power, 492.
— universal ideas, 492.
— general ideas and roots, 492.
— none formed on imitation alone, 497.
— the primum cognitum and primum appellatum, 512, 516, 519.
— knowing and naming, 520.
— and reason, 522.
— words express general ideas, 522, 526.
— natural elimination, 526.
— word and thought, 527.
— natural selection of roots, 532.
— nothing arbitrary in, 534.
— origin of and confusion of tongues, 535.
Language, Science of, modern date of the, 1.
— — names for the, 1.
— — meaning of the, 2.
— — practical character of the, 10.
— — of importance in political and social questions, 12, 27, 81.
— — one of the physical sciences, 21, 29, 80.

Language, Science of, realm of the, 25.
— — Dr. Whewell on the classification of the, 28 n.
— — as an historical science, 32.
— — independent of history, 44.
— — India and Greece only countries where we can see the origin of the, 88.
— — Empirical stage in the, 88, 90.
— — classificatory stage, 123.
— — Hervas' catalogue of works on the, 143 n.
— — importance of the discovery of Sanskrit to the, 162, 234, 313.
— — value of comparative grammar in the, 236.
— — languages on which it is founded, 445.
— — list of works on the, 446.
— — historical element in the, 530.
Languages, number of known, 25, 25 n.
— literary, are artificial, 55, 75.
— classification of, 80, 81, 136.
— are all in one sense mixed, 81.
— teaching of foreign, a modern invention, 93.
— reason why the Greeks never learnt foreign, 93.
— 'The Mountain of,' 94.
— historical study of, 130.
— genealogical classification of, 135 n, 235, 239.
— in Europe and Asia, tests for reducing to certain families, 239 et seq.
— genealogical classification not applicable to all, 241.
— radical relationship of, 242.
— morphological classification of, 370, 385, 390.
— families and classes of, 385.
— modern, built up from the ruins of ancient, 386.
— distant relationship among, 387.
— all, reducible in the end to roots, 390, 492, 512.
— polysynthetic, 444.

INDEX.

Languages, problem of the common origin of, 455, 472, 473.
— are either radical, terminational, or inflectional, 457.
— once settled, do not change their grammatical constitution, 462, 463.
— political or state, 467.
— may become dissimilar in grammar, yet be cognate, 469.
Langue Romane, 236.
Laokoon, 524.
Laos, 447.
Laotse, 396.
Laps, or Laplanders, 430, 431, 434.
— their habitat, 434.
Larme, 54.
Lassen, 190 n, 194 n, 196, 231.
— on Pehlevi, 284 n.
Latin, classical, one of the many dialects of Latium, 60, 74.
— and Neo-Latin, 74.
— changes in, according to Polybius, 74.
— the old Salian poems, 74.
— provincialisms of Cicero, 75.
— stagnation of, on becoming the language of civilisation, 75.
— translation of Mago's work on Agriculture, 105 n.
— nautical terms, 105 n.
— Ælius Stilo's lectures on, 115, 115 n.
— grammar, Cæsar's work on, 116.
— genitives, 125, 334.
— and Gothic, similarity between, 139.
— and Sanskrit, similarity between, 221, 228.
— and the Langue Romane, 236.
— and Greek, genealogical relation between, 238.
— the future in, 348.
Layamon, 35, 132 n.
Legge, Professor, 197 n.
Leibniz, the first to conquer the prejudice that Hebrew was the primitive language, 149.
— how to spell his name, 149 n.
— first applied the principle of inductive reasoning to the study of language, 150.
Leibniz, his letter to Peter the Great, 151.
— his labours in the science of language, 152, 157 n, 158, 377 n.
— his various studies, 153.
— claimed an immortal soul for brutes, 486.
— on the formation of thought and language, 515.
Leitner, Dr., 287.
Leland on American dialects, 67.
Lenormant, 397.
Lepcha, 447.
Lepsius on African languages, 450.
Lesbos, dialects of, 56.
Lesghian, 448.
Lettic and Lettish, 267, 268, 270.
Letto-Slavic, 267, 270, 288.
Leusden, on Hebrew and Chaldee words in O. T., 376 n.
Lewis, Sir G. C., on the theory of Raynouard, 237.
Li, in Chinese, 461.
Libra, 105 n.
Libretto of an Italian opera, number of words in the, 377.
Libyan, 449, 451.
Lilac, 36.
Linguistique, 1.
Linnæan system, important to science, 16.
Lion, Arabic names for, 388.
— its many names, 526 n.
Lipmann, 292 n.
Literary languages, origin of, 70, 467.
— — inevitable decay of, 76.
— — influence of, 77.
Lituanian dialects, 69 n.
— language, 267.
— oldest document in, 267.
Lives, the, and their habitat, 438.
Livius Andronicus, 108, 137 n.
— translated the Odyssey into Latin verse, 108.
Livonia, 267.
Livonians, dialect of the, 268, 430, 431.
Locative, formation of the, in all Aryan languages, 331.

INDEX. 565

Locative, in Chinese, 128, 330.
— in Latin, 332.
Locke, John, on language as the barrier between man and brutes, 14.
— on the origin of language, 31, 512.
— on universal ideas, 491.
Log, or Lok, plural in Hindi, 51.
Logology, 1.
Logone, 450.
Lohitic class of languages, 445, 447.
Lokrians, the, 137 n.
Lönnrot, 437.
Lord, 132, 277.
Lord's Prayer, published in various languages in the sixteenth century, 144 n.
Lottner, Dr., 390.
Loud, 501.
Lourdement, 52.
Loved, 129, 130, 243, 350, 352.
Low German, 244, 244 n, 246–248, 252, 258, 259.
Lucilius in the house of the Scipios, 111.
— his book on Latin orthography, 116.
Lucina, name for the moon, 11.
Lucius Cincius Alimentus, 107.
Lucretius, 74.
Luna, 11.
Lusatia, language of, 270.
Luther on astrology, 9.
Lycian, 453.
Lycurgus, his travels mythical, 96.

MÂ, to measure, 6, 382.
Mâba, 450.
MacCrindle's Ancient India, 196 n.
Macedonians, ancient authors on the, 137 n.
Macedo-Roumnic, the, 260 n.
Machina, 105 n.
MacMurdo, 191.
Madam, 341.
Magadha, 172.
Mâgadhí or Pali, 167, 168, 172, 174, 179, 182.
— the root of all languages to the Buddhists, 146, 146 n.

Mâgadhí alphabet, 176.
Magar dialect, 447.
Maggi, Prof., 209 n.
Magi, the, 281.
Magis and Plus, 40.
Mago, his book in Punic on Agriculture, 97 n.
Magyars, the, 435.
Mahabachiam, commentary on the Vedas, 214.
Mahâbhârata, 178.
— translated for Akbar, 205, 205 n.
Mahârâshtrí, chief Prakrit dialect, 167.
— used by the Gainas, 168.
Mahâvansa, 174.
Mahinda brought the Buddhist sacred books from Magadha, 174.
— monastery founded by, 175.
— his translation of the Arthakathâs, 183.
Mahmud of Ghazni, invites Alberuni to India, 201.
Mainôgî Khirad, 282.
Malade, 388.
Malaic class of languages, 452.
Malayalam, 446.
Malta, Arabic dialect of, 322.
Man, to think, 525.
Man and brutes, faculties of, 483, 485, 489, 511, 521.
Man, Isle of, dialect, 265.
Mâna, 11.
Mandaeans, or Nasoreans, 318.
Manchu tribes, speaking a Tungusic language, 407, 469.
— grammar of, 443.
— imitative sounds in, 507 n.
Manetho, his study of Greek, 97.
— his work on Egypt, 97, 98.
— his knowledge of hieroglyphics, 97.
Mani, the moon, 4.
Manka, his translations from Sanskrit into Persian, 200.
Mankba, the physician, 201.
Mankind, 51.
— common origin of, 474.
Mâno, moon, 5.

INDEX.

Manual, 37.
Manuscripts of Hanxleden, and Paolino da S. Bartolommeo, 218 n.
Marâ*th*î, 171, 180, 182.
— genitive in, 120 n.
Marcellus and the Emperor Tiberius, 39.
Märchen, dialects of, 59 n.
Marco della Tomba, 217.
— — never saw a MS. of the Veda, 217.
Mars, 106.
Marsh, on the proportion of Saxon to Latin words in English, 84 n.
Marshall, knew Sanskrit in 1677, 212 n.
Marta, 524, 525.
Mâs, Mâsa, 6.
Masora, idiom in which it was written, 317.
Massmann, 250 n.
μάσθλη, 402.
Matanga, a Buddhist, 197.
Mâtram, 6.
Maulána Izzu-d-din Khalid Khani, his translations from Sanskrit into Persian, 203.
Maximinus on Ulfilas, 307.
— on the Council of Aquileja, 307.
Mayil, 190 n.
Mayûra, 190 n.
Mazdeism, 280.
Measurer, moon, 4.
Measuring-rod, 104.
Median inscriptions, 398.
Medians, 296 n.
Medical treatises, Sanskrit, 201.
Megasthenes' visit to India, 195.
Megiscrus, published the Lord's prayer in forty languages, 144 n.
Mehlhorn, on Greek dialects, 60.
Meis, 5.
Melancthon, on astrology, 9.
Melanesian languages, 452.
Même, 54.
Mên, 5.
Mêna, 5.
Menander, his study of Greek, 97.
— his work on Phenicia, 97.

Mendaïtes, or Nasoreans, their 'Book of Adam,' 318.
Mênôths, 5.
Mensch, 525.
Mensis, 6.
Ment, origin of the termination in French adverbs, 51.
Mente, in Spanish, 53.
Mênû, moon, 5.
Meshcheräks, tribe of the, 416.
Messapian inscriptions, 262.
Messerschmidt's travels in Siberia, 68, 158 n.
Metal, same words for, in all Aryan languages, 356.
Metalepsis, really dialectical, 60 n.
Metaphrastic formation of phrases, 456.
Methodius, 268.
Métron, Greek, 6.
Mexico, languages of, 452.
Mezzofanti, 24.
Michaelis, 192 n.
Micronesian languages, 452.
Middle English, 131.
— German, 244 n, 245, 246 n, 248.
— Franconian, 247 n, 248.
Miklosich, 269, 288.
Mills, Dr., 276 n, 278, 278 n.
Milton, number of words used in his works, 379.
Minayeff, 191 n.
Minerva, 106.
Mingrelian, 448.
Ming-ti, Emperor of China, introduced Buddhism into his Empire, 196.
— sent officials to India to study Buddhism, 197.
Mint, Har Mint, 296 n.
Minsi, or tribe of the Delaware Indians, 65 n.
Misfortune, many names for, 526 n.
Mishna, 317 n.
Missionaries, help they can give as to unwritten languages, 62.
Mithridates, 24.
Mle*kkh*a, the same as Walh and Beluch? 93, 93 n.
— how used by Hindus, 140.

Moabite language, 320.
Moallakat, or 'suspended poems' of the Arabs, 321.
Mœsia, settlement of Goths in, 298.
Moffat, Dr., on South African dialects, 69.
Mohammed ben Musa, his translation of the Indian treatise on Algebra into Arabic, 201.
Mohammed Sultan Thanesari, one of Akbar's translators, 205 n.
Möller, 353.
Mommsen on Greek names in Latin, 105, 105 n.
— on Oscan, 262.
Môn or Talaing, 448.
Môna, mônan, 5.
Monad, 5.
Monboddo, Lord, on language as the barrier between man and brutes, 13, 14.
— his 'Ancient Metaphysics,' 155 n, 225 n.
— on the discovery of Sanskrit, 225.
— on the relation of Sanskrit to Greek, 227.
Mongolian, grammar of, 443.
— Chinese words in, 475 n.
Mongolic dialects, entering a new phase of grammatical life, 68.
— class of languages, 398, 407, 408, 411.
Mongols, their original seat, 407.
— three classes of, 407.
— their conquests, 408, 410.
— empire dissolved, 410.
— their present state, 411, 412.
Monosyllabic languages, 384, 391, 461.
Month, names of moon used in the sense of, 5.
Moon, antiquity of the word, 4.
— Bask and other names for, 4.
— a masculine, 4, 5.
— the measurer, 4, 6, 522.
— the daughter of Mundilföri, 5.
— father of the gods, 5.
Mora, mayûra, peacock, 191.

Moravia, devastated by the Mongols, 410.
Mordvines, the, 436.
Mordvinian, 430, 431, 444.
Morphological classification, 370, 385, 390, 401, 455.
— — of Prof. Hunfalvy, 393.
Morris and Skeat, 131 n.
Morrison, 376 n.
Mortal, 525.
Moses, the Judæan, founder of a kind of Magic, 279.
Motu dialect, 453.
'Mountain of Languages,' 62, 94.
Much, and very, 40.
Muhammed ben Ibrahim Alfazâri, author of the greater Sind-hind, 199.
Müllhauer, 204 n, 208 n, 211 n.
Müllenhof and Scherer on Teutonic languages, 258.
Müller, Dr. E., 184.
— C. and T., 195 n.
— F., 288, 446.
Munda languages, 447, 448.
Mundelföri, 5.
Murad II, 420.
Murmi, 447.
Murray on roots, 530.
Myth, 11.
Mythology, real nature of, 10.
— instead of science of language, 1.

N, 242 n.
Nabateans, 318.
— work of Kuthami on 'Nabatean Agriculture,' 319.
Nadiston, 346.
Næbbe, 347 n.
Næfth, 347 n.
Næron, 347 n.
Nævius, contemporary of Plautus, 74, 108.
Nâga, 447.
Naipâlî, 171, 180.
Nakib Khan, 205 n.
Namáz, prayer, 83.
Namdev, the poet, 181.
Name, 519.

Naming a thing, 521.
Nard, 194 n.
Narsingh Mahta, the poet, 182.
Nasoreans, or Mendaïtes, 318.
National languages, origin of, 70.
Nature, immutability of, in all her works, 32.
— Dr. Whewell on, 33.
Natural selection, 526, 530.
Nausea, 105.
Navis, 105 n.
Nay, 341.
Nebuchadnezzar, his name stamped on the bricks made in his reign, 386.
Negro races, language of the, 450.
Νεμέτζιοι, the, of Constantinus Porphyrogeneta, 93 n.
Neo-Aryan dialects, 179.
Neo-Latin dialects, 262, 263.
Ne rechi, 346.
Nerjamês, 252.
Nestorians of Syria, 320.
Neutri and neutrius, 39 n.
New Academy, 112.
New High-German, 247, 248.
New Testament, translated for Akbar into Persian, 205.
Nicobar islands dialect, 453.
Nicolai and the Empress Catharine, 160 n.
Nicopolis, battle of, 420.
Niebuhr, 192 n.
Nieder-Deutsch, 244.
Niemiec, Polish name given by the Austrians to the Turks, 93, 93 n.
Nissen, 245 n.
Niston, 347 n.
No and nay, as used by Chaucer, 341.
Nobili, Roberto de, 209.
— first European Sanskrit scholar, 210.
Noble, 367.
Nogái tribes, 415.
Noiré, 528 n.
Nolde, 347.
Nöldeke, 280 n.

Nomad languages, 399.
— indispensable requirements of, 402.
— wealth of, 72.
Nomadic tribes and their wars, 429.
— — their languages, 429.
Nominalism and Realism, 12.
Nominative and accusative, 125.
— — in Chinese, 126.
— not a case, 337.
Noricum or Nyrax, 264.
Norman words, proportion of, to Saxon, in English, 83.
Norrænish, 253.
Norris, 397.
Norse Sagas, imagery in the, 72 n.
North Indians, 129 n.
Northern French, 261.
Norway, dialects of, 55, 253.
— the two Eddas, 254.
— poetry of, 255.
— the Iliod or quida of, 256.
Norwegian language in Iceland, stagnation of, 78.
Nouns, the first words, 31.
— and verbs, distinction between, 91.
— and verbs known to Plato, 100.
— all express one out of many attributes, 418.
Nuba, 450.
Number, 91, 102.
Numerals in Greek, Latin, and Sanskrit, 227.
— in the Finno-Ugric class, 441.
Nûmus, 105 n.
Nyle, 347 n.

OAR, 364.
Oaths of Strassburg, 261.
Obliged, 36.
Obsolete words and meanings since the translation of the Bible 1611, 36.
Oceanic languages, 452.
Odyssey translated into Latin, 108.
Oersted on reason, 520.
Of, 330.
Oggi, Italian, 54 n.
Ogham inscriptions, 265.

Oigob, 450.
Oldenberg, Dr., 174.
Old High-German, 247 n, 248, 252.
— — more primitive than Gothic, 252, 252 n.
Ölöts or Kalmüks, 407, 411.
On, in on dit, 524.
Onagurs, 435.
'One o'clock,' like, 71 n.
Onkelos, Targum of, 317.
Onomatopoieia, theory of, 494, 497, 504.
Ophir of the Bible, 187-192, 192 n.
— Vulgate and Septuagint translation of, 192.
— in Arabia, 192 n, 194 n.
— in Africa, 193 n.
Oppert, Dr. J., on the word Avesta, 273 n.
— — on the Turanians, 397.
Optics, a physical science, 22.
Opu'st for opus est, 75 n.
Ore, 356.
Organic languages, 392.
Origen, on Hebrew as the primitive language, 145.
Origin of language, problem of one common, 455 et seq.
Oriyâ, 171.
Orkhan, son of Osman, 420.
Ormazd the Zoroastrian, mentioned by Plato, 275, 275 n.
— discovery of the name Auramazda in the Cuneiform inscriptions, 275.
— origin of the name, 276, 277.
Orm, 35.
Ormulum, 132, 132 n.
Oromazes and Oromasdes, 275, 275 n.
Oruj, 85.
Os, of Ossethi, calling themselves Iron, 296.
Osa, 450.
Oscan language and literature, 262.
Osman, Osmanli, 420.
Osmanli language, 82, 412, 418.
Ossetian language, 448.
Ost Frisians do not speak Frisian, 57.
Ostjakes, the, 435.

Ostjakes, dialects of the, 68, 430-432.
Otyi, 450.
Owl-glass, stories of, 370.

PACIFY, 134.
Padre Pedro, 207.
Pain d'épices, 372.
Painting, history of, 22.
Paisâkî, 167.
Paktyes of Herodotus, 287.
Palestine, early intercourse with India, 187-124.
— foreign languages in, 321.
Pâli, considered by the Buddhists the root of all languages, 146, 174, 174 n.
— the oldest Prakrit, 168, 178.
— of the Tripitaka, 168.
— Vedic forms in, 169.
— the language of Buddha, 174 n.
— its meaning in the Mahâvansa, 174 n.
— called Gina-vakana, or Tanti, 174 n.
— its agreement with Sinhalese, 183.
Pallas, Professor, and the Empress Catherine, 160.
Pampeluna, discussion at, on Bask, 149 n.
Panœtius, the Stoic, at Rome, 111.
Pânini, Sanskrit grammar of, 124, 163, 165, 169, 178, 182.
— called also Sâlâturiya, 203 n.
Pânînean Sanskrit, 179.
Panjâb, 186, 194.
Panjâbî, 171, 180.
Pañkatantra, the, 199.
Pannonians, 138 n.
Pantomime, story of the king and the, 509.
Paolino da San Bartolommeo, first Sanskrit grammar published by, 157, 216, 219 n, 220 n, 224 n.
Paradise, various languages supposed to have been spoken in, 149 n.
Pârsî, 285.
Parsis, or fire-worshippers, the ancient, 274.

INDEX.

Parsis, their colony in Bombay, 274.
— their various emigrations, 274 n, 289.
— their ancient language, 233, 274.
— their ancient books, 280.
Parthian rulers of Persia, 284.
PAS, 366.
Pascatir race, 439.
Passive, 117.
Pasu, 522.
Patagonians, 452.
Pater, 134.
Patois, 55.
Paul, 353.
Pazend texts, 285, 286.
Peacocks, 190, 191.
— name for, in Hebrew derived from India, 190, 193 n.
— exported to Babylon, 191.
Pecunia, 360.
Pecus, 360, 522.
Pedro, Padre, missionary at Calicut, 207.
Pegu, language of, 448.
Pehlevi translation of Sanskrit fables, 198.
— the Zend-Avesta in, 273.
— language, 281, 282, 283, 285, 286.
— inscriptions in, 281, 281 n.
— texts, 282.
— called Zend, by the Parsis, 283.
— coins, 283.
— inscriptions of Ardeshir, 283.
— origin of the word, 283.
— how still read, 284.
Pelasgi, Herodotus on the, 136 n.
— Pischel on the, 136 n.
— Dionysius of Halicarnassus on the, 137 n.
— as ancestors of both Greeks and Romans, 264.
Pentecost, day of, 141.
Percussion, 49.
Père, 54.
Perfect, formation of the, in the time of Wycliffe, 535.
Pergamus, Greek MSS. sent to, 100.
— scholars at, the first critical students of Greek grammar, 102.

Perion, his work on language, 144 n.
Perkins and Stoddart, 320 n.
Perm, 435.
Permian tribes and language, 430, 431.
Permic branch of the Finnic class, 430, 435.
— tribes, 435.
Persia, influence of, on the Arabs, 83 n.
— origin of the Turkman or Kasilbash of, 414.
Persian language, 82.
— — influence over Turkish, 82.
— Themistocles studied, 95.
— the ancient. *See* Zend.
— subsequent history of, 282, 286.
— alphabet, 284.
— local dialects of, 286.
Peru, languages of, 452.
Peshito, 319.
Peter the Great, letter of Leibniz to, 151.
Phenician, closely allied to Hebrew, 320.
Phíghár, astronomical tables of, 199.
Philistines, language of the, 320.
Philolaos, his guess on the motion of the earth round the sun, 19, 20.
Philology, science of Comparative, 21–23, 80, 232, 234.
— an historical science, 22.
Philostorgius on Ulfilas, 307, 309.
Phocæans discover Italy, 105 n.
Phonetic corruption, 47, 50, 51, 53.
Phonology, 1.
Phrygian, some words the same as in Greek, 138.
Physical sciences, 2, 22.
Phytology, 3.
Pig's nose, 365 n.
Piper, 249 n, 252 n.
Pisâka countries, 167 n.
Pischel, on the Pelasgians, 136 n.
— and Bühler, on Prakrit, 170 n.
Plants, migration of, 44.
Plato, knew of nouns and verbs, 100.
— on the origin of Greek, 137.
— on Zoroaster, 275.
Platt-Deutsch, 57, 244, 245, 247.

Plautus, Greek words in his plays, 108.
— his plays adaptations of Greek originals, 108.
Pleiades, 6.
— their name in Zulu, 6 n.
Pliny, on the dialects in Colchis, 62, 62 n.
— on Zoroaster, 99 n, 279, 280.
Plough, 364, 365 n.
— words for, in Sanskrit, 365 n.
Plural as first formed, 50, 533.
— in Chinese, 51, 532.
Plus and magis, 40.
Pluviæ, 7.
Pococke, 388 n.
Poisons, Hebrew treatise by Zanik, on, 200 n.
Poland, language of, 269.
— invaded by the Mongols, 410.
Polabian dialect, 270.
Pole, 7.
Polish, oldest specimens of, 269.
Polybius, on the changes Latin had undergone in his time, 74.
— in the house of the Scipios, 111.
— on the Veneti, 138 n.
Polygenetic theory, Pott on the, 475 n.
Polyhistor, Alexander, pupil of Crates, 115.
Polynesian dialects, 63, 452.
— missionary dialect, 64.
Polysynthetic languages, 444, 455, 456.
Poncel, T., 389 n.
Pongue, 450.
Pons, Father, his report of the literary treasures of the Brahmans, 215.
Pooh-pooh theory, 507.
Porca, 365 n.
Porphyry, 488 n, 491 n.
Porte, the High, 420.
Portuguese, 260.
Postel, 144 n.
Pott, Professor, his 'Etymological Researches,' 232, 252, 291, 304, 305, 428 n.
— his various works, 305.

Pott, his advocacy of the polygenetic theory, 475 n.
Pragâpati, 203 n.
Prakrit idioms, 166-173, 179.
— grammatical, 166, 168, 169, 174, 179, 182.
— used for poetry, 166.
— ungrammatical, 169, 177, 179.
— modern plays in, 169.
— three elements in, 170.
— grammars, 178.
Prâkrita equation, 168.
Prâkritas, the literary dialects, 171, 179, 180.
Prakritic dialects, 180, 182.
— four divisions of, 180.
— and Sinhalese, 183.
Prâtisâkhyas, the, of the Brahmans, 124, 132 n, 164.
Presbyter, 131.
Prescriptions, origin of the signs for, 8.
Prete, Italian, 132 n.
Preterites, 352, 353.
Prichard, 397.
Priest, 131.
Primum appellatum, 516.
— cognitum, 519.
Priscianus, influence of his grammatical work on later ages, 121.
Probus, the grammarian, 121.
Pronouns, personal, 101, 468.
Prora, 105 n.
Prospective, 369.
Protagoras, his attempt to improve the language of Homer, 40.
Provençal, modern, 173.
— the daughter of Latin, 236.
— not the mother of French, &c., 236.
— the oldest poem in, 261.
Provincialisms, 55.
Prussian, Old, language and literature, 267.
Psammetichus, linguistic experiment of, 480.
Ptolemæus Philadelphus, and the Septuagint, 98 n.
Ptolemy, importance of his system of astronomy, 17.

Ptolemy, his mention of Abiria, 191.
Ptōsis, meaning of, in the language of the Stoics, 118.
Publius Scipio, 107, 109.
Punic language, 97 n.
Pushtu language, 287.
Pyrrha, 11.
Pyrrhon, went to India with Alexander, 95 n.
Pythagoras, his travels mythical, 96.

QUATREMÈRE, 148 n, 316 n.
— on the Ophir of the Bible, 191 n.
— on Ari in Armenian, 296 n.
Quida, 256.
Quinsy, 523 n.
Quintilian, on the changes in Latin, in his time, 75.
— on the omission of final s in Latin, 75 n.
— on learning Greek, 104.
— contemporary of Flaccus, 121.
— on the faculty of speech, 481.
Quittance, une, 135.
Qurân, Arabic of the, 322.

RABE, 499.
Rabbi Jona, or Abul Walid, author of the first Hebrew Grammar, 89 n.
Rabota, 363 n.
Radical, or substantial elements in words, 50.
— stage of language, 391, 393, 457, 461.
Radicals. *See* Roots.
Rae, Dr., on rapid changes of language, in small communities, 65.
Rájmahals, 446.
Rájputâni, 171.
Râmâyana, translated for Akbar, 205, 205 n.
Rask, Erasmus, his studies of Zend, 233, 274.
— on Scythian languages, 397.
Raucus, 501.

Raven, 499, 503.
Raynouard, his labours in comparative grammar, 236.
— criticisms of his theory of the Langue Romane, 236, 252.
Realism and Nominalism, 12.
Reason, 492, 521.
Red Indians, languages of the, 451.
Regeneration, dialectic, 54.
Regere, 362.
Regular fizzer, a, 71 n.
Reinaud, M., on the Sindhind, 200 n.
— on Alberuni's Indica, 202.
Remus, 105 n, 364 n.
Rémusat, 196 n, 197.
Renan, M., 318, 320, 376 n, 388 n, 526 n.
— on the Nabateans, 319.
Répit, 367.
Respectable, 366.
Respite, 367.
Revel, dialect of Estonian, 438.
Rex, regem, 129.
Rhêma, 100.
Rhenus, 519.
Rhetoric, 118.
Rhines, 519 n.
Rhys, 266, 266 n.
Richardson's dictionary, 523 n.
Rig-veda, the, 89 n.
Ritter, 194 n.
Rivus, 518.
Roberto de Nobili, 208 n.
Roccha, published the Lord's Prayer in twenty-six languages, 144 n.
Roche, Ladevi, 30 n.
Rolon dialect, 450.
Romance languages, their Latin origin, 74, 133, 236.
— modifications of, 260.
— their origin in the ancient Italic languages, 262.
Romane, the Langue, 236.
Romanese language of the Grisons, 261.
— translation of the Bible into, 261 n.
— lower or Engadine, 261 n.
Romàni, or Walachians, 260 n.
Romànic, where spoken, 260 n.

Romanic or modern Latin, 260.
Romans, their use of the word barbarian, 139.
Rome, language of, changed very rapidly, 74.
— Greek first taught by Dionysius Thrax at, 103.
— influence of Greece on, 104, 107.
— laws of, derived from Greece, 107.
— Greek civilisation, influence of in, 110.
— religious life of, more Greek than Roman, 112.
— expulsion of Greek grammarians and philosophers from, 112, 115.
— compromise between religion and philosophy at, 112.
— wide interest shown in grammatical studies at, 114.
— the name, 300.
Rook, 593.
Roome, 36.
Roots, well known to the Brahmans, 89.
— or radicals, 358.
— necessarily monosyllabic, 372.
— classes of, primary, secondary, and tertiary, 372.
— in Semitic languages, 374, 383.
— 1706 in Sanskrit, 375.
— 461 Aryan roots in English, 375.
— 500 in Hebrew, 376.
— 450 in Chinese, 376, 376 n.
— 600 in Gothic, 376.
— 250 in Modern German, 376.
— 1605 in the Slavic languages, 376.
— demonstrative and predicative, 358, 377, 380, 383.
— in Turanian languages, 383.
— all languages reducible in the end to, 390, 492, 512.
— three forms of speech may be produced by the free combination of these elements, 391.
— the radical stage of language, 391, 393.
— never obscured in Turanian languages, 405.
— combinations of different, 455.

Roots, of different families cannot be compared, 457.
— and general ideas, 492.
— origin of, 494.
— bow-wow theory of, 494.
— pooh-pooh theory of, 507.
— are phonetic types, 527.
— Heyse and Noiré's views on, 528 n.
— number of, almost infinite at first, 529.
— natural selection of, 529.
— full and empty, 530.
Rosen, 231, 233.
Rosenkranz, his definition of language, 511.
Roth, H., 212, 216.
Roumania, language of, 260, 260 n.
Roumansch, or Romanese, 261.
RU or KRU, 500.
Rückert's Lectures, 397 n.
Rud, 501.
Rudra, god of thunder, 89 n.
Rufen, 501 n.
Rug in rugire, 501.
Rumor, 501.
Rûna, 501.
Rûnen, 501.
Russia, swayed by the Mongols, 408, 410.
Russian government encourages study of languages, 158.
— branch of Slavonic languages, 268.

S for th, 37.
— in Sanskrit equals Persian H, 54 n, 344.
— final, omitted in conversation, 75 n.
— in 3rd person singular, 86, 344.
Saba in Arabia, 193 n.
Sabaean civilisation, 322.
Sabius, not found in classical Latin, 106 n.
Saccharine, 505.
Sachau on Alberuni, 201, 202.
Saemund, Sigfusson, his collection of Icelandic songs, 256, 257 n.
Saeternus, 106 n.

574 INDEX.

Sagard, G., on the languages of the Hurons, 65.
Sage, 106 n.
St. Albans, Book of, 72.
St. Basil on names, 30 n.
St. Hilaire, Barthélemy, 174 n.
St. Jerome on Hebrew, 145.
— — his letter from the Goths, 251.
Sakha or Yakuts, 416.
Sakuntalâ, 182, 220 n.
Sâlâturiya, 203 n.
Saleh, Indian physician to Harun-al-Rashid, 200.
Salian poems, and later Latin, 74.
Sâlihotra, 203 n.
Sâlinâtha, 203 n.
Sâlotar, his work on veterinary medicine, 203.
Sâloturiya, 203 n.
Salotri, 203 n.
Samaritan, 318.
Samouscroutam, 214.
Samoyedes, the, 406.
Samoyedic, 398, 406.
Sandal wood, 189, 191, 194 n.
Sânkhya, work on the, translated by Alberuni, 202.
Sanscruta, 209.
Sanskrit, formation of adjectives in, 120 n.
— grammar, 124.
— lists of remarkable words or Ganas, 124.
— and Greek, similarity between, 157.
— grammar, first, 157.
— importance of the discovery of, 162, 234.
— language, history of, 163, 179.
— doubts as to its age and authenticity, 163.
— modern plays in, 169.
— mixed, 170.
— and the language of Asoka, 173.
— reduced to writing, 177.
— inscriptions, 177.
— literature, renaissance of, 178.
— accounts of, given by the Jews, 186-192.
— at the time of Solomon, 186.

Sanskrit, Greek accounts of, 193, 195.
— Persian accounts of, 194, 195.
— Chinese accounts of, 196, 198.
— Arab accounts of, 199.
— texts discovered in Japan, 197 n.
— study of, kept up under the Mogul Emperors, 206.
— European missionaries learn, 207.
— grammars, original, 215, 216.
— knowledge of, possessed by Hauxleden, 218, 219 n.
— genealogical relation of, to Greek and Latin, 220, 226, 234, 237.
— Lord Monboddo on the discovery of, 225.
— studies of Frederic Schlegel, 229.
— relation of, to Iranic languages, 273.
— formation of the locative in, 333.
— number of roots in, 376.
— and Greek, coincidences between, accounted for, 467.
Santhals, 447.
Sapius, 106 n.
Sapta Sindhavah, 194.
Saragurs, 435.
Sarayu, 301 n, 302.
Sassanian dynasty, established the authority of the Avesta, 280.
— — Persian language of the, 281, 283, 295.
Sassetti, Filippo, 209, 220.
Saturnus, 106, 106 n.
Sauraseni, prose Prâkrit dialect, 167, 168, 179, 182.
Savage tribes, rapid changes in the languages of, 35, 65, 66.
Savitar, 106 n.
Saxon words, proportion of to Norman in English, 84, 84.
— Continental, Low German, 244, 247.
— Upper, 246 n.
Saxony, dialects of, 246 n, 248.
Sayce, Professor, 526 n.
Scaliger, I. I., his 'Diatriba de Europæorum Linguis,' 145 n, 157 n.
Scandinavian branch of the Teutonic languages, 253, 258, 259.

Scandinavian, East and West, races, 254.
— literature, 254.
Scape, 382.
Scaurus, the grammarian, 121.
Sceptic and bishop from the same root, 367.
Schaffarik on Slavonic languages, 267.
Scheler, 135 n.
Schifo, 362.
Schisma est generis neutri, 39.
Schlegel, F., his Sanskrit studies, 229.
— his 'Language and Wisdom of the Indians,' 229.
— his work taken up in Germany, 231.
— on the origin of language, 46, 46 n, 328.
Schlegel, August W. von, his 'Indische Bibliothek,' 232.
— his criticism of Raynouard's theory, 237.
Schleicher, 28 n, 46, 252 n, 253 n, 268 n, 269 n, 270, 290 n, 534 n.
Schleiden's 'Life of the Plant,' 21.
Schmerz, 523.
Schmidt, his one root, 476 n, 530.
— Dr. K. E. A., 119 n.
Schömann, 119 n.
Schott, 468.
Schweizer-Siedler, 106 n.
Science of language, names for, 1.
Sciences, uniformity in the history of most, 2.
— empirical stage, 3.
— must answer some practical purpose, 8.
— classificatory stage, 14.
— theoretical or metaphysical stage, 18.
— physical, impulses received from the philosopher and poet, 18.
— difference between physical and historical, 22.
Scioppius, 115 n.
Scipio, P., his history of Rome, 107.
Scipios, their influence on Latin, 74.
— the Cosmopolitan Club, at the house of the, 112.

Scythian language, learnt by the Medes, 94.
— words mentioned by Greek writers, 297.
— races of Rask, 397, 398.
Scythians, the, 429.
Sea, 522.
Second, the, 242.
Seigneur, Sieur, 242.
Sein, 242.
Seljuks, 418.
Semarchos, his embassy to the Tukiu tribe, 413.
Semi-Saxon, 131.
Semitic family of languages, 33.
— — study of, 143, 313.
— words in Persian, 284.
— constituent elements of the, 313, 324.
— — divisions of the, 314.
— Aramaic class, 314.
— Hebraic class, 320.
— Arabic class, 321.
— Nöldeke's article on, 323 n.
— classes, intimate relations between the three, 324.
— languages have triliteral roots, 383.
— Berber dialects, 390, 449.
— and Aryan, the only true families of speech, 385.
— Japhetic and Hamitic, old division of languages, 460.
— genealogical table, 538.
Senart, 164 n, 174 n, 177, 178, 266 n.
Senior, the title, 342.
Septuagint, the, and Ptolemæus Philadelphus, 98 n.
— used by Ulfilas, 249.
Serpent, 523.
— many names for, 526 n.
Servian dialects, 268.
Setubandha, the, 178.
Sevmek, 426 et seq.
Shaft, 382.
Shûhûn Shâh, 284, 284 n.
'Shahnâmeh,' 286, 297.
Shakespeare, total number of words used in his plays, 379.

Shambalas, their one case, 336.
Shan, 447.
Shapen, 37.
Shen habbim, 190.
Shi, ten in Chinese, 47.
Shilhe, 449.
Shilluk, 450.
Ship and shape, 382.
Shunt, 37, 37 n.
Siamese, 445, 447.
Siberia, Tungusic tribes of, 407.
— Turkic tribes in, 416.
— dialects of, 416.
Sibylla, or Sibulla, 106 n.
Sibylla of Cumæ, her oracles written in Greek, 106.
Siddhânta, 168, 200 n.
Sigfusson. See Saemund.
Sigismund, the Emperor and the Bohemian schoolmaster, 39.
— defeated by Bayazeth, 420.
Silesia invaded by the Mongols, 410.
Silesian dialects, 246 n, 248.
Silloner la mer, 364.
Sindhi, 171, 180.
Sind-hind, meaning of, 200 n.
Sindhu, 195, 344, 519.
Singpho, 447.
Singular and plural, 102.
Sinhalese, 182, 183.
— an Aryan dialect, 182.
— agreement with Pâli, 183.
Sir, 341.
Sister, 53.
'Skalda,' the, of Snorri Sturluson, 257.
Skalds, the, in Norway, 256, 257.
Skanda-Purâna, 208 n.
Skeat on English roots, 375.
Skeat's Dictionary, 83 n.
Skeptikos, 366.
Skeptomai, 366.
SKU or KU, 418.
Slavery, justified by the Science of Language, 12.
Slavinia, the ancient, 260 n.
Slavonic tribes settled in Mœsia, 260 n.
— languages, 268, 270.

Slavonic, ecclesiastical, or ancient Bulgarian, 268.
Slovenian language, the, 269.
Smara, love, 523.
Smart, 523.
Smith, Adam, on the origin of language, 31.
— on the formation of thought and language, 512, 514.
— Sidney, on the superiority of man to brutes, 483.
Snorri Sturluson, his prose Edda, 254, 256.
— — his 'Heimskringla,' 256.
— — his 'Skalda,' 257.
Sofir, Coptic name for India, 192.
Soho, 451.
Sôl, 5.
Sol, the sun, son of Mundilföri, 5.
Soliman crosses the Hellespont, 420.
Soliman-shah, 419.
Solomon, Sanskrit in the time of, 186.
— his fleet of Tharshish, 187.
Somâli, 449, 451.
Soug-yun, the Chinese pilgrim to India, 197.
Sonrhai, 450.
Sorbs, the, 270.
Soto, 450.
Soul, 485, 522.
Sound, few names formed by the imitation of, 506.
Soupçon, 368.
Spake, 37.
Spanish, 260.
SPAS, 366.
Spea, offshoots of the root, 366.
Specere, 366, 369, 371.
Special, 371.
Species, origin of the Latin, 370.
Specify, to, 371.
Specimen, 372 n.
Specious, 372 n.
Spectator, 372 n.
Speculare, 369.
Speech, the Supreme Brahman, 89.
Spëha, 370.
Spelunca, 517.
Spence Hardy, 146 n.
Spezereien, 372.

Speziale, 371.
Spezieria, 371.
Spiegel, 277 n, 278.
Spices, 361.
Spirit, 522.
Spite, 368.
Spy, 366.
Squirrel, 505.
Srotriyas, 164.
Sru, to hear, 501.
STAN, 504 n.
Stanislas Julien, 126 n, 127, 461 n.
Stars, fixed, 7.
— travelling and non-travelling, 7 n.
Statéra, 105 n.
Steinthal, 495 n, 528 n.
Steinschneider, 200 n.
Stevenson, 182.
Stewart, Dugald, on the origin of language, 31, 477, 512.
— — his doubts about Sanskrit, 185.
— — on the affinity of Greek and Sanskrit, 229.
Sthavira school, 175.
Stilo, L. E., 115, 115 n.
Stilus, 104.
Stirrup, 505.
Stoics, philosophy of the, in Rome, 112.
Strabo, on Timosthenes, 62 n.
— on the barbarians, 137 n, 138 n.
Strachey, 199 n.
Strahlenberg, his work on the North and East of Europe and Asia, 158 n.
Strassburg, oath of, 261.
Struggle for life, 525.
Stunner, 71 n.
Sturluson. See Snorri.
Suahili, 450.
Suanian, 448.
Substantives in Chinese, not declined, 126.
Sucre, 503.
Sûdra as opposed to Ârya, 291, 292 n.
Suetonius, 111 n, 115.
Sugar, 505.
Suidas, 103 n.
Sulh, 365 n.

Sulla knows Greek, 111.
Sumero-Accadian, 315, 398.
— — affinity of the inscriptions, 398 n.
Sun, a feminine, 4, 5.
— and moon, of different genders in different nations, 4, 5.
— meaning of, 522.
— names for, 525.
Sunna, 5, 5 n.
Sunne, 5.
Sunnia and Fretela, 251.
Sunnô, 5.
Suomalaiset, the, 436.
Suspicion, 368.
Susruta, Sanskrit medical work, 200.
Süssmilch, 480 n.
Sutledge, 300.
Sûtras, Sanskrit of the, 163, 165, 179.
Svasar, sister, 54.
Swabia, dialects of, 248.
Swedish language, 78, 253, 254.
Sword, many names for, 388, 526 n.
Syl, 365 n.
Sylt, dialectic names of the island of, 57.
Synonymes, 257, 388, 525.
Synthetic languages, 456, 470.
Syria, origin of the Turks of, 418.
Syriac, used by Laban, 316.
— translation of the Bible into, 319.
— literature, 320.
— meaning of Peshito, 319.
— revival and present state of, 320.
Syrjänian, 430, 431, 435.

TAHITI, rapid changes in the dialects of, 63.
Taic class of languages, 445, 447.
Talaing, 448.
Talitha kumi, 317.
Talmud of Jerusalem, and of Babylon, 317, 317 n.
Tamasheg, 451.
Tamen, 345.
Tamulic languages, 190 n, 398, 446, 472.
— belong to the Turanian family, 472.
Tanti, 174 n.

Targums, language of the, 316.
— most celebrated, 317 n.
Tarikh-i-Badauni, the, 205 n.
'Tarikhu-l-Hind,' the, of Alberuni, 201.
Tatar tribes, 407, 416.
— conquered by the Mongols, 408.
— terror caused by the name, 408.
— or the Golden Horde, 408.
— a term of reproach, 409.
— tribes of Siberia, 416.
Tataric language, 407, 409.
— sometimes used in the same sense as Turanian, 408.
Tavastian, dialect of Finnic, 436.
Tcheremissians, 430, 431, 436, 444.
Tchetchenzian, 448.
Tea, how pronounced, 37 n.
Tear and larme, 54.
Teda, or Tibu, 450.
Telugu, 399, 446.
Tenne, 450.
Tender, 505.
Tennis, 505.
Terence in Scipio's house, 111.
Terminational stage of language, 391-396, 461.
Terminations, Horne Tooke, on grammatical, 357.
Terminology of the Greeks and Hindus, coincidences between, 123.
Testament, the New, translated into Persian, 205.
— Old, number of words in the, 379.
Teutonic class of languages, 45, 243.
— English, a branch of the, 45, 243.
— no Proto-Teutonic Grammar, 247, 258.
— Table of, 259.
Th as a termination replaced by S, 37.
Thamudic Inscriptions, 321.
Tharshish, Solomon's fleet of, 187.
Themistocles, his acquaintance with Persian, 95.
Théodicée of Leibniz, 153.
Theoretical stage, 18, 87.
Theos and Deva, 157.

Thin, 505.
Thomassin, 147.
Thommerel, M., on the Saxon and classical words in English, 84.
Thorpe, 242.
Thrace, old name of, 298.
Thracians, 137 n, 160 n.
Thum, 382.
Thunder, 504.
Thuringian dialects, 246 n, 248.
Thush language, 448.
Tiberius Gracchus, his knowledge of Greek, 107.
Tiberius, the Emperor, and the grammarians, 39.
— his knowledge of Greek, 111 n.
Tibetan, how adjectives are formed in, 120 n.
— and Burmese, relationship between, 445.
— a Gangetic language, 447.
— tones in, 476 n.
Tiger, 71 n.
Tigré language, 323.
Timosthenes, quoted by Pliny, 62 n.
Timur, Mongolian empire of, 410, 420.
Tjam language, 448.
To, 336.
Todas, 446.
Tokei, peacock, 190 n.
Tooke, Horne, 30 n.
— on grammatical terminations, 357.
— on the interjectional theory of roots, 508.
Torgod Mongols, 411.
Trade first encouraged interpreters, 95.
Trente, 53.
Tri-ūr-ēs, 364.
Trinchera, 132 n.
Tripitaka, 168.
— Pāli, of the, 169, 174, 175, 178, 182, 183.
Trumpp, 287 n.
Tso, Tseu, in Chinese, 394 n.
Tshuana, 450.
Tuareg, 451.
Tulsī Dās, the poet, 182.
Tulu, 399, 446.

INDEX.

Tulu, verbs in, 428 *n*.
Tungusic idioms, new phase of grammatical life of the, 69.
— class of languages, 398, 407, 443.
— geographical limits of, 407.
— grammar of, 444.
Turanian class of languages, 34, 325.
— origin of term, 292, 397.
— races, 297.
— names mentioned by Greek writers, 297.
— speech, component parts of, 383.
— languages, a terminational or agglutinative class, 396.
— class, divisions of, 396.
— the name, 396, 397.
— civilization, 397.
— languages, characteristic features of the, 400, 401, 456.
— peculiarly subject to dialectic regeneration, 404.
— group, account of the, 406 et seq.
— South, 444.
— coincidences in, 468, 469.
— author's letter on the, 469, 471.
— relation of the, to the Aryan and Semitic languages, 470, 473.
— genealogical table, 539.
Turk or Tu-kiu, 413.
Turkic related to Finnish, 389.
— class of languages, 398, 408, 409, 412.
— tribes, known to the Chinese as Hiung-nu, 412.
— grammar, 421.
— profuse system of conjugation, 425, 428, 443.
Turkish language affected by imported words, 82.
— Persian and Arabic words in, 82.
— two classes of vowels in, 399.
— grammar, ingenuity of, 421.
— its advance towards inflexional forms, 470.
— a synthetic language, 470.
Turkman, or Kasil-bash of Persia, 414.

Turks, history of the, 413.
— Justinian's embassy to the, 413.
— of Siberia, or Tatars, 416.
— of Asia Minor and Syria, 418.
— origin and progress of the Osmanlis, 419.
— spread of the Osmanli dialect, 418, 419.
Turner, Sharon, on Norman and Saxon words in English, 84.
Turuk, 409.
Turvasa, the Turanian, 297.
Twenty, 48.
Twice, 49.
— how formed in Chinese, 48.
Twisleton on Ophir and Tarshish, 187 *n*, 189 *n*, 191 *n*, 192 *n*.
Tycho Brahe, 19.

UGGAYINÎ, 174.
Ugly, 524.
Ugrian, North and South, 431.
Ugric branch of the Finnic class, 392, 398, 430, 432.
— distribution of the, 435.
Ugro-Tataric branch, 396, 398.
Ugry, 435.
Ulfilas, names used by him for sun and moon, 5 *n*.
— his life, and Gothic translation of the Bible, 249-251, 307.
— writers on, 307.
— date of his death, 308, 309.
— his birth, 309.
— and his Goths, 309, 310.
— at Nicæa, 311.
— Auxentius on, 311.
Umbrian language and literature, 262.
Umlaut, 534.
Upanishads, some of them probably composed for Akbar, 205.
— translated by Dàrà into Persian, 207.
— translated into French by Anquetil Duperron, 207.
Upendro Bhanj, the poet, 182.
ὑπόδρα, 368 *n*.
Upper Franconian, 247 *n*.

Upper German, 244 n, 246 n, 247 n.
— Saxon, 246 n.
Ural-Altaic division of the Turanian languages, 396, 398, 406, 443.
Uralic languages, 428.
Urals, Greek trade to the, 95.
— languages spoken there, 95.
Uran'hat tribes on the Chulym, 416.
Uranos, 107.
Uraon-Kols, 446.
Urdu, 181.
Urdu-zabân, the proper name of Hindustani, 429.
Uriya, 180, 182.
Urogs, 435.
Usbeks, history of the, 414.
Uzvârish, 285.

VAISYAS, 292.
Vâk, goddess of speech, 89 n.
Valerius Maximus, 111 n.
Vand, 374.
Vans Kennedy, 204 n.
Vararuki, oldest Prâkrit grammarian, 166, 167, 168, 169, 178, 182.
Varro, de Re Rust., on Mago's agricultural work, 97 n.
— his work on the Latin language, 115.
— librarian to the Greek and Latin Library in Rome, 116.
Varuna, 362.
Vasco da Gama, takes a missionary to Calicut, 207.
Vedas, the, 124.
— dialect of, a later Sanskrit, 124, 182.
— geographical horizon of the, 186.
— translation of, objected to by the Brahmans, 205.
— story of Feizi, 206.
— not understood by the Brahmans, 214.
Vedic Sanskrit, 163, 179.
Vei or Mando, 450.
Veinte, Spanish, 53.
Velum, 105.
Veneti, 138 n.

Venti, Italian, 53.
Vepses or North Tchudes, 431, 436.
Verbs, the first words, 31.
— no terminations for the persons in Mongolian, 68.
— terminations for the persons beginning among the Buriätes, 69.
— and nouns known to Plato, 100.
— formation of the terminations in Aryan dialects, 337, 402.
— modern formations, 344.
— in Turkish, 425-428.
Verbum, 89 n.
Vergiliæ, 6.
Vernaculars of India, 171, 179-182.
— derived from grammatical Prâkrits? 182.
Verrius Flaccus, 121.
Very and much, 40.
Vibhakti, cases in Sanskrit, 124.
Vidame, 342.
Viden for Videsno, 75 n.
Vigfusson, 362 n.
Viginti, 48, 49, 53, 227.
Villari, 482 n.
Vinninalis, porta, 6 n.
Vininius, 6 n.
Vimsati, 48, 49, 50.
Vincent, 192 n.
Vingt, 50, 53.
Virgarius, 6 n.
Vocabulary of a labourer, 377.
Vocalic harmony, 398, 406.
Vogulian, 430.
Voguls, the, 432, 435.
Volga-Baltic division of the Finnic branch, 434, 436.
— Greek merchants on the, 95.
Voltaire on the Ezour-veda, 211 n.
Votes or South Tchudes, 436.
Votian, 430.
Votjakes, idiom of the, 431, 436.
— habitat of the, 436.
Vowels, change of, in Hebrew, 534.
Vrika, 365 n.
Vuk Stephanovitch Karajitch, his Servian grammar, 269.
Vulcanus, 106.
Vyûkarana, Sanskrit name for grammar, 124.

INDEX.

WAGON, word for, in the Blackmoor Vale, 365 n.
Waitz, Professor, 307.
Walachian language, 260 n.
Waldeck, S. F., on the Delaware Indians, 65 n.
Walh, same as Welsh, 93.
Wandala, the, 450.
Warren Hastings, 223 n.
Washington and the Empress Catherine, 160.
Weber, A., 183.
Weisse, on the proportion of foreign words in English, 84 n.
Welsh, 93, 264 n, 265.
— or French, 253.
Wends, language of the, 270.
Werdin, Johann Philip, 216.
West, Dr., 273 n, 282 n, 283.
West-Teutonic, 258, 259.
Westergaard, 174, 278, 397.
Western Hindi, 171, 181, 182.
Whewell, on the science of language, 28 n, 33 n, 479 n.
White Huns, 413.
Wilkins, Mr., 225, 228, 231.
— translates the Bhagavadgîtâ and Hitopadesa, 220 n.
— on the affinity between Sanskrit and Greek, 226.
Wilson, 203 n, 220 n, 231, 275.
Windic or Slavonic languages, 267, 270.
— divisions and subdivisions of, 267.
Windisch, 353.
Windischmann, 288, 524 n.
Winidæ, the, 267.
Wisdom, weisheit, 389.
Witsen, Nicolaes, the Dutch traveller, his collection of words, 151 n, 157 n.
— on Tataric and Mongolian languages, 156 n.
Wolof, 450.
Word, 89 n.
Words, 300 only used by labourers, 377.
— express general ideas, 522.
Wright, J., 534 n.

Writing, introduction of, 172.
— down the languages of savage races, 173.
— first attempts at, in India, 176.
Wycliffe, mode of forming the perfect in the time of, 535.

XANTHUS, on the age of Zoroaster, 279.
Xavier, Francis, his work in India, 208, 209.
— his gift of tongues, 208.

YACUB, his astronomical work, 200.
Yakuts, tribe of the, 416.
— dialect of the, 399, 417.
Yŭska, 504 n.
Yates, 220 n.
Yazygos, the, 260 n.
Ye, distinct from you, 37.
Yea and yes, as used by Chaucer, 340.
Yeast, 522.
Yes, 341.
Yesm and Year, 338.
Yezd, 274.
Yoga, work on the, translated by Alberuni, 202.
Yonaka language, 146 n.
You and Ye, 37.

ZABAD, inscription of, 322.
Zand, 273 n, 283.
Zanik, author of a Sanskrit work on poisons, 200 n.
Zarathustra, 278, 278 n, 279.
Zend, 273 n, 283, 285.
— Rask's study of, 233.
— Burnouf's study of, 233.
— Haug's, 273 n, 278, 283.
— West's, 282, 283.
— the language of the Magi, 281.
Zend-Avesta, language of the, 273.
— translated into Greek, 98.
— Anquetil Duperron's translation, 233, 274.

Zend-Avesta, Rask's and Burnouf's labours, 233, 274.
— antiquity of, 280, 281.
— the words Zend and Zend-Avesta, 273 n, 283.
— editions of the, 278.
— authority of the, for the antiquity of the word Arya, 293.
Zenodotus, 100.
— his restoration of the article before proper names in Homer, 101.
— the first to recognise the dual, 102.
Zeus, original meaning of the word, 11.
— and Jupiter, 106.
Ziegenbald (or -balg), 219 n.
Zimmermann and Catharine the Great, 159.

Zoroaster or Zarathustra, his writings translated into Greek, 98.
— Plato mentions, 275.
— his principal doctrine, 276.
— his Gâthas or Songs, 278.
— is not the same as garadashti in the Veda, 278 n.
— age in which he lived, 279.
— his Logia, 279.
— known to Plato and Aristotle, as a teacher, 279.
Zoroastrian world, 293.
Zoroastrians. *See* Parsis.
Zull, 365 n.
Zulu, 450.
Zuolz, 365 n.
Zvârish, 285.
Zwanzig, 50.
Zweite, der, 242.

www.ingramcontent.com/pod-product-compliance
Lightning Source LLC
Chambersburg PA
CBHW021226300426
44111CB00007B/439